OTHER BOOKS BY THE AUTHOR

The Kabbalah
(Feldheim / Jerusalem 1975; 2 editions)

Originally published in French as
La Cabale
(Payot / Paris 1960)
2nd edition 1972
3rd edition 1979
4th edition 1983

Published in German as
Die Kabbala
(Francke Verlag / Bern & München 1966)

Published in Spanish as
La Cábala
(Ediciones Martinez Roca S.A. / Barcelona 1976)

Published in Italian as
La Kabbala
(Carucci Editore / Roma 1980)

Israël dans le Temps et dans l'Espace
(Payot / Paris 1980)

Published in German as
Israel in Zeit und Raum
(Francke Verlag / Bern & München 1984)

Sagesse de la Kabbale
(2 volumes: Stock / Paris 1986-87)

Israel
in Time
and Space

ISRAEL

FELDHEIM

ALEXANDRE SAFRAN

in Time and Space

essays
on basic themes
in Jewish spiritual thought

Jerusalem / New York

Originally published as
Israël dans le temps et dans l'espace
Thèmes fondamentaux de la spiritualité juive
Payot, Paris 1980

Published in German as
Israel in Zeit und Raum
Grundmotive des jüdischen Seins
Francke Verlag, Bern & Münich 1984

Translated from the French by
M. Pater and E.M. Sandle

English edition published 1987
ISBN 0-87306-432-1

Copyright © 1987 by
Alexandre Safran

All rights reserved

No part of this publication may be reproduced,
stored in a retrieval system or transmitted,
in any form or by any means,
electronic, mechanical, photocopying, recording or otherwise,
without prior permission in writing from the publishers.

Philipp Feldheim Inc.
200 Airport Executive Park
Spring Valley, NY 10977

Feldheim Publishers Ltd.
POB 6525 / Jerusalem, Israel

Printed in Israel

"What's mine is thine!"

To Sarah,
my wife;

Esther and Joseph,
Avinoam and Edith,
my children;

Gabriel and David,
my grandchildren

---

*"May the Torah never leave you,
neither you, nor your children,
nor your children's children,
from henceforth
and unto all eternity."*

Foreword

It is incumbent upon me to express my gratitude to Mr. and Mrs. Bruce Rappaport of Geneva, who out of their love for the spiritual values of Judaism have promoted the publication of this volume. They have done so with the same willingness as in the case of my previous work, *The Kabbalah*. And once again they have called on the good services of Feldheim Publishers, a firm which I have reason to hold in high esteem.

It is a further pleasure for me to thank Rabbi Israel Cohen for the labor that he, with such skill and devotion, has put into the making of this book.

A.S.

Preface

Most of the articles brought together in this volume draw their inspiration from a mode of thought which the masters of Jewish mysticism have been elaborating since its beginnings. Indeed as early as in the Sefer Yetsirah, reflections on life, the world, time, and man were grouped according to a plan which related to three different orders of reality, described by the three terms *olam, shanah*, and *nefesh*. These words signify the "World," or the universe of space, the "Year" or the universe of time, and the "Soul," or the psychic and spiritual human universe. The outward appearance of these three universes gives us superficial information about the different aspects of our lives. But above all it draws our attention to the essence of that life and the unity of its history, that profound unity that is difficult to grasp without intelligence or the perceptions of our senses.

Thus these three principles of life — *olam, shanah*, and *nefesh* — conceal their essence. Their being remains hidden; it eludes all intellectual curiosity, rational analysis, or material investigation. For the Creator "chose" these three vehicles of life "for Himself." He "acquired" them in order to use them in the conduct of history: they are both the messengers whom He has instructed to announce His Glory and the vessels He created to spread the knowledge of His Will.

Only the "chosen" members of humanity, *segulat adam*, who call these three principles to witness and share in their life, are able to understand their depth. It is with purity in their meditation that these chosen ones study the Torah, the precursor of the three principles and guarantee of their continuing existence, for the sake of His Name, without regard for self. It is with Godliness in their behavior that they apply the commandments of the Torah according to its strict requirements and give attention to its innermost directions. In that way they serve God out of love, rather than for the hope of reward. Equally they put themselves unselfishly at the service of their neighbors. The love which they extend leads to knowledge and profound devotion. This love comes from the love which unites the three principles of life with the supreme Principle (or Source) of Life—with God.

The chosen ones who diligently seek to know the three principles of life try to pierce to their depths, find their "center"; they pause in their midst, till they can detect their "kernel," locate their "origins," to go down to their "roots" and finally reach the heart of each of them.

According to the Jewish mystics, the heart of the *olam*, the spatial universe, is the Land of Israel, whose inner heart is Jerusalem; the heart of the *shanah*, the temporal universe, is the Shabbat, whose inner heart is *Yom Kippur*, the Day of Atonement; the heart of the *nefesh*, the psychic and spiritual universe of humanity, is the people of Israel, whose inner heart is the *tsaddik*, the righteous man. Finally, the three hearts of the *olam*, the *shanah*, and the *nefesh* are joined to the "Heart of the World," to God.

It is incumbent upon *Yisrael amiti*, the true Israelite, upon the *adam kasher*, the upright man, upon the *Yeshurun*, the just people of Israel, to make every effort to reach the heart of each of these three factors of life and to look for the relations that exist between them and find the divine "knot" that unites them.

The heart of these three primeval and determinant factors of life forms the "beginning," that is, the origin, and the "end," that is, the outcome of everything. That which exists in the history of Space comes from the heart of the *olam*; that which moves in the history of Time comes from the heart of the *shanah*; and that which acts in the history of Humanity is reflected in the heart of the *nefesh*.

The Land of Israel, the Shabbat, and the People of Israel unite to form a single heart: the heart of all things and all men. The heart, "a sensitive but most enduring organ," never ceases to beat, it never ceases to supply all the other organs. It fulfills its task with devotion and fortitude, for it is itself nourished by the Heart of the World: it is in permanent touch with God—even more, "it is the portion of the Lord."

God is "hidden and exposed," "closed and open"; the People of Israel, the Land of Israel, and the Shabbat are also "hidden and exposed," "closed and open." That is why the "exposed," that is, the relational, has something in common with the "hidden," the intrinsic.

Such are the teachings that are lavished upon us on the long road of the Kabbalah, along which there are strong lamps to lighten our path.[1] They flash brightly from the "Book of Splendor," the Zohar. But they also shine out from the works of the great interpreters of Jewish mysticism—the Ramban and the Maharal, the Or Hahayim and the Sefat Emet, and finally Rav Kook and Rav Ashlag.

The articles in the first part of this work are devoted to the inner nature of Jewish Time, the Jewish man and the Jewish People, the Land and the Diaspora of the Jews, their identity, personality, purpose, and finally their place in Eternity.

The "hidden" and the "exposed" come together in this book, in an attempt to seize globally what it means to be a Jew, considered both in its substance and in its multiple forms of expression.

A.S.

Geneva, 18 Elul,* 5746 (anniversary of the births of Rabbi Israel Ba'al Shem Tov and Rabbi Shneur Zalman of Lyady); September 22, 1986.

---

*18 Elul is also the birthday of this book's author.
In the Holy Tongue, the author's name is articulated *Shafran* and spelled with the Hebrew letter, *shin*. —[Trans.]

I

The inner nature of Israel

"God requires the heart"

1

People of Israel and Land of Israel

*Israel, "heart of the nations" /
Erets-Yisrael, "soul of the universe"*

The basic ideas of Judaism

The main dynamics which constitute the economy of the inner life of the Jewish people and the land of the Jews, the factors of Jewish life which are manifestly at work in the history of the world, bear the names: God, Torah, Israel and Erets-Yisrael (Land of Israel).

These basic ideas are the constants in the history of Israel. This is the way in which they are understood in the authentic, Jewish, religious tradition, both ancient and modern, which forms a unity from this point of view both in the field of thought and in that of existence. We who are the believing Jews of our generation can bear witness to this: We understand that which seems ancient in modern terms and we live it in the present; we understand that which seems modern in ancient terms and we relive it as in the past.

Israel, God's possession

The roots of the community of people living on this earth, which the Torah generally calls Israel and which Jewish post-biblical literature normally calls Israel or *Knesset Yisrael* (the assembly of Israel),[1] are not to be found in this world which is so deeply affected by its presence.[2] They are to be found beyond this world.[3] The sap of these roots feeds the trunk which springs from them, the crown of which reaches up to the world beyond. Just as each Jew, as he bears witness to his attachment to the community of Israel[4] and walks[5] "on its paths," is a "son of the world to come,"[6] so Israel, *Klal Yisrael*, which remains as a whole[7] firmly "attached to its God"[8] and "walks in the paths of the Lord," is all the more a people of the world to come.[9]

As the "shoot which God has planted in this world"[10] as a people,[11] "of which He is proud,"[12] Israel is a people of God.[13] It is not a people which explains its constitution, traces back its existence or bases its personality on material, earthly possessions or even on cultural, spiritual possessions which it might consider its own, which it has inherited, acquired or produced. Israel is a people because its relationships to all kinds of possessions are governed by God and determined by the relationship it has with God.

The foundations of Israel's relationships with everything that affects it on earth are defined by the clauses of a covenant.[14] This covenant[15] was concluded between God and Israel, between God who chose Israel[16] and Israel who was chosen by God, but also between Israel who chose God[17] and God who was chosen by Israel. This agreement between two partners who are, in fact, unequal[18] is conditional[19]; but it has an element of equilibrium and permanence to be found in the unconditional oath[20] of the Divine Partner to His human partner.[21] However, although it is the associate of God, its Friend,[22] Israel in itself is nothing; it has no *atsmiut*, no personality of its own.[23] But there is adequate compensation for this shortcoming.[24] In exchange for Israel's giving up its own personality, this latter has gifts of an exceptional quality because it is linked to the Root,[25] to the personality, to the "I," the *Anokhi*, of God.[26]

Moreover, Israel imparts its advantage to all who come into contact with it. For their benefit it reflects the *atsmiut* of God in which its own personality shares.[27] Israel becomes a receptacle[28] into which the Creator abundantly pours His blessing so that Israel may distribute it in turn to others. Israel possesses nothing;[29] it is not even in charge of itself. Israel has no *metsiut*, no "existence" of its own; it is "God's possession." Nevertheless, it is its own master[30] and can use its possessions only because, being itself "God's possession,"[31] God's heritage,"[32] it takes the responsibility of making these possessions available to others. Thus its poverty[33] is transformed into true wealth.[34] Because this wealth does not only serve the one who claims to possess it; it is made available to serve all who are interested in it.[35] Israel's poverty is beneficial; its wealth is advantageous and useful to others.

This is why Israel "belongs to God;" it is entirely God's.[36]

Israel is the *segulah*,[37] the jewel which God "created,"[38] "made,"[39] "acquired" for Himself; God draws it from the royal treasure which He has available to use for momentous ethical and universal purposes.[40] By taking this particular jewel out of His hidden treasure on high, by "choosing" it so that it can illuminate the earth, God declares that "the earth belongs to Him," the whole earth.[41] Because of the value He imparts to Israel,[42] by the holiness[43] He bestows on it and which remains its own,[44] by means of the grace that He grants it by giving it the Torah[45] which provides it with a clearer, living knowledge of the Creator[46] and a more complete, direct vision of His works,[47] He wants Israel to feel the need to approach Him[48] and to accept His sovereignty:[49] "the yoke of His kingdom."[50] He wants Israel to proclaim its Creator and Master in this world[54] by the care[51] it itself shows for nature[52] and for the grace[53] which He grants it. He wants Israel, by its being[55] and its merit,[56] by the firmness of its character and the rightness of its conduct,[57] to be capable of making God and His will known in this world,[58] to be the "first[59] to enthrone God as King"[60] in this world.[61] He wants Israel with its love of God to persuade humankind to love God, "to love the Name of the Heavens."[62] He wants Israel, by its attitude to the world, by its behavior in the world, by its position in the world, to convince "the nations that they are nothing compared to God,"[63] that they are subject to His judgment, that the possessions which they spend their energies on are not really theirs[64] but belong to God who made them, who created everything, "who acquires everything,"[65] "to whom the universe and all that it contains belongs," "the earth and all who dwell in it."[66] The proof is to be found in Israel,[67] in what it is and in what it no longer is,[68] in what it has and in what it no longer has.[69] If Israel owns a portion of the earth, it is because God has given it to this people.[70] If Israel has a share of genius, it is because it has received it from God.[71]

**Israel is the people of God
because it senses that
it is in relationship with Him**

Israel is therefore the people of God[72] not only because it knows that it comes from Him,[73] "it is part of its God,"[74] but above all because it senses[75] that is has a special relationship with Him:[76] "a cord links Jacob with his God."[77] Israel is the people of God because it wishes to walk "before Him," to proclaim Him, "to be with Him," to accompany Him, "to be after Him" and to follow Him.[78] Israel is the people of God because it consents to act for Him: to "be His witness."[79] By existing, acting, suffering and rejoicing, Israel attests to the existence, to the action, to the suffering and to the joy of God.[80] For Israel only belongs to God and does not belong to itself; it has no authentic existence of its own, with all the attributes which this implies, except in God and for God.[81] Its God does not only give it an idea of His existence; He does not only tell it that He conceived and created it specially;[82] He does not only bring it to sense that He predestined it even before conceiving and creating it;[83] He does not only teach it that after making it he "knew,"[84] chose and shaped it; He does not only give it the sense that for Him it is a Person, the Person;[85] since He destined it to cooperate with Him, He reveals that He considers it a Torah, the Torah.[86]

A holy people and a community of holy people by keeping the Torah

For Israel, God becomes a Torah, a Teaching which instructs it in how and why to act.[87] God Himself is realized for Israel's sake in the Torah[88] so that Israel can realize itself through the Torah and, according to the Torah, do what God requires it to do:[89] to carry this Torah into the world, to make it known to the world,[90] to encourage it to accept the "simple Commandment" from which the basic ethical commandments ("the seven commandments which relate to the children of Noah") are derived, as a consequence of the recognition of God's sovereignty and the reality of His law.[91]

It was God Himself who in the past led the first man to a knowledge of this basic law, the principle of the Torah, and who proposed it to his descendants; but they rejected it.[92] Then it was God Himself who later made known the Ten Commandments, the essence of the Torah,[93] to all of the nations[94] and invited them to keep them; but they rejected them on the pretext that the Author was preaching in His own interest "in order to receive honor!"[95]

So God called upon Israel, a community of people, to personify the Torah among mankind:[96] "Thanks to the Torah and to Israel, He says, the world will be saved." To this end He required Israel to become a "holy people," dedicating itself to Him, aware of its innate predisposition to holiness and of its immediate duty to sanctify itself;[97] He required Israel to constitute a "holy people,"[98] a community of "holy people who belong to Him" exclusively and who, in this way, live a whole life as individuals and as a people, keeping the Torah as a whole.[99] He commanded Israel to follow the Torah and thus to imitate Himself,[100] God, the Author, Himself a Student[101] and the Executor[102] of this teaching. He instructed "the whole community of the children of Israel and said to them: Be holy! for I am holy, I, the Lord, your God."[103] Israel was to be holy among men as God is holy everywhere. Israel was to be holy in its universality and its particularity, just as God is holy in His omnipresence and His uniqueness.[104] Israel was to be holy as God is holy in the imparting of the wealth of its goodness[105] and in preserving the nature of its being.[106] But, in order to attain to this degree of effective and pure holiness, Israel has only one means: keeping the Torah. It will safeguard its life if the Torah becomes its substance and gives it meaning.[107] This will guarantee its survival by linking it with God, the Giver of the Torah.[108] Indeed, before He gave the Torah to Israel, God "concentrated" Himself[109] in the Torah,* in this very concrete expression of His will in relation to the world in the midst of which He has set Israel. He made the Torah the soul of Israel; He made "the soul of the Torah the root of the soul of Israel," so that Israel's will would not only freely but also necessarily rejoin the will of the Creator. God, Himself the soul of the world, "the breath of the world,"[110] made the Torah into the soul of Israel so that the Torah would serve the world, the people who dwell in it,[111] whereupon they would become good as God intended when He created them — "the work of His hands,"[112] as God intended when He created the Torah — "the work of His fingers."[113] God created the world in order to do good to His creatures, to give them goodness;[114] He created the Torah to teach men the true good which He, their Creator and their Father, knows is good for them.[115] "Thus God created the world from a perspective of Torah!"[116]

In order to serve as an intermediary of this good in the world, Israel must not only attach itself in practice to the Torah but identify itself existentially with it through an active faith:[117] Every Jew, when he acts according to the Torah, must become a shining letter of it,[118] and the whole people of Israel, acting to radiate the Torah, must be clothed as if with a luminous scroll of the Torah, must itself be transformed into a *Sefer Torah*, a scroll of the Torah.[119]

The Torah, God's spiritual instrument
for the creation of the world,
and the *mitzvot*, man's practical instruments
for the perfection of the world

God uses Israel as an instrument[120] in order to realize His designs in this world. Israel uses the Torah in order to carry out God's designs for this world.[121] Thus Israel acts in this world and for this world. It makes use of the Torah which itself served as "blueprint" and instrument in the hands of God to create the world.[122]

God prepared the Torah with Israel in mind[123] so that Israel could

---

* Before the creation of the world God "concentrated" Himself (within bounds, as it were) in order to create it.

make use of it in its human activities leading to the completion of the Divine act of the creation of the world.[124] But, in order for Israel to represent the Torah and for the Torah to express Israel, it is not enough that Israel adopt the Torah as the guide for its life; Israel has to take it into itself, into its heart, "into its entrails," "allow it to enter its blood;"[125] it has to amalgamate it into its own life. So will the Jew bring every moment of his life in line with the appropriate observance of a provision of the Torah; Israel will see to it that the history of its life in the world coincides with the history of the Torah in this world.

Israel must identify itself with the *mitzvot*, the Divine "commandments" contained in the Torah.[126] When observed, the *mitzvot* are designed to give life to every limb and member of a Jew's body when he acts for and in accordance with the Torah; they are intended to provide a substance of true life and of active spirituality for each of his days: the components of the human body and the units of human time correspond to the number of *mitzvot*.[127] For this reason, for Israel, in its historical life, and for the Jew, in his daily life, the full name of the Torah is *Torah umitzvot*, Torah and *mitzvot*.[128] The Torah constitutes God's spiritual instrument for the creation of the world; and the *mitzvot* constitute man's practical instrument for perfecting the world. *Torah umitzvot*, Torah and the *mitzvot* together, merge and cooperate to preserve the world.

The Torah as a whole is to be lived by Israel to serve as an example to other nations. The *mitzvot* as a whole will be kept by the Jews in all the realms of their life, both moral and material, in all the realms of their personal, community, individual, social, national and international life; and thus they will provide models for the rest of mankind.

The People of Israel and the Land of Israel, foreseen together in the Creator's plan, deserved to be chosen by God

However, in order to fully live the Torah, in order to observe the *mitzvot* completely,[129] Israel needs a favorable location.[130] God has provided this; He pre-established it. As He did for Israel, He planned for the site to be well set into the earthly world; as He did for Israel, He pre-established it, well anchored in the supra-terrestrial world.[131] This place is called Erets-Yisrael,[132] the Land of Israel.

Israel and Erets-Yisrael belong together in God's plan.[133] "The Holy One, blessed be He, said to Moses: The Land is dear to Me and Israel is dear to Me; I will cause Israel which I love to enter the Land which I love; the one goes well with the other."[134]

But, together, Israel and Erets-Yisrael have also deserved to have been chosen by God. "God examined all the nations and He found that only the generation of the desert was worthy to receive the Torah; God visited all the countries and He found only the Land of Israel worthy to be given to Israel."[135]

Parelleling His earlier choice of Israel, by choosing Erets-Yisrael, God then proclaims that the whole earth and all that it contains belongs to Him.[136] By choosing Israel and Erets-Yisrael, God demonstrates not only that He is entitled to determine what happens in this world which belongs to Him as "seems right to Him,"[137] but above all that He is interested in this world, in the nations which inhabit it and in the countries which constitute it: He "seeks" them in their own interest. By "keeping" Israel and Erets-Yisrael, God shows through them to all the nations and to all the countries that He keeps them all with the People and the Land of His choice: He makes His blessing available to all through the intermediary of these two.[138]

These four factors—God, Torah, Israel and Erets-Yisrael, which are presented to us together by the Tradition, will of necessity meet when it is a question of putting God's plan into action: of bringing the Torah to life in men and causing men to observe the *mitzvot* on earth, in order thus to prepare the establishment of the Kingdom of God in this world.[139]

These four factors come together with the same purpose: realizing the intention which God had when He created the world: making the will of God reign in it; they meet, but they do not always compulsorily or simultaneously cooperate. When Divine Providence reveals itself to men, it nevertheless leaves room for human freedom to manifest itself; and when Divine grace reveals itself to men, it waits for human merits to come to light. (In God's vision, the generation of the desert was worthy to receive the Torah but not to enter into the Promised Land!)[140]

The People of Israel is called man because it is the life force of man; the Land of Israel, Erets-Yisrael, is called the Land because it is the life force of the Earth

Therefore Israel receives Erets-Yisrael in order to live the Torah, the "life force of the world," "to keep its statutes and respect its laws."[141]

Israel is the man and the people *par excellence*.

Israel "is called man" because it is the life force of man;[142] Israel is called the people because it is "the heart of the nations," as the Zohar and Rabbi Yehuda ha-Levi (12th century) described it.[143]

Israel first appeared in the thinking "of the Creator before He created the world." It therefore seems "natural" that Israel, the "life force of the world," the "personality" and conscience of the world, should receive Erets-Yisrael, the land *par excellence*,[144] as a gift from God.

Erets-Yisrael is called *erets*, land, without further addition,[145] because it was central in the conception of earth's Creator: He caused the rest of the earth to proceed "from it"; He rested the whole earth upon it and made it into "the navel of the world," its "life force" and the "source of its life."[146] For this reason, ever since it was established as the Land of Israel, Erets-Yisrael has remained "at the center of the earth," at the "center" of the spiritual concerns of the whole of humankind.[147]

Together Israel and Erets-Yisrael work out a way of living the Torah and a way of following the *mitzvot*, the religious commandments of the Torah, from which all other people and all the other nations of the earth are called to benefit.[148]

People, societies and states are invited to come closer to Israel and to Erets-Yisrael in order to discover themselves there in whatever they may still have of the spiritual, to find themselves in whatever they may have of the Divine, and to re-value and set free these holy, original elements which they have distorted and stifled in themselves.[149] People and nations are called to discern their own being in its authenticity in Israel and in Erets-Yisrael. For Israel, according to the words of Maharal, Rabbi Yehuda Löw of Prague (16th century), is *ha-adam shebe-adam*, "the man in man"; Israel is the *adam*, "the Man" *bo mekupal kol ha-adam* "in whom all of man is contained," in which every man is contained; in which is the hidden "root" of every nation, as Rabbi Yehuda Arié Leib of Gur (19th century) added; and Erets-Yisrael, which the Sages of Israel call *tevel*, simply "the world," *metubelet bakol*—"is seasoned with everything" to be found in the world.[150]

Under the influence of the Torah which they come to look for in Israel and in Erets-Yisrael, for it originates there, lived and observed in its fullness, people and nations bring their own souls out of the prison in which they had incarcerated them and establish an affinity with their Divine source.[151] Indeed, the nature of the three factors—the Torah, Israel and Erets-Yisrael—which they come to investigate is already supernatural; it is holy and separate, rising above nature while also penetrating into it and transfiguring it; it is holy by being linked to the transcendent, supra-spatial and supra-temporal origin of Divine holiness. By fulfilling their calling on earth, these three interdependent factors help man, who challenges them, to bring his reason, once it has come to grasp what it is in essence and what its destination should be, in line with the Divine Reason which is ready to nourish it.[152]

The authenticity of
the Torah of Israel
can only be declared in Erets-Yisrael

The organic inter-relationship of the Torah and Israel, even attaining complete identity, could only originate and develop in Erets-Yisrael.[153] The creative authenticity of the Torah can only be declared in Erets-Yisrael and can only be influential on the world and spread through the world originating from Erets-Yisrael.[154]

The *mitzvot* contained in the Torah are laid down for Israel to observe in Erets-Yisrael.[155] The initiative for the execution of certain *mitzvot*, including some of the most important, is directly incumbent upon the State of Israel and its duly consititued bodies.[156] Erets-Yisrael itself, the Land of Israel as such, is subject, just like the people of Israel, to specific *mitzvot, mitzvot hateluyot baArets, mitzvot* which depend on the Land; these constitute the *hovat haArets,* "the duty of the Land."[157] In observing them, Israel (Israel in the individual sense and Israel in the collective sense: each one of them and the two together have the one name — Israel!) is called upon to cooperate with its partner the Land. And the Land as such, fertile and "inhabited," will endure only as long as these *mitzvot* are kept.[158]

God requires the Land to observe these *mitzvot* because the Land, like the People, has its own personality;[159] therefore it has rapport with God, its Master, who loves and nourishes it, "who sends it the rain in due season,"[160] and who demands its faithfulness. The "Land" is able to meet these demands and respond because it is an *erets* — "land," "country," "State" — which "desires;" *rotsa* — which even "runs:" *ratsa* — to meet its Friend "in order to do the will of the *Makom* — of the Place," namely of God.[161]

God takes the name
Makom, "Place," and identifies Himself
with the "place" of Erets-Yisrael

God, indeed, adopts the name *Makom*,[162] "Place," in order to show not only that He has special rapport with Erets-Yisrael, with this Place, this *Makom,* which He assigns to Israel[163] and which He "chooses"[164] just as He chooses Israel; He calls Himself *Makom,* "Place," because He identifies Himself with the *makom,* the "place," of Erets-Yisrael. God Himself, the Undiscernible, the Immaterial, who transcends space, "who contains the whole universe within Himself," because He is *Mekomo shel olam*,[165] "concentrates" Himself in Erets-Yisrael[166] and there becomes

Himself *Makom*. God, the *Makom*, reveals Himself above all in Erets-Yisrael, in the "Place" where He is most resident,[167] where His "vision penetrates"[168] deeply.

Erets-Yisrael is the *makom*, the "place" where one is able, if one so desires, to grasp directly and immediately the "residing presence of God," the *Shekhinah*, provided that Israel lives there fully, "dwells" there, is "established" there, "devotes itself there to the Torah."[169] The *Shekhinah* in fact dwells within people and acts in time; it does not dwell in space, separate from human time. The *Shekhinah* dwells in a space by virtue of the people who dwell there being worthy "to receive the face of the *Shekhinah*." It "resides among them,"[170] that is, among the children of Israel who, "because they live in Erets-Yisrael, are in a position," in effect "to work," "to perform the *mitzvot*," "to build" a "Divine sanctuary" and a human dwelling at the same time and in the same place.[171]

It is on his return to Erets-Yisrael that Jacob acquires the name Israel

In this way God establishes His domicile in Israel. This people has more than the advantage of providing a *ma'on*, a "dwelling" for the *Shekhinah*. "By living in Erets-Yisrael" and there accepting "the yoke of the Kingdom of the heavens," Israel identifies itself with the *Shekhinah*, with the *Malkhut*, the "Divine Kingship." When the latter is realized in the human universe of Israel, it identifies itself with the Kingship of Israel (which, for its part, forms part of the Divine Kingship and effaces itself before It).[172] Then the *Shekhinah* adopts the very name of the *Knesset Yisrael*, the name of the "Community of Israel."[173]

God dwells in Israel because Israel, living in Erets-Yisrael, lives in the Torah and according to the *mitzvot*.[174]

"The name of God is sanctified" thanks to Israel: having received its holiness from God, Israel gives it concrete shape by observing the *mitzvot* and returns it to God "strengthened in this way."[175]

The holiness of Israel and the holiness of God meet, coincide and confirm one another; they become identical.

It is on his return to Erets-Yisrael that Jacob receives the name "Israel": it is there that "he sees the Divine Being face to face."[176]

The Divine Name *El*, which God so "singularly" inserted into the name of Israel, is spread by virtue of the Torah lived by Israel and of the *mitzvot* which Israel observes in Erets-Yisrael. The Divine Name infuses the whole name of Israel,[177] the whole name of Yehuda:[178] It covers it completely; It even goes beyond that: Yehossef.[179] Thanks to Israel, established in Erets-Yisrael, the Name of God becomes "unified," it overcomes all who disparage It,[180] and can finally reflect the realization of the intention which God had when He created the world, *BeHiBare'am*: to see the world accept for itself the "rule" of God, to see it cause "the Kingdom of the heavens" to descend upon itself and thus "to unite" the two kingdoms, the terrestrial and the celestial, into one.[181] "On that day God will be One and His Name will be One."[182] God is realized through the acceptance of His Name, of his Rule and His Will by mankind of whom Israel is the essence, by the nations of which Israel is the heart, by the countries of which Erets-Yisrael is the center.

**Because it neglected the Torah,
the people of Israel were forced
temporarily to leave Erets-Yisrael;
nevertheless, it remains Israel's possession**

In Erets-Yisrael, Israel identifies itself with God because it is there that it can best identify its will with the Will of God. And, in response, God identifies Himself with Israel by identifying the Name of the *Shekhinah* with the name of *Knesset Yisrael*.[183]

But when Israel in Erets-Yisrael "abandons the Torah,"[184] that is to say, it slackens the bond of cause and purpose[185] which unites it with the Land, the Land detaches itself from its People.[186] Then Israel is forced to abandon Erets-Yisrael. Nevertheless, it does not renounce it;[187] it does not separate itself from it[188] because the relationship between Israel and Erets-Yisrael belongs primarily to the order of the inner, inseparable essence, before belonging to the outer, juridical order; according to law, "the land can never be taken away from its owner."[189] Israel does not lose its right of possession because God, when punishing Israel, never takes away its rights to the land having bestowed[190] it in perpetuity;[191] He only exiles it from it so that it can return to it purified.[192] In fact, Israel cannot waive possession of Erets-Yisrael because one cannot waive a human commitment and a Divine promise;[193] one does not part with a human heritage and a Divine gift.[194] Indeed, Erets-Yisrael belongs to the categories of Jewish history which are both imposed "by the strong hand" of God and granted "by the grace" of God to the Jewish people,[195] which are both bequeathed by the fathers and redeemed by the children, that are simultaneously transmitted by the fathers and renewed by the children.[196]

Moreover, Israel could not set itself free from its bonds with Erets-Yisrael even if it wished to, because "it would find no rest among the nations."[197] Just as Israel was unable, even in the Golah, in the time of Ezekiel, "to be like the other nations" or to liberate itself from the yoke of the Torah, it will never be able to set itself free from the "bonds of love" which bind it to Erets-Yisrael.[198]

Israel remains the human title-holder of Erets-Yisrael forever; its historical right to the land has never been withdrawn. Israel remains forever the human proprietor of the Land which belongs to God[199] and which He has granted irrevocably to His People.

Israel also constantly exercises its rights.[200] Even after the destruction of their State, the supreme expression of which was to be found in the destruction of the Temple of Jerusalem,[201] some children of Israel, some organized Jewish communities, persisted in Erets-Yisrael, bearing the gall of the most bitter trials: they obstinately expressed the unbroken, physical presence of Israel. And as for Erets-Yisrael, its spiritual presence was strongly expressed in the broken heart of all Israel scattered among the nations. Israel did not forget it; indeed, it became more fervently attached than ever.[202] And the Land responded to the faithfulness of the People. Erets-Yisrael, deprived of its glory and stripped of its greenness, put on the clothes of widowhood;[203] but, by this very state of desertion, by this "desert" condition, it demonstrated that Israel was still very much alive in its eyes[204] and that its separation from Israel was only temporary. By way of proof: Erets-Yisrael neither resigned itself to a state of widowhood nor celebrated a marriage with any other than Israel; Erets-Yisrael is a widow who does not allow the other nations of the earth to make it fertile;[205] it remains obstinately "arid" while awaiting its husband who is only temporarily absent[206] but who has never repudiated it.* Erets-Yisrael lives in the heart of Israel because Erets-Yisrael is the "bride of its youth." Erets-Yisrael did not exchange Israel for another people; Israel did not

---

* There is the striking example of this indestructible, therefore essential, bond between Israel and Erets-Yisrael which is a unique example of history of humankind. After the destruction of the Second Temple of Jerusalem, Israel lived for almost two thousand years as a people while waiting to go back to Erets-Yisrael as the Land of Israel. After a break of nearly two thousand years in the exercise of its formal rights to political sovereignty over Erets-Yisrael, at the end of the 19th century Israel laid claim to the recognition by the nations of the world of its inalienable, biblical rights to this land. It returned to the country as a national entity, fertilized the land, rebuilt its towns and, in the 20th century, demanded that the nations of the world acknowledge this activity of national reconstruction and confirm the restoration of the Jewish State.

exchange Erets-Yisrael for another country.* Israel and Erets-Yisrael remain inseparably united to each other,[207] because both of them remain united with God.[208] And God did not exchange His people for another,[209] nor will He exchange His country for another. God stays with His people "in distress"[210] and He stays with His "desert" land.[211] God goes into exile with His people: His "*Shekhinah* is in the Golah;"[212] His holiness "dwells in the midst of defilement."[213] But God also demonstrates His special presence in an Erets-Yisrael in desolation[214] and, in particular, in a Jerusalem "in ruins" which remains "steadfast in its holiness," *bikdushatam heim omdim*: the "*Shekhinah* does not move at all from it"[215]: in devastation Erets-Yisrael keeps its holiness which belongs to the order of "eternity": *kedushat olamim*.

The abandonment of Erets-Yisrael is thus not a true abandonment, either by Israel or by God. While Israel as a nation was compelled to abandon the country, that was because it had neglected the Torah and the observance of its *mitzvot* in Erets-Yisrael.[216] However, Israel does not abandon its God.[217] In order for Israel to remain in Erets-Yisrael, God had proclaimed before Israel went into exile: "I would have preferred Israel to abandon Me and to have kept My Torah!"[218] For, if it had done so, Israel would have kept its God entirely.[219] "By living in Erets-Yisrael," by living there according to the Torah and its *mitzvot*, Israel indeed "is like one who has his God." However, "by living outside of the country," *huts la-Arets*, even if it follows the Torah and observes the *mitzvot*, Israel "is like one who does not have his God."[220]

**In Exile, Israel underwent
a painful apprenticeship to
the Torah and the *mitzvot***

God is only truly God when Israel is fully "His witness,"[221] when Israel is living by the Torah and according to the *mitzvot* in Erets-

---

*An undeniable confirmation of the faithfulness of Israel to Erets-Yisrael: the failure of the various attempts in the 19th and 20th centuries to find a "territorial" solution to the "Jewish problem" outside of Erets-Yisrael. There was the effort made by the Jewish philanthropist, Baron Hirsch, to get disinherited Jews established in Argentina as a national, agricultural group, but this failed. The seventh World Zionist Congress refused to accept an offer from Great Britain to create a national entity for a Jewish state in Uganda, even for the Jews who were fleeing from suffering and persecution. The Jewish population of the Soviet Union in its totality resisted the pressure exercised on it by the authorities of that country to set up an autonomous Jewish region in Birobidzhan, an area of the USSR on the frontier of north-east China.

Yisrael.[222] The *Golah,* the dispersion, disfigures the Torah and distorts the *mitzvot;* their implementation is adulterated because of the harmful influence exercised on them by a milieu which "does not keep the *mitzvot,*" which does not live in subjection to the authority of the God of the Torah. Despite itself, Israel serves "foreign gods" in the Diaspora.[223]

And yet it is in the Exile, in a new Egypt, in a Babylon,[224] that Israel painfully re-learns the Torah and the *mitzvot,*[225] in order to become worthy to return to Erets-Yisrael and recover its sovereignty over Erets-Yisrael. Yes! indeed, the faithfulness of the Land to the People never waivers: Erets-Yisrael waits for Israel to return, but on condition that it comes back equipped with evidence of its devotion to the Torah and to the *mitzvot* which it neglected in the past and, consequently, of its devotion to the Land, the place where the Torah and the *mitzvot* can be perfectly fulfilled. Because, as the Sifrei states—and Nahmanides (13th century) emphasizes this—although the Jews are required to observe the *mitzvot* outside Erets-Yisrael too, this is so that they will not forget them and will be able to perform them in the Holy Land when the day comes. It is so that they can prepare themselves by means of the *mitzvot* to execute them according to their full meaning and to the smallest detail in Erets-Yisrael.[226] Although they are implemented in an imperfect and incomplete way in the Golah,[227] the *mitzvot* themselves shape the soul of the Jews to give them the strength to tackle a fundamental ordinance, that of the *Yishuv Erets Yisrael,* the *mitzvah* of the resettlement, reconstruction and provision of Erets-Yisrael.[228] The *mitzvah* of *Yeshivat Erets Yisrael,* of "dwelling in Erets-Yisrael," is itself "equivalent to all the other *mitzvot.*"[229] There are historical circumstances in which the *mitzvah* of *Yishuv Erets Yisrael* constitutes the main preoccupation of Jews; a special concentration on this *mitzvah* may even cause a slackening in the observance of the other *mitzvot.*[230] There are moments in history when this *mitzvah* takes precedence over the others[231] so that the latter may thereafter come to full fruition. When observed with fervor and self-sacrifice, this *mitzvah* of *Yishuv Erets Yisrael* can promote the reconciliation of Israel with Erets-Yisrael and express the ardent and concrete response of the people to the expectation of the Land.

When it welcomes Israel, strengthened by the *mitzvah* of *Yishuv Erets Yisrael,* the Land, the *Erets,* prepares itself to welcome God, to greet the *Shekhinah,* in Its "fullness," in Its residence, in Zion. When it consecrates itself in love to the consummation of the *mitzvah* of *Yishuv Erets Yisrael,* Israel opens up the way to the triumph of all the other *mitzvot* in Erets-Yisrael which are closely linked to the first. And, as a consequence, Israel prepares the way for the glorious return of God into His earthly City only when the earthly City, "the Jerusalem below," has been rebuilt by men, by Israel, will God "come back" to the heavenly City, the cosmic City, "the Jerusalem above,"[232] "Jerusalem, the metropolis of the world."[233] The material and then the spiritual reconstruction of Erets-Yisrael by Israel constitutes a prior condition for the glorious return of God to the world as a whole, "to the world which He created according to His will," but from which men dared to exclude Him by their sins; they dared to "repel the feet of the *Shekhinah*."[234] The presence of the *Shekhinah* in a devastated Erets-Yisrael and the sparks of the *Shekhinah* scattered in the Golah during the wanderings of Israel "will be united," "will be made whole,"[235] to constitute the Unity of God and to make the majestic and unique Name of God heard throughout the world.[236]

In the Diaspora the Jews also observe the *mitzvot* so that non-Jews can have an idea of what the Torah is like; they can begin to learn the elementary *mitzvot* and surmise what the *mitzvot* will be like when Israel observes them in Erets-Yisrael.[237] Because Erets-Yisrael is really the only country in the world in which the Torah is the Torah, in which the Torah is understood and followed, a Torah translated into the clear and concrete language of the *mitzvot*:[238] "There is no Torah like the Torah of Erets-Yisrael."[239]

In the Land of Israel God is God by virtue of the doing of His will as revealed in the Torah.[240] The Land of Israel is the only country in the world in which the God of the Torah is the "God of the Land," the "God of the Earth," *Elohei ha-arets*,[241] and it is from there that He will extend

The "root" of every being
is inherent in the name which it bears

These then are the constant factors of Jewish life with their own dynamics: God, Torah, Israel and Erets-Yisrael. God is fulfilled in the Torah; Israel is fulfilled in Erets-Yisrael. God is realized and becomes authentic for man in the Torah; Israel is realized and becomes authentic in Erets-Yisrael firstly for itself and then for the nations and the whole of mankind. For the world, the realization of God is the realization of the Torah; for the world, the realization of Israel is the realization of Erets-Yisrael.

The dynamics of these constants, their *merkavah*,[243] their "chariot," originates in something static, in an original state of "repose,"[244] of *menuhah*, of "present," of *hoveh*; it becomes involved in the changing, successive meanderings of time, of becoming, of the *hithavut*, although it aspires "to return" to its stable point of departure, to the *menuhah*.

The authenticity of a being, the "root" of a being, of every being, is to be found in the name which it bears;[245] it tries to manifest itself; it cuts itself a path and breaks out into the confusion of the outside world; but it hopes nevertheless to leave it again in peace with its "fullness" strengthened, with its "wholeness" confirmed; it constantly tends to rejoin its "inner point."

Thus the history of a name illustrates the history of a being.[246] Originally, the being received the name which fitted its soul, which was to correspond to its assigned task in this world. However this "radical," initial name can only make itself known to itself and the surrounding world to the extent to which its bearer deserves it: the being is refined in the fire of trials, there it is transformed and enriched, it is perfected and strengthened, in order to finally acquire its true, full name. This name, which seems new, is merely the name which was hidden in the depths of the being; once it leaves its static form, the name reveals its dynamism to the world in the authenticity of its personality when fully living out its calling.[247]

The Bible and the Talmud provide eloquent examples of this; they invite us both directly and indirectly to interpret names, to discover their roots, to reveal their meanings — in other words, to pay attention to their history.[248] For in fact, the history of man is really the history of his name, and the historical stages of humankind are defined by the names of the men who determined them: *adam, gever, enosh, ish*. Their main characteristic may be of a biological or a spiritual nature;[249] the various names express either the ambition of their bearer to "resemble" the higher, Divine world, *adameh leElyon*,[250] to raise himself up to it, or his tendency to descend to the lower, animal, Edomite world of "ashes," "blood" and "bile" by succumbing to it: *adam, eifer, dam, marah*.[251]

Thus man is in a position to forge or to destroy his name.[252] His calling is to give names to every being, to the society in which he lives, to himself and even to God,[253] because it is the Creator who gave man this formidable capability, the faculty of giving names.[254] Thus He granted man the clairvoyant power[255] which enables him to administer himself and to administer the world,[256] to influence the destiny of the world and even, up to a certain point, that of God in this world.[257]

But man can use every gift he receives from God as seems best to him. Man can also lose the aptitude which the Creator has given him to see clearly and, hence, to act rightly;[258] by his misbehavior he can dim his vision and distort his action. Then his name is obscured and emptied of its original content,[259] stripped of its initial potential.[260] On the other hand, if man remains master of his intellect and uses his heart intelligently, if his approach is successful, he brings his original name to life, he makes its initial content real, he makes it original and effective.[261] God will confirm the privileged position of this man as a being who "gives himself his own name."[262] Such a man "deserves" his name; God confirms it by "determining it as a new name," which means by revealing it in the fullness[263] by which it was conceived and for which it was intended.[264] Then God links His name with that of the man,[265] and thus associates His action with that of the man. God allies Himself with the man; He cooperates with him.[266] The history of this man becomes the history of his name united with the name of God.[267] The history of Abraham and of Israel are symbolic of this union. By cooperating with God, man, who was made by his Creator, "makes himself," creates himself, causes his own being to be expressed in all its authenticity. When he cooperates with God, man, who received the Torah from God, "makes the Torah himself."[268] Consequently this man receives his true, full name which witnesses to the truth and fullness of his being.[269] When he receives his name from God, man, in turn, "attributes" to his God the name which suits Him;[270] in this way he constantly witnesses anew "the acts" of God, who by way of recompense, tells this man that He, God, is "as if He, man, had made Him!"[271]

The encounter between the human and Divine names thus shows the complementarity of human action and Divine action.[272] God crowns man's merit: by confirming his name[273] He confirms him, as He did in the case of Jacob, as it were, as the ruler of this world.[274] When man "proclaims the name of God" he invests his Creator with His "Kingship" over this world.[275]

**God deliberately puts His name
into that of Israel.
Their common name reveals
the common nature of
their historical identiy**

We have already seen that its was God Himself who taught Israel to set its own name in movement, in action, into practice. God sets the example. By giving the Torah to Israel, God identifies with the Torah even in His Name: He is called *Rahmanah*.[276] And the Torah which comes from God identifies with God even in its name: it too is called *Rahmanah*. *Rahmanah*, "God, is good," because His Teaching enables us to be good.

Thus the Zohar can state: "God, the Torah and Israel constitute a unity!"[277]

Israel deserves to be called by the name of God because it pleases God to be called by the name of Israel.[278] "Jacob was called El" already.[279] Israel, into which God deliberately puts His name, glorifies Him in the world.[280]

Jacob is unique,[281] because he is the only one of all earthly beings that God, the Unique One, "the Master," "the God of the world," "the God of all flesh," "singled out" from "those whom He sent into this world:" He linked His name with his.[282]

In this way God proclaims that He has a direct, personal relationship with Jacob; He has extended Himself; He has given Jacob a "key" in order to reach Him.[283] Still more: He makes His Divine identity clear in the identity of Israel "who is righteous," in the identity of *Yeshurun. Ka-El Yeshurun*: "Yeshurun is God-like!"[284]

"God has associated His great name with that of Israel."[285] He linked Himself with Israel through His name. "This fact reminds us of what a king did who had a small key to open his treasure. The king said to himself, "If I leave the key as it is, it might get lost. I shall attach it to a small chain." So he had a small chain made and attached the key to it. "If the key gets lost," he thought, "it will be recognizable by means of the chain to which it is attached."

"The Holy One, blessed be He, spoke in the same way: If I leave Israel as it is, it will be in danger of being swallowed up by the nations of the world. In order to avoid this, I will put my name into it, I will link mine with Israel and it will live."[286]

Thus Jacob becomes Israel.

In its activity on earth, Jacob thus raises himself to the level of Israel, capable of supra-terrestrial activity while still on earth.[287] But, in its historical experience, Israel does not cease also to be called Jacob.[288] The latter's ladder reaches up to the heavens; but it does not part with the earth; it continues to stand on the earth. The earthly Jacob is the same as the heavenly Israel. It is one, struggling on the earth and aspiring to the heavens.[289]

Therefore Jacob becomes Israel.[290]

In order to achieve this, Jacob had "to observe all the *mitzvot*" in a brutal and hostile world and, thanks to those *mitzvot*, to come close to God and attach himself to Him.[291] Israel had to wish "to live in the light of the King," which means to live "in the light of the Torah."[292] But there is a danger that the light of God may blind the man down below and the light of the "Torah of the heavens" may dazzle man on earth.[293] Therefore the Jew binds himself to the *mitzvot* of the Torah, to implement them in the material world in which he lives. At their "source" these *mitzvot* are "Divine lights" (reflections of God's light), made by means of human action to clothe themselves[294] in material acts in this world. By binding himself to the *mitzvot*, the Jew binds himself to their "roots" and thus attaches himself to God.[295]

Israel bears the name of Erets-Yisrael and Erets-Yisrael bears the name of Israel

Thus Israel's attachment to its God is the result of action. Where? Above all at a place on the earth which, like Israel among the nations, is holy in origin and in purpose; a place which Israel is called upon to sanctify by the deeds which it performs there in harmony with the activity of God. In this Israel will come to identify itself with this "place" (with which God has already identified Himself by taking the name *Makom*) and to bear its name.[296]

Israel bears the name of Erets-Yisrael; and Erets-Yisrael bears the name of Israel.[297]

"All nations shall count you happy, for you shall be a land of delight, says the Lord of Hosts." Through the mouth of the prophet Malachi God gives Israel the title: *Erets heifets*, "Land of delight," the land of His "desire,"[298] because He loves both Israel and Erets-Yisrael. He "chose" both of them because He has a yearning for them and desires to keep them: therefore they belong exclusively to him.[299] For this reason, when God gives Erets-Yisrael to Israel, He proclaims: "I am offering that which belongs to Me to the one who belongs to Me," *sheli lesheli!*[300] But God also describes Israel as "land of delight" because both the people and the land appeal to God, and thus to His Name and to His Torah; they endeavor to be worthy of their Master, their Possessor, their Inspirer, their Legislator; they are concerned to make themselves a people/land "of delight," of Prophecy and the Law, of Faith and Science, through whose intermediary "the name of the Heavens will be loved" in the world;[301] and they in fact succeed: they are deemed fortunate for this by all the nations.

The Tradition proclaims *Yisrael nikra erets*, "Israel is called land."[302] Israel is given the name Erets-Yisrael, Land, in which it can realize itself by performing the *mitzvot* of God's Torah in time and space.

Velemor leTsion ami ata, "Say to Zion (God exclaims), 'You are my people!'" From this verse of the Book of Isaiah,[303] the Zohar "derives the teaching that Israel is called Zion": *Yisrael ikra bishma deTsion*, and it adds: *lemihavei shutafa imi*, "so that it will be My associate": so God declares. He addresses Israel and calls it *ami*, "My people," and He summons it to come to Him by saying: be *imi*, be "with Me," be My associate, My colleague, My partner![304]

The concept of a people based on the concept of the people of Israel

Furthermore, by giving us this significant insight into the identity of the names—and hence of the functions and tasks—of Israel and Erets-Yisrael, the Zohar thus informs us of its concept of people, of every people, by virtue of its concept of the people of Israel. For, as we have already said, Israel is the origin, the prototype, of a people, just as it is the origin, the prototype of man,[305] although neither Israel nor Adam was chronologically the first of creatures or of peoples. For that which is perfect arrives later, or even arrives at the end: Adam at the end of the creation; Israel after the other nations had been constituted; the Torah twenty-six generations after the creation of the world; the Messiah at the end of time![306]

In order to express its concept of a people and to formulate its philosophy of the Hebrew term *am*, which means "people," the Zohar provides us with a bold interpretation of the verse of Isaiah (51:16) quoted above, when it dwells on the word *ami*, "My people," and it goes on to exhort us, *al tikrei ami ela imi*: "in this text of the prophet, do not read the word *ami*; read (it as) *imi*; in other words, do not read "My people"; read "with Me!"

However, when it authorizes us, even invites us, to make a slight change in the pointing of the word *ami*, composed of only three letters, the Zohar does not presume, and would not even think, to abolish the original vowel point "a" and replace it with the vowel point "i." On the contrary, the Zohar respects the traditional, massoretic punctuation, which it finds in the text of Isaiah, and not only maintains it but reinforces it,[307] inviting it to accept a cognate punctuation. For, from the Zohar's point of view, the latter expresses the complete meaning of the word *ami*. When they read this verse of Isaiah, the masters of the Zohar can hear God speaking to Israel and calling out: to be a "people," *am*, you must be "My people," *ami*; in other words, you must be "with Me," *imi*.[308]

Am comes from *im* and leads up to *amit*;[309] "people" comes from "with" and leads up to "colleague." And there is only one "with" which is valid; there is only one "colleague" who is sincere; there is only one "associate" who is reliable; that is the Lord God.[310] There is only one "with" which can "teach" us, which can "advise" us how to act so that our actions will be right, "righteous," and make us able to live as the people with God, to live as "Israel," to live as a "righteous" people, as *Yeshurun*, as a people of God; and that is the Torah. For the Torah reflects the "distant" (but certain) counsel of God and provides us with the immediate guidance of the *mitzvot*.[311]

Thus there is only one "with" which is able to teach us how to live with an other, near or far, whether an individual or a group, whether through our contact he becomes a personality or a community: and that too is God. As we live with Him, fear Him and "learn to fear Him," we learn not to dread anyone, we learn to live in peace with "him who is far and with him who is near," and even to love our neighbor—because it is God who comes to both of us, who comes between us to bring us closer to each other, who calls us and who listens as we speak to one another. For us this other is more than a *re'a* who faces us and "links" himself with us, "associates himself" with us and "agrees" with us (but who is also liable to change his attitude and adopt the stand of *ra*, a "wicked man," in relation to us!) [312] For us he becomes an *amit*, who is identified in his root, *im*, "with" us, who stays with us and completes us.[313] "Do not harm one another, *amito*, but fear your God! For I am the Lord your God. Obey My edicts, observe and follow My laws, and you will dwell in the *land* in safety."

In this way Israel is both the man of God and the people of God, because it consents to be with Him. Israel welcomes His friendship, it acknowledges His nearness, it consents to His company, it approves of His direction, to follow Him simply on the path which He indicates and to walk in the light of the Torah.[314]

Every nation can become a people of God like Israel

Israel discovered that God had given it the task of "keeping His vines";[315] it is responsible for the Divine Throne, the *Kisseh HaShem*, which the King has set up on the heights of Jerusalem in the center of His Palace, meaning, in the middle of Erets-Yisrael, the Land which is itself at the heart of the "inhabited world."[316] How great, therefore, is the responsibility of this guardian of the Divine inheritance! For, indeed, it is "from Zion, this center of beauty, that the Lord shines"; it is from this "high" place that one can "see the Kingship of God throughout the world!"[317]

And yet, although it has the prestige-laden function of guardian of God's vineyards, of all His vineyards, Israel often has to "go down" among the nations to bring to their countries, despite their ingratitude, the message of God.[318] While it enjoys the much-envied rank of Guardian of the Divine Throne in its own country, from which it invites the nations to "go up" to "the mountain of God, the House of the God of Jacob, to follow His paths there," to see His glory there,[319] Israel nonetheless proclaims to the nations of the earth that each one of them can become truly a people, an *am*, if it takes the trouble to be *im*, to be "with" God.[320] Just like Israel, every people can become a people of God. Every people can "attach itself"[321] to Israel, to emulate it: For Israel is spiritually omnipresent; and hence every country can appeal and draw inspiration from Erets-Yisrael[322] because it "stretches" spiritually "into all the countries."[323]

Israel is already the people of God, and it will be even more so when the other nations are converted to God (not to Judaism!), to "attach themselves to the Lord and become His people."[324] Israel as a people is already a "kingdom of priests,"[325] and it will be even more so when God is able to "choose priests" from other peoples[326] who place themselves in His service and, consequently, in the service of His creation.[327] The House of Israel is already the House of God, and it will be even more so[328] when the houses of the other nations decide to join it while still keeping their own architecture.[329] Then God will be able to say even of Egypt: "Blessed be My people of Egypt!"[330] Israel is already blessed[331] because the Name of God, which it acquired in the "struggle," in the "suffering," in the "hardship,"[332] is already inscribed in its own name, in that of its country and throughout the Torah.

Thus Israel will be even more the people of God when the other peoples, following its example, become the same. Israel, the blessed people from the beginning, will become so even more, because it will receive a *tossefet berakhah*, an "additional blessing,"[333] when "all the families of the earth are blessed in it."[334] When Israel, the priest, imparts the benefit of its *berakhah* to others, its "blessing," (and others become prepared to rejoice at this) the blessing will grow in intensity. When one gives to others, one receives more than one had before. Israel will receive an additional blessing, a *tossefet berakhah*, from the Divine Giver, the Source of blessing, because, as it fulfills its historical calling in this world, it will take history with it into "the world to come."[335]

The Torah, Israel and Erets-Yisrael,
issuing from a trans-historical world,
descend to a temporal world and
aspire to return to their source after
accomplishing their historical mission

Midrashic literature emphasizes at many points the continuation and fulfillment of the temporal history of Israel in an eternal, radiant history of Israel in the world to come.[336]

While it is temporal, the history of Israel is of an eternal nature; despite the torments which it has to undergo; it is already "eternal," that is, "holy," because of the eternity and the holiness with which it is connected: for from eternity and holiness it emerged and became; such are its origins.[337]

The Torah, Israel and Erets-Yisrael do indeed come from God.[338] "The Torah of life,"[339] "the people of Israel which is alive"[340] and "the lands of life"[341] spring from the "source of Life," from God, and live with Him, in the source of Life.[342] Because they are anchored in God, they live a true life.[343] The "tree of life" of the Torah,[344] the "tree of life" for Man, for Israel,[345] have their roots in the "lands of life" of Erets-Yisrael.[346] Having come from a trans-historical, supra-temporal world, they descend[347] into a historical world of human action which unfolds itself in time, in order to realize themselves in it and to bring about the realization of God Himself within it.[348] The Torah, Israel and Erets-Yisrael come from God and bring with them the light[349] and the perfume of *Olam HaBa*, the "world to come."[350] By realizing themselves in this world, they introduce *me-ein Olam HaBa*, they give men a foretaste of the world to come, that is, of the world which precedes and which follows this one.[351] However, realization is not yet fulfillment; therefore they aspire to reach the world to come, to return to it.[352] But, in order to get back to their "source," to return to their "root," they have to deserve it.[353] In order to "return" up there, they must first make a success of their historical mission down here.[354] If they are successful, the time in which they act will begin to transform itself down here into eternity.[355] The Torah, which on earth symbolizes the "garment of the Holy One, Blessed be He," will then be able to rejoin its essence on high which is part of the Deity Himself.[356] Israel, which serves down here as the "residence of the *Shekhinah*," will be able up there to rejoin its essence on the threshold of the Deity Himself. Erets-Yisrael, which serves down here as the "Palace of the King," will be able up there to rejoin its essence which is cognate with the *hekhal*, the Temple of the Deity Himself.[357] The *Torah min ha-*

shamayim, the Torah which came down from the heavens, will thus be reunited with the *Torah bashamayim*, the celestial Torah.[358] The Israel which came down from the heavens will thus again meet the celestial Israel. Erets-Yisrael which came down from the heavens will thus again meet the celestial Erets-Yisrael. So the "Jerusalem from below" will again meet its "corresponding city from above," the celestial Jerusalem. However, in order for God to preside over these encounters, it is necessary for the Jerusalem below first to regain its full significance as the Sanctuary of God, the King of Israel, and as the Metropolis of Israel, the People of God. "I shall not enter the Jerusalem on high — declares God — before I enter the Jerusalem below!"[359]

In the vision that Tradition has of life — of life in its true completeness, which does not begin or end down here — there are three inter-related concepts: the Torah,[360] Israel[361] and Erets-Yisrael;[362] the factor which joins them to one another and unites all three of them is the concept of *Olam HaBa*, of the world to come."[363]

The outside world has difficulty in comprehending the inner nature of the Torah, Israel and Erets-Yisrael

Certainly, by truly realizing themselves down here, most often in trials and always in search of the knowledge of God from Whom they stem, the Torah, Israel and Erets-Yisrael individualize their own existence. They begin by discovering their own character, their own inner nature, and come to a knowledge of themselves, of each one and all together. Thus the Torah of God becomes the Torah of Israel, *Torat Yisrael*;[364] and thus the People of God becomes the People of Israel, *Am Yisrael*;[365] likewise, the Land of God becomes the Land of Israel, Erets-Yisrael.[366] They take cognizance of themselves steadfastly; to a certain extent they are in charge of themselves. Their awareness of being nothing, *ayin*,[367] in themselves and through themselves is not diminished by the outer "I," *ani*, which they wear in the eyes of the world.[368] In fact, they always remain the humble creatures of their powerful Creator.[369] By their existence and their actions they proclaim the glory of God, of the "Holy One of Israel who is their majesty";[370] they convey the honor of God who is "their strength."[371] As the "armies of God,"[372] they declare that God is "their standard";[373] as God's flock,[374] they wear the yoke which the Shepherd has placed on their necks; they follow theur Shepherd with "the sagacious intelligence of man and yet with the innocent candor of an animal."[375]

However, those around them, who live completely immersed in the material world,[376] do not understand them and even go so far as to despise them; for they, both people and nations, are accustomed to judge other men and all things, institutions and states, and even ideas, by their material appearance[377] and successes. Their sole basis is the passing, psychological effects[378] which this appearance and these successes have on them; for they themselves, people and peoples, like to be respected and honored for these visible attributes, for their outward appearance, in other words, for their power, their greatness and their extensive domains.[379]

People and nations approach the Torah, Israel and Erets-Yisrael in their own way. They do not consult their inner selves in order to approach the inner nature of the Torah, of Israel and of Erets-Yisrael with serenity, in an attitude of "spiritual objectivity."[380] They do not first set aside the heavy weight of materialism which bears them down in order to perceive the refined spirituality which penetrates into the material—itself circumscribed—of the Torah, of Israel and of Erets-Yisrael. But, in order for two beings to really understand one another, there is no other way of coming closer together than that of the inner life. If this invisible way is lacking, misunderstandings will flourish, passions will be rampant and will cause hostility. This rule, which should govern relationships between the representatives of different ideologies and, in particular, interpersonal, international and interstate relations, becomes an inescapable necessity when one is dealing with an approach to the Torah, to Israel and to Erets-Yisrael.

Each[381] of these physico-metaphysical categories—the Torah, Israel and Erets-Yisrael—has its own personality, its *penimiut*, its inner nature, its *mistorin*, its mystery.[382] They are not easily disclosed nor lightly surrendered to others.[383] They do not reveal them totally to the surrounding world because they know that those around them cannot grasp either their reality or the meaning of their existence, indeed, do not even want to comprehend them, and when they claim that they do, they say so only in order to distort them. Indeed, do not the Torah, Israel and Erets-Yisrael, although they are in this world, come from a hidden, reserved, "separate" world,[384] an infinite and therefore incomprehensible world, a world which totally "differs" from ours?

The Torah, Israel, and Erets-Yisrael therefore certainly value the preservation of their integrity—but this is in order to serve[385] others better with all the authenticity of their being. They set the others the example of their own identity and faithfulness to themselves; they endeavor to perfect the image of their own identity by raising it more and more towards its original model and bringing it ever closer to the Divine Image of which they are bearers.[386]

The Torah achieves its totality thanks to Israel. It is Israel which reveals its initial and ultimate, initiating[387] and immediate, theoretical and, above all, practical dimensions, by means of the *Aggadah* and the *Halakhah*, in the oral Torah. It is Israel alone which, in its trials,[388] is constantly refining the *Torah she-beal peh*, the oral Torah, by study and continual practice. By this means, Israel is able to understand and at every moment to practice the "whole" Torah, both written and oral.[389]

The written Torah entrusts the secrets of its original, Hebrew language only to the Hebrew people.[390] When using it, Israel knows that in this "holy language the world was created";[391] it knows that the observance of the Torah, which justifies its existence and its links with Erets-Yisrael,[392] was conceived[393] with the letters of this language that was used for the creation of the world.

The oral Torah, for its part, reflects the mental processes which pertain to Israel and lead up to its complete observance in Erets-Yisrael, it reveals its "mystery" only to Israel and consequently constitutes the covert side of Israel's life; it contains the "mystery" of the covenant between God and His people, Israel.*[394]

Israel, for its part, refuses to be mingled with the other nations: "this people lives on its own."[395] And Erets-Yisrael — as we have seen[396] — prefers to remain a desert, uncrowned, and refuses to be cultivated and restored to its sovereign glory by any other than Israel.

Which of the three categories —
Torah, Israel or Erets-Yisrael —
should take precedence?

Of these three creations by God — of these three objects in His hand which, by virtue of the calling He assigned to them, became three subjects, each with its own personality and will — which one takes precedence? Of these three categories, "which one comes first?" *Mi kodem lemi?* From the chronological point of view, "Israel was the first to

---

*In the Middle Ages the Church, which interpreted "the mystery of Israel" in its own way and was unable to penetrate into the spirit of the oral Torah or judge it objectively, directed the arrows of its doctrinal and material anti-Judaism against the Talmud, the written expression of the oral Torah. It condemned the Talmud on many occasions; it decreed its "destruction" and had it burned on the public squares of the towns of Europe.[397]

arise in the Divine Thought";[398] the Torah came before the creation of the world;[399] and Erets-Yisrael constituted the central, fundamental point of the earth.[400]

Yet, from the point of view of importance and finality, which of these three creations by God takes precedence?[401]

With the prophet Eliyahu, we would well say that "Israel takes precedence."[402]

Israel performs the most important function in combining these three factors of Jewish life, by acting in the history of the world. For, while the Torah establishes the relation between its two partners and between the two together and God;[403] while Israel links all mankind with God; and Erets-Yisrael, the Land of Israel, links the Earth with God—the primacy among these three factors, all of which refer to God, belongs to Israel.[404] Indeed, without an Israel linked well to the Torah and to Erets-Yisrael the world would not exist.[405] Before Israel was born, the existence of the world and its survival depended entirely on the natural order established by the will of the Creator and on the general manifestation of Divine generosity. After the appearance of Israel in history and, in fact, already after the revelation of God to Abraham, Isaac and Jacob in the Holy Land, the existence of the world and its survival have come to depend on the observance of the *mitzvot* of the Torah which God graciously granted to Israel and which Israel can fully perform only in Erets-Yisrael. By granting the Torah to Israel, God has raised the dignity of humanity, of which Israel is the paradigm, and the dignity of the Earth, for which Erets-Yisrael is the spiritual source and center. In order to exist and in order to survive, the world no longer receives embarrassing alms, "a piece of humiliating bread,"[406] from the hands of its Creator, but a gift justified by the merit of the one who accepts it.[407]

**The appearance of Israel/Erets-Yisrael
as a bonded unit
marks the beginning of the open history
of humanity and of the earth**

When the history of Israel and of Erets-Yisrael begins, a fundamental change takes place in the life of the world and in the life of humankind. The era of natural development in a closed cycle, apparently free and independent but nonetheless fixed, tragic and chaotic—natural development in the life of men and of the earth—comes to an end. It gives way to a new age, to a history which is open but nonetheless ordered, ethically free and full of promise, which has meaning and purpose for humankind and for the world. The period "of the Torah" begins.

Until God joined together Israel/Erets-Yisrael, until the proclamation of their union over which God Himself presided, until the publication of their marriage contract—the Torah which God Himself wrote—God placed His trust in man.[408] This is why He only gave him a succinct knowledge of the things which He specially wanted him not to do.[409] Consequently, He only communicated to man and to mankind at large His reactions to what they should not do, reproaching them indirectly for not having taken account of the "counsels"[410] of the reasoning and reasonable conscience which He implanted in them.[411]

The history begins with His revelation to Abraham, in connection with his departure for the Land;[412] He did not specify the Land by name, intending to "designate it to him," to Abraham: *asher ar'eka*, "which I will show you," He told him—so that in addition to deserving it he could demonstrate whether he could discover it intuitively because of His affinity with it.[413] The history continues with His revelation to the Patriarchs and to their descendants both in and outside the promised Land;[414] by means of such partners of His, God clearly made known to men and to human societies what He wanted them to do, what He wanted them to be and what He wanted them to become. He thus indicates to men and to nations the paths that they should follow and the service that they should perform in the world. From then on, it is no longer only a task of having dominion over wealth and exploiting it; God spells out a calling in the world and a service to the world.[415]

Before revealing Himself to Abraham, God left many generations to act as they pleased; He only called them to order when they failed. Now, because He is "disappointed"[416] by their selfish conduct, God wishes to recall them to His orders, to re-establish their link with Him. He does so by giving a man, "a great man,"[417] a mission for the first time.[418] This mission is not of a prohibitive, limiting and preservative kind,[419] like in the past at the time of Noah; it is constructive, open and universal[420] although it is expressed in the actions of one man and of the course to be taken by his future descendants and by the fate of his future land.[421]

And indeed, starting with His revelation to the Israelites, taking into account their anticipated entry into Erets-Yisrael,[422] God uses them to make known to men and to human societies the clear and detailed instructions[423] that He has bestowed particularly on the people of Israel and the Land of Israel. The provisions which He publishes and proclaims to all, reveal to the world all what He wishes men and nations to be and to become.

God offers the Torah to all on condition that they accept it in its totality,[424] in its material-spiritual unity. But Israel is the only one to accept it on these conditions;[425] it commits itself to following the Torah everywhere and to realizing it in Erets-Yisrael. Thus God gives Israel and Erets-Yisrael[426] a mission to fulfill in His name among the men and the nations of the earth. They are to convince them by the example they themselves will set in the course of the process that starts with the promulgation of the Torah and its authority. Israel and Erets-Yisrael undertake to do this although they know the price they will have to pay—suffering. The promulgation of God's Torah on *Sinai* does indeed cause the release of *sinah*,[427] the hatred of the nations of the world for the people of God. The nations of the earth cannot forgive Israel for accepting what they judged so unacceptable; they resent that Israel undertook to achieve what they did not and do not want to achieve: the Torah in its totality—the Torah in its unity, which admits of no dualism between body and spirit; the Torah in its integrity which rejects any compromise with other religions and any concession to the brutal demands of instinct. Therefore the nations of the earth continue to attack the People of God, the People of the Torah, whose penetrating gaze is embarrassing, whose persuasive voice is disturbing, whose very presence is irritating.[428]

When they attack Israel, the nations of the earth in fact want to attack God whose Torah they have refused and whose sovereignty they have rejected.[429] "They hate Israel because they hate God." "When they rise up against Israel" the nations of the earth "rise up against God." But they can only deal severely with Him and get to Him through Israel. And indeed, as the prophet of Israel says, "If anyone touches Israel, it is as if he were touching the pupil of God's eye."[430]

By engaging Israel and Erets-Yisrael in His service,[431] God takes them into His protection, His "guard."[432] In the exercise of their universal functions the People of God and the Land of God thus remain indestructible[433] and their essence incomprehensible. Like God, the pure incomprehensible Essence, the Torah,[434] Israel and Erets-Yisrael which are pure in essence remain unconquerable. "Israel cannot be conquered because God cannot be conquered."[435]

God has "chosen" Israel and Erets-Yisrael so that they may transmit to mankind and to the earth His message about man and humanity, about statehood and the earth. He "concentrated" Himself in them, because He already "loved" the Fathers of Israel whom He "knew" in the Land of Israel.[436]

Indeed, over a long period of "degradation"[437] of men and of the earth, in the midst of humanity's corruption, the Patriarchs and their descendants,[438] the Hebrews, maintained, studied and cultivated the "humanist Tradition" as God intended it to unfold. He communicated its principles to *Adam*, man, the living being related to *Adamah*, the Earth, but whose "head reached the heavens."[439] Man handed on these principles to his descendants who remained true "men." And they later transmitted this divinely inspired "humanism" by study and implementation to the heads of the academies, the *batei midrash*, like those of *Shem* and *Ever*.[440] The bearers of the "name," *Shem*, the "Hebrews," disciples of *Ever*, and finally the Children of Israel, safeguarded the survival of the "Tradition," of the "Torah" even before the Torah was given, before Sinai. The main center and "focal point," where the Tradition, the Torah before the Torah, was carefully preserved and studied, was situated during the "chaotic" period in the midst of a country that was holy but defiled by those who held it by natural right, the Canaanites. It was to become Erets-Yisrael as soon as it had been freed "from the sins of its inhabitants"[441] and sanctified by the *mitzvot* of Israel. It was in Erets-Yisrael, and above all, in its *Yeshivah*,[442] that the Tradition, the pre-Sinaitic Torah, continued to be taught during the "chaotic" period before it was solemnly revealed on Sinai.[443]

Divine Presence and human freedom

God's action is not arbitrary.[444]

The Torah, Israel and Erets-Yisrael only came into operation effectively as "Jewish" factors in the Divine economy after God had offered to make them universal, to make them common to all men and to all nations by inviting them to consent to them freely. He asked the rational, universal Conscience to subscribe to the ideal of the Torah;[445] he invited the community of nations and of peoples to accept the ideals of Israel and of Erets-Yisrael.[446] It was only after the failure of this universal approach[447] that God decided to "narrow down" the Torah, Israel and Erets-Yisrael,[448] to "concentrate them" within themselves, in their own authenticity, so that they could be of greater interest[449] for others because of their own achievements, by the example that they could set.[450] From this nucleus God would one day "expand"[451] them to their universal dimension, where they would regain their original, cosmic dimension.[452]

God "foresaw" the Torah, Israel and Erets-Yisrael;[453] but, when He "pre-established" them in His Divine plan for historical action, this did not mean that, up to a certain point in history, He curtailed the freedom of people and nations to act as they thought best. On the contrary, He encouraged them to do so.[454]

Divine providence is in harmony with human freedom.[455]

Thus, before giving the *Torah* to Israel, God offers it to all the nations.[456] (In order to forestall any accusation of discrimination from the nations of the world,[457] God even gave the gift of prophecy to Balaam, the non-Israelite,[458] so that he could use it for the benefit of humanity; but the "seer" presumed to use it to the detriment of others,[459] as proved by his obstinacy in cursing Israel, the "heart of humankind.")[460]

Before giving shape to *Israel*, God wrote its potential in the heart of hearts of every man and of every nation so that they could invoke it, adopt it and even identify with it.[461]

Before He allowed Israel to enter Erets-Yisrael, God gave the non-Israelite nations,[462] especially the "seven nations" living in the land of Canaan,[463] the opportunity to display by appropriate behavior on their part the original holiness of the Land.[464] But the Canaanites proved themselves insensitive to the particular, "distinct" nature of this holy Land which "does not suffer sins"[465] and does not tolerate sinners;[466] they showed themselves callous to this Holy Land's refusal to live and prosper under the rule of a law other than that of the Torah. So they defiled this country by their dissolute living and the abominations they committed in it.[467] But when the sins of its inhabitants reach a degree of saturation[468] which makes them unbearable, the Holy Land rejects "the seven nations" from its midst (bosom); it "vomits" them.[469] Then the Holy Land opens itself to Israel, which it awaits with nostalgia because it will consecrate it.[470] Israel, which was waiting in distress to enter the Holy Land,[471] "returns" to it to sanctify it.[472] Thus Israel restores Erets-Yisrael to God, its only owner; and the *Shekhinah*, the Presence of God, dwells in Israel.[473]

When it expels "the seven nations" from its midst because of the atrocities they have heaped upon it, Erets-Yisrael prefigures the final attitude which the earth will adopt to its inhabitants who "fill it with their wickedness" and stain it with their iniquites. When men have "corrupted the earth before God"[474] so much that their accumulated sins reach a point of saturation, the earth will feel obliged to reject the sinners.[475] Israel, whose clear vocation is *teshuvah* and whose one and only desire is a "return" to God, will channel the confused currents of the nations' *teshuvah*;[476] it will centralize the various tendencies of men in a "return" to God.[477] Israel will lead the inhabitants of a "land filled with the knowledge of God"[478] back to their Creator.

By helping Israel to be Israel
and by helping Erets-Yisrael to be Erets-Yisrael,
the nations of the world help God to save them

God wants to restore men, nations and countries to their original status by enabling them to discover in themselves their initial dispositions to good.[479] He wants to save them, through helping them "by His grace" to save themselves "humanly."[480]

To this end He sets before them the human, personal and communal, national and territorial, earthly model of Israel and Erets-Yisrael.[481] They should examine it; they can approach it;[482] they will even be able, if they wish, to identify with it.[483] "By helping Israel" to be truly Israel and by helping Erets-Yisrael unequivocally to be Erets-Yisrael, the people of the earth, the nations of the world, "will help God" to save them.

So God, the "God of all flesh,"[484] proceeds to "separate" the children of Israel[485] from all the other people. He "brings this people out of the midst of the other peoples." He reserves it for Himself so as to make it available to the other nations.[486] "One day, a king came down to his estates and discovered that his garden, so pretty in the past, was full of thorns. Looking sadly at the thorns, he discovered a rose among them; he picked it, smelled its perfume and it comforted him." Similarly God created the world. After it had been lived in by many successive generations, He looked to see what had become of it. He saw the succession of generations of wicked men: the generations of Enoch, of the flood and of the Tower of Babel. In great distress He thought of destroying this world. But when he saw that there was a rose, Israel, He picked it and smelled its scent, and, at the time when Israel accepted the Ten Commandments on Sinai, He was comforted by it. When the children of Israel declared at Sinai, "We will follow and we will hear"[487] the commandments of God, the Holy One, blessed be He, said, "It is thanks to this rose, Israel, that I will spare the garden; it is thanks to the Torah and to Israel that the world will be saved!"[488]

God, "the God of all the earth," thus proceeds to separate the Land of Israel from the other lands.[489] When "the whole earth was filled with the wickedness"[490] of men, the portion of the earth which was to become the Land of Israel was relatively less affected by it and, according to tradition, it was in part spared the punishment of the flood.[491]

God reserves the Land of Israel for Himself,[492] fixing "His eyes upon it permanently,"[493] because He has exposed this country to the eyes of all the other countries by virtue of the nature He has granted it, the position He has given it in the world and the calling He has set before it.

By separating Israel and Erets-Yisrael in this way from the other people and countries, God causes people and nations to question the meaning of the creation of the world and of mankind.[494] By giving them a glimpse of the Torah, Israel and Erets-Yisrael, He helps them to find an answer to the questions which they are led to ask.[495]

When "creation" emerges from the "chaotic" age,[496] it begins the first stage of its history, the period of the Torah,[497] which should lead it to the ultimate goal, the era of the Messiah.[498] Enlightened and sustained by the Creator, creation begins its severely difficult and tortuous work of "perfection"; it emerges from its "chaotic" meanderings, from its astral fixity, from its "astrological beliefs,"[499] to acquire "foundations"[500] and become "historical." "The heavens and the earth" begin by "re-creating themselves," *BeHiBare'am*, by themselves "creating," "giving birth" to human, ethical "events" and to human, historical actions.[501] The natural phenomena are transformed into "genealogical" developments, *toladot*,[502] historical events. Nature gains access to the level of history. God, the Creator of nature, then presents Himself to the world and to mankind as the God who is also in control of historical events, *HaShem Elokim*.[503] He speaks to "man," to Abraham, the only one[504] to personify man.[505] Thanks to the vision and deeds of Abraham, creation moves on from the stage of created nature to that of creative humanity.[506] In Abraham, "father of a multitude of nations"[507] because he is himself the "root of the people of Israel"[508] and the first title-holder to Erets-Yisrael, the transition from nature to history takes place:[509] *Be-Hi-Ba-re-a-m* leads to *A-v-ra-ha-m*. Abraham the Hebrew brings the human race to a discovery and then to an understanding of the significance of creation, of *BeHiBaream*.[510]

By his "knowledge of the Creator,"[511] by his intuition for the Torah,[512] by his following of the Torah before the Torah,[513] by laying the foundations of the people of Israel in Erets-Yisrael,[514] by prefiguring the history of Israel in Erets-Yisrael and in the world,[515] Abraham sets in motion the ethical, historical, Torah-type universally relevant action[516] of the potential Israel and the future Erets-Yisrael. He thus opens up the direct, albeit troubled, course of the history of all men, all peoples and all countries.[517]

Despite the characteristic uncertainty of the process of history, Abraham already perceives the messianic signs[518] of the "new heavens" and the "new earth" which emerge from the "genealogy of the heavens and the earth"[519] begun under his inspiration. The contours of the "new heavens" and the "new earth" are already discernible on the horizon; they can be seen through the storms and the lightning which leave their imprints upon them. In the eyes of all mankind they represent the fruits of the cooperation between "the God of Abraham" and the "progeny of Abraham which loves God."[520]

The physical covenant of circumcision and the spiritual covenant of the Torah express the full bond between God, the Torah, Israel and Erets-Yisrael

God reveals Himself to Abraham individually in the Holy Land and by a *mitzvah*, which was to be confirmed by the Torah[521] later on Sinai, He bids him set the material "seal"[522] and inscribe upon his flesh the physical "sign" of His covenant with him and his posterity.[523] God prescribes circumcision for Abraham and his descendants in order to establish forever[524] not only the link between Him the Hebrew patriarch, and his race,[525] the future Israel, but also and at the same time the link between Himself and the land of Abraham's "peregrinations," the future Erets-Yisrael.[526]

Thus God informs Abraham and, through him, all men — "the multitude of nations" whose spiritual father he is,[527] the whole world whose "captain" he is,[528] — concerning the final goals He is pursuing in creating the world (which from this moment under Abraham's direction and responsibility starts its process of perfection, its period of preparation for the Torah) and in setting man, the human race, within it.[529] "If there were no circumcision, the heavens and the earth would not have been created";[530] "if the blood of the *berit*, the covenant (by circumcision), did not exist, the heavens and the earth could not survive."[531] Thus God enlightens Abraham[532] and, through him, all men, all nations, about the motives which inspired the designation of a special place for Israel among the peoples and for Erets-Yisrael among the countries.

God reveals Himself to Israel collectively before it enters Erets-Yisrael and requires it to keep with Him the spiritual covenant, the *berit*, the Torah and its *mitzvot*[533] which it will have to follow in Erets-Yisrael.

Thus God informs Israel and, through it, all men, all nations and the whole world of His purpose in creating the world (which from this moment, under the direction and responsibility of Israel, starts its process of perfection, its determinative period in the Torah[534]) and in setting man, the human race, within it. "If there were no Torah, the heavens and the earth would not have been created and could not survive."[535] God thus enlightens Israel and, through it, all men, all nations, about the motives which inspired the choice of a special place for Israel among the nations and for Erets-Yisrael among the countries.[536]

By the physical covenant of circumcision and the spiritual covenant of the Torah, God establishes the integral, total, material and spiritual bond between the Jew, the people of Israel and the Land of Israel.[537]

The covenant of the circumcision is a *mitzvah* of the Torah "equivalent to all the other *mitzvot*."[538] For this reason, as the Gaon of Vilna observes, the *mitzvah* of circumcision is simply called *berit*, "covenant," because when added to the other six hundred and twelve *mitzvot* (the numerical value of the word *berit* is 612) it makes the number 613, the total number of *mitzvot* in the Torah.[539]

The covenant of the Torah is also aggregate[540] because the Torah contains all the *mitzvot*; and the single *mitzvah* of the "study of the Torah" is of the same value as all the other *mitzvot* combined.[541]

The covenant of circumcision and the covenant of the Torah[542] have consequences for the existence of the world, because of Israel's responsibility among the nations and the position of Erets-Yisrael among the countries.[543]

God planned the creation of the world with reference to the organic, structural bond which was to exist between the Torah, Israel and Erets-Yisrael.

The Torah, Israel and Erets-Yisrael are primordial elements, conceived before the creation of the world

The bond which was to unite the three individual realities in this world — the Torah, Israel and Erets-Yisrael — can be identified even before the creation of the world. These three categories had already established a fundamental relationship, a reciprocal system of references, between themselves in the eternity that preceded the creation of the world. The Torah, Israel and Erets-Yisrael were to descend from eternity into the world. In this world they were to remember the bliss of their original abode [544] and to endeavor to share it with the country of their adoption. However, during their sojourn down here, they were to experience a great yearning for the eternity of their origins, but since they have been called to act in this world and to work for its fulfillment, they have to stay, but not merely as strangers who feel no attachment and have no interest in the needs of the world and its aspirations; on the contrary, they are to participate fully in its life. Accordingly the Torah, Israel and Erets-Yisrael have shared directly, since before the creation of the world, in the very process of its creation. In this they have cooperated; they have consulted together about its birth and its life. They are "genetically" related to this world. The concern which they show during its existence is an expression of their parental relationship to it.

Indeed, the Midrash[545] sees the Torah, Israel and Erets-Yisrael as three constitutive, complementary elements of the Divine ordering of the world. They are all primordial elements, *reshit*,[546] which were conceived by God at the very beginning, long before He created the world, before the moment of creation came, before the time of the material creation was born: *bereshit*.[547]

The Torah,[548] Israel[549] and Erets-Yisrael[550] were conceived by God from the very beginning so that each of them, by setting its own example, could make the world aware of the purpose which God was pursuing in creating it: that it should find fulfillment to the glory of its Creator.[551] These three "initial" elements will thus be "the first" to accept "the Kingdom of heaven."[552] Each one of them will promise its own *reshit*, its own "first fruits,"[553] to God; thus they will teach the world also to dedicate its own "first fruits" to God, recognizing by this initial act of allegiance the principle of the sovereignty of God[554] and, consequently, undertaking never to forget that everything belongs to God[555] and that all that it receives from Him should serve the accomplishment of His will.[556]

The Torah, Israel and Erets-Yisrael were conceived by God at the very beginning so that each of them could be a *reshit*, an archetypal, spiritual, decisive and exemplary element for the existence of other beings yet to be born. They were conceived at the very beginning with a view to the future material existence of the world, *bishivil*,[557] so that all three together could enable the physical world to subsist and contribute to its duration.[558] For the world was to subsist only by virtue of the infusions of "holiness," the spiritual content, which these three "holy" entities were to provide as they were instructed by God. The world was to survive because of the ethical significance and historical purpose which God had determined for it before He created it and which He revealed at the beginning of its creation. These three "capital" entities (which are therefore able to influence the organism of the whole world) immediately accept the responsibility, in the principle of their own volition, which they often bear against their will.

The *tnai*, the Divine "condition,"
governs the life of
the Torah, Israel and Erets-Yisrael

The *tnai*, "the condition," is one of the characteristics of the Jewish, biblical and talmudic conception of the world and of history: God lays down conditions of a spiritual order so that the world can endure;[559] God prescribes conditions of a moral order for humankind so that it can survive.[560]

The first, original Divine *tnai*, which causes a disquieting, human "doubt" and arouses an uncertainty that is nevertheless creative salutary and human, runs through the history of Israel like a trail of fire. The brief, pointed word of warning, consisting of only two letters, *im*[561] (or sometimes *ki*),[562] is scattered throughout the texts of the Bible; and the legal term, *tnai*, often stands out in post-biblical documents.[563]

Certainly, the *tnai*, the Divine "condition," governs the life even of these three factors, the Torah,[564] Israel[565] and Erets-Yisrael.[566] But, however harsh it may be, this Divine "condition" is firmly counterbalanced by the *havtahah*, the reliable Divine "promise," which reassures and results in a *shevuah*,[567] a precise, reliable Divine "oath,"[568] which consolidates the "faith," the *emunah*, of Israel in God who is *Ne-eman*, "Faithful."[569]

Israel not only places its trust in "God, the faithful King" by accepting "the yoke of the Kingdom of the heavens"; it entrusts its existence to Him. It relies on Him both in the rapture of joy and in the joy of suffering which it receives from Him.[570]

We can see *tnai* and *havtahah* as two components of the covenant, the *berit*, made between God and Israel[571] (and the latter, in its pact with God, commits not only itself but also its two other companions, the Torah and Erets-Yisrael).[572]

Despite the freedom of movement, choice and decision which the pact with God confers on Israel, the *tnai* makes Israel an object in the hands of its Master.[573] Naturally, it is a precious object, a *segulah*, a "jewel,"[574] but it is still an object like any other thing acquired by and entirely at the disposal of the *Koneh Hakol*, the "Acquirer of all."[575]

However, above all else, the *tnai* also makes Israel a *kinyan*, an "acquisition" of exceptional "value."[576] The *Koneh Hakol*, the Owner of everything,[577] only grants the epithet *kinyan* to His great and masterly works such as the Torah, the heavens and the earth, Abraham, Israel or the *Beit HaMikdash* (the Sanctuary of Jerusalem, the supreme center of Erets-Yisrael).[578] God devotes special attention to these *kinyanim*[579] because He is "proud" and "jealous" of them: proud to have made them and jealous of their fidelity to Him. God gives these *kinyanim*, these creatures, "the works of His hands of which He is proud,"[580] a creative drive He intends to be worthy of His own creative drive, which is motivated by the desire to do good.[581]

The *kinyanim*, the "value acquisitions" of God—the Torah, Israel (whose "root," "sign" and first historic and Messianic expression is Abraham) and Erets-Yisrael (whose "origin" in the place of the *Beit HaMikdash* and whose ultimate aim is the building of the *Beit HaMikdash*)—are given the mission of exalting the "heavens and the earth," raising them to a level of value aware of itself.[582] Among the *kinyanim*, the "value acquisitions", Israel occupies the most important place and is entrusted with the most decisive role.

It is precisely this Divine *tnai*, related to the Divine *havtahah* and with it constituting the terms of the covenant[583] between God and Israel, which makes God Himself, the God of Israel, into an "acquired subject" of Israel, a Divine subject acquired by His human partner.

Irrespective of the realization of the *tnai* by Israel, God declares that He Himself is the *kanui*, the "subject acquired" by Israel![584]

Israel entrusted itself to God and, consequently, God entrusted Himself to Israel. God is the Guardian of Israel; but Israel is the guardian of God![585]

The impossibility of destroying Israel

Israel thus has an advantage over its two partners, the Torah and Erets-Yisrael, because of the three it is the acting partner, consciously and humanly active. However, Israel depends on the two others, not only for its self fulfillment but also for its life. Israel would in fact succumb if it were no longer to evolve in the living waters of the Torah,[586] just as a fish succumbs when it is taken out of water.[587] On the other hand, as Maimonides (12th century) gravely points out, and his statement has considerable halakhic significance, Israel would no longer be a people if there were no more Jews in Erets-Yisrael. According to this austere Doctor of the Law, the absence of Jews in the Land of Israel would mean *kilayon shel haumah*, "the disappearance of the (Jewish) nation."[588] And Rabbi Moses ben Maimon goes on to state: "Only the children of Erets-Yisrael have the right to be called *kahal*,"[589] a Jewish holy community.[590] (A similar halakhic judgment was pronounced by a famous authority of the 19th century, Rabbi Moses Sofer, the author of the *Hatam Sofer* responsa.[591]) But Maimonides adds forcefully, "The annihilation of this nation is impossible" because there is the *havtahah*, the promise of God, may His name be blessed, which guarantees the perpetual survival of Israel.[592] The annihilation of Israel even in Erets-Yisrael, despite its limited area, is impossible; convincing proof is the unbroken presence of Jews in the Land of Israel despite the difficulties for them to live there. As for the extinction of Israel in the world, that is excluded precisely because of the physical resilience of the Jewish people in the Diaspora.[593] The Jewish population of a region may be destroyed; the Jews of a country may be expelled from it. But the fact is that Israel cannot be "annihilated" because God cannot be overthrown.[594]

"I, the Lord, do not change, and [hence] you, children of Jacob, have not been destroyed."[595] Israel does indeed live and does not change. In essence, in its fundamental structure, it is always the same.[596] Since its "inner being," which due to its original,[597] spiritual, holy nature does not change,[598] is linked to God[599] who never changes, Israel is therefore eternal.[600] Even the name of Israel[601] does not change because God has linked His name with that of Israel.[602] Just as God's name is eternal,[603] so Israel's name is eternal.[604] "One nation" may come and another may go; one decree against Israel may be promulgated and another may disappear; but Israel does not change or disappear,[605] it is not destroyed and it will never be destroyed[606] because "attached to the Lord, its God, it will always live as surely as it lives this very day."[607] And the "covenant" which unites Israel with its God "is eternal," "will never be broken," "is irrevocable";[608] it is a "covenant of salt":[609] salt does not change.[610] So God remains faithful to His covenant, His promise, His oath "to keep Israel upright."[611] "God does not abandon His people or desert His heritage."[612] The confirmation of His unbreakable attachment to Israel is to be found in the fact that Israel is alive: despite the torments which it constantly undergoes, it cannot be felled.[613] "Every weapon forged against it will be ineffective!"[614]

The Divine love for Israel is a love of the world

God keeps His promise and honors His oath not only because of His "everlasting love" for Israel but also for love of the world of which Israel is "the heart."[615] His *ahavat olam*, His "everlasting love," of Israel is *ipso facto* a love of the *olam*, of the whole "world."[616] God cannot allow Israel to disappear because, if Israel disappeared, the world would disappear.[617] But God, of His own accord, would not cause the world to disappear during the period of time which He has granted for it to exist.[618] Did He not promise, did He not "swear" after the flood, "never again to curse the earth because of man, and never again to strike all living creatures as He had done"?[619] Nevertheless, the world must *deserve* to survive. And it is incumbent on Israel to provide it with this merit.[620] This is why God "compels" Israel at the foot of Sinai to accept the Torah. For had Israel not accepted it, not only would it have been "buried" on the spot; the whole world would have collapsed.[621] Israel, the conscience of humanity, is therefore obliged to survive: it becomes the guardian of the Torah in order to ensure that the world is safeguarded.[622]

Indeed, if Israel disappeared, the world would collapse.[623] And even if the world continued to survive beneath its ruins, "it would return to its chaotic state of *tohu vabohu*,"[624] to the natural, primal, prehistoric state before the revelation of the Torah.[625] God created the world "in order to do good to His creatures."[626] God loves His creation; He wishes to "rejoice over the work of His hands"; He loves His creatures, "His very own handiwork";[627] He is waiting for "them to constitute the joy of their Creator." "God does not will the death" of humanity, even if it is already nearly "dead" because of its sins. He does not let it die. He wants it to return to Him "in order to live."[628] He wishes the world to continue to exist. And, to this end, he entrusts the world to Israel's guardianship; He gives it a most vital mission: to save the world from perdition.[629] When Israel undertakes this weighty responsibility, it remains "God's witness,"[630] a witness to God's love for the world; Israel remains the witness, the guarantor, the one responsible for the survival of the world. In order to succeed in its difficult task, Israel is the first[631] to begin the movement of *teshuvah*, of "return" to God. It continually pursues this ideal and brings it to its highest expression directing it towards the coming of the Messianic era,[632] thus heralding the establishment of the Kingdom of God in the world.[633]

Israel, the man and people of *teshuvah*,
shows men and peoples
the way of the "return" to God

Teshuvah, the "return" to God, restores man, whose sins have alienated him from God[634] or who was forced by the sins of others[635] to depart from God, to the state of a "new creature"[636] before his Creator. He finds himself in the state of amazement and spiritual commitment in which Adam, the first man (who contained in his soul the souls of all the people to come after him), found himself at the moment when God placed him in this world and entrusted it to him.

This is the state to which the Jew returns when making his *teshuvah*. Moreover, the Jew and Israel who "do *teshuvah*" find themselves again in the situation of wonder and spiritual commitment in which the six hundred thousand Israelites (the "roots" of the Jews who were to be born thereafter) found themselves when the Torah was promulgated[637] at the foot of Mount Sinai.

The *ba'al teshuvah*, the man of *teshuvah*, is aware of his responsibilities to his own generation and to past and future generations; the Jewish "master of *teshuvah*" knows that he "alone" can contribute to the *teshuvah* of Israel as a whole; Israel "doing *teshuvah*," is aware that it can have an influence on or even determine the *teshuvah* of the whole of humankind,[638] and each of them, as he "returns" by *teshuvah* to God, sees himself[639] in the ambience of that reinvigorating wonder in which mankind, the Jews, the people of Israel and the whole of humanity will find themselves at the time when the "horn," the *shofar* of freedom and of supreme *teshuvah*, resounds in the world, announcing the establishment of the kingdom of God.[640]

The desire for *teshuvah* is inherent in the Jewish soul.[641] Even before the creation of the world, God breathed into Israel the breath of *teshuvah*. Thus *teshuvah* (God's saving sign coming from a spiritual world) will animate Israel (itself from a spiritual world) when it acts in this material world so that the world, with the people and nations which dwell in it, will "return to God." Although it is a desire[642] which burns in Israel in many forms, *teshuvah* is also the object of a formal *mitzvah*,[643] a Divine commandment, which instructs Israel to act and fulfill it. The clear-sighted action of *teshuvah* makes Israel still more aware of the force of "doing *teshuvah*," the force of leading the world back towards its Creator. It is true that *teshuvah* is the condition for the deliverance of Israel;[644] but this Divine *tnai* is accompanied by a *havtahah*, a Divine "promise," an assurance, that despite the obstacles it will encounter, Israel will finally[645] be able to perform the supreme act of *teshuvah*[646] bringing ultimate salvation to all mankind.[647] Israel will carry out the task which it has been given of lifting the world to the level of a *kinyan*, a Divine "value acquisition," as intended by its Creator at the time of its creation. Following the example of Abraham, its father, Israel will then present the world purified and enlightened[648] to the One and only Divine Creator. The world as a whole, having been made aware of itself, will go back up to God by the ladder of Erets-Yisrael.[649]

The body of man, of Adam, was made of dust which the Creator collected from all parts of the world; but his head was made of the dust which He took from the place where the Altar of Jerusalem was to be built.[650] When man's thinking has been purified, it will find its way to God through the "gates" of Erets-Yisrael.[651] The first man saw the light of day in Erets-Yisrael;[652] the human race will see its salvation in Erets-Yisrael.[653]

The world will go back up to God by the light of the Torah, the charter of the universe,[654] within which each person will finally recognize his place.[655]

Israel, the *makneh* ("conveyor"), will cause the world to be "acquired" solemnly by the One who is *Koneh Hakol*, the "Acquirer of all."[656]

At the moment of supreme *teshuvah*, the *Koneh Hakol* will acquire *everything* anew; all creation will have the value of a special acquisition and be inspired by the awareness that: "every creature will understand that it was He who created it"[657] and will voluntarily ascend to Him.[658]

The daily life of Israel itself constitutes a life of *teshuvah* and is a call to *teshuvah* for others.[659] Once a year, however, Israel, the man and the people, solemnly proclaim their vocation of *teshuvah* before the whole world; then the world is exhorted to follow them on the path which leads to God.

On New Year's Day (Rosh Hashanah—"the head of the year")[660] Israel celebrates the creation of the world, and specifically the creation of man.[661] On that day, according to the Kabbalah, the world relives its own birth, and thus, above all, man should relive his own birth and become conscious of it.[662] That is the day on which Israel, appearing before the Creator as His creation, scrutinizes itself, submits to His judgment and performs its *teshuvah*; it performs this in the sight of the world and invites the world's collaboration in establishing the kingdom of God.[663] (Ten days later on Yom Kippur, Israel performs *teshuvah* in greater depth, in the depths of its own inner being.)[664]

On the day of Rosh Hashanah Israel humbly observes how widespread is the creative Power of the great and distant God; but at the same time it also listens earnestly to the call addressed to it by the same God, who is good and near, which says, "Enthrone Me" as your King.[665] *Elokei Yisrael*, the "God of Israel," is *Melekh*, "King of Israel";[666] *Malkhuto bakol mashalah*,[667] "His Kingship" will impose itself on everyone, first by means of the awe of His rule, *mashalah*, which it inspires; and thereafter it will be accepted by everyone with joy.[668] The King of Israel, recognized as "King of the whole earth"[669] "will then reign over all—*vetimlokh al kol ma'assekhah*—from the heights over Mount Zion...."[670]

Israel can never forget itself because
it is linked to God who keeps it in
a state of permanent awareness

The Jew, and especially the *tsaddik,* the righteous man, who is "the heart of Israel"[671] because he bears its responsibilities, who is "the foundation of the world" because he guarantees its life;[672] the Jew who loves God and responds to God's love for him, is thus called upon to love the Torah, the observance of which is the condition for the existence of the world.[673] In order for this love of the Torah to be effective, the Jew is called upon to love all Israel which only collectively is able to perform all the *mitzvot* of the Torah.[674] In order for this love of Israel to be effective, the Jew is called upon to love Erets-Yisrael, the only place in the world where Israel's consciousness is keen and alert, where its "heart is awake," the only place in the world where Israel assumes its "full stature"[675] because there it is able to perform *all* of the *mitzvot,* whether personal or communal, individual or social, commercial or agricultural, national or international.[676]

In the Golah, the Diaspora, the slowing down of his vital functions, his spiritual sluggishness or physical suffering often make the Jew lose sight of the creative significance of the *mitzvot.* In the Golah these take on a rather severe, prohibitive character and their aim becomes mainly to prevent the Jew from "falling asleep," to arouse him from his stupor and protect his "inner nature," his personality, from the harmful or hostile influence of the outside world.[677] But in Erets-Yisrael the task of the *mitzvot* is to enliven "the waking heart" of the Jew, to liberate his inner nature, his personality, to bring it directly, existentially and absolutely into contact with the inner essence, the personality, of Erets-Yisrael.[678]

In the Land of Israel when observing the *mitzvot* the Jew "does not forget himself,"[679] he does not go to sleep.[680] He knows that, in all that he does, he is standing before his Master, God of the Heaven and Earth, God of Israel, God of the Torah. About all of these three subjects/objects God says "they are Mine!" They were "Mine" and "with Me" before they existed down here, while they are down here, and finally they can be "Mine" and "with Me" "in the world to come."[681]

For the Jew who is inspired by the Torah and supported by the *mitzvot,* the ideal state of "rest," of *menuhah,*[682] which he can attain in Erets-Yisrael[683] is basically a permanent state of tension and of "daily" action, a state of watchfulness, of alertness,[684] prefiguring the ideal, Messianic state, the "day"[685] when his senses keep themselves awake and are spiritualized, when his hands working the land are spiritualized, when his body resting on the Earth becomes "spirit," becomes "soul."⁶⁸⁶ Forgetting oneself as a result of forgetting God and the Torah, the forgetfulness brought about by tranquillity, satisfaction, opulence,⁶⁸⁷ the "security" which "the Land"⁶⁸⁸ provides and which causes the most serious sin, that committed by negligence,⁶⁸⁹ is an attitude no longer thinkable in Erets-Yisrael.⁶⁹⁰

For the Jew, his pleasure, his possessions, constitute grounds for serene, spiritual "joy"⁶⁹¹ for which he "trembles" as he finds himself before God.⁶⁹² In all that he thinks, in all that he undertakes, in all that he does, he "remembers" that he is the "son of the King,"⁶⁹³ "that he stands upright"⁶⁹⁴ and "serves the King in His own Palace."⁶⁹⁵ He recalls why the King gave him access to the *Gan-Eden* which is identical with Erets-Yisrael⁶⁹⁶ and why God set him there: "to till it and care for it" in conformity with His "commandments to act" and with His "orders to abstain."⁶⁹⁷ He also remembers why God "drove him out" of it, so that he could come back purified by the testing.⁶⁹⁸

If the Jew fails to observe the *mitzvot* in Erets-Yisrael, he can only partially forget himself. Certainly, a departure from the *mitzvot* in Erets-Yisrael itself has serious consequences. The demands of this country are inexorable. However, even in these difficult circumstances, the *zikaron*, the "memory," of the Jew remains sound:⁶⁹⁹ in its hidden, inner nature it remains almost intact. It never completely fails; it merely weakens on the periphery. The *zikaron* never lets the Jew down even when he is forgetful. For in fact, the Jew never forgets his God; he does not forget his Torah;⁷⁰⁰ he does not forget his People, Israel; he does not forget his Land, Erets-Yisrael: he cannot "forget" his City, Jerusalem.⁷⁰¹ The oath not to forget Jerusalem governs him spiritually and even physically; it is stronger than he; it has possessed him completely and for ever.*

For this reason the Jew cannot totally alienate himself from himself. (As for Israel, it can never depart from itself nor become a stranger to itself⁷⁰² because it is bound to God by its "hidden inner nature" which keeps it in a state of permanent watchfulness.) As he cannot completely forget himself, the Jew can also not sin irremediably.⁷⁰³ (As for Israel, it cannot forget itself at all; because in order to remain Israel it must not forget its God. And, indeed, the Jew does not forget Him. Even the admonitions addressed to him by the Torah in this connection are evidence of this. They contain the seeds of future blessings;⁷⁰⁴ the

---

* Indeed, the Jew of our time, in 1967, spontaneously and eloquently bore witness to this, when the City of David returned to the sovereignty of Israel, demonstrating how powerful and complete the force of this several thousand years old oath is over his being.

"admonished" are called *banim*, "sons,"⁷⁰⁵ "children,"⁷⁰⁶ and, according to the accepted halakhic⁷⁰⁷ judgment of the famous Tanna Rabbi Meir (2nd century),⁷⁰⁸ no matter what they do they remain the "children of the Lord their God."⁷⁰⁹*

Consequently, in essence, in its inner nature, in its totality, Israel as a people never sins finally and irrevocably: "the people as a whole is righteous."⁷¹⁰ This is proved by its eternal, indestructible, holy survival. Its defects are only external;⁷¹¹ its sins are merely accidental,⁷¹² but the heart of its being, the "Israel bound" to God, remains holy,⁷¹³ pure, invulnerable from external forces, beyond the reach of alien influences;⁷¹⁴ its "root" which is planted in God remains untainted.⁷¹⁵

Ahavat HaShem, the Jew's love for God, therefore finds its counterpart and expression in *ahavat haTorah*, in his love for the Torah, in *ahavat Yisrael*,⁷¹⁶ his love for Israel, and in *hibat haArets*, his love for the Land⁷¹⁷ (in *ahavat Erets-Yisrael*, his love for Erets-Yisrael).**

The unique character of Israel
is beneficial to all those
who are honestly prepared to benefit from it

In order to pursue its continuously desired path to come voluntarily closer to God in ever greater intimacy, and in order to follow its way, ever and always a way of *teshuvah*, of conscious return to God, for to Him all the paths of *teshuvah* of all men converge,⁷²⁰ Israel must apply itself to the Torah and devote itself to Erets-Yisrael. It does so even when it "descends" into the Golah. For it is "dispersed" there in order thereafter to better "gather" itself, enriched by the experiences which it has undergone there and by the "sparks of light" which it accumulated.⁷²¹ It will also be better able to teach others by example, the benefits of recognizing, trustingly and without jealousy,⁷²² "the distinctive

---

*This same Rabbi Meir, a great "defense attorney" of Israel, said of the non-Jew who "devotes himself honestly to the study of the Torah, that he is worthy of the same respect as the *Kohen Gadol*," the high priest of the Temple of Jerusalem.⁷¹⁸

**Rabbi Akiba, the illustrious teacher of the Halakhah and the Aggadah (2nd century) "symbolizes" by his teaching, his life and his death as a martyr a combination of these three forms of *ahavah*. For Rabbi Akiba all of these manifestations of "love" are summarized in the following principle of Leviticus: "you shall love your neighbor like yourself," which, according to him, constitutes "the great principle of the Torah." However, the precept of love of one's neighbor is itself only the end result of the precept of Deuteronomy: "you shall love the Lord, your God, with all your heart and soul and strength."⁷¹⁹

character," "the uniqueness,"[723] "the solitude"[724] of Israel, which is willed[725] and guaranteed by God and is yet in harmony with all men, all peoples and all creatures.[726] In fact, this "particularity" of Israel is "radiant," like that of God who orders and protects it; it is beneficial to all those who are sincerely and honestly disposed to benefit from it.[727] Israel, like Abraham, its "root,"[728] spreads out in the world though remaining "alone in the face of all,"[729] "isolated among the other peoples";[730] it reaches out into the world while still keeping its own Land "separate," rejecting any "Canaan-ism," any "haggling"[731] over the unique nature of this land. For Israel carries the Torah everywhere, makes itself available for better or for worse to everyone. It does so in order to be better able to help men and peoples, "all flesh,"[732] in time to ascend[733] of their own initiative to the Residence of God in Jerusalem, to "see God,"—to contemplate His glory there; to go up to the source of the Torah in Jerusalem, and there to meet *de visu* and *de facto* the realities of the Torah, of Israel and of Erets-Yisrael as they flourish freely in the "sight of God."[734]

The *reshit*, the beginning, virtually contains the *ahrit*, the outcome

In the Jewish tradition, Israel constitutes not only an earthly but a universal necessity, being part of the universal context of the Torah and of Erets-Yisrael.

These three entities with their universal dimensions, as they proclaim the *reshit*, configuring that which preceded the beginning of time, reveal the Divine "thought" that was responsible for the conception and then for the creation of the world, and the introduction of historical time, for the start of the Messianic process.[735]

Reshit, in the sense of beginning, implies *ahrit*, both the precise and the potential outcome, inscribed on it and prescribed for it by the Creator.

The *reshit* potentially contains the *ahrit*,[736] because the former was conceived with the latter in mind; the *reshit* was planned with a view to its outcome in mind—"for the sake of its purpose."[737] The *reshit* contains its own light, which is already "the light of the Messiah," *oro shel Mashiah*.[738] God has "hidden it"[739] in the *reshit* so that it can reveal itself in the *ahrit*,[740] in "the future yet to come"[741] but already beginning[742] to appear.[743] In the meantime, "the sparks" of the lights of the Messiah keep appearing little by little,"[744] and their brightness will spread until they unite and burst into the great and perfect "illumination of the Messiah."

"The end of the action is to be found in the beginning of the thought."⁷⁴⁵ God is its architect. "I am God and there is none like Me. From the beginning, from the *reshit*, I have proclaimed the things of the future,⁷⁴⁶ the *ahrit*, and long beforehand, that which has not been done." "I speak, My decision remains, and I accomplish all that I will."⁷⁴⁷ Yet it is a man, called by his Creator to be free, in His image, who accomplishes *in nearness to God* all that God wills. However, by his wickedness, man, "God's associate," can also by his wickedness temporarily prevent the execution of the will of God, just as he can speed it up by his zeal.⁷⁴⁸ Howbeit: "Who performed, who achieved all this? He, who from the beginning, *calls the generations into existence*, I, the Lord, who am the First and will yet dwell with the last."⁷⁴⁹

God does not cease
revealing Himself through the *reshit*

Divine Revelation through the three constructs of *reshit*, Torah, Israel and Erets-Yisrael, on which the world was "founded," is a continuing process.

In truth God reveals Himself to man by constantly revealing Himself in these three entities of *reshit*,⁷⁵⁰ giving them a historical character⁷⁵¹ and assigning to them their Messianic vocation.⁷⁵² The Divine revelation through the *reshit* will not cease until the *reshit* becomes *ahrit* and until the *ahrit* becomes *reshit* again.⁷⁵³

God's revelation in the three *reshit* is historical not only because it took place totally at a precise moment in history, at the moment of the *reshit*, and because it will be repeated fully at a precise moment in history, the moment when the *ahrit* rejoins the *reshit*. It is not only historical because it marks the whole of history between *reshit* and *ahrit*. It is historical above all because it takes place continuously, in different degrees and forms, before the eyes of those who are prepared to see it; it is apparent to those having the perspicacity to grasp it. The revelation takes place "today";⁷⁵⁴ it "is repeated everyday" for those who have ears to attune to its "echoes" and eyes to catch its reflection.⁷⁵⁵ Every day, indeed, God renews the *reshit* for man's sake and, in cooperation with him, whether he will or not, He prepares the *ahrit*. To the *tsaddik*,⁷⁵⁶ the righteous, the revelation does not appear as a repetition of something ancient; it is a new revelation: "he values it as if it had been *given* to him this very day";⁷⁵⁷ he experiences it as if it were an actual *reshit*, the *ahrit* of which he can already and positively sense,⁷⁵⁸ since the future is already inherent in the present.

In each one of us God is seeking for the *tsaddik*, the righteous, who is both idealist and realist. As he hears God's word, this righteous man realizes in wonderment at every moment that "God is again creating the world"[759] which He once brought to life by His word.[760] But, living in this world and when he "turns back to God," feeling day by day like one who is "newly born,"[761] this righteous man also knows that the three entities of *reshit*, which presided over the birth of the world, and continue to determine both its existence and its final purpose, are themselves renewed each day by the creative word and in the ceative act of God.

Indeed, this righteous person, this Jew, is fully aware and realizes with his whole being that God "gives the Torah to Israel this very day."[762] He gives it to Israel so that the Torah can safeguard its life but also that it may "attract" the world to itself by the "ways of peace"[763] — so that it may "spread" through this world with gentleness, without coercion; so that it can come closer to nations and human beings, to each one according to their affinity to it and their capability to understand and adopt it. This righteous man, this Jew, now praises God because He is *Noten haTorah*, He is at present the Giver of the Torah.[764]

This righteous man, this Jew, knows that, by giving the Torah to Israel at the present time, God makes Israel into "a people this very day," into His own People. This Jew praises God because at the present time He chooses His people "with love," *Boher be-amo Yisrael be-ahava*, so that the people will "proclaim His unity with love."[765]

This righteous man, this Jew, knows full well that, by choosing His people and assigning it its own task, God "is now giving" to Israel His land which He had already given to the fathers of the children of Israel: *HaArets asher HaShem Elokehem noten lahem* — because this land is itself called to make known the unity of God. So this righteous man, this Jew, gives thanks to God, now, for the gift of the Land.[766]

The historical, universal and exceptional importance of the simultaneous manifestation of the three *reshit*

These three *reshit* reveal themselves every day. However, it is not every day nor in every generation that the revelations of these choice and Divine gifts take place simultaneously, at the same moment of the day, at the same point in history.[767]

There are select times when God allows these three entitites to reveal themselves concurrently. Those extremely significant periods provide a wealth of teaching.[768]

The three *reshit*, the Torah, Israel and Erets-Yisrael, are intuitively aware of the exceptional importance of their joint manifestation. They intuitively sense the striking ethical impact brought about in the world by their collective appearance. They feel the spiritual greatness of such a moment in history. Rather than proving the existence of God, explaining His conduct and interpreting His teaching, the Torah, Israel and Erets-Yisrael devote themselves to making the King "visible" in His splendor, pointing Him out even to children and exclaiming, "Here He is, it is He, our King, for whom we were waiting," "He is coming." Thus they prepare themselves to proclaim aloud the unity of God. He in turn causes everyone to sense His immediate, personal Presence and the unity of His Name, by enabling them to discern His direct and undeniable Divine Acts.[769]

So the Torah, Israel and Erets-Yisrael are aware of the great and serious responsibility laid upon them at such a moment in the life of the world and of the cosmos.

At a turning point in history like this, these three entities themselves gain a greater awareness of the inner forces at their disposal and of the miraculous capacities with which they were endowed by the Creator. They have preserved these inestimable faculties within themselves over long periods of history; they have transmitted them by invisible channels to succeeding generations, each one of whom has enriched them with its own original contribution[770] and marked each one with its own personal seal. Nevertheless, the fundamental nature of the Torah, Israel and Erets-Yisrael, increased and enriched as it is in the course of time, has rarely surfaced at the same time to express itself and act simultaneously and effectively.

The moment does finally come, however, when these latent and matured forces emerge into the light to reveal themselves.[771]

That which is "hidden" in the Torah, the *nistar*, then becomes obvious to the mind; it "unveils itself," becomes *nigleh*, visible.[772] That which is "hidden" in Israel, the *nistar*, then manifests itself with vigor and amazes the world; "unveils itself"; it too becomes *nigleh*. That which is "hidden" in Erets-Yisrael, the *nistar*, then rises up with power and makes an impact upon other countries; it "unveils itself," it too becomes *nigleh*.[773] This process of *hitgalut*, this *nigleh* in process,[774] prepares for the revelation of the glory of God: *Veniglah kevod HaShem*, "then the glory of God will be manifested."[775]

"Then those who are righteous in heart will hear it, see it and rejoice."[776] But those who are wicked "will hear and become angry"; they will be puzzled by what they hear; they will grieve at what they see.[777] Although they call on the name of the Lord and lay claim to His

Word,⁷⁷⁸ they vent their anger upon Israel which means they lose their temper with God.⁷⁷⁹ Yes, they are irate because He shows them that His Torah is true;⁷⁸⁰ they are exasperated because He requires them to recognize that, in truth, "He is in the midst" of Israel.⁷⁸¹ They take offence because He causes them to see with their own eyes "that he is entering Zion"⁷⁸² to reside within it, "It will no longer be called forsaken and its land will no longer be called desolate, because its land will have a bridegroom."⁷⁸³ Instead of proclaiming the truth,⁷⁸⁴ the modern Amalekites "are troubled"; they shut their eyes to the evidence, the goodness,⁷⁸⁶ the greatness of God;⁷⁸⁷ they refuse to admit that Israel has the right to receive this manifestation, this goodness, this greatness of God. They rebel against God in this way; they will not tolerate a God who proclaims, "For the love of Zion I shall not keep silent; for the love of Jerusalem I shall not rest until its justice shines like the light of day."⁷⁸⁸ Therefore they attack Israel, Erets-Yisrael and the Torah, or what they call the Bible.

The rigid spiritual/material dualism into which non-Jews have locked themselves⁷⁸⁹ prevents them from receiving a "Torah of life," one, unified, comprehensive Torah of life.⁷⁹⁰ They would like to see the Bible—which they choose to call simply the "Book"—as "pure" in its sublime spirituality, "purified" of its too concrete and practical elements, emptied of its too "material," too "political," too "immediate" truths. Proud and hard of heart, like Pharaoh,⁷⁹¹ the Amalekites⁷⁹² do not want to hear about a "God who is true";⁷⁹³ they challenge Him because He dares to "attest to the *Emet*, the truth and the loyalty to Jacob, and the *hessed*, the grace, to Abraham, which He had sworn to them from the days of old."⁷⁹⁴

In view of the "comforting" proof of God's faithfulness to them⁷⁹⁵ and, at the same time, faced with the wrath⁷⁹⁶ unleashed by those who, "detesting" God in their heart of hearts, breathe out their "hatred"⁷⁹⁷ against His Torah, His People and His Land, because these three jointly proclaim the Divine truth and together enjoy the Divine grace⁷⁹⁸—faced with this situation that is both comforting and testing, the Jewish people closes its ranks.

Just as at the climax of the revelation, on Sinai in particular,⁷⁹⁹ Israel continues to affirm its unity, its *ahdut*,⁸⁰⁰ without fear and without hesitation. It proclaims its unity in God, in *HaShem Ehad*; it proclaims its unity in the unity of God; and it does so not only by virtue of the *Yihud HaShem*, of its awareness of the unity of God and the experience it has of this, but above all by virtue of what it makes of it in the present, living now in the reality of this unity.⁸⁰¹ Israel is also a witness to the unity of a "people which is one" by being gathered "in the Land," *goi ehad baArets*. Indeed, the unity of Israel is strengthened when it rests on the Land;[802] it is the latter which, by means of its needs, its demands and its attraction, makes it into a "communalistic," active unity.* However, this unity does not depend on material organization; it is governed by the *penimiut*,[804] the "inner life" of Israel; it is made up of Jewish souls of all the ages[805] because it is based on the impregnable "hidden Jewish point" which, with God as its foundation, expresses itself by its profound attachment to the Torah.[806]

The House of Israel is "a nation unlike others" and "a land unlike others"

The Torah makes Israel into a nation which is not "like others,"[807] confirming that it is the "people of God" and giving it a particular status;[808] the Torah makes Erets-Yisrael into a land which is not like others,[809] confirming that it is "God's heritage,"[810] likewise with a special status.[811]

In order to conquer and keep the Land of Israel, the people of Israel realizes that it must make reference to the Torah.[812] It is indeed only the Torah which gives it a right to this land and entitles it to set aside the accusation of usurpation.[813] Never, not even in the most adverse circumstances, was the right of Israel to Erets-Yisrael derived from the natural "law" of the nations,"[814] from the right of conquest, of habitation and of utilization of territory. The "natural" right of Israel, a natural, miraculous people, to Erets-Yisrael, a natural, prodigious land, is derived from the one supernatural right[815] written into the supernatural Torah of God who grants the Land of Israel to the People of Israel.[816] God gives this Land expressly to Israel.[817] He grants it only this Land and no more than this Land.[818] He forbids it to extend this Land beyond the frontiers laid down in the Torah.[819] He prohibits it from acquiring lands in other countries in different parts of the world.[820] Yes, Erets-Yisrael could "extend[821] in the future over the whole world,"[822] albeit spiritually; it could make its presence felt in peace throughout the world by the

---

* How eloquent is the example provided over the past few years (1970-1971) by the Jews of the USSR. For decades they have been kept away from the Torah and separated from their fellow believers in the world. And now, encouraged by the existence of the State of Israel, they are becoming aware of their historical Jewishness and daring to claim their right to go to the restored Land of Israel, "to return to the historical Fatherland of their people," in order to live their Judaism freely and fully there, studying the Torah and fulfilling the *mitzvot*.

beneficial influence which it would exert. Erets-Yisrael would rise "above all other countries" so that they could contemplate it from afar as a shining example.[823]

The Torah grants Israel a right to Erets-Yisrael, but even more, in a *mitzvat asseh*, a formal "commandment which orders an action," it makes the "conquest," the "settlement," the "administration" of Erets-Yisrael (*kibush Erets-Yisrael, yeshivat Erets-Yisrael, yishuv Erets-Yisrael*)[824] into a duty which is incumbent on Israel alone—on every individual Jew.[825] Israel's possession of Erets-Yisrael is not a political, social, economic, national or military fact brought about by force;[826] it is not an imperious act of human beings who call down the "Divine grace" upon it to sanctify it. Israel's possession of Erets-Yisrael is primarily a Divine gift, formally contained in the Torah. This gift of Divine grace has resulted in human beings taking charge of the land, at first individually and symbolically but in a positive manner by Abraham, the pioneer who "traverses" the Promised Land;[827] then in an individual symbolical but spiritual manner by Moses who "saw" the Land from afar,[828] and finally, concretely and collectively, and in a total, material and spiritual manner by the people of Israel. These become the proprietors of the Land of Israel. However, to become the proprietor as a consequence of a Divine gift and as a result of human action[829] is only authorized at a moment when the sins accumulated by the inhabitants of the Land of Canaan have reached a saturation point which the Holy Land can no longer tolerate.[830] Equally, this same entry into possession is only sanctioned after the Canaanites have rejected the Israelite calls to peace,[831] for this act of possession is not a Divine arbitrary act;[832] it is humanly justifiable.

Holiness and the sanctification of the Land of Israel

After entering into Erets-Yisrael, into this land which is "holy" by nature,[833] Israel consecrates it, "sanctifies" it by acts of a religious and ethical character.[834] These acts are prescribed for it by the Torah in precise *mitzvot*. The "sanctification" which Israel contributes to the Land confirms, completes, puts into practice and, to a certain extent, conditions the "holiness" granted by God to Erets-Yisrael.[835] The holiness implanted by God in the Land of Israel waits for Israel to take it beyond its state of "noble" potential and to "reinforce" it by its action of sanctifying the land.[836] In this way Israel introduces holiness into the movement of everyday life; it causes it to circulate as a force in "the world of action."

However, once this action of human sanctification loses its force and, as a consequence, the Land of Israel becomes desolate, it is the Divine holiness[837] that assumes a protective role: it envelops the Holy Land and preserves its holy essence in its own depths.[838] Human sanctification is then reduced to symbolic acts, both material and spiritual, performed by the children of the Land in sorrow, at a far distance from it. Their sincere "motive" then transports them in thought to an Erets-Yisrael which is truly holy;[839] their pure *kavvanah* transports them to live there again, especially as individuals, through its "memories"[840] recalling times past when the Land was fully sanctified. They pray[841] throughout their lives for the renewal of the process of sanctification of Erets-Yisrael. The important moments marking the beginning, the flowering and the end of the life of a Jew — birth, marriage and death — are registered within a prayer in which the Jew asks to see the Land "reconstructed," Jerusalem "restored," and the *avodah*, the "service" of total sanctification, both cultural and ethical, re-established to its full extent.

Eight days after his birth, the Jewish male is "introduced into the covenant of Abraham, our father," the founder of the People and of the Land of Israel. It will be incumbent on this Jew, as soon as he is able, to observe the Torah and the *mitzvot*, which will teach him how to contribute to the "sanctification" of the Land. At the marriage ceremony, the "blessings" invoked upon the young Jewish couple are articulated against a background of creative, "sanctifying" "joy" whose dwelling place is Zion and Jerusalem.[842] After the burial of a Jew, the members of the family receive from their co-religionists proof of their participation in their mourning and as an expression of their consolation, the wish that God, "the *Makom*, might comfort them among all those in mourning for Zion and Jerusalem." The mourning for Zion and Jerusalem is just as genuine as the mourning of a Jewish family which has lost one of its members; and the consolation of a Jewish family in its affliction, its future "joy," can only be found in Zion and in a Jerusalem, comforted, rebuilt — in the midst of a reconstructed Erets-Yisrael.[843] Erets-Yisrael will again rejoice over the offerings of "sanctification" which will be brought by the Jews re-establishing the *avodah* in the *Bet HaMikdash*, in all its spiritual and material aspects.[844]

The recognition by the "nations of the world" of the specificity and legitimacy of the bond between the Torah, Israel and Erets-Yisrael

The *umot ha'olam*, "the nations of the world," will bear witness to their own good faith and to the sincerity of their own belief in God when they truly recognize the specificity of the bond established by the Torah between Israel and Erets-Yisrael.[845] History has never ceased to contribute its confirmation of this bond, most often in a painful way. "The nations of the world" will thus demonstrate that they have overcome the "jealous," venomous,[846] "Amalekite"[847] element which remains within them; that they have "set free" the "Israelite" element that was waiting to express itself in the depths of their being.[848] By accepting the evidence of the unique interrelationship and interdependence of Israel and Erets-Yisrael, the "nations of the world" will no longer attempt in vain, by their peculiar ideological approach, to enclose the joint phenomena of Israel and Erets-Yisrael artificially in a dialectic, materialist or spiritualistic system. Taking a realistic approach, they will abandon their desire to see the people of Israel "spiritualized," and "disembodied," by considering it politically dead; and the Land of Israel "secularized," "Canaanized," "Palestinized," by considering it religiously dead.[849] They will recognize that the People of Israel and the Land of Israel are linked with the Torah, which "came from heaven"[850] and is implemented "not in heaven"[851] but on earth in daily human life.[852] On the one hand, they will recognize that, by its structure, the people of Israel constitute a *goi kadosh*,[853] "a holy nation," a State with a physical "body," *gev, geviya*,[854] living on earth and having terrestrial needs—but precisely because it has a body, this people is compelled and desires to be holy[855] by sanctifying its bodily life.[856] On the other hand, they will recognize that this *goi kadosh*[857] is at the same time an *am kadosh*, a "holy people"[858] that lives with God[859] and hence belongs inevitably to another, holier, world, vastly different from this one.[860]

Finally, the *umot haolam* will recognize that the Land of Israel is "a holy land." On the one hand, its physical aspect is "hallowed" by Israel; on the other, it is holy because here on earth it reflects a sublime spiritual region which is vastly different from the earth on which we humans dwell.[861]

In the vision of the Kabbalah, the People of Israel and the Land of Israel are one, both on the horizontal plane and on the vertical plane. Because they are simultaneously *ila'a* and *tata'a*, they have an upper structure which projects into a lower structure and *vice versa*; and thus they consitute a whole.[862]

Obviously, it is difficult for the "nations of the world" to grasp and define such structures.[863] As nations, their sole objective is to be firmly established in this world and to remain here. Their criteria for judging the value and importance of a nation belong only to the material and rational order;[864] even their desire for mystical understanding relates only to individuals and not to human communities. Their approach to nations is derived exclusively from this world within which they struggle to exist.

The horizontal and vertical unity of the People of Israel and the Land of Israel[865] seems strange and alien to the "nations of the world." It arouses their hostility because they do not like to be reminded that their own existence is only earthly, material and political.[866] So they rebel against this "other"[867] symbolized by the People of Israel and the Land of Israel, which, like the "Torah of God," derive from Sinai. They endeavor, most often by the use of force,[868] to separate the People of Israel and the Land of Israel from the Torah of God. Sometimes they use "persuasion"[869] to bring Israel to abandon the Torah of life, the unifying Torah. They invite them to be like themselves,[870] promising them the transitory possessions, favors and pleasures of *Olam HaZeh*, of this world of which they claim to be masters,[871] in exchange for the eternal Torah. But Israel firmly resists both their threats and their promises.[872] It confronts them with its unshakable faith[873] in "the end," the *ahrit*, the *sof*[874] of material domination in this world,[875] and the beginning of the rule of the spirit,[876] of *Olam HaBa*, the "world to come," whose dawning is already visible in this temporal world[877] although its perfection awaits the world of Eternity.[878] Before "the nations of the world" Israel never ceases to profess its profound belief that their present existence is following a path towards a denouement which will eventually overtake it.

Each time that the Torah, Israel and Erets-Yisrael are manifested together in the world a supreme denouement can be expected and should be hoped for.

Solidarity of Israel and shared reponsibility of the Jewish People

At the great moments in history, when the Torah, Israel and Erets-Yisrael manifest themselves together, the Jewish people as a whole unites in a burst of fervent solidarity.[879]

Because of its constructive character and its creative, universal consequences, this solidarity goes far beyond a purely defensive unity or kind of mutual assistance in misfortune.[880] It is brought about by the pressure exercised on the Jews by the enemies of Israel. The Jews respond to it by their "participation in the suffering of the community" and by their efforts to alleviate this suffering.

At the great moments in history, when the Torah, Israel and Erets-Yisrael manifest themselves together, the Jewish people expresses its devotion to the Torah; it declares itself "responsible for all the children of Israel";[881] where every Jew is born, "whether he be born there or whether one day he hopes to be there,"[882] it demonstrates its attachment to Erets-Yisrael and to Zion.

(From the point of view of the Halakhah, the principle of *arevut*, of the solidarity of the people of Israel and of the shared responsibility of the Jews, came into effect in all the realms as soon as Israel accepted the Torah and the *mitzvot* on Sinai and, above all, as soon as the Israelites crossed the Jordan to enter into Erets-Yisrael in order to study the Torah and to follow the *mitzvot* there.[883])

However, it is only an active minority of Israel that concretely attributes significance to the Torah and works to uphold it effectively;[884] it does so by means of an intense *limud haTorah*, an idealistic study of the Torah, and by a conscientious *shemirat hamitzvot*, a strict observance of the *mitzvot*.[885] An active minority of Israel also effectively attributes importance to Erets-Yisrael so that it can display its strength; it does so by *yishuv haArets*, the intrepid clearing, assiduous reconstruction and courageous defense of the country.[886]

Nevertheless, Jews throughout the world, all of them, bear witness ardently to the *messirut nefesh* (a term which cannot really be translated from Hebrew into any other language because it is so full of the Jewish existential secret), bear witness to a "gift of the soul"—and not merely of the body—demonstrating a spirit of total sacrifice.[887] They affirm that they have resolved to express the feelings in the depths of their souls as clearly as possible; their *ahavat HaShem* which results in *ahavat haTorah*, *ahavat Yisrael* and *hibat haArets*, their love of God which stimulates their love of the Torah, their love of Israel and their love of Erets-Yisrael.[888] They are resolutely determined to devote their burning love, this ardent brazier of love, to the honor and service of the moment which reveals the union of the three entities related to their God. For they know that the Torah, Israel and Erets-Yisrael unite not only for the deliverance of the Jewish people but in order to contribute to the preparation of the salvation of the entire world.[890]

There is a tree of love, from which the energetic response of the Jews springs to the solemn, simultaneous challenge flung at them by the three entities which characterize Jewish life. It is not an expression of the emotions, however powerful that may be. It is a concrete and visible demonstration of the *messirut nefesh* of which the Jews are capable at great moments in their history.[891] They demonstrate this specifically Jewish virtue of *messirut nefesh* in order to perform three *mitzvot* which, because of their urgency, Rav Kook (1864-1935) called *mitzvot kolelot*, total, all-embracing *mitzvot*, correlating the Torah and *kiyum Yisrael veErets-Yisrael*, the enduring existence of Israel and Erets-Yisrael.[892]

Contemporary reflections

Following the tragic catastrophe that overwhelmed them in modern times, the Jews, in particularly characteristic style, have grasped the interdependence of these three *mitzvot* relating to the survival of Torah, People and Land, each one of which could henceforth hardly exist without the others.

The fear which recently gripped the Jews of the whole world (in 1967), faced with the danger of the extermination of Israel in Erets-Yisrael itself, was quickly dissipated thanks to the miracles which God, "the guardian of Israel," graciously performed for His people in its struggle to survive. In the soul of the Jews terror was replaced by the shining apparition resulting from the creative, sovereign encounter of the Torah of God, the people of God and the Land of God.[893] In it they discerned clearly what their prophets and Sages have only enabled them to glimpse for thousands of years, namely the beginning of the rule of the Torah of Israel, restored in Erets-Yisrael and there they can detect *ipso facto* the dawn of the rule of God over the whole earth. Indeed, the active, visible rule of God in the world is inconceivable without the rule of the Torah of Israel in Erets-Yisrael[894] and especially in Jerusalem, the "City of Eternity." This City represents the Throne of God; it radiates the Torah throughout the world, to incorporate the people of Israel: for it is the symbolic "center of the Land" of Israel.[895] And the dominion of God in the world will be fulfilled in the re-establishment of the "rule of the House of David" in Jerusalem.

For this reason, restored to freedom in the City of David, the Jews are "comforted."[896] They are encouraged by the Psalmist of Jerusalem to call out to the peoples of the earth, saying to them, "Praise the Lord, all nations, extol Him, all you peoples; for His love protecting us is strong, the Lord's constancy is everlasting. O praise the Lord!"[897] There the Jews

58 • THE INNER NATURE OF ISRAEL

hope to hear the voices of many nations,[898] as foretold by the prophets of Israel,[899] who exhort the nations with these words: "Come, let us go up to the mountain of the Lord, to the house of the God of Jacob; He will teach us His ways and we shall walk in His paths. For the Torah will come forth from Zion and the word of the Lord from Jerusalem."[900]

2a

EXILE AND REDEMPTION
Galut — Exile — a specifically Jewish phenomenon
its universal, cosmic reference
and its meta-historical dimension

The unique nature of the Galut and of the history of Israel

The Jewish Exile — Golah or Galut — is a unique historical phenomenon just because it is Jewish. It constitutes one of the fundamental aspects of the history of Israel, which is itself a history unique in all its aspects.

The Galut is historically unique primarily because it relates to Erets-Yisrael:[1] one single country, the Land of Israel, is both the point of departure and the point of return. This is why the Midrash[2] states that there is only one "exile" that can be called Galut — that of Israel, for it is the only people which, having left its country, must of necessity return to it: it is just as certain that it will return to that country as it is certain that it left it.[3] In fact the Midrash states that "*HaKadosh Baruch Hu* — The Holy One, Blessed be He — said to Moses, 'I have said to Jacob, their father' (the father of the Israelites), 'I will go down with you to Egypt, and I myself will bring you back again without fail.' (Gen. 46:4). 'Behold, I came down here (to Egypt) to bring my children up again, as I said to their father, Jacob. And whither shall I bring them up? To the place from which I brought them out, the country which I swore to their fathers to give to them.'" (Ex.R. 3:4).[4]

The return to Erets-Yisrael is thus assured, both as regards its subject, the People of Israel, and its object, the Land of Israel; the latter has never been finally taken away from the former even when Israel sinned; the former will never be annihilated, even if they "have committed sins."[5] "If Israel goes into exile, it will return to Erets-Yisrael." Israel therefore will continue to exist as Israel while in exile; it will continue to exist with its own identity and inner integrity. This will remain intact in spite of possible "external" errors that Israel may have committed.[6] Israel will be able to return as Israel to its own country, Erets-Yisrael. How truly history bears witness to the trustworthiness of this Divine guarantee.[7]

Thus Israel alone knows the meaning of the Galut; lives through it and re-emerges from it, for it "will never be lost." Israel alone is a people of the Galut, on the one hand because of their exceptional ability to adapt themselves amid other nations, and on the other hand because of their persistent obstinacy in wanting to remain constantly and enduringly themselves. Though any Jew as an individual may become assimilated during Exile, as a community the Jewish people is non-assimilative;[8] they do not wish to become assimilated within the nations among whom they live; they can be distinguished from the others by their behavior; they "keep their covenant with God." For this reason the Midrash concludes, "Even if the nations of the world are exiled, their Galut is not a true Galut."[9] Israel *cannot* let themselves be assimilated by the nations whose "guests" they are because they find no "tranquility" among them.[10]

The Sages of Israel used the following metaphor to express the reality of Jewish exile: "Israel is like oil; just as oil does not mix with water, Israel does not mingle with the other nations."[11] Even Balaam, the non-Israelite, said they were "a people that dwells alone, that does not account itself one with the nations" (Num. 23:9).[12] Israel's peculiarity, which is its privilege, is accentuated by the isolation within which "the nations of the world" confine it. In doing so, they reinforce Israel's identity which centers around its point of departure and its return—Erets-Yisrael. And in its turn Erets-Yisrael is centered, like the People of Israel, on the Torah of God which makes the Land of Israel God's Land and the People of Israel God's People: "Israel lives in security, the tribes of Jacob *by themselves*, in a land of corn and wine....Happy are you, *people* of Israel, peerless, set free; the Lord is the shield that guards you" (Deut. 33:28-29.)[13] This special situation of peculiarity and isolation is in fact vital so that Israel can maintain its own existence in the midst of other nations and with their goodwill.

Exile and diaspora

Indeed, the Jewish Galut is not only exile but also *pizur, pezura, tefutsa, tefutsot*; it is also "diaspora."[14] It is a diaspora or dispersion with a symbolic meaning. For this dispersion is found, according to the Midrash, in the four great and powerful "kingdoms," which according to the Maharal and Sefat Emet[15] are opposed to the Kingdom of God. It is also a dispersion with a purpose, for it is spread to the *"four* corners of the earth," to the *"four* winds of the earth," conveying there, according to the Zohar, the Ari HaKadosh and the Maharal, the message of God; Israel transmits this message in the name of God, the name expressed in essence by the *"four* letters of the Tetragrammaton."[16]

The Jewish Galut is thus imprinted upon Israel's flesh and upon the spirit of other peoples, upon Israel's existence and upon the life of the nations, upon Israel's history and upon that of the peoples of the world—upon the life of humanity itself. Simultaneously the Jewish Galut and deeply marks them all.

Above all, the Jewish Galut has also a supra-historical character, a meta-historical dimension: it has a metaphysical value. It is not only desired by God; it involves God in the fate of Israel ("the salvation of Israel is the salvation of God"!), and thereby in the fate of the world, to which He is bound—Israel being the intermediary.[17] Indeed God goes with Israel into exile; He is present there in His *Shekhinah*.[18] And so by His own exile God signifies to every man that he (man) is himself in exile.

In truth Israel's Galut makes man aware of the fact that, although he may be living in his own country, he is in reality in exile; in turning away from God Who is close to him but whom he ignores, and in turning away from Israel, the people of God, who are close to him but whom he keeps at a distance, regarding them and treating them as "strangers"—this man is really cutting himself off from his own country, turning away from his own people, separating himself from his neighbor and finally dividing himself from himself, from his inner being.[19]

The Jewish Galut, by its special nature, and its unusual character, by its very "exclusiveness," not only has a universal dimension because of its vast geographical extent, but it contains above all a lofty human significance "because of the questions it arouses in man."[20] In truth, the exile of the Jews ought to excite in the minds of their "rulers" a serious range of problems that are religious, spiritual and moral; it ought to lead them to an earnest consideration of their own humanity, to a thorough examination of their relationship with God, with their environment, both natural and social, and with each other. In fact in the Jewish Galut, the Maharal observes—in this situation which is "forced," "un-structured," "a-substantial," "special" and yet "provisional," "confused," which is "abnormal," "against nature" but also "supernatural"—there exists a "providential" factor which is called upon to awaken, to arouse and so to educate the conscience of every human being living on "God's earth."[21] (Four centuries after the Maharal, Albert Camus, with his own particular perspective, and the writers of the Jewish-American school, with their particular perspective, have tackled the theme of the Exile and the Stranger.)

Israel's slavery in Egypt, prototype of all the exiles

The Jewish Galut thus cannot be regarded simply as a judgment of God upon Israel for their sins.[22] (Christian theology which has lent credence to the idea that the Jewish exile began with the destruction of the Second Temple in 70 A.D., *after* the death of Jesus—and as a consequence of it!—has no foundation in history.) In reality *Galut Bavel*, the Babylonian exile, began with the destruction of the first Temple, that is, six centuries before *Galut Edom*, the Roman exile. By the time the Second Temple was destroyed the Jewish Galut had already become a matter of great importance.

Jewish religious doctrine sees the beginning of the Galut in the *Shibbud Mitsrayim*, the slavery of the Israelites in Egypt. The enslavement of the "children of Israel" in the land of the Pharaohs, according to Rabbi Yitshak Luria, marks not only the beginning of the Jewish galuyot, but is the very symbol, properly speaking the model, the "prototype" and "equivalent" of all the exiles.[23] This is the reason, states the Rambam, why the people of Israel were prohibited from returning to Egypt,[24] for, as Israel, they had already completed their exilic task there, as the Ari HaKadosh observes, both as regards their own life—having been purified, and as regards the Egyptians—having led them to "know God."[25]

The Galut of the Israelites in Egypt remains for ever the symbol of all the other exiles, all the *Shibbudim* of Israel in the *Malkhuyot*, the "Kingdoms" by each of which in turn Israel was later oppressed.

In fact Egypt, by its very name, *Mitsrayim*, is still the typical example of the country, state or nation that persecutes Israel. *Kol haMalkhuyot Nikrau Al Shem Mitsrayim, Al Shem SheHayu Metsirot LeYisrael.* "All the (oppressor) kingdoms," says the Midrash, "are called by the name of Mitsrayim because they have oppressed Israel."[26] Indeed the *Galut Mitsrayim* is a model of *tsar*, of human beings being kept in "straits," by the *tsara*, "sufferings" both physical and moral which are inflicted by the *tsorer*, the "enemy" of God and of mankind upon the men they had enslaved—and from whom they exacted forced labor. The *Galut Mitsrayim* was a model established by the *tsorer mitsri*, the "Egyptian enemy," from which its successors profited. By putting the Israelite boys to death, by intending to exterminate the Israelite "race," by having "every new-born male child thrown into the river,"[27] the *tsorer mitsri* demonstrated to their successors how to implement a veritable genocide. This infamous example and other criminal plans for the annihilation of Israel were later to be taken up, expanded and "brought to perfection" over the centuries by the *Mitsrayim* in all the *Malkhuyot*. These plans were to be "systematically" improved and carried out in accordance with "scientific methods," notably by the *Tsorer HaYehudim* of our time, Adolf Hitler, and his henchmen and "collaborators."

A punishment disproportionate to the sin

To be sure, seen in relation to the order of the visible world, the *Galut* is a direct consequence of Israel's transgressions against the Torah; it is the result of Israel's immediate or long-term disobedience towards God, the Lawgiver of the Torah. The sudden event of the Galut is represented in the Talmud and Midrash in simple, incisive terms: "The Israelites sinned and went into exile," "Israel angered God and left to go into exile."[28]

Israel sinned. But their sin was a "sin of greatness": *Het SheBeGadlut*.[29] Their sin is judged not in relation to its intrinsic importance (that is, its gravity), but rather on account of the greatness of the sinner, their innate capacity for abstaining from sin and, as the Shelah HaKadosh observes, because of the greatness of their ancestors, their "forefathers," of the *avot*.[30] If the sins Israel committed had been committed by other nations, they would not have brought down on those peoples a Divine judgment so prompt or so severe as that suffered by Israel, says the Midrash.[31] Nor is there any comparison between the sins of the "nations of the world" and those of Israel: the former are always more numerous, more grievous and more continuous, says the Maharal.[32] However, the prophet Amos had already warned Israel in these words, "It is you alone whom I have singled out among all the families of the earth, wherefore I demand a reckoning for all your errors!"[33]

Israel's severe chastisement is thus not in direct proportion to the gravity of their sins; on the contrary, it is clearly disproportionate. God Himself recognizes this in saying to Israel, "The sufferings that I have caused you are not in accordance with your deeds."[34] Israel's excessive and exemplary punishment is the consequence of the "advantage" and "privilege" which is entailed in their being "chosen" *by* God; it flows from their special, direct and permanent relationship with their God; it is the result of the particular position they occupy in the world, where they must serve as "witnesses." In fact God "watches" Israel in the least of their acts; He makes them responsible to Himself for the smallest infraction of the rules of living that He has prescribed for them. "When one occupies an important position and is distinguished by his abilities, God punishes him for the least thing, as He punished Moses our master," writes the Maharal.[35] The Talmud and Midrash had already affirmed that "the Holy One, Blessed be He, requires of the just, of the *tsaddikim*, those who are gathered around Him, that they be extremely meticulous in carrying out His commands. He follows their behavior with scrupulous attention and reproaches them for any violation of His prescriptions, even by so much as a hair's breadth."[36] "God metes out punishment to the just for the slightest error, whereas He punishes the wicked only for serious faults."[37]

Thus God is particularly rigorous in punishing Israel, this "people" of whom He says by the word of His prophet Isaiah that He is "proud of them" and that His children are "all of them just."[38] "He punishes them, not to make them suffer, but to bring back to life the fundamentals that they have neglected in their own life."[39]

Punishment and love

Indeed how could God wish to cause suffering to the people of whom He Himself says that He "loves them as the apple of His eye," that "He loves them with an everlasting love" and that "His goodness towards them will not fail?" Would God take pleasure in causing suffering to Israel "whom He loves more than all the nations"? How could He bring suffering to "Israel, His eldest son," "whose sufferings He counted as His own?"[40]

Nevertheless God chastises Israel; but, as He Himself declares, "if He chastises him, it is as a father chastises his son,"[41] "for he whom He loves the Lord chastises as a father chastises the son who is dear to him."[42] Moreover, God too suffers when He metes out punishment to Israel! According to the Talmud, God exclaims concerning the Exile of Israel, "Alas, because of their sins I have exiled My children among the peoples of the world. I have ruined My house, I have burnt My palace. Woe to the Father who has exiled his children! Alas, that they were driven away from their Father's table!"[43] God is not only wounded by Israel's exile; He is full of remorse in His "lamentations," as they are perceived in the Midrash and handed down to us. God cries out in His sorrow, sharing the sorrow of Israel, "O how I would love the children of My people to be with Me in Erets-Yisrael, however much they defile it! O how I wish that

Israel might be with Me in Erets-Yisrael, even though they disobey Me."[44]

Thus it cannot be that God takes pleasure in punishing Israel in order to make them suffer. He does so out of love for their ultimate good.[45] It is precisely because He loves Israel, because He says to Israel, "You are the children of the Lord your God,"[46] that God *chooses* for Israel, His *chosen* people, the punishment of Exile.[47] He chooses *this* punishment in accordance with the spirit and the letter of His covenant with Israel. In fact this punishment will demonstrate even more clearly His love for Israel and His presence among them. For it is the punishment of Exile, and in particular the Dispersion,[48] which clearly shows that it is the Father who is punishing His child and is yet not leaving him to perish. The assurance is given — by the very prophet who announced the exile — that the "remnant of Israel" will live to experience "the salvation of His people," "brought back, and gathered together from the ends of the earth, and led once again to the abundant springs." In truth, the Lord says, "I am a father to Israel, Ephraim is My first-born!"[49]

Had God wished only to punish Israel out of mere love of punishment, He could have done so on the spot, in their own country, in Erets-Yisrael itself, and there brought about their death and disappearance.[50] But God "does not desire the death of a sinner; rather that he may turn from his way so that he may live."[51] This is why He chooses for Israel the punishment of exile, so that Israel may live. The characteristic of *Jewish* exile is that it shall persuade Israel and indeed the whole world, by means of the very punishment itself, that it is impossible to annihilate the Jewish people. In fact, "God sends Israel into exile, yet He swears He will not leave them there."[52] He watches over the Jews in their torment but never abandons them.[53] In the Torah God had clearly stated, "Yet even then, when they find themselves banished in their enemies' land, I shall not have rejected nor spurned them, bringing them to an end and so breaking My covenant with them, because I am the Lord their God."[54] And the wise men of Israel clung to the last words of this Divine statement to emphasize the strength and validity of God's promise to Israel: "I am the Lord their God" — that is to say, "In future no nation or culture will be able to put Israel in subjection for ever." Experience has shown and history demonstrates that during the various exiles Israel has in the end remained indestructible. In Egypt, during the enslavement of Israel, God had proclaimed to Moses, *"Ehyeh asher Ehyeh"* — "I will be what I will be." And the wise men of Israel found in this statement, of the future, something of the personality of God and His links with Israel an irrefutable promise of the Lord; "I will be with them in their present distress, I who will be with them in their servitude under other rulers."[55] And in truth, "because I, the Lord, do not change, you also, children of Jacob, have not been destroyed!"[56] A link was established between the Lord "Who is in exile with Israel," and Israel who find themselves with God in exile; it is a link which cannot be broken, for one of the partners is the Eternal One and the other has its roots in the Eternal, and what is eternal, as the Maharal observes, does not change.

Galut (exile) and Israel's continuing survival

It is precisely in His choice of exile as Israel's punishment that God "removes" Israel from the "natural," "normal" order of the life of the nations; He removes them from the usual, visible, natural-historical order and places them "outside" in a "non-visible" area.

Before making the covenant with Abraham and bringing him the *bessorah*, the "news"—both of the land which He promised to his descendants and the exile which He proclaimed for his children (these two forecasts made up one single and unique *bessorah*!), God caused "Abram" "to go outside"; "He led him out" and said to him, "Look now towards heaven."[57] Thus He showed to the first Hebrew (according to the Talmud, the Zohar and the great Hebrew Bible commentators)[58] that He was putting him, Abraham and with him his descendants, Israel, outside the natural order; He was raising him, and with him his descendants, above that order: placing Israel in direct subordination to Himself.[59] He was placing them under personal obedience to Himself, or to use Rashi's expression,[60] "God took him out of the sphere of the world and carried him up above the stars. That is why the Biblical text uses the verb *habet*, which means 'to look down from above.'"

The status of Israel in the world, in history, was thus not to be a part of the established *natural* order, the preconceived order of succession and repetition in history, but part of the order of a conceived, miraculous *creation*: of the order of a creation which is continuous and "is renewed every day by the grace of God's goodness."

The exile (Galut) and in particular the dispersion (Pezura) of Israel, therefore, is not so much a reflection of God's retributive justice as it is a witness to His Divine mercy towards Israel. If there had not been this extraordinary mercy, asks the Talmud, "how could this people have been able to exist on its own amid so many hostile nations?"[61]

Normally exile consigns an exiled people to destruction, whether through death by violence or by other means. The deportees of the past were condemned to die either by being physically exterminated or by the elimination of their identity; they would all in time die a "natural" death. Thus it is that the "nations of the world" succeed one another and mingle with one another. They absorb one another: those who are invaded are absorbed by the invaders; the invaders are absorbed by those they invade.[62]

This did not happen with Israel. When God announced to Abraham the "frightening" decision concerning the Galut, the exile and dispersion of Israel, at the same time He gave him a guarantee "against annihilation," an assurance of continuation and survival.[63] And in addition He affirmed that the personality of Israel would not only be preserved but be strengthened as a result of their suffering in exile;[64] the suffering would make the character of the "stiff-necked people" even firmer, more resolute and unshakable.[65]

Thus there is an intimate connection between Israel's obvious eternal quality, active continuity and fruitful existence and God's eternal quality, His active continuity and His creative existence in the world. Though the historical circumstances that intervene may vary, neither God nor Israel "change" their original essence, their mutual relationship, the redemptive goal they extend to one another; and so, in the words of the prophet Malachi,[66] the unbroken survival of Israel is directly connected with the eternal nature of God;[67] it is experienced in the association of God with Israel, who find themselves always on the way to redemption. "Yes, I shall be with you, says the Lord, to save you; though I make an end of all the nations whither I have scattered you, yet will I not make an end of you; I will chastise you as you deserve, but will not eradicate you altogether" (Jer. 30:11).[68]

"Behold, I, the Lord God, have my eyes on this sinful kingdom, and I will wipe it off the face of the earth. Yet I will not wipe out the family of Jacob root and branch, says the Lord. For lo, I will command, and I will shake the house of Israel to and fro through all the nations as a sieve is shaken to and fro—and *not one grain* shall fall to the ground.... On that day I will restore David's fallen tabernacle; I will repair its gaping walls and restore its ruins, and I will rebuild it as it was long ago.... Behold, a time is coming, says the Lord, when the ploughman shall overtake the reaper, and he who treads the grapes, him who sows the seed.... I shall bring back the captives of My people Israel; they shall rebuild the devastated cities and live in them, they shall plant vineyards and drink their wine, make gardens and eat the fruit. Then will I plant them on their own soil, and they shall never again be uprooted from the soil I have given them. The Lord your God has spoken" (Amos 9:8-15; see Ibn Ezra and Radak *ad loc.*).

In the view of Montesquieu, and later Oswald Spengler, Paul Valery and Arnold Toynbee, "civilizations are transitory"; as one civilization fades, it gives place to another. In the sight of the Torah, the Talmud, the Midrash, the Zohar, in the view of Rabbi Yehuda HaLevi and the Maharal, when through their sins the "nations of the world" reach "the fullness of the measure," the height of corruption, when they reach the lowest depths of "decadence" — they die and vanish "naturally."[69] Israel itself, being in exile, "ascends and descends" like the angels Jacob saw in his dream, "but never sinks completely," "is never annihilated"; "Israel endures forever!" exclaims the Midrash Tanhuma. "The arrows launched against Israel are all used up ... but yet Israel is not exterminated." "The sufferings inflicted on Israel run out, and Israel is still alive."[70] Israel is in exile, scattered, but returns as Israel to its own country, Erets-Yisrael, as God promised Abraham and Moses.[71]

Abraham sought to know whether his descendants "would be worthy" to be entitled to possess the Promised Land forever, if they should disobey God and the Torah.[72] (Rashi writes: "When Abram asks, in relation to the Promised Land, *Bama eida*, 'Whereby shall I know that I shall inherit it?' [Gen. 15:8], it is not that Abram was asking God for a sign, but asking, 'Let me know how my sons may be worthy to keep it.'") And it was the patriarch himself who, on the advice of God, "chose the punishment of exile" for his descendants if they should be disobedient to God and transgress against the *mitzvot* of the Torah; he himself "chose" for them the punishment of being dispersed in the "kingdoms of their persecutors." The chastisement of exile is painful, but it will inevitably come to an end, says the Maharal.[73] So Abraham was assured of the continuing survival of Israel in this world and its eternal existence in the world to come.[74]

After undergoing the ordeals of circumcision and the *Akedah* (the "binding of Isaac"), Abraham received God's confirmation that no sin of his descendants would make Israel disappear or prevent their return to Erets-Yisrael; in addition God promised Abraham the final, complete, Messianic salvation of Israel.[75] As for Jacob, who like his grandfather was anxious about the "worthiness" of his children and their future relations with God and Erets-Yisrael, he in his turn received the Lord's assurance that "his children will outlive all the 'kingdoms' that persecute them"; Israel will exist for ever, to all eternity.[76]

Today and for ever Israel stands firm, for they are before the Lord their

God. And Rashi states, "You (you Israelites) have often displeased God, but yet He has not exterminated you and you have been always in His presence."[77] It could not be otherwise. For "you who have bound yourselves to the Lord your God, you must all be living today!"[78]

"Sufferings of love"

Israel suffers in exile. Bound irrevocably to the Lord their God, they nevertheless succeed in neglecting "the covenant of the Lord God of their fathers ... and the Lord has taken them from their soil in anger, and cast them into another country as can be seen today."[79] The Exile is indeed Divine punishment, and Israel suffers in Exile. "It is true," says the Talmud, "that there is no suffering without sin,"[80] yet "there is no suffering that God causes Israel to undergo which has not its origin in God's love for Israel and is not for the good of Israel," as is stated in the Midrash and confirmed by the Shelah HaKadosh.[81]

While it is a faithful interpreter of Jewish optimism, the Midrash believes that in fact "there is no life, no real life, without suffering." It is in the counsel of the wise King Solomon of the Bible that the Sages of the Midrash (and later Rabbi Nahman of Bratslav) find justification for this religious existentialist conception. Indeed in the Proverbs of Solomon we find written, "Correction that leads to instruction is the path of life."*[82]

Tradition adds its weight to this idea of the Midrash (although, on the other hand, sayings in the Midrash celebrate life's happiness). "Abraham began" his life "with suffering." Isaac even asked God for it. Jacob bore suffering for the greater part of his life."[83]

Yet Israel, which has already been terribly tested over a long period, like Jacob, does not "seek" suffering.[84] Their fundamental hope is to "observe God's laws and live in them."[85] But if suffering comes, they accept it, welcome it calmly, in "silence," and even consider it valuable. "Suffering is loved" by Israel — 'havivim yessurim' — for "it atones for sin more than sacrifices do" and above all because it is the visible sign of the

---

* "Man is born to famine," "to trouble," cries Eliphaz in the book of Job (5:7). The Maharal, in meditating on human misery (but not forgetting human greatness), concedes the truth of this cry by the interlocutor of the Biblical personification of tragedy — tragedy not in the Greek sense, since Job's is not the result of fate, or the caprice of the gods, and what is more it does not paralyze human action! Even Hermann Cohen, the modern apologist for the Hebrew prophets' active optimism, observes that fundamentally "suffering is revealed as being man's essence.... If you wish," he says, "to know what man is, know him in his suffering." (*Die Religion der Vernunft aus den Quellen des Judentums*, Leipzig, 1919, p. 171.)

covenant that God wishes to make with Israel. Thus He wishes suffering to seal or "carve" the covenant — '*berit keruta*'; and consequently "He causes His Name to rest on him who suffers."[86]

And so Israel regards the sufferings that overwhelm them as "sufferings of love" which they receive "with joy."[87] They know that suffering will remove their sins and above all they feel that "thanks" to it they "come closer" to God and place themselves, even here below, "under the wings of the *Shekhinah*," under the protection of the immediate Presence of God; they will find there their ultimate shelter in the realms above, in the "joy of the world to come," which is "reserved" for them, which "awaits" them.[88] Thus the *Shekhinah*, here below, is "with them in their distress"; "it goes with them everywhere in their exile (Galut)"[89] ... (as we have already said) and the Exile is Jewish because Israel suffers there. (This is why "the nations of the world, even if they are exiled, are not in Galut, for they do not suffer as Israel does".)[90]

The anguish that Israel endures, especially in the Galut, "in no way prevents them from praying to God"; on the contrary, suffering "incites them to pray," in fervent entreaty.*[91] It must not be expected that the sorrows and in particular the sorrows of Exile drive Israel to rebel against God or provoke them to "deny" God. Quite the contrary. When the "nations of the world" ask, "Where is their God?"; when the "nations of the world" urge them to repudiate a "God who does evil" — Israel replies by complete submission to God, by giving to Him their whole being; they "sanctify" and glorify "His Name." Israel feels God closest precisely at the moment when they call to Him with the profound cry of the Psalmist: *Eli, Eli, lama azavtani*, "My God, my God, why have You forsaken me?" It is in that very moment that Israel feels, with utter

---

* Myriam (now Mrs. Myriam Schönberger, living in the State of Israel) was 13 years old when she was deported from Hungary to Auschwitz by the Nazis. When they arrived at the extermination camp she and her friend, Ruth, who was the same age and from the same country, were separated from their parents. The parents died in the crematoria. Myriam and Ruth, who belonged to the group of "twinned children," were chosen by Mengele, the infamous "doctor" at the extermination camp, to be subjected to his cruel "scientific" experiments. Myriam recalls that "we had with us (at Auschwitz) a book of prayers that we had brought from home. At home we had been taught to read Hebrew. We always prayed (in Hebrew), without understanding very well what was written (in the book of prayers). In Auschwitz this book of prayers was our only source of hope, our only comfort. One day the woman guard whom we had nicknamed 'the Snake' because of the way she behaved, snatched the book from our hands, boxed our ears and shouted, 'After all that's happened to you, do you still dare to believe in God?' She hid the book, but Ruth managed to find it again and so we got it back..." (*Ma'ariv*, Tel Aviv, 19 January 1979).

conviction, that God will not leave them!⁹²

In their agonies, especially those of exile, Israel feel themselves even more drawn towards God and experience an ever closer attachment to Him. "Fleeing from Him they run to Him," wrote Rabbi Shlomo ibn Gabirol; "they persist in wanting to be near Him, even if they think God is trying to drive them away from Him," says Rabbi Mendel of Kotsk.* Israel takes refuge with Him; they bind themselves to God, trust in God with total faith;⁹³ thus they can discern even more clearly His "hidden" face which, though it seems to be "angry," is really filled with love and compassion; thus they see that this apparently "angry" face is really the sad face of a "father" who punishes his son, who temporarily "drives him away from his house" and "from his table," but follows him with his eyes, "watches him," "protects him," waits for him."⁹⁴ So suffering ceases to be suffering. Exile ceases to be exile.

This *emunah*, this unshakable "faith" in God has in our day also inspired Jewish believers, the victims of Nazi oppression, during their march towards death. Before the eyes of their executioners, legions of Jews dug their own graves or went into the gas ovens of Auschwitz singing the Jewish hymn of faith: *"Ani ma'amin..."* — "I believe..."

Very moving, but supremely characteristic, are the *Divrei Torah* ("Words from the Torah") addressed by Rabbi Kalonymos Shapira to his followers in the Warsaw Ghetto between 1940 and 1942. The manuscript of these "Words" was discovered in the ruins of the Ghetto in

---

* Even earlier Rabbi Bahya ibn Pakudah had written, "If he overwhelms them they give thanks; if He defeats them they are patient and simply feel greater love, greater surrender. A 'pious man' rose in the night and said,
O my God You have left me to hunger,
You have left me
In the Shadows of the night,
Abandoned.
But if by Your sovereign glory
You should consume me in flame and fire,
Let nothing grow in me but my love for You,
My joy in Your bosom.
And Job too said,
Though He slay me yet will I trust in Him (Job 13:15).
The Torah expresses this offering of self thus:
Thou shalt love the Lord thy God
With all thy heart and all thy soul (Deut. 6:5),
(even if He demand your soul of you, TB Berakhot 54a)."
(*Hovot Halevavot*, from the translation by André Chouraqui, *Introduction aux Devoirs des Coeurs*, pp. 583-584.)

1956 and published in Jerusalem in 1960 under the title *Eish Kodesh* ("The Fire of Holiness"). The following is an extract: "... Truly there is no reason for questioning God ... It is true that sufferings like ours only happen once every few hundred years. But how can we claim to understand God's actions, or be unfaithful when we do not understand them? If we cannot understand the mystery of a single blade of grass made by God, how could we understand spiritual things; how could we grasp His thought (praise be to Him)? How could we wish to grasp with our intelligence what He (praise be) knows and understands? ... but this is what we say: we must offer Him our souls, our beings, not letting our *emunah*, our faith in Him be shaken. We believe with a perfect faith that all (that He does) is just; that all (that He does) He does out of His love for Israel."[95] "We have the faith," the martyred Rabbi said, "that all God does for us, even when He strikes us, all is for our good."[96]

As a complement to this declaration of faith made in the very "fire" of suffering, here is part of a letter, the last sent by Rabbi Kalonymos Shapiro's namesake, Rabbi Shraga Shapiro, to his friends at the end of 1943; he was at that time in a Nazi extermination camp: "As you see, the words of the Bible are being fulfilled in me: 'While I was on the way, the Lord led me' [cf. Gen. 24:27] .... I am glad of this, for a Jew should learn to serve God in any situation. I say it here, and we all say it in our prayer, '*Ashreinu ma tov helkeinu!*' 'How happy are we! How fair is our lot!' People will say that it is hard to understand this phrase from the liturgy in the circumstances in which I now find myself. But in truth, is there any people (like the people of Israel) who wherever they go, wherever they find themselves, are able to take all their goods with them, namely the Torah and the *mitzvot*, or are conscious that God (blessed be the Holy One) is with them? And so, why be troubled? I am happy. Individuals greater than we have accepted suffering for the faith with joy, and as for how can I not appreciate (this privilege)?"[97] The Rabbi was here referring to the famous Tanna Rabbi Akiba who was renowned for his love of God, the Torah, Israel and Erets-Yisrael, and was tortured to death by the Romans in the second century. The Talmud thus describes his death:[98] "'Happy are you, Akiba,' his companion said, 'to have been seized for the sake of religion' ... When they led Rabbi Akiba out to be tortured it was the hour for the reading of the *Shema*, the Jewish profession of faith (Deut. 6:4), 'Hear, O Israel, the Lord our God is One.' While they were tearing away his flesh with iron tongs, he was welcoming the yoke of the kingdom of heaven. 'Master,' his disciples said, 'the ordeal is enough.' 'All my life,' he replied, 'I have been tormented by not having been able to put into practice literally the words, "Thou shalt love the Lord thy

God ... with all thy soul," that is, even at the cost of your life, and I used to ask myself, "When shall I be able to fulfill this precept?" How happy I am today to be able to fulfill it!' He drew out the word *ehad* (one) until he had given up the ghost. A heavenly voice was heard to say, 'Happy are you, Rabbi Akiba, for your spirit left you while you were uttering the word *ehad* (one).'"*

Galut and purification

In the Mishnah Rabbi Akiba recalls the words of the Torah that the children of Israel are "the children of the Lord, their God," and it is he, Rabbi Akiba, who calls on the children of Israel in the Mishnah to count themselves "happy to be able to *purify* themselves before their Father who is in heaven."[100]

"God does not destroy the progeny of Israel, but He punishes them by purifying them," writes the Gaon of Vilna.[101]

Galut mekhaperet avon. "Exile purifies (Israel) of its sins," and "the generation that shall see the coming of the son of David (the Messiah) will have been melted down and remolded again and again."[102]

In fact, since the *Shibbud Mitsrayim*, the slavery in Egypt, Exile has meant for Israel a means of being "melted down" — *tseiruf*, "cleansed" — *zikukh*; a process of refinement and clarification — *beirur*; a road to restoration — *tikkun*.[103]

"Cleansing" (*zikukh*) through exile is a painful but health-giving process not only of education, healing and regeneration, but also of creation.[104]

God puts Israel "in the crucible" to refine it like gold, so that it comes out purified of its imperfections and restored to its real worth. The process of refining confers its reality upon the nation as it does upon gold, and gives it strength and durability. "The fire of the furnace purifies Israel," says the Maharal; "it gives it purity and spiritual strength."[105]

The purpose of the Galut, therefore, is to "put an end to sins" and "not to put an end to the sinners."[106] Liberated once and for all from the malign influence of its sins, Israel is not only left alive; in turning again to

---

* In the Middle Ages, and especially during the time of the Crusades, and the Inquisition, when Jews suffered terrible tortures and went to the stake, they welcomed their martyrdom for the faith uttering the words of the *Shema* "with joy" following the example of Rabbi Akiba. Simon Bernfeld in his *Sefer HaDema'ot* (Book of Tears) quotes many instances of such deaths "for the sanctification of the Name" of God, *Al Kiddush Hashem*.[99]

God, the Giver of life, Israel is restored to a new life,[107] a real life, full and lasting; this life surpasses in worth the life Israel led before it sinned, which was a "tested" life;[108] it is better in quality; a spontaneous life, it is "much" closer to the Source of Life than it was in the past at the dawn of creation.

"When these things have befallen you, the blessing and the curse of which I have offered you the choice, if you and your sons take them to heart there in all the countries to which the Lord your God has banished you, if you turn back to Him and obey Him heart and soul in all that I command you this day, then the Lord your God will show you compassion and restore your fortunes. He will gather you again from all the countries to which He has scattered you. Even though He were to banish you to the four corners of the world, the Lord your God will gather you from there, from there He will fetch you home. The Lord your God will bring you into the land which your forefathers occupied, and you will occupy it again; then He will bring you prosperity and make you more numerous than your forefathers were" (Deut. 30:1-5).[109]

Thus Israel is inspired in its wanderings and sufferings by a new, compelling breath of life; Israel has conquered its faults and emerged victorious and strengthened both spiritually and materially: "Israel has established its heart in God and observes the commandments of the Torah down to the soles of its feet,"[110] everything that is physical in them, all that is materially close to the earth is become spiritual. Having tested Israel in the crucible of affliction, "the crucible of iron," and "withdrawn them from the furnace, in order to fulfill the promise He made to their forefathers, to give them a land flowing with milk and honey," God assures them that "He has made them His heirs, they are His people and He is their God; His glory He has not given to another." Israel, who made a covenant with God, and swore to Him that they will not exchange Him for another God, respect their oath; they realize that God, Who made a covenant with them and swore not to exchange them for another people, has likewise respected His oath.[111]

Responsibility of Israel's persecutors

It has to be acknowledged, therefore, after this process of *zikukh* (purification) and *teshuvah* (return) of Israel to God, which, as the Midrash and the Zohar say, is in fact "Pharaoh drawing near" to the children of Israel to destroy them — *Phar'oh hi-kriv* — this has "brought them to the *teshuvah*, the road of return" to God — *kariv lon liTeshuvah*! For when "the Divine punishment overtook them, the children of Israel in their distress could only turn to God," "lifting their eyes to Him," "pouring their hearts out in silent prayer" before Him.[112]

And must it not be acknowledged, with the Talmud, that when Israel does not of its own accord carry out the *teshuvah*, "The Holy One blessed be He raises up against them a king whose edicts are as severe as those of Haman (who sought to destroy all the Jews living in the kingdom of Ahasuerus), so that in this way Israel does perform *teshuvah*"?[113]

Indeed, God has "the olives pressed so that the oil runs out."[114] God "had Israel chained," and then later freed them to make them into an emancipated people, "liberated not only from physical pain, moral suffering, and material slavery in exile in the 'kingdoms,' but also from the metaphysical agony of death." The people of Israel thus acquire a genuine liberty; they are "free, in keeping the commandments of the Torah";[115] they are free in this world, in keeping the commandments of the Torah which come from another world, and which assures them life without end in "the world to come."

It is certainly true that Pharaoh and the Assyrian, "rod of Mine anger," Haman and the rest, were instruments used by God to "bring back" Israel to Himself when His people tried to escape from Him; He "raised up" despots against Israel to make the people of the Torah observe the laws prescribed in the Torah, and so to ensure the survival of the world, its continued existence.[116]

However, this service which was "voluntarily" and even "gleefully"[117] rendered to God by the Pharaohs and their successors, gave them no authority to usurp the place of God and set themselves up as judges over Israel; it gave them no authority to interpret the thoughts of God, for "their thoughts are not My thoughts and their ways are not My ways, says the Lord."[118] Haman and his successors could not arrogate to themselves the "right" and much less assume the "duty" to carry out the "sanctions" of God against Israel and themselves "punish" Israel "in the name of God" (or "to fall upon Israel under the pretext of avenging the death of a god!"). This "service" which they hastened to render to God and which God *did not ask of them*, in no way exempted them from their moral obligation, or absolved them from making proper use of their "free will."[119] Their power and duty was to act towards Israel as towards any other person or nation, according to the "seven commandments" that God had ordained for the "sons of Noah" and made known to them — which He has engraved on the conscience of every man. The fact is that these fundamental Divine commandments contain the implication not only of respect for the Creator but also respect for His creatures and especially for the human being, his faith, his possessions, and his life.[120]

God thus holds the Pharaohs, the Assyrians, the Hamans and their successors responsible for their misdeeds; their crimes perpetrated against Israel will in no way be absolved.

It is true that "God said to Abraham, 'Know this for certain, that your descendants will be aliens living in a land that is not theirs; they will be slaves and will be held in oppression....But I will punish that nation whose slaves they are'" (Gen. 15:13-14).

Pharaoh and the Egyptians would, in fact, be punished by God, inasmuch as the proclamation made by God to Abraham, as well as the warnings, the *tokhahot* given to Israel about the *galuyot* they would undergo if they violated the Law of the Torah (Lev. 26 and Deut. 28), did not state the names of their persecutors.[122] No invitation was extended to them to oppress and enslave Israel; nor was any "justification" provided for the griefs they inflicted on this people with such joyous persistence. The proclamation made by God to Abraham about the enslavement of his descendants did not rescind the freedom of action of Pharaoh[123] or his successors who manifest so violently their hatred towards Israel; the Divine proclamation does not excuse the crimes they commit against this people. Tyrants overpower Israel with so many sufferings because they themselves "sin and wish to do evil to Israel who are in their country," and "God never orders man to do wrong" to his neighbor: so states the Rambam emphatically.[124] "God therefore judges the people who enslave" Israel, "and also," say the Midrash and Rashi, "the four kingdoms which enslave Israel." They will themselves disappear "because they have associated themselves with the enslavement of Israel."[125] The proclamation by God of Israel's oppression does not free their future persecutors from their duty and ability to act in conformity with the Divine command to love one's neighbor. These tyrants and nations that oppress Israel will therefore be punished on "the Day of the Lord"[126] for their sins, which are numerous and grave because they have not respected the "seven commandments of the Sons of Noah." In addition they will be punished for having caused Israel terrible suffering, because he who makes Israel suffer makes God suffer. They themselves have made Israel suffer because they hate the people of God; therefore, they will be punished because those who are the enemies of Israel are the enemies of God; they will be punished "measure for measure," taking account of the evil they have done to Israel.[127]

In fact, Pharaoh, the Egyptians and those who come after them will be punished also for their ingratitude towards the people of Joseph, the people of the various "Josephs" who have helped them in times of difficulty;[128] they will be punished for the massacre of Israelite children;* they will be punished for their inhuman exploitation of the physical strength of their Israelite slaves;[129] they will be punished for the moral humiliation and religious persecution they have inflicted on Israel.

God will "bring retribution on those who hate Him," says the Bible. For, as it is written in the Ramban, "those who have done so much evil to Israel did it not for 'the name of Heaven,' but out of hatred of the Holy One, blessed be He. They bore Israel hatred not because — like themselves — Israel committed the sin of idolatry, but because Israel did not act like themselves, because Israel served the Holy One (blessed be He) and kept His commandments; because they faced death for Him, every day. It is out of hatred for the Holy One (blessed be He) that they have done so much ill to Israel; they are therefore indeed 'His enemies' (enemies of God)."[130]

Knowledge of this Divine love and justice gave David authority to address God in these words: "Pour out Your wrath over nations which do not know You and over kingdoms which do not invoke You by name; see how they have devoured Jacob and laid waste his homesteads" (this was indeed the only goal they pursued in attacking Israel). "Do not remember against us the guilt of past generations.... Help us, O God our savior, for the honor of Your name.... Why should the nations ask, 'Where is their God?'" "O God, be neither silent nor still, for Your enemies are making a tumult, and those that hate You carry their heads high. They devise cunning schemes against Your people.... 'Come, away with them,' they cry, 'let them be a nation no longer, let Israel's name be remembered no more.' With one mind they have agreed together to

---

* In the Warsaw Ghetto (between 1940 and 1942) Rabbi Kalonymos Shapira wrote, "The continuing existence of Israel in this world is effected thanks to the children. This is why the first enemy of Israel, Pharaoh, fell upon Israel's little children; he gave the order, 'Every newborn boy is to be thrown into the river' (Exod. 1:22). Thus Israel's enemies are always particularly cruel towards the little children, either massacring or forcibly converting them. Today we can also see with stricken hearts how the cruelty they employ in killing our children exceeds anything one could have imagined.... Our whole existence in this world we owe to our children and grandchildren; and when the murderers destroy them they destroy us, they destroy our very existence. That is why in our prayers we say, 'Our Father, our King, have pity on *us* and on our *children*,' for they, our children, are not just themselves; it is we who are in them.... And indeed it is amazing that the world still exists after hearing so many children's cries and soaking up so many children's tears.... It is amazing that this world has not turned to water.... It is amazing that the world still stands as if this was none of its concern" (Quoted in *Ani Ma'amin*, by Mordehai Eliav, page 247).

The number of Jewish children massacred by the Nazis was more than one million.

make a league against You. . . . Heap shame on their heads, O Lord, until they confess the greatness of Your name. . . . So let them learn that You alone are Lord, God Most High over all the earth."[131]

David, the minstrel of God's mercy, allowed himself to call on God in such heartrending tones, for God Himself afterwards declared by the word of His prophet Zechariah: "I am very jealous for Jerusalem and Zion. Full of anger am I against the nations that enjoy their ease, because while My anger was but mild, they heaped evil on evil. Therefore, these are the words of the Lord: I have come back to Jerusalem with compassion, and My house shall be rebuilt in her."[132] David calls on God in such imperative tones because it is God Himself who "makes the nations of the world swear not to oppress Israel excessively, not to let their yoke weigh on them too heavily."[133]

"Nevertheless, do not regard
your oppressor with horror"

It is true that David and all Israel asked God to "behold and see" His people groaning under the sufferings inflicted on them by their enemies; they were thereby pleading with Him to take action against those who were oppressing them.[134] However, the very fact that they asked God to act against their persecutors meant that the Israelites refrained from acting for themselves and by themselves, meaning in their own right,[135] against those who had done wrong to them; they would not themselves "avenge" the tribulations of which they were the victims.

With David, Israel besought God that the "sins"—*hata'im*—of their persecutors might "disappear" so that the crimes they were perpetrating against Israel would end, but the Talmud observes that they did not ask God to "make the sinners—*hote'im*—disappear," or let the criminals perish; if the sins disappeared "there would be no more wicked people."[136] That would be enough.

It is for God, therefore, the Supreme Judge, to weigh men's actions, punish the wicked and "avenge the blood of His servants"[137]—"for justice belongs to God,"[138] says the Bible. Indeed "justice belongs to God." "It is for Him to establish a system of rights among His creatures, for He created them so that equity and justice should reign among them," says the Ramban (Nachmanides) in his commentary on this verse from Deuteronomy.[139]

As for Israel, "the servant of God," if he is not in a position, materially or physically, to defend himself against those who rise against him or prevent the crimes being planned against him,[140] "he gives his body to those who strike him and his face to those who insult him,"[141] "he stretches out his neck towards those who would cut his throat";[142] he finds his "strength in being trespassed against without trespassing."[143]

Therefore is it for God to chastise the "Pharaohs," the "Egyptians," the "Edomites," all the numerous "enemies of Israel," should he deem it imperative to do so.

Israel itself received God's express command "not to hate them." This same God who rescued them from slavery in Egypt and saved them from annihilation by the armies of Edom, clearly commanded in the Torah: "You shall not regard an Edomite as an abomination, for he is your own kin; nor yet an Egyptian, for you were strangers in his land" (Deut. 23:8).

In commenting on this verse Rashi wrote, "You shall not hate the Edomite; you shall not hate him at all, even though you may have the right to hate him because he came out against you with raised sword." Yet more: the Edomite—though wishing to destroy Israel—has always remained "his brother" in the eyes of Israel because in fact they have "both the same Father, the same God who created them,"[144] the same God who "in that day," in the days of the Messiah, will be recognized by all nations as the "One God."[145]

"You shall not hate the Egyptian." Though it became—in the words of God Himself in the Decalogue[146]—"a house of bondage" for Israel, the "land of Egypt" had nevertheless been for the first Israelites, Jacob and his family, a country where they lived as "guests" of Pharaoh and the Egyptians.[147] Thus the Sages of Israel say, "You must not cast mud into the well from which you have drunk, for it is written in the Torah, 'You shall not hate the Egyptian, since you were sojourners in his land.'"[148]

"You shall not hate the Egyptian," wrote Rashi, "even though he threw your son into the Nile" (even though, as the Midrash[149] relates, "Pharaoh, being stricken with leprosy, had the little children of Israel massacred so that he could bathe twice a day in their blood"). "You shall not hate the Egyptian." "Why? Because they gave you shelter in your time of need, in the time of famine, under Joseph."

In other words the memory of the suffering inflicted on you by the Edomites, O Israelite, should not make you harbor feelings of hatred against them. And the pains inflicted on you by the Egyptians during your enslavement in their land, O Israelite, should not wipe out all feeling of gratitude to them for having given you food during the time of famine in Canaan. Rashi says also in quite a different context, "In the very place where a man is judged for his misdeeds, his good and just actions must also be remembered."[150]

The lesson to be learned from the slavery in Egypt: "You shall love the stranger as yourself"

"Not to hate the Egyptian" is only the first step towards the love which Israelites must learn to bear them.

Referring to the period when Israel was enslaved in Egypt and recalling to the Israelites their own experience as strangers in that land, the law of the Torah not only forbids them to hate the Egyptians, but requires them to love all strangers. This requirement has religious, historical, psychological, even existential motives which lie in the fact that the Israelites were themselves strangers in Egypt, "themselves and not only their ancestors."

In fact, the Mishnah teaches (and Jews acknowledge this teaching on Passover night), "In each generation, every Jew must think of himself as if he himself had been liberated from the slavery in Egypt, as it is written (in the Book of Exodus): 'And you shall say to your son, This commemorates what the Lord did for me when I came out of Egypt.'"[151] Every generation of Israel, all Israelites in every age are thus directly affected by the slavery of Israel in Egypt and by the Exodus of Israel from Egypt. Consequently the Torah says to every Israelite, to every Jew, "You shall not oppress the alien, for you know how it feels to be an alien; you were aliens yourselves in Egypt" (Exod. 23:9). And the Torah goes even further in its requirements relating to respect for aliens, since it goes so far as to command all Jews throughout the ages, "You too must love the alien, for *you* were once aliens in Egypt" (Deut. 10:19).

In the plan of Divine Providence the slavery of Israel in Egypt had an object which was educative, religious and moral. "You shall not deprive aliens and orphans of justice nor take a widow's cloak in pledge. Remember that you were slaves in Egypt and the Lord your God redeemed you from there; that is why I command you to do this" (Deut. 24:17-18).

If there are constant reminders to the Jew in the Torah that he was a slave in Egypt and that God released him, it is so that he shall appreciate true *liberty*, that which is intrinsic, and not simply extraneous *liberties*, which are forever changing. It is also so that he may convert his status of slave of Pharaoh into that of a free servant of God;[152] that he may aid any man deprived of liberty in regaining it, and finally so that he may assist one who does not yet know the meaning of liberty and wishes to acquire it. This is why a considerable number of *mitzvot* (injunctions) in the Torah, including the most important religious commandments of an ethical nature, make reference to the slavery of Israel in Egypt and to the Exodus from that country.

Among these commandments are two *mitzvot* linked with the "Exodus from Egypt" which were prescribed for Israel even before they had left the land of the Pharaohs. Acceptance by Israel of these two *mitzvot* constituted in a way the precondition necessary for their liberation from slavery in Egypt: the *mitzvah* relating to the way in which the celebration of the feast of Pessah, Passover, should be kept, "in memory of the Exodus" from Egypt[153] (which was still in the future), and the *mitzvah* concerning the liberation of slaves (in the future Hebrew state!).[154]

The Jew is enjoined to love his neighbor, as he is taught by "the great priniciple of the Torah":[155] "Love your neighbor as yourself" (Lev. 19:18). After forbidding him "to hate your brother in your heart" (Lev. 19:17) (knowing that he is capable of "controlling" it), the Torah step by step progresses along the road to educating man, by commanding the Israelite to love his neighbor, whether this neighbor be "near or far,"[156] for the Torah knows that the Creator has engraved the faculty of loving on the human heart.

And the Torah goes on: It affirms the force and importance of this cardinal principle by making it a further precept to love the stranger.

As regards loving one's neighbor, the Torah asks the Jew to turn his attention benevolently *towards* his neighbor, to direct his love *towards* him (in Hebrew: *le-rei'akha*, in the dative case, or literally "to your neighbor,"[157]) so that his neighbor may be able to see the love which comes *to* him, in his direction and embrace it. As regards loving the stranger, the Torah enjoins the Jew to "love him" (in Hebrew: *Et Hager*, "the stranger," in the accusative[158]); in return the stranger must acknowledge a love that reaches out to envelop and hold him fast.

It is characteristic that in the Torah the grammatical construction of the precept to love the stranger should be identical with that of the precept to love God.[159] The Torah thus reveals that these two precepts are equally important; both the one and the other are expressed in the accusative case: *Et Hager* and *Et Hashem* (Deut. 10:19 and 6:5). To love God, the great and all-powerful Other, whom man can consider as the Being, both furthest removed, yet closest to himself, is of equal value to loving the stranger, loving the small and the weak, the "other" whom man sees coming towards him from afar and who possesses the ability to make him conscious that he himself is "a stranger on earth"[160] — so much so that in order to become a "resident" he has to rely on the support of God, the Other. Now it is upon the human face of the "other," the "stranger" — he who can become the closest "neighbor," the true brother to him who adopts him—that as a mark of privilege God imprints His Divine image. It is thanks to this "other" human being, whom man "admits" into his inner life, into his innermost being, that man can gain access to the inner life and immanence of the Divine, transcendent Other. The wise men of Israel go a very long way towards equating loving God with loving the stranger. In particular we can hear their conviction that "hospitality is of greater value than welcoming the Divinity" expressed in the astonishingly daring adage: *Gedolah Hakhnassat Orhin MeHakbalat Penei Shekhinah*: "It is more important to bring guests" (*Orhin*, *Oreah* is the stranger, the man who is traveling: *Orah*) "into your house than to greet the face of the *Shekhinah* (the Divine Presence)!"[161]

It is Abraham, "lover" of God and lover of "traveling" men who provides the wise men of Israel with an example so that they dare to profess such teaching: teaching which gives loving the stranger priority over loving God. In fact "it was God (who was at Abraham's door) whom Abraham asked to wait so that he might welcome the travellers" (Rashi, referring to Gen. 18:3). Abraham knew well that God not only approved his seemingly disrespectful attitude towards Him but expressly commended it. Does He not say of Himself that He "loves the stranger" (Deut. 10:18)? God invites those who wish to love Him, says the Ba'al Shem Tov, to love first those whom He Himself loves. In welcoming "the travellers" first and afterwards greeting the Divine *Shekhinah*, Abraham was nearer to the *Shekhinah* than he had ever been before.

Jews grieve over the sufferings endured by their oppressors

When the day of Divine Judgment finally comes, God Himself will feel anguish at having to punish the "Pharaohs," the "Egyptians," the oppressors of His people Israel. For the Creator "has pity" on His "human creatures"[162] even when they rebel against Him.

"I will take vengeance on My adversaries, and bring retribution on My enemies," says the Lord.[163] But is the "vengeance" of God really vengeance? Decidedly not.[164] "I take no pleasure in the death of him who dies," says the Lord, the Eternal One; "turn again and live" (Ezek. 18:32).

In the Psalms, King David declares, "The Eternal One is a God of vengeance";[165] and the Talmud comments: "When punishment is necessary," in the Hebrew, the term "vengeance" comes between two

Names of God which both represent Divine mercy.[166]

The punishment that God inflicts on the wicked and the perverse "devourers of Israel,"[167] therefore, does not constitute in itself an act of vengeance; it is not inspired by a feeling of vengeance and does not fulfill a vengeful intention; on the contrary it is derived from mercy and tends towards mercy. It should be looked upon as an act intended to teach a lesson, an act of correction intended for those who are its object, so that they shall not continue their horrifying activities; it is meant to discourage others who might be tempted to undertake similar villainous actions.

The goal of Divine punishment is to show men that "there is a Judgment and there is a Judge," who is "true."[168]

The punishment God inflicts on men, or on peoples, who "deserve it," whether they be Jews or not, is not in contradiction with His love for them. It is not inflicted for love of punishment, but for love of man, of humanity.

The *Shirat HaYam*, the "Song of the Sea" (Exod. 15) contains the hymn sung by "Moses and Israel" in God's honor after they had miraculously crossed the Red Sea. The Midrash says that God was particularly appreciative of this great ode made in His honor by Israel, the first such praise dedicated to Him by a whole people; it was the first ode in which a whole people made God known to the world.[169] It pleased God, this hymn which expressed all the gratitude of Israel towards Him and their joy at having been saved. Nevertheless at the moment when the angels (who are always associated in heaven with the hymns which Israel offers on earth to God) were intoning a *shirah*, following Israel's example and in solidarity with them, a "song" to glorify God for having saved Israel from drowning, God interrupted them, according to the Talmud, hurling at them the following resounding reprimand: "The works of My hands (My creatures the Egyptians) are drowning in the sea; how can you say the *shirah* (sing hymns in My honor)!?"[170]

Yes, God punished the Egyptians who in their chariots were implacably pursuing the Israelites newly freed from the chains of slavery. God punished the Egyptians, it is true, but He did so against His will, for the Egyptians were still to Him His creatures, "the works of His hands"; He even promised the people of Egypt that "He would give them in that day," in the time of the Messiah, "His blessing and say: Blessed be My people of Egypt!"[171] This people would by then have accepted His sovereignty and acknowledged His law.

God did not consent to the angels singing to His glory at the moment when His creatures the Egyptians were perishing. They were indeed perishing by their own fault but their suffering, says the Zohar, made their Creator suffer.[172]

Israel itself suffers through the suffering of its enemies. At the moment when Israel thanked God for the benefits he had lavished on them in saving them from the hands of their Egyptian oppressors, Israel was thinking sadly of these same oppressors whom God had punished for their misdeeds. On Passover night, during the solemn *Seder* meal, the Jews commemorate "the deliverance of their ancestors and their own deliverance from slavery."[173] Then, in that hour of joy, from their full cup, symbolic of their rejoicing, they allow a few drops of wine to fall, symbolic of their tears of compassion in memory of the Egyptians who underwent the painful punishment of God, at the end of Israel's slavery in Egypt, concurrent with their leaving the country.

During the feast of Passover,
Israel celebrates its deliverance from Egypt
and not the Egyptians' defeat.

The Sages of Israel point out that, in relation to the feast of Passover, which commemorates the exodus of the Israelites from Egypt, the Torah does not use the word *simhah*, "joy," whereas in regard to the feast of Sukkot the Torah mentions the concept of *simhah*, three times, and also alludes to the notion of *simhah* in connection with the feast of Shavuot.[174]

How can we explain that this notion of "joy" is missing from the feast of Passover, when it is the first of the "three feasts of pilgrimage" — Shavuot and Sukkot being the other two — the feast that celebrates an outstanding event of national salvation in the history of Israel?

The Sages of Israel justify the absence of the term *simhah* in the Biblical description of the feast of Passover by saying that it is not right to speak of *simhah*, "joy," even when it is a case of an important event of salvation, if this event is linked with human suffering or the death of human beings.

Certainly Passover recalls first of all the freeing of the children of Israel from the chains of slavery and the way in which they were saved from annihilation. But in recalling these extraordinary wonders we must also remember distressing facts connected with them: the Egyptians suffered the "plagues" which God inflicted on them because they had oppressed His people, and then the Egyptians "perished in the sea" when they pursued the Israelites as they were leaving Egypt (Exod. 14). How then can we rejoice in our salvation, ask the Sages of Israel, when we know that it was not without human suffering? It is not fitting that we should rejoice even when "sinners perish": for, as a virtuous woman, Beruryah, wife of Rabbi Meir (in the 2nd century), said in the Talmud,[175] we only wish the "sins" to disappear, but not the sinners (Psalms 104:35). Certainly it happens that "when the wicked perish there is rejoicing" in the world (Proverbs 11:10), for the "glory of God" is seen therein; or in other words, one thereby comes—like Pharaoh—"to know God," and to recognize His absolute power both in Nature and in History. But God Himself who punishes the wicked "does not rejoice when the wicked fall," says the Talmud.[176] For how could He, the Creator, the Builder, rejoice, asks the Maharal, "when there is injury, annihilation, destruction?"[177]

Therefore there cannot be "joy" for the Israelites when human beings are suffering, though they be enemies; there is no place for rejoicing when one recalls that enemies have suffered. The Torah and then the Mishnah have already stated this strongly, teaching us, "When your enemy falls, do not rejoice, and when he succumbs, let not your heart be glad; lest the Lord see it and it displease Him."[178]

Indeed, it does "displease Him." We have seen it; God forbade the angels to manifest their joy at the time when Israel miraculously crossed the Red Sea: He would not accept the *shirah*, the hymn, the paean of praise they wished to sing in His honor in the heavens above to "respond" to the *shirah* being sung by Israel on the earth below (Exod. 15). Israel on earth had a "duty to thank God for the miracles He vouchsafed to *them*"[179]—therefore they sang the *shirah*; but the angels above were not to do so. How could they do so when they saw that, while Israel was saved, their "enemies," "the chariots of the Pharaoh and his army" pursuing Israel to destroy them, "were drowning in the Sea of Reeds"? That is why God censured the angels, saying to them, "The works of My hands (My creatures, the Egyptians) are drowning in the sea, and you, you dare to say the *shirah*!?"[180]

After the crossing of the Red Sea, "Moses and the children of Israel sang the *shirah*"; they sang it with enthusiasm, impressed by the greatness of the miracle. But throughout the centuries that have followed that event the Jews have continued to live each day in the "memory of the Exodus from Egypt" and the "parting of the Sea of Reeds." They still feel at all times, and especially during the feast of Passover, during the *Pessah Dorot*, during the "Passover of the generations," the need to give free rein to their feelings of gratitude to God who freed their ancestors from slavery and delivered them; they regard it as a duty to recite, during the religious ceremonies at Passover time, the *Hallel*, the special chapters of "praise" to God (Psalms 113-118). The Talmud[181] calls these "Songs of Praise"; *Hallela Mitsra'a*, the *Hallel HaMitsri*, the "Egyptian Hallel," for "it is read during the feast of Pessah" and it concerns above all "the Exodus from Egypt." The Talmud[182] also calls them by the simple, but oh how majestic, name of *shirah*, "hymn," which reminds us of the *shirah par excellence* "sung by Moses and the children of Israel" after crossing the Sea of Reeds. (Because of its importance this *shirah* is included in the daily liturgy).

But we see that religious Tradition and Law prescribe that the *Hallel* be recited "in its entirety" only during the religious ceremony on the first day of Pessah (in the Galut, in the countries of the Diaspora, the "entire" Hallel is also recited on the second day of Passover which "duplicates" the first day celebrated in Erets-Yisrael, in the Land of Israel). Indeed the first day of Pessah recalls the actual day of the "Exodus from Egypt"; it recalls the *Pessah Mitsraim*, the Pessah experienced by the ancestors of the Israelites in Egypt itself during one day when they ate *matsot*, "unleavened bread." The Israelites of all "generations," of all times[183] celebrate the *Pessah Mitsraim* during the *Pessah Dorot*, and therefore recite on the first day of Pessah the *Hallel Shalem*, the "entire *Hallel*"; they "thus thank God for the deliverance of their fathers and for their own deliverance from Egypt."

On the other days of Pessah, especially on the seventh, which recalls the day of the crossing of the Red Sea, Tradition and Law require the Jew to moderate the tone of the *Hallel*, to lessen the intensity of expression, that is, to "reduce" the number of chapters to be recited, to omit some of its *Mizmorim*, its "songs" and during the religious services on those days to recite only *Hatsi Hallel*, "half the *Hallel*," an incomplete, partial *Hallel*.[184] For the above reasons the Law does not authorize Jews to recite the *Hallel Shalem*, the "*whole Hallel*," during the days following the first of Passover.

Thus Pessah constitutes an exception in relation to Shavuot (Pentecost) and Sukkot, the two other feasts forming parts of the cycle of the "three feasts of the pilgrimage." Whereas during all the days of the Feast of Sukkot and of the Feast of Shavuot (including the second day of the latter in the Galut), the *Hallel* is said "in full" during the religious services, the days of the Feast of Passover do not all enjoy the same favor on the liturgical plane. The reasons are clearly indicated by the Sages of Israel; they are the sufferings of the Egyptians, the defeat of the "enemy," the participation of Israel in the sufferings of their "enemy."[185]

❋ ❋ ❋

It seems to us that we should transcribe a passage from the book *Meshekh Hokhmah* here. In these lines the celebrated Torah commentator Rabbi Meir Simhah Kohen of Dvinsk (who is also the great commentator on Rambam's *Mishneh Torah* in his book *Or Sameah*) shares with us his reflections on the meaning of certain Jewish feasts. Taking as the basis for his reflections the Biblical prescriptions on the subject of the feast of Pessah, the erudite "expositor" writes: "One must understand the meaning of the *mitzvot* of the 'commandments' of (God), blessed be He.... All peoples celebrate days of victory, and they celebrate them on the same day as the defeat of their enemy. Israel does not follow the same procedure. They do not rejoice in the fall of their enemies nor do they celebrate it with joy, for they are enjoined: 'Do not rejoice when your enemy falls... lest the Lord see it and it displease Him' (Prov. 24:17-18). The Bible requires man to raise himself to such a level of morality that he cannot rejoice in the fall of his enemies. Such a joy is not pleasing in the eyes of God (and what is displeasing in God's eyes should be displeasing in the eyes of man). That is why during the feast of Pessah we celebrate only the fact that God brought the children of Israel out of the Land of Egypt, and not the fact that God punished the Egyptians. There is no feast in Israel to commemorate the fall of their enemies! Thus the feast of Hanukah also finds justification only in the miracle of the olive oil (in the Temple of Jerusalem), in the purification and dedication of the House of God (the Sanctuary in Jerusalem) and thus in the manifestations of Divine Providence and protection bestowed by God on his people, the House of Israel. And we but light the candles of Hanukah during the week which bears that name to recall the miracle which was not very well known outside the Temple where it happened. (The Talmud[186] tells us: 'After the Hasmoneans had got the better of the enemy, a search was made in the Temple and only a single flask of oil was found bearing intact the seal of the High Priest. The contents of this flask would have been enough for one day at the most—but a miracle happened and it burned for eight days.') So we do not celebrate during the feast of Hanukah the Maccabeans' celebrated victory, which might make people believe that we were taking pride in our ancestors' physical strength and military strategy (in reality they overcame their powerful enemies because God helped them).[187] No, we are commemorating above all, that miracle which can only be due to the hand of God, that God of Israel who leads His people by miraculous and supernatural ways of His special Providence. We observe the same attitude in relation to the feast of Purim. We are not celebrating Purim as the day when Haman (the 'enemy of the Jews' in the 'kingdom of the Medes and Persians') was hanged (on the orders of his King, Ahasuerus), nor as the day when the enemies of the Jews in that country perished, for these events do not constitute a subject for rejoicing for the people of Israel; but we celebrate Purim as 'the days when the *Jews* had *rest* from their enemies' (Esther 9:22). The joy of the Jews comes only from the fact that God saved them from annihilation....As for the Egyptians who (following the Israelites who were escaping from Egypt) were drowned in the sea on the seventh day of Pessah, the Sages of Israel stress that God does not rejoice in the fall of the wicked. That is why He commanded the Israelites, while they were still in Egypt, to celebrate the seventh day of Pessah. Thus He showed that the Israelites would not celebrate that day because of the drowning of the Egyptians, for He prescribed the feast of the seventh day of Pessah for His people *before* the Egyptians were drowned in the sea....In truth it is written, 'When your enemy falls, do not rejoice.' "[188]

The Torah, in commanding the Israelite, or man, "You shall love your neighbor—*le-rei'akha*—as yourself: I am the Lord" (Lev. 19:18), uses for "neighbor" the term *rei'a* or "friend." Indeed any man, no matter who, is—whether by his physical being or ethical calling—the *rei'a*, friend of others (the *rei'a* to whom "he should do no wrong").[189] According to examples given in the Bible, every human being should regard his fellow man as his "*rei'a*" thus his "brother," independent of whether he shares with him spiritual, social, political or indeed any other interests (Gen. 29:4; Num. 20:14; Kings I 9:13). Truly, are they not both "made in the image of God" (Gen. 1:26-27; 9:6)? Are they not both the creatures of "God Who is their common Father, Who has created them" (Mal. 2:10)? Is God not addressing them both in asking them to love one another, in reminding each of them, "I am the Lord your God" and upon which Rashi comments,"I am your God and his God"?

By the term *rei'a* the language of the Hebrew Bible teaches us that every man is supposed to be the "friend" of every other man, even though one knows that he is also capable of becoming at any moment his adversary and even his "enemy." Thus the Israelite *rei'a* can become the adversary of another Israelite, and the non-Israelite (in this case the Egyptian) *rei'a* of the Israelite can become his oppressor—a *ra*, a "wicked" person—and hence his enemy.[190] However, even though he becomes the "enemy" of the Israelite, the Egyptian always remains for the latter, virtually and ultimately,[191] a *rei'a*, a friend. Indeed the *ra* is always capable of regaining the letter *yod*, his *Yod* which he eliminated from the central place it previously occupied in *r-ei-a*; the *ra* is always able to reinstate, in his heart, the *Yod* represented by the symbolic *tsere* vowel, which is the sign of the humanizing Divine[192] Presence within him. He thus become conscious of the beneficial, salutary effect which the *Yod* exercises upon him, upon his whole being; the *ra* is thus always capable of ceasing to be *ra* and turning again into a *rei'a*: yes, the "wicked one" can again become "fully" a "loving person" and so a "friend."

The *rei'a*, the neighbor, like the "person far off," is the object of the love preached by the Torah in the precept of love for one's neighbor.[193]

Nevertheless in the Hebrew Bible the precept to love one's neighbor does not remain merely something preached. It is true, this precept constitutes in the Talmud, according to Rabbi Akiba (second century), "the great principle of the Torah."[194] But this precept is itself a *mitzvah*, a religious "commandment." Inscribed in the heart of the Book of Leviticus, it is surrounded by a number of *mitzvot*, prescriptions, laws. These show the Jew how to apply, in the varied circumstances of individual and collective daily life, the "principle" of love for one's neighbor; how to apply this "principle" to the benefit of every man, every *rei'a* whether he be, as he should always be, a "friend," or whether he becomes, as he can become, temporarily an "enemy."[195]

Even more, in their religious laws the Torah, and after it the Talmud, not only judge the "enemy" worthy of understanding but consider that even the "beast of the enemy" merits man's attention. Thus we read in the Second Book of Moses: "When you come upon your enemy's ox or donkey straying, you shall return it to him. When you see the donkey of your enemy (lit. *Sona'akha*, "someone who hates you"—though, you may not hate him) lying helpless under its load, you shall take care not to abandon it; you must give him a hand with it" (Exod. 23:4-5). Moreover—the Jew is instructed by the Talmud to lend his aid to the beast of his "enemy" rather than to the beast of his "friend." Why this preference? Because in acting in this way once, then "four or five times," the Jew will be implementing his own education; he will come to weaken, conquer and finally suppress the antipathetic reaction that "the one who hates him" arouses in him. In view of this generosity, his enemy will not be long in becoming once more his "friend."

This is how the Talmud formulates this legal requirement and expresses this advice which, one would say, belongs to "depth psychology": "If you have to help your friend to unload his beast and your enemy to load his beast, it is commanded—by a *mitzvah!*—that you help your enemy so that you can surmount your evil inclinations." Furthermore, the Talmud says, "You are obliged to unload the beast of your enemy even if he is not with his animal."[196]

2b

The Galut — Israel's exile
Divine providence and human liberty

Essential reality and final objective

The Galut is not simply the consequence of Israel's transgressions;[197] nor is it only a punishment; or just the "ordeal by fire" through which Israel's errors are pardoned; or just the "crucible" in which Israel is "purified" of its sins.[198]

The Galut was "provided for," "predestined," "determined" by God well before Israel could have "voluntarily" or "freely" committed the sins for which exile is the punishment. It is the manifestation of a "marvelous, Divine Providence."[199] It is not only a historical event which came to pass, but exists as an essential, "compelling" reality: a *hekhreah*, as it is called in the language of the Maharal.[200] The temporary absence of the people of Israel from their country, Erets-Yisrael, is a *hekhreah* which, according to Rav Kook, calls forth in *consequence* another *hekhreah*: the return of Israel to Erets-Yisrael.[201]

The Maharal and Sefat Emet vigorously affirm that "the Galut thus does not arrive by accident"[202] (and every "sin of Israel is only an accident"![203]), "but it is essential." Exile is predetermined in the *cosmic* order established by the Creator. In fact God "created the Galut," states the Talmud[204] and *consequently*, again according to the Talmud, "the *gathering in of the galuyot* is as important — as 'memorable' — as the day on which the heavens and earth were *created*."[205] Now, as the Divine creation of nature has as its final — spiritual, ethical, historical and Messianic — objective the *geulah*, salvation, therefore "the Galut and the *geulah* constitute a principle which effects the order of the universe itself," writes the Maharal.[206]

The Galut is thus engraved in the cosmic-historical scheme of God; it is a part of the Divine plan for the *particular* history of Israel, the significance of which is *universal*, it is assigned to Israel whose structure is *specific* and whose vocation is universal.[207]

Between the times of the beginning and the fulfillment, between Genesis and the Messiah — Abraham

The Galut and its historic evolution, as well as the "return" to God, *teshuvah* (the instrument broadly and specifically linking both the "first" serene times of the Creation, and the "debased," troubled times of the Galut and the "final" serene times of salvation), have their foundations in the pre-cosmic, infinite worlds and in the undefined, prehistoric world of Israel and of humanity.

The Midrash illustrates this idea in its cogent words on the first verses of Genesis.

The teaching of the Midrash is as follows: The Torah says,[208] "In the beginning God created... but before the world was created, God had created *Shemo shel Mashiah*, the 'name of the Messiah,' and *teshuvah*, 'the return' to God."[209] ("The *name* of the Messiah," that is to say, the Messianic principle, ideal aspiration, or expectation; and *teshuvah* itself should occur immediately after the creation of man and be utilized by him to reach the Messianic, sabbatical age. In fact Adam had recourse to it a few hours after being created, on the eve of the Sabbath; thus Adam serves as an example to future generations.)

Again the Torah says,[210] "The earth was without form, *tohu*, and void, *bohu*, and darkness, *hoshekh*, was upon the face of the deep, *tehom*." And the Midrash interprets it thus, "*Tohu* is the kingdom of Babylon; *bohu* is the kingdom of the Medes; *hoshekh* is the kingdom of Greece; *tehom* is the kingdom of wickedness (Edom)."[211]

These conditions of chaos and darkness, of the abyss, are the *typical* conditions of the transient, Galut civilizations into which, in the course of its history, Israel has been led away, in which it has found itself in the past and in which it still finds itself.[212] Israel was dragged into exile by Nebuchadnezzar, king of Babylon (in the 6th century B.C.E.), by Ahasuerus, king of the Medes and Persians (in the 5th century B.C.E.), by Antiochus Epiphanes, the Greco-Syrian king (in the 2nd century B.C.E.) and thereafter by the autocrats of the Roman Empires, both pagan and Christian.[213]

Then the Torah says,[214] "And the spirit of God moved upon the face of the waters." The Midrash defines this, "It is the (watery, primordial, 'purifying') spirit of the King, the Messiah."[215] This King is the opponent of dark, wicked despots. He manifests himself first as the herald of the first triumph of the light; later he will affirm the final victory of the light. For, the Torah continues, "God said, *yehi or*, let there be light."[216] "*Yehi or — zeh Avraham* — this is Abraham," states the Midrash. "Indeed, Scripture states, "*Mi he'ir*, [it is I, God] who have raised up one, *mimizrah*, out of the East, who is met by justice where his footsteps."[217] And the Midrash interprets: "Do not read this as *he'ir* (with the letter *ayin*), 'has raised up, awakened,' but rather *he'ir* (with the letter *aleph*), 'has made radiant, illumined.'[218] He has illumined the world by permitting it a glimpse of the Messianic justice,[219] by making it feel the beneficence of Abraham,[220] and allowing it to hear the footsteps of the Messiah."[221]

The primeval light, after it was eclipsed by the darkness of man's tyranny, after being "hidden" by God, made its "new" appearance in Abraham: The first Hebrew patriarch is the depository of the redemptive light of Divine origin which gives illumination; he sheds upon human activities an emancipating light that "heals."[222] Abraham is the promise and hope that this beneficent light will be diffused universally. Paradoxically, Abraham himself receives the Divine pronouncement of Israel's *galuyot* and in himself feels deeply the "dark anguish" which they cause; but it is also Abraham himself who receives the Divine proclamation of a shining *end* to the darkness of the Galut; he receives not only the prophecy of the end of the Galut but also that of the *geulah*, salvation.[223] This is much more than a deliverance; it is the final objective of creation: the liberation of the Word that created light, and the coming forth of the Light from its obscurity; it is the union and synchronism of Word and Light, as they were at the beginning of creation.

The Jewish Galut, a mission to the universe

The Galut is an essential element in the Divine plan of Salvation. It is part of the "hidden designs of Divine wisdom," said Rabbi Yehuda HaLevi.[224] In order to realize His intentions, which governed the creation of the world, God uses Israel, His people.[225] The people of God are an instrument in God's hands, not only in Erets-Yisrael, in the "Land of Israel" which He gave to this people, but also in the *Tefutsot Yisrael*, the "dispersions of Israel" into which He sent them.[226] Indeed Israel's exile also constitutes a *tefutsah* (dispersion), a *pezurah* (scattering) of Israel among the nations. For Israel is the "one people" — *goi ehad* — of the one God — *HaShem Ehad*, of that God Who is the "God of the Land" of

Israel[227] and at the same time the God of "all the earth."[228] So Israel proclaims God's will to the world, both from within its own country as well as from within other countries.

Rabbi Yitshak Luria, the Ari HaKadosh, teaches that the *galuyot*, Israel's exiles, are "necessary" for the world, at different periods of its development, in successive epochs of its history.[229] By existing, creatively, in different parts of the world, Israel is able to help men and nations rid themselves of their own states of exile, of which they may not even be conscious. Indeed spiritually they are in exile though at home in their own countries, to which they have become enslaved. Now, under their dark and unclean "crust," these countries of exile "hide" some *nitsotsot*, Divine "sparks." These are scattered, strewn in confusion throughout the world because of the *Shevirat HaKeilim*, the "breaking of the vessels" which could not withstand the superabundance of light poured into them at Creation on account of Adam's first sin which agitated the order of the world.[230] By studying the Torah and observing the *mitzvot*, Israel is able to "free" these "holy sparks" from their "prisons," to "liberate" them from their place of "detention," "raise" them from their "fall" and bring them on the road of "return" to their "root."[231] Thus Israel contributes to the *tikkun*, the "restoration" of cosmic harmony, which has been disturbed and disorganized, during the periods of exile. In carrying out its duty, its task of "gathering together the holy sparks strewn all over the world" which were abandoned through the sins of men and nations,[232] Israel brings close the time for the "gathering in of the *galuyot*," that is the ingathering of its own exiled people, dispersed throughout the world, and their return to their "source of blessing," Zion, in Erets-Yisrael.

This is why the Galut was provided for by God, *a priori*, before Israel's experience, even before the formation of Israel as a people. It was the object of a *gezerah*, a Divine "edict," a Divine "decree" which was foreseen, pre-destined, pre-ordained and pre-determined, before Israel began its historical career, before it was "free" to act, and consequently to be guilty of possible transgressions, to bring upon itself the punishment of exile, and so provoke the Galut.[233]

In His all-embracing, cosmic Providence, God "designated" Israel for the Galut, because He chose them "to reconcile Himself to His world," which is always ready to turn away from Him. God "chose" Israel on this cosmic,[234] eternal level before "choosing" them on the level of historical, temporal events—namely at a precise historical moment and in a precise topographical position, on Sinai[235]—for precise historical periods, in a precise region, Erets-Yisrael.[236] It is Israel's "election" on the cosmic level which preconditions, implies and imposes, as an inescapable necessity, its "election" on the historical, national-religious and universal-religious plane.

Israel's election and Israel's Galut

The Jewish Galut is therefore regarded as a *gezerah*,[237] a supreme decision by God, "carved" and "fashioned" by Him *a priori* and engraved not only in the Jewish historic, national, human and universal schema, but even in the cosmic grand design established *a priori* by the Creator. He "created the Galut."

God is guiding this order, established at the two connected levels of Nature and of History, towards a manifest finale: the raising up of the world to the Creator, by the raising up of man, agent both of nature and history. The Galut must therefore lead to the *geulah*, exile must lead to salvation, "for the Galut and *geulah* depend upon the same principle, which affects the enigma of the cosmos and its order," as the Maharal says.

In order to carry out this difficult but "necessary," painful but "salutary" operation, of raising the world towards the source, bringing the world back to God; in order to lead the world back from Galut to *geulah*, the Creator "chose" Israel.[238] That is why "from before the creation of the world, God designated Israel to receive the Torah" ("in His thought before the creation of the world, God had the intention to create Torah and Israel.")[239] "He therefore chose Israel so as to give them the Torah." He chose Israel so as to put at their disposal the Torah, itself created before the creation of the world, the "instrument" which He had used for creating the world and which Israel would use for "bringing light" into a dark world, for restoring a world that was disordered. The Torah would constitute the link between Nature and History.[240] For as Israel observes and fulfills its *mitzvot*, particularly those which are synergistically concerned with *teshuvah*, the Torah will bring the Galut on a sure course back to the *geulah*.[241]

This "election" of Israel is not a privilege bringing material advantages; it does not allow the "chosen one" to consider himself superior to others; on the contrary, it is a very heavy burden, bringing with it not only serious material disadvantages, but also, and above all, harsh sufferings.

Prefiguring his descendants in Israel, Abraham was "chosen" by God for the Galut. (He himself experienced it, in Egypt!) The first patriarch was "known" by God — meaning he was "loved" and "chosen" by Him.[242] After him, Israel, his posterity, has been "known" by God — that is to say, "loved" and "chosen" by Him; God keeps them in His sight in order to watch over them with the strictest justice and goodness.[243]

Israel is thus "compelled" to suffer and realize the Galut; they are obligated to take it upon themselves. That is why "Jacob 'went down into Egypt,' compelled by the (Divine) Word,"[244] and "lived there as a stranger"; and "the Egyptians treated (his descendants) iniquitously, oppressing them, and imposing a heavy servitude on them."[245] When they left "for the bitter Galut" in Egypt, writes the Noam Elimelech, "Jacob sought to alleviate and to decrease the severity of the (Divine) decrees," but also to engage in a work of *tikkun*,[246] the restoration or regeneration of Egypt.

Israel is thus brought to bear the pangs of the Galut in spite of themselves, above all since they do not find that they have "deserved" it.

The dialectic of the Galut:
Divine coercion and human freedom

The dialectic of the Galut moves over a wide arc; it swings between, on the one hand, God's "compelling" Providence, God's will that His "heavenly justice" — *dinei shamayim* — should remain for the time being beyond human grasp — *hekhreah*;[247] and on the other hand God's manifest Revelation, His will that His justice, visible to human eyes, should be understood — *bidei adam* — immediately: *veyissartikha lamishpat*[248] "I will punish you according to the Law — in proportion".

The first part of the dialectic of the Galut, Providence, is supra-rational; it is all-embracing and conceals a long-term Plan of God; it "hides" the reward of the righteous, the tremendous good "reserved" for them in the future, in the "world to come."[249] The second part, Revelation, is completely visible; it is partially comprehensible, and it immediately controls human error by adminstering *onesh*: chastisement.

Thus the Galut is situated between the meta-historical, unfathomable Providence of God, and the phenomenon of historical reality in which Israel lives from day to day. The Galut is placed between God's omnipotence and man's miserable, uncertain state, between God's reassuring merciful Power and Goodness and man's limited, conditioned liberty.

Truth to tell, God "envisaged" Israel's exile before the latter "in their human liberty" (itself dependent of God, its Creator) gave way to the temptations of the world (also created by God). The Sages of Israel, in their defence of Israel, victim of the Galut, have even dared to argue that God, the "Awe-inspiring," the Supreme Judge, searched for *alilot* —

reasons for accusing Israel so that He could condemn to this exile an Israel, a people much more "predetermined" in its acts than it is "free" in its options.[250]

In truth, God had "made provision for" Israel's Galut even before this people came to "sin" and thus to "justify" its exile.[251]

God "decreed" the Galut *a priori*—by a *gezerah*, by a "trenchant" decree. He had pronounced the sentence of Galut upon Israel before any member of that people had ever been accused of any transgression against the Torah and consequently condemned.[252] Furthermore, God took the decision on Israel's Galut even before Israel had received the Torah. He "made known" His decision to the first Hebrew patriarch, Abraham, the Man,[253] who had committed no sin, at any rate none intentionally,[254] although it must be admitted that "there is no righteous man on earth who always does good without fail."[255] On the contrary, Abraham stood out from his own generation as well as the generations preceding him,[256] as the "first" of the truly "righteous,"[257] the "first believer" who would become "the father of the believers,"[258] the "head of the believers."[259] As we have seen it was "to Abram that God said: Know this for certain, that your descendants will be aliens living in a land that is not theirs; they will be slaves, and will be held in oppression there for four hundred years" (Gen. 15:13). Thus God foretold to the "father" *par excellence*, Abraham (*par excellence*[260] because he transmitted his virtues both to his children and his distant posterity[261]), that his descendants would have to live in a country not their own, and that they would be enslaved and oppressed.[262] Now these descendants were not yet born; they were therefore virtually innocent.[263] And moreover, in the distressing picture of the impending Galut which his children would have to suffer in Egypt, God allowed Abraham the "father" to see, "with anguish," all the darkness of the *galuyot*, the successive exiles which his descendants would have to face.[264] "Abraham our Father," the father *par excellence*, feels not only, as is natural, his children's and grandchildren's suffering but also that of all his descendants till the "last of the generations"!

The prediction of the Galut, made to Abraham and no other, holds the attention of the Maharal, as it also held that of the Talmud[265] and the commentators on the Torah. How can God convey this portentous message to none other than "Abraham whom He loves"?[266] It is true that Abraham is reproached for the question he dared to put to God, "How can I be sure that I shall possess (the Promised Land)?" (Gen. 15:8). He put this question even after receiving the Divine affirmation, which was clear: "I am the Lord who brought you up out of Ur of the Chaldees to give you this land to occupy." But must one see in this "question" put by the "first believer" a wavering of his faith in God, and of his trust in the Divine Word?

Bama eida, "How shall I know?" This unfortunate phrase of Abraham's indicates a desire — so understandable and human — to "be sure," to "know" as much as possible about the thing which concerns himself and his posterity. Yet, it is objectionable in the eyes of God, He who "chose Abraham" because "he had faith in the Lord."[267]

Indeed this question of Abraham's calls forth God's retort: *Yadoa teida*, "You shall know it for certain."[268] "You shall know it for certain that your descendants shall live in a strange land, where they will be enslaved and oppressed" (Gen. 15:13). "Measure for measure!" And yet more. In His reply God is not content to merely employ the same verb used by Abraham in his question; He repeats and emphasizes it, so as to drive home to Abraham the Galut of his children. Truly the Talmud[269] sees in that imprudent question of Abraham's, *Bama eida*, one of the causes of the Galut of the first Hebrew patriarch's descendants.

However, most of the great Torah commentators, such as Rashi, Ramban, Abravanel[270] and Seforno, pardon this unfortunate question of Abraham's. They do not discern in it any wavering of the *emunah*, the "faith" of the man whom Ramban calls *Shoresh HaEmunah*,[271] "the Root of the Faith." In spite of this momentary error, they praise the "upright," "unconditional," constant faith of him whom God Himself invites to be "upright."[272] They do not admit the possibility of a weakening of faith even for an instant in this "great man," one of the "giants" of the faith. They make every effort to demonstrate that by his question, *Bama eida*, Abraham was not asking God for an *ot*, a tangible "proof" of the fulfillment of His promise (although it is true that a later request by King Hezekiah for an *ot* was to "cause the Galut of his children!")[273]

God's promise satisfied Abraham. In putting to Him the question, *Bama eida*, he was not asking Him for an explanation regarding that promise. But he knew that a Divine promise should also be "merited" by those who benefit.[274] The question *Bama eida*, far from reflecting the slightest doubt, the least uncertainty in the patriarch's heart touching the unbelievable nature of the Divine promise, was a sign rather of a doubt or uncertainty concerning the merits of his children. Would they prove themselves to be "worthy" of the generous Divine promise? It was on account of their behavior that his heart was filled with uncertainty and even with anxiety. He wondered if his children "would always deserve" to possess what God had promised to *him*. Besides, in the Talmud, which "accuses" Abraham of having caused his children's Galut by putting the question *Bama eida*, we learn (on the same page!) that Abraham trembled, "he shuddered with anxiety" concerning his own faith, about which he was not sure. But what true man of faith can say he is satisfied and sure of his own faith?[275]

Nevertheless, other great interpreters of the Torah, such as the Maharal, the Moharan[276] (Rabbi Nahman of Bratslav), the Mikhtav MeEliyahu[277] (Rabbi Eliyahu Eliezer Dessler), do not exclude a certain weakening of faith on the part of Abraham at the moment he posed the question *Bama eida*. They do not therefore unreservedly excuse the unfortunate expression of the patriarch who, because of the "greatness of his faith," ought to have weighed each and every one of his words. Given the exceptional quality of his faith, even a small lapse could have disastrous consequences for him and his descendants. Thus the Galut of Israel could be attributed to this infinitesimal error, this inadvertance of their ancestor.

The dialectic of the Galut:
From Talmud to Tosafot,
from the Maharal to
the Gaon of Rogachev

The Maharal, cleaving through the ample discussions on the subject of the dialogue between Abraham and God (Gen. 15) and consequently through the disconcerting contradictions which feed the dialectic of the Galut of Israel, clears the pathway for his own thought on the theme of the exile of the Jewish people. As usual he does it with great ease and much originality, although he was preceded by so many other exegetes, notable the Tosafists in concise comments, and Abravanel in broad dissertations. He remains an astonishing dialectician, although so many masters of Jewish thought after him, up to the Gaon of Rogachev, have plowed through this same problem area and enriched it with their reflections.

The Maharal's reflections on this difficult theme run through all his writings in particular his *Netivot Olam*, *Be'er HaGolah*, and *Perushim LeAggadot Hashas*; however, he concentrates his reasoning in his *Gevurot Hashem*. There he writes in particular, "One can say that God has led Abraham's descendants into exile because Abraham was not strong enough in his faith."[278] Indeed the Maharal points out in addition that "the man who changes part of his faith for even one minute is already straying from its faith. Even Abraham, chief of the believers, in saying *Bama eida*, 'How shall I know?' was straying from his faith."[279] Rabbi

Nahman of Bratslav reinforces the impression given us by the Maharal by writing in this connection, "When Abraham did damage to the faith, it was detrimental to the heritage of the Land (of Israel), for this Land depends on the faith, the [pure] *emunah.*"[280]

In *Gevurot Hashem* the Maharal continues, "Abraham was not punished for his sin; on the contrary, in accordance with the Divine promise he died 'in good old age' (Gen. 15:15)![281] Why then is his sin visited upon his children, who themselves have not sinned?"[282] He replies: Abraham was the beginning and the mainstay [root and stem] of Israel, and everything derives from the beginning.[283] (In a different connection Ramban puts forward a similar view.[284]) Once Abraham was not entirely perfect, that sin first found in him who was, and remains, the root also appears in his descendants who are the branches.[285]

"That is then the reason why God brought the descendants of Abraham into the Galut. He led them there so that in exile they would acquire *complete* faith, in learning to know the power exercised by God.

"We do, however, have the right to ask ourselves this: Was Abraham's sin really so grave that it brought in its wake so severe a punishment for his descendants?" The following is the reply, writes the Maharal: "It was laid down for all time that the existence of God should be made known on earth; for what value could the world have if God is not known? It was laid down for all time that the Name of God should be sanctified on earth. However, some sin or other was needed so that this necessity could be realized, for the exile had to happen in any case."

The Shelah HaKadosh observed earlier, and well before him Rashi made the same declaration,[286] that "a *gezerah*, a Divine 'decree,' will in any case be fulfilled." But since there can be no suffering without sin, it was consequently imperative that a sin, however minute, should occur, as both Abravanel and the Maharal observe, so as to bring about the Galut.[287]

In truth Ramban, who calls Abraham *Shoresh HaEmunah*, "the Root of the Faith," finds in the patriarch, though his faith was "ten times tried," some "involuntary" faults with no bad intentions, which nevertheless could provoke and even justify the Galut for his descendants. For example, the mistake made by Abraham of "going down into Egypt" voluntarily, because of the famine then prevailing in Canaan (he did not have sufficient faith in the God who "feeds His creatures"), provided a motive for the "enforced" exile of his descendants *in Egypt.*[288]

So a slight inattention, an inappropriate attitude, an unreasoning gesture, an improvised meal, an unjustified weeping,[289] just as much as a grievous sin such as that of the spies who being sent to explore the land of

Canaan which God had given to the children of Israel betrayed a lack of "faith" in the promise and power of God![290] — such apparently innocent behavior and grave national misdemeanors are both capable of provoking the Galut, making it descend perforce upon future "generations."[291]

In fact, says the Maharal, "the Galut and enslavement did not find Israel in a state of perfection. That is why a minor slip-up caused a situation that was unavoidable."

※ ※ ※

The Torah tells how, after the explorers had returned to the wilderness from the land of Canaan, "the people passed *that* night in weeping" (Num. 14:1). That night, according to tradition, was the night of Tishah be-Av, the ninth day of the month of Av. It was on that very same date, centuries later, that the destruction of the first and second Temples in Jerusalem occurred.

The Talmud and Midrash comment on the verse which speaks of the weeping of "that night" in these terms: " 'You broke out in unjustified tears,' said the Holy One (speaking to the generation of the explorers of the Land of Canaan); 'I Myself will designate *this* same night as a night of tears for future generations!' In *this* very hour the *gezerah*, the 'final judgment' was pronounced that the *Beit HaMikdash* (Temple of Jerusalem) should be destroyed and that Israel should leave to live in exile, Galut, among the nations. As it is written (Ps. 106:25-27), 'They muttered treason in their tents and would not obey the Lord. So with uplifted hand He swore to strike them down in the wilderness, to scatter their descendants among the nations and disperse them throughout the world.' " And the Midrash concludes, "The (all-powerful) Hand was uplifted against the uplifting of the (feeble) voice."[292]

What a concatenation of events, what linking of the generations! "The generation of the wilderness" was guilty before God on a precise date, and it was the cause not only of its own punishment on that same date but also a decree of punishment for future generations![293] Those generations, though, would be guilty enough[294] before God to "justify" the decision taken concerning them: *Banekha Hatu VeGalu*!

"God visits the sins of the fathers upon the children," say the Bible and the Talmud, in regard to children "who follow the fathers' bad example."[295] For it is the same God, the same people of Israel, and the history of their dealings which are reported in the Torah, in the Bible.

The History of Israel, "the holy people," is always, in every epoch of its existence, a biblical, a holy History.

To return to the initial causes of the Galut, the Maharal asks the following question: "Could one say that Israel became exiled because of the sin of Joseph's brothers in selling Him (Gen. 37)?"[296] But did Joseph himself not provoke his brothers' violent reaction against him?" The consequence of that reaction was that they sold him to the Ishmaelites, who took him off to Egypt. And so, the Shelah HaKadosh observes, "the descent of Joseph into Egypt was the beginning of the Galut in Egypt!"[297]

The Talmud underlines the existence of small mistakes that have grave consequences. Thus it cautions parents to treat their children with fairness, and requires them "not to make a distinction between their children."[298] To support this requirement the Talmud gives as an example the relations between Jacob and Joseph and his brothers, and says, "Because Jacob gave to Joseph two shares more than he gave to his other sons, they became jealous, and events unfolded and followed one upon another—*Nitgalgel HaDavar*—in such a way that our ancestors went down into Egypt (in Galut)." "Nevertheless," the Maharal says, "this is contrary to what is written in the Scriptures, according to which the Holy One, Blessed be He, said to Abraham, well before the tribes (descended from the sons of Jacob) were born, 'Know this for certain, that your descendants will be aliens living in a land that is not theirs, where they will be enslaved and oppressed' (Gen. 15:13)." The Tosafists had earlier made the same observation in connection with the passage from the Talmud mentioned above; they wrote, "Even if Jacob had not discriminated between his children, the *gezerah*, the Divine decree of Israel's exile, was already in existence." The Maharal, quoting the Tosafists, adds in his commentary on the same Talmud passage, "And yet a strong cause was necessary for the *gezerah* to be brought into operation, for the very serious Divine decision to be fulfilled decreeing the descent (of our ancestors) into Egypt. And this serious cause was provided by Jacob's discrimination between his sons."[299] And the Maharal makes the thought more precise elsewhere:[300] "Although the *gezerah* of Hashem, Blessed be He, (God's decision) that Israel should be enslaved by the nations, had already been given, He had sent ahead of them one man, Joseph, 'who had to be sold' by his brothers, 'until the Word would be fulfilled.'" Rashi had earlier remarked that Joseph was "'sent ahead' so that the Word of the Holy One (Blessed be He) might be fulfilled, so that His *gezerah* might be carried out, and events followed one upon another—*SheYitgalgel HaDavar*—in such a way that the sons of Jacob went down to Egypt (into exile)."[301] "One can see, therefore," the Maharal continues, "that the sale (of Joseph by his brothers) took place so that the descent (of Israel) into Egypt would follow, as our Sages tell us in the Talmud,[302] in commenting on a verse of the Torah."[303] "Israel's bondage in Egypt made the selling (of Joseph by his brothers) inevitable, and not the reverse!"

The Gaon of Rogachev, Rabbi Yosef Rozin, master of halakhic thought, helps us define the interaction between God's absolute freedom of decision and man's freedom of action.[304] There is a relationship and complementarity between the providential supra-rational determinism of God who *knows* everything, and the relatively rational and natural determinism of man, who *wishes to know* everything. The two determinisms nevertheless belong to the world of freedom. They are manifested not only at the historical level but also on the plane of the Halakhah, the plane of practical and ethical application of the Torah in everyday living, right down to the small things of daily life.

In daily life incidents occur. To those who experience them they seem to be of a strictly personal, family character; only their immediate significance is seen and perceived. On the other hand, in the perspective of Providence, Divine, hidden, and as yet incomprehensible, they are called to play a determinative historic role. For these incidents concern the history of Israel, and by that fact have a universal bearing. This is how the case of Joseph should be considered—he who was at the start of the "descent of Israel into Egypt."[305]

To illustrate its philosophy of Jewish history, the Midrash takes one of the stories about Joseph as its motif. This is the story (Gen. 43:1-6):

"The famine was still severe in the land (of Canaan). And when they had used up the corn they had brought from Egypt, their father Jacob said to his sons, 'Go back' (to Egypt, where Joseph was, though his father did not know it) 'and buy a little more corn.' But Judah replied, 'That man' (Joseph!) 'plainly warned us that we must not go into his presence unless our brother' (Benjamin!) 'was with us' ... and Israel said, 'Why have you done me *this wrong*? Why did you tell the man that you had yet another brother?'"

On this Biblical foundation the Midrash develops its theme and says, "We are told things that are true and we respond with trivialities: 'And Israel said, Why have you done me *this wrong*?' No, Jacob never said anything trivial. But it is God, the Holy One, Blessed be He, who is saying, I Myself am working to install his son (Joseph) as king in Egypt, and he (Jacob) says, 'Why have you done me this wrong.' The prophet of Israel is referring to this when he exclaims (Is. 40:27), 'Why do you complain, O Jacob, and you, Israel, why do you say, My plight is hidden from the Lord and my cause has passed out of God's notice?'"[306]

From "old Jacob's" "momentary" annoyance and his complaint "today" were to be born his great joys of "tomorrow," but Jacob did not know this. Above all he did not know that the family incident which had erupted over Joseph was the start of great historical developments. He was to learn this only when the *Ruah HaKodesh*, "the spirit of holiness," inspired him.

What a difference, however, between the limited human horizons and the wide-open Divine horizons! What a difference, too, between the "subjectivity" of both the passing griefs and fleeting pleasures of man, and the "objectivity" of the hopes of enduring salvation that God is shaping for the Man *par excellence*, for Israel!

The Midrash again, with the help of an example taken from the Bible, and as before in an ironic way, reveals to us the serious side of its historical-philosophical conceptions. Now this example is found in a Biblical episode which, according to the Talmud and the great Torah commentators, is intentionally[307] placed in the very heart of the recital of the "descent of Joseph into Egypt" and his first experiences in the land of the Pharaohs. In between two chapters dealing with Joseph in Egypt is inserted chapter 38 of the Book of Genesis. This tells an apparently "irrelevant" fact. Judah, Joseph's brother, who played an important part in the rediscovery of the brother who had been "sold" meets Tamar. Now from this meeting was to spring a line of descent which led directly to the birth of David, the Messiah-King, ancestor of the Messiah, "son of David."[308]

In the course of this brief meeting, Judah committed "a sin through ignorance";[309] Tamar committed one "with a good intention," *LeShem Shamayim Nitkavnu*: "the intention" that inspired their act and determined it was consecrated "in the Name of Heaven."[310] God sees it; He even "facilitates"[311] this free human action, for He *knows* what will be the result: "the Kingdom of the House of David," "the Messiah-King."[312]

This is how the Midrash depicts this strange situation:

"It happened that *at that time* Judah left his brothers..." (Gen. 38:1). Thus the Torah introduces the chapter which speaks of the meeting of Judah and Tamar, "precisely at that time when people were concerned about Joseph." And the Midrash comments: " 'For I *know* my purpose *for you*' (Jer. 29:11). The founders of the tribes (the sons of Jacob) are occupied with selling Joseph. Joseph is occupied with his fasting. Jacob is occupied with his hunger. Judah is occupied with taking a wife. And the Holy One, Blessed be He, is occupied creating the light of the Messiah. 'It happened that at that time Judah left his brothers...' 'Before the onset of labor she gave birth' (Is. 66:7). Before the birth of the first oppressor (of Israel) the final redeemer is born!"[313]

"It happened that at that time," when Judah was engaged in his discussions about Joseph, not only was the Galut born but the *geulah* too was inaugurated. Indeed, "at that time," following her meeting with Judah, Tamar gave birth to Perez, who was the direct lineal ancestor of David.[314]

Here is an example of the interaction between Divine Providence manifested, acting with absolute freedom, and mankind with obscured vision, acting with limited freedom. But their development and co-operation leads to salvation.

* * *

We should no longer be astonished that the Maharal goes a very long way in his argument about the *gezerah*. He bases it on Talmudic texts which allow one to say that the fulfillment of one *gezerah*, a plan of God's, may make another *gezerah* necessary by which Israel will *apparently* commit a sin, so that it can accomplish its *teshuvah*, "return" to God,[315] for in turning again to God, it will come back "renewed," "raised up" and even "closer" to its Creator.[316] It would in that case be a matter of what the Talmud calls *Mitzvah HaBa'ah BaAverah*, "a good action that comes about through a bad action,"[317] or *Gedolah Averah LiShmah*, "a transgression committed with a good intention."

But indeed such an *averah* is only *apparent* — *Mithaze Kahet*; in truth such a sin is not real, as is demonstrated by the great masters of Jewish mysticism and especially the Ari HaKadosh and Rabbi Moshe Alshekh (who place the meeting of Judah and Tamar in this category).[318] The Talmud had earlier affirmed that "he who says that Israel (and some illustrious sons of Israel, including David) sinned, is mistaken." For they only sinned to teach the world about *teshuvah* and its efficaciousness. Israel only sinned to offer the world the example or model of *teshuvah*, the 'return' to God."[319]

However, the *gezerah*, the "decree" by which God "binds Himself"[320] to act against Israel, leading them, for example, into exile, is not necessarily of a painful nature; it may also be a pleasant one.[321]

Viewing it always in the general interest of Israel and the world, and looking at it from the viewpoint of final salvation, the *gezerah* does not foresee for Israel only painful measures like the Galut; in point of fact it also comprises measures that are "gracious," protective, nay, indeed leading to salvation for man, for Israel and for Erets-Yisrael.[322]

Thus to Israel God declares, "What can I do? I have already pronounced a *gezerah*; I have already established a decree, whereby you (the children of Israel) are My children!"[323] And regarding Erets-Yisrael, the Land of Israel, God declares to Abraham, "I have given this land to your descendants."[324] The Midrash analyzes the purport of this statement and finds, "He does not say, 'I *shall give* this land to your descendants,' but 'I *have given* this land to your descendants; I have already given it to them and it is theirs.'"[325]

Nevertheless, this Divine *gezerah*, constant, unshakable, irrevocable, in the sense that it represents the *shevu'a*,[326] the "Oath" of God, does not thereby become less dynamic when it comes in contact with man, with Israel; it does become mobile, for it must by its very nature "allow things to develop" and follow one after another. *Nitgalgel HaDavar*. Indeed, the Creator has favored man with the gift of liberty so that he will use it, even to go against His own *gezerah*: *mevatlin gezerah!*

Gezerah Min Hashamayim and *Koah HaBehirah Alei Adamot*: "The Divine Decree from Heaven" and man's "Freedom of Choice on Earth"

The Galut is therefore a *gezerah*, a "cut" that God makes in Israel's body. He engraves the *gezerah* of the Galut in Israel's flesh, just as by circumcision he has commanded the "sign" of His "covenant with Abraham" to be engraved in the flesh of a Jew, the sign of Abraham's "integrity;"—likewise he made Jacob lame in the hip even while raising him to the rank of "Israel," the "invincible."[327] With strict compassion and merciful severity that He engraves the terms of this Covenant, this *gezerah*, in Israel's spirit, the strength of which comes from the nature his Creator has granted him. The *gezerah* is really a decree that God "carves" in the rock of this people, Israel, in the rock that God, Who is called The Rock of Israel, has Himself constructed and shaped, so that they should have "the strength" to endure this painful "cut," this severe wound, in their body; so that they should have the strength to resist the vicissitudes to which He exposes them. This is why He adapts this *gezerah* to the people's capacity to resist in the *various* circumstances of the *galuyot*. For He Himself has endowed them with these capabilities since their creation, when the phenomenon of exile itself was inscribed in the cosmic blueprint. For He, the Creator, "knows his path and He knows his resting place."[328]

Of course God knows man, for He created him; He knows Israel for

He created them; He "understands" and "foresees" their actions, which "He permits them" to carry out.[329] But in making Man, in creating Israel, He made them know that "they are unique in the universe"[330] because He "has given them free will."[331] If man wishes to take the path of goodness to be righteous, that depends only on him, if on the other hand he wishes to take the path of wrongdoing to be wicked, that is also open to him, "do not let yourselves be convinced," writes Maimonides, "by the view held by stupid people that the Holy One, Blessed be He, decrees (*gozeir*) for every man, even from his birth, whether he should be righteous or wicked; that is not the case. In fact every man has the possibility of being righteous, like Moses our Master, or wicked like Jeroboam....And no one forces him or predetermines (*gozeir*) his behavior....The Creator does not predestine (*gozeir*) man to be righteous or wicked. If this priniciple is accepted, it follows that the sinner himself brings about his own ruin."[332]

In his praise of self-determination in the twelfth century, that "cold" rationalist, Maimonides, is joined by the "warm" pietist, Rabbi Ya'akov Yossef of Polnoy, disciple of the founder of the Hassidic movement, Rabbi Israel Ba'al Shem Tov, in the eighteenth century. The famous author of *Toldot Ya'akov Yosef*, likewise strongly affirms that "every Jew can attain the level of Moses our Master"[333] without, however, being able to reach the level of Moses as a prophet, a level that no one can achieve.[334]

The daring affirmations of the Rambam (Maimonides) and Rabbi Ya'akov Yosef reflects the basic principle of equality in the Jewish religion. The latter is not content—as Rabbi Moshe Alshekh underlines—with "holy personalities" who shine among the Jewish "community," but requires that the whole "community," the "whole community of the children of Israel," be "holy."[335] Moreover, these affirmations confirm that the principle of human self-determination is at the very foundation of the Torah, which says: "Behold this day I offer you the choice of a blessing and a curse. The blessing will come if you listen to the commandments of the Lord your God which I give you this day, and the curse if you do not listen to the commandments of the Lord your God" (Deut. 11:26-28). This too is characteristic of the ethical conception of the Talmud which states, "Everything depends upon Heaven, except the fear of God."[336]

Nevertheless, the same Maimonides, who remains the most illustrious representative of the Jewish philosophy of free will, recognizes that at the national communal level of the *people* of Israel, free will is very restricted. Nor did he, a doctor and a psychologist, fail to recognize that free will can be gravely affected, in the case of an individual, by "innate" and "social" factors![337]

But the *gezerah* exists. God has "inscribed" it deeply into the life of His people. Its effect on the existence of Israel is hard. In his *Igeret Teiman*, his famous "Epistle to the Jews of the Yemen," Maimonides strongly asserts that the *gezerah* shapes Israel's destiny; it is predestined for them. In this letter the Rambam brings light and comfort to his fellow believers struggling in the shadows of distress, but he does not hide from them — he even emphasizes — the seriousness and the influence of the *gezerah* in the life of the people of Israel: it is this which will assure the *geulah* their deliverance from the pangs of the Galut.

That "cold" rationalist, the Rambam, pleads the bitter cause of the *gezerah* of the Galut with the same warmth and emotion which the Jewish mystics such as Rabbi Yehuda HaLevi, Rabbi Moshe Alshekh and Rabbi Israel Ba'al Shem Tov, convey to us when they speak of the Galut.

Certainly the *gezerah* has the unchangeable character of a Divine decree, a *shevua*, an "oath." It remains what it is. The Sages of Israel have taught us this.[338] Therefore Israel should accept it. And in fact Israel lives through the *gezerah*, through the entirety of Galut, courageously and nobly. But it was given on condition (so the Sages of Israel teach us, emulating the prophets) that Israel engages not only in self-questioning about the meta-historical, "hidden," genesis of the *gezerah* of the Galut, but also about the immediate "visible" historical motives which *unleashed* it; that Israel asks, like Jeremiah, *Al Mah*, "Why?" "For what reason?" "What was the cause of all that is happening to us?" And it was given on condition that they ask, like the Sages of Israel, *Mipnei Mah*, "Why?" "For what purpose?" "Where will all that is happening to us lead us?"[339] In admitting that there is a cause and an end purpose for all that is happening to Israel, in taking an active interest in them, participating consciously and consientiously, *Mah Lechah*,[340] the Jew exercises his free will even in relation to the *gezerah*. Thus it is possible to reconcile the apparent contradiction between the Rambam's theses on the completeness of the individual Jew's free will (as he expounds it in the "Shmoneh Perakim," the *Yad HaHazakah*, and the *Moreh Nevukhim* — "Guide to those who have gone astray"), and the same thinker's argument on the restricted free will of the Jewish national community, as he presents it in the *Igeret Teiman*.

It is true, the Sages of Israel and especially Rabbi Yohanan ben Zakkai preach the submission of Israel to the *gezerah* which inaugurated the Galut; like the prophet Jeremiah they exhort the Jewish people not to reject "by force" the universal domination of their oppressors, in as much as the latter allow them to study the Torah and apply its *mitzvot*; they (the Sages) ask the Jewish people to recognize the solemnity of the Divine "oath"[341] concerning the dispersion of Israel among the nations — temporary in character even if prolonged; they recommend that Israel consider the "kingdoms which enslave them" as being "established by a decree of Heaven:" *Uma Zu Min HaShamayim Himlikhuha*.[342]

However, the Sages also teach that the Divine *gezerah* neither completely contradicts nor totally abolishes human free will; consequently man, Israel, retains his right to contest, object, disagree, and even to oppose; and above all he retains his right to spiritual acts likely to lead to the *geulah*, to deliverance. Free will is no less safeguarded when it is precisely a question of a *gezerah* which concerns a *tsibbur*, a "community," the community of Israel; such a "*gezerah* is not signed";[343] it is not sealed, it is not final.

For the *tsibbur*, thanks to its constitutional assets, and above all to the qualities inherent in it, is capable of unexpectedly effecting its *teshuvah*, the "return" to God. The *teshuvah* of the *tsibbur* thus makes the *gezerah* inoperative, taking away from it the historical, immediate opportunity necessary for it to be put into operation.

Indeed the *yahid*, the "individual," has greater difficulty in finding the way of *teshuvah*, than the *tsibbur*, the community of Israel which has long experience of relations with their God. Furthermore, the prayer of the *tsibbur*, the "community," is welcomed by God more than that of the *yahid*, the individual.[344] It is the people of Israel, the community, the "*eida*," who publicly bear witness to God, who can solemnly sanctify "the Name " of God,[345] who proclaim God's sovereignty in the world. For it is to the people of God in its totality that God revealed Himself in order to give them the Torah, and in the people of Israel united at the foot of Mount Sinai were included all the future generations of Israel.[346]

The *gezerah* is thus not entirely inconsistent with free will. That is why, even as far as the *yahid*, the "individual" is concerned, after the verdict that follows the "*gezar din*," the judgment, though the *gezerah* be signed and sealed it can always be revoked, modified, "averted" or "postponed" — *ma'avirin* — and even "annulled" — *mevatlin*, and, finally, "torn up" — *mekarin*. If Israel wins favor, He who has pronounced the *gezerah*, God, is ready to abrogate it.[347]

But such an invalidation of the *gezerah* in *Beit Din shel Ma'alah*, the "Tribunal on High," cannot be considered unless the motives for the annulment are valid. If man, that is Israel, has "sincerely" used the means available to obtain a postponement or even a repeal or cancellation of the *gezerah*, this can be considered on High and hoped for on Earth. What are these means? Prayer, charity—including justice—and above all *teshuvah*, a "return to God."[348] It is this return which both conditions and embraces prayer and charity, which both engenders and brings to a successful conclusion prayer and charity. The latter have value only if they are undertaken and carried out as the *mitzvot* of the Torah, as the commandments of God, which must be observed in the context of the other *mitzvot*. Return to God is therefore primordial and ultimate; it is thanks to the return that a "change"[349] in the *gezerah*, the verdict, and a "reversal" of the *kelalah*, the "curse,"[350] can be obtained.

But a return "to God" must not be considered only as an improvement of the relations between man, Israel, "and his Creator," leading to reestablishment in His confidence. The *teshuvah* is meant also, and above all, to bring about an improvement and a reestablishment of relations between a man and his neighbor, and between the individual Jew with his people. The return to God precedes and consolidates the "reconciliation" of man with others, with him who is called to be his "friend," his "fellowman," claiming the same Creator. Without this human reconciliation, *teshuvah* is not only incomplete but totally worthless. It is not a *teshuvah* to God. For God Himself attributes a greater importance to this "reconciliation" between men than to the reconciliation between man, Israel, and his Creator. He makes the *former* a condition for the *latter*, in the domain of relations between the Jew as a human being and his Creator. This priority can be seen especially in the laws of *teshuvah* on the Day of Atonement,[351] but it is also evident in the domain of relations between Israel and Erets-Yisrael and the God of Israel.[352] Thus the "cause" of Israel's first Galut in Egypt is to be sought in the "hostility of Joseph's brothers" towards him; Israel's Galut in Babylon after the destruction of the first Temple of Jerusalem was limited in time; it lasted only 70 years[353] because the Israelites, though they offended God in His Land, behaved charitably towards one another; conversely, the Galut in Edom, after the destruction of the second Temple of Jerusalem, is the longest[354] for it was "caused" by the "enmity"[355] which reigned among the Jews in the Holy Land.

Complete *teshuvah*, when a man becomes reconciled with God, and, thanks be to God, also with his fellow man, is the supreme expression of human freedom. It leads to love: a man's love for God, and the love of man for his fellow man thanks to God. Such a *teshuvah* is capable of influencing the *gezerah*, as much on the individual level of the Jew's relations with God as on the community level of Israel's relations with God. The *teshuvah* of King Hezekiah, his return to God, following his prayer and his charity, serves as a model, in the eyes of the Sages of

Israel.³⁵⁶ It changed the *gezerah* concerning Hezekiah's person and his life; and it changed the *gezerah* concerning Hezekiah's people and their safety. It meant the prolongation of the King's life and the avoidance of exile for his people.

Though it is a "predetermined" *gezerah*, the Galut can thus always be averted. To this truth the admonitions of the Torah are directed in the *tokhahah* as well as in the warnings both visible and audible given by the prophets and Sages of Israel.³⁵⁷ Through the appeals made to Israel by these *tsaddikim*, these "righteous" men, God warns His people what awaits them, and He Himself asks them to "act" so as to "modify" His *gezerah* in order to avert catastrophe. The "changing of human action," *Shinui Ma'asseh*,³⁵⁸ the change of direction that man prints on his action, the accomplishing of this action for the sake of the "Name of Heaven," can bring about a "changing" of the *gezerah*.

Thus the revelation of the *gezerah*, the making public of this "hidden" verdict, is by no means an incitement to fatalistic resignation or a "wait-and-see" attitude, but on the contrary an invitation to saving action.³⁵⁹ The Torah states this clearly: "Because they forsook the covenant of the Lord the God of their fathers which He made with them when He brought them out of Egypt... the Lord uprooted them from their soil in anger... and banished them to another land.... There are things *hidden*, and they belong to *the Lord* our God, but what is *revealed* belongs to *us* and our children... so that we shall 'act' — *la'assot* (so that we observe all that is prescribed in this Law)" (Deut. 29:25-29).

Teshuvah may "hasten" or "retard" the arrival of the Galut, so that it happens in conditions less severe than those that were "intended." But once the *gezerah* has been put into effect and the Galut has begun, the "merit" of the *teshuvah* can "lighten" the burden of the exilic slavery; it can "shorten" the length of exile that was originally "intended" (the example of the "slavery in Egypt" is still edifying); it can "bring forward" the expected "date" of the *geulah*, of deliverance.³⁶⁰ "If" Israel "merits" — *zakhah* — if Israel even achieves a *zikukh* (purification) before the time anticipated, which makes them worthy of *geulah*, salvation, the Messiah will come. "*Mashiah*, the Messiah, may even come *hayom*, 'today,' if you will hear His voice," the voice of God, assure the Sages of the Talmud.³⁶¹

The Divine "determinism" concerning the Galut is thus itself subordinate to the conditions imposed upon it and the "limits" imposed upon it by human free will. It is a determinism which is in suspense, conditional — *Zekhut tolah*; it depends, in spite of its all-powerfulness, on precarious human freedom. It is thus a determinism which is not frozen or static, but open to the initiatives of Israel and notably of him who personifies Israel, the *tsaddik*, the "righteous" man.

Thus it is that God is disposed not only to suppress the *gezerah*, but to submit Himself to a *gezerah* of human origin! It is the *gezerah* of the *tsaddik*, the righteous man (and even of the simple Jew "who observes the Sabbath," strictly and joyously, and even of the simple Jew "who respects one *mitzvah* in its fullest sense!")[362]

Afilu HaKadosh—Baruh-Hu—gozeir gezerah, hu mevatlah. "Even if the Holy One, Blessed be He, decrees a *gezerah*, (such a righteous man) is able to cancel it," exclaims the Talmud.[363] Such a *tsaddik* succeeds in "dominating" God! (It was the ambition of the Hassidic *tsaddik*, Rabbi Levi Yitshak of Berditchev[364]—an ardent defender before God of the Jewish people in distress, and accustomed to "bringing cases before God"—to oblige Him"[365] to honor His pledges to His people Israel!)

What an astonishing dialectic is that of the Galut of Israel.

On the one hand this Galut represents a *gezerah* of God, a *gezerah* which is made specially with a view to the "missionary"[366] and "exemplary" vocation of Israel's exile: this people is in exile so that the world may learn, through Israel, through the miraculous example of its life and conduct, to have a better knowledge of the existence of God the Creator of the world, and a better understanding of His intervention in human History. The Galut of Israel thus represents a universal "necessity"—*hutsrakh*, as the Ari HaKadosh has said; Israel must be dispersed among the peoples so that they can directly and immediately perceive the Existence and Presence of God.

On the other hand the Galut represents the punishment that God inflicts upon Israel. But the Hassidic author of the *Sefat Emet*,[367] and the most erudite author of the *Beit Halevi* both affirm (as does the Ari HaKadosh) that, if Israel had not sinned, it would not have had to go into exile in different parts of the world, there to witness to God before men and peoples, but the latter would have come to them in the Land of Israel so that Israel "could teach them their ways" and teach them "the word of God," as was "envisaged" and "promised" for the messianic period.[368] The beginning, the creation, would at once have been merged with the end, the Messianic Age, without having to pass through the Galut, in its Messianic progress, painfully climbing back towards the Beginning. Potentially the free will of Israel, of man, could have deflected the *gezerah* of the Galut. But this did not happen. For "sin caused" the Galut: *Garam HaHet*! In exchange, "the reward is proportionate to the suffering," to the punishment patiently endured, the labor diligently sustained: *Lefum Tsa'ara Agra*.[369]

The *gezerah* is a *hok*, a law.
The *hok* of Galut, Torah and Nature

God uses the same terms to designate the origins and the mandate concerning the Galut, the Torah and Nature. The identity of these terms signifies that they are all His works, and are all under His authority. His "constraining" Providence concerning Israel's Galut, His "constraining" Will concerning the promulgation of the Torah; His "wisdom" concerning the establishment of Nature, all three are expressed by the word *gezerah* and the same word is even explained by its synonym, by the word *hok. Gezerah gazarti, huka hakakti.*[370]

The Legislator of the Torah, the Creator of Nature, the Lord of the History of Israel, God, announces by His *hok*, His "law," the coming into force and the result of these three acts, Torah, Nature, History.[371] The Torah which precedes the creation of Nature; Nature which is at the service of the Torah; and finally the History of a people which—especially in the Galut where the imperative requirement is *teshuvah*, "return" to God—links Torah and Nature to their common Author.[372] The Torah, Nature and History all have a permanent character. Nevertheless, History, expressed in Israel's life-journey, must include the Galut, of a temporary character—for this is an instrument, to achieve a purpose. And the laws of Galut are included in those of History—"conditioned by them.

For the *hukim*, "laws," which govern these three domains proceed from the same *hok*, the same law and are called upon to amalgate with it.

In truth, God proclaims, *Zot Hukat HaTorah*, "This is the law of the Torah!"[373] and He declares, "These are the words of the Lord who *set the sun* for a light by day and *hukot* (laws, ordained rules for) the moon and stars for a light by night.... If these *hukim*, if these *laws* vanish out of My sight, only then could the race of *Israel* cease for evermore to be a *nation* in my sight..." "These are the words of the Lord: If I had not made my covenant with the day and night, and if I had not established *hukot*—the *laws of the heavens and the earth*, I would also spurn the descendants of Jacob and David.... For I will *bring back their captives from exile*" (Jer. 31:34-35; 33:25-26).

And so the *hok* instituted by God simultaneously governs the Torah, Nature and the Galut.

Galut, Torah, Nature, have their origin in the *Mahshavah*, the Divine "thought" which was responsible for their "creation";[374] that Thought prescribes their "laws" over which It "keeps watch" and whose observance It guarantees. But this Thought should not be classified in rational human categories. The Reason of God is supra-rational, without being anti-rational. It allows man to use his reason, with which the Creator has endowed him, and to think about the Divine Thought and thus to be persuaded, thanks to his own reason, about the justness of the Divine word. Thus the Prophet Isaiah says: "As the heavens are higher than the earth, so are My ways higher than your ways and My thoughts higher than your thoughts."[375] Therefore, the Sages of Israel add, "Do not seek out that which passes your understanding; do not seek out what is hidden"; do not seek for the "roots" of things. However, "you are permitted" to seek for the "reasons" behind the events of history[376] and particularly those of the Galut, the "reasons" underlying the phenomena of Nature, and the "reasons" fundamental to the precepts of the Torah — the *Ta'amei HaMitzvot*. You may seek to explain what *is*, what is created, legislated, given by God; it is even recommended to you to try to "understand," "as far as you are able";[377] but on the other hand you are "compelled" to accept all the ordinances as you accept the laws of Nature; but you are also "free" to adopt them, apply them, according to the capabilities and requirements of your own *person* and the *social* circumstances in which you live. However, if you apply them, apply them because they constitute a *gezerah* of God[378] and not because they satisfy, at least in part, the judgment that you have formed about them, for your judgment is relative, and far, very far, from approaching the absolute — so that most lucid "seeker," the Rambam, acknowledges.[379]

Consequently you have only to listen to God's proclamation which says, "I have pronounced a decree, a *gezerah*; I have promulgated a law, a *hukah* and it is useless to contest their worth; it is futile to rebel against them; it is superfluous to question their utility; this will become evident particularly 'in the future.'" *Ein LeHarher Ahreya*. "There is no cause to conceive illusory ideas about them."[380] The laws of God are just. For all of them emanate from the Thought of God. Now His Thought engenders your own thought, illuminates it and extinguishes it; His Thought precedes and follows you; it is eternal and so all-seeing; it is therefore all-embracing.

In truth, the prophet of Israel asks, "Who has measured the waters in the palm of his hand, or with its span measured the limit of the heavens? Who has gauged the dust of the earth? Who has set limits to the spirit of the Lord? *What counselor stood at His side to instruct Him?* With whom did He confer to gain discernment? Who taught Him how to do justice or gave Him lessons in wisdom? Why, to Him nations are but drops from a bucket, like a grain of dust on the scales" (Is. 40:12-15).[381]

Therefore may He demand of you, O men, O peoples, both submission

THE GALUT — ISRAEL'S EXILE • 115

to His power and confidence in His wisdom.

He conceived the world before creating it, and consequently, "He has mapped out *laws* which will not change";³⁸² He conceived the Torah before promulgating it, and consequently He "compelled" Israel, "on Mount Sinai,"³⁸³ to accept this Law which "will not change."³⁸⁴ He conceived the ultimate goal of the History of Israel (and *ipso facto* that of Humanity) before it began, and consequently He included in it the *law* of the Galut (an impermanent law but one firmly fixed in the general law of History) which He subsequently imposed on Israel, so that the Galut would mark, at its "finale," the "ultimate goal" of History, the salvation of Israel and Humanity.

Interrogation and silence

The Galut, Torah and Nature are Divine "conceptions"; each individually, and all together they "appeared in the beginning in the Thought of God," in His *Mahshavah*.

However, you may find you have "questions" about their "rightness," and being disquieted you may sometimes wish to ask their Author for an "explanation" about the "unmerited sufferings," "the unjust punishments" and the absence of equitable "rewards" that you see around you; you may feel the need to ask Him, in the words of Moses, "Why do the righteous suffer and the wicked flourish?"³⁸⁵ And if at a given moment you are indignant about a deed, or an event, which seems unjust (and which nevertheless derives from the "order" of these laws) and if you dare question Him about this, says the Talmud, the reply is not delayed; it can be clearly heard. A commanding voice comes from highest Heaven, admonishing you with the voice of authority that halts you, saying, "*Shetok! Kah Ala BeMahshavah Lefanai!* — Be silent, for the fact (which you have observed) has thus risen up before Me, in My *Mahshavah*,"³⁸⁶ in My Thought, while Silence reigned in the world of Nature (as it was to reign in the world when God promulgated the Torah and "spoke on Sinai; "then," says the Midrash, "*Hishtik Kol HaOlam*, God made the whole world *silent*, so that the creatures should know that there is no one apart from Him."³⁸⁷ In reality "nothing exists without Him" and "all the creatures take their being only from the truth of His being"³⁸⁸).

Thus God conceived this fact which you, O man, raise in your "objection," before any human voice could be heard nor any "spoken" complaint could be uttered. He inscribed the *gezerah* of this deed from the beginning, in the same order of Thought, *Mahshavah*, that was responsible for the creation of the Torah, of Nature, of Israel.

You recognize, then, the inadequacy of your human judgment, and you are silent. But like Abraham you receive the "reward" for your silence.[389] And you speak again. Not to complain, but humbly to proclaim the *Tsiduk HaDin*,[390] the Divine "justification of the judgment." You recite this Biblical verse which is at the basis of the *Tsiduk HaDin*: "The Rock, His work is perfect, *tamim*" (when one regards it in its "totality," which goes beyond the immediate present); "for all His ways are just" (as one will recognize when one is able to understand *Omek HaDin*, all the "depth of judgment"); "a faithful God" ("Who will reward the righteous for their piety in the future world, and though He may delay the date, He will in the end keep faith") (Rashi on Deut. 32:4).

Jewish martyrs who recite this verse measure the future; they are in another world which is not at all far from them; "it is a few steps away" and they refrain from "the slightest thought" that is "critical" about the justice of the "measures" taken by God regarding themselves; they forbid themselves the least thought of "discontent": *Ein LeHarher Aharei Midotav*.[391]

The *tsaddik*, the righteous man, suffers in sympathy with God's suffering

The *yissurim*, the "punishment" of the Galut which these Jews "feel" as "sufferings," are in their eyes the result of a Divine decree which the Creator and Lawgiver, the Lord of History, Who is "all-seeing," Who "sees the whole," has promulgated for the "good" of all people, for all times.[392]

As for the *tsaddik*, the "righteous man," the Jew in exile, he feels in the Galut not his own sufferings but the "suffering" of Him Who, "bound by the laws," the *gezerot*, which He has proclaimed, is Himself "compelled" to apply the "verdicts" which He has reached concerning human beings. The *tsaddik* therefore suffers for God and not for himself; he suffers because God suffers in sympathy with his sufferings. For he knows, he feels that God "is with him in suffering." That is why he "weeps" with Him in the "mysteries" of his intimacy with Him—*BaMistarim*.[393]

Thus the *tsaddik*, the righteous man, prays for God; he prays "that the Galut of the *Shekhinah*," the Divine Exile, may end; he prays for the "deliverance" of the *Shekhinah* from the Galut.[394] And when he prays for the deliverance of Israel from the Galut, he does it because he knows that the deliverance of Israel from the Galut will at the same time mark the deliverance of the *Shekhinah*. For in himself he has a profound sense of the Presence of the *Shekhinah* in the Galut.³⁹⁵

Above all, the *tsaddik*, perceiving this Divine Presence and feeling His close and comforting nearness, "clings to his God," unites himself with Him, identifies himself with Him. Has he need of anyone other than Him? Having Him, he has everything, and he has everything with joy. Little by little, therefore, the pangs of the Galut fade completely. The Galut not only dissolves from his mind and ceases to exist, but he is already living in the beginnings of the *geulah*, the deliverance; he even feels the foretaste of salvation. He feels it with the joy that comes to him from contemplation of the "perfect work" of God: the Torah, Nature, the existence of Israel, its History, including the "former" Galut. He tastes the delights offered by the "study of the Torah," *Talmud Torah*; "prayer in community," *Tefilah BeTsibur*, in the "love of Israel," *Ahavat Yisrael*, in the *Bet HaKnesset*, in the "House of Assembly" for study and prayer, for the glorification of the Name of the *Borei Olam*, of *Noten HaTorah*, of *Elokei Yisrael*—for the sanctification of the Name of the "Creator of the World," the "Giver of the Torah," the "God of Israel."

The *tsaddik* already experiences deliverance in the present; he already feels salvation itself, the *geulah*. The Maharal and the Sefat Emet bring us the evidence of this.³⁹⁶

The Galut and its task of unifying the Torah, Nature and History

To describe the domains of the Torah, Nature and Galut and assign them their tasks, God uses the same vocable, *hok*; in the lexicon of the Sages of Israel this word is synonymous with *gezerah*. It must be considered, therefore, that between these three domains which all have the same origin there is a correlation which might lead to their identification with one another.

This correlation comes from the fact that they have as their Author the same Lawgiver, the same Creator, the same Lord of History. It is God; the one and only God.

But this one and only God, in accomplishing His work which originally was unitary, gradually diversified it as each part developed and acquired a certain autonomy. However, being one in its origin (and remaining one in its whole), His work is required to recover its initial unity.

The task of "unification," of *Yihud*, falls to Israel, "the one and only people," *Goi Ehad*, which proclaims to the world the *Yihud HaShem*, the "unity of the Name," the oneness and uniqueness of God. Israel is the incumbent of the mission to "unite" the worlds of Torah, Nature and History, to the glory of their Author; to make them rise again from the temporal state to which they have descended back to the Source, on the threshold of Eternity from which they came; to restore them to their Root; to make them "turn again" to God.[398] Now to this end Israel uses the Galut (a severe and effective instrument) in which it finds itself; it uses this galutic, "dispersed," "divided" world in which it is disseminated;[399] it uses it to overcome the fragmentation and divided state of humanity and so to accomplish the Whole, to achieve Unity.

In doing so Israel rises above its status as a created being to that of a creator; that is to say, one who creates in unity. From creature (though truly God's Handiwork, in which He takes pride![400]) Israel becomes "the partner of the Holy One, Blessed be He, in the work (task) of the Beginning."[401] He is worthy of the title of co-creator, for, like Abraham, he is leading "the Divine work of the Beginning," which has become diversified, back to the Beginning, to Unity. Thus he is carrying out "the intention which was the Creator's at the moment of Creation": to receive on its return to its Source the work which He sent forth. Israel thus completes the work of God, the work that He began so that it might by the grace of the Divine Creator be completed by the labor of the human creator, *La'asot*.[402] Reflecting on this cosmic, historical and Messianic process, in which Israel is the principal and recognized agent, the Sages of Israel affirm that "the gathering together of the galuyot is as important as the day on which the heavens and the earth were *created*."[403]

Now the Galut is, by its origin, its essence and its very goal, linked with Erets-Yisrael. (God prophesied the exile to Abraham at the same time as He promised him the "Land"; Israel was born as a future nation at the very moment the "land" was born as the future Land of Israel.) It is thus proper that Erets-Yisrael, the place designated *ab origine* for the gathering together of the galuyot, for the *Shivat Tsion*, the "return of the Jewish people to Zion," should be the place where *teshuvah*, the return, of Israel to God[404] should end "in song,"[405] where the return of the world to God should be celebrated with gladness.

It is in this Country where, according to the Gaon of Vilna, "the heavens and the earth embrace," where, according to Rabbi Menahem Mendel of Kotsk, "the Earth rises to heaven and heaven descends to Earth"; where, according to the Hidushei HaRim, "the land is called to become heaven and heavens are called to become land"—it is in this country that the ultimate union of Torah, Nature and History will take place. The Torah will there attain its practical concrete expression, and Nature will find its ideal spiritual realization. Consequently the *hukim*, "laws," of the Torah and of Nature will unite in the same unique *hok*, in the same unique "Law" from which they emanated. The Galut having dissolved, its laws will be re-absorbed into those of Erets-Yisrael and in particular in the *Mitzvot HaTeluyot BaArets*; the latter will be finally and totally joined again to the Laws of the Torah and Nature, and together they will be united in the same *Hok*, the same "Law" of God, the one and only God Who reigns over "all the united worlds." Once Israel is reestablished in its own country, its History—which from then on will exemplify the History of Humanity reconciled with God and at peace in itself—will rejoin the stability of the Torah and of Nature; the laws of History will link up with the laws of the Torah and Nature and all of them together will be united in the collective *Hok*, the collective Law which, simultaneously and harmoniously, governs the Torah, Nature and History.

The detailed *ta'amim*, the particular "reasons" for all the laws of the Torah, of Nature and of the History of Israel, will appear in the future in all their clarity and they will harmonize with one another;[406] they will be unified in the general, all-embracing Reason of the *hok*, which will then be revealed in its full brightness. The Reason, the *Ta'am* of the *hok*, will thus give Man, the Jew, the fundamental understanding of all the *hukim*, all the "laws." Reason will not only be grasped by human intelligence; it will equally be felt by the human senses, in its *Ta'am*, its revitalizing "taste." This union of reason and the emotions expressed by the *ta'am* constitutes the reward of the Jew, of Israel who has functioned as the protagonist of exile, paving the way to Messianic times.

Geulah through Galut: Galut leading to *geulah*

We have said that Israel's Galut in Egypt is the "root," the prototype of all Israel's *galuyot* in the world;[407] it is virtually the "sum" of all the *galuyot*. Consequently the "exodus from Egypt," Israel's deliverance from slavery, is the root, the prototype and, according to the Hida and the Sefat Emet,[408] the "preparation" for all Israel's deliverances, *geulot*, from the various *galuyot*.

Just as Israel's "going down into Egypt" into the Galut necessarily implies "Israel's exodus" from Egypt, *Yetsiat Mitsrayim*, so the "wanderings of the children of Israel in the wilderness after leaving the land of Egypt," *Mas'ei B'nei Yisrael*,[409] prefigure the "march" of the children of Israel in the "wilderness of nations," *Midbar HaAmim*,[410] in all the *galuyot*, symbolized by their exiles in the "Four Kingdoms." It demands their re-entry into the Promised Land.[411]

When He foretold to the children of Israel the first Galut (the Galut in Egypt, though this is not specifically mentioned), which implies all the other *galuyot*, God said to Abraham, "Know that I will scatter them; but know also that I will gather them together again. Know that I Myself will make them slaves; but know also that I Myself will save them."[412]

The certainty of Israel's deliverance from the galutic pangs thus well and truly exists. God has not only promised to liberate the children of Israel from the horrors of the *galuyot* but, says the Midrash, "He has sworn that, as He saved Israel from the first exile in Egypt, He will save them from the (last) Galut in Edom."[413] The Midrash supports this assertion with the Divine words communicated to the people of Israel by the prophet Micah: "I will show you miracles, as in the days when you came out of Egypt."[414]

Israel's coming out of Egypt remains the "root" and prototype of the miracles of all Israel's coming out of *galuyot*. The proof, according to the same Midrash and, according to Rabbi Joshua in the Talmud, is the date of the "future"—and thus final, ultimate—deliverance of Israel from all its *galuyot*; it will coincide with the date of the coming out of Egypt. *BeNissan Nig'alu; BeNissan Atidin Liyga'el*.[415] The "spring" month of Nissan, the month of Israel's "coming out of Egypt," the month of the celebration of Pessah, will always be called *Hodesh Shel Geulah*, the month of deliverance, of salvation. A correlation is established between the four biblical expressions foretelling the deliverance from exile in Egypt, *Arba Leshonot Shel Geulah*"; the four cups of wine, *arba kossot* at the *Seder*, the festive meal on Pessah night; and the foretelling of the *galuyot* in the four kingdoms, *Arba Malkhuyot*."[416]

However, the "future deliverance," *HaGeulah HeAtidah*, from the Galut of Edom will also be *HaGeulah HaAharonah* the final deliverance and will exceed in importance and in value the "first deliverance," *Ha Geulah HaRishonah*, from the *Galut Mitsrayim*.

Indeed the Mekhilta writes, "In future Israel will no longer speak of the exodus from Egypt, for it is written (Jer. 16:14), 'The days are coming, says the Lord, when men shall no longer swear "by the life of the Lord who brought the children of Israel up from Egypt" but "by the life of the Lord who brought the children of Israel back from a northern land and from all the lands to which He had dispersed them" and I will bring them back to the soil which I gave to their forefathers.' "[417]

Moreover, the "future deliverance" will be the "definitive," the "ultimate," *Teshuat Olamim*: "there will be no other *shibbud*, no other enslavement, no other Galut after that."[418]

But the essential fact is that the "future deliverance," that from the

Edomite Galut, will be due above all to *Itaruta DiLetata*, a state of readiness coming from below, which is to say a Divine grace earned by Israel living on earth, having been long tested and purified in every part of its essence.[419] Deliverance from Egypt on the other hand was due above all to *Itaruta DiL'eila*, a state of readiness coming from on high, to a celestial grace not wholly merited by Israel on earth.[420] That is why God was "obliged" to liberate Israel from their Egyptian slavery "in haste," *BeHipazon*,[421] so as to avoid the risk of a catastrophic worsening of the situation; whereas the deliverance from the last Galut will be "without haste," *Lo BeHipazon*, as the Prophet Isaiah foretells, "But you shall not come out in urgent haste nor leave like fugitives, for the Lord will march at your head, your rearguard will be Israel's God" (Is. 52:12). At the time of the "future deliverance" God Himself, the *Go'el Yisrael*, the "Savior of Israel," will liberate them; He alone,[422] for He will not employ a messenger, as He used Moses in Egypt: "He will be His own messenger."[423] For, as the prophet Isaiah puts it, "Yes, the Lord is our Judge, the Lord is our Lawgiver; the Lord is our King, to Him we owe our salvation" (Is. 33:22). As for the Messiah, according to the description given us by Maimonides (Rambam, Hilkhot Melakhim, XI and XII), he is a descendant of David who will "reestablish" the kingdom of his ancestor; "who will build the *Bet HaMikdash* (the Temple of Jerusalem) and assemble the scattered remnants of Israel".[424] He is thus a spiritual head, a king, and a temporal commander of Israel "upon whom the spirit of sanctity rests," "who studies the Torah and keeps the *mitzvot*"; he is also a spiritual leader for the whole world, preparing them for God's service, so that they all will invoke the name of the Lord, and worship Him with one heart, as the prophet Zephaniah foretold (Zeph. 3:9).

Galut, the cause of the *geulah*

Thus the Galut bears witness to the *geulah*; exile firmly attests to redemption. The Galut is not only the sign but also the "cause" of the *geulah*, as the Maharal and the Kedushat Levi emphasize: *HaGalut Hi HaSibah LiGeulah*.[425]

As we have seen, the Galut is a phenomenon situated outside the natural, normal order of the life of the nations. God has appointed for each nation a country which is suitable for it. To Israel He assigned in a special way the country best suited to it, and this country alone; moreover He has destined this country for Israel in the immutable *cosmic* order. Separated from its country, therefore, Israel finds itself in an abnormal state which upsets the order of the world; this state therefore can only be temporary, for the order of the world, initiated by the Creator, cannot and should not be permanently disturbed. The Maharal believes that it is fitting that the *geulah*, a phenomenon which like the Galut is supernatural, should reestablish the normal order willed by the Creator, and put an end to the Galut which the Creator introduced only temporarily into the world.[426] So Israel *should* be brought back to Erets-Yisrael and be reestablished in the Land of Israel; and simultaneously "the gathering in (of Israel) from the midst of the peoples among whom they were dispersed," the *necessary* return of Israel to its own country will also mark the "free and willing return (of Israel) to the Lord their God" (Deut. 30:2-3).

Thus the Galut itself creates the *power* which invokes the *geulah*; exile makes this deliverance possible. The Galut is thus the very cause of the *geulah*. This is why the Jerusalem Talmud affirms that "the very day when the *Bet HaMikdash* (Temple of Jerusalem) was destroyed, the Messiah was born."[427] At the moment when the Galut begins, when the Galut appears, the Messiah is born, and there arises the one who shall personify[428] the end of the disorder caused by the Galut; and by implication he shall mark the *tiukun*, the "restoration" of Israel to its normal life and the restoration of Humanity to a life such as the Creator willed, and for their sake, desired it from the "beginning" of Creation.

Galut, the preparation for the *geulah*

The Galut "prepares" the way for the *geulah*; exile is the *hakhana* of deliverance; it first has to prepare the way in the minds of those very Jews who "suffer" exile. The Galut has to become "unbearable" to Israel, from the spiritual aspect above all because of the spiritual and religious "deprivations" which it involves. The danger of a prolongation of the exile grows when Jews come to find it easy to "tolerate" the Galut; spiritually they bear it complacently, morally they become accustomed to it and even say they are "happy" with it.[429] This is why, says the Sefat Emet[430] in the name of the Hidushei HaRim, in promising the children of Israel "to relieve them of of the burdens of Egypt," *Mitahat Sivlot Mitsrayim* (Exod. 6:6), God also "promises" them that He will act in such a way that they themselves will not wish "to tolerate," *Lisbol*, the Galut in Egypt: that they themselves will reject the *Sivlot Mitsrayim*; that they will become disgusted by them, and from this inward rejection of the Galut by Israel, concludes the Sefat Emet, comes the *geulah*, salvation. The Kedushat Levi[431] had earlier given the same interpretation of this verse of the Torah. The teacher of the Hidushei HaRim, Rabbi Menahem Mendel of Kotsk, observes in this connection that, in foretelling the Galut of his descendants to Abraham God did not give the name of the country to which they would be exiled, but told him only that "they will be in a country which will not be their own" (Gen. 15:13). Israel ought to *know* that any country in which they find themselves is not their own, for in truth it is not theirs, so that they will not forget Erets-Yisrael, their country of origin.

The children of Israel, writes the Hatam Sofer,[432] ought to consider themselves to be in exile as did the sons of Jacob in Egypt who, when they arrived, presented themselves to Pharaoh and said, *LaGur BaArets Banu*: "We have come to sojourn in this land"[433] and not to settle here indefinitely.[434] Indeed the verb *LaGur* means to stay as a *Ger*, "a stranger," as one who looks upon himself as a stranger.[435] In truth the heart of Jacob's sons remains in Erets-Yisrael: they hope to go back there. They feel themselves in Galut because they know they must return to Erets-Yisrael.

"The very principle of the Galut is to remind us that we must return to Erets-Yisrael," exclaimed the Shelah HaKadosh (and this reminder effectively contributed to his decision to "go up" to Erets-Israel).

This "reminder" of Erets-Israel (especially the command "not to forget Jerusalem"[436]) has two aspects; its nature is both sentimental and practical. It is sentimental, for the fact of being "prevented" from returning to Erets-Yisrael reinforces the "will" in the mind of the exiled Jew, of Israel in exile, to regain his country, says the Shem MiShemuel. The fact that he "is far away" from the country which is his, observes Bnei Issakhar, awakens in the mind of the exiled Jew, of Israel in exile, the "wish" to return to Erets-Yisrael, to "find once more his well-beloved" land.[437]

This "wish" not only expresses the reaction of a man held apart from his well-beloved; it can also correspond to the "wish" of a man who, having gone of his own accord to a foreign country and feeling far from his wife, ardently wishes to rejoin her; this wish for "reunion" which overcomes a husband after a temporary absence from his wife is roused by separation. Indeed, observes Bnei Issakhar, and like him several other eminent representatives of mystical thinking, the distance that separates the lover from his beloved increases the desire of the former to rejoin the latter; but the distance itself increases in the latter a desire corresponding to that of the former.[438] For the two, Israel and Erets-Yisrael, are both *dodim*, "lovers," who love and seek each other as do the "lovers" in the Shir HaShirim, the Song of Songs.

This is another aspect of the dialectic of the Galut, revealed to us by the Jewish mystics: the *Hibat HaArets*, the "love of the Land" of Israel.

Abraham himself, observes the Shelah HaKadosh, was tested on his journey to Egypt by a feeling of nostalgia, of searching, of impatient waiting for Erets-Yisrael.

The Torah tells us that "Abram went down into Egypt" and then "Abram went up out of Egypt" towards the land of Canaan (Gen. 12:10 and 13:1). Separation from the well-beloved, from the Promised Land, increased the degree and quality of his love, for "separation induces nostalgia, and nostalgia increases love," is the observation, full of remarkable psychological acuity, of the Shelah HaKadosh and after him of the Toledot Ya'akov Yosef and of the Bnei Issakhar.[439]

For these "lovers of Zion," the Galut thus fulfills a positive, creative function in the life of Israel and Erets-Yisrael: for the Jews, for Israel, it renews, keeps alive and above all increases "the love of the Land" of Israel, *Hibat HaArets*.

On the other hand, the "reminder" of their link with Erets-Yisrael, the reawakening of their need to return to Erets-Yisrael, which is felt by Jews individually and Israel collectively in the Galut, are induced by negative factors. These are the enemies of Israel who despise and scoff at every expression of Jewish sentiment, and the "nations of the world" who are hosts to the Jewish people in dispersion, who make the life of the Jew and of Jewish communities in exile hard and "bitter." Now it is this "bitter" existence, the fate of Israel in the Galut, "which forms the beginning of the *geulah*, of their deliverance," writes the Sefat Emet.[440]

The school of the Galut

On the temporal plane the Galut "prepares" the way for the *geulah*.

On the meta-temporal plane this preparation for the *geulah*, for deliverance, and salvation itself by way of the Galut, is primal; it is of the utmost importance.

Thus the "slavery" of the Israelites in Egypt "preceded" and "introduced" the revelation on Mount Sinai which was "Messianic" in character[441] and "prepared" the way for the presentation of the Torah.[442] Indeed, tried by a severe regime of slavery the former slaves of the Pharaohs "learned to appreciate a life of freedom and were ready to exchange their status as 'slaves of slaves' for that of 'servants of God.'" In making the transition from *Avdut Par'oh* to *Avodat HaShem* the Israelites showed themselves to be "worthy" to receive the Torah;[443] they had "earned" it. Now it was Israel's undertaking to respect the

Torah which justified the entry of Israel into the Promised Land: God has given Israel this "Land so that His Laws and His Torah may be kept there."[444]

Later in the course of history, it is the successive purifications in the Galut which prepare the people of Israel for their "return to Zion" in a state of physical and spiritual completeness, which will be marked by the coming of the Messiah. His entry into Jerusalem will signify the arrival of the "days of the Messiah," the coming of the era of salvation for Israel and the whole of humanity.[445]

Galut and *geulah*: want and plenty

Because of its lack of consistency, its disordered, "chaotic" nature, the Galut is to be regarded as a *he'eder*, as a want, a lack, an absence. But "absence is the cause of presence," *HaHe'der Hi Sibat HaHavaya*, observes the Maharal.[446] "As the night precedes the day, so want, non-being, precedes being." The Galut, being a "state of absence of emptiness," precedes and indeed produces the *geulah*, which is "reality," "substances," "as darkness precedes and produces light."[447]

Indeed in the Talmud and Midrashim, the Galut is designated by the name of *hoshekh*, "darkness"; it is compared with "night," *lailah*; whereas the *geulah* is called *or*, "light"; it is compared with "day," *yom*, and with *shahar*, "morning."[448]

Just as light emanates, is born, and emerges out of the dark, so the *geulah* emanates, is born, and emerges out of the Galut.[449]

Thus the Galut produces the *geulah*; the first is the *Siba*, the cause of the second, teaches the Maharal.

The *geulah* materializes out of the Galut; Israel counts the years that separate it from the *geulah*, from the beginning of the Galut, from the destruction of the *Bet HaMikdash*. For Israel has been expecting it since the beginning of the Galut.[450]

What is more, the darkness of the Galut helps us to "distinguish" even more clearly and "to appreciate" with even greater understanding the "light" of the *geulah* "which is good." As it is written, "God saw that the light was *good* and He *separated* the light from the darkness" (Gen. 1:4).

The darkness of the Galut precedes the light of the *geulah*, notes the Shelah HaKadosh, so that it shall better underline, emphasize and enhance the daylight of the *geulah*, the benefits of deliverance. "One does not know the advantages of the light," he says, "except by the depth of the shadows, and by distinguishing the light from the darkness. This is why the Torah says, 'Abram went down into Egypt... and Abram came up out of Egypt.'⁴⁵¹ It was in coming up out of Egypt and returning to the Promised Land that Abraham understood in depth that 'light is far superior to darkness' (cf. Eccl. 2:13)."[452]

Nocturnal visions foretell the Galut

The Galut is compared to night; it is referred to as "darkness" (cf. Gen. R. 2:5).

The Divine prophecy of the Galut, as slavery, or exile, is made by God to Abraham in a *vision* by *night*. The fulfillment of this prophecy is entrusted, and "commanded" by God to Jacob in "a vision by *night*." Abraham and Jacob are "filled with anguish" when they learn the "news" of the Galut; but God comforts them, in assuring them of His presence with them, in promising to be with their descendants, with Israel, in the Galut. Abraham and Jacob accept the Divine decision concerning the Galut and God's personal involvement with Israel in the Galut; they accept it with a complete "trust," with total confidence in the Divine Word, a confidence which is nevertheless not without "fear" (cf. Gen. 15:6; 28:20).

God conveys to Abraham "the news of the Galut" which his children will have to endure in a vision by *night*. He asks him to "look at the starry sky"; "*as the sun was going down, VaYehi HaShemesh LaVo,* a trance came over Abram, and then a *terror*, a deep *darkness* came upon him" (according to Rashi this was "an allusion to the anguish and darkness of the Galut," of exile). God said to him, "do not be *afraid*, Abram; *I am a shield to you.*" Abraham "put his *trust* in the Lord" (Gen. 15).

When Jacob was constrained to put into execution the Divine plan concerning the Galut for Abraham's descendants, God (*Elokim*, the God of "Power") spoke to him and through him "to Israel (to all Israel) in a vision by *night* and said, 'Jacob! Jacob!' " (this repeated call to him by name, according to Rashi, is a sign of love, a mark of God's affection for Jacob), "and he answered, 'Here am I.' God continued, 'I am God, the God of your father. Do not be *afraid* to go down into Egypt.... *I will go down with you* to Egypt, and I Myself will bring you back again' (Gen. 46:2-4)."

It was at *Be'er Sheva* (Beersheba) that Jacob made the preparations for his departure for Egypt. It is true, *this* departure of Jacob into exile was to take him to a country where his well-beloved son, Joseph, was viceroy. To fulfill the Divine decision concerning the Galut of Abraham's posterity, the Sages of Israel say, "Our father Jacob ought to have gone down into Egypt in chains, but his merit brought him favor" so that he arrived there under less arduous conditions.⁴⁵³

However, Jacob had already tasted the "bitter" reality of the Galut when he fled from Esau. On that occasion he had left for an exile where no viceroyal son awaited him with affection; there he was received by the crafty Laban. Nevertheless, for this personal Galut which was a preliminary to the true Galut "of Israel" that began in Egypt, Jacob "set out from *Be'er Sheva*" (as for Egypt). And as it was a matter of a Galut, "he reached a place where he spent *the night, because the sun had set — Ki Va HaShemesh.*" It was during the night that he had the *vision*, the "dream" in which God said to him, "Behold, *I am with you* and *I will protect you* wherever you go and will bring you back to this land, for I will not leave you until I have done all that I promised you" (Gen. 28:10-15).

How remarkable is the coordination of all these texts (today one would call it a "structuralist" arrangement)! They complement and explain and support one another.

It is necessary to add that, according to Tradition, it was Jacob "who initiated *evening* prayers," the purest expression of "trust during the night," the trust of the Jew "who can rely only on his Father in Heaven!"⁴⁵⁴

The darkness of the night
and the rising of the sun

In addition the *geulah*, deliverance, rises like the dawn from the blackest darkness of the Galut; before the dawn breaks the darkness of the night grows deeper; before the *geulah* appears, the darkness of the Galut becomes dense, oppressive, stifling, impenetrable.⁴⁵⁵ The prophets and Sages of Israel teach us, *Ve'Eit Tsarah Hi LeYa'akov, Umimenah Yivashe'a.* They say, "When the time of distress (is the most trying) for Jacob, deliverance will be the result."⁴⁵⁶

Whenever Israel's Galut will appear to humans to be heavier than ever before, the *geulah* shall be very close. In a galutic situation which is inextricable, confused, with apparently no way out and no hope, the glimmer of the *geulah* will suddenly and unexpectedly appear; it will break out "with a bound," as at the end of the slavery in Egypt, over barriers which have seemed insurmountable.

In truth, the story of Israel's deliverances, of the supernatural *geulot* which end supernatural *galuyot*, is a story made up of disconcerting "surprises," *KeHeref Ayin*, of swift, unforeseen "reversals," *VeNahafokh*, as in the time of Esther.⁴⁵⁷

When Israel is at the edge of the abyss (as it was formerly at the edge of the Sea of Reeds[458]), Divine intervention suddenly manifests itself, takes Israel under its wings ("picks them out of the dungheap and makes them leap over the abyss").[459] "When we were cast down, He remembered us" (Ps. 136:23). When Israel is at the lowest point, God remembers them, raises them up, and Israel is reborn to a new life.[460]

The experience of ancient history shows that "the increased burden of slavery" in Egypt precipitated the liberation of the Israelites.[461] The experience of recent history shows that the dazzling restoration of the Hebrew state sprang from the dense smoke of the crematorium oven of Auschwitz.

The miraculous re-establishment of the Jewish State will certainly be inscribed in a particularly striking way in the history of the Jewish people which is already phenomenal. Nevertheless it does not yet point to the advent of Messianic times. Some fundamental precursory signs[462] are missing, both in the State of Israel itself and in the world in general. However, the terrifying prehistory of the State of Israel, as well as its own short but painfully significant history, recalls some of the harsh aspects which, according to the prophets and Sages of Israel, are characteristic of the most important epochs in the history of the Jewish people. Some dare to call these aspects "pre-Messianic;" others insist on contesting this description. Undoubtedly it is proper to beware of being too positive on so delicate a subject as that of pre-Messianic (not to speak of Messianism itself); it is fitting to maintain, as Maimonides advises us (Rambam, Hilkhot Melakhim[463]), an extreme caution concerning a subject on which, he says, even the Sages of the Talmudic times did not dare to make pronouncements of a precise nature, these things being so much wrapped up in allusions and hidden in the inner meaning of the Torah....

What is certain, however, is that the re-establishment in 1948 of Jewish national sovereignty in Erets-Yisrael constitutes an act of Providence, *unique* in the history of humanity. After almost 2,000 years of exile, Israel, the dispersed people, exists; it has preserved and even deepened its original religious identity and its initial link with the Promised Land, and consequently it is able to return there and on that sacred soil reconstruct its State.

This extraordinary happening is a "sign" to which God has caused the people of Israel and the whole world to give serious attention. It is sending "signals" to Israel and to humanity, who as always experience jointly, *nolens volens*, the great turning points of history. Now they all find themselves at a major turning point....[464]

As for the "coming of the Messiah," according to the Sages of Israel it will be preceded by the "sufferings of the Messiah," *Hevlei Mashiah*, just as the birth of a child is preceded by the pains of labor, *Hevlei Leida*.⁴⁶⁵

Certainly if Israel is worthy of it and "reveres God's word," the promise made by the Prophet Isaiah will be fulfilled, and, "before being in labor she has given birth; before the pains seized her, she has been delivered of a male child" (Is. 66:5-7).⁴⁶⁶

Good is the final objective of the Galut

Divine wisdom, always incomprehensible, ordained and decreed the Galut and the sufferings that follow, for the sake of a supreme objective and for the ultimate welfare of mankind, say Rabbi Yehuda HaLevi, Abravanel, the Maharal, Shelah HaKadosh, the Gaon of Vilna, Kedushat Levi, the Sefat Emet and Rav Kook. "The blessing will not arrive immediately, but its goal is the good," and "even the basis of evil is composed of what is (ultimately) good."⁴⁶⁷

In ordaining the Galut and putting His decision into action, God makes known to those who will be affected by it that "in the end the *geulah*, deliverance, will come," *Sofan Liyga'el*. The fulfillment of this *havtahah*, this promise of God for "the end" will coincide with Israel's own efforts to achieve *teshuvah*, return to God: *Hivtiha Torah SheSof Yisrael La'Assot Teshuvah*. This "final *teshuvah*," of which the Rambam and the Ramban speak, "will help" God to fulfil His promise.⁴⁶⁸

The community of Israel thus lives in a state of "waiting" for these latter days in its "faith" in the coming of the Messiah."⁴⁶⁹

Of course a Jewish person suffers, but his faith assures him that, in the *Olam HaBa*, in the "world to come," he will see with total clarity the reasons for the Galut and his sufferings, and that he will experience there the gladness and the joys that follow the Galut and its pains.⁴⁷⁰ His faith strengthens him again in the hope that in the *Yemot HaMashiah*, the "days of the Messiah," the people of Israel will understand the grounds for the Galut — and will then experience its happy consequences, both material and spiritual.⁴⁷¹

The *tsaddik*, the righteous man, can already glimpse, through the Galut's darkness, "the light which is hidden in the very shadows of the Galut": so the Sefat Emet assures us.⁴⁷² "When I sit in darkness [I see that] God is a light to me" — just as the prophet Micah⁴⁷³ has expressed it — and he understands what the Midrash says about these words of Micah: "Through the darkness gleams the light; through anger — mercy; through narrow confinement — enlargement; through separation — restoration."⁴⁷⁴

The *tsaddik* in the Galut is conscious of living close to his God, who through His *Shekhinah* is Himself "present" in the Galut.[475] The immediate "Presence" of the *Shekhinah* is for him a guarantee that there in the Galut already shines the hidden light of the *geulah*, salvation. The *geulah* is not only inaugurated at the beginning of the Galut, but it continues to develop progressively, *Kim'a Kim'a*,[476] little by little. The Galut itself is already the *geulah*, states the Sefat Emet,[477] although the *geulah* be still hidden, observes Rav Harlap. "The *geulah* could not even be manifest," he says, "without the Galut as intermediary, for the Galut is predestined to be the body of the *geulah*, which is its spirit. The Galut itself is predestined to shelter and increase the light of that spirit which is the *geulah*."[478]

The Maharal, Shelah HaKadosh, and the Kedushat Levi[479] go so far as say that the Galut is not only the cause and an omen of the *geulah*; it is also witness to it.[480] The fulfillment of the biblical curses relating to the Galut constitutes as they did for Rabbi Akiva,[481] a proof that they will be "reversed" and "transformed" into the blessings of the *geulah*. The curses are not only preceded and followed by blessings, but they already include within themselves the blessings—so states the Zohar HaKadosh—and that is so thanks not only to the "promise" of God, but also to the "merits" of Israel.[482]

Divine power and mercy

The curses and blessings thus form a unity. In the eyes of the Zohar, Divine power and mercy form a unity.[483] The Galut and the *geulah* form a unity in history, just as night and day constitute a unity in Nature, as it is written, "Evening came and morning came, the first day" (Gen. 1:5). But darkness and light have their source in the same *One* God, the God of History and of Nature, "who makes the light and creates the darkness; it is He, the Lord, who makes all these things," who "made the *earth* and created the *men* who people it" (Is. 45:7,12).

The *din*, the Divine "power" which envelops the darkness of the "night," and the *rahamim*, the Divine "mercy" which envelops the light of "day," have their origin, say the Jewish mystics, in the same God, who is both the God of Power, *Elokim*, and the God of "Mercy," *Shem Havayah* (the Tetragrammaton). He "built the earth on the foundations of His gracious mercy,"[484] "He estblishes the earth by His rigorous justice"[485] and "He combines love with justice"[486] to make the world so that this earthly planet may remain in existence.[487]

HaRahum Umakdim Rahamim LeRogez[488]

Yet power has its roots in mercy.[489] That is why "God has created the remedy before the wound exists; He has prepared the cure before the injury occurred"; "He caused the birth of the savior before the oppressor was born."[490] That is why, say the Sages of Israel again, the *geulah* comes to pass both "through distress," *tsarah*, and "through mercy," *rahamim*.[491] Also, states the Kedushat Levi, "power is only justified because it in its turn engenders mercy."[492]

In reality the Divine "anger" *veils* "clemency;" for clemency is charity which is only hidden, says the Midrash, paraphrasing the words of the prophet of Israel (Hab. 3:2)[493] when he prays God to "remember" His clemency in the midst of His wrath: *BeRogez Raheim Tizkor*. For there is no Divine power which does not include mercy, states the Zohar; it draws its strength from it. *Leit Dina DeLa Havu Bei Rahamei*.[494] With God, "power—from the outset—comes with grace," and "in truth His power is grace," the Zohar teaches, and after it the great masters of Jewish mysticism, such as Rabbi Hayyim Vital, the main disciple of Rabbi Yitshak Luria: *HaDinim HaElyonim Hein Atzman Mamtikin Otan*.[495]

Veil and transparency

"In every kind of suffering, whether physical or moral," writes R. Ya'akov Yosef of Polonoye in the name of his master, Rabbi Israel Ba'al Shem Tov, "the man who is attentive can distinguish the Name Himself, blessed be He; but He is enveloped in raiment. When the man becomes aware of this, the raiment is removed, the concealment ends and the suffering is stopped. All the heavy *gezerot* thus are cancelled..."[496] The Gaon of Vilna shares this view with the Besht.[497]

But why does God conceal Himself? R. Ya'akov Yosef finds the answer to this serious question in the verse which says, "I will hide My face completely," *VeAnokhi Haster Astir Panai* (Deut. 31:18). "God hides Himself so that man shall not easily find out that He is there," R.Ya'akov Yosef believes.[498] And the Teachers of Hassidut add: "God hides Himself to incite man to search for Him." Long ago Amos[499] exhorted his co-religionists to do this: "Seek the Lord and you shall live." For the 'Hassidim the *hester*, the "concealment" of God "under different garments" (this is how the Tikunei HaZohar presents it[500]) is a testimony of the love of God for Israel. God wishes that He and Israel reciprocally "seek one another" so that their mutual love will be revealed, writes

Rabbi Avraham of Slonim.⁵⁰¹ "If man knew that everything comes from God, there would be no veil at all," states the Sefat Emet.⁵⁰²

"He who understands that in the Galut there is a *Pekidah*, a sign, pointing to salvation, but that this *Pekidah* is hidden, *BeHastarah*—he is ready for the *geulah*, for deliverance."⁵⁰³ For the *tsaddik*, God withdraws the veil which separates Him from him so that even in the Galut he can glimpse the *geulah*. Being very close to him, "God has already given him the keys to the *geulah*..."; so we are taught in the Sefat Emet.⁵⁰⁴

As for the "average" Jew, *benoni*, "fearing" God but incapable of discerning the *Pekidah* of the *geulah* under the veil of the Galut,⁵⁰⁵ not even knowing that the veil exists? Must he wait till the end of the Galut to discover the hidden "reasons" for Israel's exile? For him the veil will not easily be lifted; and even if a particular *Nekudah*, a particular "point" under the veil does appear to him, in the *hester* of the Galut, the Sefat Emet⁵⁰⁶ considers that this point would also be "hidden."

Only the actual arrival of the Messianic era will allow him to understand the profound motives for the Galut, and even to "see" them clearly. When he has justified by the *Tsiduk HaDin*, all "the things which he had not understood in this world,"⁵⁰⁷ he will then be able to grasp them clearly, in their *totality*. Being now in a position to consider the whole, in its entirety, and to put together in one unity the past, present and future—this "whole," including "suffering and death," will seem "good"—indeed "very good"—to him, as it was in the "enlightened" eyes of Rabbi Meir.⁵⁰⁸ He will become aware that a veil prevented him from "seeing" these realities clearly; that darkness was only veiled light; and that, now the veil has disappeared, everything has become transparent and lucid.

"Then the glory of the Lord shall be revealed, and all *flesh* shall *see* it together" (Is. 40:5).⁵⁰⁹ The flesh in its spiritual state shall see what Moses was unable to see completely,⁵¹⁰ and what the *tsaddik* who does not undergo any trials in this world only succeeds in perceiving at the moment when he is separated from life on earth.

Illuminated by the immense good, *Rav Tuvkha*,⁵¹¹ which is reserved for those who fear God, he will understand that the Galut, with all the suffering that it brought, was for the good.⁵¹² To that which he thought to be but an excess of evil in this world, in the Galut, there will be corresponding excess of good in the world to come, in the true reality.⁵¹³ God who was able to provide for him in this world some ephemeral pleasures, will prove Himself able to give him unsuspected, unimaginable and above all, eternal bliss.⁵¹⁴

Convinced at last that the goal of the Galut was for his ultimate good, he "will thank" God for having made him "suffer." Like King David, he "will give thanks" to God, his Deliverer, "for having heard my prayer," *anitani*[515]; which the Sages also interpret as meaning "for having made me suffer." Like Isaiah,[516] he will thank God "for having made His anger flame out against him, for His anger is ended and He has consoled him," and he will be able, as during the Pessah Seder, "to bless God for the bitter herbs," the *maror*, which he ate during his slavery in exile...."[517] He will praise God, who is "All Good and Beneficient" — the God who is *Kulo HaTov VeHaMeitiv*.[518]

The "faithfulness of God,"[519] in His goodness, His wisdom, will at last be wholly manifested to him.[520]

From Golah to geulah, from exile to redemption

"The root of the *geulah* is in the Galut," writes the Sefat Emet,[521] to which observation there is much midrashic support. Indeed the letters of the word *geulah*, "salvation," are also in the *golah*, "exile." One has only to add a single letter, *aleph*, which has the numerical value of one, to the letters which form the vocable *golah* to make the word *geulah*.

Rabbi Yehoshua of Ostrova[522] said that when Jews learn to take seriously the meaning of the *aleph*, the *one* and only God, and know that it is He who is the *Alupho Shel Olam*, the "Master of the world," Israel will be able to see the *aleph*, the *one*, interposed in the word *golah* and shaping it into a *geulah*.[523]

Of course, in order for the mutation of the *golah* into *geulah* to take place, Israel needs God's "supreme grace." But if Israel is worthy of this, the "help of Heaven" is available.[524] Now the *aleph* is ready to intervene and to use its *unifying* power, the Maharal teaches us.[525] God will gather the *four* letters of the word *golah*; He will gather together the parts of the *golah* "dispersed" to the "*four* winds of the world," will elevate them and make of them *one geulah* and lead them back to the source, whence they originated and whither they are bound, Erets-Yisrael, and more specifically, Jerusalem.

The word *golah* contains four letters, and when the *aleph* is introduced as a second letter, it occupies a central position linking the two halves of the word *golah* and forming it anew into *geulah*. In *geulah* the *five* letters which make up this vocable, and which symbolize the "*Five* Books of the Torah," draw together to make "one single band which accomplishes the will of God," *LaAssot Retsonkha BeLevav Shalem*.

3

Jerusalem, heart of Israel / heart of the world

Jerusalem, the place where God and man,
God and Israel, meet

To the highest possible degree Jerusalem represents the history of the world and of man, of Israel and of mankind, the history of the relationships which exist between them in the light of their relationships with God. It reflects the purity of the heavens on the earth and it witnesses to the value which the earth has in the heavens. For it was there, in Jerusalem, at its innermost point, that the heavens and the earth were born; it was from its "foundation stone" that "the world was constructed."[1] Thus Jerusalem became both "the gate of the heavens"[2] and "the navel of the earth."[3] From Jerusalem, from this central point, a *kav emtsai*,[4] a "central line," rose up into the heights and established the celestial City, the *Yerushalayim shel ma'alah*, with its Sanctuary above, the *Beit HaMikdash shel ma'alah*, as its focus; from this same central point a *kave emtsai*, a "central line," went downward and established the Earthly City, the *Yerushalayim shel matah*, with its Sanctuary below, the *Beit HaMikdash shel matah*,[5] as its focus. Along this *kav emtsai*, this central line, dwells the *Shekhinah*, the Divine Presence, and from here it spreads its glory throughout the world, "fills the earth"[6] and leaves "no place exempt from it";[7] from this *kav emtsai* on which it resides the *Shekhinah* descends until it reaches the heart of each Jewish entity, individual and communal, national and territorial. It descends until it reaches the most intimate consciousness of Israel and of Zion, and especially of Israel in Zion: *tsahali varoni yoshevet Tsion ki gadol bekirbeikh Kedosh Yisrael*.[8]

So Jerusalem, the meeting-point between the heavens and the earth,[9] "where the heavens and the earth embrace,"[10] is the chosen place for the encounter between God and man, between "God who wishes to have a dwelling-place down in the world below" and man, the earthly creature "of below," who nevertheless belongs to the extra-terrestrial, "higher" world "of above" and whose actions have repercussions which go beyond the limits of the earth.[11] In this way Jerusalem becomes the initial and final meeting-point between God and Israel, as Israel signifies he personification of man "in whatever the latter has which is 'perfect,' 'being the Man in Man,' whose soul is 'embedded within the Throne of the Divine Glory.' "[12]

With the history of Israel as its mediating force, Jerusalem therefore constitutes the essence of the history of nature united with that of the history of mankind; Jerusalem is the expression of God Himself in His relations with nature and mankind.

Indeed, it was from a particular "point," a *nekudah*,"[13] that the universe was born, and this point, Jerusalem, "which is situated at the center of the world,"[14] still constitutes the center of the spiritual concerns of mankind. The world should be interested in Jerusalem because it is the center of Israel's permanent spiritual radiance;[15] even when Israel is physically and temporarily displaced in the world, it is not spiritually detached from its original and ultimate home, from Zion.

Jerusalem must continue to be the point towards which mankind's spiritual attention is directed—because it was at that place that God came to man, and spoke to him for the first time: "He called to him." It was at Jerusalem[16] that God asked Adam the famous question, *ayeka*?[17]—"Where are you?"—thus questioning him about his conception of the position which he held in the universe and about the attitude that he intended to adopt to the Master of the universe; and since that time God has been addressing this same question from Jerusalem, *ayeka*, to man wherever he may be. Again Jerusalem should continue to be the point towards which mankind's spiritual attention is directed because at this point, after retreating from God, man "came close" to Him again for the first time, thus accepting His sovereignty and bringing Him the "offering," the *minhah*,[18] of his gratitude. So at this place, at Jerusalem, the relationships are established between God and "Israel who is called Man"[19] *par excellence*; and this place serves as an intermediary in the development of the relationships between God and Israel in the world, until they are finally linked to their source of unfolding, Jerusalem. At that time the relations between God and all men will have been clarified by the establishment of the Divine Kingdom throughout the earth, with Jerusalem as its metropolis.[20]

When he leaves Jerusalem,
man transports God into the world

It is from Jerusalem that Adam set out into the world. As man sets out from Jerusalem, he takes God into the world; he transports the Deity everywhere; he makes the *Shekhinah* present among men. Man is the *merkavah*[21] of the *Shekhinah*: he is the "chariot" of God. "The whole earth is full of the glory of God,"[22] while man aspires from everywhere to the place from which he comes.[23] Wherever he is and whatever he does, Adam, whose "body was made from dust gathered from all over the earth," tends towards this central point, this site of the *mizbeah*, of the altar, of the future of Jerusalem, because "his head was made of dust found beneath the *mizbeah*."[24] Wherever he may be, man "thinks of Jerusalem, he turns towards the mountain of Moriah, which has borne this name from the beginning of time, because it was from those heights that "the great teaching" about man was "to proceed into the world"[25] — his vocation and his relationship with God.[26] "Wherever God causes His name to be invoked, He *will come* to man and bless him"; wherever man finds himself,[27] he allows God to remind him of this truth and acts accordingly. Although He is everywhere,[28] God, who is *Mekomo shel olam*, "the Place of the world,"[29] *will come* to the man of the *makom*,[30] of the place, *par excellence*; He will come, equipped with the Teaching proclaimed at this "place which He chose,"[31] and invite man to direct his thoughts and his words to this same place. This is why, when he recites his prayers the Jew faces towards Jerusalem.[32]

When he turns his heart towards Jerusalem,
man, especially the Jew,
hallows the whole earth

"Turning his heart towards Jerusalem,[33] towards the House of holiness and sanctification,[34] towards the Holy of Holies,"[35] man, and the Jew in particular, will, again, more and more sanctify the whole earth, which was called by its Creator from the beginning to be holy by virtue of the sanctification it would receive from man's action. In it man will sublimate, and spiritualize, everything God gives him and all that God permits him to do, in order to enjoy it by consecrating it, and returning (to Him), partially at least, whatever is best in it,[36] as a gift to God, thus enabling mankind to benefit from it. This joy[37] leads man first and foremost to himself, to his inner self, to his own consiousness, to his own being and, through and together with his fellowman,[38] towards The

Being, to God, so that he thus becomes "worthy" of the *Shekhinah*, for which he himself also becomes "the dwelling."[39] This joy and gratitude[40] towards God illuminates and guides man everywhere in the world as he continuously makes his way towards the epicenter of the inhabited world,[41] in which Jerusalem is situated, wherein exists the past and future Sanctuary with its celestial equivalent.[42] It is in heaven above "the City of righteousness"[43] that the *Shekhinah*, the Divine Presence, wishes to be known as *Tseddek*, "justice," in order thus to be reflected in its earthly dwelling where men live and thus radiate throughout the earth of mankind[44] so that it then becomes God's dwelling-place.[45] For this to happen man must also will it[46] wherever he may be; therefore man must make his thinking and action converge in the direction of this place of predilection, Jerusalem, which has been responsible from the beginning for "the light called into being in order to radiate throughout the world."[47] But if he does not will it, man severs himself from this central point,[48] this ideal and radiant center, known as Jerusalem. Consequently he severs himself from God who, for His part, certainly wishes to exert His effective influence, His beneficial action, on the universe starting from this central point, this point of equilibrium. So man dares to "repulse the *Shekhinah*" from this world, to send God back "to the distance of the heavens."[49] Thus man breaks the contact between the heavens and the earth, by disregarding, despising and damaging the very place where the contact was firmly established; by maligning that place which belongs to him in the heavens, man damages the City of God in the heavens. Henceforth God will never go back to the celestial Divine City, the Jerusalem on high, until man returns respectfully to the earthly Divine City, the Jerusalem below, thus to "permit" the re-entry of God Himself: "I shall not make My return to the Jerusalem on high before I make My return to the Jerusalem below!" declares God.[50]

Will man make this double return a possibility? Has he not already built himself a false Jerusalem?[51] Yes, this man is self-sufficient; he proclaims himself the owner of that which, as he says, he has acquired and of that which, as he claims, he will yet prevail by his own strength, as if he were his own creator, had made himself, and could do what he pleased with others. He considers that it is no longer necessary to thank anyone for what he receives; he believes that he no longer needs to account for his actions. He "fears" no one. He is self-made.[52] He progresses not by God but, as he believes, by himself. He receives the possessions which he enjoys not from the hands of God, but so he claims, from his own hands.[53] His rejoicing in God and for God, his joy in man, is transformed into pleasure from himself and for himself,[54] into a pleasure he obtains from others. Man sins because he goes away from God,⁵⁵ away from his fellowman and from that which he still has of value in himself. He is sad because he is alone.⁵⁶ This is how man's exile⁵⁷ and the dispersal of mankind began.⁵⁸ In the past man continued to think of the place *par excellence, HaMakom*,⁵⁹ and acted according to its requirement, where he was. The places through which he passed constituted a periphery⁶⁰ which "was fed from the blessing" of the universal center.⁶¹ So to that he felt an attraction and around that he gravitated. As soon as man stopped thinking of the place *par excellence* and no longer acted in accordance with its requirement, all the places where he was then became exiles—dry, shadowy, chaotic, confused, impure, profane dispersals—because they were detached from the center. Nevertheless, every exile, by the very fact of being an exile, also implies the possibility of gathering back; every dispersion, by the very fact of being a dispersion, inherently implies the possibility of reassembling.⁶² In every exile lies the kernel of deliverance: *golah* (exile) differs from *geulah* by one Hebrew letter: *alef*.⁶³ Enlarged, fulfilled by this one letter, *golah* becomes *geulah*. Every sin already contains the seed of repentance.⁶⁴ Every departure from God also implies the desire for a voluntary return to Him or the necessity of a forced return to Him.⁶⁵

After fleeing from God, man runs to Him: "from You, to You," he cries.⁶⁶ In the long run man cannot be self-sufficient. He yearns for God. He wishes to come before his Creator again. But where?⁶⁷ At the site where Adam was created,⁶⁸ at the very location where he committed his first sin and where the means "of obtaining forgiveness for it" are available,⁶⁹ at Jerusalem—by definition the place where the exiles gather again, the place of re-inclusion for those who withdrew from its true radiance.⁷⁰

**Jerusalem, made sacred in the first place
by the will of God,
is afterwards hallowed by the merits of man**

After the expulsion of Adam from the Jerusalem *Gan Eden*, after the exile of Cain and dispersal of the generation of the tower of Babel, the first to attempt to prepare the way back to Jerusalem was *Malki-Tseddek*,⁷¹ the ruler whose very name indicates that he was a just king:⁷² He could be nothing else: he was the king of *Shalem*, of that site called "integrity," of the Jerusalem of the future. He had left his own country for Jerusalem to serve God, and became, as the Torah relates, "a priest of God Most High." Tradition identifies *Malki-Tseddek* with *Shem*, son of Noah,⁷³ and thus with the very person who, together with Ever, enabled the Hebrew patriarchs to understand and transmit the pure faith.[74] But *Shem* who is *Malki-Tseddek*, who certainly recognized the sovereignty of the "God Most High, creator and proprietor of heaven and earth," was merely a precursor of the first Hebrew patriarch, Abraham, who proclaimed this omnipotent Ruler as his own God, the God who communicates with man,[75] the "Lord"[76] to whom Abraham brings the world close, "brings" "the heaven and the earth," as an offering.[77]

And, indeed, Abraham was the first to launch an authentic, genuine, decisive movement of return to the origins of man. Abraham, the father of the Hebrew people and the spiritual father of a "host of nations,"[78] inaugurates the real journey of the Hebrew and of mankind in general whose point of convergence is Jerusalem.[79] To begin with, on his own initiative,[80] or more precisely on the initiative of his father,[81] he turns away from his birthplace,[82] from an environment which is materially rich, from a periphery which for him in truth, is not very far removed from the center. He turns towards the "country which is at the very center of the world" in the spiritual sense of the phrase.[83] His initiative is reinforced[84] by God's order to "proceed" firstly "towards himself," *lekh lekha* towards his own consciousness,[85] and then towards the country which, without its being named,[86] he is to discover by means of the attraction which it will exert on him:[87] God will show him this country in himself, in Abraham, in his own merits: *ar'eka*.[88] This country he is to hand down to his chosen descendant, his son Yitshak, as the latter will to his chosen descendant, his son Yaakov.[89] This country acquires a specific, precise, national worth and, at the same time, takes on a vast, universal, human significance. At its heart this country, the "center of the world," comprises "the most precious point of this center," the mountain Moriah. Towards the mountain, designated now by no name[90] Abraham is to make his way, equally by God's order, to discover there, by his intuition, the Place, *HaMakom*, the place *par excellence*. No explicit name is given him; Abraham must discover it for himself[91] — by identifying the spiritual traces of Adam and of Abel who made offerings there to God, and of Noah and his sons[92] who there brought, "raised up," sacrifices, *olah*,[93] to God. The Lord confirms Abraham's discovery[94] and there Abraham erects *ha-mizbeah*, the Altar *par excellence*,[95] which already at one time had been built there by his own efforts.[96] This place, Moriah, is in Jerusalem. It is indeed the essence of Jerusalem,[97] the site of the *Beit HaMikdash*: the Sanctuary.[98] This place was established with a view to its future vocation, *al Shem he-atid*:[99] it will be called by its full, true name: *Yerushalayim*.

One far greater than Abraham, God Himself, will give this place a name, its full name,[100] without this name being as yet clearly understood. Originally sanctified[101] by the will of God and later by the merits of man,[102] this place is to receive a fitting appellation. God gives it this name, as He does whenever He wishes to indicate the calling of the bearer of a name.[103] But the name Jerusalem, like that of the Torah, will only formally come into use when *all Israel* deserves it, accepts it, submits to it. When all Israel is established on its land[104] which its king will have conquered,[105] then Jerusalem will become Jerusalem.[106] David[107] was to influence this name, not only with his personality and with that of his immediate successor son, Solomon,[108] who was called to build that which would constitute the true worth of Jerusalem, the *Beit HaMikdash*.[109] David was also to cast his influence, far in advance, with the personality of his distant son, *Mashiah ben David*, the Messiah who would be his descendant[110] and would be called to fulfill the vocation of Jerusalem, to complete its work.

Yerushalayim, a plural form: shows the holiness of that city is due to the collaboration of God and man

Nevertheless, Abraham too made a major, decisive contribution to the establishment of the name of Jerusalem. When he set a supreme, unique example there of faith and trust through the *Akedah* of Yitshak,[111] the patriarch gave this place of trial a name: *Hashem yir'eh*,[112] "God will see." The Divine eye will alight not only on the place[113] because it has been "chosen" by the Lord—*HaMakom asher yivhar*[114]—but above all it will alight on the one who comes there,[115] because he "is searching" —*tidreshu*[116]—the one who will always return there as if he were coming for the first time, *hayom*, "today,"[117] to see God there, *Hashem yir'eh*;[118] the one who will do what is necessary there for "God to make Himself seen" by the man who is worthy of Him (to the extent to which a human being can do so during his lifetime).[119]

To this personal name of God who seeks for man, and who observes him at close range, *Hashem yir'eh*, that Abraham gave to this place and which God accepts, God adds the name *Shalem*, "of integrity," which was used by a man, a righteous man, *Malki-Tseddek*, to describe this place as the one where man, as he seeks his personal God wishes to live in integrity before the Lord.[120] By putting these two names together, *Hashem yir'eh*[121] and *Shalem*, God Himself creates the name *Yerushalayim*.[122] This word *Yerushalayim* is in the plural[123] to indicate that the holiness of this City is due to the cooperation which takes place within it between God and man; between God who "shows" Himself to man and man who "fears"[124] God and seeks to live with integrity in His "sight";[125] between God whom man "causes to descend" towards him[126] and man whom God causes to rise up towards Him.[127]

If man neglects his share of this task of co-operation, God withdraws into His heavens

In our tradition, the holiness of Jerusalem does not belong to the static category of "areas sacred" in themselves; it is not part of the class commonly known in other religions by the name of "holy places."[128] In the view of Judaism, the holiness of Jerusalem is due to the active, constructive cooperation[129] which takes place between God and man.[130] It is realized and renewed through the activity of creative cooperation between God and man.[131]

If man fails in this work of cooperation, God withdraws into His heavens[132] and leaves man to struggle alone in his dispersion (although the *Shekhinah*, the Divine Presence, follows the Jew into the Galut).[133] Then the site itself, chosen by God as a place of holiness,[134] sees its holiness impaired, and is distressed[135] because man no longer recognizes its worth. Indeed, its original holiness is affected,[136] like that of Israel, by the merits of those to whom it is entrusted.[137] If the merits of its users diminish, the sanctity of the area (the local holiness) is affected.[138] It is reduced but it does not disappear: "holiness remains upright."[139] But it is disturbed,[140] especially at the point where its initial intensity was strong. "Everything that is holier than the rest is more impoverished than the rest":[141] Jerusalem suffered more than the rest of the Country. Israel too suffers more than other nations when it offends against the will of God,[142] especially when this "holy nation,"[143] the sensitive "heart of the nations,"[144] is at Zion,[145] the sensitive, vulnerable delicate "center of the world."[146]

Israel faithfully carries Jerusalem in its heart, retains its identity in exile thanks to Jerusalem

However, Israel continues to exist. Although it may be far away from Jerusalem, scattered throughout the world, because of the sins which it had committed in this holy City, Israel lives because Jerusalem, this City which is indestructible in essence, remains alive within it. Israel carries Jerusalem in its heart with exemplary fidelity; it bears no resentment against Jerusalem for not having accepted it with its iniquities, because

Israel knows that "the City of justice[147] does not tolerate iniquity."[148] On the contrary, Israel remains fundamentally attached to the Torah of Zion; it remains painfully attached to the Messianic ideal[149] of the ingathering of the exiles to Jerusalem, which then adumbrates the ideal of the rebuilding of the *Beit HaMikdash*, of the House of holiness and of sanctification.[150] Individuals or nations that are driven out of their country or leave it of their own accord, become detached from it and forget it. Israel is not like that in the course of time. In exile,[151] it swears not to forget Jerusalem;[152] in exile, it still lives in Jerusalem, in the ideal Jerusalem of its heart.

Though Israel descends into the Galut because of its own faults,[153] it does so in order to ascend from there to Jerusalem.[154] In exile, it keeps its identity thanks to Jerusalem,[155] not merely thanks to its nostalgia for Jerusalem[156] but above all due to its own conception of Jerusalem. The relationship between Israel and Jerusalem is certainly profound and mystical. But it is also given, ordained, demanded and imposed "with a strong hand"[157] by the Master of the world, the God of Israel, the God of Zion. He causes the people of Israel to endure by means of Jerusalem, and he causes Jerusalem to last for the sake of the people of Israel. This is an unquestionable sign of their common destiny, of their mutual interdependence.[158] Despite all the vicissitudes which have unleashed themselves on the people of Israel in the course of the millennia, it has not been possible to destroy Israel: "the remnant of Israel" survives, it is indestructible, because God lives in it: "I, the Lord, do not change; and you, children of Jacob, have not been consumed!"[159] Despite all the invasions and dominations to which Jerusalem has been subjected in the course of the millennia, the City is "eternal":[160] in it remains "the trace of the House of our holiness." This is the *Kotel HaMa'aravi*, the western Wall of the *Beit HaMikdash*, which has not been destroyed although it could have been in the course of the centuries.[161] Like Israel, it is a witness to the validity, the reliability, of God's promise: the Eternal swore that Israel would not be annihilated;[162] "the Eternal swore that the *Kotel HaMa'aravi* will not be destroyed,"[163] for the *Shekhinah* is ever in *ma'arav*, in the west.[164] And both of them stand, endure. For the *Shomer Yisrael*, the Guardian of Israel, is standing behind them. The *Shekhinah*, the Presence of God, never leaves Israel;[165] "the *Shekhinah* never leaves the *Kotel HaMa'aravi*,"[166] declare the Sages of Israel, basing this on a verse of the *Shir HaShirim* which says: "Behold, there He stands behind our wall."[167]

The phenomenon of Israel is expressed in the phenomenon of Jerusalem

Generation after generation of Jews have confirmed, by their tears shed over these stones to which their hopes were directed from afar, this truth which the Midrash based on a verse of the Bible. They have *believed* in this truth and, for them, this truth has been more solid, more sure, than any tangible reality.[168] And, now, in our own days, we can *see* this truth; we are experiencing the validity of the *havtahah*, of the Divine promise: Behold, He is there,[169] He is standing behind the Wall;[170] He is waiting for us; He comes out, He appears: we see Him with our own eyes[171] as He sees[172] and welcomes us and thus prepares to return totally, and finally, to Zion.[173] The heroes who took the Wall by assault and liberated it from its nineteen years of solitude and captivity burst out sobbing the moment they reached it. A heart opened up to them behind the stones which they embraced.[174] There they perceived the voice of[175] "the One who is behind the Wall"; it was before Him that the hardened warriors burst into tears,[176] like innocent children when finding their mother again after being separated from her: "As a mother comforts her son, so will I myself comfort you, and you shall find comfort in Jerusalem."[177] During those overwhelming hours of 28 Iyar 5727, Jews from everywhere, from the Land of Israel and from the Diaspora of Israel, rose up "like one man and with one heart"[178] to gaze at and then to flock towards this Wall.[179] How can one explain the haste with which hundreds of thousands of Jews, on hearing the news, came to the Wall to pray there, to shed a tear or to place a kiss there? Is there a rational explanation, in our so-called rationalist age, for this Jewish phenomenon?[180] No. It is the irrefutable proof of the supernatural character of the history of Israel, of the profoundest depths of its life.[181] It is the phenomenon of Israel expressed in the phenomenon of Jerusalem. It is the very real experience of an event long awaited, patiently yearned for, and so long unfulfilled.[182]

Jerusalem personifies the unity of Israel

The re-unification of Jerusalem is not an event of human dimensions; nor is it an event of national dimensions, however grandiose they may be. This episode belongs to the wholly inexplicable uniqueness of Israel and of Jerusalem, and of their unifying function within the universe. Genuine contact between the innermost point of the Jew, the "heart of Israel," and that other focal point, the "heart of Jerusalem," was finally re-established.[183] As Israel re-vindicated its authentic self, it again recaptured the true nature of Jerusalem and what is required of it by its essence.[184] Israel, all Israel, found it again, since in order that Jerusalem be recovered whole, it was necessary for *all* Israel to share in it. The unity of Israel was the primary condition for the construction of the *first* Temple in the past; it will be the condition for the re-establishment of the *third* Temple, the final and eternal one.[185] And this unity, which until recent times was still weak, has been strengthened with an impressive force which came from within under the direction of the consciousness of Israel. This unity has been comprised *all* Israel because "the City demanded it." When it resolutely manifests its will to recuperate the sovereignty of Israel, when it decides to adorn the head of Israel with its crown, Jerusalem is the City which "unites" around it all "Israel,"[186] all the children of Israel "together," into one fellowship."[187] Indeed, Jerusalem personifies the unity of Israel:[188] this "City was never divided among the tribes" of Jacob.[189] In it all the generations of Israel meet;[190] at *all* times it is *all* to *all* Israel. It is true Jerusalem especially when Israel, whose conscience it determines, again becomes worthy of it by its inner unity;[191] then it is that Jerusalem, inwardly united within itself,[192] again becomes worthy of Israel by means of its outward unity.[193] The two together, *one* Israel and *one* Jerusalem,[194] thus mutually rediscover one another in that which they share of truth, of eternity: for they rediscover one another in Him, the Eternal, the true God, the God of Israel, the King of Zion, in His Torah from Zion, in His word from *Yerushalayim*.[195] Israel and *Yerushalayim* "thus deserve one another mutually";[196] their mutual attraction is more than sentimental, since they need each other for the sake of the fulfillment of their common vocation to evolve Jewish existence further.[197] By this very fact, it is a vocation of universal consequence,[198] indeed of cosmic consequence,[199] and, even more so, a Divine mission,[200] because "Jerusalem will be called"[201] "heart of the world,"[202] the "Throne of the Eternal."[203]

4

Jewish time: sabbatical time

The Torah teaches the right use of time

Judaism is based on a particular concept[1] of time, that of Sabbatical time. "The order of time presides"[2] over the Torah—over the Divine Teaching of Judaism; it governs and regulates the life of the Jew which is arranged in turn according to the order of the Torah.[3] The chronology of the positive mitzvot—of the religious prescriptions—fits into the order of time;[4] and transgression of the negative mitzvot—of the religious prohibitions—upsets the order of time.[5]

The Torah with its mitzvot, its religious regulations, teaches the right use of time.[6] "Do you want to succeed in your vocation to be a Jew?" Rabbi Menahem Mendel of Kotzk[7] said one day to one of his disciples. "You must know what you can and what you must and must not do with your time. In brief, act in such a way that you do not have time to commit a sin, that you do not have time to make an error with time."

Now, not making an error with time means, first and foremost, not miscalculating time: "Teach us to count our days!"[8] Man on his own, with his concept of time, is led to compute time, to assess its subdivisions and appreciate their irreversible uniqueness. By virtue of his "determinative" responsibilities, he is capable of "acquiring" the world, "his own world," the whole world "in one hour"; but he is also able to lose his own world and the whole world in an hour, as the Talmud says and as Rambam emphatically underlines.[9]

However, in keeping count of time the Jew does not and should not do as do other humans. He does and should count it differently in order not to succumb, as a consequence of false calculation or a lack of calculation, either to the avarice of life or to the anguish of death, or yet to the indifference brought about by apathy.

To safeguard the clear calculation of time and to ensure its success, the Mekhilta instructs the Jew to count the days with reference to the Shabbat. Commenting on the verse of the Bible, "Remember the Shabbat day to keep it holy,"[10] through the words of Rabbi Yitshak, the Mekhilta instructs the Jew by saying to him, "Do not count (the days) as others do, but count them rather with reference to the Shabbat."[11] In this way Rabbi Yitshak was informing the Jew, "You should know that the Shabbat comes at the end of your count of the days and not at the beginning."[12] "It comes at the end of your activity because it constitutes the finality of a finished work."[13] "It is the ethical objective, the *takhlit*,[14] of work that you will resume after interruption." "With the energy which this interruption will have given you, you will continue to work according to a plan that has been drawn up for you, with a meaning which has been conveyed to you, by One who has preceded you and who will follow you,[15] who has provided you with the materials for your work, the energy to undertake it and, above all, the ability to rest from it and to return to it."[16] "Spiritually,[17] at the beginning of creation, He Himself followed the order which He suggested to you, and He has generously pursued the aims[18] which He set before you at the end of His primordial work: goodness, blessing, and holiness, the blessing being found within holiness."[19] "He also offers Himself to you so that you may have Him with you during your work: He offers Himself to you so that He may have you with Him during His rest."[20] "He grants you the privilege of reaching Him and, still more, of bringing to Him, to the Holy One, the human offering of your sanctification." "Be holy, for I am holy—I, the Lord, your God; keep my Shabbatot!"[21]

"*Zakhor et yom haShabbat lekadesho*... Remember the Shabbat day to keep *Him* holy." But the word *Shabbat* in Hebrew is feminine.[22] The Torah should read *lekadesha* but it says *lekadesho* because, according to one commentator on the Torah,[23] it is God Himself, the creator of the Shabbat, whom we are called to keep holy by our remembering the Shabbat.[24]

"Respect the Shabbat of your God as if all your work were already done"

The rhythm which should be characteristic of the Jew's life is that of six units of time[25] for work and one unit for rest.[26] Six days of practical work (the meaning of the verb *avod*)[27] which stretches over a defined, visible and divisible area, and then one day when the work which could have been continued is interrupted (the meaning of the verb *shavot*);[28] but one interrupts it as freely[29] as one began it, in order to examine it, as Philo says,[30] asking ourselves, according to the Sefer Hahinukh,[31] whether it is in line with the designated ethical purpose. If it is not so, then according to the teaching of the Shelah Hakadosh[32] and of Rav Kook,[33] *teshuvah*, calm repentance, is recommended for the eve of the Shabbat as a contribution to the *tikun*,[34] the restoration of the imperfect human work. However, if the work matches up to the ethical demands of the Creator, like Him we shall appreciate it with joy, as the Sheiltot affirms.[35]

In any case, on the Shabbat day the Israelite is to consider the work done during the six preceding days sufficient. The Torah tells us, "You have six days to labor and do all your work."[36] And the Mekhilta asks, "Is it possible for man to do all his work in six days?" "Yes," it answers, "Respect the Shabbat of your God as if all your work were already done!"[37]

Erev Shabbat, on the eve of the Shabbat, the Jews says "Enough" to his work, just as the Creator, looking at the skies which continued to expand at the end of the six days, said to the world, *dai*, "Enough:" "enough" to expansion, "enough" to development, "enough" to growth. "Enough!" because the world, as the Midrash says,[38] was in danger of collapsing if its dimensions became excessive.[39] And the Sages of Israel continued the lesson, "Respect the Shabbat, O Man! Stop your work, even if you have the impression of not having earned sufficiently." "Put your trust in me," says your Creator. "Draw on My account and I shall pay."[40]

By strictly observing the *ha'amadah*, the cessation of *tenuah*, of movement, as Rabbi Yehuda Halevi[41] and the Maharal[42] point out, man in tranquility testifies to the highest degree to his likeness to the Creator. By refraining from the pursuit of his material labors on the seventh day he releases himself from the pressures of his greed, he sets himself free from the *avdut*, the slavery,[43] into which an excess of work,[44] *avodah*, could have led him. He does not regret what he does not have, he appreciates what he has: he is content with it because he is "satisfied" with Divine generosity.[45] By transforming his hard, enslaving, alienating work of *avodah*, of *avdut* (cf. Exod. 1:14), into agreeable, liberating activity, *avodat Hashem*, "service of God" (cf. Exod. 3:12); by ceasing to be a

By virtue of its identification
with the Torah and with the Shabbat
Israel becomes a cosmic factor

The passiveness[51] which we observe on the Shabbat is only apparent passiveness.[52] Rambam, the codifier who annotated the legal framework for the Shabbat, attributes to it the characteristics of both a *mitzvat asseh* and a *mitzvah lo ta'asseh*. The verb *tishbot*,[53] which instructs the Jew to make a break in his work on the seventh day, is a *mitzvat asseh*, an active mitzvah, despite the impression it may give of causing passiveness, of not working;[54] whereas the *lo ta'asseh kol melakhah*, "you shall not do any work"[55] of a material, creative kind,[56] is the *mitzvah lo ta'asseh* which is effectively negative, because it prohibits the Jew from working on the Shabbat.[57]

We thus imitate our Creator, who ceased His material work on the seventh day; in other words, He added nothing more from the material order[58] to the work done during the six days—in order "to rest Himself," *va-yinafash* (a reflexive verb),[59] in order to "reflect" on the work done and especially, as pointed out by the Or Hahayim,[60] the Bnei Issakhar[61] and the Sefat Emet,[62] in order to create the soul, the *nefesh*, which this work needs, and the repose, the *menuhah*,[63] to which it aspires.[64]

This soul, which God *created*[65] by the *va-yinafash* on the seventh day, will be able to function in a creative, active way so that the material work which had been interrupted can recommence and continue.[66] If this soul had not been created by God on the seventh day, all the material things produced during the first six days would not have survived; they would have remained in their material form like a *guf beli neshamah*, "a body without a soul."[67]

For this reason—and this is how we understand the comments of the Zohar and the Tosafot[68]—at the end of the description of the process of Genesis the Torah says, "On the seventh day God ceased from all the work He had done"[69]—on the seventh day and not on the sixth day. Indeed, it was only on the seventh day, by virtue of the soul which He gave to the world, that God completed His work of creation.[70]

By suspending his material work for a unit of time, during the seventh day, Shabbat, man is also able to concentrate on his inner self,[71] *va-yinafash*, thanks to the creative force of the *menuhah*, by means of the *nefesh* with which the Creator endowed the seventh day. He builds up his reservoir, as Rabbi Yehuda Halevi put it, a *mitstayedet*[72] (reserve), which, by analogy with the Divine *va-yinafash*,[73] should make it possible for man to pursue, foster and direct all his material labors.

Furthermore, according to the Zohar, the soul, which God created in His *va-yinafash* and gave to the world on the seventh day, is the *raza de-Shabbat*, "the mystery of the Shabbat," which at the same time is the *raza d'oraita*, the mystery of the Torah and also the mystery of Israel.[74] This *raza* will enable Israel, the People of the Torah, to ensure that on every

Shabbat cosmic life will begin again, that the world will continually be recreated (a creation which God conceived "while contemplating the Torah").[75] Israel will ensure this by the novelty that it will find every Shabbat as it reads the Torah[76] and especially the *parashat hashavua*, the weekly section of the Pentateuch.[77] It will ensure this by virtue of its own sabbatical renewal[78] which will be produced by its observation of the mitzvot of the Torah concerning the Shabbat—mitzvot which embrace all of the other mitzvot of the Torah.[79] Thus Israel will ensure a kind of *hiddush ha'olam*, a recreation of the world, a renewal of the world after the Shabbat, by the *hiddushei Torah*, by the new light it itself contributes to the Torah[80] through its profound study of it.

In such wise, writes the Bnei Issakhar, relating his thoughts to those expressed in the Or Hahayim, the Talmudic saying should be understood which states, "He who prays at the start of the Shabbat and recites the text *vayehulu* (from the begining of the second chapter of Genesis: 'Thus heaven and earth were completed with all that they contain. On the seventh day God ceased from all His work'[81])—he who recites this text on Friday evening is considered by the Torah to be an associate of God in the work of the original creation."[82] By proclaiming respect for the Shabbat, man joins himself to God to enable His work to survive, to recommence and to continue.

By virtue of its identification with the Torah and the Shabbat, Israel becomes a cosmic factor and plays a determinative role in the administration of the cosmos.[84]

The Shabbat will be
what one has succeeded in making of it
during the "preparation" period

The regulation of the cosmos,[85] as understood by the Sages of Israel, corresponds to the regimen of the Torah, and this in turn corresponds to the life of man and, in particular, of the Jew.[86] This regimen is based on a ratio of six to one[87] which is a relationship between the activity of reflection and reflection on the activity. The relationship between the *vita activa* and the *vita contemplative*, which is described by Philo,[88] is in fact a relationship of equilibrium, a compensation for the tangible, material *quantity* of the six "physical" days by the *quality* of the one day, the "day of the soul,"[89] which appears to be ethereal but is in reality full of substance. Indeed, the number seven, as the Maharal says, is a round, "whole" number; the *shevi'i*, the seventh, is the sign of *sevia (sova)*, of "satiety."[90]

The Shabbat constitutes the end of the six days of labor. It is their *sikum*: it comprises the sum total of the thoughts and actions of the Jew during the preceding six days. It represents the tangible result[91] of his efforts during this period of tension. And thus it brings calm to man, as he is "liberated" from tension.[92]

The value of the mitzvah of the Shabbat rest will depend on the extent to which the mitzvah of work was implemented during the six days (work for six days of the week is also a mitzvah).[93] Thus, as understood by Jewish mysticism from the Zohar to the Sefat Emet,[94] the Shabbat will become that which one has succeeded in making of it during the "preparation" period, the *hakhanah*, which preceded it. According to certain halakhic authorities, the *hakhana*, the spiritual and material, ethical and aesthetic preparation for the sacred Shabbat,[95] is not only indispensable to the observation of the mitzvah of the Shabbat;[96] it constitutes in itself a *mitzvat asseh*.[97] The *hakhanah* does not only relate to the "preparations" "on the eve of the Shabbat,"[98] it also embraces all the activity of the Jew.[99] Whether he be stringent like Shammai or gentle like Hillel, or be he a simple Jew bent on his everyday tasks, the practicing Jew of the "pre-Shabbat" relates all his thinking "to the Shabbat." He awaits the Shabbat for the fulfillment of all his desires,[100] and dedicates all that he finds good and beautiful to the Shabbat, "in honor of the Shabbat," "in the name of the Shabbat," *likhvod Shabbat, lesheim Shabbat*.[101]

> The days of the week do not
> even have names of their own;
> they all refer to the Shabbat

For the Jews time is therefore sabbatical time.[102] It is influenced by the Shabbat, either by the days which precede it or by the days which follow it.[103] The Hassidim say that the Shabbat is the *hemdat hayamim*, the day "which all the other days desire" or hope for.[104]

Rashi, in his commentary on the Gemara,[105] teaches us that the days of the week are divided into two categories: *kamei shabta* and *batar shabta*. The last three days of the week "precede," await, the Shabbat;[106] the first three days of the week "follow," are linked to, the Shabbat.[107] All of the days of the week look towards the Shabbat, look forward to it or are inspired by it. They derive their strength from the Shabbat[108] and "their" blessings "depend" on the blessing which the Shabbat gives them.[109] For this reason, the activity in which we engage during the week only acquires its full worth when seen in ultimate relation to the Shabbat.[110]

The days of the Jewish week do not even have names of their own, observe Ramban and Abarbanel.[111] They all refer to the Shabbat and they all meet again in the Shabbat. Without the Shabbat they would not exist.[112]

Our possessions belong to us to the extent to which we recognize that we belong to God

Thanks to the Shabbat we are aware that all that we are, have, do or transform is only possible because the universal proprietor, *Koneh Hakol*, has endowed us with capacities to plan our activities, to select them and to complete them in order to benefit His creatures as He does, *leheitiv labriyot*.[113] All that is temporarily at our disposal is merely an instrument, a *keli*,[114] as both the Hassidim and the Ba'alei ha-Mussar would say, which God put into our hands for our use in order to do good, to share it and then to bequeath it to others.

The *Shabbat bereshit*, the Shabbat of the Beginning, and its corollary the *Shabbat ha-arets*, "the Shabbat of the earth,"[115] the Shabbat of space, teach us that our possessions only belong to us to the extent to which we recognize that, in fact, we belong to God, that both what we are and what we have belong to Him. "When you belong to Me," God says to us, "this belongs to you."[116] The symbol of this kind of Shabbat, as the Sefat Emet put it, is the *bitul ha-yesh*,[117] the nullification of what we are and what we have, before Him, our Creator: like Abraham,[118] we bring to Him the sacrifice of all that we have.

And we bring this sacrifice to Him on the day when we *are* more than on other days,[119] when we have more than on other days.[120]

The Shabbat enables everyone to feel that they are equals for at least one-seventh of their lives

The effective observance of the Shabbat would offer all human beings the possibility of spending at least one-seventh of their lives in a state of approximate economic, social and cultural equity, because during the Shabbat, which is a *yoma de'oraita*, "a day of the Torah," the Jewish ideal of universal, permanent adult education becomes a concrete reality.[121] In this way the cultural gap[122] between the members of the same community is considerably reduced.

Rabbi Yehuda Halevi[123] and the Rambam, Rabbenu Bahya and S.D. Luzzatto,[124] express the wish that the Shabbat should enable people to feel for one-seventh of their lives that they are equals, in order to prepare for the Messianic, complete and universal Shabbat.[125]

The *mitzvah* of Shabbat observance is equivalent to all other *mitzvot* of the Torah

The Shabbat is the sign by which the Jew witnesses[126] to his belief in what is termed, in Jewish religious thinking, the *hiddush ha'olam*, namely the creation of the world from nothing.[127]

In its description of Creation, *Bereshit*, the Torah uses the term *bara*, which refers to the Divine creation *ex nihilo*.[128] But, says the Rambam,[129] if there is a creation there must therefore be a Creator, *Elohim*. Creation *ex nihilo* is the fundamental basis of our faith in God. If, however, by ignorance or absurdity, one accepts the idea which Rav Kook[130] calls obscure and confused, of the *Kadmut ha'olam*, of the eternity of the world, meaning perpetuity, there would no longer, according to the Rambam,[131] be any room for faith; there would be no more room, according to the Rambam,[132] for the Torah; the open paths of faith in the *Adnut HaBorei*, the sovereignty of God, would be obstructed, according to the Hafetz Hayim.[133]

Consequently the Sages of the Talmud consider the *mitzvah* of the Shabbat, which is derived directly from *Bereshit bara Elohim*,[134] the first verse of the Torah, to be the equivalent of all the other *mitzvot* of the Torah.[135] This is the way in which the Ramban[136] explains the high number of regulations concerning respect for the Shabbat, because basically it is a question of respect for the Torah as such. Therefore the Rambam, at the end of his Hilkhot Shabbat,[137] in line with the other codifiers, lays down what the Talmud[138] posits and Rashi[139] cites, namely that the Jew who flouts the Shabbat deliberately and publicly should be stigmatized as an idolater because he denies the principles of *Hiddush ba'Olam* and of *Borei Olam*, the principle of *creatio ex nihilo*, of the absolute, voluntary creation by the Creator.[140] These are the principles which lead to faith in *Hashgahah* and *Nevu'ah*, faith in the Providence of God and in the prophecy of His messengers.[141]

Three proclamations of the Shabbat:
(1) the Shabbat of the primordial time;
(2) the Shabbat of the giving of the Torah;
(3) the Shabbat of the time to come

When listing the reasons which justify respect for the Shabbat, Rabbi Yossef Karo in the Beit Yossef[142] put the concept of *Hashgahah*, Providence, first and then the concept of *Torah min haShamayim*, the revealed Torah. Why? There is careful reasoning behind this choice of order by one of the greatest masters of religious codification. It becomes clear to us in the light of the way the Shabbat is presented in the Midrash.

There are three proclamations of the Shabbat, says the Midrash, that of *Shabbat bereshit*, the Shabbat of the Beginning of the Creation; that of *Shabbat matan Torah*, the Shabbat of the giving of the Torah, of the revelation of the Torah on Sinai; and that of *Shabbat shele'atid lavo*, of the future, the Messianic Shabbat. The Tur[143] adopts this triple view of the Shabbat and thus explains the content and meaning of the three "central" Shabbat prayers[144] which consecrate the *kedushat haYom*, "the holiness of the day," of Shabbat.

The Gaon of Vilna,[145] for his part, understands this triple sabbatical order less as a chronological and scriptural sequence than as an interweaving of motives. Indeed, *Shabbat bereshit*, the Shabbat of the Beginning, leads up to the Messianic Shabbat of the future. The letters of the word *reshit*—*beginning*, can be rearranged into the Hebrew word *she'erit*—*remnant*. The concept of *She'erit Yisrael*, the remnant of Israel, symbolizes the salvation of Israel and the final *ge'ulah*, that will also be Universal Salvation, when the world will be renewed as in the Days of the Beginning (Micah 2:12, 5:6,7). As for *Shabbat matan Torah*, the Shabbat of the promulgation of the Torah, it is this which creates the link between the *Shabbat bereshit*, the Shabbat of the Beginning, and the *Shabbat shele'atid lavo*, the Shabbat of the future. It is this, the *Shabbat matan Torah*, which constitutes first the goal of the Shabbat of the Beginning[146] and secondly the necessary condition for the Messianic Shabbat, by virtue of the Torah accepted and adopted by Israel on Sinai. Was not the creation planned with a view to the advent of Israel and revelation of the Torah?[147] And will not the coming of the Messianic age be made possible by Israel's observance of the *mitzvot* of the Torah?[148]

For this reason the revelation of the Torah, which gives expression to the revelation of the creation of nature in *Bereshit bara* ("In the beginning God created...") took place, according to the Talmud, on Shabbat,[149] the day which commemorates the *Shabbat bereshit*, the Shabbat of the

Beginning. The *Shabbat matan Torah*, the Shabbat of the revelation of the Torah, marks the completion of the *Shabbat bereshit* but also, and above all, the *tikkun*, the restoration of that which all the Shabbatot which have succeeded one another from *Shabbat bereshit* to *Shabbat matan Torah* have been unable to achieve. But *Shabbat matan Torah* also constitutes the indispensable means of access to the Messianic Shabbat, *Shabbat shele'atid lavo* of the future.[150] The *Shabbat matan Torah* is therefore the center, the heart, of the three Shabbatot, because it was through it and in it that Israel was chosen to exercise its religious vocation which is simulataneously cosmic and universal.

Why is it the *Shabbat matan Torah* which brings about the *tikkun*, the restoration of what all the Shabbatot since the *Shabbat bereshit* have been unable to achieve?[151] Because on the *Shabbat bereshit* the Word of God came forth[152] as a soliloquy, a monologue:[153] No real partner was there in a dialogue, no real *ata*,[154] no human "thou," to respond to the Divine affirmation *Anokhi*, "I." "And yet it was I, *Anokhi*, says the Lord," speaking through the voice of Isaiah, "I made the earth and created man upon it."[155] Adam, however, did not pay sufficient attention to this affirmation addressed to him by *Anokhi*, the God of Creation, and did not respond to it correctly:[156] On the very eve of the Shabbat on which he was created he committed his first sin![157] However, the Sages of Israel say that Adam was created on the eve of Shabbat in order to perform his first *mitzvah*, that of the Shabbat itself, immediately.[158] Humbled by sin and eventually saved by the Shabbat itself,[159] which teaches him the ways of *teshuvah*,[160] Adam is no longer capable of being a true partner in God's dialogue, and his descendants were to be still less capable (with the exception of the Hebrew patriarchs who, according to Tradition, observed the Shabbat).[161]

Shabbat kodesh hallowed by God
will henceforth be "sanctified"
by man via the *kiddush*

It is for this reason that in the Book of Bereshit, when referring to the seventh day, the day of rest, God speaks as *Elohim*,[162] the impersonal, "strict" God, Creator of nature: *Elohim begematria ha-tevah*.[163] The name of the Shabbat itself is not yet used, it is simply referred to as the *yom ha-shevi'i*, the "seventh day" of Creation. The possibility of man observing the Shabbat is only potentially expressed by the verb *shavat*[164] which the Creator puts into effect in His own way,[165] but it is only a proposal set before man; man has not yet given it its personality. Only in the Book of

Shemot, which records the promulgation of the Torah, does the Shabbat of God also become the Shabbat of man.[166] The "holy Shabbat" (*Shabbat kodesh*), which "God makes holy" (*mekadesh haShabbat*),[167] will henceforth be "sanctified" by the *kiddush*, by the "sanctification" which it receives from man. Indeed, this man has "prepared" himself in order to merit the Shabbat; he has attracted and "called" it towards himself; he has "invited" and received this Divine host into his home: he has "sanctified" it.[168]

The *Anokhi* of the God of the Torah, with which God opens the Decalogue,[169] thus finds a true partner in man, the true man for whom God was waiting, Israel:[170] *atem beru'im adam*....[171] Israel becomes the *ata*,[172] the human "thou," who is opposed[173] to the *Anokhi*, to the Divine "I," not as a rebel but as "God's fellow worker in the perfection of the initial creation," as the collaborator foreshadowed at the end of the *ma'assei bereshit*, the account of the creation of the world, in the *vayehulu*,[174] who now takes up his duties on Mount Sinai.

This is why it is only in Sefer Shemot that the word *shabbat* occurs clearly as a noun. It was called into being and will remain alive thanks to Israel.[175] It will only be called "*Yom haShabbat*," states the Maharal, when Israel observes it insofar as it is God's Shabbat.[176] God offers it to Israel as a sign of love,[177] gives it to Israel as a *matanah*,[178] a "gift:" a *matanah* received on the day of *matan Torah*,[179] the very day on which He makes Israel the gift of the Torah.[180] Israel receives the *matanah* of the Shabbat; it commits itself to respect it, to treat it with care,[181] to regard it as an approved *mitzvah*.[182] The Jew calls the appointed *mitzvah* of the Shabbat *oneg*, "delight:" "And what does 'delight' mean?—*oneg Shabbat*, the delight of the Shabbat!"[183]

As the *shomer Shabbat*,[184] the guardian of the Shabbat, and the *meshamer Shabbat*,[185] the trustee of the Shabbat, Israel rehabilitates Adam, the *hoteh erev Shabbat*, sinner on the eve of the Shabbat. In Sefer Shemot, God speaks to Israel as a personal God when offering them the Shabbat, using the *Shem Havayah*, expressed by the Tetragrammaton, the symbol both of the supratemporal Origin of Creation and of the guiding Principle of historical Time.[186] But above all He speaks as a personal God who, when communicating His commandments to His people, grants them His *mitzvot*[187] because He loves Israel; and Israel, in turn, responds, accepting the Shabbat out of love for God.[188]

The *Shabbat bereshit* inspires *fear* in men (the Zohar discerns two words in the term *bereshit: yera Shabbat*,[189] and formulates the exhortation "to fear the Shabbat!") because it is addressed to their *reason*[190] and refers to the power of the Creator, of a distant God; so the *Shabbat bereshit* is transmuted into a Shabbat of love[191] which establishes itself in our hearts, *be-ahava uveh-ratson*: this is the love of the Creator, His "intimate" love,[192] the love of God who is close to us, the love of God for Israel which opens itself up to His goodness: *ahava unedavah*.

Shabbat bereshit, the Shabbat of Genesis, of nature, is then transformed into the Shabbat of the Torah,[193] set out in parashat *Ki tissa* of our Sefer Shemot.[194] Here God expresses the wish that not only the children of Israel as individuals should witness by the Shabbat to their Creator, to His creation and to the particular place in Time which He has reserved for the Shabbat, but that a whole nation, "the community of the children of Israel," should witness by the Shabbat to the unity of God and to the special place which He has reserved for Israel in the World.[195] *Shabbat bereshit*, in which God had inscribed the natural "sign of the covenant" between Himself and humankind[196] who were unable to conceive the greatness of the Shabbat, is transformed in Sefer Shemot into a Shabbat *ot*, a "sign," a spiritual sign of the covenant,[197] of the *berit* between God and Israel.[198]

The convenant is incarnate in the *mitzvah* of the Shabbat which is equal to all the other *mitzvot* of the Torah.[199] The word *berit*, which means "covenant," is the numerical equivalent of the six hundred and twelve *mitzvot* which, with the *mitzvah* of the Shabbat, make up the total of the six hundred and thirteen *mitzvot*. Furthermore, the covenant of God with Israel implies the perenniality of Israel in *berit olam*: "an everlasting covenant."[200] Thus the Shabbat becomes the sign of the perenniality of Israel and Israel ensures the perenniality of the Shabbat.[201]

In fact, as the Sages of Israel point out, in the world there are "three partners who witness to one another: Israel, Shabbat and God."[202]

The marriage contract between the Shabbat and Israel is written in the Torah

Rabbi Shimeon bar Yohai, who so greatly loved the Shabbat,[203] has informed us in a famous story, preserved for us by the Midrash, that at the moment when the world was created the Shabbat said to God, "Master of the world, you have given a partner to each of the other days of the week, but I have none." God replied, "The community of Israel will be your marriage partner." And when Israel was at the foot of Mount Sinai to receive the Torah, God said to it, "Remember what I said to the Shabbat: the Community of Israel will be your marriage partner; this is why in the Ten Commandments I say: Remember the Shabbat day to make it holy."[204] For in ancient Hebrew usage, to "marry" someone is expressed as *le-kadesh*, to make holy."

The *kiddushin*, the "holiness," of the conjugal union between Israel and the Shabbat was proclaimed at the foot of Mount Sinai.

The marriage between Israel and the Shabbat[205] was celebrated at the moment when the Torah was promulgated, the marriage contract is written in the Torah. The Torah is the marriage certificate.[206]

The two spouses accept their mutual responsibilities according to the law of the Torah. Thus, while "the Torah is the essence of life," "the origin of the Torah is the Halakhah," as the Maharal emphasizes,[207] because the Halakhah is the living rule which teaches us how to observe the *mitzvot* of the Torah in our lives. By means of its practical regulations, the Halakhah determines the actuality of the Shabbat[208] and creates the true spirit of Shabbat which is both "pleasure," spontaneity, and "law," constancy.[209]

The Jew who observes the Shabbat is called by the Sages of Israel *shomer Shabbat kehilkhatah*, by the Sages of Israel, an observer of Shabbat according to its Halakhah. This is how the Jew cultivates the Shabbat, and it is also, in turn, the way the Shabbat cultivates Israel: *Shomer Shabbat kehilkhato*. For *shemirat Shabbat*, the observance of Shabbat, is based on reciprocity: the words *shemirat shabbat* implicitly contain the mutal commitment of Israel and the Shabbat: *kehilkhato* and *kehilkhatah*.[210]

**The children of Israel
live the Shabbat in their home**

This reciprocal, loving regard of the two partners, Israel and the Shabbat, for each other, can only fully become a reality in the family home in which the *zug*, the Jewish couple[211] lives together, in which the constancy and spontaneity of the Shabbat harmonize, and where the continuity and renewal of generations of Jews are confirmed.

The Zohar makes a remark which is of capital importance for understanding the Shabbat. In the fundamental text concerning Shabbat the Torah tells us, "The children of Israel will therefore be faithful to the Shabbat and keep it for all generations, *ledorotam*."[212] And the Zohar, simply but daringly, reads the word *ledorotam*, "for their generations," as *bediratam*, in their home, "in the house where they live."[213]

What a profound insight! The children of Israel live the Shabbat in their home because the home, the *reshut ha-yahid*, the private domain, is the domain of the *Shekhinah*, of the Presence of God who dwells among them.[214] The *reshut ha-yahid* is the place of union, *ahdut*, return, of coming back to oneself, tenderness and tranquillity, concentration and meditation, reflection: It is Jerusalem: it is salvation. Whereas the *reshut ha-rabbim*, the public domain, the road, the highways, are the place of disunion, of *peirud*, going out, haste, insecurity, irritation, alienation, confusion, dispersion: It is the Galut: it is the Exile. It was Rabbi Moshe Alshekh[215] (who belonged both to the kabbalistic school of Rabbi Yitshak Luria and to the halakhic school of Rabbi Yossef Karo) who particularly suggested these ideas for reflection on these two fundamental concepts of the Halakhah relating to the Shabbat: *reshut ha-yahid* and *reshut ha-rabbim*.

There is a close relationship, one might say a relationship of cause and effect, between the love for and veneration of the Shabbat and that of parents, and *vice versa*.[216] In the Decalogue, the commandment to respect one's parents follows that of respect for the Shabbat; and in Sefer Vayikra the respect of parents precedes that of the Shabbat.[217] By living the Shabbat in the home, according to the Halakhah to promote the spontaneity of our behavior and joy in our interpersonal relationships,[218] we shall ensure the harmonious continuity of the generations.[219]

In the Sabbatical law, tenderness and severity,
freedom and discipline
dwell together in mutual harmony

The practice of the *dinim*, the laws, concerning the *hadlakat ha-neirot* (the "lighting of the candles" for Shabbat),[220] the *kiddush* (the "sanctification" of Shabbat over wine) and the *havdalah* (the prayer at the conclusion of Shabbat by which the "distinction" and the "separation" is made between Shabbat and the working days), and many other details—and I mean details—whose majestic and meticulous beauty makes them into solemn acts, prepares the Jewish man and the Jewish woman so that they can experience what the Sages of Israel say about the family Shabbat and what the Halakhah sees in it: a home in which "the Jew and the children of his household harmonize"[221] in mutual affection and understanding.

The loving and enlightened observance of these *dinim*, as modern Jewish thinkers like Hermann Cohen[222] and Franz Rosenzweig[223] write with feeling, confers on the parents an authority which the children sincerely desire to emulate, and on the children a personality which is liberally reinforced by their parents. In the Sabbatical law sensitivity and rationality, spontaneity and orderliness, the new and the old, conviviality and cohesion, tenderness and severity, freedom and discipline live together in constructive and fruitful harmony.[224]

One has to be well aware that the Jewish home cannot become the centre of Jewish life, and therefore of sabbatical time during the week, unless the regulations of the Halakhah are accepted with love and followed punctiliously. There are laws concerning *hotsa'ah*, and *tehumin*, provisions limiting the transport of objects, the movement of persons, the distances to be covered during Shabbat.[225] All these regulations, which are certainly restrictions, exist in order to reinforce the attachment to the Jewish home,[226] to promote the cohesion and unity of the Jewish family. The Halakhah does not allow us physically to distance ourselves from our homes once the eve of Shabbat begins.[227] And if we do so on Shabbat itself, to the extent and in the manner we are authorized, this permission is granted within sight of and for the sake of our home.[228]

An event recorded by the Midrash[229] about Jacob is very characteristic. When he arrived in a town on the eve of Shabbat the patriarch, father of a large family, devoted his first attention to his "house"[230] and laid down the limits which could not be crossed on Shabbat: *kava tehumin*. And when the Halakhah proceeded much later to draw up its regulations governing the limits allowed for the respect of the Shabbat, it stipulated that distances in town should be "measured with reference to the family home.[231]

The undeniable force of the Shabbat throughout the centuries and millennia and in the midst of different civilizations, when it is observed in the full Jewish way, is undoubtedly due to the fact that the sincere acceptance of the idea of the Shabbat must be accompanied by its practical observance, regulated by the Torah and, in particular, by the oral Law.[232] We do not call the Jew who keeps the Shabbat *zokher Shabbat*, a Jew who "thinks of the Shabbat," but *shomer Shabbat*,[233] a Jew who "keeps the Shabbat in practice."

Two key words govern the Halakhah of the Shabbat: *zakhor* and *shamor*

The two key Hebrew verbs which govern the Halakhah and inspire the Aggadah of the Shabbat. These two words are *zakhor* and *shamor*: "remember," think of it, and "keep," observe it. The first of these verbs introduces the commandment to keep the Shabbat in the first version of the Decalogue: "Remember the Shabbat day to make it holy!" evoking the cosmic event of the creation of the world. The second of these verbs introduces the Shabbat commandment in the second version of the Decalogue: "Keep the Shabbat day holy!" referring to the historic-social event of the liberation of the Israelites from their slavery in Egypt.

The most extensive and most significant comment which the Sages of Israel make on these two different and complementary terms used by the Decalogue to express the commandment to respect the Shabbat is that of the Talmud which says: *Zakhor veshamor be-dibbur ehad ne'emru.*[234] At the moment when the Decalogue was revealed, the two verbs *zakhor* and *shamor* were pronounced as one single word. However, the interpretation by our Sages of the identity of these two verbs goes beyond the concrete description of the miracle of that revelation. Above all it teaches us that only that which is observed in practice can be considered to be respected by thought: *Kol sheyeshno bi-shemirah yeshno bi-zekhirah.*[235] The thought itself must become manifest and to this end it must be accompanied by a material act. You are required to "remember to keep the Shabbat day holy." Therefore, the Talmud exclaims: "Remember it by sanctifying it over a cup of wine,"[236] by reciting the Kiddush, and drinking a substantial amount, a sufficient *shi'ur* of wine.[237]

Now we can understand why the mother of Rabbi Zakkai, a poor Jewish woman who did not have enough money to buy the Kiddush wine for her son, sold the *kipah she-al roshah*, the headscarf which she wore, to obtain the small sum necessary for the Kiddush wine of her illustrious son.[238] This suggests that one who was supposed to teach the laws of Shabbat to others was not sufficiently capable, in his mother's eyes, of focusing on the Shabbat unless he had a cup of wine before him.[239]

"The nations of the world" have only adopted the "idea" of a day of rest

The commands *zakhor*, "remember the Shabbat day," and *shamor*, "keep the Shabbat day," go together in the Torah. The *hame'aneg et haShabbat* and the *ha-meshamer et ha-shabbat*, "the one who pleases the Shabbat" and "the one who keeps the Shabbat," go together in the Talmud. They make up the unity of the Shabbat for Jews who, individually, are *shomrei Shabbat vekorei oneg* and, collectively, are *am mekadeshei shevi'i*, "the people who sanctify the seventh day" of the week and thus transform it into a Shabbat.

The harmony between these biblical and talmudic expressions and the harmonization of their meanings constitute the essence of the Jewish Shabbat; and it is thus that we sanctify the name of God in the world.[240]

The world needs this particular testimony. Israel has the obligation, according to the Rambam, by virtue of the *mitzvah* of *kiddush haShem*, of the "sanctification of the name" of God,[241] to "make known to humanity" the "true" concept of God and of His relationships with the world and with humankind. Consequently, Israel is called upon to instruct humanity about the true authoritative concept of the Shabbat and to enlighten it by its own radiant observance of the Shabbat.[242]

The Sages of Israel were right to say that, for the time being, "the nations of the world" have chosen only the *zakhor*, have only adopted the idea of a day of rest once a week.[243]

Israel, however, has a revolutionary concept of God. Israel knows of one single, spiritual God— creator of the world and ruler of His creation.[244] And thus Israel has an objective concept of the unity of the cosmos and its creatures, both animate and inanimate.[245] What follows is a comprehensive idea of the unity of humanity which should be reflected in the harmony between human beings and domestic animals and in ecological harmony in general: Israel has a concept of justice linked with the ideal of love and thus a concept of human creativity, freely developed, and with its self-discipline, freely accepted.[246] And so Israel understands the dignity of labor, freely chosen, undertaken, pursued and then suspended; the ethical purpose of work; it perceives the freedom of human personality and of the necessity of social equality. And finally Israel holds to the idea of the "kingly"[247] freedom of man based on the obedience he owes to his Creator and His ethical commandments. For all these reasons the Shabbat remains a universal institution.[248] Especially by means of its inner essence, by its soul which links time with eternity, as the Ramban underlines,[249] it remains "the very foundation of the world." And Israel, for its part, by keeping the Shabbat as a Jewish Shabbat makes itself worthy of the supreme reward: It merits its own deliverance and hastens the universal Messianic salvation.[250]

By keeping the Shabbat as a Jewish Shabbat, "distinct," with *havdala*,[251] Israel "draws the divine benediction over the whole world," because that is its task. It is the Sefat Emet,[252] none other than one of the most ardent hassidic individualists, who extols this vocation of Israel. Indeed, Jewish individualism is the most feithful servant of Jewish universalism, above all because of its constancy in respect for the command *shamor*:[253] to keep and guard the Shabbos.

The Messianic Shabbat will be
the result of the sum total of
the Shabbatot kept by Israel

Every Shabbat Israel hears God saying to it: "You, children of Israel, by observing the laws of Shabbat have enthroned Me as King in this world!"²⁵⁴ The Messianic Shabbat will be the result of these weekly enthronements brought about by Israel.²⁵⁵

Toward the end of each Shabbat day, during the prayer of Minhah, the Jew, sensing the love of God to the highest degree — *ra'ava dera'avin*;²⁵⁶ expresses his desire to see the coming of the One Messianic day²⁵⁷ when Israel as One²⁵⁸ redeemed by God in a final deliverance²⁵⁹ will make it possible for God to be acknowledged as One King²⁶⁰ in One united world.²⁶¹ The mystery of the Shabbat which is *raza d'ehad*,²⁶² the mystery of unity, will then finally be unveiled, understood and accepted, and identified as "The Day which is entirely goodness," "The Day which is entirely Shabbat."²⁶³ And then Israel will recite the "hymn for the Shabbat day"²⁶⁴ and will exclaim:

"How good it is to praise God!"²⁶⁵

5

Jewish identity

*being and becoming a Jew/
individual and community*

**Having been "made" initially by Another,
the Jew is in a position
"to remake himself"**

Jewish identity is an asset granted by the Creator to the individual whom He causes to be born a Jew. This gift, which is itself a constraint, has an effect until the end of his days on that person whom God, by the unfathomable mystery of His will, has placed within "His people, the house of Israel."

Rendered Jewish, "made" a Jew, by the irrevocable decision of the Creator, the man is invited independently to consider the condition which is already his own, to joyfully consider the asset which the Creator has made available to him by fixing "Jewishness" within himself: he is called to accept it, to develop it, to enrich it, in biblical terms to "choose" it, to "live" it every day of his life:[1] he is called to become a Jew by choice.

The Jew by birth is invited to become a Jew and thus to deliberately confirm the decision taken about him by his Creator. Although he was initially "made" by Another, the Jew is then in a position "to remake himself."[2] In this way he voluntarily justifies the will of the One who created him a Jew. He "sanctifies" His will[3] by a persistent search for His comprehensive, educative, inspiring spirit which is manifest in the Torah, and by the daily observance of the details of His wishes which come together in the living unity of His *mitzvot*.

**The Jew does not submit to his identity:
he cherishes it as a vocation**

Thus the identity of this Jew is not established by others, by non-Jews who at times attribute it to him despite himself, who apply it to him when he often tries to hide it or even to reject it. He is not reproached for this identity by such as Sartre describes,[4] who seek to use it as a stigma with most of the faults attributed to the Jews as hereditary. Although it may not be outwardly displayed, this identity is nevertheless expressed with dignity and courage by its bearer and owner; for the Jew discovers it with "freshness" and interest in the genetic, spiritual heritage of which he is concurrently heir, transmitter and progenitor. He does not submit to his identity; he grasps it as a vocation. It is not that which others, non-Jews, attribute to him with hostility and contempt. It is rather that which attracts the admiration—even if it is tinged with a "Bileamite" enmity[5]—of those who, when they look at him, must exclaim: "See how beautiful the behavior of this Jew is, how pleasing his actions are and worthy of imitation!"[6] In fact, they can "read the name of God on him."[7] Such a Jew "sanctifies the name of God in this way," because in his identity—zekhut—by virtue of the "merit"—which this identity gives him, he identifies with his God—having already identified himself with the Torah of his God. Such a Jew bases his identity on the identity of the One whom he cannot grasp; and rather than attempting to comprehend Him from afar with his own puny intelligence, he loves Him very closely with his whole being. He experiences Him so closely that he exclaims: "*Ze Eli veanvehu!*" "Behold, it is my God whom I glorify"—by fulfilling the *mitzvot* in His honor, by following along His way, by going forward according to His laws:[8] by being fully what I am and thus consciously becoming what I become; and by thus participating fully by myself and consciously in myself in beautifying the lives of others, all of whom are children of God in a world which belongs completely to God.

A duty to become a Jew this very day as if he were not yet a Jew yesterday

The Jew, when he awakens each morning and marvels at the creation which the Creator "renews each day by His goodness" and which man is called to "complete"[9] each day by his actions, finds he has been created anew himself and discovers, to his great joy, that he has been born a Jew. For this reason, his first blessing is to thank his Creator "for not having made him a non-Jew!"[10] He immediately devotes himself with confidence, to perfecting himself, to "making himself a Jew," during the day which he begins with a hymn of gratitude dedicated to his Creator. Now it is up to him to avail himself of the strength which God offers him in order to be capable of accepting the Torah which seems "new" to his eyes; it is up to him to avail himself of the strength given him by God in order to begin to observe the *mitzvot* "as if they had been communicated to him this very day."[11]

Yes, it is the Jew's duty — and opportunity — to become a Jew this very day as if he were not a Jew yesterday.

Rabbi Jacob Isaac of Przysucha (1776-1813) was called *haYehudi haKadosh*, "the holy Jew," because, according to the Hassidim, he became a Jew each day, he changed for the better every day, he constantly made progress in "his service to God," as one who changes and progresses from a stage where he was not yet a Jew to a stage where he becomes one.[12]

No claim to a Jewish identity without a claim to the Torah and the *mitzvot*

You may say, and rightly — that the portrait of the Jew which we have drawn is of the ideal Jew, of the perfect man, the one whom the Sages of Israel call *adam kasher*,[13] the man ready ... always to become more of a man, the Jew ready always to become more of a Jew. This is certainly true. "But," you may also ask, "are there many Jews who belong to this category or are they merely rare examples, or do they even simply constitute a very unusual model for a Jew, like the "holy Jew," *haYehudi haKadosh*?" Only God, who "knows the thoughts" of man, who "sees the heart" of man,[14] can answer these questions. What we can say is that no Jew can consider himself outside of the Torah and the *mitzvot*, or claim a Jewish identity without, consciously or subconsciously, appealing to the Torah and the *mitzvot*. We also know that no Jew exists who has never had an opportunity, whether or not he looked for it, when he could not have become a Jew by the free or compulsory fulfillment of a *mitzvah*.[15] For only thus can his fundamental Jewish existence acquire worth, meaning, by his becoming a creative Jew, with a promising future, fruitful and rich in unforeseen consequences for himself, his family and his descendants.[16]

There is no Jew "who has not reserved a *mitzvah* for himself"

In fact, there is no Jew who does not have "his hour," the hour of truth, the hour of a *mitzvah*; who does not have "his moment of good will" when he is incited or even attracted by a *mitzvah*, even if his original intention was not to fulfill it as a *mitzvah* for its own sake, *lishmah*.[17] There is no Jew "who has not reserved a *mitzvah* for himself" "who does not observe a *mitzvah* to its true extent," claim the Sages of Israel. There are even Jews who, while observing several *mitzvot*, choose one to give it special attention. They have a "predilection"[18] for a *mitzvah* which relates more closely to "the root of their soul"[19] and speaks particularly to their spiritual affinities. In fact, it is easy for the Jew, in order to "make himself a Jew," to be interested in or challenged by a *mitzvah* which is within his scope among the numerous *mitzvot* of the Torah. They are indeed numerous because they cover the individual, communal, social, national, territorial and universal life of the Jew. The Jewish mystics, and especially the Ba'al haTanya,[20] teach us that it may happen that a Jew, even if quite accustomed to observing the *mitzvot*, becomes enthusiastic about a *mitzvah* without even describing it as such—and devotes himself spontaneously to fulfilling it with *messirut nefesh*, with a devotion amounting even to "offering up his life." The true life experience of many Jews confirms it, particularly in our own age of *kiddush haShem*, of martyrdom, through the "sanctification of the Name" of God. Indeed, there is probably no Jew who does not show, either by his thinking or his words or his actions, though he be unwilling to state it, that he has an active and deliberate or at least sentimental share in *ahavat Yisrael*, in love for the People of Israel; that he has a share in Erets-Yisrael, in its development and its defence; that he has a share in the Torah of Israel. According to the *mekubalim*, the Jewish mystics, he has the equivalent of a letter in the Torah—the best among us have only asked God to "grant them a share in His Torah"—consequently, he has "a share in the God of Israel."[21]

A *mitzvah* is never isolated

By having a share in Israel, in Erets-Yisrael, in the Torah of Israel, in the God of Israel, by holding onto just one end of these fundamental values of Judaism, the Jew holds onto everything; by holding one end of the string, the Hassidim tell us, the Jew is attached to the whole string.[22] By performing one *mitzvah* initially, even without relating it to an obvious, religious intention, the Jew of the *lo lishmah* can begin to express and evolve his hidden Jewish potential. He gains the ability to fulfill this *mitzvah* and eventually many more *mitzvot* as well, *lishmah*, with a firm and enlightened will to serve his God. In fact, a *mitzvah* is never isolated, many other *mitzvot* "depend on it." Each of the *mitzvot* has an inner link with the organic unity of the other *mitzvot*: "one *mitzvah* attracts another *mitzvah*," and so on.[23]

So many *mitzvot*: hence their observance by so many different Jews

Rabbi Hananyah ben Akashya said: The Holy One, blessed be He, wanted to grant Israel some signs of His goodness (wanted to increase the merits of Israel) and therefore gave it a rich Torah and numerous *mitzvot*.[24] The Rambam, in his commentary on the Mishnah, writes about this, saying, "Since the *mitzvot* are numerous, it is not possible for the Jew in the course of his life not to fulfill at least one completely; and by fulfilling this *mitzvah* he vitalizes his existence by this action."[25] The author of *Ikarim* adds, "One *mitzvah* alone would have sufficed to give the Jew his perfection, but in containing many *mitzvot*, the Torah wills the good of the Jew. It wills that each man in Israel should have his own merit and acquire his own right to the world to come—by performing at least one of the *mitzvot*. The *mitzvot* are not intended to be a heavy burden; they rather reflect God's desire to grant Israel this favor to offer the children of Israel many ways of acquiring human perfection. So the large number of *mitzvot* makes possible their observance by different Jews.

If this were not the case, all Israel could not have merited the world to come through the Torah; it would have been the destiny of one man from each town or each generation. Instead the truth is to be found in what the Sages said: "All Israel have a share in the world to come"—which expresses the idea that "all the children of Israel will attain to one of the degrees of the world to come."[26] Along these same lines *Or HaHayim* writes in his commentary on the Torah, "The children of Israel mutually grant one another their respective merits, for the Torah was given so that it could be observed by Israel as a whole: each Jew acts according to his own abilities and each Jew enables other Jews to benefit from his own merits. God has given us 613 *mitzvot*. No single Jew can observe them all. Look at the *Kohen*, the *Levi*, the *Yisrael*.[27] There are *mitzvot* which concern the *Kohen*; there are *mitzvot* which concern the *Yisrael*, yet the Torah is fulfilled because of the bond which unites Israel as a whole; it enables the one to benefit from the other. This is why the Torah states, 'The children of Israel did all that God had ordained,' it attributed to everyone the works of each one and of all. *All* Israel did *everything*."[28]

Shared responsibility with other Jews because of the *mitzvot*

One fundamental principle governs Jewish life, and its halakhic significance is considerable: the common responsibility of all Jews. Within the People of Israel, each Jew identifies with the other because of the *mitzvot*.[29] Any Jew is responsible for other Jews; each Jew must identify with his community. But Israel, as an entity, also has its own personality, which is made up of the total of the personalities of all Israelites. Similarly, at a level beyond our reach, the soul of each Israelite conceals the soul of Israel as a whole. Even the souls of Jews, who to us seem "empty, are full of *mitzvot*," because there is a hidden, inviolable relationship between the individual Jew and the community Israel. The individual Jew, our Sages point out, has the same name as the community Israel: the one and the other are Israel.[30]

Jewish identity only when one "does not separate himself from the ways of the community"

Jewish identity belongs, according to the Talmud, to one who "performs the acts of his people." Jewish identity, from the point of view of the Halakhah as presented by the Rambam, belongs to one who "does not separate himself from the ways of the community" and "does not reject the yoke of the *mitzvot*" completely. Jewish identity belongs to one who "makes himself an integral part of *Klal Yisrael*, the whole of Israel, by means of the *mitzvot*." And, even before he composed his Mishneh Torah, Rambam went on to write, "It is a *mitzvah* to love one who makes himself an integral part of *Klal Yisrael*, even if his transgressions are due to his desire for the material things of this world."[31]

Every Jew is responsible for the Judaism of his fellow believers

By virtue of the *mitzvah* of *ahavat Yisrael*, of love of the People of Israel, every Jew has the duty of being concerned with the spiritual development of the other Jews in his neighborhood; he is expected to contribute to the strengthening of the conscious and effective Jewish identity of his neighbor, whether he be directly in contact with him or farther removed from him: he is personally responsible for the Judaism of his fellow Jews, which means, in authentically Jewish terms, for their life in the spirit of the Torah and in the observance of the *mitzvot*.[32]

The Jewish soul is inexhaustible in essence

One *mitzvah* demands of every Jew to love every other Jew without distinction; and if he is obliged not to approve or even to disapprove of something which is not right in the behavior of some of his fellow believers, he must nevertheless love them, according to the *mitzvah*, "for the sake of the good which is hidden in them": so the Tanya[33] instructs us. Indeed, each Jew conceals an unexploited fund of goodness; in each Jew there is an inexhaustible source of living vitality which may spring up surprisingly at any moment and convince us that the Jewish soul is inexhaustible in essence,[34] that it is full of unexpected potential, that it is loaded with "holy sparks" which can break free from their isolation, "gather themselves together from their dispersal," unite to form a shining torch and to transform themselves into a flame — powerful flame of the Jewish faith. (The example provided in recent years by Soviet Jewry is eloquent witness to this!) The Jewish soul comprises "part of the Divinity above"! Who can grasp it? It is so bewildering. Who can discern its energies? Are they not awe inspiring?

Israel is always the same

In this people Israel every Jewish soul is integrated, bound, so that it can live its own authentic life![35] Who can comprehend the reality of Israel? Who can fathom the existence of Israel? Both the one and the other are beyond any hypothesis or calculation. Since its birth Israel has been the same and yet each time it becomes new, original, singular, prodigious, its actions take place in this world and endure far beyond this world.[36]

Like its God, "who linked His name with it," Israel remains singular and unique.[37]

II

The inner spirit of Israel

"Enlighten our eyes in Your Torah"

1

The people of Israel and the land of Israel

The people of God:
the terms of a dialectic;
internal dynamic and external repercussions;
complementary themes and categories

Let us postulate some significant themes.

God of Israel and "God of all flesh"; King of Israel and King of the Universe. People of God and God of the peoples. God who chooses Israel, and Israel the people chosen by God; Israel, the people who choose God, and God chosen by the people of Israel.

The gratuitous selection of the Hebrew Fathers, and the gratuitous selection of the people of Israel. The unmotivated choosing of the Hebrew Fathers, and the justified deserved election of Israel. The deserts of the Fathers, and the love of the people. The characters of the Fathers and the characterisics of the people.

The election of the minority, of the poor, and the weak, and its influence on the majority, the rich, the powerful. Human deprivations and Divine proprietorship. The wilderness and the promised land. Grace and labor.

The total human covenant—physical and spiritual, and the total Divine covenant—historical and spiritual. The conditional covenant of unequal parties, the human and the Divine, and the unconditional oath of the Divine master craftsman in favor of His human partner to the contract: The contractual obligations, human and Divine: human obedience and Divine commitment; human acceptance and Divine promise.

Divine providence and human liberty. God's mighty hand compelling

Israel to be the people of God, and the free will of Israel to become and to remain the people of God.

Israel's self-abasement before God and its obstinacy in relation to other peoples; dependence in relation to God and independence in relation to men; servant of God and "not the servant of servants."

The special status of Israel among the nations, and Israel's participation in the life of nations. Israel acts in the world, in taking action upon itself; it becomes a blessing for all the families of the earth, in being itself a blessing; it serves others in being submissive to God. It demonstrates to others its adherence to the will of God, by entrenching itself behind the walls of the Law; it opens itself generously to the world, by isolating itself within the "four cubits of the Law."

The Torah which separates Israel from the rest, and the Torah which presents Israel as an example to the rest.

The incorruptible nature of the people of Israel and the circumstantial faults of the children of Israel.

The essential holiness offered by God to the people of Israel, and the holiness acquired by the children of Israel, who hallow themselves in God by imitating His acts of impartial goodness.

The merit earned by the good deeds of the people of Israel invoked in favor of their recalcitrant children; the merit earned by Israel's righteous men invoked in favor of the rebellious people.

The people of Israel forced to serve God; the children of Israel consenting to serve. The people of Israel who serve God by worshipping His Name in Erets-Yisrael, the Land of Israel; the children of Israel who serve God in hallowing His Name in the *Tefutsot-Yisrael*, the dispersions of Israel.

The exemplary service of the House of Jacob to the community; the exemplary service to the State of the "kingdom of priests;" the exemplary individual service of the children of Israel, of members of the "holy nation."

God, the King of the people of Israel and Father of the children of Israel. The people of Israel, servants of God, and the children of Israel, children of God. Israel son and servant, son or servant of God. The passing shortcomings of the children of Israel, and the eternal love of their Father, the God of Israel.

Fear and love. The fear of God, Lord of Israel, and the love of God, Friend of Israel.

Though at times they were not worthy of the honor of being "His people," the children of Israel exist nevertheless as "children of the living God."

God has linked His Name with that of Israel. The enemies of Israel, enemies of God, will never succeed in erasing the name of Israel.

God, the Inward Spirit of the world, is immutable; Israel, the inward spirit of the peoples, is indestructible.

God, the Heart of the universe, determines its life; the Righteous Man, the heart of Israel, determines its life; Israel, the heart of the nations, determines their life.

God's faithfulness towards Israel: He does not abandon them; He does not exchange them for another people; Israel's faithfulness towards God: they do not deny Him, they do not associate other gods with Him. Yet more, Israel proves its devotion to God by the total giving of itself, even to the sacrifice of its life *al Kiddush Hashem*, "for the sanctification of the Holy Name". It is the supreme act by which Israel demonstrates its identification with God, with His Cause; it is the ultimate act by which Israel testifies to its absolute consecration to its vocation to make God known in the world. *Kiddush Hashem* is the sovereign act by which Israel proclaims to the world the oneness and the truth of God, the unity and the cogency of His ethical teaching.

The aberrations of Israel and Israel's correction. God's "hiding of His face" and the loving search for His children by their Father. He follows them into Exile, "He remains with them in their sorrow;" their sorrow is His sorrow. They always remain "His children, whether or not they do His Will."

Chastisement and love. Chastisement inflicted out of love, to purify, instruct or heal; and chastisement inflicted as punishment for sin.

Israel's frequent punishment and Israel's preservation from being exterminated.

Chastisement disproportionate to the fault; intensified punishment because of the status of the offender, "the chosen of God," "the son of the King," with particular commitments towards his Lord.

Chastisement foreseen and chastisement deserved.

The sufferings of Israel and the guilt of the peoples who make them suffer purely out of hatred for them and their God. The Father is vexed when people disdain His son in the period when he has been "banished from His table"; the King becomes angry when people maltreat His servant "when he has been carried away among strangers."

The sufferings of Israel, "servant of God," because of the sins of others. "The righteous man is held back because of the sins of his generation;" he admonishes their heedlessness; he intercedes for their redemption, their salvation. Israel, the essence of humanity, calls upon humanity to return to God after straying away from Him, after being lost in a dispersion without a name. Israel appeals to humanity, which is concentrated in and surrounded by Israel, to repent through them and with them; they summon humanity to return to itself and to God.

The Golah of Israel, the Jewish diaspora: physical dissemination and spiritual gathering together; apparent weakening of identity and intrinsic strengthening of identity; inadequate means for action and an increasing desire to act.

The Golah, visible and immediate reality, invisible and metaphysical mystery.

The Golah, punishment and mission. The proportional magnitude of the punishment and of the mission; the vast extent of the final dispersion, that Israel may be present among many and powerful peoples and so awaken their conscience.

The Golah, which is a fall and an alienation, is itself a motive for recovery and re-convergence. The Golah, nostalgia and hope; sorrow at separation and expectation of reunion; separation from the Lord's hearth, and restoration to the Father's House.

Return to God, return to the "palace of the King," resulting from the spatial and organic unity of the generations and the forbearance of God.

Humanity in suspense and in action; patient waiting for deliverance and assiduous action to obtain it. Human preparation and Divine assistance. Punishment reduced and deliverance brought forward.

Israel's spontaneous and inevitable return. Israel's free and unerring return. Return chosen freely by Israel and return imposed or promised by God in His Grace.

Israel's honor restored is God's honor restored. The salvation of Israel is the salvation of God.

The relation between the Torah and Israel,
between the letters of the Torah and the Jews;
the symbolic value of the numbers six,
sixty and six hundred thousand

"God granted the Torah to Israel. The soul of Israel constitutes the body of the Torah" and "the Torah constitutes the root of Israel's soul." "Israel constitutes the six hundred thousand letters of the Torah: thus Israel is the Torah, for each Israelite is a letter of the Torah. "So say the Shelah HaKadosh, the Kedushat Levi and the Likkutei Moharan. The letters which form the name Yi-s-ra-e-l are the first letters of the words *Yesh Shishim Ribo Otiot LaTorah*, "there are six hundred thousand letters in the Torah." In fact there are more. But according to mystical tradition, six hundred thousand root-letters are to be found in the Torah. These basic letters correspond to the six hundred thousand root-souls, which are the souls of the root-Jews, the foundation of the people of Israel. Each root-Jew possesses a root-letter in the Torah; this gives him support, for his soul is animated by the corresponding letter of the Torah. The Jew who has his letter in the Torah becomes aware of it through earnest study of the Torah and the earnest application of the *mitzvot* of the Torah. (Moreover, not only the Israelites but the "four corners of the Land of Israel" have a letter in the Torah; both Israel and Erets-Yisrael are thus identified with the Torah.)

Jews who are less perfect than the root-Jews in the study of the Torah and in the observance of the *mitzvot* benefit from the "sparks" scattered by the *mitzvot* amid the Jewish people; they attach themselves to the "branches" which the "root-Jews" cause to grow in the garden of the people of Israel; they occupy the "blank" spaces in between the six hundred thousand root-letters of the Torah. (Indeed it is on the blank space of the Torah that the six hundred thousand root-letters are written: thus there is an organic, substantial intercommunication between all the components of the Torah.) Each Jew without distinction thus has his share in the Torah and the *mitzvot*, writes Rashi. Any Jew may succeed in taking upon himself a letter in the Torah: so we are assured by the Tanya and the Sefat Emet.

The numbers six, sixty and six hundred thousand are "perfect and unitary," "complete and general" numbers, according to the Maharal's definition. When Israel had attained the number of six hundred thousand adult men on departing from Egypt—and not one Israelite "was missing" from this number—Israel was capable of receiving at Sinai the Torah from which not one letter "was missing," thus becoming the root-people, the people of Israel, the people of the Torah, God's messengers in the world, as the Maharal and Shelah HaKadosh observe. (Indeed, adds Rav Kook, the number of six hundred thousand is the obligatory number necessary for the people of Israel to proclaim God in the Land of Israel.)

The corporal body of six hundred thousand standing below Mount Sinai in order to receive the *Aseret HaDibbrot*, the Ten Commandments, the essence of the Torah, represents not only a unitary number of Jews but all the genrations of Israel, all the "branches" that were to sprout from this stem. These *Shishim Ribo*, these initial "six hundred thousand" Israelites, form the quintessence, the foundation, the roots of the people of Israel of every age.

Moses, "the great scribe (of the Torah) of Israel" for all time, held within his soul the souls of the six hundred thousand Israelites who were his contemporaries, who had come out of Egypt and were present at the revelation on Sinai; he understood the six hundred thousand letters of the Torah as they were understood and "commented upon" by his six hundred thousand contemporaries, and as they would be "interpreted" "in the future" in the course of the centuries and the millennia. In truth each of his six hundred thousand contemporaries made his personal "interpretation" of the Torah (for the Torah is both eternal and contemporary, communal and personal).

There were six hundred thousand Israelites when they were liberated from slavery in Egypt, and when their liberty, their identity, was proclaimed through the Torah on Sinai. Consequently, there is no "generation" in Jewish history, there are no large Jewish "populations," "large communal units" which can number less than the basic number of six hundred thousand. This number is the qualifying, basic number of the whole people of Israel when it undertakes, for its own sake and for humanity, any great, determinative, historical, messianic tasks. Indeed it is the number which corresponds to the essential character of the "people of God." "These national conditions" (of ever numbering six hundred thousand), "established at the beginning of our existence as a people, have changed in no way during the course of time," states Rav Kook, "for the foundation of our nationality depends on the Eternal One, the God of Israel, whose name is inscribed in ours, and whose word is forever. This is why the same number that in the beginning contained the sum of opinions and values (of our people) now too is sufficient to re-establish our national stature. And the population which, not only in the Galut but also in Erets-Yisrael, will form the required number of *Shishim Ribo* (six hundred thousand) will be the beginning (of the renewal) of the House of Jacob, to witness that Israel is a people before God.

In fact, in the modern history of Israel, about six hundred thousand formed the *Yishuv*, the Jewish community in Erets-Yisrael in 1948 when the State of Israel was proclaimed.

The number six, basis of the number six hundred thousand, already has a fundamental importance in cosmic history and consequently in the messianic history of mankind (six days of creation before coming to the Shabbat, and consequently six millennia of existence for the world before coming to the seventh, the messianic Shabbat). The number six has a vital function in the expression of the faith of Israel. The "Shema," the Jewish profession of faith—verse four of the sixth chapter of Deuteronomy—has six words; in the basic structure of the oral Torah, the Mishnah, which enables us to fill out the written Torah, one finds six "orders," and in the Talmud, the development of the Mishnah, there are sixty treatises.

The number six plays an important role in the modern history of the Jewish people. Six million Jews were massacred in Europe between 1933 and 1945, and their martyrdom led directly to the establishment of the Jewish State in the Land of Israel; six million Jews living in the United States provided massive aid for the restoration of the Jewish State in Erets-Yisrael.[1]

2
Exile and redemption

The Hebrew verb *gur* means "to sojourn" in a place
both as a stranger and as an inhabitant;
the Jew is a "stranger and an inhabitant,"
both in the countries of other nations,
in the Diaspora, and in his own country, Erets-Yisrael;
man, par excellence Jewish,
the Jew, par excellence man,
is both "stranger and inhabitant" on this earth

God used the verb *gur*, "to sojourn," when He spoke to Isaac, asking him "to inhabit" the land of Canaan, "to live there permanently," *Gur BaArets HaZot*, and on no account to leave it (Gen. 26:3). In their turn, the Hebrew patriarchs used the verb *gur* to let us know that they "inhabited" this country, the Land which had been promised them by God (Gen. 35:27).

Now the noun *ger*, which means "stranger," "pilgrim," is connected with the verb *gur*, which means "to inhabit" one's own country in a permanent way, "to gather one's possessions together" in one's own house!

In truth, the Hebrew patriarchs and their descendants after them, the Jews, even while living in their own country, Erets-Yisrael, knew that they were at the same time *gerim*, "strangers." When Jacob arrived in Egypt from Canaan and introduced himself to Pharaoh, he said, "The years of my wanderings—*megurai*—have been a hundred and thirty, the days of the years of my life have been few and hard, and they have not equalled the years of my fathers, the days of their wanderings—*megureihem*" (Gen. 47:9). Thus Jacob used the noun *magur*, which means "wandering" but also "stay," to show Pharaoh how the years of his life—divided between the "flight" to a country which was not his own and the "stay" in his native land, in his country, had all been difficult and harsh. Indeed the letters which make up the word *magur* are the same as those that form the word *magor*, which means "fear," "anguish," "terror," as Abravanel[1] has remarked, commenting on an earlier verse of the Bible concerning Jacob (Gen. 37:1). However, Jacob used the same noun, *magur*, to intimate to Pharaoh that his grandfather, Abraham, who had lived in the Promised Land, and Isaac, his father, who had lived nowhere else but in the Promised Land, had had like him the feeling of living like *gerim*, like "fearful" "strangers."[2] There is therefore a certain similarity between these extreme situations of "wandering-sojourning," the *megurim* of Jacob, Isaac and Abraham —which nevertheless are dissimilar from other points of view. One can discern an allusion to this similarity in the interpretation given by Targum of Yonathan ben Uziel of this Biblical verse (Gen. 47:9) which contains an autobiographical sketch of the patriarch Jacob.

Undoubtedly there is a relation to be established between the inner meaning of *gur* and *ger*, and *magur* and *magor*.

In truth, the Hebrew patriarchs all consider that the country, their country, which they "inhabit," does not really belong to them, nor does it belong to their descendants, their nation, nor their State; this country belongs exclusively to God. Yes, God declares concerning their country, the land of Israel, the Promised Land: "The Land is Mine, for you are coming into it both as strangers and as settlers: *Gerim VeToshavim*" (Lev. 25:23).

In fact, on arriving in the Promised Land Abraham acknowledged himself to be "a stranger and a settler: *Ger VeToshav*" (Gen. 23.4). And on arriving in Egypt from the Promised Land, according to Rashi, Jacob told Pharaoh (ad Gen. 47:9): "All the days [of my life] I have been a stranger in the land—*BaArets*." (*BaArets* means both "on earth" in general and in the Land of Israel in particular.) David also considered himself "a stranger in the country" over which he was king: *Ger Anokhi BaArets*, because as a man he considered himself to be a "stranger on earth" (Ps. 119:19). Israel, the Man, knows that every man is both a "stranger" and a "settler" on this earth, and that he is more of a stranger than a settler.[3]

This is why the same verb *gur*, which means "to settle" permanently in any place or country, also means "to sojourn" temporarily as a *ger*, as a "stranger" in different places and different countries.

When speaking before Pharaoh, when they came from Canaan to Egypt, the sons of Jacob said to him (Gen. 47:40, "We have come *to stay* (*LaGur*) in this land." They had come not to remain there permanently, but "to stay temporarily:" *LaGur*.[4] They had come *LaGur*, to accomplish what God had foretold to Abraham: "Know this for certain, your descendants will be strangers (*Ger*) in a land which is not theirs" (Gen.

15:13). Indeed their "stay" in Egypt would be that of a *ger*, a "stranger," of a man who is not only looked upon as an "alien" by the people of the country he has come to, but also looks upon himself as an "alien."[5]

Faithful to its ethical conception of man, in whom it sees both a stranger and a settler, the Torah uses the verb *gur* (which means "to inhabit" one's country peacefully, enjoying liberty and stability) concerning the *Ger* (which means the "stranger," whose existence is generally marked by insecurity and all kinds of privation)! Indeed, the Torah commands (Lev. 19:33-34): "When a stranger (*ger*) *settles* (*yagur*) *with you* in your land, you shall not oppress him" (he ought to feel at ease *with* every one of the inhabitants, to whom the Torah also says (Lev. 25:35-36): "Your brother shall live *with* you; you shall assist him as you would a stranger or a settler and he shall live with you." "He shall be treated as a native born among you, the stranger who settles—*HaGer HaGar*—with you and you shall love him as yourself, for you have been strangers in Egypt."

Since the Land of Israel is, by right and in fact, the Land of God, the Jewish citizen who is virtually a *ger*, a "stranger," should consider the *ger*, the "stranger" who comes to it formally as a stranger, as an "inhabitant" of the country. He will benefit not only "with you" from the protection of the State, which assures him respect for the rights common to every man because he is created "in the image of God," the Sovereign of the Land of Israel, but he will also enjoy the personal love ("with you") that each Jew ought to show him because of his own love for God. "I am the Lord, your God!" Hermann Cohen, the German-Jewish thinker, states, rightly, that Jewish "national" structures "serve as a basis for love for the stranger, who himself constitutes the foundation of love for one's neighbor."[6]

The *Sukkah* — "dwelling" — in both wilderness and Erets-Yisrael;
the dwelling of the Jew on earth;
to be erected by nations in time to come
to lead to the *Sukkah* of bliss "in the world to come."

In autumn every year, "in the rainy season," Israel celebrates the festival of Sukkot, the festival of "Booths." This feast commemorates the booths in which God caused the Jews to dwell when He brought them out of Egypt to lead them to the Promised Land.

Indeed, the Torah says, "The Lord spoke to Moses and said: Speak to the Jews in these words: On the fifteenth day of this seventh month the festival of Tabernacles [begins, and lasts] for seven days....You shall dwell in *Sukkot* for seven days, all who are native Israelites, so that your descendants may know that I made the children of Israel dwell in *Sukkot* when I brought them out of Egypt. I am the Lord your God" (Lev. 23:33-34, 42-43).

To celebrate the festival of *Sukkot* (also known as the feast of Tabernacles) in conformity with the command of the Torah, Israel must live for several consecutive days in *Sukkot*, which means, according to the Talmud's phrase, in "temporary dwellings," *dirat arai*.[7] To comply with this requirement of the Torah, it is not enough for the Jew to build an arbor and to spend a day in it, for example, thus symbolically reproducing his ancestors' rough type of dwelling in the wilderness. The *mitzvah* of the *Sukkah* cannot be reduced to such a short-lived action, such a transitory stay, to a mere imitative gesture. What the Torah asks of the Jew is to build a *Sukkah* and go into it, in order to relive, concretely, the conditions that his ancestors knew during the decades that followed their exodus from Egypt.

To fulfill the *mitzvah* of the *Sukkah*, the Jew is not to be satisfied with commemorating the historical events or reproducing the topographical conditions of the past; he must experience, effectively and existentially, what his forebears experienced during those events or under those conditions in the past. The Jew thus fulfills the *mitzvah* that "God gave him to sit in his *Sukkah*," *LeiSheiv BaSukkah*, which according to the Sages of Israel means, "to sit in it as if he were living there": *Teishvu Ke'ein Taduru*.[8]

In order to have the feeling that he is living in the *Sukkah* as if in what the Torah calls a "permanent dwelling," a *dirat keva*, the Jew must live there for a whole week. Indeed, "for seven days the (Jewish) man regards his house (as his) temporary (dwelling) and his *Sukkah* (as his) permanent (dwelling)."[9] This is why the Sages of Israel decree that "only a *Sukkah* (which is inhabited for) seven days warrants the name of *Sukkah*!"[10]

In this way, by an experience he has felt personally, the Jew proves that he is reliving the experience felt by his forebears.

Nonetheless, this faithful reconstruction, in a material and spiritual sense, by Jews of every age, of the state in which their ancestors lived, does not take place during the spring or summer season which follows the date of the "exodus of Israel from Egypt."[11]

(The commemoration of the exodus from Egypt takes place during the festival of Passover, *Pessah*, in the month of Nissan in the spring; this commemoration also takes place in accordance with biblical laws and halakhic rules which prescribe that Jews shall relive in a concrete way the situation of their ancestors, the Israelites, when they were freed from slavery in Egypt. The Jews are required during the feast of Pessah to eat *matsot*, unleavened bread, so as to put themselves in the place of their ancestors who, when they left "in haste" the country of their enslavement—and during their slavery—ate *matsah*, the "bread of affliction." The *matsah* which all Jews without exception eat during the feast of Pessah, is the bread of the poor, the bread of "strangers"; the *Sukkah* where all Jews without exception live during the *feast* of Sukkot, is the dwelling of the poor, the hovel of the "strangers."

In truth, God asks Israel to celebrate the feast of Sukkot "so that your descendants," as He says, "may be reminded how I made the children of Israel live in *Sukkot, when* I brought them out of the Land of Egypt" (Lev. 23:43). Thus in prescribing the *mitzvah* of the *Sukkah*, the Torah only alludes to the season when God brought Israel out of Egypt: *Be-Hotsi'i*;[12] it does not refer specifically, as it does elsewhere, to the *day* on which God brought Israel out of Egypt: *BeYom Hotsi'i*. The festival of Sukkot is thus not linked by the Biblical injunction to the exact date of the exodus from Egypt.

Therefore it is in autumn, and not in spring or summer, that the Jew performs the *mitzvah* of the *Sukkah*. He fulfills the Biblical injunction concerning the building of the "temporary dwelling" and living in it, at the time of the year when most people prefer to stay at home in solidly-built houses; they are not at all inclined to "set up house" in tents or booths at that season.

In the wilderness the *Sukkah*, the "booth," sheltered Israel from the burning sun by day and from the cold by night;[13] it protected them from the snakes that swarmed there. In the Promised Land, in Erets Yisrael, and wherever Israel has lived in the course of its history, the *Sukkah* has not served any practical, useful purpose for them. On the contrary, built during the wet weather season, the *Sukkah* in which the Jew lives during the Feast of Tabernacles is intended only to enable him to carry out a *mitzvah*, an "order of God," a "decree of the King." By entering the *Sukkah*, by depriving himself of warmth and domestic comforts, the Jew "blesses" God for having "ordered him to sit in the *Sukkah*;"[14] by doing this he clearly demonstrates his will "to realize the will of his Creator,"[15] that is, his desire to fulfill the *mitzvah* and nothing else. Indeed everything he does there, everything there which makes him rejoice, is in relation to the fulfillment of the *mitzvah* concerning the *Sukkah*.

Moreover, the *mitzvah* to "sit in the *Sukkah*, which impels the Jew to live in a concrete and existential way in a situation similar to the conditions experienced by his ancestors in the wilderness, has as its aim above all to teach the Jews that they also, like their forebears, cannot count on "their own strength and the power of their own arms." In any circumstances whatsoever they must trust in God alone and place themselves under His protection so as to be sheltered from the vicissitudes of existence, just as their ancestors did in the wilderness; the latter were compelled by the circumstances of their life in an "arid land" to be constantly in search of God; they were forced by the harshness and barrenness of their natural surroundings to seek and pray from Him, the Creator of nature, some sort of shelter and refuge.[16]

Indeed, God heard the prayers of the Jews in the desert. On the one hand, He "surrounded" them with *Sukkot* that were spiritual, immaterial, composed of Divine "clouds of glory": *Ananei Kavod*; and on the other hand, He had them "make material *Sukkot*": *Sukkot Mamash*.[17]

Sheltered by the *Sukkot* in the depths of the desert, the Jews turned their gaze to Heaven; through the interstices of the flimsy roofs they raised their eyes to God; they turned their prayerful, trusting and grateful thoughts to Him.

Like his ancestors wandering in the "wilderness of the Land of Egypt," the Jew of every age, wandering "through the desert of peoples,"[18] seeks the "protection" of God through the *Sukkah*. In truth, God constitutes for him a "providential" redeeming *Sukkah* which "covers his head with His protection."[19] God is the *Sukkah*.[20] (The numerical value of the Hebrew word *Sukkah* is equal to the numerical value of the letters in the Hebrew names of God, the Tetragrammaton and "My Lord": 91.)[21]

However, this "act of grace" of God is "merited" by the "work" of man. The Jew "makes" the *Sukkah* and it is "through action that he fulfils the *mitzvah*: *Asiya Ossa Mitzvah*."[22] The Jew erects the *Sukkah* with his hands. That is why he also has the right to rejoice in the labor of his hands: he has the privilege of entering wholly into the *Sukkah*; he enters it not only with all his soul but with all his body. The *mitzvah* of the *Sukkah* is unusual, observe the masters of religious thought: the Jew enters it with his whole body, for the law requires of him that he be wholly there.[23]

The *mitzvah* of "living in the *Sukkah*" and the *mitzvah* of "living in Erets-Yisrael" empower the Jew to let himself be completely embraced[24] by the object which serves for the realization of his religious duty. The *Sukkah* and Erets-Yisrael permit the Jew to be contained entirely in them: his body and his soul are found both in the *Sukkah* and in Erets-Yisrael, remarks Rabbi Eliyahu the Gaon of Vilna.[25]

In addition, both in the *Sukkah* and in Erets-Yisrael the Jew is aware of the *Hashgahah*, the Divine Providence which watches over and touches the people of Israel and the land of Israel. Living in the *Sukkah*, through the branches which form the frail roof of his "tent," the Jew can see the stars;[26] he can thus direct his gaze towards Heaven, the Divine Heights. Living in Erets-Yisrael, "turning his eyes to the Heights," the Jew meets the gaze of God there, for Erets-Yisrael is, according to the testimony of the Torah, "a land which the Lord your God watches over; the eyes of the Lord your God are continually upon it from the beginning of the year to the end." The Gaon of Vilna bases his thought about the similarity existing between the *mitzvah* of "living in the *Sukkah*"—*Yeshivat Sukkah*—and the *mitzvah* of "living in the land of Israel"—*Yeshivat Erets Yisrael*—on the verse of the Psalms (76:3): "*Vayehi BeShalem Sukko UMeonato BeTsion*: His tent is pitched in Salem (Jerusalem) and his dwelling is in Zion." And again, the Gaon of Vilna observes, just as Jacob received the description of *Shalem*, "whole," "entire" ("physically, materially and spiritually"),[27] when he arrived in Erets-Yisrael, so the Jew acquires the quality of *Shalem* when he enters the *Sukkah* (with all his body and all his soul). And, the Gaon of Vilna adds, just as the Jew must "act" personally to fulfill the *mitzvah* of *Yeshivat Sukkah* by "making" the *Sukkah*—*Ta'asseh VeLo Min HeAssui*,[28] so he must "act" personally to fulfill the *mitzvah* of *Yeshivat Erets Yisrael* and *Yishuv Erets Yisrael*, by "doing" his best for the "peopling" and "developing" of Erets-Yisrael.

According to the Zohar, the Jew who recognizes himself to be "of the stock of Israel" and wishes to penetrate into "the mystery of the faith," will thus succeed in finding shelter in the *Sukkah* in "the shadow of the faith," *Tsila DiMeheimnuta*.[29]

Detached from his house, separated from his wealth, the Jew is no longer able to say, "It is my own power, it is the strength of my arm which brought me these riches!"[30] For being in the *Sukkah*, the Jew will attempt rather to find "the spirit of holiness," *Ruah Hakodesh*, which if he merits it he will find there, writes Rabbeinu Bahya.[31] There he reveals himself to God so as to be "covered" by Him; there he trusts himself to God so as to be "surrounded" by Him. Like King David in Jerusalem, he prays to God to "shelter him in His *Sukkah*," to "envelop" him, to "protect him in His tent."[32] After "making" his *Sukkah* himself "with his own hands," after "acting" himself so that the *Sukkah* is "erected" and "lived in" by himself, the Jew can hope to deserve to welcome there the *Ruah HaKodesh*, "the spirit of holiness," and to greet there the *Ushpizin* the "guests," the "fathers" of the people of Israel, arriving from another world to him, in his *Sukkah*.[33]

* * *

Nevertheless, the *Sukkah*, the booth, is not only the "temporary dwelling" of Israel in the "wilderness of peoples," in the Galut, in the *Tefutsot Yisrael*, in the "dispersions of Israel," where the Jewish people live without any "permanent home"—*dirat keva*, where they live as if "in a booth," in a humble *Sukkah*, the height of which is restricted,[34] the interior of which is "filled rather with shadow than with sunshine,"[35] and the roof of which is "covered with branches," "torn from the earth."[36] For these are the halakhic requirements concerning the *Sukkah*, prescriptions which in the eyes of the Jew living in the Galut possess a symbolic meaning. The *Sukkah* is not only the fragile "temporary dwelling" where the Jew of the Galut, disinherited, deprived of human succor, finds himself compelled to rely upon God, for "there is no other possibility but to rely upon our Father in heaven."[37] The *Sukkah*, the booth, also constitutes the "permanent home" of Israel "in his Land," *BaArets*, in his own Country, in Erets-Yisrael. In truth, the Land of Israel is only a *Sukkah*; it is a *dirat arai*, a "temporary home;" it is a *Sukkah*, having the same religious, spiritual and moral meaning as the *Sukkah* "in the wilderness," *BaMidbar*, as the *Sukkah* in the "wilderness of peoples," in the Galut.[38]

Even Jacob, when he returned from exile, from the country of refuge, when he returned to the Promised Land, to the "country of his fathers," the future Land of Israel, "made *Sukkot*"[39] and, according to the Zohar, celebrated the festival of Sukkot.[40] (In "erecting *Sukkot*," Jacob "built himself a House:" *Bayit*. The House of Jacob, his Home, his Homeland, is a *Bayit*, because it is only a *Sukkah*![41] On the road which brought him back to his country, before he reached the town of Shechem, the first name that Jacob gave to a place was *Sukkot*. It is the first topographical name designated by Jacob, at the moment when the Erets, the country of his Homeland, appeared once more before his eyes![42]) Much later Joshua, coming from the wilderness and entering Erets-Yisrael at the head of the people of Israel, had *Sukkot* built so that Israel, having reached their country, could celebrate the festival of Tabernacles.[43] King Solomon, at the peak of his glory, arranged for the celebration of the inauguration of the Temple of Jerusalem to coincide with the *Hag*, the "Festival," the feast par excellence, that is to say, the festival of Sukkot.[44] The dedication of the Temple marked the consecration of the realization of the supreme religious goal of the entry of Israel into Erets-Yisrael![45] The city of Jerusalem itself was built by David because it was intended to contain the Temple;[46] therefore, according to the Zohar, "Jerusalem is a *Sukkah*!"[47] Finally, Ezra and Nehemiah, "returning to Zion" at the head of the Jews "coming back from captivity" in Babylon, had *Sukkot* built, so that Israel, reinstated in their Country, could celebrate the Feast of Tabernacles.[48]

Why was there this constant recalling of the importance attached to the building of *Sukkot* and the celebration of the festival of Sukkot when Israel first entered into and when they returned to their Country? From the example of Jacob—the patriarch who lived through both the suffering of being separated from his country and the joy of returning to it,[49] who acceded to the title of *Israel* upon his return "to his father's house,"[50] on his return to his own Country—the Israel of every age knows that neither taking possession of the Land, their land, the land of Israel, nor their installation therein, are sufficient for them to consider themselves safe from trouble. Indeed, the land of Israel is not theirs, it is not Israel's, but it is the land of God. God has categorically declared to the children of Israel: "The land is mine and you are living with Me as strangers and settlers—*Gerim VeToshavim*" (Lev. 25:23). The land and its people, Erets-Yisrael and Israel, belong to God, live with God. It is why He required every settler, every native-born, every *citizen* in Israel, "*Kol HaEzrah BeYisrael*," "to live in *Sukkot*," in tents during the seven days of the Feast of Tabernacles, "so that your descendants may be reminded (says the Lord) how I made the Jews live in *Sukkot* when I brought them out of Egypt. I am the Lord your God" (Lev. 23:42-43). The Sages of Israel add, "*HaEzrah BeYisrael*, the citizen of Israel shall live in the *Sukkah* during the period of the festival of Sukkot, and, with him in the *Sukkah* shall also live the *ger*, the stranger in Israel."[51]

It is characteristic that the Biblical *mitzvah* of the *Sukkah* is particularly and expressly for the *Ezrah*, the "citizen." Indeed, in the seventeenth century Rabbi Hayyim Alfandari observes that the *Ezrah*, the native-born, enjoying all civic rights and his livelihood assured, may consider himself master in his own country, architect of his own fortune, proprietor of his own house; and therefore safe from all trouble. That is why the *mitzvah* is addressed particularly to him telling him, "Although you are an *Ezrah* and because you are an *Ezrah*, leave the dwelling that you think of as yours, go into the *Sukkah*, enter the 'tabernacle' and lift your eyes to the heavens and remember the words of Ecclesiastes: 'If you see the poor oppressed and right and justice violated ... [know] that there is One Who is *higher* than those in high authority and He *keeps watch* over them. ...'[52] Know that you are the descendant of those whom God brought out of Egypt, from the house of bondage, and whom He made dwell in tents, in *Sukkot*, in the wilderness."

The inhabitant, the native citizen, proprietor of his own home in his own country, thus must bear witness by the *Sukkah* to his sense of the brotherhood of man, of social equality, and of moral solidarity with "the stranger sojourning in his country" who on arrival has no home of his own.

The Jew bears the same witness to human brotherhood, social equality and moral solidarity with the stranger on the Shabbat, by respecting the commandment of the Decalogue which bids him "rest, you and the stranger within your gates."[53] He bears similar witness during Pessah, at the Passover Seder, when he observes the Biblical precept which in memory of the exodus from Egypt requires that "the stranger like the native-born" shall partake of "the bread of affliction"[54] and eat "unleavened bread—*matsot*."[55] The *Ezrah* thus recognizes that the exercise of his civic and religious rights is closely linked with the fulfillment of his human and religious duties: the latter consist in the first place in the recognition of the fundamental rights of the stranger and, in particular, his right to work and rest, to food and shelter, "to bread and clothing,"[56]—rights which he should enjoy out of absolute respect of his human dignity. In truth, "all men are born equal in dignity and rights."

"The citizens, the native-born, though they possess palaces, must live (during the Festival of Sukkot) in tents, must freely choose of their own accord to sojourn in the *Sukkah*, and this just at the season of the year when they are gathering in the harvest and their barns are full of all kinds of wealth. This is just the time when they should say to themselves, 'It is not our hands which have brought us this fortune,' for in living in the *Sukkah* they will thank God for having *given* them this (country as an) heritage and houses filled with all kinds of wealth." Thus writes the author of the Hizkuni, commenting on the Biblical precept concerning the festival of Sukkot.[57]

It is not only at the time of their installation in their own land that Israel is bidden to remember through the *Sukkah* that this land is not their own but belongs to God, that this land is only a *Sukkah*; but particularly when this country, Erets Yisrael, reaches an exceptional degree of achievement, as in the reign of David; when this State touches the height of its spiritual glory and material prosperity; then this whole land becomes truly a *Sukkah*: "the realm of the House of David"—*Malkhut Beit David*—receives the name of "*Sukkah* of David"—*Sukkat David*! Indeed, "the realm of the House of David" is only a frail "tent," which God the Sovereign of this land protects and succours. And when Israel, having sinned against the "God of this Land"—*Elokei HaArets*, is temporarily expelled from the land and becomes exiled in the Galut, they will pray to God to "raise up again the *Sukkah* of David which has fallen."[58]

The *Sukkah* of the Galut will become a *Sukkah* of the Restoration, for the Exile calls forth Redemption.

Just as Erets-Yisrael received the title of *Sukkah* in the time of its "first splendor," in the period of the proto-messianic glory during the reign of King David,[59] so the land of Israel will be called *Sukkah* with even greater justification in the ultimate age of Davidic glory, in the final messianic age, at the time of the coming of the "Messiah, son of David," *Mashiah Ben David*. Erets-Yisrael will then become the true *Sukkah* of the inextinguishable glory of Israel; it will be clothed "with pride and splendor," for "then the Lord will create over the whole breadth of Mount Zion a cloud...a bright flame of fire...every place will be covered by a canopy. It shall be a *Sukkah*" (Isa. 4). "This will be the *Sukkah* of the clouds of Divine glory—*Ananei Kavod*—the radiance—*Meorot*—of the (Messianic age) to come—*LeAtid LaVo*," comments Rabbeinu Bahya on this verse of Isaiah.

In the wilderness, after the exodus from Egypt, Israel benefited from the *Sukkah* composed of *Ananei Kavod*, the heavenly "clouds of glory," the "clouds of Divine grace." These clouds, according to the Zohar, were also called *Ananei Aharon*, "Aaron's clouds,"[60] for they were due to the "merit" of Aaron, the High Priest, the man of goodness,[61] "who loved peace, and all God's creatures."

Analogous to the *Sukkah* in the wilderness, the *Sukkah* of the Messianic age will be the "*Sukkah* of Peace;"[62] but it will be a *Sukkah* of *shalom* which ultimately will be a peace of "truth," "justice" and "love," a "peace" which will be "complete"—*Shalom: Shalem*—and consequently irrevocable. Of course this peace will be the expression of Man's will for peace, but it will above all be "made" by God, "the Lord of Peace;" it will be *His* work; it will be "sealed" by Him "Whose seal is Truth." Peace, therefore, will itself be a *Sukkah*.[63]

Then God "will spread a *Sukkah* of Peace over His People, the House of Israel and over Jerusalem."[64] The "City of David" will be restored as a Sanctuary; it will become that which was ordained from the beginning of the world: the Place where the "House of Holiness," the *Beit HaMikdash*, the Temple of Jerusalem, would be built. The Temple of Jerusalem is the place wherein the *Ruah HaKodesh*, the "spirit of Holiness" dwells; it is manifested there in particular abundance during the festival of Sukkot,[65] and it is revealed no matter when and no matter where in the world, during this same festival, to him who deserves it, in his own *Sukkah*.

The creation of the world was envisaged by the Creator in the light of the building of the *Sukkah* in Jerusalem and with a view to the teaching which the *Sukkah* is called to bring to the world. Indeed, say the Sages of Israel, "from the beginning of the creation of the world, the Holy One, blessed be He, has erected a *Sukkah* in Jerusalem and has prayed there *Kivyakhol*: if one may dare to use the phrase). He has said: May the wish be that I see My House (the Temple of Jerusalem) built here as it will be written in the Psalms of David (76:2): 'In Salem also is His tabernacle and His dwelling place is in Zion.' "[66]

* * *

From time immemorial the "nations of the earth" have been accustomed to rely on their material strength, on the power that their States afford them; they are accustomed to take pride in the riches which their lands provide them. In the messianic age the "nations of the earth" will show their good sense by recognizing the vanity of their strength and the stupidity of their pride; they will prove their good faith in admitting the absurdity of their hostility towards Israel, which has constantly reminded them that their power and riches were vanity.[67] How will they make known, these "nations of the earth," their moral change of direction and their spiritual conversion? The Sages of Israel say it will be by carrying out the *mitzvah* of the *Sukkah*, that "little *mitzvah* which exists and is called *Sukkah*;"[68] that *mitzvah* which Jacob, "little Jacob,"[69] carried out in the past; that *mitzvah* which Israel, "the smallest of all the peoples,"[70] is still carrying out. Indeed this is the people which God "has joined to Himself," which He "loves," because, as the Talmud states, "when He grants it greatness, it humbles itself before Him, just as Abraham, Moses, Aaron and David humbled themselves before Him, whereas the nations of the earth, when He grants them greatness, they rebel against Him, as did Nimrod, Sennacharib, Nebuchadnezzar and Hiram."[71] How will they, the nations of the earth, demonstrate their recognition that God alone is great? By celebrating the festival of Sukkot in Jerusalem. For as the prophet Zechariah foretold, "All who survive of the nations which attacked Jerusalem shall come up year by year to worship the King, the Lord of Hosts, and to keep the pilgrim-feast of Tabernacles. If any of the families of the earth do not go up to Jerusalem to worship the King, the Lord of Hosts, no rain shall fall upon them....This shall be the punishment of Egypt and of any nation which does not go up to keep the feast of Tabernacles."[72]

To date, the "nations of the earth" have never made the spiritual journey up to Jerusalem to celebrate the festival of Sukkot. They are still prisoners of their power, captives of their pride; they are still in rebellion against the greatness of God.

Indeed, it is rather thought provoking to see that the "*nations of the* earth" which have long dominated the world, and particularly the Christian *nations*, have adopted some of the great Jewish festivals and adapted them to their own religious conceptions; but they have not adopted the autumnal festivals, known as Rosh Hashanah, Yom Kippur and Sukkot. Rosh Hashanah and Yom Kippur signal the renewal of life for man and for humanity, for society and nations, by an examination of conscience, both individual and collective, with a historic, messianic focus; by a personal and communal confession of sins; by individual and collective repentance, also in a historic and messianic perspective. Sukkot, indeed, having—according to Abudarham—a historical and messianic relevance, is a denunciation of the absurdity of human pride, both personal and communal. These three autumn festivals (Rosh Hashanah, Yom Kippur and Sukkot), whose crowning point is the festival of Shemini Atseret (an eighth day added to the seven days of Sukkot[73]) and Simhat Torah (the festival of the "Joy of the Torah," of the joy felt by the Jew in studying the Divine Teaching and the Observance of its commandments)—these festivals find no place in the Christian calendar; they are notably absent from it.

However, according to the Talmud, acceptance by the "nations of the earth" of the festival of Sukkot, in its authentic meaning, will be the sign of their rational, sincere and true submission to God. It is only then that they will be entitled, with full justification, to cry with Zechariah, the prophet of the festival of Sukkot, "then the Lord shall become King over all the earth; on that day the Lord shall be one Lord and His name the one name."[74] For the prophet Isaiah had earlier foretold it: "Then man's pride shall be brought low, and the loftiness of man shall be humbled, and the Lord alone shall be exalted on that day."[75] Power and material strength will no longer have any value,[76] "for the earth shall be filled with the knowledge of the Lord as the waters cover the sea."[77]

The Jew prepares for the arrival of "that day" with loyalty and patience, each year leaving his "normal dwelling place," his comfortable house, to live for a week in the "temporary dwelling place" of the *Sukkah*. Thus he reminds himself and the world how precarious and illusory is the material strength of man, but how constant and firm is his power when he recognizes the power of God; how fragile is his power when he trusts in himself but how sure his power is when he trusts in God, when he puts his confidence in his Creator and places himself in close touch with Him.

Every year, for a full week, the Jew "sets up house" in the modest *Sukkah* and proves that he can be "happy" with few belongings; he does not seek for possessions that are "superfluous." Like Jacob, the man of the *Sukkah*, and the generation of those who dwelt in *Sukkot* in the wilderness, he looks for the "protection" of God and asks of Him only to satisfy his most elementary material needs: "to be fed and clothed."[78] As he declares himself satisfied with "what is strictly necessary," that is to say, his well-being; as he feels safe "today," like the generation of the "manna" and the "*Sukkot*" in the wilderness, "he is not anxious about tomorrow;" he is full of confidence about the future, for he has faith in Him Who, "day after day,"[79] provides basic needs for all His creatures; more than ever he considers himself "rich" and "rejoices in what he possesses."[80] The Jew is neither worried by anxiety nor attacked by envy; he is not tempted to take that which does not belong to him; like Jacob of old, the man of the *Sukkah*, the man of the *Ohel*, the man of the "tent," he rejects anything that could be regarded as *gezel*, larceny or pillage.[81] The Hatam Sofer observes that he is therefore at peace with himself, for being an "honest man" "he has everything," "he lacks nothing."[82] He is even able to give this peace to others, for being a generous man, since God gives him wealth in *excess* of what he needs, he shares it with those who need it.[83] As the Ba'al HaTanya remarks, this state of peace does not weaken or prevent him from the act of "giving and receiving," or from taking an active part in everything that may contribute to the "development of the world," *Yishuv HaOlam*, and its economic development. It does not prevent him either from tasting the joy of knowing himself to be the possessor of what he has "honestly" acquired, like Jacob of old,[84] by his own toil—the possessor of that which represents the "fruit of his labor," "the work of his hands." In fact, the Torah acknowledges the Jew's right to "private property"—the Torah to which all Israel listens "during the festival of Sukkot" at the end of every seventh year, at the time fixed as a year of *Shemittah*[85]—which is the symbol of the Torah idea of social justice.[86] This property, according to the Ba'al HaAkedah, should first of all provide a decent life for everyone, "the necessary minimum" for his livelihood and housing. But the Torah requires from the Jew that he consider his property within its limits, within the limits imposed upon him by his consciousness of the sovereignty of God, the Creator, Who is the sole Owner and Master "of everything on the earth and all it contains:" *Koneh Hakol*.

To keep this consciousness alive, the Torah ordains that the Jew shall live seven days each year in the *Sukkah*. And this shall be in autumn, at a time of year when the Jew in the Land of Israel "is gathering in the fruits of the earth."[87] It is the season when the Jewish farmer *brings home* the harvest; it is the time when he *gathers into his home* all his wealth; it is the time when he *brings indoors* and surveys with satisfaction all his stores, everything he *has*; it is the time when he takes comfort in the support of what he *has*, what he possesses *naturally*, what nature has brought him. It is exactly at that season, in that season of natural plenty, that the Jew as an ordinary human is tempted to take pride in what he *has*. Then the ordinance of the Torah steps in, bidding him not to be too much occupied with what he *has*, with what he claims to have, but to be preoccupied above all with what he *is*, what he is and what he ought to be. It recommends him, therefore, to *leave his house*, go *out of doors*, go to the *Sukkah*, to *sit there* for a whole week, so as to have time to reflect on the illusion of *having* and the reality of *being*; to take time to look *up to the Heavens*, "towards God,"[88] from whence may come his *"salvation;" "towards his Fathers,"* whom he should take as an example for his conduct.[89]

Just as God "led Abraham out" and made him and his descendants "leave," "go outside" of every "natural expectation," in order to make His Covenant with him, in order to show him the great goals of the History of Israel—so God "leads out," "makes the Jew leave" his house and leads him into the *Sukkah* and there has him celebrate the festival of Sukkot, that festival which Abraham celebrated. By the rules which it establishes for the *Sukkah*, the Torah, places the Jew "outside nature," while at the same time bringing him as close as possible to nature, inviting him to appreciate the gifts and respect the "bounties"[90] of nature, and preaching to him a life style which is natural, simple and healthy. (Does not the *Sukkah* bring to the Jew and through him to the whole world, a true *ecological* message?)

* * *

Hag HaSukkot, "the festival of Sukkot" which the Jew celebrates "outside," in "tents," coincides with *Hag HaAsif*, "the festival" of the harvest which the Jew "brings home" into his barns.[91] The "seven days of Sukkot" correspond to the "seven species" of agricultural produce for which Israel, the land of Israel, is particularly noted. It is not only a matter of the simultaneous celebration of *Hag HaSukkot* and *Hag HaAsif*, but more of an identity between these two modes of Jewish festival. What unites them is "joy." Joy, rejoicing par excellence, characterizes them, fills them and makes them, according to Jewish tradition, a "season of joy," *zeman simhatenu*. And in addition this "season of joy" which extends over the seven days of Sukkot culminates in an eighth day of joy. This last day, Shemini Atseret-Simhat Torah,[92] consists "exclusively" of rejoicing, of pure joy, experienced by the Jew "before God:"[93] "During this festival of the 'year's end,' God says to Israel: I am 'keeping' you with

Me! This is an expression of God's love. As a royal Father, He invites His children to a feast for a certain number of days. When the time comes for them to bid their Father farewell, He says: My children, I pray you, stay with Me one more day; your leaving makes Me sad."[94] (In the Galut lands of the Diaspora, this last day of "enhanced joy" extends over two days, during which the Jew prays to God that He will make him worthy to experience again, with intensity, the joy of this festival of the year's end, concentrated into a single day in Erets-Yisrael, especially in Jerusalem.)

Indeed the Torah "commands" the Jew by a *mitzvah* to celebrate the *Hag HaSukkot*, the *Hag HaAsif*, in joy.[95] The Torah says to him: "You shall keep the pilgrim festival of Tabernacles for seven days after you have brought in the produce from your threshing floor and wine press. *You shall rejoice* during your festival, you and your son and daughter, your manservant and maidservant, as well as the Levite, the stranger, the orphan and the widow who are within your gates. You shall keep the seven days of the festival in honor of the Lord your God, *in the place which He will choose* (in Jerusalem); for He, the Lord your God, will bless you in all your harvest, and in all the work of your hands, and you shall be entirely filled with joy" ("on the evening of *Shemini Atseret*").[96]

How can the Torah "command" the Jew to rejoice? Is this not "a thing that depends on the heart" of man? Is it not a movement of the soul which "only the heart can decide"?

Certainly, in the season when the Jew celebrates *Hag HaSukkot* and *Hag HaAsif*, joy can be caused and justified by the satisfaction of seeing the fruits of his labor; but is the sight of these material things sufficient to fill him with joy, a full, complete joy? No. The Torah, which knows the soul of the Jew, considers it has the right to "command" him to be joyful, to command him to have a sentiment which is generally produced by the emotions and "entrusted" to the heart. For the Torah knows that the joy which the Jew feels on this day of Sukkot is "in honor of the Lord." This joy, which thus has a double motive—both spiritual and material, may lead the Jew to experience it "before the Lord his God," in His Presence. And "the Presence of God, His *Shekhinah* manifests itself in joy!"[97]

When he observes the *mitzvah* of joy during the festival of Sukkot, when he "rejoices for seven days before the Lord his God" as the Torah commands, the Jew is "assured" by the Torah itself[98] that on Shemini Atseret-Simhat Torah he will experience absolutely, and exclusively, a pure, "unique" joy;[99] he will "be wholly given up to the joy" before God.

The joy which is brought to the Jew by the sight of his harvest, in its richness; the joy that the soul of the Jew feels in his gratitude to God

Who has "blessed" him by "giving," by granting him an abundant harvest; all this joy engendered as much by material as by spiritual motives, is likewise transformed into true joy.[100] The Jew then feels, in all its authenticity, that "unique" joy of Shemini Atseret-Simhat Torah. Thus after the "preparatory" experience of the joy of Sukkot, celebrated *before* God, and in search of Him, the Jew feels a "sublime" joy, celebrated privately *with* God, and in communion with Him.

The joy of *Shemini Atseret-Simhat Torah* is "purely" religious; no longer is there any link with any material element, no longer a tie to any material symbol; neither the *Sukkah*,[101] nor the "four species" from the world of plants which the Jew "blesses" during Sukkot.[102] It is a totally sublime joy, coming from God and His Torah and directed towards God and His Torah. It is exclusive: *Ah Sameah; it is nothing but joy.*[103] It is *the Simhat Torah*, "the joy of the Torah." It is a double joy, expressing both the joy of the Torah in belonging to Israel, and teaching them the path of life, and the joy of Israel in possessing the Torah and receiving its "lessons for life," its teachings which assure them life and survival."[104] It is thus a joy "before God," "in His Presence," lived in communion with Him. Israel rejoices in God, in Him Whose gracious will has been "to choose Israel in order to grant them His Torah," Whose gracious will has been "to favor Israel with the gift of the Torah which is the embodiment of His will."[105]

* * *

However, this rejoicing should not be exuberant;[106] it should be serene and clear; it should even be austere, for it is a joy that the Jew feels "before God" Whom he knows to be present, and very close to him; it is a joy that he experiences in God; it is a joy which surrounds him like "faith," which "surrounds him like wisdom,"[107] which shelters him like a Sukkah, in the present circumstances, or like a *bayit*, like a "house."[108]

Now in emphasizing the "joyful" character of this festival, and in reference to it, the Torah mentions "three times" the idea of joy, of *Simha*.[109] And of the three pilgrim festivals Jewish tradition names the festival of Sukkot as "the time of our joy," *zeman simhateinu*.

And yet—what a paradox—during Sukkot and Shemini Atseret, during these festivals of joy, the Jew reads the Book of Kohelet. Tradition invites the Jew in these days of rejoicing, to reflect seriously on "the words of the Speaker (Kohelet), son of David, king in Jerusalem."[110] It is Solomon, the wise king, who tasted abundantly of all the pleasures of this world; Solomon "and no other," says the Midrash,[111] who puts at the very start of his meditations the adage, "Vanity of vanities, says Kohelet, vanity of vanities; all is vanity!"[112] These words, apparently reflecting a skeptical attitude towards life, should not, however, decrease the creative urge of the Jew, nor diminish the joy which it may bring him. For the creativity of the Jew may be conceived and executed both with the design as well as with the objective which the Creator prescribes for it. Indeed, Kohelet *ends* with one decisive exhortation; "Let us hear the *conclusion* of this whole discourse: Fear God and keep His commandments, for this is the whole of man. For God will bring every work to judgment."[113]

According to the Talmud,[114] this closing passage in the Book of Kohelet is in perfect harmony with its beginning: "the beginning and the end of the book do not contradict one another; both are statements of the Torah, *Divrei Torah.*" "The beginning of this Book which says, 'What does man gain from all his labor and his toil here under the sun?' does not refute the end of it which says, 'Fear God and keep His commandments, for this is the whole of man'" ("for that is the goal of the creation of the world," adds the Talmud). Without doubt, the beginning and the end of this Book mutually confirm and strengthen one another, for, without this end, without this final goal towards which human endeavor must tend, must seek to reach, "all is vanity."

Thanks to the reading of the Book of Kohelet, the joy which the Jew feels during the days of *Hag HaSukkot* and *Hag HaAsif* becomes a serene, calming joy; it is considered controlled, measured, moderated: it is not a lighthearted gaiety. This joy is of the kind which the Talmud preaches (and which Rabbeinu Bahya evokes in connection with Sukkot), quoting the verse in Psalms (2:11) which says, "Serve the Lord with fear and rejoice with trembling." At the very time he surrenders himself to *joy*, at the very time he is in communion with God in the *love* of his Creator, the Jew does not forget that the distance between himself, the creature, and his Creator is immense; so he trembles, in *fear* of God. This fear and love must lead the Jew to the respect and love of his fellow man.[115]*

* * *

It is in the midst of these apparent contradictions that the Jew celebrates the festival of Sukkot. It is not so much that during these days of joy he feels sorrow at being only a transitory creature on this earth,

---

* From Biblical and post-Biblical times up to the era of the Hassidim and the Ba'alei HaMussar, Judaism has always been opposed to both excessive joy and excessive sorrow. Fundamentally optimistic, it has always been able to avoid the excesses of the human

where his activity is likely to vanish into oblivion for want of an ethical objective; it is rather that during these days of meditation he has a feeling of joy at knowing himself able—in the image of his Creator—to conceive and direct, with intelligence and love, an activity which has "good," *Tov*, for its objective, for the benefit of others, "for the good of God's creatures." Such activity therefore allows man, the Jew, the creature, himself to become a creator; he has the qualities needed not only to prevent his activity from "vanishing like smoke," but to have it inscribed on an enduring and imperishable foundation.

It is precisely because he is in the *Sukkah*, because he is living in a "temporary dwelling," close to nature, that the Jew lives there in peace and security. He lives there in all simplicity, without being tempted by luxuries. However, he lives there in pleasant surroundings, in a setting embellished with all kinds of things which in a modest and peaceful way illustrate the ideal of "beauty" exemplified by the "*Sukkah* itself: *Noi Sukkah*."[119] This ideal is represented during the festival by the "four

---

psyche and set a working balance between the two contradictory states of the human spirit.

In joy, Judaism reminds mankind of the uncertainty and finite nature of his physical existence; in sorrow, it reminds mankind of the lasting nature of the effects of spiritual actions. Joy and sorrow must be united in serenity; they should complement one another in a thoughtfulness which embraces both the precarious condition as well as the majestic vocation of humanity.

Thus the Talmud itself, in the passage we have mentioned above, tells us:[116] "When Mar, son of Ravina, celebrated the marriage of his son, he saw that the Sages were very jolly; he had a glass of great value fetched, which had cost 400 zuz, and broke it in their presence and thus put an end to their mirth. Rav Ashi, for the same reason, did the same. When the marriage of Mar, son of Ravina, was being celebrated, the Sages asked Rav Hamnuna Zuta, 'Why do you not sing us a song?' 'Let me remind you,' he said, 'that we all have to die!' By these sad words he meant that marriage has as its principal aim the procreation of children for the perpetuation of the race; therefore, though on the one hand the marriage itself is a happy occasion, it reminds us that we are mortal. On the other hand, since by marriage we are fulfilling a *mitzvah*, the first in chronological order of the *mitzvot* of the Torah,[117] we fulfill the *mitzvah* with joy.

From the above, perhaps, stems the Jewish tradition (taking its origin from the verse in Psalms 2:11 that we are to rejoice with trembling") which requires that during the ceremony of the *Huppah*, the canopy, which consecrates his union with "his heart's choice," the *Hatan*, the bridegroom, be dressed in *sargenes*, the *kittel*, the "white clothes" of death (the burial clothes of Jews—all identical—are white and plain, *takhrikhim*). Jewish tradition also requires that during the *Huppah* the *Kalah*, the bride, for the same reason should wear a white dress. At "the height of their joy" the *Hatan* and the *Kalah* are dressed in white to remind them and their guests that they are all poor mortals; at the same time the guests invited to take part in the marriage festivities are in duty bound to behave towards the bridal pair as if they were royalty; their religious duty is "to make the *Hatan* and the *Kalah* happy."[118]

species" of plant origin which are linked with the *Sukkah*, and especially by the *Etrog*, which the Torah calls *Peri Eits Hadar*, "Fruit of the Beautiful Tree" (symbolizing the spiritual and moral "Abrahamic" beauty of the Tsaddik, the "righteous man" who is "beautiful before His Creator" and "in the eyes of men" because of his "Torah and his good actions").[120]

As Rabbeinu Bahya has already told us, the Jew lives in the *Sukkah* enveloped in "the spirit of holiness," the *Ruah HaKodesh*, and consequently from the *Sukkah* he looks out with an eye full of benevolence towards others, far and near, *Ayin Tova*, as explained by the Ba'al Hiddushei HaRim.

The *Sukkah* requires the Jew to "know"[121] that "in this world" he lives in a "temporary dwelling" and that here "joy" cannot be complete; that his "permanent abode" is in the "world to come" and that the "true joy"[122] awaits him there, if he deserves it. Thus the Jew's true *Sukkah* is to be found in the "world to come;" it will be such as the Jew will have "prepared" in this world. In the *Sukkah* "in this world," called the "antechamber," the Jew prepares for the *Sukkah* "in the world to come," called the "palace."[123] The Jew who "has rejoiced" in the *Sukkah* here on earth "before the Lord his God" will be worthy to "welcome" "the Presence of God," the *Shekhinah*, and to "rejoice with it" in the *Sukkah* on high. There he will meet with the *Ushpizin*, the "guests," the "fathers" of the people of Israel, whom he has only envisioned and idealized in the "preparatory" *Sukkah* "in this world;" he will be one of their company and converse with them; he will "rejoice together with them in the splendor of the *Shekhinah*."

If the Jew, in his *Sukkah* "in this world," knows how to "prepare" his *Sukkah* in the "world to come," he will live there a life of "spiritual richness that never ends" and "even while living" he will see the face of the *Shekhinah*, he will see the Divine light that will neither blind him nor crush him, but on the contrary will comfort him by its gentle brightness: "He will rejoice there in the brightness of the *Shekhinah*, in the brightness of the Divine Presence."[124] There his love for God will be "free from all fear," *BeLa Dehilou*, affirms the Zohar; his "understanding of God will be for him a delight," concurs Rabbeinu Bahya. Truly "he shall delight in the Lord," "he shall find pleasure in the Almighty." Thus he will discover the "secret of faith" in its entirety.[125]

In the *Sukkah* in the "world to come," "the Holy One, blessed be He, will rejoice with His children (the Jewish people), as He rejoiced in the past with Jacob, when he sat in his *Sukkah* ('in this world'). How great therefore is their merit! How great is their share in this world and in the world to come!" exclaims the Zohar.¹²⁶

But to get there, to reach the *Sukkah* of the "world to come," the Jew first builds with patience and confidence his "preparatory" earthly *Sukkah* in this world;" he knows that his "*Sukkah* links earth to heaven."¹²⁷

Then, the *Sukkah BaMidbar*, the "*Sukkah* of the desert," of the Galut, and the *Sukkah BaArets*, the "Sukkah in the Land," in Erets-Yisrael, will have become the *Sukkah LeAtid LaVo*, the "*Sukkah* of the future," the Messianic *Sukkah* here on earth, opening into the heavenly *Sukkah* of the hereafter. "The darkness will become the light of day," "death will be abolished,"¹²⁸ and life will be "nothing but joy;" an eternal life, an eternal joy.

3
Jerusalem, heart of Israel/ heart of the world

Jerusalem, center of the world

"Jerusalem is the heart of the world."[1] Jerusalem is "at the center" of the world, of Erets-Yisrael, and specifically of Judea. "Within the core" of this center is the *Beit HaMikdash*, the Sanctuary. There is a profound relationship between this center and its core, on the one hand, and between the center of the nations—the people of Israel—and its core, its "heart"—the *tsaddik*, the righteous man, on the other. There is a close relationship between these centers, spatial, terrestrial and human, and the extratemporal center, the Shabbat (which also has its "core"). In the economy of the world, of humanity and of time, the center and the core constitute that which is essential and innermost, spiritual and freely given, balanced and righteous, sacred and, therefore, truly vital.

The role of Jerusalem in history is primordial; it too is essential and therefore truly vital.[3]

The peoples of the world recognize the religious value and spiritual importance of Jerusalem.[4]

The kings of the earth, the world's men of power, would like to possess some part of the city of King David.[5]

That is why Jerusalem, being historically Jerusalem of the Jews, is the object of jealousy, quarrelling and strife on the part of so many nations of the world.[6]

Jerusalem links heaven and earth

"Gate of the heavens,"[7] Jerusalem is the place which links earth to heaven.[8] Jerusalem is the place that Jacob saw in the dream (Gen. 28:12-17) in which he received the "good news" concerning the Land which was promised to him and to his children. The ladder which Jacob saw in his dream "hung over the site of the *Beit HaMikdash*," the future Sanctuary of Jerusalem.⁹ That ladder therefore links heaven to earth; it joins the two extremes and makes of them one whole on earth.¹⁰

The world is virtually contained in Jerusalem

It was from Jerusalem that Jacob was called to spiritualize and to "hallow" the whole world, the latter being virtually contained wholly within Jerusalem,¹¹ just as a person's being is contained in his soul.

Like the Hebrew Patriarchs who experienced the revelation of God in the Holy Land, the righteous man, the *tsaddik*, is the "chariot" of God in the world; he is the vehicle who makes known throughout the world the God who is manifest in Erets-Yisrael.¹²

Jerusalem is the Sanctuary

Jerusalem was founded not only because of its own immediate importance, but above all because of its future purpose.¹³

The essence of *Yerushalayim* is the *Beit HaMikdash*, the Sanctuary, and "the *Beit HaMikdash* (the House of Holiness) is the essential part of *Yerushalayim*;¹⁴ it is the quintessence of all the Land of Israel."¹⁵ *Yerushalayim* is only hallowed on account of the *Bayit* (the "house," the House of Holiness).¹⁶

"In reality *Yerushalayim* and the *Beit HaMikdash* form but one whole, a unity."¹⁷ "*Yerushalayim* is the heart and the *Beit HaMikdash* is the head."¹⁸

The Jew prays towards Jerusalem

The Jew utters his prayers in the direction of Jerusalem.¹⁹

"They shall pray to You turning towards the land which You gave to their fathers, facing the city which You chose and the house which I have built in Your honor." "They shall pray in this place." (So Solomon prayed at the dedication of the Temple of Jerusalem.)²⁰

"If the Jew at prayer is outside the Land of Israel he must turn his heart towards this Land; if he is in *Erets Yisrael* he must turn his heart towards *Yerushalayim*; if he is in *Yerushalayim* itself, he must turn his heart towards the *Beit HaMikdash*; if he is in the *Beit HaMikdash* he must turn his heart toward the *Bet Kodeshei HaKodashim* (the Holy of Holies)."²¹

When he turns towards Jerusalem in his prayer the Jew turns his "heart" to the Holy City,²² for it is his heart that prays: the Jew serves his

God with the "vitality" of his heart.[23] Therefore "he speaks to the heart of Jerusalem;"[24] he speaks to the heart of Jerusalem with "words of love."[25] If he is able to speak in this way in his "inward spirit," such a Jew at prayer is himself called *Yerushalayim*.[26]

The *Beit HaMikdash* is above all else a holy House to the extent that it is a House of holiness: a House where holiness reigns because "people" enshrine it there.[27]

There is a progression in the way the Jew's thought travels in prayer: first of all it turns to Erets-Yisrael, then towards Jerusalem, then towards the Sanctuary, then to the Holy of Holies, and finally to the Throne of Glory.[28] Prayer "advances step by step."

Indeed the holiness of the Holy Land increases the nearer it is to Jerusalem, to the Mountain of the House (of the Lord) The *Har HaBayit*, to the Holy of Holies and finally the Throne of Glory: it follows a progression of focalization and concentration.[29]

Sinai and Moriah:
Sinai is the place of God's word and man's listening;
Moriah-Jerusalem is the place of
the mutual quest of God and man

The mutual desire to meet at Jerusalem governs the creative collaboration between God and man.

"Holiness dwells in the *heart* of the world, that is, in Jerusalem."[30] But it dwells there because the *heart* of Israel *desires* that God dwell there. And it is in order to respond to that desire of Israel that God makes His *Shekhinah* dwell in Jerusalem.[31]

BeKhol HaMakom ... "Wherever I cause My name to be invoked, I will come to you and bless you" (Exod. 20:24). *BeKhol HaMakom*, in the place where the "soul" of man, like that of David, *coltah*—"desires and pines for the courts of the Lord,"[32] God comes and causes His *Shekhinah* to dwell there: He comes to the "holy place," to the *Beit HaMikdash*, the House of Holiness, and there blesses Israel. "This shall be His place of desire,"[33] for Israel desires Him in this place.[34] Indeed "the *Shekhinah* of God is found in the *Beit HaMikdash*, because of His love of Israel!"[35]

Sinai is the place of God's Word and man's listening; Moriah-Jerusalem is the place of the mutual quest of God and man.

The *Beit HaMikdash* was not built on Mount Sinai, the place where the grace of God was revealed in giving His Torah to man, to Israel. On Sinai the collaboration of God and man occurred at God's initiative, and was brought into being primarily by the action of God. From Mount Sinai

God "descends" towards man.[36]

The *Beit HaMikdash* was built on Mount Moriah, the Place of the *Akedah* of Yitzhak, the place where the total devotion of man to God was shown; on Moriah the collaboration of God and man was established at God's initiative, but it developed due primarily to the action of man. From Mount Moriah man "ascends" towards God.[37]

Sanctified by man's action, Mount Moriah exceeds Mount Sinai in value, hallowed though it is by God's action. After God had revealed himself, first in the "burning bush," in the *sneh*, prelude to Sinai, and then on Mt. Sinai itself, that "place" ceased to be a "site of holiness."[38] That "place" was "holy ground" only as long as Moses stood there, as long as the man Moses, "standing on it," found himself in a relationship with God. It ceased to be holy ground from the moment when that relationship between God and man was severed. The mountain of God, Sinai, "lost" its holy character after the revelation of God had taken place, after God "withdrew," breaking His relationship with man: the holiness of Sinai was linked exclusively with the particular event.[39] Whereas Mount Sinai was indicated by God in advance to Moses and to Israel with extreme "precision" as *the* mountain in the Sinai desert,[40] in contrast, *one* of the mountains of the land of Moriah was discovered, by Abraham to be *the* Mount Moriah.[41] After the *Akedah* of Yitshak the mountain of Moriah "retains" its holy character; it is always "existent in its holiness." Distinguished by the initial sacrificial action of man and by those sacrifices which succeeded it, Moriah continues to be a holy mountain, a "mountain of holiness," "a mountain of God's holiness,"[42] for man by his action holds God there for evermore: the holiness of Moriah is "permanent."[43]

How characteristic is the fact that it is precisely after the revelation on Sinai that commands were given such as, "You shall make an altar of earth for Me" (quite simply of earth),[44] "in whatever place I cause My name to be invoked, I will come to you and bless you."[45] This "place" will forever be *HaMakom*, the place which God will choose, and on it will be established "The House of the Choice," *Beit HaBehira*.[46] Nonetheless, "in whatever place" that man wishes it, he "can set aside a special place for praying" and communing with God.[47] Thus God leaves the initiative for sanctifying the place to man. Moreover, the consecration of the place by God, which chronologically precedes its human santification, yields to the latter: the places consecrated by God *follow* man to the place where he sanctifies *himself*. Consequently it is man who "sanctifies" the "holiness" of the place where he is.[48] Moriah moves so as to follow the *man*, Jacob.[49] Sinai, God's mountain, moves so as to join

Moriah, the mountain of God and *man*.⁵⁰ Indeed, "Moriah becomes Sinai,"⁵¹ the Tossafists write. (It also happens that man sanctifies a place chiefly by his *personal* holiness; he thus precedes and even determines the initial choice of the place of heavenly consecration. For example: the Israelites at the foot of Sinai!)⁵²

Rabbi Hayyim Halberstam of Zanz (1793-1876), famous scholar of Hassidic thought and of Halakhah, author of Divrei Hayyim, asks "Why was the *Beit HaMikdash* built on Mount Moriah and not on Mount Sinai, the mountain where God gave Israel the Torah?" He answers, "Because it was on Mount Moriah that the Jew put his head on the block and offered his life for the honor of Heaven. Is there anything greater than that?" Indeed Mount Moriah symbolizes the whole history of the Jews, which is a history of *Messirut Nefesh*, the "offering of the soul," the offering of one's life for God; this mountain thereby symbolizes the whole history of Israel, for it is only a history of *Kiddush Hashem*, the "santification of the Name" of God. In recognition of this, said the Gaon of Vilna, "the *Shekhina*, the Divine Presence, dwells permanently on Mount Moriah, in Erets-Israel, but it has no permanent place on Sinai."⁵³ "Sinai was initially the place where the 'marriage' of God and Israel was consecrated; Jerusalem-Moriah is, maritally speaking, the place where their continuing, authentic joy was consummated.⁵⁴

The *Akedah* of Yitshak, never the "Sacrifice of Isaac"

Chapter 22 of the Book of Genesis is generally given, in the non-Jewish world, the title of "The Sacrifice of Isaac". However in Jewish tradition this chapter is known by the name of *Akedah*. The term *akedah* has its roots in the word *VaYa'akod*, which is to be found in the same chapter (Gen. 22:9) and means "and he bound" (Abraham "bound his son Isaac and laid him on the altar").

In being willing to sacrifice his son, Abraham demonstrated his faith in a manner more majestic and impressive than Isaac himself.⁵⁵ The ordeal of Isaac was less terrible than his father's; it is easier for a believer to "offer himself up" to his God than to "sacrifice" his well-beloved son. Moreover, the act that Abraham was ready to do is called *nissayon*, "ordeal,"⁵⁶ whereas that which Isaac was ready to undergo is called *akedah*. If Abraham's act of faith is not called "sacrifice," it is not only because the sacrifice of Isaac did not in fact take place but indeed because God had not explicitly commanded such a sacrifice.

In truth, God *"does not command"* human sacrifices. "He declares," (according to the Talmud's commentary on the words of the prophet

Jeremiah, 19:5), " 'I never intended that Isaac, son of Abraham, should be sacrificed.' "[57]

Therefore it is with justification that Rashi (*ad* Gen. 22:2) observes, " '*VeHa'Alehu Sham LeOlah* — *VeHa'Alehu*: bring him up.' God did not say to Abraham, 'Sacrifice him (Isaac).' That is something the Holy One, blessed be He, never wished. He wished only to have Isaac *lifted up* — *LeHa'Aloto* — on the mountain so as to give to his person the nature of an *olah* (of an offering — which one 'lifts up' to God).[58] And once He had caused him to be *lifted up*, He said, 'Take him down.' "

Moreover, Abraham, even while he was meticulously preparing to execute God's command, said to the servants who were with him, "We will come back" (Gen. 22:5).[59] "He prophesied that both of them (Isaac and himself) would return" (Rashi, *ad locum*). This is also the reason why, observes Rabbi Menachem Mendel of Kotsk, the Torah says "Abraham stretched out his hand and took the knife to kill his son" (Gen. 22.10). Why "stretched out his hand?" Because as a rule Abraham's hand did by itself whatever God asked him to do, without being forced. For Abraham (the numerical value of the letters composing his name "Abraham" is 248), having enthroned God over the 248 organs and limbs of his body corresponding to the 248 "active commandments" of the Torah, had reached the state in which his limbs executed God's orders of their own accord.[60] Now in the case of the *Akedah*, Abraham found himself compelled to "force" his hand to act, for it felt that God's intention was not that Isaac be sacrificed, but only "lifted up" as an *olah*, an offering to God.[61]

The *akedah* was in fact *urged* by God upon Abraham (for He said to him, "Take your son, I beg you — *na*" — Gen. 22:2), to "let the world know" (*yadati*: *hodati*) and to "let the future Israel know," "how far *in fact* Abraham's faith in his God went."[62]

Seeing and fearing; fear and love; fear and peace of mind

When the written Torah and the Talmud[63] prescribe to *Yisrael* the "ascent" to Jerusalem, to the place "chosen by God" for the bringing of offerings, as in the chapter on the *Akedah*, the words *yireh*, *yiraeh*, *reiya* (all concerning "seeing") occupy important places; the idea of *yir'ah*, "fear" of God,[64] is also attached to these words. Indeed the word *yir'ah*, "fear," is written exactly like the words *yireh*, *yiraeh* and *reiya*. These three words only differ in their vowels, for the letters in all three are the same.

Speaking of the *Beit HaMikdash*, to stand on the very site where the

Akedah happened,⁶⁶ the Torah uses equally—as in the case of the *akedah*—both the verb "to see:" *yeraeh, le'iraot*,⁶⁷ and the verb "to fear:" *tirau*:⁶⁸ "Fear My sanctuary—*mikdashi*." (The commandment concerning the building of the Tabernacle in the wilderness⁶⁹ contains the term *mikdash* and is the scriptural basis for Israel's obligation to build the *Beit HaMikdash* in *Yerushalayim*.⁷⁰)

All the same, "you are not obliged to fear the sanctuary (in itself), but Him Who commanded (respect for) the sanctuary!"⁷¹

The purpose of the *akedah* (as indeed the purpose for the Jew visiting the *Beit HaMikdash*⁷²) was to lead Abraham, the man who loved God,⁷³ to the state of being the man who "fears God": *yerei Elokim*. The reward of the *akedah* ordeal, said the Lord to Abraham by the word of His angel, consisted in the fact that "from now on I know—*yadati* (I knew, I know, I make known in you, I make known to all men through you) that you fear God, that you are a *yerei Elokim*."⁷⁴ The road to Mount Moriah thus led Abraham to the *mora*, the "fear" of God!⁷⁵ Moses also was to receive the supreme reward for his devotion to God in the title given him by the Torah of *eved Hashem*, "servant of God,"⁷⁶ that is, the man "fearing God," the "servant who serves his Master" through *mora*, through "fear."⁷⁷

Among most men the fear of God is unformed and primitive;⁷⁸ it is only at a late stage that it becomes a sign of man's earliest and ultimate wisdom.⁷⁹ Only this fear born of wisdom leads man to the love of God.⁸⁰

With Abraham (but not with Job⁸¹), with the man who knows that "he is standing before God," the love of God, a love which is completely detached, leads to the fear of God, an enlightened fear.

Such a man finds his self-realization in his attitude to God; he finds his own fulfillment in being close to God; his "self-identity," finally, in God: *VeYahed Levavenu LeAhava UleYir'a Et Shemeha*. To the extent to which such a man comes close to God, he accepts with ease the *Mora Shamayim*, the "fear of Heaven," the fear which he feels *in relation to* Him, the fear which comes to him because of the distance which *separates him from* Him; but which simultaneously brings him even closer to Him.⁸² Moreover, that fear is heightened by the very near Presence of God, which arouses in him who feels it genuine *Yir'at Shamayim*, a fear that comes directly and immediately from God Himself. Therefore, this fear is not primitive or natural, or simulated, but it is rather rational and serene; its aim is not to repel man, to discourage or humble him, but to raise him still nearer to God. It is an exalted fear, *yir'a ila'a*, a sublime fear, *Yir'at HaRomemut*, it is the supreme fear: it brings stability to man; it makes him conscious on the one hand of the nearness of God which benefits him, creative man, who lives in the light of his Creator; and on the other of the distance which separates him, the creature, from his Creator. This fear does not weaken man's love for God or his "attachment" to God; on the contrary it reinforces and deepens them, for this fear of God is highter than love for God, while at the same time it is founded upon that love and merges with it.[83]

The man who has arrived at this degree of fear of God is "whole;" he fears only God; he would find difficulty in fearing anyone other than God—or fearing something for himself. He fears only God: he is holy; he lacks nothing.[84] Therefore, he is *Yareh VeShalem*; he is "reverential and whole." He is "the whole man:" *Adam HaShalem*.[85]

This wholeness which man attains thanks to his fear of God brings him inner balance, "quietness of mind," *menuhah*. Now "*Menuha*, that is *Yerushalayim!*"[86]

A "holy" place is determined by God's sovereign will
but only partially shown by Him to man;
it is man who is called upon freely
to identify it and "sanctify" it

"The Lord said to Abram, Go to the country that I shall show you. If God did not tell him from the outset what country it was, this was in order to make it more desirable to him and to be able to reward him for every word which he obeyed."[87]

Abram had to discover for himself the country where the "root" of his soul was to be found.[88]

VaYissa Avraham Et Eynav VaYar Et HaMakom MeiRahok. "Abraham looked up and saw the place—*HaMakom*—in the distance" (Gen. 22:4). Abraham by his own intuition identified the place which God had not clearly indicated to him; he saw "a cloud clinging to the mountain." Isaac also saw the cloud, while the servants with them saw nothing special: they "saw only a barren-looking place."[89]

It was in this way that Abraham discovered the mountain about which God had said that "He would show him," but which in reality He only described vaguely as "one of the hills in the land of Moriah."[90] Indeed it was the right mountain that Abraham "saw," the one which God intended for his purpose. Abraham's vision proved to be correct. Abraham's discovery corresponded with God's intention.

A similar phenomenon was to occur later in the same place. David and Solomon were making preparations for the building of the *Beit HaMikdash*, the Temple of Jerusalem, but the exact position of the future

Sanctuary was not given to them. Nevertheless the position "appeared"—*nir'a*—to David, due to his "prophetic" intuition: he perceived it, like Abraham before him, on the same "mountain," "Moriah."[91] And later still, on the "return to Zion" of the Jews coming back from exile in Babylon, the rebuilding of the Temple, the building of the second *Beit HaMikdash*; was to require extensive researches on the part of the leaders of Judah so that the exact place could be identified where the *mizbeah*, "altar," had stood. These investigations were necessary in spite of the detailed descriptions of the Temple that the prophet Ezekiel had prepared for them.[92] And finally, concerning the final rebuilding of the Temple, the third *Beit HaMikdash*, although the Book of (Ezekiel) Yehezke'el indicates the "dimensions," as does also the Mishna of Middot, there are no clear details as to how to understand the "Writing of the Hand of God;" there are no indications on how to identify once more the different places on the "Hill of the Holy House" which will serve for the supreme worship of God.[93]

A *holy* place is *determined* by God's sovereign power but not revealed fully by Him to man. It is the latter who is called upon to identify it *of his own free will*, to "perceive" it, to develop it, to "sanctify" it. In the search for the "place," divine prophetic grace only comes to man's aid if he is sustained by his own merits. These result from his exact performance of the *mitzvot*, from the activities he enters into and perseveringly pursues, from his fervent recital of prayers and from the sufferings he has patiently borne, the "ordeals" he has courageously undergone with the sole aim of finding the "place."[94] The ultimate holiness of the "place" is therefore conditional: it depends directly upon the attitude that men have towards it as much before they have found it as afterwards. It is man that makes the (holy) place continue to be holy."[95]

The meeting of the inward spirit of Abraham
and that of the Promised Land;
the descendants of Abraham are chosen
by God's providence

"Go to the country that I *shall show* you: *Ar'eka*" (Gen. 12:1). God would show the country to "Abram." He would look at it with his inward, spiritual eye. Only then would the land reveal to him its particular, temporal, and spiritual character. The inward spirit of "Abram" and that of the Land would meet in accord. That is why "Abraham," who had a claim to this country, saw in it something which Ephron the Hittite (cf. Gen. 23) did not see. The latter looked at it as a landscape like any other and considered first of all the advantages it would bring him. Now, this country revealed its true identity, its intrinsic and personal value to Abram who understood them and thereby showed himself worthy of them; it revealed them to him whose soul found its "root" in the depths of its soil and the height of its skies: the country revealed them to Abraham, and through him to Israel.[96]

Abraham had to bequeath the Promised Land to his heir, who was repeatedly and in precise terms designated to him by God, "in" the person of his son Isaac—*beYitshak* (Gen. 21:12); and he in turn would transmit it to his heir in the person of his son *Ya'akov*. These heirs were chosen providentially and impartially by the will of the Creator, but also by reason of the loyalty they were to demonstrate. By choosing Abraham, God himself showed his heirs under what conditions their loyalty would have to be exercised. They accepted these conditions as well as the "ordeals" they would have to undergo in connection with the possession of the Land of Israel ("slavery," restricted enjoyment, possible exile—*galut*).[97] The *Berit*, the covenant, concerned only Abraham, Isaac and Jacob.[98]

"I took your father Abraham from across the river, and I led him all through the land of Canaan, then I multiplied his descendants, and I gave him Isaac. To Isaac I gave Jacob and Esau; I gave Esau the mountain of Seir for his possession" (without putting him to the test of the *galut*!); "but Jacob and his sons *went down* to Egypt" (to undergo there the tests of the *galut*)...."And I gave you a Land" (Josh. 24:3-4, 13).

Search and discovery

"You *shall seek for—tidreshu—* His dwelling in the place the Lord your God will choose....And it is there that you shall go" (Deut. 12:5). And the Sifrei adds, "*Search* and you shall find; and afterwards the prophet will tell it to you (will confirm it to you)." "But search and do not wait for the prophet to tell it to you; search and you shall find; if you search I promise you will succeed in getting there."[99]

"You shall go to search for the place in his honor," the place "where" 'He is to be found,' where His *Shekhinah* shall take up residence."[100]

Man, the Jew, goes to this place to *search* for God, and God comes to meet him, in the "land that God *searches for—doresh*" (Deut. 11:12).[101]

Tidreshu Et HaDoresh: search for Him who is looking for you! God and man meet after searching for one another.[102]

Tidreshu UBata Shama. "You shall search for the place which the Lord your God has chosen to receive His name." It is in looking for this place that "you will reach it" (Deut. 12:5).

Indeed, "*Tsion* must be *searched for*:" "*Tsion* has need of *derisha*, of being sought."[103] *Tsion* must ceaselessly be questioned, challenged.[104] "*Ask*: where is the road that leads to the House of the Lord?"[105] Jerusalem cannot be reached except by searching for it: it cannot be gained "except after a long quest," by long supplication and regular prayer.[106] Jerusalem can be found by him who desires it, if he strives long and patiently to reach it and if he obtains the merits that make him worthy to reach it.

This is why God did not reveal to Abraham at once which was the country to which he should go, to receive it as a gift from His hand;[107] it is also the reason why, later, He did not show him the exact place for the altar on which he was to "lift up" Isaac as an offering.[108] Because the orders that God gave to Abraham did not lend themselves to any very precise method of applying them they constituted *nissyonot*, "ordeals," for the Hebrew patriarch, which would make it possible to demonstrate in the eyes of the world how complete was his faith in God, how great his capacity to endure the most harsh suffering so as to fulfill the tasks set him by God.[109] It was only after a long march that Abraham found the Land,[110] that he discovered the place for the *Akedah*.[111] Certainly these discoveries were made spontaneously; equally they were not without difficulties. Jacob himself in turn "labored" for a long while to identify "the Place."[112]

Choice and confirmation;
the original choice by God
and the actual choice by man

To the people of Israel God commanded the building of "The Chosen House," of His choice, on the spot that He would choose, but without indicating where it would be.[113] It would not be astonishing if this place were in Jerusalem, the very place where Adam, Abel, Noah and above all Abraham had worshipped and served God.[114] Nevertheless, the exact place, the definite site where Israel would celebrate divine worship was not revealed: they must "search for it," and consequently "earn it."

Neither was the exact location of this spot revealed to David, though he was called upon to "lay the foundations" of the *Beit HaMikdash*, and to make preparations for the building of the Sanctuary in Jerusalem.[115] David would only know for certain the place intended for this building and its boundaries after having taken great pains to discover them, and after having shown himself worthy to receive God's precise directions about the exact positioning of the future Temple, including the method of its "inauguration."[116] God would only make His choice clear at the moment when man's worthiness justified it; He let it be known when David had demonstrated his capacity to "sanctify" the place by his righteous words and deeds.[117] He let it be known at the moment when David was able to disclose the pristine "holiness" that God had imprinted on this place. By man's *free* intervention this place then became *raoui*, worthy of being what God had "intended" it to become.[118] God's choice is thus fulfilled by man. The merit of man confirms God's choice. The actual choice of man corresponds to the prior choice by God. The two choices meet as one. The active, creative maintaining of the concord between them is alone able to ensure their common immortality.[119]

Holiness and sanctification;
Divine choice and human choice

To bring into effect the intrinsic holiness which the Creator has imprinted upon Jerusalem, man's santifying presence is required. Originally the holy place was *consecrated* by the will of God; thereafter it is sanctified by the merits of certain men (and of the generations that succeed them). The holy place has been hallowed by the "sanctifying"—*kiddush*—"words" and "actions" of men such as Abraham, Isaac and Jacob, David and Solomon, and later the prophets and righteous men, priests and sages.[120] In hallowing the holy place, the "sanctifiers" have added to its holiness.[121] Each of them has marked it with the particular seal of his personality.[122] In addition, each of them has himself become a sanctuary (like Jacob, who became a "House of holiness").[123]

The Torah says Jacob "came to a certain place where he halted for the night. He took one of the stones of that place to make his pillow and passed the night there. He had a dream...And Jacob rose early in the morning, took the stone which he had placed under his head, and set it up as a monument. And Jacob made a vow...'This stone that I have set up as a monument shall become the House of God' " (Gen. 28 vv. 11, 18, 20, 22). And the Zohar specifies: "This stone is the *even shetiyya*, the stone on which the world was built."[124] This stone is the stone on which the altar would be built, on which Yitshak had been "bound" for his "sacrifice."[125] This stone is the stone on which "the Temple of God would rise," the *Beit HaMikdash*, in *Yerushalayim*.[126]

Rashi makes this comment on the account in the Torah: "When Jacob passed the site for the Sanctuary (for the future *Beit HaMikdash* of

Jerusalem), why did God not hold him back? If he himself had not had the idea of praying in the place where his fathers had prayed (perhaps because of his modesty?),[127] would Heaven have had to stop him there? He went travelling on as far as Harran, as the Talmud says. And the text proves it: Jacob left Beersheba to go to Harran (Gen. 28:10). Arriving in Harran he said to himself, *'Is it possible that I passed the place where my fathers prayed and that I did not pray there myself!'* He decided to turn back; he had already reached Bethel when the earth moved towards him. (It was the Sanctuary itself which came to Bethel to meet him. Jacob called Jerusalem *Bethel*: the House of God.)"[128]

Jacob, and his fathers before him, loved to pray in a place already "sanctified by prayer." Abraham prayed at "the very place where the altar was that he had erected earlier."[129] And Isaac went out to meditate in the field (Gen. 24:63), "in the same field that Abraham had bought and where he had prayed."[130]

Rabbi Avraham of Slonim writes: "So that the *Shekhinah* (the Divine Presence) could reside on earth, the *avot* (the Hebrew patriarchs) inscribed sign after sign on the earth: each put his *reshimah* (his 'mark') there. The principal residence of the *Shekhinah* is on Mount Moriah. And Abraham, by the holiness of his deeds and his ordeals, by the *akedah* (binding Isaac on the altar where he 'lifted him up'), inscribed there the first sign, in calling that mountain 'the mountain of God' (Gen. 22:14). Isaac had the merit later to reinforce this sign, which he called *sadeh* ('field,' cf. Gen. 24:63). After them Jacob had the merit to call that place *bayit* ('house,' cf. Gen. 28:19; TB Pessahim 88a). David and Solomon in their turn had the great merit to build the *Beit HaMikdash* (the Temple of Jerusalem) on the place where this Mountain was. And in the future, the royal Messiah will have the merit to see raised on this Mountain the House of God, the *Mikdash* which will never be destroyed."[131]

"The Lord your God will choose the place for His dwelling" (Deut. 12:11).

The place was originally selected by the Creator from the beginning of the world. But He will choose it finally when men merit it enough to choose it in their turn. When God's choice coincides with that of man, *HaMakom*, that place, the place par excellence will be finally "chosen." Men will build there the *Beit HaBehira*, "the Chosen House."[132]

God "chooses" the City "and man *builds* there the House in honor of the Name" of God (cf. I Kings 8:48).

"The holiness of the House of Eternity does not apply to the building unless the place (where it stands) has been chosen according to the word of God; this same holiness does not apply to the place (chosen according to the word of God), if the building (of the House of Eternity) is not erected there by man," wrote Rav Kook.[133]

The place of the *Shekhinah* depends on the man who receives it, asserts the Maharal.[134]

The *Shekhinah* is to be found at the *Kotel HaMa'aravi* (the Western wall of the Temple of Jerusalem), for it is a hill that everyone looks towards, where everyone calls upon God, say the Sages of Israel.[135]

Shekhinah BeMa'arav. The Presence of God manifests itself on the West side of the Temple of Jerusalem.[136]

The Presence of God manifests itself on the West side of the Temple of Jerusalem. But "God, for His part, has no *Makom*, has no geographical position; His contour cannot be outlined by any frontiers. However, on the part of him who receives the Presence, these dimensions do exist, for he can only receive It in a place specially destined for the purpose and with such reception in mind. Although 'the heavens and the heavens of heavens do not contain Him,'[137] and they cannot contain His glory, nevertheless all these things are necessary so that the signs of God's love can be received and understood by those to whom they are directed. For God is to be found in relation to those who are there. He shows Himself to them, if they deserve to receive His glory. However, the *Shekhinah*, the Presence of God, dwells down here on earth, for those who live down here form a *hashlamah*, a complement to the Presence. And every complement, by definition, serves to fulfill the thing that it completes: the last complement of all is thus doubly a *hashlamah*. That is why the *Beit HaMikdash* is situated on the territory allotted to the tribe of Benjamin (the youngest of Jacob's sons) and the *Shekhinah* is manifest in the lot of Benjamin who himself was a *hashlamah*, that is also why the *Shekhinah* manifests itself at the *Kotel HaMa'aravi*, the Western wall of the Temple, for it is on the West side that we see the horizon last, just as it appears first in the East," writes the Maharal.[138]

The sanctity of the place is a result of the sanctity of human conduct. Jerusalem is a holy city because its inhabitants, *Nekiyei HaDa'at SheBeYerushalayim*, are concerned with the "purity of their thought," the generosity of their actions, the decency "of their behavior": in a word, with saintliness.[139] *Ki HaMikdash VeHaMizbeah VeYerushalayim — HaKol Hu LeAdam, Ki BeAdam Hu HaKol*. "For the Sanctuary, the Altar, and Jerusalem are all for Man; and Man contains everything," exclaims the Maharal.[140] And Rabbi Shemuel Shmelke Horowitz of Nikolsburg emphasizes: "*HaAdam Nikra Beit HaMikdash, Yerushalayim. Man is called House of Holiness, Jerusalem.*"[141]

The holiness of Jerusalem results from the active collaboration between

God and Man, between God and the *tsaddik*, the "righteous" man.¹⁴²

The conduct of the Jews who live in Jerusalem, "The Gate of Heaven," should be of a "heavenly nature": *Melekhet Shamayim*, according to the demands of the Tosafot,¹⁴³ activities which God demands and which man consecrates to the *Da'at Hashem*, to the "knowledge of God," to the purity of family life as well as to the good of the community. That is why the credibility of the Jew is increased by the fact that he lives in Jerusalem; he enjoys the credibility of the man who lives in the "Palace of the King," who lives in God's presence, who fears God and serves Him with joy. The children of Israel in Jerusalem fear God and are upright before the Holy One blessed be He: — *MiB'not Yerushalayim, Eilu Yisrael, Yereim UShelemim LeHaKadosh Barukh-Hu*," writes Rashi.¹⁴⁴ In Jerusalem the inhabitants do not persist in sin and the young people are little inclined to do wrong; they are all more open to *teshuvah*, more disposed to "return" to God.¹⁴⁵

The sanctity of the place both calls for and in return fosters the sanctity of man.¹⁴⁶

Man is the true holy place that God desires

Man, if he deserves it, may become the "dwelling of God." It is he, man, who is worthy to be the true "holy place" that God "desires" to establish in this world: *Ohel Shiken BaAdam*: "He had set up the tabernacle in man" (Ps. 78:60). Thus the heart of man can be transformed into a Sanctuary: he is capable of containing God.¹⁴⁷ The man who has a "heart" no longer has need of a "place", for he is the "place of the world" — the Divinity dwelling in his heart.¹⁴⁸ This is why God commands the children of Israel: "Make for Me a sanctuary — *mikdash* — so that I may dwell in their midst — *betokham*" (that is to say, not in the midst of *it*, the sanctuary, but in the midst of *them*, the children of Israel!¹⁴⁹).

The Ramban, therefore, affirms, "The men who rise to a high degree (of holiness) are themselves the dwelling of the *Shekhinah* (of the Presence of God).¹⁵⁰

And the Maharal emphasizes: "Man himself can be regarded as a sanctuary, for man is comparable to a house, and if he is holy, he is regarded as a veritable House of holiness: *Beit HaMikdash Kadosh*."¹⁵¹

And Rabbi Shemuel Shmelke Horowitz of Nikolsburg adds: "*Adam HaShalem Nikra Beit HaShem*: the perfect man is called the house of God."¹⁵²

Yes, declares Rabbi Hayyim of Volozhin, "The man who is sanctified by fulfilling the *mitzvot*, the commandments of God, becomes a true Sanctuary—*Mikdash*—and God dwells within him!"[153]

The divine salvation of the heavenly Jerusalem depends on the human salvation of the earthly Jerusalem

"The Holy One, blessed be He, has said, has sworn: 'I shall not make My return to the Jerusalem on high until I have made My return to the Jerusalem on earth below,' 'until Israel has made its return to the Jerusalem below.' "[154]

The divine "salvation" of the heavenly Jerusalem depends on the human salvation of terrestrial Jerusalem by the Community of Israel. When the Community of Israel is "in its place" in the terrestrial Jerusalem, "God will return to His place, to Zion." Then the children of Israel will exclaim, "This is our God whom we trusted to rescue us, this is the Lord in whom we hoped: let us rejoice and exult because of His salvation." And the Zohar completes this quotation from Isaiah (25:9) with these two characteristic words: *BeYeshuato, Vadai*: "Surely, because of His salvation."[155] In the Jewish conception, "the heavenly Jerusalem" is not free "so long as the present Jerusalem and its children are enslaved"; "the Jerusalem on high is like a desert as long as the Jerusalem below is like a desert."[156] The liberation of the Jerusalem on high, and with it the liberation—as it were—of God, can only happen if the Jerusalem below, is freed together with Israel. Indeed the two Jerusalems are but one.[157]

However, Jerusalem on high and its *Beit HaMikdash* will not be rebuilt except with the "work," the good deeds, of the *tsaddikim*, the "righteous" of this world. For let us not forget that they too have suffered through the misdeeds of the *reshaim*, the "wicked" of this world. It is because Jerusalem on high and its *Beit HaMikdash* were thus "destroyed that the Jerusalem here below with its *Beit HaMikdash* became vulnerable and it was possible for them to be destroyed."[158]

"The Holy Name is not complete on high—the Holy One, blessed be He, is not called 'great'—until the Community of Israel is united with Him, as it is written: 'Great is the Lord in the city of our God' (Ps. 48:1): with the city of our God."[159] "In swearing that He will not make His return to the Jerusalem on high before He has made His return to the Jerusalem here below, God testifies that He prefers the Jerusalem here below to the Jerusalem on high, for 'He loves to dwell among us,' 'His people and His heritage'."[160]

God does not question man
about his territorial position
but concerning his moral position

"And they heard the voice of the Lord God walking in the garden in the cool of the day. The man and his companion hid from the presence of the Lord God among the trees of the garden. And the Lord God called the man and said to him, 'Where are you—*Ayeka?*' He answered, 'I heard Your voice in the garden, and I was afraid because I was naked, and I hid myself'" (Gen. 3:8-10).

God asks Adam not about his earthly position, but rather about his moral position. He does not ask him, "*Eifo ata?*—What place are you in?" (He knows that very well, for He Himself is everywhere and can determine the place exactly since He is speaking to Adam!) But He asks, "*Aye-ka?* What is your position in relation to Me?" God does not wish to "take Adam by surprise" with this question, but to "begin a dialogue with him" on his relationship with God. "You were so close to Me; do you now want to move away from Me? But where are you now, solitary, anxious, and afraid? You are not in your place, the place I assigned you in this world in order to care for it. Take note what you have done and what you have become by avoiding the task which is yours. Do you think that, having committed this fault, you can hide from Me like a child who hides behind the door so as not to face his father whom he has disobeyed? Think about what you have done, take responsibility for your actions. Lift your eyes to Me, come close to Me, restore the thing you have spoiled and begin again 'like a new-born child.'"

That is what was and will always be the meaning of that single word *Ayeka*, as it was understood by the Gaon, Rabbi Eliyahu of Vilna, and his contemporary, the Ba'al HaTanya, Rabbi Shneour Zalman of Liady.[161]

אַיֶּכָה / אֵיכָה
"Where are you?" / "How I pity you!"

Man, who because of his sin "hides from the face of the Lord," is "a fugitive and a wanderer on the face of the earth."[162]

The divine challenge, *Ayeka*, "Where are you?" (Gen. 3:9) demonstrates man's loss of identity. God knew well where Adam was, but in asking him "*Ayeka?*" He meant "What has become of you, Adam? Where is your heart turning?[163] Have you not neglected your responsibilities? You have gone so far from Me! How I pity you — *eikha!*" (Lam. 1:1).

By His *Ayeka* God confirms that Adam is solitary—*badad* (Lam. 1:1)—in an isolation that will lead him into exile (cf. Lam. 1:3). Those who see him are "astonished—*eikha*!—at what has become of him and what he has become—all because he fled from God and "hid" from Him. After having to listen to the divine interrogation, *Ayeka?*, man finds himself inexorably drawn into a situation where he has to listen to the exclamation *eikha* uttered by both God and men.[164]

The words *ayeka* and *eikha* have the same spelling and can only be distinguished from one another by their vowels. The *ayeka* of the Book of Genesis foretells the *eikha* of the Book of Lamentations. Were it not for this foretelling, the Book of Genesis could have written *ayeka* without the letter *he* at the end (from the grammatical point of view this letter is not indispensable: it is only added to give additional meaning).[165] If the Torah says *ayeka-h* with *he* at the end of the word, it is because the *ayeka*, the astonishment, the reproach, the warning, and the lament, are a prelude to the pitying, to the *eikha-h* which has, and must end with, a *he*. Indeed the Zohar writes,[166] "The Lord God called to the man and said to him, '*Ayeka*: where are you?' (Gen. 3:9) God desired Adam to understand by this allusion—*remez*—that the *Beit HaMikdash* (the Sanctuary of Jerusalem) would be destroyed and that people would then weep (and cry out), '*Eikha yashva badad*: alas, see how she sits solitary!' (Lam. 1:1)"

Galut, a specific dimension of Jewish history; Jerusalem, the memory of Israel

The Galut, exile, is a specific dimension of the history of the Jewish people. "Non-Jews are never in Galut. Even when they are exiled outside their own country, their "Exile" is not a Galut. But for Israel (the children of Israel who in exile do not assimilate the customs of those who surround them), their "Exile" is a *Galut*, as it is written (Lam 1:3), '*Galta Yehuda...*'" (Lam.R. 1:29).

One of the great scholars of both Hassidism and the Halakhah, Rabbi Abraham of Sohatshov (19th century), wrote in his Responsa: "In spite of the fact that at present Israel is in Galut, the place of the children of Israel is always in *Erets-Yisrael*. When we are in any other country, we are considered to be *golim*, people in Galut, for our place is in *Erets-Yisrael*. Therefore, we have the religious obligation, the *mitzvah*, to live there, and even if we do not yet live there we must be considered as being all in *Erets-Yisrael*, for our place is in *Erets-Yisrael*."[167]

"If ever I forget thee, O Jerusalem, may my right hand forget itself.

May my tongue cleave to my palate, if I do not always remember thee, if I do not place Jerusalem at the summit of all my joy!" (Ps. 137:5-6—see Tosafot, *ad* TB Avoda Zara 3b). For the Jew, to think of Jerusalem means to think of God; "Remember the Lord from afar, and call Jerusalem to mind" (Jer. 51:50). In remembering God, Israel asks Him in the same Psalm also to remember Jerusalem (Ps. 137:7).[168]

In reality, since the destruction of the Temple, Jerusalem has become Israel's active, creative memory. It governs the whole life of Israel as a people and of the Jew as a person.

Three times a day the Jew prays for Jerusalem. "God of Mercy, return to Your city, to Jerusalem, as You have promised; rebuild it in our day, and live there, and may the throne of David soon be re-established there. Praise be to You, O Lord, Who will rebuild Jerusalem." "O Lord our God, may Your people Israel and their prayers be acceptable to You. Bring back the holy service to the sanctuary of your House." "Let our eyes see Your return to Zion through your mercy! Praise be to You, O Lord, Who will re-establish the resting place of Your glory in Zion."

In the thanksgiving after every meal, the Jew says, "Have pity, O Lord our God, upon Your people Israel, Your city Jerusalem, Zion the home of Your glory and that great and holy House on which Your Name rests!" "Raise again, soon in our days, the walls of Jerusalem, the holy city. Praise be to You, O Lord, Who by Your mercy will rebuild Jerusalem!"

At the end of the solemn meal on the evening of Pessah, the Jew expresses this wish: "Next year in Jerusalem!"

The central section of the liturgy of Yom Kippur, the Day of Atonement, is a recapitulation of the *avodah*, the "worship service" of Yom Kippur formerly celebrated in the Temple of Jerusalem.

In the course of the year, "three weeks" of recollection, "nine days" of mourning, three (four) days of fasting are dedicated to Jerusalem.[169] One of them, Tishah be-Av, the ninth day of the month of Av, is stamped with particular sorrow. On that day Jews commemorate the destruction of the first Temple and of the second Temple of Jerusalem. "The atmosphere of Tishah be-Av", in synagogues and Jewish homes, faithfully recalls the atmosphere described at the beginning of Psalm 137: "By the rivers of Babylon, there we sat down; yea, we wept when we remembered Zion." During the religious service for the end of the day of Tishah be-Av, Jews repeat this moving prayer: "O Lord our God, console the afflicted of Zion and Jerusalem, console this city of mourning, full of ruins; console this widow weeping for her children scattered, her palaces destroyed, her glory faded, her country forsaken. Enemy legions have invaded it; they have massacred Your people Israel and in their fury they have slaughtered the faithful servants of the Most High. Weep, Zion, shed your bitter tears. Lift up your voice, Jerusalem! My heart breaks at the remembrance of those massacres; my bowels are harrowed by the tale of those martyrs. O Lord, by fire You have destroyed; by fire You will rebuild, as it is written (Zech. 2:5), 'I will be a wall of fire round her, says the Lord, and a glory in the midst of her.' Praise be to You, O Lord, who will comfort Zion and rebuild Jerusalem."[170]

The Jew never ceases to weep at the remembrance of Zion.[171] When a Jew wishes to express his condolences to a fellow Jew who is in mourning, he makes no separation between this one's private sorrow and the greater mourning: the mourning of those who weep for Zion and Jerusalem.

But the Jew's happiness is also tempered by thoughts of Jerusalem; his happiness is incomplete, because Jerusalem has not yet been completely rebuilt. The Jew "at the height of his happiness" (cf. Ps. 137:6) at his own marriage ceremony acknowledges that his joy is not complete; he breaks a glass in remembrance of the ruined Temple of Jerusalem and prays for its restoration.[172] So also the "enterprises," the "constructions" of a Jew are marked by the "remembrance of the Destruction of the Temple," *Zeikher LeHurban*. To show that his house will remain unfinished as long as the House of Jerusalem is not rebuilt, the Jew leaves a cubit of his own house unfinished: "it is not whitewashed."[173]

Since the destruction of the Temple of Jerusalem, the Jew has the feeling that he himself is incomplete, he is not whole. He aspires to "wholeness," and "wholeness" is *Yerushalayim*. He aspires to "fullness", and "fullness" is the *Beit HaMikdash*.

The choice of David was made with the choice of Jerusalem in mind

God chose David and Jerusalem simultaneously. In designating David, sweet singer of His glory—and his descendants—He made His definitive choice of the person to be the King; in designating Jerusalem He made His definitive choice of the seat of Royalty, which is both the place for the divine dwelling, for Royalty, and for the terrestrial capital of the Kingdom. Before the selection of David, the definite choice of Jerusalem could not be made.[174]

Consider the order of the verses that follow: "For the love of David... the Lord swore to David an oath which He will not break: 'A prince of your own line will I set upon your throne'.... For the Lord has chosen Zion and desired it for His home" (Ps. 132:10-13). "The choice of the line of David was made with the choice of Zion in mind."¹⁷⁵

It was not possible, therefore, to build the *Beit HaMikdash* (the Temple of Jerusalem) before the birth of David for the Messiah was to be a descendant of David.¹⁷⁶

Identity of Jerusalem and Israel; Israel is called Zion.

There is an identity between Jerusalem and Israel.

In the Galut the Jew keeps his identity thanks to Jerusalem.

"Now there was living in Susa a Jew—*yehudi*—named Mordecai ....He had been deported from Jerusalem—*Yerushalayim*—among the captives—*HaGola*—carried away" (Esther 2:5-6; cf. Jer. 29:4, Obad. 1:20).

"From the day that Israel was carried away from Jerusalem out of the Land (of Israel: into Galut), he has not lifted up his head." Removed far from Jerusalem the Jew bows his head; "comforted" by the restoration of Jerusalem, of the House of Holiness, he lifts his head again, for he is "comforted" by the hope of Israel's "salvation."¹⁷⁷

Thus the "remembrance of Jerusalem" helps to preserve the identity of Israel, of the Jew in captivity.

Besides, since the beginning of their common history Israel and Jerusalem have been one. Their formal relationship is to be seen in their names, which are synonymous, and in their essential identity which is unchangeable. This identity which is buried within their "hearts,"¹⁷⁸ leads to a profound relationship between the two hearts,¹⁷⁹ between "the heart of Israel" and "the heart of Jerusalem."

This mysterious correlation between the immutable essence "of Israel," and the "essence" of Jerusalem, which is equally immutable, has also been established between Israel, the "Jerusalem" of the nations, and Jerusalem, the "Israel" of places, countries, cities.¹⁸⁰

For Israel and Jerusalem are both "chosen" by God: the one to serve Him as an instrument in the unfolding of time, the dynamic orientation of history; the other to serve Him as a dwelling place, a fixed point, a center for the whole wide world.¹⁸¹⁻¹⁸²

Israel is called Zion.

Jerusalem personifies both the Land and the People of Israel. *Vatomer Tsion: Amra Knesset Yisrael Lifnei HaKadosh Barukh Hu...* "Zion said," (Is. 49:14): "The Community of Israel said to the Holy One, blessed be He..." (TB Berahot 32b).

Thus Zion is Israel. Zion, whose heart is the *Beit HaMikdash*, is identified with Israel, whose heart is in the *Beit HaMikdash* of *Yerushalayim*.[183]

Long before it was constructed, the Temple of Jerusalem was the concretization of the great ideal of the Patriarch Jacob, which he hoped to see fulfilled:[184] that this Temple would serve to unite the hearts of the children of Israel and bring them close to their heavenly Father.[185]

During the period when the Temple stood, Jerusalem was the unifying factor of the people of Israel. The *Aliya LeRegel*, the "ascent" of Jews to the Temple in Jerusalem at the time of the three pilgrim feasts,[186] reinforced their national and religious unity.[187]

Even after the destruction of the *Beit HaMikdash*, the site and the actual ruins of the Sanctuary continued to exert a unifying influence upon Israel, isolated and dispersed in the *Gola*; they were a true source of hope and faith.

Indeed, Jerusalem embraces both the geographical dimension of *Erets-Yisrael*, the Land of Israel, and the historical dimension of *Am Yisrael*, the People of Israel.

In the name of *Yerushalayim* is expressed the territorial entity, *Erets-Yisrael*. "Beneath the stones of the *Kotel HaMa'aravi*, under the weight of the West wall of the Temple of Jerusalem is concentrated the nucleus of the holy places; all the holiness of Jerusalem is concentrated there,"[189] the whole religious entity of Israel is contained there.

The name of God rests both on Jerusalem and on Israel (cf. Dan. 9:19).

Zion is the mountain of God (cf. Is. 2:3); Israel is the people of God (cf. Exod. 7:4; Ezek. 36:20); the Land of Israel is the Land of God (Ezek., *ibidem*).

In God, Zion is Israel (cf. Zohar I 84b; 242a). And "through the Torah," issued from Zion,[190] "all the Community of Israel is found in Jerusalem" (cf. Zohar III 20:1). That is why, the Sages of Israel state, "Zion is called Israel;" their identity is complete: it is external but above all internal, for, God Himself said to Zion, "You are My People!"[191]

It is upon this unity, this identity that the whole body of Jewish liturgy is founded. It emphasizes the interpenetration of these three realities: The people of Israel, Erets-Yisrael and Jerusalem. In the New Moon and Festival prayer, Jews say: "Our God and God of our fathers, may the remembrance of us and of our fathers, the remembrance of the Messiah, son of Your servant David, the remembrance of Jerusalem, Your holy city, and the remembrance of all Your people Israel, arise, approach and come before You; may they be favorably received for our salvation, so that we may enjoy Your grace and peace."

The interpenetration of these three realities, Israel, Erets-Yisrael and

Jerusalem, was already manifest at their emergence into being,[192] as well as throughout their history;[193] it becomes more profound in their salvation.[194] For they have one and the same destiny; they belong reciprocally to one another, and they share a common hope.[195]

The interpenetration of these three realities of Israel, Erets-Yisrael and Jerusalem means that each of them embraces the essence of the other two. Thus Jerusalem personifies the essence of the people of Israel;[196] Jacob-Israel personifies the essence of the Land of Israel, and the Land of Israel, "Erets Yisrael as a whole", is concentrated in *Yerushalayim*, in Jerusalem.[197]

During the course of successive phases of history, all the enemies of Israel, from Hadrian and Constantine, through the Crusades and the Muslim conquerors, down to those of today, have tried obstinately to separate Jerusalem, and consequently Erets-Yisrael, from Israel. By doctrinal or theological arguments and disputes, as well as by brute force, they have tried to substitute their projections for the ideas of "Israel," Erets-Yisrael ("Palestine") and "Jerusalem." Yet they have never succeeded in touching the very kernel of the interpenetration of the three Jewish realities, Israel, Erets-Yisrael and Jerusalem. This kernel remains impenetrable, indestructible.

Israel, in Erets-Yisrael, and especially the Jews in the Galut, preserve a life-long nostalgia for Jerusalem, for the Temple of Jerusalem:

"My soul yearns, yea, even pines for the courts of the Lord; my heart and my flesh sing for joy to the living God. Even the sparrow has found a home and the swallow a nesting place for her young. (As for myself, I dream of) Thine altars, O Lord of hosts, my King and my God. Blessed are they that dwell in Thy house, and never cease from praising Thee!" (Ps. 84:3-5; cf. Ps. 63:2-3; Ps. 102:15)

It is this profound nostalgia which will lead to the rebuilding of Jerusalem. To Israel, to the Jews, "her stones will be dear and they will cherish her dust."[198]

The *Aliyah*, the "ascent":
the Jewish people's history is always
the history of the "ascent" to Erets-Yisrael
and in particular to Jerusalem

Aloh, "to ascend," is the verb which signifies the march of Israel, as a people, and that of the Jew as an individual, to *Erets-Yisrael*, to the Land of Israel, and in particular to *Yerushalayim*, to Jerusalem.

The last word in the Hebrew Scriptures is *VeYa'al*, "Let him go up"—"with God," to Jerusalem, to the House of God.[199]

The whole of the Torah is the history of the "ascent" of the Hebrew patriarchs and of the people of Israel, and with them, of God Himself, to Erets-Yisrael and in particular to Jerusalem; it is the history of the "descent" of the Hebrew patriarchs (except for Isaac) and of the people of Israel—and with them, God Himself—into the Galut, exile; it is the history of the "re-ascent" of the Hebrew patriarchs (except for Isaac) and the people of Israel—and with them, God Himself—to Erets-Yisrael and in particular to Jerusalem. And the history of the Jewish people, which gives a perfect reflection (with an astonishing consistency, in spite of the differences of circumstance and situation) of the history of the *Avot*, the patriarchs,[200] and of the biblical people of Israel, is always the story of the "ascent" to Erets-Yisrael and in particular to Jerusalem, of "going down" into exile and the "re-ascent" to Erets-Yisrael and in particular to Jerusalem.

The Torah begins with the words, *Bereshit*, "in the beginning God created the heavens and the earth." And Rashi begins his commentary on the Torah with the following words: "Rabbi Yitshak said: The Torah should have begun in this way: 'This month shall be for you the first of months' (Exod. 12), since it is the first *mitzvah* prescribed for Israel (the *mitzvah* of the celebration of Pessah, Passover). Why begin with *Bereshit*? (We find the explanation in Psalm 111:6): 'God showed His people what His strength could do, bestowing on them the lands of other nations.' For if the peoples of the world should say to Israel, 'You are robbers, it is by violence that you conquered the lands of the seven nations' (who lived in the land of Canaan), the reply will be, 'The entire world belongs to the Holy One, blessed be He. It is He who created it and He has given it to whom He sees fit (cf. Jer. 27:5). By an act of His will, He gave it to these peoples, and by another act of His will He took it back so as to give it to us.' "

The Hebrew Bible ends with the following verse: "Thus said Cyrus, King of Persia: The Lord the God of Heaven has given into my hands all the kingdoms of the earth, and He Himself has charged me to build Him a house at Jerusalem in Judah. To every man of His people now among you, I say, the Lord his God be with him, and let him go up: *VeYa'al*."[201]

For Israel in every age, the "going up," every re-ascent, is centerd upon Erets-Yisrael, and the "going down" is going into the Galut.[202] In "going up" to Erets-Yisrael and in particular to Jerusalem, Israel and the Jew "ascend" spiritually, for Erets-Yisrael, and especially Jerusalem, has a "higher" situation than any other place in the world.[203]

"You will go up three times a year to enter the presence of the Lord your God" (Exod. 34:24 *et al.*). The Jews who "go up" to Jerusalem on the occasion of the three pilgrim feasts acquit themselves of a religious obligation and fulfill the *Mitzvah D'Aliya LeRegel. Yisrael Olin LeRegel.*[204] The Israelites who "go up" to Jerusalem to present "the first-fruits of all the fruits of the soil,"[205] acquit themselves of a religious obligation: *Ma'alin Et HaBikkurim*, "they bring up the first-fruits" to Jerusalem.[206] The Jew who sets out for Erets-Yisrael, who goes to Erets-Yisrael to settle there, is nowadays too called an *Oleh*, the man who "goes up."[207] In the *Halakhah*, especially in marriage and family law, the term *ma'alin* ("they bring up") plays an important role (the husband can ask the wife and the wife can ask the husband to agree that their family place of residence should be Erets-Yisrael and particularly Jerusalem[208]).

The *aliya*, the "ascent" to Erets-Yisrael, is therefore a religious "ascent." In fact, in "ascending" to Erets-Yisrael and particularly to Jerusalem, the Jew is fulfilling a *mitzvah* of *Yishuv Erets-Yisrael*, a *mitzvah* for the strengthening and re-establishing of the Land of Israel.[209] That is why the Torah uses the verb *alo*, "to ascend," when it speaks of the road that leads Israel to Erets-Yisrael.[210] The "ascent" to Jerusalem, situated on Mount Zion, the city "out of which the Torah comes and from which the Word of God goes forth" is in the first place a physical "ascent" but it is also a religious, spiritual and moral "ascension."[211] Even to "look" at the Promised Land from afar, as Moses had to do, one must "ascend" so as to be able to "contemplate" it.[212]

Thus *aliya* has always signified in Hebrew the religious, spiritual and moral elevation of the person who "ascends." Israel, Jews, "ascend" when they go to Erets-Yisrael and in particular to Jerusalem; they "ascend" when they bear witness to their God by respecting His precepts.[213] As regards law and religious practice, there is an *Aliya LaTorah*, an "ascent to the Torah;" when the Jew is called to pronounce "the blessing of the Torah" over the Torah scroll, he is called *Oleh*. As regards mystical belief and faith, there is *Aliya* to the heavens by the soul of a righteous person who lives in this world; there is *aliya* in the heavens by the soul living in the after world.

All the *aliyot* have their origin in the *aliya* to Erets-Yisrael and particularly in the *aliya* to Jerusalem, "The Gate of Heaven," whence the Jew's soul flies more easily than elsewhere to the spheres above.

**In Jerusalem, the city of *Shalom*, Peace,
God is served with Joy;
in Jerusalem, the city of *Shelemut*, Perfection,
man must be perfect before his God**

In Jerusalem, City of *Shalom*, of Peace, God is served with joy (Zohar III 118a).

"Great is the Lord and highly to be praised, in the city of our God, His holy mountain. O beauty of panorama, joy of the whole earth, the mountain of Zion. God lives in His palaces!" (Ps. 48: 2-4):[214]

"The *Shekhinah* (the Divine Presence) rests only upon one who fulfills the Mitzvot with joy,"[215] and the true service of God can only be fulfilled with joy.[216] The *Beit HaMikdash*, in Jerusalem, is the source of joy, of a joy which is holy and bestows holiness.[217] There the *Shekhinah* dwells in fullness as man serves God there in fullness. There God shares man's joy and there man shares God's joy. There the joy of man is pure: it is the joy of the "perfect" man (*shalem*), who brings *shelamim* in honor of his God. There the joy of man is the expression of his being in its entirety, achieved in the nearness of God. When he derives joy there, he is "deriving" it from the *Ruah HaKodesh*, the "holy spirit."[218] Therefore his joy is serene, marked by the fear of God,[219] the veneration of the heavenly King. The fear that a man feels there draws him close to his Creator;[220] that is why he that comes to the City of Jerusalem to serve God cannot be sad, for he feels within himself the truth of what is written in the Book of Psalms.[221] On the other hand, man in mourning is excused from bringing offerings, for "his heart is not with him," he is not perfect, he is not joyful.[222] Such a man humbly accepts God's decision, and awaits the opportunity to serve God another day in Jerusalem, with joy.[223]

Jerusalem is the City of *Shelemut*, Perfection.[224]

In Jerusalem, therefore, man wishes to be *shalem*, "perfect," before the Lord his God.

In the prayer which King Solomon recited for the dedication of the Temple of Jerusalem, the term *shalem* appears again: *VaHaya Levavkhem Shalem Im HaShem Elokenu* "And let your heart be perfect — *shalem* — in (loyalty to) the Lord our God, to walk in His statutes and to keep His commandments, as at this day" (I Kgs. 8:61).

Man is an organic unity: in Jerusalem he is "perfect" — *shalem* — in the rational and moral sense of the word. Reason commends to him the fear of God (*Moriah* leads to *mora*, the "fear" of God[225]); his "heart" commends to him the love of God (he does that which He whom he loves, loves him to do: he keeps His commandments with love).[226]

In *Yeru-shalem*, *Malki-Tseddek* looked at the external "integrity" of the place and the behavior which the place demands of one who would live there. As for Abraham, he saw in *Yerushalayim* what *Hashem Yireh*, what God knew He would see in this place, in its essence, even before it had been created. Abraham, Isaac, Jacob and their descendants would in their turn "see" inwardly what God saw there "in His providence" from the beginning: they would see God there as He wanted to be seen in His "providential" appearances—*Hashgahah*—to Israel. *Hashem Yiraeh*, "God will be seen" in this place, "on this mountain," where Israel "will be seen." *Hashem Yireh* leads to *Hashem Yiraeh* (Gen. 22:14).[227]

The Jew who "ascends" to the Sanctuary of Jerusalem goes there "to see" God and also "to let himself be seen" by God. He goes there to make himself worthy of "being seen" by Him; he presents himself to be appraised by God, for he "does not go empty-handed," he testifies to the integrity of his consciousness and the generosity of his actions as a Jew, both the one and the other being dedicated to the "Lord, the Eternal, the God of Israel."[228]

Malki-Tseddek looked at the sacred place in a superficial way; his survey took in the immediate, he appraised only what was visible, even though the visible reflects the invisible. Abraham's intuition perceived the intrinsic quality of the holy place: its pre-cosmic,[229] physical and metaphysical, historical and metahistorical significance. It penetrated its hidden sacred mysteries both in the immediate and ultimate future.[230]

Jerusalem — salvation and justice; salvation and truth; salvation and return to Zion

Salvation and Justice.

"You (Jerusalem!) shall be called the home of righteousness, the faithful City. Justice shall redeem Zion" (Is. 1:26-27).[231]

Resepct for justice was the cardinal condition which governed the choice of Jerusalem as the future capital of the Land of Israel, of the Land which God had promised to Abraham. For God said, speaking of the first Hebrew patriarch, "If I have taken special care of him, it is so that he may charge his sons and his family after him to keep the way of the Lord, doing what is right and just" (Gen. 18:19). "It is justice, justice—*tseddek, tseddek* ('justice' twice over) that you must seek so as to live and possess the land which the Lord your God is giving you" (Deut. 16:20; see Ramban *ad locum*).

The rebuilding of the *Beit HaMikdash* (of the Temple of Jerusalem) will be done when the just man and justice—*Tsaddik VaTseddek*—are united, writes the Shelah.²³²

Salvation and Truth.

Rabbi Eliyahu, Gaon of Vilna, teaches: *Takhlit HaGeulah: Geulat HaEmet*: "The ultimate aim of *redemption* is the redemption of *truth*." The prophet Isaiah proclaims this aim when he says, "Break forth in shouts of joy, sing together, ye ruins of Jerusalem! For the Lord has taken pity on His people and *ransomed Jerusalem*" (Is. 52:9), Jerusalem which is called the "City of *Truth*" (Zech. 8:3). And the Gaon continues, "The aim of the redemption of truth is *Kiddush Hashem*, 'the sanctification of the name' of God." That is why, the prophet Isaiah adds, "The Lord has bared His holy arm in the sight of all nations and the whole world from end to end shall see the salvation of our God" (Is. 52:10).²³³

As long as salvation has not come, Truth remains hidden.²³⁴ When salvation comes, "truth shall spring out of the earth" (Ps. 85:12). This springing up, this discovery and revelation of truth, is the advance signal of salvation, writes the Maharal.²³⁵

Salvation and Return to Zion.

The Objective of salvation is to see the children of Zion return to Zion. The supreme objective of salvation is expressed in the hope that these children, having returned to Zion, will have the privilege of "seeing" God, the "God of truth who redeems them,"²³⁶ of "seeing" their "King" arrive in Jerusalem, of "seeing" the *Shekhinah* residing in Zion.

Jews pray daily, "God of mercy, return to Your city, to Jerusalem," and they hope that "their eyes may be able to see His return to Zion." In this way they will attain the real aim of their own return to Zion: "They will sing praises to the Lord who dwells in Zion" (Ps. 9:11); when? "When it is His wish that His *Shekhinah* returns to Zion."²³⁷ Then "God will speak to Israel and say: Here, My light is your light and your light is My light: I and you, we shall shine in Zion, for it is said (Is. 60:1), 'Arise, shine, for thy light is come and the glory of God is risen upon thee.' "²³⁸

Unity of Jerusalem, Israel and God

The unity between God, Israel and Jerusalem is perfect, state the Sages of the Torah. "Israel is called Zion," and "Jerusalem is called by the name of God."²³⁹

The Zohar (III:93b) writes, "When Israel is in Jerusalem here below (on earth) it is called *one*, as David declared, 'And is there *one* nation in the land—*BaArets*—like Your people, like Israel?' (2 Sam. 7:23). In the

Land it surely constitutes *one* nation: but together with the Land it (Israel) is called *one*."

"The Inheritance which the Lord your God gives you (O Israel)" (Deut. 12:9): both the Sifrei and Rashi (*ad locum*) emphasize, "this 'inheritance' is Jerusalem!"[240] Why? "Because the title of 'inheritance' which belongs to the whole of *Erets-Yisrael* (the whole of the Land of Israel) derives its strength from the source of holiness which is found in Jerusalem, the place where it is revealed. This marvelous rank of *nahala* (inheritance) was never confirmed before Israel arrived in Jerusalem."[241]

However, the common responsibility of all Israelites (both jointly and individually) began from the time when they crossed the Jordan.[242] For, as Rabbi Avraham of Sohatshov noted, quoting the Maharal, "Being reserved for Israel alone, Erets-Israel makes of Israel who live there one single man. That is why, when they entered Erets-Yisrael, the Israelites became wholly united with one another,"[243] and consequently all Jews are partners in the possession of their common inheritance, in the *nahala* of *Erets Yisrael*.[244]

Yerushalayim HaBnuyah, KeIr SheHubra La Yahdav. Jerusalem is built as a city of harmonious unity (Ps. 122:3). *Ir SheHubra: Ir SheMehaberet Yisrael Ze LaZe.* Jerusalem is a city which unites Israel, which unites the Jews with one another.[245]

Yahdav means both uniqueness and unity.[246] The *yahdav* of Israel, the people unique and unified around Jerusalem, meets the *yahdav* of Jerusalem, the city unique and unified around Israel.

"In the Jerusalem here on earth, Israel is called one," says the Zohar.[247] Indeed Jerusalem especially, and more particularly the *Beit Hamikdash* during the pilgrim festivals, unifies Israel.[248] *Yerushalayim HaBnuyah.* The "Jerusalem which is built" (Ps. 122:3), the Jerusalem which is rebuilt, which is re-unified, calls — according to Rashi — for the "consolation" of Israel, the "ransom of Israel," and thus it contributes to the re-uniting of the Jerusalem above with Jerusalem here on earth.[249]

KeIr SheHubra La Yahdav. Then "Jerusalem is at unity with itself: she carries here center within her."[250]

Yerushalayim HaBnuyah, KeIr SheHubra La Yahdav: Ir SheHi Ossa Kol Yisrael LaHaverim. Jerusalem is the city which unites all Jews into a bond of friendship.[251]

Thus Jerusalem personifies the unity of Israel.[252] "In Jerusalem Israel is called 'one,' 'one people.'" *BiYerushalayim Ikrun Yisrael Ehad: Goi Ehad.*[253]

Jerusalem as a whole belongs to Israel as a whole. That is why Jerusalem is not part of a territory belonging exclusively to one tribe. "All the tribes are partners in Jerusalem; each of them has its share in the city." Moreover, David himself, when he bought the threshing floor which was to be the site of the Temple, asked all the tribes to contribute towards the purchase of the ground, which was originally in the territory of the tribe of Benjamin.

In fact, on the *Har HaBayit*, the Hill of the House, there are twelve gates, which correspond to the twelve tribes of Israel.[254]

To illustrate the fact that Jerusalem was national property, that in effect the city belonged to the whole population of the country, "the inhabitants of Jerusalem did not have the right to charge any fee for the rooms or the beds" which they put at the disposal of pilgrims who flocked to the Capital during festivals. "Houses in Jerusalem are not rented," the religious law states categorically, "for they belong to the tribes!" Indeed the law of property did not exist in Jerusalem. Legally the houses in Jerusalem did not belong to their owners! The citizens of Jerusalem were therefore obliged to put their apartments at the disposal of their guests free of charge; and indeed they did so very generously — it often happened that they put up their guests inside the house while they themselves — the owners! — "went outside to sleep."[255]

The prior condition for the *redemption* of Israel, for which Jerusalem is the symbol, is the *unity* of Israel, the union of the Jews.[256]

The prior condition for the *salvation* of Israel, for which Jerusalem is the symbol, is the "love of Israel," the love of one's fellow Jew, and so the love of Jerusalem.[257]

The Maharal observes[258] that the middle radical of the three letter verb *ga'al*, "has redeemed," is an *aleph* ($=1$), the symbol of unity. Similarly, when the Community of Israel achieves its unity here on earth and becomes *aguda ahat*, a single band, it will make itself worthy of redemption and of becoming the chariot of the Kingdom of Heaven Above, as it is written (Deut. 33:5): "Thus He became king of Yeshurun, when the chiefs of the people were gathered together and the tribes of Israel were one union."[259]

Not only is the unity of Israel the prior condition for the reign of God in this world; even more, it is due to this unity that "the Throne of God is established on High; that is why it is written, 'He has built in the heavens His sublime dwelling and founded His vault — *agudato* — upon the earth' (Amos 9:6)." When does He build His dwelling in the heavens? asks the Midrash; and it replies, "When His vault — *agudato* — His unity, is founded upon the earth."[260]

And Rashi[261] writes, "The Holy One, blessed be He, is 'King in Yeshurun' (in Israel), when (the children of Israel) are united in a single band. When peace reigns among the children of Israel, God is their King."[262]

So it is necessary that the unity of Israel here on earth should be felt, should be experienced by Israel as unity in God. Only then will Israel's unity be capable of contributing to its redemption by the Messiah.[263]

"Great is the Lord in the City of our God" (Ps. 48:2). "When is He great? When he resides in the city of our God!"

"When is the Holy One, blessed be He, called great?" asks the Zohar, and replies, "When He is in the city of our God, *united* with the Community of Israel. Then He is great in the city of our God, *with* the city of our God."[264]

For the love of God for Israel to manifest its powers of salvation, the Jews' "love of Israel" must not fail.

The destruction of the *Mikdash Sheini*, the second Temple of Jerusalem, was caused by *sin'at hinam*, the causeless hatred (of Jews by Jews); this sin is the greatest of all sins: it is in itself the equivalent of the three most serious sins (which a Jew has no right to commit, even to save his own life).

This is why the Galut which followed the destruction of the *Mikdash Sheini*, the Galut of Edom (the Edomite, Roman, Nazarene Galut) is the longest of the Galuyot: the sin of *sin'at hinam* has not yet been fully expiated. The three most serious sins which caused the destruction of the first Temple, including the sin of trespassing against God, were atoned for relatively quickly in the 70 years of captivity in Babylon; only the sin of trespasssing against man, trespassing against a fellow Jew, *sin'at hinam*, is more serious in the eyes of God then the sin of trespassing against Himself!

Is it necessary to add that the *Galut Edom*, being also the greatest in extent geographically, needs a longer time for Israel to accomplish its "mission," the mission of the Jewish exile: to carry the Word of God to "the nations of the world," to let them know His divine purpose and loving will, which is "to do good" and "to make peace."[266]

"If we have been ruined, and if along with us the world has been ruined, because of *sin'at hinam*, gratuitous hatred, we shall be rebuilt and along with us the world will be rebuilt, thanks to simple *ahavat hinam*, gratuitous love: the love that comes down from the summit of the Rock: 'I will be gracious to whom I will be gracious, and will show mercy on whom I will show mercy' (Exod. 33:19)"—thus writes Rav Kook.[267]

The universal, messianic vocation of Jerusalem, the "Throne of the Lord"

In the messianic age, "Jerusalem will become the spiritual metropolis of all Countries."[268] "At the end of time," Jerusalem will become the spiritual capital of the nations: "And many nations (each retaining its identity) will come, saying: let us ascend the Mountain of the Lord to the House of the God of Jacob."[269]

In this House of God, in the Temple of Jerusalem, the Jews will pray and like their ancestors before them will bring offerings for the good of all the other nations (represented by the "seventy races"). This is why Jerusalem, like God, like the Torah and Israel, has 70 names.[270]

"Oh, if the nations had known how good for them was the *Beit HaMikdash*! They would have ringed it with fortresses to protect it!"[271]

In Jerusalem, capital of the Land of Israel, site of the "House of the God of Jacob," the governments of other countries will meet and deliberate; "they will march to its light." Then "Jerusalem will be expanded"; it will expand its spiritual influence over all countries, for the latter will "surround it." "Finally Jerusalem will be stretched out to the highest places" in the other world; its influence will be able to reach the "Throne of divine Glory:" *Kissei HaKavod*.[272]

"Its neck is like the Tower of David."[273] Jerusalem is called "neck" because it joins the world below and the world on high.[274]

"In those days Jerusalem will be called *Kissei Hashem*: Throne of the Lord. All the peoples will assemble together in Jerusalem, in honor of the Lord."[275]

This Throne here below, set up in the place chosen on earth with the utmost care, will be a symbol of the establishment of the Kingdom of God in the world of History; this throne here below will correspond to the throne above, established outside the confines of History.[276]

The united Jerusalem here below will be one with the united Jerusalem on high: the two Jerusalems will be united in God.[277] Jerusalem being thus united in peace, the world here below and the world on high, all the worlds,[278] will sing together to the glory of the One and Only God.

Thus "Jerusalem will be the light of the world, as it is written,[279] 'And the nations will come to thy light.' And who will be the light of Jerusalem? The Holy One, blessed be He! As it is written,[280] 'The Lord will be for thee an everlasting light.' "[281] "The light of God which shines in Jerusalem" is indeed that of the light of Israel, in *Erets-Yisrael*,[282] for it is due to Jerusalem and the *Beit HaMikdash*, that Erets-Yisrael has been given by God to Israel. Indeed, all the Land of Israel derives its strength from Jerusalem, and Jerusalem derives its strength from the *Beit HaMikdash*.[283]

In the messianic age, all the Land of Israel, all the "country of holiness," *Erets HaKodesh, Admat HaKodesh*,[284] will be looked upon as "Jerusalem, the City of holiness," *Ir HaKodesh*,[285] and the City of Jerusalem will be called *Beit HaMikdash*, "House of Holiness," "House of Sanctification."[286] As a result the whole of Erets-Yisrael will become *Kissei Hashem*, the "Throne of the Lord."

How rich in teaching and in hope are the reflections of the late Chief Rabbi of modern Erets-Yisrael, Rabbi Avraham Yitshak HaKohen Kook (1865–1935), recorded long before the formal proclamation of the State of Israel. In one instance he wrote: "The State does not constitute the happiness of man. I speak of the usual State, which is not much more than a large insurance company. Nevertheless the State which from its very foundation is an ideal State, will set forth in its constitution supreme ideals, which are those of the welfare of its citizens. Such a State will truly be on the very highest rung on the ladder of happiness. And such a State, the *Medinat Yisrael* (the State of Israel) could become. It could become the basis of the *Kissei Hashem* (the basis of the Throne of God in the world), whose greatest desire would be that 'the Lord shall be One (only) and His Name be One' (Zech. 14:9), for this is truly supreme joy. It is true that so great a joy has need of long explanations for its light to be seen in these somber days. However, it does not, therefore, cease to be the greatest joy."[287]

The ultimate and enduring words of this visionary, "utopian" text of Rav Kook's correspond to words we find in the Zohar.[288] There too the wish links up with the statement, and prayer grows into certainty. These words are as follows: " 'In those days Jerusalem will be called the Throne of the Lord.'[289] . . . Thus it is written,[290] 'On that day the Lord shall be One (only) and His Name shall be One.' Blessed be the Lord for evermore. Amen and amen. May the Lord reign for evermore. Amen and amen!"[291]

Tsion and Yerushalayim
Zion and Jerusalem

Although *Tsion* and *Yerushalayim* are synonymous terms, nevertheless they constitute "two categories" that are different but complementary.

In general these two names are used for the mountainous region in which lies the capital of all the Land of Israel and of Judea in particular. There *Tsion* is the Mountain, the country area; *Yerushalayim* is the city, the City of David. "*Tsion* is the Mountain."[293] "*Tsion* might become a country area."[294] "*Tsion* is a well of living water in a countryside."[295] "*Yerusahlayim* is the City."[296]

However, the moral, spiritual and religious meaning of these two terms, *Tsion* and *Yerushalayim*, is more important than their physical, geographical meaning. In the realm of the spirit there is mutual correspondence, harmony and accord betwen *Tsion* and *Yerushalayim*. "*Tsion* is mercy;[297] *Yerushalayim* is justice."[298] "*Tsion* is the place from which *Yerushalayim* receives its blessing."[299] But "*Tsion* receives its blessing from on high and, together, *Tsion* and *Yerushalayim* form but one whole."[300] The Gaon of Vilna, studying the relationships between *Tsion* and *Yerushalayim*, observes that "the face of *Tsion* is one of grandeur;" nevertheless it is united in an absolute unity with *Yerushalayim*.[301] Rabbi Yitshak Aizik of Sovalk, commenting on these words of the Gaon of Vilna, finds in *Tsion* "the grandeur of the fear of God," *yir'a* whereas in *Yerushalayim* he sees "majesty," *malkhut*, which in this case is not merely divine but also human, and specifically "Davidic" (the latter being at the service of the former). "Here *Yir'a* and *Malkhut* are joined in pleasantness."[302]

Tsion as outlined by the Gaon of Vilna and his disciple, Rabbi Yitshak Aizik of Sovalk, can clearly be visualized. It seems to us to be inspired by an idea from the Talmud, for there the verse from the Psalms, "The Lord loves the gates of Zion more than all the dwellings of Jacob" (Ps. 87:2) is interpreted by the Sages of Israel as follows: "God loves the gates of *Tsion*, for they rise above the rest and are 'distinguished' — *HaMetsuyanim* — by the Halakhah (by the Law which is studied there and serves for the correct application of the commandments of the Torah)."[303] The greatness of *Tsion* thus rests on the fact that it is *metsuyenet*, "distinguished," by the Torah which is fervently studied there and from there radiates throughout the world.[304]

As for *Yerushalayim*, the description of it by the Rabbi of Sovalk brings us close to Rav Kook's conception of its splendor.

In the vein of Rabbi Shelomo Alkabez of Safed, author of the Sabbath hymn *Leha Dodi*, Rav Kook salutes in this renowned city of God the Sanctuary, the City of the divine Torah. But while he celebrates the fullness of its sanctity, he also salutes it as the Capital of human royalty, the City of David: he praises the glory of the Psalmist-King.[305] As for the difference between *Tsion* and *Yerushalayim* and their rapport, Rav Kook defines them thus: "*Tsion* and *Yerushalayim* stand side by side. From the beginning of our history the name '*Tsion*' has been used particularly to express the idea of our royalty, our material strength, which is certainly holy for it serves the holy purposes of our people which are and will be for evermore those of a kingdom of priests and a holy nation (Exod. 19:6) for the entire world. As for the name 'Yerushalayim,' it expresses the purpose of our holiness in itself; it demonstrates the supreme, idealist aspiration of our national being both with regard to ourselves and with regard to the whole of humanity. The site of the *Beit HaMikdash* (the Sanctuary of Israel), to be the future House of Prayer for all people, the place where the great Sanhedrin met, whence came the Torah and from which it will come again for all Israel—it is all of this which is denoted by the name 'Yerushalayim.' "[306]

The interpretations of *Tsion* and *Yerushalayim* offered us by the Zohar (III 262b) and the masters of Jewish religious thought are certainly varied, but they are always complementary. *Tsion* and *Yerushalayim* form an inseparable couple, symbolizing father and mother, the patriarchs and matriarchs, intelligence and wisdom. Thus the Shelah HaKadosh, Rabbi Yeshayahu Horowitz, saw in "*Tsion*" the inward point where splendor and majesty merge: "*Tiferet U'malkhut*."[307] Rabbi Shemuel Shmelke Horovitz himself believes that *Tsion* symbolizes the external aspect of man at prayer, his moving lips, while *Yerushalayim* personifies the internal aspect of man at prayer, his heart.[308] However, the Gaon of Vilna remains the master who carries the reflections on the relational symbolism of *Tsion* and *Yerushalayim* to their pinnacle: he finds in them a numerical symbolism of the letters that form the names of God.[309] Indeed, without going into the details of the figures, Rashi had previously written, "*Tsion* is the name of the Holy One, blessed be He."[310]

As for Rabbi Yona of Gerona, who studied the divine arithmetic closely, he stated that the numerical value of the letters forming the words *Mishkenei Elion* ("dwellings of the Most High") is the same as the value of the letters forming the word *Yerushalayim*: i.e., 586.[311] The words *Mishkenei Elion* come from verse 5 of the 46th Psalm of David in which he exclaims: "There is a river, whose streams make glad the city of God, the holiness of the dwelling place of the Most High."

4
A survey of "Jewish time / Sabbath time"

Shabbat:
Source and prerequisite of holiness

It is in connection with Shabbat that the Torah first introduces the idea of holiness: the first account of Genesis is crowned with the words, "And He blessed (the seventh day) and made it holy" (Gen. 2:3).[1] Prior to that God had given His blessing to the animals as well as to man and woman, so that they might multiply (Gen. 1:22, 28). To the latter He gave His blessing in words that He addressed to them personally and directly.

The procreative instinct, both animal and human, is blessed by the Creator, for He does not want His creation to continue as a wasteland (see Is. 45:18). Yet the aspiration, the need for holiness arises only in connection with the Shabbat: man and woman are asked to adopt it voluntarily and to respond to the call of their own free will.

Without suppressing it, holiness raises man above instinct: it refines him, ennobles him, offering him an ethical goal. It is holiness which sets the seal upon the union of a Jewish man and woman, and in particular marks their conjugal union during Shabbat.[2]

One can only be holy by being good. By making Shabbat the quintessence of goodness, for man's sake, God has also made it the quintessence of holiness.[3] For man, holiness is a striving to achieve his intention to do, in all his thoughts, words and actions, what is good for himself and good for others; to do what is good as the Creator conceives it and wishes it.[4]

God and Israel create the Shabbat, its Divine holiness and its hallowing by man

Created by God, the Shabbat is "established and *exists*;"[5] accepted by Israel, the Shabbat *lives*: even more, it becomes Israel's creation: " 'And the children of Israel shall keep the Shabbat, to *make* the Shabbat' (Exod. 31:16). For he who keeps the Shabbat should be thought of as if he had *made* it."[6]

The Shabbat is *holy* because of its Divine, extra-temporal nature (cf. Gen. 2:3). God "transmits" it, entrusts it to the Jew so that the latter will "hallow" it and perfect its holiness in the human, ethical, temporal world (cf. Exod. 20:8; Deut. 5:12). Sent by God, coming from eternity, the Shabbat is welcomed and introduced into time by the Jew, who creates out of it the quintessence of time. Israel thus becomes a "collaborator with God in the work of Creation" where time and eternity are conjoined: God is the Creator of the Shabbat, and after Him and with Him Israel is the creator of the Shabbat!

God, the Shabbat and Israel

The collaboration between the three partners, God, Shabbat and Israel, leads to their total identification: "Shabbat is the Name of God"[7] and "the congregation of Israel is called Shabbat."[8] The Shabbat, which is the "Name of God," strengthens the inner unity of Israel (just as it affirms the inner unity of each individual Jew).

Israel is one, for its unity-oneness rests on the unity-oneness of God; Israel reflects God's unity-oneness to the world.[9]

Ner Shabbat, "The Shabbat candle," the privilege of the Jewish wife

Lighting the candles at the beginning of Shabbat is the duty incumbent above all upon the Jewish wife, the Jewish mother.[10]

By carrying out the *mitzvah* of *ner Shabbat*, the commandment to light the Shabbat candles, the Jewish wife is making reparations for the fault of Eve who, by inciting Adam to commit the first sin, "*extinguished* the soul of the first man,"[11] "put him in darkness. She brought about discord between God and His human creation; she caused disagreement between Adam and his descendants; she thus aroused dissension between the generations, who suffer as a result of the first man's first sin; she awakened disturbance in human behavior; she created the confusion between good and evil."[12]

The *nerot Shabbat*, the Shabbat candles which the Jewish wife lights in her home, are intended to re-establish the peace that was destroyed by Eve's fault in the original home of the first married couple. She lights these candles for *shelom beto*, to ensure the peace of her husband's home,[13] for which she is responsible, being the personification of this same home: "the wife is the home!"[14]

Through the light, both material and spiritual, that she brings into the house at the beginning of Shabbat, the Jewish wife re-establishes for its duration (and if she is deserving, like Sarah, from one Shabbat to the next)[15] peace between body and soul;[16] she establishes "holiness" in the house, which is after all the meaning of Shabbat.[17] This brightness without confusion, making way for pure desires, expresses the holiness which comes about in a wholeness without contradictions. Thanks to the fulfilling of the *mitzvah* of *ner Shabbat* by the wife, the Shabbat becomes an act of "reparation" for the sin of "the tree of the knowledge of good and evil:"[18] the Shabbat, therefore, becomes wholly "good."[19]

As she lights the *nerot Shabbat*, the "Shabbat candles," the Jewish wife, "priestess of the house,"[20] summons peace into it and welcomes it. For the Shabbat is *shalom*: it is called "peace"; it is greeted as peace, perfect peace in the worlds above and below.[21]

On *leil Shabbat*, Friday evening, the Shabbat eve, the Jewish husband and wife assume priestly tasks in their home. However, the ceremony which the wife performs at the beginning of Shabbat is more important than that which falls to the husband, the priest of the house. If their financial means are not sufficient for them to obtain both the wine for the *kiddush* (the "sanctifying" of Shabbat, recited generally by the husband on Friday evenings) as well as the candles for the *nerot Shabbat*, religious law gives priority to the purchase of the candles, *Mishum Shelom HaBayit*, "for the sake of peace in the home." There is no real peace in a home that has no *ner Shabbat*.[22]

As she lights the Shabbat candles in her home on Friday evenings, the Jewish wife brings joy to it. And if "the home is joyful on Shabbat eve, the *Shekhinah* (the Divine Presence) is there. It says, This home belongs to Me: 'Yisrael, it is in you that I glory!' But if (the home of a Jew) is not joyful (on Shabbat eve), the *Shekhinah* departs, and the angels with it, and bad temper comes in and the Name of God withdraws from between the man and woman; they remain side by side like *Esh VaEsh* (like 'fire with fire'), and the food becomes unclean."[23]

The Talmud[24] sees the source of harmony, of peace between man and wife (two elements by their very nature opposed to one another), in the presence of God with them. His Name (a part of the Tetragrammaton itself) constitutes the hyphen between them; He raises them out of the world of nature, and so of adversities, to the world of the spirit, and so of unity. Thus, as man and woman become spiritually united, they draw near to God, to the One.

Man is called *ish*; woman is called *isha*. The *yod* (=i) in *ish* and the *he* (=a) in *isha* are the letters *Yod* and *He* in the Tetragrammaton, the paramount Name of God. If a married couple is worthy, this part of the Name, *Yod He*, is with them; *Ish VeIsha, zahu Shekhinah benehem; lo zahu, eish okhlatan!* If not, it withdraws and the man and woman, *ish* and *isha*, deprived of these two letters *yod* and *he* (which give them at the same time both their identities as individuals and their identity as a couple), stripped of the Name of God, having rejected the "Presence of God," the unifying, pacifying Presence—the man and woman live alone together. They remain *esh* and *esh*, they remain face to face like "fire" and "fire": ready to attack one another, ready to join forces, not in the enjoyment of a deepening love, but "devouring each other" in fleeting pleasure: they annihilate each other.[25]

Light, not fire! The beginning of Shabbat comes in light, by the lighting (generally by the wife) of the *ner Shabbat*; the end of Shabbat comes in light, by the lighting (generally by the man) of the *ner havdalah*, of the "candle of the distinction" "between the seventh day and the six days of labor." During the *havdalah* prayer, the blessing of *Borei Me'orei Ha'esh* is recited: God Who "creates the light of fire" is praised. "The fire" lit on Saturday night, *Motsaei Shabbat*, the termination of Shabbat, marks the beginning of the civilizing, industrious activity of the week; but this fire itself which the Creator has put at our disposal and which He teaches us to obtain for ourselves is also a fire of *light* which is illuminating and non-destructive; it is equally a fire of holiness which ennobles those "things" which man is preparing to make.[26]

As she lights the *nerot Shabbat* and diffuses her home with the soft light of Shabbat, the Jewish wife remembers the prohibition concerning Shabbat which in the Torah is given peculiar emphasis: "You shall not light any *fire* in any of your dwellings on the Shabbat day."[27] This definite prohibition with regard to a physical act is assumed not only by the mystics[28] but equally and with great insistence by the halakhic legislators to relate also to the field of human relationships. "It is forbidden to light any fire" of discord, and above all not in the homes, which ought to be dwellings of peace; and above all not on the Shabbat day, the day of peace,[29] preparing the way for the peace of the coming week. It is the day of cosmic inner peace,[30] preparing the way for the peace of the world to come.

The Kiddush: the prayer of the "sanctification" of the Shabbat

We perform the *kiddush*, we recite the "sanctification" of the Shabbat to give concrete form on Friday night to the *mitzvah* which bids us to consecrate our *thoughts* to the Shabbat: *zakhor*.[31]

Through an agreeable act of "joy"[32] — drinking wine, in "moderate" quantity — "we evoke the 'remembrance' of the splendor of the day and we establish in our *hearts* the truth of the creation of the world *ex nihilo*;"[33] by the same act we evoke the "remembrance" "of the exodus from Egypt," for the latter reminds us of the *Hashgahah*, the special Providence with which God benefits His people, Israel.[34]

In the *kiddush* for Shabbat, *Zikaron LeMa'assei Bereshit* and *Zeikher LiYetsiat Mitsrayim*, the remembrance of the work of creation and the recalling of the exodus from Egypt are mentioned side by side.

For, both in leading to and in implementing the exodus of the Children of Israel from Egypt, God lavished on His people miracles so extraordinary that they were equal to those that He performed to create the world. Through the *Shibud Ma'arakhot*, through a "mutation in the systems of the Universe," God made the Israelites understand, after having "brought them out of the land of Egypt, out of the house of bondage," even the miracle of the Creation, at which man could not be present.[35]

This is why the *Kiddush HaYom* (the most important "kiddush of the day" is that of Friday night[36]) is commanded by the term *zakhor* — "remember!" It contains in it both the remembrance of the *creation* of the world and that of the *exodus* from Egypt: the two events demand from us a *zeikher*, that is, a "commemoration" which is also participation, a "recalling" which brings the past to the present. Through the use of the word *zekhirah* the Torah asks us (after we have experienced the exodus from Egypt and thereby the Creation itself) to "remember"[37] both of these two events, Creation and exodus.

The *kiddush* of Friday night, a spiritual idea, crystallizes by word and action the *thought* of the *zakhor*[38] and *leads* us to the *observance* of the *shamor*.[39] The *zakhor*, free and open, leads to the *shamor*, the observance, which effectively frames and minutely regulates all our acts during the Shabbat.

The *zakhor*, as Rabbi Shneur Zalman of Liady says at the very end of his *Kunteres Ahron*,[40] represents the *penimiut*, the inwardness of the *mitzvah* of the Shabbat,[41] and the *shamor* represents the *hitsoniut*, the external aspect of the same *mitzvah*.

The *zakhor* is a *mitzvat asseh*, a positive, active *mitzvah* and like every *mitzvat asseh* it is obeyed, as the Ramban[42] remarks, out of *love of God*; whereas the *shamor* is a *mitzvah lo ta'asseh*, negative, prohibiting;[43] and like every *mitzvah lo ta'asseh* it is obeyed out of *fear of God*.[44] Nevertheless a *mitzvah lo ta'asseh*, if it is influenced by the love of God produced by a preceding *mitzvat asseh*, can be obeyed with ease. The *shamor*, the *Shamor Et Yom HaShabbat*, is not restricting but pleasant, for it has been instilled in the heart of the Jew beforehand by the *zakhor*. The Zohar, and subsequently the Sefer Haredim and the Or HaHayim,[45] say that the *shamor* responds to the impatient waiting of Jews who wish to see the arrival of Shabbat. They take as their scriptural basis for this interpretation of the *shamor* the biblical verse which makes us feel Jacob's earnest love for his son Joseph, awaiting the fulfillment of his dreams which is described by the verb *shamor*: *VeAviv Shamar Et HaDavar*.[46]

Moreover, the *shamor* can equally well lead to the *zakhor*.

Indeed the *shamor*, the observance of one Shabbat in *practical* ways, prepares the Jew, spiritualizing and purifying him,[47] for the coming of the next Shabbat. Such a Jew arrives refined at the threshold of the new Shabbat, the awaited guest; he is capable then of reaching the "inwardness" of the *mitzvah* of the *zakhor*.

Zakhor leads to *shamor*; and *shamor* leads to *zakhor*; they form one whole: *Zakhor VeShamor Kahda Mithabran*.[48]

So this oneness of the *Zakhor VeShamor*, of the *mitzvat asseh* and *mitzvah lo ta'asseh*, which relates to the *mitzvah* of the Shabbat,[49] becomes the source of oneness of all the *mitzvot*,[50] that is to say, the source of the blessing that the Jew recites before proceeding to perform a *mitzvah*, a Divine commandment: "Blessed be Thou, the Eternal One, King of the universe, Who hast sanctified us by Thy commandments..."

Observance of the Shabbat is organized by the married couple together

In a Jewish home the Shabbat is welcomed and inspired by the married couple, a duality which harmoniously tends toward unity and therein finds its complete realization.

Kol issha Shabbat kaful...[51] "The whole of the Shabbat observance, from biblical times the Temple of Jerusalem,[52] down to the present day, is double," organized by the team of husband and wife. This duality is a reflection of the vital role of the couple in the home.

Two candles brighten the Shabbat table, and before them are placed two loaves, *lekhem mishne*, to be blessed; they are intended to recall the two biblical principles which govern Shabbat observance: *Zakhor VeShamor*. *Zakhor*, "Remember," and *Shamor*, "Observe": the one (Exod. 20:8) the masculine principle and the other (Deut. 5:12) the feminine principle,⁵³ and both inscribed in the two tables of the Law.⁵⁴ The two verbs *Zakhor VeShamor* complement each other in the unity of the Shabbat, in the light of the hope of messianic times, the times of universal brotherhood. The two *Shabbatot*, the "Shabbat here below" (terrestrial) and the "Shabbat on high" (celestial) will then form one perfect sabbatical whole.⁵⁵

That the welcoming of Shabbat in a Jewish couple's home has been successful is attested by *two* angels who visit it on Friday evening.⁵⁶

The Shabbat home is a place of heavenly glory

"See, the Lord has given you the Shabbat! Therefore on the sixth day He gives you provision for two days. Let everyone stay where he is; let no one go out from his habitation—*mimkomo*—from his place on the seventh day" (Exod. 16:29).

"'*Mimkomo* is an allusion to what is written in Ezekiel 3:12: 'Blessed be the glory of the Lord from His place: *Mimkomo*.' This is why the man who puts on his heavenly crown does not leave his place (on the Shabbat day)...'Let him not go out from his habitation, his place: *mimkomo*, (on the seventh day) for it is the place of holy glory.'"⁵⁷

The *kiddush*, the "sanctification" of the Shabbat, must be pronounced in the place where the family Shabbat meal is eaten, "in his house."⁵⁸

"And I will give rain to your land, in its time—*BeLeilei Shabbatot*—on Shabbat eve, when everyone is at home."⁵⁹

The most propitious "time" for conjugal union in holiness of thought, purity of love and "Shabbat joy" is the night between Friday and Saturday, the night of the "Shabbat which is holy," the "Shabbat which is the mystery of unity."⁶⁰

Respect for God, for the Shabbat and for one's Parents

"The commandment to respect—*kibbud*—one's father and mother is equal to that of respecting the Shabbat—*Kevod Shabbat*."⁶¹

A Jew must *honor* the Shabbat and *honor* his parents: *VeKarata LaShabbat Oneg, VeKhibadeto* (Is. 58:13); *Kabed Et Avikha Ve'et Imekha* (Exod. 20:12, Deut. 5:16).⁶²

Therefore, the respect—*kavod*—due to one's parents is comparable to the respect—*kavod*—due to the Creator: *Kabed Et Avikha Ve'et Imekha*

("Honor thy father and mother"); *Kabed Et Hashem* ("Honor the Lord;" Prov. 3:9).[63]

The very fact of having parents, and having the parents that we have, not those we might have chosen, leads us to the respect we owe to our Creator who holds "the keys" of life, the secret of life.[64] Indeed there are "three partners" ruling over the birth of man: "the Holy One, blessed be He, the father and the mother."[65] "The Holy One says (to the father and mother of the future child), 'Let us make man.' "[66]

However, if parents ask their sons or daughters to profane the Shabbat, they should not obey their parents, for both parents and children owe respect to their Creator, which the observance of the Shabbat demonstrates.[67]

It is Jacob's example which the whole family of Israel follows in celebrating the Shabbat

"To Israel, Thy people, Thou has given the Shabbat, with love: to the posterity of Jacob whom Thou hast chosen" (prayer for the morning of Shabbat). "Abraham rejoices in this day; Isaac is full of happiness; Jacob and his sons celebrate it by taking rest" (prayer of Shabbat afternoon).

The prayers put the emphasis on "the posterity of Jacob," "Jacob and his sons," who constitute the people of Israel; the celebration of Shabbat by the *whole family of Israel* began with them (for Ishmael, the son of Abraham, and Esau, Isaac's son, did not celebrate the Shabbat).[68]

Oneg Shabbat — the delight of the Shabbat

The *mitzvah* which commands people to take kindly to the Shabbat is called *Oneg Shabbat*, "the delight of the Shabbat," "Command and "enjoyment" meet and complement one another to form a whole: the unity of the affectionate respect for the Shabbat.

"What does 'this delight' consist of?" ask the Sages and they reply: "When Isaiah says (58:13), 'You shall call the Shabbat a delight,' I know that it means the *oneg Shabbat*, the delight of Shabbat."[69]

The concept of the *oneg Shabbat* is a specifically Jewish one, both aggadic and halakhic in its scope. It means the spiritual "pleasure" (including material and physical pleasure, which is raised to the level of sublime joy) which the Shabbat offers to the Jew, involving the totality, the fullness of his being, in body and spirit, for man is one[70]. It also signifies the pleasure that the Jew offers to the Shabbat, personified in: "Give pleasure to the Shabbat," "honor it";[71] indeed it is the Shabbat personified which is praised in Isaiah 58:13: "You shall call the Shabbat 'delight'—*oneg*—(you shall call it '*oneg*' when you address it): 'holy of the Lord,' (it is) 'honorable' and you shall honor it."

VeKarata LaShabbat Oneg: you shall speak to the Shabbat, you shall "call" it, you shall "summon" it, you shall "invite" it.[72]

On the basis offered by this verse of Isaiah, the sages of Israel build the the magnificent aggadic and halakhic edifice of the *oneg Shabbat*. Itself a quality and a reality, the *oneg Shabbat* ends by being what it *ought* to be and what it *is pleased* to be, if it is preceded by another quality and reality: *kevod Shabbat*: "the honor of the Shabbat," the honor owed to the Shabbat.[73]

The *kavod* owed to the Shabbat includes both the spiritual preparations for the welcoming of Shabbat, e.g. reading and studying of the weekly portion of the Pentateuch and its traditional Aramaic translation and also the material preparations for welcoming the Shabbat such as purchases, etc. Thus the Jew prepares himself spiritually and materially during the week to welcome this special guest, and in increasing measure as the day approaches. On the eve of Shabbat the Jew prepares his person also "in honor of the Shabbat" (he "washes" his body, he puts on "clean clothes"; thus he "hallows" his body, he spiritualizes it). By these final pre-Shabbat actions he makes a sign everywhere of the change he is making around him and within him in honor of the Shabbat. Indeed there should be both a visible and perceptible "difference" between his customs, attitudes, "step" and "word" on a weekday and his behavior on the Shabbat day.

On the Shabbat day the Jew is different from what he is on weekdays. He is different; he is better. His being and his appearance are "different"; they are "radiant"; they are not like what they are on the other days of the week.

To be different on the Shabbat day, in the presence of the Shabbat, the Jew prepares his family surroundings, his home, his dining room, his bedroom, to be ready for the arrival of the "Shabbat Queen": the house is spruced up, the furniture is tidied, the "table is laid," and the "bed is prepared."

Everything having been done "in honor of the Shabbat," every Jew—man, woman and child—goes to meet the Shabbat, to welcome the Shabbat "bride."

Then the *oneg Shabbat* begins.

The pleasure that Jews give to the Shabbat and that the Shabbat in turn gives to Jews is typified by the lighting of the candles, by joyful prayer, by zestful study of the Torah, by friendly talk, peaceful behavior, soft singing, individual meditation, meeting at the synagogue, and also by "bringing guests into the house," above all those in need; by "eating with joy," "in proper order" and "at the proper time," "delicious Shabbat dishes"; by sweet drinks; by conjugal union in serene and trusting love.

All these actions, and any other "permitted" action performed for the "joy of the *mitzvah*," constitute the *mitzvah* of the *oneg Shabbat*, and contribute to the fulfillment of the religious *obligation*, the purpose of which is Shabbat *pleasure*. This pleasure is not merely an ephemeral enjoyment, but is prolonged beyond this world in which both Israel and the Shabbat have their origins. In this world, this *oneg* is obtained both by "learning the Torah" and "eating," by "going to Synagogue" and "staying at home," by "contemplation" and "sleeping," provided all is done "for the sake of the *mitzvah*," and in combining all these activities, the Jew "makes the Shabbat day a joy which is entirely Torah"![74]

Truly, the intention of the Torah is that the *oneg Shabbat* shall determine the quality of life of Jewish husbands and wives, of Jewish families, and of the Jewish people, in holiness. The *oneg Shabbat* is measured not by quantity, but by the quality of the way it is realized, the "intention" that governs it, the "heart" which stimulates it. The quantity of "Torah" or of "provisions" that the Jew has available for fulfilling the *mitzvah* of the *oneg Shabbat* is of little importance; what matters is his consciousness of the *mitzvah* he is realizing to the best of his ability given his capacity and his means. "Even if a Jew eats very little, if he eats it with joy for the sake of Shabbat he is fulfilling the *mitzvah* of *oneg Shabbat*." "It is better," writes Rabbi Yehuda He-Hassid (in the 13th century), "to eat vegetables on the Shabbat (in a house) where love reigns between a man and his wife and the members of his family than to eat beef in discontent" (cf. Prov. 15:17). On the other hand, Jews who are filled with *oneg Shabbat*, *medushnei oneg*, will not suffer on account of their abundance, for they will enjoy them in holiness and therefore in moderation (cf. Ramban, *ad* Lev. 19:2; Prov. 13:25), and at the same time in the purity of their relationships with themselves and their families.

The *oneg Shabbat* is a "joy" which is full but serene, and wise in the ways of holiness. Thus it leads a Jew to live it in the presence of, and indeed in communion with, Him Who is the source of holiness: "if you call the Shabbat a day of joy, the *holy* day of the Lord . . . then you shall *find your joy* in the Lord" (because of Him Who gives you the Shabbat; with Him Who favors you with His goodness) (Is. 58:13-14; Zohar II: 88b).

The *oneg Shabbat* therefore can only be visualized with the whole and interdependent use of man's spiritual and physical faculties: both body and soul are involved, and both together. The Zohar (II 47a), in commenting on the verse from Isaiah (58:13) on which are based both the Jewish ideal concerning the *oneg Shabbat* and its reality, says, "*Oneg Shabbat*: *oneg*, the delight of everything, delight of the mind and of the body, delight (of the world) on high and (of the world) below." Experience of the *oneg Shabbat* bears out that "the soul of the Jew comes from the world of heavenly pleasure, from the *Olam HaTa'anug* of which it is part."[75] The Jew searches for this *ta'anug* in this world, and the Shabbat day produces it for him.[76]

Shabbat/Pessah/sanctuary.
Holy Day and Holy Place.
The Power and the Leniency of the Shabbat Laws

It is above all in reference to the observance of Shabbat and Pessah, the festival of Passover (there is an inner, formal relationship[77] between the motivation and celebration of these two solemn occasions) that the Torah uses the vigorous verb *shamor*: to observe (assiduously), to keep (meticulously).[78] The word *Shamor*, *HiShamer*, denotes a *mitzvah lo ta'asseh*, a religious prohibition.[79] And most of the laws relating to the Shabbat contained in the Mishnah Shabbat are in the nature of restrictions, are *mitzvot lo ta'asseh*.

Thirty-nine types of principal, productive "activities" are forbidden on Shabbat. The *Torah She'Be'al Peh*, the oral Law, establishes the principles of these productive, transforming, civilizing activities ("considered," "constructive" "finalizing" activities), taking for a model the activities required for building the Tabernacle, the *Mishkan*, in the wilderness.[80] The thirty-nine principal forbidden activities (*Avot-melakhot*, "parent-activities"), "produce" other activities (*Toladot*, "offspring-activities") which are likewise forbidden on Shabbat.[81] There is a close relationship between the Biblical prohibitions relating to the Shabbat and those relating to the building of the Tabernacle (cf. Exod. 31 and 35). The sanctity of the Shabbat takes precedence over the sanctity of the *Mishkan*; the holiness of the day takes precedence over the holiness of the place. The sanctuary could not be built nor yet exist if the Shabbat was not respected.[82] The Shabbat is able in any place to bring man into a personal relationship with his God, independently of the *Beit HaMikdash*—*bekhol moshvoteikhem* (Exod. 35:3; Lev. 23:3); in its own precise position the latter cannot serve to bring about a rapprochement between man and his God, if the Shabbat is profaned.[83]

The Shabbat comes from on high; the *Beit HaMikdash* is raised from below. The *Beit Hamikdash can only help the man who has sinned to come closer to God* (the *Mishkan* was built after the sin of the golden calf!).[84] But the Shabbat enables man to communicate directly with God, without any intermediary; it enables even a sinful man to communicate with God, even one who is guilty of the grave sin of idolatry.[85] Such a man, who has strayed away from God, when he "observes the Shabbat," *ipso facto* he acknowledges the existence of the Creator, His works, His sovereignty over creation, over all created beings, and thus over himself, his very being, over his possessions, all of which he submits to Him.

The oral Torah, based on the written Torah, has elaborated the Shabbat laws with extreme precision;[86] they are "mountains which hang on a thread." The bases of this legislation are found in particular in the seventh chapter of *Massekhet Shabbat*, the Talmud treatise on Shabbat. The Shabbat legislation is coherent and systematic, consistent and unified; it is constructed methodically, following logical rules, so as to reflect the actual order of life.

The juridical strictness and regard for regulation which govern the establishing of the *Lamed-Tet Melakhot*, the "thirty-nine activities" forbidden on Shabbat, are realized in minute detail by the strictness of the requirements concerning *shemirat Shabbat*, observance of the Shabbat. In the case of the *shomer Shabbat*, the Jew who observes Shabbat, however, this strictness does not diminish the fervor which he puts into the conscientious execution of the requirements, nor does it lessen the refreshing effect which performing them has on his spirit. On the contrary, for him they constitute a *Tal* (Tet-Lamed), a revivifying "dew," a foretaste of the messianic "dew," redemptive, "luminous," the "dew of resurrection," the "dew of life."[87]

Pikkuah Nefesh, safeguarding human life,
takes priority over observance of the Shabbat laws

The identification between the three partners, God, Shabbat and Israel,[88] has for its primary objective respect for life, and particularly the safeguarding of human life. The primacy of life springs from the existence of a scale of values which determines the respective importance of the sanctity of place, time and life.

If one compares the *Beit HaMikdash*, the "sacred place," the Sanctuary of Jerusalem on the one hand and the Shabbat, the "sacred time," on the other, the latter takes priority over the former. The sanctity of the

Mikdash takes second place to the sanctity of the Shabbat. The Divine command to build the *Mishkan* in the wilderness, and later the *Mikdash* in Jerusalem, yields place to the Divine command to respect the Shabbat: "The building of the *Mikdash* does not have priority over Shabbat." "Jerusalem (its Temple) was destroyed on a Shabbat because the Shabbat had been profaned there."[89]

The sanctity of human life (of the spirit) is not only greater than that of the Sanctuary of Jerusalem, but it exceeds that of the Shabbat period, and this leads the Mekhilta to vigorously enunciate a fundamental halakhic and aggadic principle: "It is written (Exod. 31:14), 'You shall keep the Shabbat, for it is a holy day for you — *lahem*'; *lahem*, it is to you that the Shabbat is entrusted, and not you to the Shabbat." In fact, the text reads literally, "To you the Shabbat is transmitted (put in your hands)."[90] This statement is obviously of considerable import, its power exceeds that of the adage which says, "The Shabbat was made for man and not man for the Shabbat." For the Mekhilta continues, "It is written (Exod. 31:16), 'The children of Israel shall keep the Shabbat (perpetuating it from one generation to another)'; one Shabbat may be profaned for him (for man) so that he may be able to observe many Shabbatot."[91]

The Shabbat is holy. However, of all things known in this world the greatest sanctity is that of life, particularly human life, for it is in the human spirit that the transcending, Divine sanctity, from which all sanctity derives, receives its own immanence;[92] the *Shekhinah*, the Divinity of the Holy One, blessed be He, is present in the sanctity of the human spirit: *VeShakhanti BeTokham*. Man is the *Maon LiShekhinah*, man is the home of the *Shekhinah*.[93]

From this derives the principle of *Pikkuah nefesh dohe Shabbat*, according to which "observance (of the well-being) of the soul sets aside the Shabbat," which is equivalent to saying that the saving of human life takes priority over observing Shabbat.[94] It is the Shabbat itself, the rules for which are shown by God in the Torah, which "authorizes" — to put it more precisely, which prescibes — the "suspension" of its own observance when human life is thereby threatened, even when there is only a faint possibility of such danger occurring: *safek nefashot dohe Shabbat* ("even when there is only the shadow of a threat to the soul"), the safety of human life sets aside the Shabbat.[95]

The greatest codifiers of Jewish religious law, Rambam and Rabbi Joseph Caro, consequently state that it is not only permitted (to a sick person, a doctor or any other person) to set aside the Shabbat laws in order to heal, but that one is compelled by a *mitzvah*, by virtue of a religious commandment of the Torah, to act thus. Even in a case where one only suspects the existence of danger to a person's health, one is obliged to set aside the Shabbat ordinances and take action to preserve the patient's health.

In fact, the definition of health is quite relative and subjective, and Jewish religious law takes this uncertainty into account. So when a sick person demands that the Shabbat laws be broken, contrary to his doctor's opinion, precedence shall be given to the patient's feelings: it is the sick person who must be listened to and not the doctor. And in a case where the patient refuses to co-operate in a transgression of the Shabbat laws which may be made necessary by his state of health, he can be forced to do so. Authorization by a rabbinical court or a halakhic authority is not required to suspend the Shabbat rules in the case of *pikkuah nefesh*. A person who is quick to take action to save a life in peril or heal a sick person "should be praised" for this meritorious act; a person who hesitates to intervene should be looked on "as if he were spilling the blood" of a human being. It is even suggested that those who transgress the Shabbat laws in order to heal or to preserve life in danger may be "the great men of Israel," so that the importance of this *mitzvah* may be made evident. "For the laws of the Torah are laws of mercy, charity and peace in the world. He who claims that to transgress the Shabbat laws for health reasons is to profane the Shabbat is a heretic," writes the Rambam.[96]

The Sages of Israel derive the principle of *pikkuah nefesh* from a Biblical verse of capital importance, for it demonstrates the objective of all the *mitzvot*, all the commandments of the Torah: respect for life. Indeed the Torah says, "You shall observe My laws and My statutes: he who keeps them shall have life through them: I am the Lord."[97]

It is on this Biblical verse which deals with the observance of all the *mitzvot* and insists on respect for life that the Sages based their interpretation of *pikkuah nefesh*, the safeguarding of life; they taught the importance of the Biblical words which require man to keep the Divine laws and statutes "so that they may find life in them," adding, "but not so that they should die because of them!"

The Sages of Israel established that the purpose of observing the *mitzvot* is the safeguarding and ennobling of life on earth; but they also add that this life, lived out here on earth in a worthy manner, will lead to the true life, that of the "future world."[99] Life here has an end; life in the hereafter has none.

The Sages of Israel were never "heretics" in the sense conveyed in the Shabbat law. They placed a man's life and health above the Shabbat, and in the man who is accomplished in the study of the Torah and practice of the *mitzvot*, in the *talmid hakham*, the *tsaddik* (the "scholar," the "righteous"), they saw the personification of the Shabbat: "the *talmid hakham*, the 'disciple of the sage,' is called Shabbat."[98]

For the Shabbat itself, though we enjoy it here on earth with all its delights, is only the prelude to the "Shabbat of the future world"; it is only the preparation for leaving behind the "working days" of the week, of the "finite" "present world," to gain the "long day" of the "infinite" "future world" of the eternal Shabbat.[100]

This is a unique religious concept; there is not even any adequate translation in other languages or other laws: "to watch over the soul," that is to say, to watch over man's life, man's health. "To watch over the soul!" For man is a man by virtue of his soul. But at the same time as being a spiritual principle, man must also be thought of in his psychic *and* physical totality: his soul is linked with his body; it is one *nefesh*. Man in his totality is, therefore, one *nefesh*, one "spiritual being."

It is quite characteristic that the principle of *pikkuah nefesh* is precisely that which finds its chief expression in the domain of Shabbat observance, to which it "runs counter"! The principle of *pikkuah nefesh* demonstrates the will to sanctify *time* as lived by man, even when it involves an apparent transgression of the laws regulating the sacred time of the Shabbat.

Shabbat observance and the precariousness of the "leisure civilization"

A Jew can only be sure of being able to respect and truly benefit from the Shabbat, both morally and physically, if he accepts and adopts it as the Torah requires: to observe Shabbat as the *Shabbat Hashem*, the "Sabbath of the Lord" (Exod. 16:25, 20:10, Lev. 23:2, Deut. 5:14), as *Kodesh LaHashem*, "consecrated to the Lord" (Exod. 31:15). Shabbat Observance is regulated by the Divinely revealed Law, *Torah Min Hashamayim*: a Shabbat law which harmonizes the hegemonic, supra-rationality of God and the autonomous rationality of man: *Hok UMishpat*.[101]

But if man looks on the Shabbat as a purely conventional, civil, useful institution and not as Divine, permanent, inalienable; if man trusts in his own intelligence or lets himself be ruled by his moods in judging the rightness and necessity of this institution; if he decides for himself what he may do and himself prescribes what he may *not* do on the Shabbat—then its observance is neither authentic nor effective. Even the most powerful and most intelligent of people will fail to enjoy a true

Shabbat rest if they do not respect its laws as permanent laws of a Divine nature. For "they will not be able to resist the temptation to indulge in leisure activities and make journeys on the day of rest."[102]

There is no *menuhah*, no real and true Shabbat "rest" unless we are ready to consider and to observe it as a *menuhah sheleimah*, "complete rest," "as God wills," "for our joy and our good."

The failure of the "leisure" civilization, that is to say of a civilization of "freedom" "to do whatever one wants, above all during one's free time," is due to the fact that the idea of rest — even if it is claimed to be of a "religious" nature — is not linked with the ordered, co-ordinated practice of Shabbat rest.[103]

The Shabbat and a weekly day of rest

"The nations of the world" have accepted only the *zakhor*, the remembrance of the day of rest (Exod. 20:8); they have adopted only the idea of the Shabbat. Yet while on the one hand they have accepted the idea of the Shabbat, on the other they have falsified its very principle, which is divine. Through the modifications they have brought into the institution of the Shabbat, by the fundamental changes they have introduced into its structure, they have removed from the "Biblical Shabbat" its pure, monotheistic character. In abandoning the Biblical day of rest, appointed by the Creator for all time, and themselves choosing a weekly day of rest, "the nations of the world" have not only erased its universal significance, but have also deprived it of its ethico-social character.[104]

The Jewish Shabbat and the Mesopotamian day of rest; the "delight of the Shabbat," and the sorrow of the *Shappatu*

The Jewish Shabbat is not like the days of rest appointed in an irregular and haphazard fashion by the ancient Mesopotamians.

The Jew consecrates the Shabbat to Him who created Nature and Who judges him to be capable of freeing himself from Nature's constraints. Moreover, the Creator considers man capable of imitating his God, permitting him in his turn to create, that is, to perfect the Divine work of creation with the ethical intention of doing good. He permits him also to cease from creation; that is, to rest, not to experience the pain of labor and not to need to work on the one day on which He Himself ended His work of Creation "and rested." For the Jew the Shabbat crowns an activity which is regarded as good, for his Creator, who is good, created with love so that "the benefits of His Goodness may be felt by His creatures";[105] Shabbat, therefore, is a source of blessing, sanctity, joy and love.

The Shabbat contrasts with the days which the Babylonians and Assyrians consecrated to Nature and to the astrological signs in which Nature is manifest: they did not dare to free themselves from this constraint. These peoples dedicated days of rest to "nature" gods, attempting thereby to win their favor and appease their anger. The Mesopotamians did no work on certain dates because they considered them unlucky and therefore dangerous; that is why on those *shappatu* days they not only avoided all work[106] but also all show of happiness. They spent the days of *shapptai*, those accursed days of rest, in sorrowing and fasting; allowing themselves no pleasure but only penitence and abstinence, for fear of increasing the wrath of the gods who were particularly prone to anger on those days.[107]

A quotation from the Midrash Tanhuma[108] can best illustrate the difference, and even more the contradiction, between the Jewish Shabbat and the Mesopotamian days of rest: "The Shabbat was given to Israel for blessing, pleasure and rest and not for grief!"

The Shabbat prayers contain no petitions

On the day when he observes the Shabbat in all its requirements, the Jew lacks nothing. For him "Shabbat is everything, is *hakol*."[109]

The prayers recited on the Shabbat, therefore, generally include no petitions.[110]

Trouble, sorrow, mourning, do not touch the Jew on Shabbat, on that day when all is light and joy in the world above and in the world here below;[111] on that day when everything is "love and gratitude," "goodwill" and "peace."[112]

The three Shabbat prayers and the three Shabbat meals

The first of the three prayer services is recited on Friday evening, at the commencement of Shabbat. It recalls the creation of the world. This is its theme: "*Atta kidashta*, You have hallowed the seventh day" (cf. Gen. 2:3) "and You have consecrated it to Your glory. It is this day which crowned the work of the creation of heaven and earth. You have blessed it above all days, and have hallowed it above all seasons, as it is written in Your Torah."

The second of the three central prayers is recited during *Shacharit*, the

Shabbat morning service. It recalls the revelation of the Torah on Sinai. These are the contents: "*Yisma'h Moshe*, Moses rejoiced at the gift of his portion,[115] for You named him Your faithful servant. You placed on his brow a splendid crown while he was before You on Mount Sinai, and He brought down the two tablets of stone on which the observance of the Shabbat was inscribed. And thus it is written in Your Torah."

The third of the three characteristic Shabbat prayers is recited on Shabbat afternoon, towards the end of the day. It recalls the messianic days when the unity of God and His name will be known. These are the contents: "*Atta Ehad*, You are One and Your Name is One.[116] 'Who is like Your people Israel, a single nation on the earth?'[117] You have given to Your people this day of rest and holiness as a symbol of glory and crown of salvation. Abraham rejoiced in this day, Isaac was full of happiness in it, Jacob and his sons celebrated it with rest, a rest granted in generous love, a true rest and one of faith, a rest of peace and tranquility, quietness and safety, a perfect rest such as You desire. Your children know their rest comes from You, and by their rest they sanctify Your name."

There is a fourth Shabbat prayer, which is recited during the *Mussaf* service which follows *Shacharit*. The three special Shabbat prayers concern events related to the *time* or duration of the Shabbat, and the fourth, "*Tikanta Shabbat*, You commanded the celebration of the Shabbat," refers to Shabbat worship celebrated in the *venue* of the Shabbat, the *area* of the Shabbat, the "*Beit Hamikdash*."

The Shabbat is one: its spiritual and material aspects make up the unity of the Shabbat![118]

Corresponding to the three Shabbat prayers are the three Shabbat meals, *shalosh seudot*: on Friday evening, at midday on Shabbat, and at the end of Shabbat.[119] These three "obligatory" meals are a part of the Shabbat programme; filled with the "taste" of the Shabbat, they become "meals of joy," "meals of faith," "holy meals"; they are a sign that the Jew participates with the whole of his being in the celebration of Shabbat.[120] The spiritual pleasure which comes to the Jew on the occasion of the three meals (reminding him of the Shabbat manna; cf. page 236), which are served and eaten in honor of the Shabbat, completes the spiritual joy he feels during the recital of the three Shabbat prayers. Each prayer is followed by a festive meal.

These three meals also recall the three Hebrew patriarchs, Abraham, Isaac and Jacob,[121] and have a basis in Exodus 16:15, which says, "Eat it (the manna) *today*, for *today* is the Shabbat in honor of the Lord; *today* you will not find any in the fields." The word *hayom*, "today" is repeated three times in one single verse (referring to the food for the Shabbat), and this led the Sages of Israel to build upon the Scriptures the Jew's "duty" to take three meals during Shabbat.[122] The word *hayom* refers to the three events of Shabbat time, recalled in the three central Shabbat prayers: *hayom*, the day of Creation;[123] *hayom*, the day of the revelation of the Torah;[124] and *hayom*, the day of the Messiah.[125]

Thus we can understand the importance attributed by the Sages of Israel to the three Shabbat meals, which—coming from the material world—are incorporated into the world of the spirit. These three Shabbat meals testify to the spirituality that envelops the human body itself with its desires and inclinations, on the Shabbat day; they demonstrate the raising of material things to the level of the spirit. They demonstrate the nature and vocation of the Shabbat itself: coming as it does from the supra-temporal world into the temporal world, it leads the latter to spiritual heights, to eternity, back to the source from which it itself comes.[126] Thus these three Shabbat meals, "prepared" "for (the sake of) the *mitzvah*, served and eaten in honor of God"—Creator, Lawgiver and Savior—are looked upon as "meals of the faith," "holy meals." The Shabbat table is therefore a table laid before God.[127] The very same Jew who, standing before God prays, and who, sitting before God, eats, becomes devoted to God, and so on the Shabbat day "returns to his source."[128]

There is a fourth Shabbat meal, taken on Saturday evening, after the Shabbat has terminated: *melaveh-malkah*. The Jew "accompanies the Shabbat queen," and recalls the prophet *Eliyahu*, the prophet of the Messiah, and King David, father of the Messiah. In this way the Jew, "having left the Shabbat" behind and on the point of "entering the week," demonstrates his unshakable faith that the spiritual messianic ideal, which has filled his soul during the Shabbat, will find a concrete, temporal realization.

By celebrating the Shabbat, man saves himself from settling into the materialist conditions brought about by continuous work

Rabbi Shemuel of Sochaczew makes this profound observation: " 'Everything that lasts less than seven days,' say our Sages, 'should be considered temporary.' That is why the Shabbat has been given to the Israelites to be celebrated once in every seven days so that there shall not be seven consecutive days of work; for that (an unbroken succession of 7 working days) might give the impression of being (something) permanent; now, six days only of work do not provide that impression of being permanent (appointed). (In observing the Shabbat, therefore, the

Jew is not settling into) the materialist condition which is brought about by (continuous) work."[129]

Shabbat, the day of knowledge

Through the strength and will that the knowledge of God gives us, we suspend our material activity during the Shabbat, but in exchange we increase our spiritual activity.[130]

The Shabbat is particularly the day of *da'at*, of "knowledge."[131]

It begins by illuminating us with the "light" of knowledge of *Kedushah*—sanctity; it ends by illuminating us with the "light" of the "knowledge of the *havdalah*"[132] The entire Shabbat is a day of knowledge which (when we deepen it) illumines for us the value of this Divine institution; it is a day of "knowledge" which "binds"[133] us to its Author, to Him Who "gives us the gift of knowledge," that is to say, the ability to "distinguish" one thing from another and even one value from another.

As a day of knowledge, the Shabbat brings us near to the source of holiness which is of God, Who says to us, "Observe My *Shabbatot* (not simply to do no work on those days, but) so that people may know—*LaDa'at*—that it is I, the Lord, Who sanctifies you," Who makes a distinction between you and others, by putting you to My service and thus to the service of My world, of all mankind.[134]

The *da'at* of the Shabbat reflects the *da'at* of Moses; God gave the gift of the Shabbat to him, on behalf of Israel, says the Talmud, "so that people may know—*LaDa'at*—that it is I, the Lord, who sanctifies you."[135]

The Shabbat *da'at* of Moses presages the Shabbat *da'at* of the Messiah.[136]

Word and Action: Word and Witness

A Jew should recite, "pronounce," the text of *Vayekhulu* (Gen. 2:1-3) audibly and standing, and in company. By reading aloud this Divine decree instituting the Shabbat, the Jew bears his human witness on this subject. He declares mankind's adherence to the respect for the Divine Shabbat; he "witnesses" to it solemnly, standing on his feet.[137]

In the Friday evening *Kiddush* in his own home, he again stands and recites the *Vayekhulu* as a witness to the Shabbat.[138] He says, *Omer: Vayekhulu*. He is thus emulating God, who "by the word"[139]—*Vayomer* (Gen. 1), created the world "without fatigue or trouble." In ceasing his human labor that is both troublesome and alienating, by reciting the *Vayekhulu*, the Jew himself becomes a "partner of God in the work of the first Creation" thanks to this verbal, spiritual act,[140] which shares the nature of the Divine word. Indeed, "the word is analogous to action," as it is written, "By the word of the Lord the heavens were formed."[141]

Speech: *Ma'amar* and *Dibbur*

Ba'Assara Ma'amarot Nivra HaOlam: "The world was created with Ten singular Injunctions" — *ma'amarot*.[142]

The Torah was revealed on Sinai in Ten "Statements" — *devarim, dibbrot*.[143]

What is the difference between *ma'amar* and *dibbur*? The *dibbur* links the speaker to his interlocutor, and the *ma'amar* is independent (for itself), for the *ma'amar* can be pronounced without being meant to be heard, although obviously it could be heard. This is the difference between *Assara Ma'amarot* and *Asseret HaDibrot*. The creation of the world was done by the *Ma'amar*, which is independent, which exists for itself alone; but the *Asseret HaDibrot* constitute the link between Israel and their Father in heaven.[144] The "*amirah* means the *ma'amar* in itself, and the *dibbur* shows the relation between him who speaks and his interlocutor."[145]

Nevertheless, according to the Sefat Emet, *amirah* means *hibbur*, "attachment," and according to B'nei Issachar, the "*amira* reveals the things of the heart."[146] Indeed in the Mishnah the expression *assa ba ma'amar* means the consecration of woman by man with "words" with marriage in view: this "word," this *amirah*, is both audible and silent, solemn and intimate.[147]

God is distant yet near: *Hu* and *Atta*, "He" and "Thou"; He and you

God Himself, as Creator, is distant; reigning in the world above, He is *Hu*, "Him," hidden;[148] and when He "reveals" Himself and allows man to draw Him down, when it pleases Him to be served by man, He becomes *Atta*, "Thou," quite close to him;[149] then He reigns in the world below.[150]

"*Lo ta'asseh kol melakha, atta*... The seventh day... thou shalt do no work, *atta*, thou..." (Exod. 20:10; Deut. 5:14). Ibn Ezra (*ad* Exod. 20:8) writes, "The word *atta* includes everyone who is included under the heading of 'a son of the *mitzvah*,' *benei mitzvah*."

God the Liberator, the Lawgiver, speaks to *atta*, the free man, who is able to obey Him, and commands him to respect the Shabbat.[151]

The Jew is a servant of God during the week and a son of God on the Shabbat

"To Israel, Your people, You have given the Shabbat, in Your love" (Shabbat morning prayer). " 'For it is a sign between Me and you.' It is a sign of great prestige between us, that I have chosen you, to give you as an inheritance, My day of rest, to make it your day of rest."[152]

God offers the Shabbat to His *firstborn*, to Israel, who serves Him with filial love and trusts in Him.[153]

During the days of the week, a Jew is "obliged" to serve His God. On the Shabbat he passes over from the obligatory status of "servant of God" to the freely-chosen status of "son of God."

On the Shabbat, a Jew is released from "showing" his "attachment" to God by the material reins of phylacteries (*Tefillin*) tied to his arm and his forehead on weekdays to demonstrate his acceptance of the "yoke of the Kingdom of Heaven." On the Shabbat, the "yoke of the Kingdom of Heaven" that the Jew accepts is entirely spiritual in nature; it is all made out of "love, good will and acts of charity."[154]

"See how much the *mitzvot* are loved, how gentle are the Divine commandments!"[155]

That which might be considered to be "the yoke of the *mitzvot*" during the week is thought of on the Shabbat as *ratson*, the free, loving, joyful wish, to fulfill. For the *mitzvah* accepted and fulfilled on the Shabbat is an *oneg*, a pleasure. Indeed on that day the soul of the Jew, by drawing upon the power of the supra-temporal Shabbat, in the Shabbat of the "world to come," is strengthened, "grows" in power, opens out, "expands" and increasingly irradiates his physical being, so that the soul helps the body itself to find in the *mitzvah* the springs of the *oneg*; the strengthened soul helps the "heart" to "taste," to understand the *oneg*. Now here below "there is no good thing which can surpass the *oneg*." And the authentic *oneg* here below, the Shabbat *oneg*, foretells the true *oneg*: that of the "world to come," of *Olam HaBa*, of the world which will come, which is already coming nearer.[156]

"The Holy One, blessed by He, gives man on the Shabbat eve a *neshamah yeterah*, a soul enriched," an addition to his own soul.[157]

Awe of the Shabbat and love of God

The "brain" registers the fear of God; the "heart" produces the love of God.[158]

Man's sense knows the fear of God; his sensibility commands him to love God.

The believing, practicing Jew always feels "the awe of the Shabbat,"[159] but this awe is not the fear of some external subject or object, such as the "fear of punishment"; it is an "inner fear," an "uplifting fear"—*Yirat HaRomemut*—raising him toward "Him who commands respect for the Shabbat."[160]

The Shabbat as a personal experience of the creative and providential revelation of God

"*Anokhi*, I am the Lord your God, Who brought you out of the land of Egypt, out of the house of bondage" (Exod. 20:2). It does not say, "I (am the Lord) who made the heavens and the earth and who made you."[161]

The man, the Israelite, to whom God is speaking, was not present at the creation of the world nor does he remember his own creation. Such a man, an Israelite, nevertheless had the privilege of having personally experienced the "creative" revelation of God in the miracles associated with the exodus from Egypt: "Israel *saw* the great power which the Lord had put forth against Egypt" (Exod. 14:31).[162] In every generation a man (a Jew) must see himself as if he himself had gone out of Egypt (so Mishna Pessahim 10:5; quoted in the Haggadah shel Pessah). That man, that Israelite, moreover enjoyed the privilege of having personally lived through the experience of the revelation of God's Torah on Sinai: he "*sees* the voices [thunderings] there" (Exod. 20:18; cf. Zohar II, 81a). Every day they should seem new in your eyes as though on that very day you were commanded regarding them.[163] The words *Sinai* and *Ayin* (eye) have the same numerical value: 130![164]

For the Israelite of the period after the exodus and the revelation at Sinai, the Shabbat which God the Creator communicates to him personally—solely in His role of a Personal God of *Hashgahah*, Providence—will be the first "great Shabbat," *Shabbat HaGadol*,[165] which will enable him to feel and to understand personally the creation of the world: he collaborates in that act, he confirms it. That act, which hitherto had preceded him in time, is now contemporaneous.[166] Henceforth, thanks to the Shabbat, he, the Israelite, has a direct relationship with the *Anokhi* who brought him out of the land of Egypt (Exod. 20:2), who concomitantly is the *Anokhi* who created the world.[167] According to Ramban, "the Shabbat is the remembrance of the exodus from Egypt and the exodus from Egypt is the remembrance of the Shabbat."[168] For the Kedushat Levi, "Pessah is Shabbat."[169]

That is why, following the exodus from Egypt and the revelation at Sinai, in parashat *Ki Tissa* (Exod. 34:18-22), the *mitzvah* to observe the

Shabbat is pointedly mentioned *after* the *mitzvah* to celebrate the feast of Pessah which commemorates the exodus from Egypt, and before the *mitzvah* of the celebration of the feast of Shavuot which commemorates the revelation on Sinai; the law concerning the Shabbat is placed between the laws concerning Pessah and Shavuot.

The Shabbat of the Covenant with Israel precedes the Shabbat of the Creation

"In future the children of Israel shall keep the Shabbat, observing it from generation to generation as a covenant forever. It is a perpetual sign between Me and the children of Israel showing that in six days the Lord made heaven and earth and on the seventh day he ceased work and rested" (Exod. 31:16-17).

The two Shabbatot, the *Shabbat Bereshit*, Shabbat of the Creation, and the Shabbat of the Covenant with Israel, the Shabbat of the Torah and the *mitzvot*, are inscribed in this fundamental text. However, in a manner that is so characteristic, the Shabbat of the Covenant precedes the *Shabbat Bereshit*, the Shabbat of the Creation!

The covenant of circumcision and the Shabbat

The patriarchs who proclaimed the oneness of God faithfully observed the Shabbat, which testified to the creation of the world by God.

Moreover, having received the *mitzvah*, the commandment of God to make a covenant with Him through circumcision (circumcision is considered a *berit*, a "covenant"), it was "natural" for the patriarchs as "Jews" to also consider the *mitzvah* of the Shabbat to be a *berit* like circumcision and on a par with it.[170]

The three patriarchs thus became the "three" great observers of the Shabbat; they taught respect for the Shabbat to their descendants who remained loyal to it even in the difficult conditions of slavery in Egypt.[171]

Manna, sign of the Shabbat

In a miraculous and visible way the manna (Exod. 16) substantiates the idea of the Shabbat: it convinces the Israelite of the reality of the Shabbat and therefore obliges him to accept its observance.[172] Moreover, manna is for the Israelite an invitation to have faith and trust in God as well as to exercise moderation in his desires and needs.[173] This invitation was not merely theoretical, but, like the "sweet waters" in the desert a short while before (cf. Exod. 15:25), it was a "test." "The Lord said to Moses, 'I will rain down bread from heaven for you. Each day the people shall go out to gather a day's supply so that I can test them to see whether they will obey my Torah or not'" (Exod, 16:4).

The test of the manna enabled the Israelite to show the strength of his faith and the depth of his trust in God, as well as the merit of his "deserts" which would make him worthy to receive Divine grace: a human test, corresponding to the Divine supra-natural, miraculous character of the Shabbat. For the Shabbat is a manifestation of the will of God, who can freely regulate the Nature He created, dispense the generous goodness of God who "foresees all that is necessary" and so good for man, with whom He deigns to enter into communication. In truth the Shabbat is a Divine institution; it is a Divine product.[174] Hitherto only the idea of the Shabbat had been revealed to the Israelites; from now on the Israelites were really to "see" the Shabbat, for they could see the gift made to them by God for the Shabbat. Hereafter this gift would serve as an immediate and future material sign of the total gift of the Shabbat, which they would "remember" and "keep" from "age to age."[175] "'*See*, the Lord has *given* you the Shabbat! That is why He will *give* you two days' food on every sixth day'.... And the people kept the Shabbat on the seventh day" (Exod. 16:29-30). The people *saw* the gift; they touched the manna. "'Each of you is to gather as much as he needs; let every man take one *omer* per head for every person in his tent' (according to the number of members in his family). The children of Israel did so. Then they measured it by the *omer*. Moses said to them, 'Let no one keep any of it till morning.' Some did not listen to Moses; they kept part of it till morning and it became full of maggots and stank."[176]

The manna which was a gift and an invitation became a gift and a limitation: a gift limited to what was strictly necessary to the needs of the day. The manna, a gift and an invitation, became a gift and an obligation: it obliged each to stand by his family, for it was only with them that he could find his "bread." The manna, a gift and an invitation, became a gift and a test: it forced man, living in the desert "from hand to mouth," in uncertainty, to put away cares for the morrow; it taught him to have faith in God: a faith, an *emunah*, which leads to trust, to *bitahon* in God.[177] The tangible, visible manna leads the Israelite to a tangible visible faith (in truth "faith," *emunah*, is "seen," *reiyah*; cf. Exod. 14:31). The exclamation of the Israelites when they saw the manna, *man hu*, "it is manna!" is transformed into a cry of faith: the letters which form the words *man hu* are the same as those which form the word *emunah*! And even if the Israelites conceived the words *man hu* as a question, "what is it?" this question, an expression of their astonishment, was quickly transformed into the affirmation of a certainty, a certainty of faith felt and experienced. Indeed, after "gathering (manna) for six days when some of the people went out on the seventh day to gather it, they found none!" (Exod. 16:26-27). In addition: when Moses challenged the Israelites saying, "See, the Lord has given you the Shabbat and therefore He gives you two days' provisions on the sixth day" (Exod. 16:29), the proof of the Shabbat was produced; it became explicit: the Shabbat comes from and belongs to the world of miracles; inserted into Nature, it goes beyond, surpasses and conquers[178] Nature. From then on it cannot be denied that the Shabbat expresses the will of God, who is Master of Nature, and that it manifests the goodness of God, who "foresees" all that is "naturally" good for man, for Israel. The Israelite, in accepting the proof of the Shabbat provided by the manna, bears witness to his faith, the foundation of which is the Shabbat.[179]

Having faith, the Israelite finds in the manna much more than what is strictly necessary for his physical needs: the manna is more than bodily nourishment. That fact that it is limited in quantity fades before its quality, which is boundless. Quality overrides quantity. And the quality consists in "blessing" and "holiness." For, to the Israelite who believes in the blessing and holiness of the Shabbat, manna brings "blessing" and "holiness."[180] Now all "that is blessing is a surplus," is abundance; and all "that is holiness is different":[181] it is uplifted. The Israelite who at the onset of the Shabbat has received an addition to his soul, his *tossefet*, his *neshamah yeterah*,[182] is able to discern the *tossefet*, the extra quality in the manna: he can detect in it a special *ta'am*, an extra "taste," an unsuspected richness of taste. And lo, the *ta'am*, the taste he discovers is to his liking, it is that which he is seeking, which he is expecting.[183] It is the *ta'am* of the Shabbat, of *his* Shabbat and of the special flavor of the Torah which goes with it. It is the *ta'am* of the Shabbat, both spiritual and material, the *ta'am* of the spiritual Torah and the material *mitzvah*.[184] This *ta'am* has been perpetuated, kept and transmitted by the manna (a food both spiritual and material); it has been "stored up for future generations" (cf. Exod. 16:32). The Jew who "enjoys the Shabbat" (*me'aneg et haShabbat*) and rejoices in the Shabbat finds this *ta'am* again in the *tavshil shel Shabbat*, the Shabbat dishes. It is the Shabbat that brings him this *ta'am*; it is personal and incommunicable like faith itself which is personal and incommunicable.[185] The *ta'am* of the *tavshil shel Shabbat* is new every time, "different," even as was the *ta'am* of the *lehem mishneh*, the taste of the "double portion of bread" on the day before Shabbat—the taste of the manna which was *meshuneh*, "different" every time.[186] The *tavshil shel Shabbat* is only a recollection, an extension of the manna, the "heavenly bread" (cf. Exod. 16:4), the "bread of the soul" which spiritualizes the Jew's body and penetrates his whole being.[187] It is therefore with justification that the Zohar calls the meal of the Jew who celebrates the Shabbat with faith and joy *Seudata DiMehemnuta*, the "banquet of faith," or *Seudata DeKudesha Berikh-Hu*, *Seudata DeMalka*, "the banquet of the Holy One, blessed be He," "the banquet of the King," whose guest is the Jew, *Shomer Shabbat KeHilkhato*.[188]

The gift of Shabbat came before the gift of the Torah

In reality, in expressing Himself through the Tetragrammaton, God gave Israel the Shabbat before giving them the Torah (cf. Shoheir Tov 92). The midrash observes that the Torah says, "See," and not "Know," that the Lord has given you the Shabbat: *natan lahem haShabbat*. It is the reason for His giving you, *noten lahem*, on the sixth day a supply of manna for two days.[189]

It is to this gift of the Shabbat, coming before the gift of the Torah, that the word *zakhor*, "remember," alludes in the version of the Decalogue in the Book of Exodus (20:8);[190] it is this same gift of the Shabbat, coming before the gift of the Torah, that is referred to in the words *ka'asher tsivkha*, "as (the Lord thy God) hath commanded thee" (the verb is in the past tense), in the version of the Decalogue in Deuteronomy (5:12).[191]

Thus God preceded the visible gift (in the spiritual sense) of the Shabbat with the visible gift of the manna (materially): God caused this gift of manna to pass "from His hand into Israel's hand!"[192] By its miraculous appearance and because the Israelites received a double portion on Shabbat eve, the manna convinced the Israelites of the Divine nature of the Shabbat. " 'See' with your own eyes that the Lord in His own glory is instructing you about the Shabbat, since on each Shabbat eve the miracle occurs by which you are given bread for two days."[193] The miracle of the manna "compels those who *see* it" to accept the Shabbat.[194] And this precious *gift* of the Shabbat was made by God to the Israelites *after* giving them the "law" of the Shabbat, so that they should know how to use it.[195]

The two *Shabbatot* which the Israelites celebrated before the promulgation of the Torah on Sinai exercised a strong edifying influence upon them; the Shabbatot made them able and worthy to receive the gift of the Torah at Sinai.[196]

The Shabbat makes Israel worthy to enter into a covenant with God at

Sinai,[197] just as the Shabbat makes the Jewish male child worthy to enter "into the covenant of Abraham" by circumcision on the eighth day after his birth, thus "after the Shabbat has passed over him":[198] "there is no circumcision without Shabbat: *ein milah belo Shabbat!*"[199]

Torah, Shabbat and Israel

"It was on the Shabbat day that the Torah was given to Israel."[200]

"The Shabbat belongs to Israel, for just as on the Shabbat day the world reached its completion, so Israel is the completion of the world. Hence Israel became a people on the Shabbat day, since the Torah which makes them a people was given them on that day. That is why the Community of Israel is considered the consort of the Shabbat."[201] These three factors, Torah, Shabbat and Israel, have descended from the supra-temporal world to accomplish their tasks and fulfill their "civilizing" activities in harmony in this temporal world. They take their place in this world temporarily but effectively, enriching it and brightening it with their presence, so as to be more deserving of their ultimate return to the supra-temporal world from which they came and to which they rightly belong. The *Shemirat Shabbat*, the "keeping of the Shabbat," thus has a double meaning: Israel observes the Shabbat and the Shabbat guards Israel. "God has given you the Shabbat so that you may keep it."[202]

"'Six days you shall labor, but on the seventh day you shall do no work. And you shall take care—*tishameru* (you shall be attentive to everything I have told you)' (Exod. 23:12-13). What is the exact meaning of the word *tishameru*, 'you shall take care'? The Torah should have said *tishmoru*, 'you shall keep.' But the expression *tishameru, vadai*, certainly, means you will be kept (protected) by the Shabbat!"[203]

The German Jewish philosopher Hermann Cohen (1842-1918) was to write with justification, "The Sabbath is the patron saint of the Jewish people."[204]

On the Shabbat the Torah was given to Israel;[205] by spiritualizing his material life on the Shabbat the Jew makes a Torah of that whole day.[206]

The Shelah HaKadosh teaches that for every Jewish soul there is the corresponding soul of a Shabbat and the corresponding soul of a letter of the Torah.[207]

The Shabbat of the individual and
the Shabbat of the community

"'For this is a sign between Me and you'; it is a sign of great prestige between us, that I have chosen you to give to you as an inheritance My day of rest for (making it your day of) rest. 'To know'—so that the nations may know—that it is I, the Lord, who sanctifies you—*mekadishkhem*."[208]

God *sanctifies* Israel by giving them the Shabbat. By this fact, respecting the Shabbat, Israel is able on its part to *sanctify* the Name of God, to proclaim the oneness of God, to announce the glory and the sovereignty of the Creator, to witness to the providence of the God of Israel and of all mankind.

People and nations ask, "Why do the Jews not work on the Shabbat?"[209] By their restraint, by respecting the Shabbat, Israel is therefore sanctifying the Name of God.[210]

Jewish respect for the Shabbat is characterized by two aspects: one personal, the other collective.[211] Consequently there is an internal, Jewish aspect and an external, universal aspect. Is this the meaning of the Biblical verse:[212] "The *children* of Israel will observe (individually)[213] the Shabbat, to make—*la'assot*—the Shabbat (collectively),"[214] to announce it to the world as a whole? This could be the significance of the Talmudic dictum,[215] "Were Israel to observe (only) two *Shabbatot* punctiliously—*meshamrin*—(the Shabbat in its two aspects), it would forthwith be relieved from suffering, it would promptly receive salvation, for it is stated,[216] 'Thus says the Lord (to those) who observe My Sabbaths—*Shabtotai* (in the plural)... And the sons of the stranger who have joined themselves to the Lord, all those who keep the Shabbat... I will lead them to My holy mountain.'" This is to say that, by making the idea of the Jewish Shabbat accepted by non-Jews, Israel will have accomplished its universal mission: to make God known as Creator and Sovereign of the world, to make the world alive to His Presence.

Indeed Israel lives for the service of God and thus of humanity. Its vocation is to enthrone God in this world and to raise the world towards God, to make men accept the justness of God's moral will and to ensure that the Divine "goal of creation" is accomplished. Israel assumes this task as guardian of the Shabbat.[217] When humanity appreciates the heritage of the Shabbat, sincerely and honestly, Israel will have accomplished its task and obtained its salvation.

The salvation of Israel thus confirms the salvation of humanity; and the salvation of humanity confirms that of Israel.

The consummation of the Divine Shabbat is the product of collaboration between God and Man

The Gaon Rabbi Yosef Ber of Volozhin (1820-1892) commented in a novel manner on the following verse (Genesis 2:3): "God blessed the seventh day and proclaimed it holy because on that day He rested from all His work which He had created so that it might be done—*la'assot*." In his Bet HaLevi he wrote, "All the work of the six days was then finished, but the creation of the seventh day will be done in the ages to come (in the Messianic times): *la'assot*. This is why the Torah requires that the children of Israel observe the Shabbat, to make—*la'assot*—the Shabbat" (cf. Exod. 31:16).²¹⁸

Although the Shabbat already serves as the foundation of the revelation of the glory of God, nevertheless the children of Israel, in observing the spirit and the *mitzvot* of the Shabbat, contribute to an even greater revelation of the glory of God until in the "ages to come" there will appear "the day which is entirely Shabbat." On that day, when "God will be One" (cf. Zech. 14:9) there will take place the inauguration of the Great Shabbat.

A similar idea (without reference, however, to the two verses from the Torah mentioned above) is expressed by the Tsaddik Rabbi Yehuda Arie Leib of Gur in his Sefat Emet (II, page 88):

"All the days were created before a single one of them dawned!" (Ps. 139:16). The Shabbat of the first week of creation, therefore, will find its own creation completed only on the Messianic Shabbat, "at the end of time." For "God blessed the seventh day... which He had created so that it might be completed: *la'assot*." This completion will be the result of collaboration between God and man. *La'assot* concerns both God and humanity.

The creation of the seventh day continues, therefore, throughout the duration of history, that is throughout the duration of the cooperation of God and humanity. It will reach its end when the Messianic Shabbat comes. Only then will the Shabbat have reached its full potential.²¹⁹

Each hour is irreplaceable

If one forgets just once to pronounce the "blessing" on one of the days of the *sefirah*, "the *seven* weeks" that are counted between the Feasts of Pessah and Shavuot (cf. Lev. 23:15-16), he no longer has the right to pronounce the "blessing" on the other days of the *Sefirat HaOmer*, "the counting of the Omer."²²⁰

Every day counts; it is irreplaceable: "forgotten," "neglected," it hinders the course of the days that follow.

Ve'im lo akhshav eimatai, said Hillel (1st century). "And if (I do it) not now, when (shall I do it)?"²²¹

Every hour it is incumbent upon a man to do a good deed, for he will be unable to do the same deed in any other hour.²²²

The days of the week are included in the Shabbat

The psalm which the believing Jew recites every day at the end of morning prayers is preceded by the affirmation: "Today is the first (second, etc.) day *in* the Shabbat."

The days of the week, therefore, are included in the Shabbat; they are concentrated, according to the Shelah HaKadosh, within the single "element" of the Shabbat, which is the root of all the days.[223]

The days of the week are called "days of Shabbat."[224] The weeks are called Shabbatot.[225] The principle of the festive days of Israel, which are seven in number corresponding to the days of the week, is virtually, and initially, contained in the very name of the Shabbat.[226]

Rabbi Abraham of Sochaczew wrote: "The Shabbat is the source of hallowed time and the festivals flow from the Shabbat. The Shabbat is the essence of holiness—*kodesh*; and a festival day is in turn a 'sacred meeting'—*mikra kodesh*."[227] This last idea had earlier been expressed by Rabbi Levi Yitshak of Berditshev, who justified it as follows: "The holiness of the Shabbat comes from God alone. That is why it is called *kodesh*; whereas the festivals are called *mikra'ei kodesh*, for Jews hallow the time by the *mitzvot* which they perform during the festivals."[228]

The source of their reflections on the *Shabbat kodesh* is found in the Zohar.[229]

The Shabbat, demarcated externally, is immeasurable in depth

A single unit (of time) for rest goes with six units for work. But this unit for rest, because it has its roots in a supra-temporal world, is greater in depth, in inner meaning, than the other six.[230] The Torah not only says, "Observe the day of the Shabbat," (Deut. 5:12), but also, "The children of Israel shall observe the Shabbat" (Exod. 31:16), where the latter word is not preceded by the word "day." Indeed the Shabbat, lived in depth, in its immeasurable inner significance, extends far beyond the length of one day. It comes from eternity and travels to eternity making ports of call in the world on the way; it is outside temporal things and at the same time assumes temporality, it establishes the link between "this world"—*Olam Hazeh*, and "the world to come"—*Olam HaBa*.

The Jew who observes the Shabbat in faith and joy prepares himself for "the world to come"; he sees in the Shabbat the model of the world to come and already tastes its flavor: *Me'Ein Olam HaBa*, says the Talmud. In this "flavor," in this *me'ein*, state the Hassidim, the Jew discovers the

Mayan Olam HaBa, "the source of the world to come." Indeed, *to'ameha hayim zakhu*, "Those who taste it have the privilege of tasting the flavor of life," of true life.[231]

The Shabbat, immeasurable in depth,[232] is defined externally;[233] it is called "law"[234] for it sets a limit to activities performed during the six weekdays; it invites man to be moderate. God Himself set the example; He is called *Shaddai*, for having allowing the world to expand for six days, He said "*dai* — enough!"[235] "He created the boundaries of the world,"[236] and is content with what He has done to attain His purpose.[237] The House of Jacob, kept within bounds on the Shabbat, becomes by this very fact the vast domain of the Shabbat *oneg*, the unbounded heritage of Shabbat joy.[238]

The Shabbat, a day of revelation and discovery

In Jewish mystical thought the Shabbat age which will end with the age of the Messianic Shabbat is regarded as a time of Divine "kingship:" *Shabbat behinat malkhut — malkhut Shaddai*.

During the Shabbat a man meditates on the consolidation of every good human activity, he "makes God his King" and "enthrones" Him, for he accepts His will during the days preceding the Shabbat by "introducing the Kingdom of heaven into the world of *assiya*, action"; thus he proclaims His Name.[239] And God for His part makes His Name known to man which man in turn will make known to the world. He causes man to understand that which he has been unable to understand before, that all His actions lead "to good." Thus God reveals Himself, in everything that He shapes with His Name: He reveals Himself both as He is and as He appears. He reveals Himself thus on the Shabbat, which is the day of the "unfolding" of the inner spirit — on the Messianic Shabbat day, which is the day of the "uncovering" of the mysteries.[240] Shabbat is thus a Day of "revelation" and "discovery," even in this world, "of the world to come," the *Olam HaBa*, that is, the world where man is able to understand the "thoughts" of God, to discover, to "see," the "ways" of God (and not, as in the past, only to "justify" them humbly).

The Shabbat offers to the Jew who is *shomer Shabbat* a foretaste of Eternity (*Me'ein Olam HaBa*), although he is still in the world of Time. In spite of his temporal nature, such a Jew is already quickened by the "breath of the Messiah" which permits him to exclaim in all conscience and consciousness: "In that day God will be King, He will be One and His Name will be One!" (cf. Zech. 14:9).[241]

The Shabbat: wholly day, wholly light

The mystery of the Shabbat will be revealed in the Messianic age, as it was in the first age of Creation, as a day which is entirely Day, entirely Light.[242]

As regards the seventh day of Creation, Genesis (chapter 1) does not say, as it does regarding the other days, "there was *evening* and there was morning," for the first Shabbat was wholly light.[243]

And as regards the Messianic day, the prophet Zechariah says, "It shall be all one day, whose coming is known only to the Lord, without distinction of day or night, and at evening-time there shall be light."[244]

The unity of the Shabbat

The Shabbat is one (a whole, a unit), for within itself, in its "interior" point, it contains all the days of the week.[245] "God completed (*va-yekhal*) on the seventh day the work which He had done, and He rested on the seventh day from *all* the work which He had done" (Gen. 2:2-3). He made "all His work" enter into (be contained in) the seventh day.[246]

The Shabbat is one (a whole, a unit) in this world of action, for in it all the *mitzvot* find their fulfillment—the *mitzvot asseh* (of action) and the *mitzvot lo ta'asseh* (of restraint)—symbolized by the two key words of the Shabbat: *zakhor* and *shamor*.[247]

The Shabbat is a unity in the cosmos, for it includes both the terrestrial Shabbat and the celestial Shabbat, which together form one entity and constitute a Sabbatical mystery.[248]

The Shabbat will yet reveal the peaceful harmony between the celestial world and the terrestrial, for it is essentially the harmonization of peace: Upon it the world will be established just as upon it the world was originally founded.[249]

In the Sabbatical, Messianic Age, the diversified world will return to its source and its unity

The world, which was one in its origin, became diversified over the course of the days of creation and even more so in the course of time. On the day of "Shabbat" the world returns—*shav*—to its root; it turns, inwardly, towards the One God: it is reunited.[250]

In the Sabbatical, Messianic times the world will return to its root, it will come back to God; but then it will return wholly, that is, it will also return outwardly: then it will become one. It will become one because humanity, and Israel in particular, will by its "unifying," ethical action, consecrated to the One God, by its act of *Yihud* in the world, contribute to the unification of the natural world and the ethical world, the material and the spiritual worlds, into one single world consecrated to the One God.[251]

By the number seven the Creation, the Torah, Israel and the Shabbat are bound to one another

The first verse of the Book of Genesis contains seven words, corresponding to the seven days of Creation.[252] The very beginning of the Torah thus hints at the purpose of the Creation: the Shabbat in the broadest sense of the term. Six days of the week find their crowning in the Shabbat; six years end in the sabbatical year *shemittah*; seven *shemittot* lead to the Jubilee year, *yovel*.[253] During the Shabbat, seven men are called to recite their blessings before the *Sefer Torah*. These seven Jews called before the Torah (into which "God looked when He created the world") correspond to the seven days of the creation of the world and the seven *"kolot,"* voices of God which were heard when the Torah was revealed at Sinai.[254]

The first verse of the Book of Genesis contains seven words, and the verse which introduces the Decalogue—the quintessence of the Torah—revealed on Sinai, also contains seven words (Exod. 20:1).[255]

The verse of the Ten Commandments (Exod. 20) which ordains respect for the Shabbat, the seventh day of the week, is the seventh verse of the Decalogue (Exod. 20:80). This verse begins with the letter *Zayin*, the numerical equivalent of which is seven: "*Zakhor*—remember the day of rest—the Shabbat—to keep it holy... That day you shall do no work, neither you, nor your son nor your daughter, nor your manservant or maidservant, neither your cattle, nor the stranger within your gates" (Exod. 20:8-10). This prohibition concerns seven categories of people. And seven categories of *Menuhah*, of "rest," are listed in the prayer of *Atta Ehad*, which a Jew recites in the *Minhah* service, on Shabbat afternoon.[256]

The significance of the number seven in the history of the world and the history of Israel

The Midrash affirms, "All 'sevenths' are beloved (by God). Of all the heavens, the seventh heaven, *Aravot*;[257] of all the lands, the seventh, *Tevel*;[258] of all the generations, that of Hanokh, the seventh;[259] of all the patriarchs, the seventh, Moses;[260] of all the sons, the seventh, David;[261] of all the years, the seventh, the sabbatical year;[262] of all the sabbatical years, the seventh, the Jubilee;[263] of all the days, the seventh, the Shabbat;[264] of all the months, the seventh, Tishri, the month of the great festivals.[265],[266] God "loves" and "blesses" the seventh: it is both "foundation" and "outcome";[267] for the seventh is the "soul," the "center," the "inner life" of all that exists, of every being: it is the *tsaddik*, the "righteous."[268] "Everything depends on the number seven."[269]

God has "selected"[270] the number seven out of all the other numbers. While it is *nivdal*, "distinguished," "apart," this number "seven," represented by the figure *zayin*, is by its very shape "open" to everything; "being open on all sides" it speaks to everyone, it is ready to offer its *mazon*, its spiritual "nourishment" to everyone.[271] God has selected the number seven and promoted it above all the other numbers; He has appointed it for a particular and universal task: He has called it to bring together the "six corners," the "six extremities"[272] of the other six days, the days of work, and to unite them under its aegis. He has called upon it to "influence" the other numbers, to "hallow" them with its own loving "holiness."

God has chosen the number seven to signify the relation which must exist between the world of Nature—seven heavens,[273] seven planets,[274] seven seas,[275] seven continents[276]—and the world of the Torah: the seven voices that were heard during the revelation of the Torah which occurred on the seventh day of the week,[277] on Sinai;[278] the seven branches of the candelabra, the *Menorah*,[279] radiating the light of the Torah.

God chose the number seven to signify the relation which must exist between the world of Nature set on seven foundations[280] and the world above Nature, divided into seven regions, having seven *heikhalot*, seven "palaces."[281]

God chose the number seven to be a sign of the relation which must exist between the world of Nature, established on seven principles pronounced before it was created,[282] and the world of Nature's intelligence, which grows according to the seven principles of wisdom.[283]

God chose the number seven to signify the relation which must exist between the world of Nature, of space supported by seven columns, and the world of ethics, of history,[284] of time, supported by seven *tsaddikim*,[285] by seven "righteous men," by seven shepherds,[286] by seven generations, seven fathers,[287] seven sons,[288] seven prophets, seven prophetesses.[289]

God chose the number seven to be a sign of the relation which must exist between the world of Nature in its kind and the world of miracles in its kind, the seven clouds of the glory of God.[290]

God chose the number seven to mark the relation which must exist between the world of Nature in its entirety, in its outward aspect marked by the seven seas which surround it, and the world of Nature in its essence, in its inward aspect, the Land of Israel surrounded by seven "seas";[291] the Land of Israel composed of seven countries which are linked to the seven countries of the "Land of Life" in heaven above;[292] the Land which Israel redeemed from the sins of the "seven nations"[293] who were occupying it, these seven nations representing a symbolic "tenth part" of the "seventy nations of the world"; the Land of Israel which is characterized by "seven species"[294] of natural vegetative bounty of which the Jews consecrate the "first fruits," *bikkurim*, which entail seven *mitzvot*,[295] and which they consume according to the norms laid down in the Torah as part of their duty to God, Proprietor of this Land.

God has chosen the number seven which He loves and hallows; and that is why He has multiplied it by the number of "holiness," which is ten.[296] He has made the number seventy, "tree of life," the meeting point between the life of man, whose life span is seventy years,[297] and the life of Israel, the people whose original quintessence was in the "seventy souls" who went with Jacob to Egypt.[298] He has made the number seventy the meeting point between the life of the people of Israel, represented by the seventy Elders, *zekeinim*, the "eyes of the community,"[299] and the life of humanity represented by the "seventy nations of the world,"[300] constituting the whole of the "families of the earth." He has made the number seventy the meeting point between the life of the Torah in the holy tongue, with "seventy faces"[301] and the life of humanity, consisting of seventy principal nations, speaking seventy principal languages.[302] He has made the number seventy the meeting point between the cosmos consisting of seventy principal worlds[303] and the Tabernacle, the Israelite sanctuary which has seventy columns around its court.[304] He has made the number seventy the meeting point between the cosmos,[305] man, Israel, humanity, whose life is governed by the number seventy[306] and Himself, Whose Presence among them, the *Shekhinah*, is manifested by His seventy names.[307]

All are linked to Him and to His "holiness" through the Jewish "sanctification" of the Shabbat: the Shabbat *kiddush* has "seventy words,"[308] representing the "seven crowns" which "ornament" the "Sabbath day."[309] The "Shabbat Day" is the "Day of Return." The Messianic "Day of the Great Shabbat" is the "Day of the Great Return." The "seventy souls" who "went down" into exile in Egypt, "went up," "returned" to the Promised Land. After seventy years of "captivity," of exile in Babylon, the Jews began their "Return to Zion."[310] After seventy major units of time, humanity will celebrate with Israel the Day of Return of the spiritual Dispersion, the moral Exile; it will come back to God; it will "go up to Zion," "climb the hill of the Lord." In the name of a humanity reconciled with God and itself, Israel will hold the Great Year of Jubilee, the Great Day of Return, after "seventy years of pre-Messianic suffering," *Hevlei Mashiah*, after "seventy years of Messianic days," *Yemot HaMashiah*.[311]

God has chosen the number seven to introduce eternity into the world of time, which is arranged in seven categories: Jubilee, sabbatical year, year, month, week, day, hour.[312] The seventh day is the Shabbat; the seventh week "after the Shabbat" which is Pessah, after the feast of physical liberation, ends with Shavuot, the feast of spiritual liberation; the seventh month of the year is Tishri, the month of the great festivals; there are seven Jewish festivals each year.[313]

God chose the number seven and He multiplied it by itself. After six days and six years of labor, of sanctifying activity and co-operation with the Creator, He allowed man, the Israelite, to reach the seventh day—which is the Shabbat Day, the holy day, "Shabbat of God" —and the seventh year—which is the sabbatical year, the "Shabbat of God."[314] He then multiplied the seven years of the sabbatical year, the *shemittah*, by seven, allowing man, the Israelite and the people of Israel, after forty-nine years of sanctifying their lives before God, to reach the special "sanctification" of the fiftieth year, which God ordains, just as He did in the case of the first Shabbat[315] as a "holy year," a year of "return."[316] This return is that of man to God and man to himself; he can then consider what is true in himself and pause where he has the right to pause. Thus the year of *Yovel*, the "jubilee year," is the year of "freedom" for man who allies himself once more with God, and also the year of equality between men, for they find themselves standing before God; it is the year that prefigures the time of Messianic "freedom." God multiplies one "Day of God," one "millennium"[317] by seven, permitting man finally to reach—after 6,000 years of more or less fruitful collaboration with Him—the seventh millennium, the "Day which is wholly Sabbath," the "Day which is wholly good." At this millennium (according to commentators on the Talmud and mystical texts)[318] everything that is ephemeral and uncertain will be transformed into "desert" or (according to other interpreters of the same basic and often contradictory texts)[319] will be looked on as "barren," and everything that is enduring and good, will be "renewed" so as to continue to exist and develop on "a higher level."[320] Then He will multiply the seven millennia by seven millennia, allowing humanity to act and to blossom under His eyes and so to reach the fiftieth millennium, which is the millennium of

Completion. This opens into the Gate of Wisdom, beyond which man will be able to see and understand "a little" of what he could neither see nor understand before.[321] The *Olam HaBa*, the "world to come," the "world which is coming," the possibility of which is perceived on earth by the "keepers of the Shabbat" on the day of Shabbat, but which is only completely realized beyond this world, will be wholly completed on earth at that *Shabbat HaGadol*, that Great Shabbat of the fiftieth millennium, at that *Yovel HaGadol*, that Great Jubilee of the fiftieth millennium. The world then will be wholly (but not definitively) spiritualized; the world will have become Torah.[322]

To reach that millennium, the "road" is "straight"[323] though difficult; nevertheless it is open to all men. The way is full of dangers; it is full of mysteries; "it is like a narrow bridge." However, the means to overcome the dangers of the journey and its anxieties, and the key that allows one to unravel the mysteries, are given in the number seven. "All the mysteries and all holy (things): all are based on the number seven, and the supreme seven is the 'world to come,'" states the Zohar.[324] To attain it, man is called upon to collaborate with his Creator, taking into account the fact that upon the "fluid" economy of this figure of plenty, seven, God has "founded" the "stability" of the world. He has, however, left man the possibility of making the world evolve, under His eye. He has given man the "freedom" to forge, under His eye, the history of this world, for the evolution of which He has "made provision"; and which will, nevertheless, take place within the bounds of this number of realization, seven. He has allowed man and the world to move towards Himself. He has made man and the world feel nostalgia for a "return" to their source. By his "merits" man can "hasten" this return.[325] However, God has reserved for Himself the ultimate date when He will act, by His grace and by His will, in order to bring about this return and in order that man's destiny and that of the universe may be fulfilled — when the time-limit He has assigned to the number seven will expire.

The life of the individual Jew, that of the people of Israel and the Land of Israel, of humanity and the earth, of the life of the whole cosmos, thus constitute a process which flows from the number seven: it is a symbol of the "source" of all existence and the beginning of all progression; it is a symbol of becoming which, after arriving at its conclusion, sets in motion a new beginning of being, a new start of becoming.[326]

Within this septenary process, both repetitive and new, successive and inventive, cyclical and original, one can observe high and low points, successes and reverses. This living dynamic is that of freedom; this selective play is that of freedom; this loving contest is that of freedom.

Within this septenary process (but neither at the beginning nor at the end) of progressive fulfillment, nothing is determined. While "everything has been foreseen," everything is also "free,"[327] while everything is linear, nothing is regular, nothing is simple, nothing goes forward without hindrances. For everything is free and man's freedom lies in his power to take initiatives—within the limits of his capacities and the means at his disposal; furthermore he can take the initiative in order to respond to those initiatives, those "lightning flashes" that come from above and which are intended for him. Everything is free: it must be so because the type of process in which man finds himself "enclosed" is ethical and quasi-historical. Man cannot be other than free, cannot act other than in freedom, which, it is true, is relative but is nevertheless a very considerable force.

To enable this dynamic of ethical, historical liberty to unfold and to be fulfilled, the number seven of blessing, of acting with love, of joy,[328] of justice, of uprightness and of absoluteness, collides with the "opposite side" of the same number,[329] that of cursing,[330] of destruction and sorrow,[331] of vanity and negativeness. In the former, the seven verses of the work of Creation, it is written "that it was good";[332] the seven blessings, *Sheva Berakhot*, consecrate the right and duty of Jewish couples to procreate.[333] In the latter, the seven vanities of the world are opposed to the seven days of Creation.[334] However, their antagonism too engenders life,[335] it causes the dynamic of life, and, in particular, ethical, historical life. Indeed from their confrontation there arises the creative unity, which moves towards the only unity absolute in itself, that of God. The unity of human activity, of human existence is, however, the result of a reconciliation, or conciliation, of contradictory impulses, ideas and forces. From the confrontation of the "seven good qualities" of humans, *middot tovot*,[336] the seven good gifts of the "Sage"[337] [which allow him to fulfill the commandments of God, such as the seven basic *mitzvot*, *Sheva Mitzvot DiB'nei Noah*,[338] eminently universal in character, or the seven *Mitzvot DeRabbanan*,[339] specially Jewish in character] with the seven bad human qualities of the "fool"[340] (which lead him to commit seven serious violations of God's edicts, *Shiv'a Gufei Avera*,[341] which drive him to perpetrate "seven abominations," *Sheva To'evot*,[342] recalling the seven synonyms for the inclination to evildoing, the *Yetzer HaRa*[343]) flows man's search for his unity, the unity of his activities and existence, for unity itself. This unity is attributable to the sublimation, the "raising up" of the seven "natural" *middot* commanded by the "seven planets" and the concretization, the "descent" of the seven "spiritual" *middot* recommended by the "seven heavens." This is a fluid unity; thus it is a state of equilibrium which is not definitive; it is a state of perfection but not final; it is a state of repose but not static. For if it were definitive, final and static it would annihilate the ethical, historical reason for existence, the meaning of life itself.

On the personal level this unity distinguishes the seventh day, which is a day of "fulfillment" after the six days of preparatory action, and the seventieth year and the years that follow it, which is a year of "enjoyment"[344] here on earth and on high, after the six preparatory units of time.[345] On the level of the individual and the communal, the universal and the cosmic, the natural and the supernatural, this unity distinguishes the Sabbath Day, every week, every seven years, every fifty years, every seventh millennium and the fiftieth millennium, or the Day of the Shabbat on high: the Day which is Day alone,[346] after six nights and days, after all the nights and days. This unity won with great struggles in the fight for the personal and the common good, harshly but also joyfully tested in the ordeal of altruistic, missionary action—marks the fusion of this last unity with the primeval, given unity. The last unity, which has been acquired, exceeds in value the first unity which, though perfect, was nevertheless given as a gift. By the unity which has been won, Messianic man comes level with the first man. But the Messiah is far superior to Adam, for he has the merit of active movement, and of victory after the fight; he has the merit of "purification,"[347] of self-purification: he has the merit of having been refined.

When Messianic man comes close to the consummation of the number seven, he pursues with ever greater intensity his work of refining (a sevenfold refinement);[348] of sublimation, of self-conquest, by deepening his self-knowledge, making himself open to others, cooperating patiently and confidently with his Great Partner. In this work Divine Grace is certainly decisive but not determinant. The ultimate unity of the number seven, that is, of *shleimut*,[349] of near-absolute perfection,[350] is a unity of *shalom*,[351] of peace which is being perfected. It is creative, prophetic, it foretells the establishing of *malkhut*, the kingship of God. This kingship, though it is a desirable fulfillment—that is, "when all the potentials and all the directives are sent into action"—is yet, above all, another *assiyah*, a developing "action," implying the beginning, inauguration, renewal of action; it constitutes a halt, prior to a fresh start.[352]

The *Ahrit HaYamim*, the "end of days," so much "hoped for," so "long awaited," will in reality be the beginning of "other days" (*Ahrit-aher*), of other, better days, always better.[353] The Presence of God, the *Shekhinah*, will be felt and experienced by men. For they will have succeeded, like the seven *tsaddikim* from Abraham to Moses, in bringing down the *Shekhinah* from the seven heavens to which It withdrew after each of the seven sins committed by man, each time to a more distant heaven.³⁵⁴ Once more the *Shekhinah* will be here on earth among men, as It "wishes" to be and as It was before Adam sinned: *Ikar Shekhinah BaTahtonim.*

When the *Yihud*, the Divine unification, the unification of the worlds, has been accomplished through man's religious, ethical and historical action, total unity will be re-established. In unity man, humanity and in particular Israel, "the people who sanctify the seventh," will celebrate the absolute unity of God. This will be revealed thanks to man's *assiyah*. The *shevuah*, the "oath" which God made not to abandon man,³⁵⁵ Israel, and the oath which Israel made at the foot of Mount Sinai (the day of *Shevuot*-Shavuot) to be faithful to God—*shevuah* having its roots in *shiv'a*, the number "seven,"³⁵⁶ in the primeval principle of subsistence and permanence—will have been accomplished. The Sabbatical, Messianic *shiv'a* indicates *kol*, the "whole,"³⁵⁷ the fullness. But this "whole" can always be more complete; this fullness can always be more full.

The unity of God is celebrated in prayer,³⁵⁸ for it is itself the outcome of the Shabbat prayer, which rests upon the principle of the number seven: it contains "seven prayers," *tefilat sheva*,³⁵⁹ and leads through these seven blessings to the "unity of blessings," the "source of blessings," *Me'Ein Sheva, Me'Ein HaBerakhot—Mayanei HaBerakhot*.³⁶⁰ The prayer celebrating God's unity is also a Shabbat prayer because of its content, for it is a prayer of satisfaction and so of thanksgiving (in the Messianic age none other than thanksgiving prayers—*hoda'a*—and thanksgiving worship—*toda*—will be employed³⁶¹). It expresses the *sheva hoda'ot*, the "seven thanksgivings," the "seven praises"³⁶² which man must give to his God: man is grateful to His Creator for the "seven blessings"³⁶³ which He granted to his soul when He placed it in his body and charged it with its earthly mission. The "seven thanksgivings," having become Messianic thanksgivings, are celebrated under "seven *huppot*," under "seven nuptial canopies,"³⁶⁴ symbolizing a procreative life beginning³⁶⁵ in a joyful union, one full of trust and confidence between God and man.

Thus the *geulah*, "deliverance" is realized, "salvation" is obtained. The *geulah* will consist of *sheva geulot*, "seven deliverances"³⁶⁶ like the seven miraculous deliverances by which God blessed His people Israel when they left Egypt. The deliverance of Israel from bondage in Egypt is celebrated by God and Israel³⁶⁷ especially during the seven days of the feast of Pessah. The Messianic union between God and Israel will be especially celebrated by the Creator and His people, the King of Israel and the people of Israel, during the "Seven Days" of joy, like the *Shiv'at Yemei HaMishteh* which the bride and bridegroom celebrate when they have been declared husband and wife.[368]

The number seven thus joins for all eternity the Creator and His Creation, God and His people: and the hyphen uniting them, is the holy Shabbat.

References, sources, and notes

ABBREVIATIONS

TB	Babylonian Talmud (Bavli)
TY	Jerusalem Talmud (Yerushalmi)
Gen.R.	Midrash Genesis Rabbah
R.	Rabbi, Rav
Rambam	Mishneh Torah (=Yad HaHazakah) by R. Moses ben Maimon (Maimonides), Hilkhot...

Preliminary Remarks

The essays in this volume were originally conceived and committed to writing without notes. In the course of time, however, as they were presented in various courses and gatherings, and as they appeared in written form in various journals and collections of lectures, with later reflection it became increasingly apparent that references to the traditional sources were necessary; and they were duly added.

A number of these sources, particularly the writings and thoughts of the Maharal, Shelah HaKadosh, Sefat Emet, Avnei Nezer, and Rav Kook, have cumulatively made us aware of a convergence between our own humble thinking and that of our revered masters — a convergence which sometimes amounts even to a similarity in the way ideas are formulated.

The sources referred to are to be found in all the "chambers" of the vast "palace" of the Torah. They represent all the domains of Jewish spiritual creativity that constitute the great, wide-ranging heritage of almost 4,000 years of vital, dynamic Judaism. These domains are both varied and complementary, embodying down the ages the sacred Hebrew Scriptures, Talmud, Midrash, Halakhah, Aggadah, Rabbinic literature, Jewish mysticism and philosophy, ethics, jurisprudence, exegesis, homiletical writings, hasidic thought, and mussar.

To faciliate use of the notes, we have adopted the concise method used by the schools of the Gaon of Vilna and the Gaon of Rogatshov. The references and sources are not limited to providing the reader with the "scholarly bases" for the texts to which they refer; they are also intended, by allusion and association, to suggest to the knowlegeable reader an explanation of many questions in Jewish law and thinking and to draw attention to views opposing those arguments which the references defend; and, as well, to open up lines of thought to kindred arguments which the references support or suggest.

Preface

1. Cf. Sefer Yetsirah III, 6; IV, 1. Zohar II, 47a; III, 221b. *Sefer HaZohar Im Perush HaSulam* V, Vayakhel, p. 60. Sifra DiTseniuta, Im Biur HaGra, *Likkutei HaGra*, p. 78. Shir HaShirim R. 5. Pirkei DeRabbi Eliezer 18. Shoher Tov, 92:2. Yalkut Shim'oni, Tehillim 139:888. *Kuzari*, III, 5. Rabbeinu Bahya on Exod. 20:8, pp. 197-98. *Perushei Maharal MiPrag LeAggadot HaShas*, II, Shabbat 118b, p. 97. Shelah, I, p. 26a. Maharsha, *Hiddushei Aggadot*, Yoma 2a; Beitsa 16a. Rabbi Eliyahu, the Gaon of Vilna, *Aderet Eliyahu*, pp. 322, 340. Rabbi Dov Baer of Mezerich, *Maggid Devarav LeYa'akov*, 20, pp. 32-33; 86, p. 149. Rabbi Nahman of Bratslav, *Likkutei Moharan*, V, 2, p. 5a; *Siddur Sha'arei Ratson*, p. 480. Rabbi Tsevi Elimelech of Dynow, *Bnei Issakhar*, I, pp. 22a, 23b. Rabbi Abraham of Slonim, *Yessod HaAvodah*, II, p. 83; *Be'er Avraham*, pp. 203-4, 215. Rabbi Abraham of Slonim, *Bet Avraham*, pp. 102, 108, 109, 146, 152. Rabbi Avraham of Sochaczew, *Avnei Nezer*, p. 125; *Neot HaDesheh*, pp. 2, 120, 136, 141. Rabbi Shemuel of Sochaczew, *Shem MiShemuel, Bereshit* I, p. 5; *Bereshit* II, p. 223; *Shemot* II, pp. 225, 246; *VaYikra*, pp. 351, 354; *Bemidbar*, pp. 347-48; *Devarim*, pp. 90, 176; *Moadim*, p. 111. Rabbi Yehuda Aryeh Leib of Gur, *Sefat Emet*, I, pp. 6, 9, 10, 81, 222, 229, 246, 247; II, pp. 79, 210; III, pp. 197-98; IV, pp. 61, 174. Rabbi Meir Simha Kohen of Dvinsk, *Meshekh Hokhmah*, pp. 147-48. Rav Kook, *Orot HaKodesh*, II, p. 303.

PART ONE

Chapter One

1. Cf. Zohar II, 90b; III, 7b; 23b; 252a. Tikkunei HaZohar, 1b; 21b; 40a. Shir HaShirim R. 1:11. See also Gen. R. 74:8; Shir HaShirim R. 4:6; Rashi on Ta'anit 8b. Cf. Ramban on Gen. 24:1. Shelah, I, p. 21b. Rabbi Eliyahu, Gaon of Vilna, *HaGra, Biur HaRa'ayah Mehemnah*, p. 35 (III, Behar 29b). *Tanya, Likkutei Amarim*, 19, p. 48; 37, p. 98; 41, p. 114. Rabbi Hayyim of Volozhin, *Nefesh HaHayyim*, I, 17, p. 17. Rabbi Shemuel of Sochaczew, *Shem MiShemuel, Devarim*, p. 210. Rabbi Yossef Hayyim of Baghdad, *Ben Ish Hai, Da'at UTevunah*, p. 72b. See also Rabbi Ya'akov Emden, *Siddur Bet Ya'akov*, I, p. 83.

2. Cf. Zohar I, 31b. Rabbi Yehuda Aryeh Leib of Gur, *Sefat Emet*, I, p. 49; II, pp. 94, 109; IV, p. 5. Rabbi Yossef Hayyim of Baghdad, *Ben Ish Hai*, pp. 132-33.

3. Cf. Hakdamat Sefer HaZohar, I, 13a; 14a. Zohar I, 25a; 47a; 97a; II, 138a; III, 7b; 12a; 26a; 29b; 170a; 218b; 219a. Zohar Hadash, Bereshit 6:4, 10:4; Balak 56:4. Hakdamat Tikkunei HaZohar 1:1. Tikkunei HaZohar, 22 (65b); 70 (138a). *Sefer HaZohar Im Perush HaSulam*, I, p. 5. *Sefer HaZohar*, HaRav Reuven Margaliot, ed., III, p. 339. HaRav Reuven Margaliot, *Sha'arei Zohar*,

p. 264. See also TB Shabbat 152b. Rashi on Hullin 91a. Targum Yonathan on Gen. 28:12. Cf. Gen. R. 68:18, 78:6. Pesikta Zutarta, Vayeitsei. Ibn Ezra on Deut. 32:8. Ramban on Gen. 2:7 and on Deut. 32:7. Recanati, Bereshit 7:2. Alshekh on Lekh Lekha and Nitsavim. Rabbi Hayyim Vital, Sha'arei HaKedushah, III. Shelah, III, 164b. Maharal, Be'er HaGolah, 3, p. 19a; Netsah Yisrael, 7, 11, Derekh Hayyim, p. 7; Perushei Maharal MiPrag LeAggadot HaShas, IV, Yevamot 63a, p. 27; Tiferet Yisrael, 1, pp. 4b-5a; 19, p. 21b; 24, p. 20b; Gevurot HaShem, 47, p. 115; 67, p. 193. R. Eliyahu of Vilna, Aderet Eliyahu, p. 16; p. 515 (Be'er Yitshak); Biurei HaGra Al Aggadot, II, Likkutei HaGra, p. 85; Sifra DiTseniuta Im Biur HaGra, 3, p. 28; 4, p. 32. Rabbi Hayyim of Volozhin, Nefesh HaHayyim, 1:5, p. 9; 1:17, p. 17; 2:17, pp. 27a-b; Ruah Hayyim, Avot VI, 3, p. 96. Tanya, Likkutei Amarim, 2, p. 6a; 19, p. 48; 37, p. 98. Iggeret HaKodesh, 7, pp. 111-12. Rabbi Nahman of Bratslav, Likkutei Moharan, 14:3, p. 19a. Rabbi Zevi Elimelech of Dynow, Bnei Issakhar, I, p. 112a; Haggadah Shel Pessah, p. 25. Rabbi Hayyim Atar, Or HaHayyim on Nitsavim, Deut. 29:17. Rabbi Abraham of Slonim, Yessod HaAvodah, p. 253, Be'er Avraham, p. 49. Rabbi Abraham of Sochaczew, Neot HaDesheh, p. 152. Rabbi Yehuda Aryeh Leib of Gur, Sefat Emet, V, pp. 36, 130, 182. Rabbi Meir Simha Kohen of Dvinsk, Meshekh Hokhmah, p. 28. Rav Kook, Olat Reiyah, II, p. 326; Orot HaKodesh, III, p. 68. Rabbi David Kohen, Kol HaNevuah, p. 68. Rabbi Yossef Hayyim of Baghdad, Ben Ish Hai, p. 27. Rabbi Eliyahu Lapian, Lev Eliyahu, pp. 138-39. Siddur HaGeonim VeHaMekubalim, III, pp. 780-81. Rabbi Yehuda HaLevi Ashlag, Matan Torah, pp. 129-30.

4. Cf. TB Berakhot 30a; Rambam, Hilkhot Teshuvah, III, 11. Rabbi Yehuda Aryeh Leib of Gur, Sefat Emet, III, p. 158; V, p. 131. Rabbi Abraham of Sochaczew, Avnei Nezer, p. 70. Rav Kook, Orot, pp. 74, 146; Orot HaKodesh, III, pp. 201, 319-20; Orot HaTeshuvah, p. 81; Olat Reiyah, I, p. 297; II, p. 2. Rabbi Baruch HaLevi Epstein, Barukh SheAmar, Avot, pp. 14-15. Rabbi Bezalel Ze'ev Safran, She'eilot UTeshuvot Harbaz, I, p. 267.
5. Cf. Gen. R. 30:11; Exod. R. 15:18; Yalkut Shim'oni, Noah 3; Rashi on Noah, Gen. 6:9. Kli Yakar on Vayelekh, Deut. 31:6. Rabbi Naftali Tsevi Yehuda Berlin, "The Netsiv," Ha'amek Davar, I, Vayehi, Gen. 48:15, p. 181.
6. Cf. Mishnah Sanhedrin X, 1 and Rambam ad loc.; TB Sanhedrin 90a; 104b; Rashi ad loc. See also TB Sanhedrin 10b; 90a-b. Rambam, Hilkhot Teshuvah, III, 6. Cf. Maharal, Derekh Hayyim, Avot III, 11, pp. 101-3. Shelah, III, p. 201a. Rabbi Yossef Hayyim of Baghdad, Ben Ish Hai, p. 133.
7. Cf. Rabbi Yisrael of Koznitz, Avodat Yisrael, p. 193. Rabbi Yossef Hayyim of Baghdad, Ben Yehoyada, II, p. 81b.
8. Cf. Deut. 4:4. Tanhuma, Ki Tissa 8. Zohar I, 207a. Zohar Hadash, Bereshit 10:4.
9. Cf. Isa. 60:21; Mishnah Sanhedrin X, 1. TB Sanhedrin 90a; Shabbat 153a; Megillah 28b; Ta'anit 22a; Ketuvot 111a; Menahot 53b. Cf. Tossafot on Ketuvot 103b. Cf. Gen. R. 6:5; Exod. R. 32:1; Shir HaShirim R. 6:16. Zohar I, 33a; 59b; 93a; 95b; 179a; 216a; II, 23a; III, 113a; 177b. Zohar Hadash, Ruth 78:4. Tikkunei HaZohar, 5 (141b). Pirkei DeRabbi Eliezer 37. Tana Devei Eliyahu Zuta 24. Kuzari, II, 14; Rambam, Hilkhot Teshuvah, III, 5; Hilkhot Issurei Bi'a, XIV, 4. Maharal, Netsah Yisrael, 15; Derekh Hayyim, Avot, pp.

2, 6, 7-8, 251; *Tiferet Yisrael*, 5, p. 8b; *Derashot Al HaTorah*, p. 41. Shelah, III, pp. 23a, 171b, 175a, 201a. Rabbi Eliyahu, Gaon of Vilna, *Biurei HaGra Al Aggadot*, I, p. 82. Rabbi Yehuda Aryeh Leib of Gur, *Sefat Emet*, II, p. 62; IV, p. 183. Rabbi Abraham of Sochaczew, *Avnei Nezer*, p. 28. Rabbi Naftali Tsevi Yehuda Berlin of Volozhin, *Ha'amek Davar*, V, Ki Tavo, Deut. 26:17, p. 108. Rav Kook, *Olat Reiyah*, II, p. 157. Rabbi Yossef Hayyim of Baghdad, *Ben Ish Hai*, pp. 133, 147; *Da'at UTevunah*, p. 110. Rabbi Barukh HaLevi Epstein, *Tossefet Berakhah*, V, pp. 106-7.

10. Cf. Isa. 60:21. Cf. Jer. 2:21; Tanhuma, Ki Tissa 8. Hakdamat Sefer HaZohar I, 13a. Zohar I, 96b. Shelah, I, 163b. Cf. also Shir HaShirim R. 7:7.

11. Cf. Exod. 6:7. Deut. 7:6, 14:2. I Sam. 12:22. I Kings 8:16. Isa. 26:2. Zohar II, 121a. Rabbeinu Bahya on Exod. 19:6.

12. Cf. Isa. 43:7; 49:3. Sifrei Vezot HaBerakhah 355 (Deut. 33:26), p. 148a. Pesikta Zutarta, Shelah (Num. 14:21). TB Yoma 86a. Esther R. 7. Tanhuma, Kedoshim 2. Midrash Lekah Tov, Shelah. Zohar I, 97a; II, 79a; 87b; III, 4b; 55a; 112a. Cf. also Hakdamat Sefer HaZohar I, 10a. Cf. Rambam, *Hilkhot Yessodei HaTorah*, V, 11. Rabbi Hayyim Vital, *Sha'arei Kedushah*, II, 4. Rabbi Nahman of Bratslav, *Likkutei Moharan*, I, 17a, pp. 21b-22a; II, 40, p. 26a. Maharal, *Gevurot HaShem*, 44, pp. 104-5. Rabbi Abraham of Slonim, *Be'er Avraham*, p. 107.

13. Cf. Deut. 11:29. Cf. also Judg. 5:11; II Sam. 6:21. Cf. Mekhilta Beshalah, Messihta DeShirah 9 (Exod. 15:16), p. 51b; Isa. 43:21.

14. Cf. Rashi on Deut. 30:19. Ramban on Deut. 28:9, 32:1. Zohar Hadash, 4:2. Maharal, *Derashot Al HaTorah*, p. 39.

15. Cf. Exod. 19:5; Mekhilta Yitro (Exod. 19:5), Messihta DiBaHodesh 2, p. 71a. Cf. Exod. 31:16, 34:27. Jer. 33:25. (Cf. also Gen. 6:18, 9:9, 11:15, 15.) Cf. Num. R. 9:54. Zohar III, 29a. Rabbi Nahman of Bratslav, *Likkutei Moharan*, 31:3, p. 43b. See also R. David Tsevi Hoffmann, *Sefer Bereshit*, I, pp. 235-36.

16. Cf. Gen. 12:2, 17:7-9. Exod. 6:7. Lev. 26:12. Deut. 4:37, 7:6-8, 10:15, 14:2. Isa. 41:8-9, 44:1-2. Jer. 30:22, 31:2, 31:32. Ezek. 36:28, 37:27. Hos. 11:1, 14:5. Mal. 1:2. Ps. 135:4. Neh. 9:7. I Chron. 17:13. Sifrei Re'eh 96 (Deut. 14:1), p. 94a. TY Yoma VII, 1; Sanhedrin X, 1. TB Berakhot 6a; 11b; Shabbat 55a and Tossafot ad loc.; see also TB Kiddushin 70b and Rashi ad loc. Gen. R. 20:16, 29:7, 44:4. Exod. R. 32:2, 47:4, 49:1, 74:9-10. Lev. R. 7:1, 36:5. Num. R. 3:2, 8:2. Deut. R. 5:6. Shir HaShirim R. 6:4. Kohelet R. 12:7. Pirkei DeRabbi Eliezer 24. Tanhuma, Ki Tissa 8; Bemidbar 17. Zohar II, 205b; 260b; III, 128a; 256a; 263b. Zohar Hadash, 49:2. Rashi on Gen. 18:19; and on I Chron. 28:10. Rambam, *Iggeret Teiman*, p. 114; see also Rambam, *Hilkhot Avodat Kokhavim VeHukot Ovdeihah*, I, 3. Ramban on Gen. 12:2; Exod. 3:15; Deut. 7:6-7, 9:4. Rashbam on Deut. 7:8; see also idem on Deut. 7:9. Rabbeinu Bahya on Gen. 11:28. Rabbi Yitshak Arama on Gen. 12:1. Alshekh on Deut. 9:4, 10:15. See classical Hebrew commentators on Gen. 15:8. Maharal, *Netsah Yisrael*, 11; *Gevurot HaShem* 8, p. 28; 24, p. 64; *Derekh Hayyim*, Avot, p. 8; V, 2, p. 167; V, 16-17, p. 200; *Derashot, Derush LeShabbat HaGadol*, p. 59; *Perushim LeAggadot HaShas*, II, Shabbat 55a, pp. 52-53 and I, Kiddushin 70b, p. 103. Shelah, I, pp. 21b-22a; 69a; 78b; 79a; 93b. *Or HaHayyim* on Gen. 12:1. Malbim on Exod. 19:5. Rabbi Samson Raphael Hirsch on Exod. 32:13. *Ha'amek Davar* on Deut. 7:7-8, p. 38; 9:4, p. 44; 10:15, p. 51. Rav Kook,

REFERENCES, SOURCES & NOTES · 285

Orot, p. 75; *Olat Reiyah*, I, pp. 60-61; *Iggerot HaReiyah*, II, p. 186. Rabbi Ya'akov Moshe Harlap, *Mei Meirom*, VI, pp. 75-76, 189; VIII, p. 74. *Sefat Emet*, I, pp. 45, 136; V, p. 136. *Avnei Nezer*, p. 82. *Shem MiShemuel*, *Moadim*, p. 207-8. Rabbi Simha Zissel Ziv, *Hokhmah UMussar*, I, p. 245. Rabbi Eliezer Eliyahu Dessler, *Mikhtav MeEliyahu*, II, p. 22. Rabbi Abraham Yaffen, *HaMussar VeHada'at*, II, Jerusalem: 5733 (1973), p. 161. Rabbi Yitshak Hutner, *Pahad Yitshak*, New York: *Rosh HaShanah*, 5734 (1974), p. 41. *Meshekh Hokhmah*, pp. 61, 328. *Siddur Rabbeinu Shelomo of Garmaise* (Worms), p. 8.

17. Cf. Deut. 26:17-18. Cf. Deut. 4:4, 6:4 (cf. also Deut. 7:6, 32:9); Josh. 24:21-22. Isa. 63:16 (see also Deut. 14:1); I Chron. 17:13). Jer. 10:16, 11:4, 30:21. Ezek. 36:28, 37:27. See also Hos. 1:9. Cf. Mal. 3:7. Ps. 16:5, 89:27, 119:57. Shir HaShirim 2:16, 6:3. Eikhah 3:24, 5:21. Sifrei Ha'azinu 312 (Deut. 32:9), p. 134b. Sifrei Re'eh 97 (Deut. 14:2), p. 94a; see also Sifrei Ha'azinu 306 (Deut. 32:1), pp. 130-31. Sifrei Vezot HaBerakhah 343 (Deut. 33:2), p. 143a; see also idem. 355 (Deut. 33:26), p. 148a. Mekhilta Beshalah (Exod. 15:2), Mesihta DeShirah 1, p. 42. TB Berakhot 6a; 48b; Pessahim 87a; Haggigah 3a; Gittin 57b; Kiddushin 70b and Rashi ad loc.; Menahot 53a. Gen. R. 20:16, 46:7. Exod. R. 36:2-3, 42:9. Num. R. 10:1, 14:22. Deut. R. 2:24. Esther R. 7. Shir HaShirim R. 1:25, 2:34, 7:16, 7:18. Eihah R. 3:3. Ruth R. 2:24. Tanhuma, Mishpatim 17; Nitsavim 1. Pirkei DeRabbi Eliezer 24. Tana Devei Eliyahu Zuta 23. Zohar II, 5b; 20a; 126a-b; III, 61a; 81a; 128a; 258a. *Kuzari*, III, 17; IV, 3. Rashi on Shir HaShirim 8:5. Ramban on Deut. 26:17-18. Rabbeinu Bahya on Exod. 25:8. Radak on Jer. 3:19. *Siddur Rabbeinu Shelomo of Garmaise*, p. 285. Maharal, *Gevurot HaShem*, 23, p. 31a; 44, p. 103; 67, p. 193; *Perushei Maharal MiPrag LeAggadot HaShas*, I, Kiddushin 70b, p. 103; *Derekh Hayyim*, Avot III, 14, p. 111. Rabbi Levi Yitshak of Berdichev, *Kedushat Levi*, p. 54a; 90b; 142b. *Sefat Emet*, IV, p. 172; V, pp. 136-37. Rabbi Abraham of Slonim, *Bet Avraham*, pp. 107, 137. Rabbi Abraham of Sochaczew, *Avnei Nezer*, p. 82. Rav Harlap, *Mei Meirom*, II, p. 47. Rabbi Meir Simha Kohen of Dvinsk, *Meshekh Hokhmah*, p. 44. Rabbi Yitshak Ze'ev HaLevi of Brisk, *Hiddushei Maran Riz HaLevi*, p. 49.

18. Cf. Exod. R. 24:1; Shir HaShirim R. 5:3. Tikkunei HaZohar, 62 (94b). See also Shir HaShirim R. 3:21. See also Rashi on Lev. 26:12. Cf. also Abrabanel on Gen. 17:4-9, pp. 222-23; Malbim on Gen. 17:2. Cf. Alshekh on VaEthanan; Maharal, *Derashot*, p. 39; Shelah, I, p. 25b.

19. Cf. Exod. 19:5, Ibn Ezra and Rabbi Samson Raphael Hirsch ad loc. M.D. Cassuto, *Perush Al Sefer Shemot*, Jerusalem: 5719 (1959), p. 156. Cf. Exod. R. 47:4.

20. Cf. Bemidbar R. 9:54. Tanhuma, Tetsaveh 6; Nitsavim 3. Cf. Ibn Ezra and Radak on Isa. 45:23, 49:18, 62:8. See also Deut. 29:11.

21. Cf. TB Gittin 57b; Gen. R. 76:1; Lev. R. 6:5. Cf. Rashi on Gen. 32:11 and Deut. 29:12; see also Rashi on Exod. 32:13. Cf. Ramban on Gen. 16:7, 22:16, 26:3; and on Deut. 9:4, 28:9, 28:42. Cf. Radak on Gen. 22:16. *Biur HaGra*, *Sefer Mishlei* 14:22, p. 88. *Mikhtav MeEliyahu*, II, pp. 21-22. *Hiddushei Maran Riz HaLevi*, pp. 20, 52, 104.

22. Cf. TB Menahot 53b. Cf. Deut. 4:7; Jer. 12:7; Ps. 145:18, 148:14. TY Berakhot IX, 1. TB Shabbat 137b; Sotah 37a. Pesikta DeRav Kahana II, 464

(Jer. 11:9). Gen. R. 41:11; Exod. R. 27:8; Lev. R. 6:1; Num. R. 10:3; Deut. R. 3:12. Shir HaShirim R. 3:21, 5:1. Esther R. 7:17; Kohelet R. 4:13. Tanhuma, Kedoshim 5; Behar 1. Shoher Tov, 4, 84, 118. Yalkut Shim'oni, Bo 13:222. Zohar I, 96a; II, 55b (Ps. 122:8); 122a; 160b; III, 7b; 77b; 96a; 277b; Zohar Hadash, Hukat 52:3. Rashi on Shabbat 31a (Prov. 27:10). See also Rambam, *Hilkhot Teshuvah*, VII, 6. Cf. Ramban on Gen. 48:15. *Perushei Maharal MiPrag Le Aggadot HaShas*, I, Sotah 5b, p. 29; II, Shabbat 137b, pp. 124-25. *Kli Yakar* on Exod. 19:4. *Bet Avraham*, p. 128.

23. Cf. TB Hullin 89a and Rashi ad loc. See TB Makot 24a. Zohar I, 48b; 238a; 240a; II, 13a; 81a. Maharal, *Netivot Olam*, II, *Netiv HaTemimut*, 1, p. 163b; *Netsah Yisrael*, 13, 30, 62; *Gevurot HaShem*, 3, 4; *Perushei Maharal MiPrag LeAggadot HaShas*, I, Sotah 5b, p. 29; 42b, p. 73. Shelah, III, pp. 176b-177a. *Tanya*, *Likkutei Amarim*, 6, p. 20. *Sefat Emet*, III, p. 191; V, p. 136. *Bet Avraham*, p. 154. *Shem MiShemuel*, *Bereshit*, I, pp. 349-50; *Haggadah Shel Pessah*, p. 95. Rav Kook, *Orot*, p. 149.

24. Cf. Tanhuma, Eikev 3. Yalkut Shim'oni, Eikev 11:874. Cf. Rashi on Hullin 89a; cf. also Rambam, *Iggeret Teiman*, p. 128. Cf. TB Ta'anit 3b. Zohar I, 177-178a (Isa. 41:14). Shelah, III, p. 178a. Cf. Maharal, *Netivot Olam*, I, *Netiv HaAvodah*, 1, p. 31. Rav Kook, *Orot HaKodesh*, III, p. 117. Rabbi Hayyim of Volozhin, *Ruah Hayyim*, Avot I, 1, pp. 3-9. Rabbi Bezalel Ze'ev Safran, *She'eilot UTeshuvot Harbaz*, I, p. 137.

25. Cf. *Sefat Emet*, I, p. 2; V, pp. 12, 136. Rav Harlap, *Mei Meirom*, VIII, pp. 108, 110. Maharal, *Netsah Yisrael*, 57; *Perushim LeAggadot HaShas*, I, Sotah 4b, p. 27; 17a, p. 49.

26. Cf. Sifra Behar 4:8 (Lev. 25:23), p. 108. TB Sotah 5a; Hullin 89a. Lev. R. 7:2, 27:5. Tanhuma, Eikev 3. Cf. Zohar III, 256b. Tikkunei HaZohar, 30 (73b). Rabbeinu Nissim Gaon on Berakhot 56b. Maharal, *Netsah Yisrael*, 30; *Tiferet Yisrael*, 10, p. 14a. Shelah, *Siddur Sha'ar HaShamayim*, p. 152. Rabbi Dov Baer, the Maggid of Mezerich, *Maggid Devarav LeYa'akov*, 132, p. 229. *Kedushat Levi*, p. 47a. Rabbi Moshe Yehiel HaLevi Epstein, *Be'er Moshe*, *Bereshit*, Tel Aviv: 5724, p. 116, and *Shemot*, p. 549. *Shem Mi Shemuel*, *Bereshit*, II, p. 244. Rav Kook, *Orot HaKodesh*, III, pp. 117-18, 155.

27. Cf. Maharal, *Gevurot HaShem*, 44, p. 103.

28. Cf. Zohar III, 152a. *Biurei HaGra Al Aggadot*, I, p. 34. *Sefat Emet*, IV, p. 175; V, p. 9. Rav Kook, *Orot HaKodesh*, III, p. 117. Rav Harlap, *Mei Meirom*, II, p. 41.

29. Rambam, *Hilkhot Shemittah VeYovel*, XIII, 12-13. HaGra, *Siddur Ishei Yisrael*, p. 42 (*Siah Yitshak*). Rabbi Yehuda HaLevi Ashlag, *Matan Torah*, Jerusalem: 5737, p. 45.

30. Cf. Gen. R. 34:11, 67:7. Deut. R. 2:24 (Prov. 24:21). Zohar I, 106b. Zohar Hadash, Noah 21:4. See also Avot IV, 1; TB Bava Batra 78b; Yalkut Shim'oni, II Sam. 23:165. Cf. *Hizkuni* on Lekh Lekha, Gen. 17:17, p. 24. *Sefat Emet*, I, p. 211. *Be'er Avraham*, p. 115.

31. Cf. Deut. 4:20, 9:26, 32:9. Joel 4:2. Mekhilta Beshalah (Exod. 15:17), Messihta DeShirah, 10, p. 51b. Ramban on Lev. 18:25.

32. On the subject of the tribe of Levi, spiritual "root" of the people of Israel, see also Deut. 10:9, 18:1-2; Exod. R. 37; Num. R. 1, 3; Pesikta Rabbati 21.

33. Cf. TB Haggigah 9b. Lev. R. 13; Shir HaShirim R. 1. Tana Devei Eliyahu

Zuta 3. Shoher Tov, 18 (Ps. 18:28; see also Ps. 113:7). Zohar III, 273b (II Sam. 22:28; Ps. 116:6; see also Zeph. 3:12). See also TB Eruvin 41b; Megillah 11a; Nedarim 64b; Avodah Zarah 5a. Exod. R. 31:11. Tanhuma, Mishpatim 11. Zohar II, 119a; III, 33b. Tikkunei HaZohar, 22 (60b). Zohar Hadash, Ki Tavo 60a. See also *Biurei HaGra Al Aggadot*, II, p. 7 (*Likkutei HaGra*).
34. Cf. Deut. 7:7 and *Ha'amek Davar* ad loc., p. 38; Deut. 10:22 and *Ha'amek Davar* ad loc., p. 52. Cf. Deut. 1:10-11. Gen. 13:16, 15:5, 22:17. Isa. 48:19. Lev. R. 27:5. Num. R. 11:1, 13:5. Kohelet R. 3:19 (Kohelet 3:15; see also Ps. 34:19). Tanhuma, Eikev 3. See also TB Shabbat 88b and *Perushei Maharal MiPrag*, II, pp. 75-77. TB Eruvin 54; Ta'anit 7a; Bava Kama 93a; Hullin 89a. Cf. *Perushei HaTorah LeRabbi Yehuda HeHassid*, p. 202. Shelah, I, p. 21b; *Siddur Sha'ar HaShamayim*, p. 520. *Meshekh Hokhmah*, p. 238.
35. Cf. Isa. 48:10ff. Cf. Prov. 3:34. I Sam. 17:14. See also Amos 7:2, 7:5. Cf. TB Eruvin 13b; Ta'anit 10a; Megillah 11a; Sanhedrin 96b-98a; Hullin 60b. See also TB Megillah 31a. Exod. R. 21:4 (Ps. 90:1, 102:1); Lev. R. 30:3. Num. R. 2:12-13, 11:1 (Isa. 29:19). Tanhuma, Hayei Sarah 8 (Isa. 60:22). Zohar I, 122b; 157a; 168a; 192b; 238a; 249b; 256b-257a; II, 43a; 232b; III, 49b; 168a. Tikkunei HaZohar, 21 (53b). Rashi on Sotah 5a. *Siddur Rabbeinu Shelomo de Garmaise*, p. 196. Maharshal, Rabbi Shelomo Luria, *Hokhmat Shelomo* on Berakhot 17. *Perushei Maharal MiPrag LeAggadot HaShas*, I, Shabbat 55a, pp. 11-12; Sotah 5a, p. 26. Maharal, *Gevurot HaShem*, 23, p. 62b. Shelah, III, pp. 25b, 178a, 183b-184a, 202b. Rabbi Nahman of Bratslav, *Likkutei Moharan*, I, 1:1, p. 1a; II, 72, p. 33a; *Sefer HaMiddot*, pp. 41-42; *Siddur Sha'arei Ratson*, p. 360. *Kedushat Levi*, p. 57b. *Bet Avraham*, p. 78. *Avnei Nezer*, p. 83. *Shem MiShemuel, Haggadah Shel Pessah*, p. 43. Rav Kook, *Orot*, pp. 160-61; *Olat Reiyah*, I, p. 386; *Orot HaTorah*, pp. 13-14. *Mei Meirom*, VI, p. 268. Rabbi Yossef Hayyim of Baghdad, *Od Yossef Hai*, pp. 209-10. Rabbi Yehuda HaLevi Ashlag, *Hakdamah, Sefer Ets Hayyim*, p. 2. Rabbi Bezalel Ze'ev Safran, *She'eilot UTeshuvot Harbaz*, I, p. 27.
36. Cf. Exod. 6:7, 19:5 and Mekhilta ad loc., Messihta DiBaHodesh, 2, p. 71. Exod. 15:16. Lev. 20:26, 25:55 et al. Isa. 43:1. Jer. 2:3. TB Kiddushin 22b; 53a and Rashi ad loc.; Bava Kama 116b. Num. R. 23:11. Tanhuma, Kedoshim 3. Yalkut Shim'oni, Yitro 19:276.
37. Cf. Exod. 19:5. Deut. 7:6, 14:2, 26:18. Ps. 135:4. See also Kohelet 2:8. Yalkut Shim'oni, Kohelet 5:572. TB Bava Batra 52a. *Sefer HaBahir*, 40, p. 18. Tanhuma, Ki Tissa 8. Ramban and Malbim on Exod. 19:5. Recanati, Yitro, p. 7b. *Derashot Maharal MiPrag, Derush Al HaTorah*, p. 41. *Biurei HaGra Al Aggadot*, I, p. 51. Rabbi Samson Raphael Hirsch on Exod. 19:5-6, pp. 194-95; *Iggerot Tsafon*, p. 77. *Ha'amek Davar* on Deut. 7:6, p. 38, 26:18, p. 108. M.D. Cassuto, *Perush Al Sefer Shemot* on Exod. 19:5, p. 156. *Bet Avraham*, p. 151. *Sefat Emet*, V, p. 182. Rav Kook, *Orot*, pp. 9-10, 94-95, 148, 167; *Hazon HaGeulah*, pp. 96-97; *Olat Reiyah*, I, pp. 236, 269, 397; *Iggerot HaReiyah*, II, pp. 186, 194; *Shabbat HaArets*, p. 9.
38. Cf. Isa. 15:21, 43:1, 44:2, 44:24. Jer. 1:5. Ps. 102:19.
39. Cf. Deut. 32:6, 32:15. Isa. 44:2. Ps. 100:3, 149:2. Cf. also Isa. 29:23, 54:5.
40. Rashi on Exod. 19:5.
41. Cf. Lev. 25:23. Exod. R. 29:3. Rashi on Gen. 1:1; Exod. 19:5; Deut. 10:14. Ibn Ezra on Exod. 19:5. *Sefat Emet*, I, p. 229.

42. Cf. Ibn Ezra on Exod. 33:21. See also TB Yevamot 79a.
43. Cf. Exod. 22:30; Deut. 14:2; Isa. 6:13; Jer. 2:3; Ezra 9:2. Sifrei Re'eh 97 (Deut. 14:2), p. 94a. TB Hullin 7b. Exod. R. 38:8. Zohar II, 121-22. *Kuzari*, I, 95. *Perushei Maharal MiPrag LeAggadot HaShas*, I, Kiddushin 70b, p. 103. *Mei Meirom*, VIII, p. 74.
44. Cf. Zohar I, 47a.
45. Cf. Mishnah Avot VI, 11; Makot III, 16. Ramban on Deut. 26:18.
46. Cf. Avot DeRabbi Nathan 4 (Prov. 2:5). Zohar II, 134b; 161b. See also TY Rosh HaShanah I, 3.
47. Cf. Zohar I, 55a; 177b; II, 87b; III, 11b; 278b. See also TB Berakhot 11b. Cf. Rabbi Hayyim of Volozhin, *Nefesh HaHayyim*, 4:32, p. 50.
48. Cf. Ps. 42:2-3, 63:2, 84:3. Cf. Shir HaShirim R. 7:16; see also Gen. R. 64:2. Cf. also TB Sukkah 45b. Cf. Zohar I, 205a; III, 112a. Zohar Hadash, 16a. Rashi on Sanhedrin 76b. Maharal, *Netsah Yisrael*, 21; *Gevurot HaShem*, 47, p. 115. *Tanya, Likkutei Amarim*, 19, p. 24. *Nefesh HaHayyim*, 1:4, p. 8. *Sefat Emet*, V, p. 78. *Bet Avraham*, p. 98. Rav Kook, *Olat Reiyah*, II, p. 2; *Orot*, pp. 48-49, 52, 64-65, 135, 138-39. *Shem MiShemuel, Shemot*, I, p. 22; *Devarim*, p. 210; *Haggadah Shel Pessah*, pp. 39, 46.
49. Cf. Yalkut Shim'oni, Yitro 19:276. Rashi on Shabbat 89a. *Sefat Emet*, III, p. 198. Rav Kook, *Orot*, pp. 139, 159.
50. Cf. Mishnah Berakhot II, 2; TB Berakhot 13a-b; Deut. 6:4. Hakdamat Sefer HaZohar I, 12a; Zohar III, 108a. See also TB Rosh HaShanah 32a.
51. Cf. Mekhilta Mishpatim (Exod. 22:30), Messihta DeKaspa, 20, p. 104a. TB Shabbat 104a; Yoma 39a. Exod. R. 38:8; Num. R. 3:2. Tanhuma, Kedoshim 2, 9 (Ps. 20:2). Midrash Shemuel 8:2. Zohar I, 62a; 77b; 88b; 142a; II, 11b; 79b; 121a-b. Ramban on Deut. 26:17. Maharal, *Tiferet Yisrael*, 7, p. 11a. *Sefat Emet*, V, 15:62. Rabbi Abraham of Slonim, *Be'er Avraham*, p. 49. Rav Kook, *Orot*, pp. 96-97; *Hazon HaGeulah*, p. 96; *Olat Reiyah*, I, p. 397; *Iggerot HaReiyah*, II, p. 186; *Mussar Avikha*, p. 84.
52. Cf. Zohar II, 121-22. Maharal, *Netsah Yisrael*, 10; *Derekh Hayyim*, Avot, p. 7; VI, p. 251; *Tiferet Yisrael*, 1, pp. 4-5; 5, p. 8a. Shelah, I, p. 69a. *Bnei Issakhar*, I, p. 112a. Rav Kook, *Orot*, pp. 49, 52, 64, 90, 96, 110, 167; *Shabbat HaArets*, p. 7; see also Rav Kook, *Orot*, pp. 93, 150; *Olat Reiyah*, I, pp. 269, 397; II, pp. 155-56; *Iggerot HaReiyah*, II, p. 186. Cf. *Mei Meirom, Missaviv LiShmonah Perakim LeHaRambam*, p. 155.
53. Cf. *Or HaHayyim* on Gen. 12:1.
54. Cf. Gen. 21:33. Isa. 29:23, 43:7, 43:21. Ps. 22:32, 102:19. Avot VI, 11. TB Sotah 10a-b; Sanhedrin 110b; Menahot 53a; Hullin 91b. See also TB Berakhot 7b. Tossafot on Berakhot 40b. Gen. R. 39:24, 43:8. Exod. R. 23:1, 23:4. Lev. R. 6. Num. R. 5:6, 14:7. Shir HaShirim R. 2:1, 2:4. Esther R. 6. Shoher Tov, 104. Yalkut Shim'oni, Tehillim 110:469. Zohar I, 40a; 90a; 189a; II, 18b; 42a; 164b; III, 22a. Tikkunei HaZohar, 3a. Zohar Hadash, 17a. *Shulhan Arukh, Yoreh Deyah*, 260. Rambam, *Sefer HaMitzvot, Mitzvot Asseh, Mitzvah 3*; *Mishneh Torah, Hilkhot Avodat Kokhavim VeHukot Ovdehah*, I, 3. Ramban on Gen. 12:8, 21:33, 22:33; and on Exod. 13:16. *Likkutei Moharan*, I, 37:1, p. 51a; II, 71, p. 32b. *Sefat Emet*, I, pp. 203, 211, 214, 216, 218, 221, 229, 245; II, pp. 65, 68; V, p. 136. *Avnei Nezer*, p. 36. Rav Kook, *Orot HaKodesh*, III, p. 106. *Siddur HaGeonim VeHaMekubalim*, III, p. 730.

Rabbi Nathan Tsevi Finkel of Slobodka, *Or HaTsafun*, I, pp. 218-20.
55. Cf. Maharal, *Derekh Hayyim*, Avot, pp. 7, 251; Shelah, *Siddur Sha'ar HaShamayim*, p. 517; Malbim on Exod. 19:5; *Bet Avraham*, p. 136; Rabbi Y.H. Ashlag, *Matan Torah*, p. 41.
56. Cf. Sifrei Re'eh 97 (Deut. 14:2), p. 94a; Sifrei Ha'azinu 311 (Deut. 32:8), p. 134a. TB Beitsa 25b; see also TB Yoma 71a. Cf. Gen. R. 41:11. Exod. R. 21:5, 37:5, 42:9, 47:4. Lev. R. 18:3. Num. R. 2:5, 3:1-2. Shir HaShirim R. 42:8. Tanhuma, Bemidbar 13. Tana Devei Eliyahu Zuta 10. Zohar II, 121b. *Kuzari*, I, 95; II, 14; 26. Ramban on Deut. 7:7. Maharal, *Derekh Hayyim*, Avot, p. 8; *Tiferet Yisrael*, 1, pp. 4b-5a; *Derashot*, p. 53; *Netivot Olam*, II, *Netiv Koah HaYetser*, p. 136b; *Gevurot HaShem*, 23, pp. 62b-63a; 44, pp. 102-3. *Siddur HaGra, Ishei Yisrael*, p. 43 (*Siah Yitshak*). *Ha'amek Davar*, I, *Petihah LeSefer Bereshit*, p. 1; on Deut. 7:7, p. 38; 9:6, p. 45; 10:16, p. 51; 26:17, p. 105. *Sefat Emet*, IV, p. 174; V, pp. 9, 78. *Avnei Nezer*, pp. 29-30, 110. Rabbi Eliyahu Lapian, *Lev Eliyahu*, Jerusalem: 5732 (1972), p. 71. *Mikhtav MeEliyahu*, II, p. 22. Rabbi B.H. Epstein, *Tossefet Berakhah*, Tel Aviv: 5736 (1976), V, p. 244. Rabbi Y.H. Ashlag, *Matan Torah*, pp. 37-38.
57. Cf. Rav Kook, *Olat Reiyah*, I, p. 236.
58. Cf. Gen. R. 43:4; Exod. R. 6:2.
59. Cf. Zohar II, 3a; *Sefat Emet*, V, p. 78; see also Lev. R. 2:4.
60. Cf. TB Rosh HaShanah 16a; 34b. Tanhuma, Ki Tissa 8.
61. Cf. TB Ta'anit 25a; see also TB Sanhedrin 20b. Cf. Yalkut Shim'oni, Yitro 19:276; Yeshayahu 43:555. Shoher Tov, 20. Rabbi Yisrael of Koznitz, *Avodat Yisrael HaShalem*, p. 210.
62. Cf. Sifrei VaEthanan 32 (Deut. 6:5), p. 73a. TB Yoma 86a; Sotah 10b. Zohar I, 230b. Rambam, *Sefer HaMitzvot, Mitzvot Asseh, Mitzvah* 3; *Mishneh Torah, Hilkhot Yessodei HaTorah*, V, 1. Maharal, *Gevurot HaShem*, 47; *Netivot Olam*, II, *Netiv Ahavat HaShem*, p. 105; *Perushim LeAggadot HaShas*, II, Shabbat 133b, pp. 23-24. HaGra, *Divrei Eliyahu*, p. 42 (Deut. 28:10). *Ha'amek Davar* on Deut. 10:16, p. 51b. *Sefat Emet*, V, p. 34. Rabbi Yeruham HaLevi Livovitch, *Da'at Hokhmah UMussar*, pp. 119-20.
63. Cf. Isa. 2:11, 2:17, 40:17. Cf. also Num. 23:9. Cf. TB Sanhedrin 39a-b. See Rashi on Exod. 19:5.
64. Cf. Jer. 9:22-23. TB Nedarim 9b; Avodah Zarah 2b. Yalkut Shim'oni, Yeshayahu 43:454. Tikkunei HaZohar, 6 (22a). HaGra, *Siddur Ishei Yisrael*, p. 46 (*Siah Yitshak*).
65. Cf. Rashi on Gen. 14:19.
66. Cf. Ps. 24:1, 50:12, 89:12, 98:7. Cf. TB Berakhot 35b. Rashi on Gen. 1:1. Rambam, *Mishneh Torah, Hilkhot Yessodei HaTorah*, I, 3-5; *Hilkhot Shemittah VeYovel*, XIII, 13. *Sefat Emet*, I, p. 5; III, p. 190; V, pp. 35, 68.
67. Cf. TB Yoma 69b.
68. Cf. Ezek. 39:23, 39:28, 39:36.
69. Rabbi Samson Raphael Hirsch, *The Hirsch Siddur*, p. 221. *Sefat Emet*, III, p. 197.
70. Cf. TB Sanhedrin 39a. *Sefat Emet*, I, p. 5; III, p. 196. *Mei Meirom*, VI, p. 294.
71. Cf. Isa. 42:1, 51:16, 59:21. Joel 3:1-2. Zech. 12-10. I Chron. 29:14. Avot III, 8. Eihah R. 2:11. Cf. Yalkut Shim'oni, Mishlei 2:832. Zohar II, 43a. Rabbi Hayyim Vital, *Peri Ets Hayyim, Sha'ar Hag HaMatsot*, 7, p. 11. HaGra,

Siddur Ishei Yisrael, p. 42. Rav Kook, *Olat Reiyah*, II, p. 356. *Mei Meirom*, VI, p. 268.
72. Cf. Num. 11:29; Deut. 29:12; Judg. 5:11; Ezek. 36:20 et al. *Kuzari*, II, 56; IV, 3.
73. Cf. Isa. 45:11 and Rashi ad loc. Maharal, *Netsah Yisrael*, 11; *Tiferet Yisrael*, 17, p. 19b; *Perushim de Aggadot HaShas*, IV, Yevamot 63a, p. 27. *Bet Avraham*, p. 98. Rav Kook, *Hazon HaGeulah*, pp. 96-97.
74. Cf. Deut. 32:9. Cf. also Sukkah 51b; 53b. Cf. Deut. R. 2:24. Tanhuma, Ha'azinu 6. Zohar I, 177b; II, 39b; 96a; 278b; III, 12a; 80b; 112b; 192b. Zohar Hadash, Bereshit 6, 74 (Jer. 10:16, 51:19). Maharal, *Netsah Yisrael*, 11; *Gevurot HaShem*, 8, 47; *Be'er HaGolah*, 3, p. 19a; *Derekh Hayyim*, Avot IV, 4, p. 130. *Magen Avraham* on *Shulhan Arukh*, *Orah Hayyim*, 224:5. Shelah, I, p. 78b; III, pp. 21b, 171a, 201a; *Siddur Sha'ar HaShamayim*, p. 517. HaGra, *Aderet Eliyahu*, p. 484. Rabbi Dov Baer of Mezerich, *Maggid Devarav LeYa'akov*, 198, p. 321. Rabbi Levi Yitshak of Berdichev, *Kedushat Levi*, p. 54a. *Sefat Emet*, III, pp. 153, 197. Rav Harlap, *Mei Meirom*, VI, p. 294. Rabbi Yossef Dov Baer of Brisk, *Bet HaLevi*, I, 35. Rabbi Yossef Hayyim of Baghdad, *Ben Yehoyada*, II, p. 81b.
75. Cf. Avot III, 14 (Deut: 14:1). Cf. Maharal, *Derekh Hayyim*, Avot III, 14, pp. 107, 111; Hanokh Albeck, *Shishah Sidrei Mishnah Meforashim*, *Seder Nezikin*, Avot III, 14, p. 367.
76. Cf. Zohar I, 95b; 195a. *Or HaHayyim* on Deut. 32:8; Rabbi Samson Raphael Hirsch on Deut. 32:9.
77. Cf. Deut. 32:9. Sifrei Ha'azinu 312 (ad loc.), p. 134b. Lev. R. 2:4. Deut. R. 2. Tanhuma, Ki Tissa 8. Tana Devei Eliyahu Zuta (Ps. 16:5). Pirkei DeRabbi Eliezer 24. Zohar II, 39b; 126a; 149a; III, 80b; 149a. See also Ramban on Gen. 2:7. Cf. *Perushei Maharal MiPrag LeAggadot HaShas*, I, Sotah 9a, p. 32. Shelah, I, p. 70a; III, pp. 171a, 175a; *Siddur Sha'ar HaShamayim*, p. 517. R. Eliyahu of Vilna, *Aderet Eliyahu*, p. 16. *Or HaHayyim* on Deut. 32:8. Rabbi Hayyim of Volozhin, *Nefesh HaHayyim*, 1:5, p. 9; 1:17, p. 17; 1:19, p. 18. *Ruah Hayyim*, Avot VI, 3, p. 96. *Tanya, Likkutei Amarim*, 19; *Iggeret HaTeshuvah*, 5, p. 95; 6, p. 96. *Sefat Emet*, III, pp. 197-98. Rav Kook, *Orot*, p. 139. Rabbi Yossef Hayyim of Baghdad, *Ben Ish Hai*, p. 247.
78. Cf. Gen. 6:9, 17:1. Deut. 13:5. TB Sotah 14a; Sanhedrin 90b. Zohar II, 160b (Deut. 27:9). Gen. R. 30:11. Zohar III, 278a. Rabbi Yitshak Arama, *Akedat Yitshak*, I, p. 117. *Mikhtav MeEliyahu*, II, pp. 179-80.
79. Cf. Isa. 43:10, 43:12. Lev. R. 6:5. Yalkut Shim'oni, Yeshayahu 43:555a. *Sefat Emet*, III, p. 197-98; V, pp. 30, 132. Rav Kook, *Orot*, pp. 18, 138, 143.
80. Cf. Ps. 91:15, 149:2. TB Berakhot 3a; Sotah 38b; Sanhedrin 46a. Exod R. 30:21; Shir HaShirim R. 5:3. Tanhuma, Shemot 14. Zohar III, 17a; 74b; 197b; 219b. Tikkunei HaZohar, 6 (23a). *Mei Meirom*, VIII, p. 86.
81. Cf. TB Beitsa 25b. Maharal, *Netsah Yisrael*, 13. Rav Kook. *Orot*, p. 50; *Hazon HaGeulah*, pp. 96-97. Rabbi Samson Raphael Hirsch on Exod. 6:7, 12:3.
82. Cf. Deut. 32:6. Isa. 42:6, 43:1, 43:7, 43:15, 43:21; 44:1-2, 44:24, 46:3; 49:1, 49:5, 54:5. Ps. 22:32, 102:19, 149:2. Exod. R. 29:6. Num. R. 11:4 (Gen. 12:2). Avot DeRabbi Nathan 1. Hakdamat Sefer HaZohar I, 13a. Zohar I, 177b. Tossafot on Shabbat 137b. Maharal, *Gevurot HaShem*, 23; *Tiferet Yisrael*,

17, pp. 19b-20a; *Derekh Hayyim*, Avot, pp. 7-8; *Perushim LeAggadot HaShas*, II, Shabbat 119b, p. 109; 137b, p. 124. Shelah, I, p. 78. Rabbi Dov Baer of Mezerich, *Maggid Devarav LeYa'akov*, 41, p. 62. Rabbi Simha Bunim of Przysucha, *Midrash Simhah*, I, p. 27. Rabbi Yossef Hayyim of Baghdad, *Ben Ish Hai*, p. 189.

83. Cf. Isa. 44:2, 46:3. Jer. 1:5. TY Berakhot IX, 3. Exod. R. 25:13. Rabbi Abraham of Slonim, *Be'er Avraham*, pp. 98, 107.
84. Cf. Amos 3:2.
85. Cf. R. Ya'akov Tsevi Meklenburg, *HaKtav VeHakabbalah*, I, *Shemot*, p. 8.
86. Cf. TB Shabbat 105a. Sefer HaBahir, 58. Exod. R. 33:1. Deut. R. 8:7 (Ps. 148:14). Shir HaShirim R. 1:32. Zohar I, 152b; II, 60a; 86a; 87b; 90b; 124a; III, 9b; 61a; 73a; 81a; 176a; 238b; 260b; 278b. Zohar Hadash, 29a. Ramban, *Hakdamah, Bereshit*; Ramban on Exod. 25:3. Alshekh on Bereshit. Maharal, *Netivot Olam*, I, *Netiv HaTorah*, 1; *Gevurot HaShem*, 8, 47; *Netsah Yisrael*, 5; *Tiferet Yisrael, Hakdamah*, pp. 2a-b; *Derekh Hayyim*, pp. 3, 93, 99, 211, 216; *Perushim LeAggadot*, I, pp. 18, 49, 81. Shelah, I, pp. 2b, 27a, 96a; III, pp. 9a, 12a. R. Hayyim Yossef David Azulay, the "Hida," *Nahal Kedumim, Beha'alotkha*, Num. 8:2. *Kli Yakar* on Deut. 33:10. *Be'er Mayim Hayyim, Yitro*, p. 123. R. Moshe Hayyim Luzzatto, the "Ramhal," *Derekh HaShem*, 4:2:2. *Toldot Ya'akov Yossef, Hakdamah*. *Maggid Devarav LeYa'akov*, 55, 56, 122, 132, 168. *Tanya, Likkutei Amarim*, 4, 35-37; *Iggeret HaKodesh*, 7, 18, 19, 23. R. Hayyim of Volozhin, *Nefesh HaHayyim*, 1:6, 4:2-3, 10, 17, 19, 24-25; *Ruah Hayyim*, pp. 29, 30, 65, 90, 96; *Likkutei Moharan*, I, 5:2; 33:4-5; 34:4; 48:1; II, 28:2; 60. R. Menahem Nahum of Tchernobil, *Me'or Einaim, Hukat*. *Hessed LeAvraham*, p. 52. *Sefat Emet*, III, pp. 26, 206; IV, pp. 44, 52; V, pp. 53, 65. *Shem MiShemuel, Bereshit*, I, p. 121; *Shemot*, I, p. 176. *Bet Avraham*, p. 234. *Ha'amek Davar* on Deut. 26:17. *Olat Reiyah*, II, p. 410. *Orot HaTorah*, p. 20. *Meshekh Hokhmah*, p. 20. *Ben Ish Hai*, p. 64. *Shiurei Da'at*, II, pp. 197-98. *Matan Torah*, pp. 129-30, 144.
87. See also TB Berakhot 11b. Cf. Zohar III, 53b.
88. See Zohar II, 87a; 124a. Ramban, *Hakdamah, Perushei HaTorah*.
89. Cf. Num. R. 14:22. Zohar III, 53b.
90. Cf. Tana Devei Eliyahu Rabba 18. Cf. Maharal, *Derekh Hayyim*, pp. 111, 120, 210-12, 220; *Netivot Olam*, I, *Netiv HaTorah*, 1; *Tiferet Yisrael*, 25.
91. Cf. TB Shabbat 55b; Sanhedrin 56b. Gen. R. 16:9, 24.5. Exod. R. 30:6. Shir HaShirim R. 1:16. Zohar I, 35b; III, 111b. Tikkunei HaZohar, 56 (89b). Zohar Hadash, Yitro 33b. Rambam, *Hilkhot Melakhim*, VIII, 11; IX; X. Ramban on Gen. 34:13. *Sefer Hahinukh*, 416. Shelah, III, p. 2a (Gen. 2:16).
92. Cf. Mekhilta 5 (Exod. 20:1). TB Bava Kama 38a. Exod. R. 32a. Zohar III, 122a.
93. Cf. Num. R. 13:15. Rashi on Exod. 24:12; Ralbag on I Kings 8:9. Recanati, Yitro, p. 8. *Or HaHayyim* on Exod. 20:1. Shelah, I, p. 11a; III, pp. 47b, 172b. *Tanya*, 36.
94. Cf. Mekhilta 1 (Exod. 19:2), 5 (Exod. 20:2); Sifrei 343 (Deut. 33:2); Yalkut Shim'oni, Yitro 19:275. Pesikta Rabbati 21:3, 31:4. Exod. R. 27:4; Lam. R. 3:3; Tanhuma, Shoftim 9. TB Shabbat 88b; Ta'anit 25a; Avodah Zarah 2b-3a. Zohar I, 25a; II, 3a; 146a; III, 91b; 122a; 192a; 193a. Zohar Hadash, Ruth, 83:3. Tikkunei HaZohar, 22 (64a). Rambam, *Iggeret Teiman*, p. 143. See also

Pesikta DeRav Kahana 5, pp. 81-82; R. Yossef Dov Baer HaLevi, *Bet HaLevi*, II, p. 41.
95. Cf. TB Kiddushin 31a; Pesikta Zutarta, Tetsaveh, 27:2.
96. Cf. Exod. 6:7; Lev. 26:12; Deut. 4:20, 27:9, 29:12. I Sam. 12:22; II Sam 7:23-24. I Chron. 17:22; Isa. 26:2. Jer. 7:23, 11:4, 24:7, 30:22-25, 32:38. Ezek. 11:20, 14:11, 36:28, 37:23, 37:27. Zech. 8:8 et al. Mekhilta 3 (Exod. 19:11); Deut. R. 7:9. TB Hullin 101b. Petihta DeRuth Rabba (Ps. 50:7). See also Zohar II, 189a; III, 149a; Num. R. 11:4. Cf. *Or HaHayyim* on Deut. 32:8. TB Kiddushin 22b (Lev. 25:55). Rabbeinu Sa'adya Gaon, *Sefer HaEmunot VeHaDeot*, 3, 7. Maharal, *Derekh Hayyim*, pp. 8-9, 99; *Perushim LeAggadot*, I, p. 64 (Ps. 68:27; Prov. 14:28); *Tiferet Yisrael*, 17; *Gevurot HaShem*, 38; *Netsah Yisrael*, 11; *Netivot Olam*, I, *Netiv HaAvodah*, 15. *Kuzari*, I, 25; 47; 87; 95; II, 56; III, 17; 73; IV, 3; 11. Rambam, *Iggeret Teiman*, pp. 132-33; see also *Mishneh Torah, Hilkhot Terumot*, I, 1-2. Ramban on Deut. 32:26, 33:4. *Orot*, pp. 21, 32-33, 50, 52, 96, 104-5, 109-10, 144, 154; *Iggerot HaReiyah*, I, p. 178. *Mei Meirom*, VIII, pp. 81-82. *Bet Avraham*, p. 151. *Sefat Emet*, I, p. 109. *Ha'amek Davar* on Lev. 26:12; Deut. 26:19. *Meshekh Hokhmah*, pp. 156, 328. *Ben Ish Hai*, pp. 84-85.
97. Cf. Lev. R. 23:3; Shir HaShirim R. 2:2.
98. Cf. Exod. 19:6, 22:30; Deut. 6:9. Jer. 2:3. TB Hullin 7b; Kiddushin 53a and Rashi ad loc. Zohar II, 121a; III, 81a. Mekhilta (Exod. 19:5-6). See also Exod. 6:7; Lev. 26:12. Deut. 27:9, 29:12 et al.
99. Cf. Deut. 28:9. Sifrei 343 (Deut. 33:2); Mekhilta 5 (Exod. 20:1).
100. Cf. TB Shabbat 33b; Sotah 14a. Lev. R. 25:3. *Sefat Emet*, III, p. 153.
101. Cf. TB Avodah Zarah 3b; Bava Metsia 86a. Gen. R. 49:6, 64:4. Deut. R. 5:11. Zohar III, 166b. *Ben Ish Hai, Hakdamah*.
102. Cf. TY Rosh HaShanah I, 3. TB Bava Kama 60b. Exod. R. 30:6; Lev. R. 35:3; Deut. R. 3:13. Pesikta Rabbati 31. *Biurei HaGra Al Aggadot*, I, p. 103. Shelah, III, p. 204a. *Sefat Emet*, III, p. 207.
103. Cf. Lev. 11:44, 19:2. Mekhilta 20 (Exod. 22:30); Sifra 1 (Lev. 19:2); Sifrei 115 (Num. 15:40). Exod. R. 15:24, 38:8. Lev. R. 24:1; Num. R. 9:4, 17:7. Tanhuma, Kedoshim 1. Zohar III, 94a. Rashi on Lev. 11:44. HaGra, *Siddur Ishei Yisrael*, pp. 365-66. *Mei Meirom, Missaviv LiShmonah Perakim LeHa-Rambam*, p. 155.
104. Cf. Lev. 11:44-45. See Isa. 6:3, 40:25, 54:5. Hasdai Crescas, *Or HaShem*, I, 2:1. Maharal, *Tiferet Yisrael*, 44. R. Moshe Hayyim Ephraim of Sudylkow, *Degel Mahaneh Ephraim*, Vayishlah. *Sefat Emet*, III, p. 153.
105. Cf. TB Shabbat 133b.
106. Cf. Isa. 57:15.
107. Cf. TB Beitsa 25b.
108. Cf. Shir HaShirim R. 1:32, Zohar III, 260b.
109. Before the creation of the world God "concentrated" so as to create it. Cf. *Ets Hayyim*, I, 1. *Maggid Devarav LeYa'akov*, 1, 71, 122, 189. *Kedushat Levi*, pp. 25b, 47a, 61a, 92a. *Tanya, Likkutei Amarim*, 4, 35. *Iggeret HaKodesh*, 7, 19. R. Nahman of Bratslav, *Likkutei Moharan*, 33:4, 49:1; *Siddur Sha'arei Ratson*, p. 207. R. Moshe Hayyim Luzzatto, *Pithei Hokhmah*, p. 24b. *Likkutei HaGra*, in *Sifra DiTseniuta*, p. 38. *Nefesh HaHayyim*, 3, 7. *Da'at Torah*, p. 67. *Lev Eliyahu*, p. 195. *Mei Meirom*, V, p. 179. See also Exod. R.

REFERENCES, SOURCES & NOTES · 293

34:1; Lev. R. 29:4.
110. Cf. Rema, *Torat HaOlah*, 2:2. *Tanya*, 50.
111. Cf. *Sefat Emet*, I, p. 9.
112. Cf. Ps. 8:3.
113. Cf. Exod. 31:11.
114. Cf. R. Hayyim Vital, *Ets Hayyim*, I. R. Menahem Nahum of Tchernobil, *Me'or Einaim*, VaYeshev. See also Avot VI, 10 and Maharal ad loc., *Derekh Hayyim*, p. 246.
115. Cf. Ps. 33:15.
116. Cf. Gen. R. 1:2. Tanhuma, Bereshit 1. Zohar I, 5a; 90a; 134a-b; III, 35a; 69b; 178a. Zohar Hadash, Bereshit 5b. Rashi on Job 28:23. *Maggid Devarav LeYa'akov*, 63. Cf. Lev. R. 35:4. Maharal, *Derekh Hayyim*, pp. 111, 210-11; *Tiferet Yisrael*, 20.
117. Cf. *Likkutei Moharan*, 36:1.
118. Cf. *Toldot Yossef, Hakdamah. Maggid Devarav LeYa'akov*, 192. *Tanya*, 37. *Bnei Issakhar, Haggadah*, p. 44. *Likkutei Moharan*, 14:3. *Nefesh HaHayyim*, 4, 11. *Avnei Nezer*, pp. 68, 70. *Yessod HaAvodah*, p. 273. *Ben Ish Hai, Od Yossef Hai*, p. 27; *Da'at UTevunah*, pp. 72a-b; *Ben Yehoyada*, II, p. 22b.
119. Cf. TB Shabbat 105b and Rashi ad loc.; Moed Katan 25a. See also TB Sanhedrin 68a; 101a; Makot 22b; Avodah Zarah 18a. Zohar III, 29b. Hakdamat Tikkunei HaZohar, 11b; Tikkunei HaZohar, 10 (25a). *Derashot Maharal*, p. 46.
120. Cf. *Sefat Emet*, IV, p. 67.
121. Cf. Maharal, *Tiferet Yisrael*, 17; *Derekh Hayyim*, pp. 17-19. *Sefat Emet*, II, pp. 89, 93; IV, p. 175; V, p. 88.
122. Cf. Avot III, 14 and Rabbeinu Jonah Geronda ad loc. (p. 50); Maharal, *Derekh Hayyim*, p. 111. Sefer HaBahir, 5. Gen R. 1:1; Tanhuma, Bereshit 1. Zohar I, 5a; 47a. Hakdamat Tikkunei HaZohar, 4b; 11b; Tikkunei HaZohar, 2 (18a). *Da'at Torah*, pp. 12-14.
123. Cf. TB Berakhot 11b. Shelah, I, pp. 43-44. Maharal, *Derekh Hayyim*, pp. 8-9.
124. Cf. Exod. R. 47:4.
125. Cf. Isa. 51:7; Jer. 31:30-32; Ps. 37:31, 40:9, 119:11. Prov. 22:18. Mekhilta 1 (Exod. 13:17). TB Berakhot 17a; Eruvin 53b-54a and Rashi ad loc.; Berakhot 18a; Ta'anit 11a; Moed Katan 21b; Sanhedrin 106b (Ps. 119:11). Deut. R. 11:5; Shir HaShirim R. 1:19. Avot DeRabbi Nathan 24:4. Tana Devei Eliyahu Zuta 14; Shoher Tov, 119 (Ps. 37:31). Tossafot on Ketuvot 104a. Maharal, *Tiferet Yisrael*, 68; *Perushim LeAggadot*, I, p. 63. Shelah, III, pp. 11a-b, 12a, 23a. *Nefesh HaHayyim*, 1:6, 4:29. R. Tsadok HaKohen of Lublin, *Tsidkat HaTsaddik*, p. 133. *Meshekh Hokhmah*, p. 258. *The Hirsch Siddur*, p. 8. *Sefat Emet*, II, pp. 61, 206; IV, p. 42. *Ben Ish Hai*, p. 118. R. Yehezkel Sarna, *Daliyot Yehezkel*, I, p. 353.
126. Cf. *Tanya*, 4, 23.
127. Mishnah Ohalot 1:8. Cf. TB Makot 23b; Nedarim 32b. Targum Yonathan Ben Uziel on Gen. 1:27. Gen. R. 12:1; Shir HaShirim R. 1:3. Tanhuma, Lekh Lekha 15; KiTeitsei 2. Zohar I, 170b; 224a; II, 25a; 118a; 162b; III, 110b; 278b. Tikkunei HaZohar, 48 (81b); 70 (130b). Zohar Hadash, Ki Tissa 44a. Rambam, *Sefer HaMitzvot*, pp. 6, 14. Cf. also Ramban on Exod. 20:8. R. Yitshak Luria, *Likkutei Torah*, p. 104. R. Hayyim Vital, *Sha'arei Kedushah*,

1:2. Maharal, *Tiferet Yisrael*, 4, 7, 17; *Netivot Olam*, I, *Netiv HaTorah*, 1. Shelah, I, pp. 22a, 26b, 27a, 370b; III, pp. 3-4, 9a, 50a, 173a, 198b, 199b. R. Eliyahu of Vilna, *Aderet Eliyahu*, p. 483; *Sifra DiTseniuta Im Biur HaGra*, p. 38 and ibidem, *Likkutei HaGra*, p. 78. R. Hayyim of Volozhin, *Nefesh HaHayyim*, 1:6; *Ruah Hayyim*, pp. 27, 29, 30. *Tanya, Likkutei Amarim*, 37, 51; *Iggeret HaKodesh*, 7. *Or HaHayyim* on Deut. 4:4. *Toldot Ya'akov Yossef, Hakdamah*, Hayei Sarah, Shemini. *Noam Elimelekh, Devarim. Hessed LeAvraham*, pp. 36a, 51b, 52a, 55b. *Be'er Avraham*, pp. 117, 170-71, 185, 188. *Avnei Nezer*, p. 156. Cf. also *Likkutei Moharan*, 5b. *Sefat Emet*, II, p. 151; IV, pp. 74-75, 78, 82, 84. R. Yisrael Meir HaKohen, *Hafets Hayyim*, p. 4; *Mishnah Berurah*, III, 1:1. R. Yehudah HaLevi Ashlag, *Mavo, Sefer HaZohar Im Perush HaSulam*, I, p. 29.

128. Cf. Sifrei 41 (Deut. 11:13); Yalkut Shim'oni, Eikev 11:461. Cf. Exod. R. 31:16. Cf. TB Megillah 26a; Kiddushin 30b; 40b; Sotah 21b (Prov. 6:23); Avodah Zarah 17b. Cf. Zohar II, 82b; 117b; 118a; III, 82b-83a; 218b. Tikkunei HaZohar, 52. Cf. R. Eliyahu Vidas, *Reshit Hokhmah, Hakdamah*. Maharal, *Derashot, Derush Al HaMitzvot*, pp. 73-93; *Hesped*, p. 15. Maharal, *Perushim LeAggadot*, I, pp. 50, 90, 93, 95; II, pp. 10, 67-68, 121. Maharal, *Netivot Olam*, I, *Netiv HaTorah*, I, 1; 5; *Tiferet Yisrael*, 13, 59; *Derekh Hayyim*, pp. 3, 119, 125-26, 211, 215. Shelah, I, p. 2b. HaGra, *Biurum Al Mishlei*, 14:27; *Al Aggadot*, I, p. 39. *Tanya, Likkutei Amarim*, 41; *Iggeret HaKodesh*, 20. *Nefesh HaHayyim*, 1:6; 4:30. *Likkutei Moharan*, 33:4. *Be'er Avraham*, pp. 211, 309. *Neot HaDesheh*, pp. 64, 88, 90-91, 239, 251. *Sefat Emet*, I, pp. 67, 231, 234, 237; III, p. 195; IV, pp. 68, 73-75, 82, 84, 99, 131; V, pp. 66, 131. *Da'at UTevunah*, p. 106a. *Bet HaLevi*, II, p. 50.

129. Cf. Gen. 26:2-5. Deut. 4:1, 4:5, 4:14, 5:28, 8:1, 11:8, 11:11, 11:22-23. Ps. 105:44-45 and Radak ad loc. Mekhilta 9 (Exod. 15:16). Sifra 6 (Lev. 25:38). Sifrei 41-42 (Deut. 11:13-14), 80 (Deut. 12:29). Pesikta Zutarta, VaYeshev (Gen. 37:1). Gen. R. 46:7. Lev. R. 36:2. Num. R. 10:3, 17:7, 23:7. Tana Devei Eliyahu Rabba 11:12. Yalkut Shim'oni, Eikev 11:860-61; Yeshayahu 53:476. Tanhuma, Behar 1; Re'eh 8. Mishnah Kiddushin I, 9. TB Kiddushin 36b-37a; Ketuvot 110b; Sotah 14a. Zohar I, 177b. Zohar Hadash, Bereshit 14. Hakdamat Tikkunei HaZohar, 2a. *Kuzari*, V, 23. Ramban on Gen. 1:1; Lev. 18:25; Deut. 4:5. Rashbam on Bava Batra 91a; 117a. Tossafot on Pessahim 113b. *Tashbats*, III, 288. Maharal, *Netsah Yisrael*, 24. Shelah, I, pp. 79b, 168b; III, pp. 172a-173a. *Or HaHayyim* on Lev. 25:1, 25:35. *Likkutei Moharan*, 20. Hatam Sofer, *She'eilot UTeshuvot, Yoreh Deyah*, 234; *Hiddushim*, Sukkah 36a. R. Ya'akov Emden, *Mor UKtsia*, p. 16a. *Orot*, p. 163. *Mei Meirom*, VI, pp. 261, 314. *Meshekh Hokhmah*, pp. 63, 269. *Ha'amek Davar* on Deut. 8:11. *Mikhtav MeEliyahu*, III, p. 191.

130. Cf. Gen. 12:2. TB Rosh HaShanah 16b; Ketuvot 112a; Gittin 57a. Num. R. 23:5. Tana Devei Eliyahu Zuta 2. Tanhuma, Mass'ei 4 (Isa. 42:5). Zohar I, 177b; 179b-180a; III, 7. *Kuzari*, I, 109; II, 8; 12; 14; 20; 50; IV, 17. Rashi on Deut. 32:43. Ramban on Gen. 10:15, 14:18; Lev. 18:25. Seforno on Gen. 12:1. Alshekh on Lekh Lekha. Maharal, *Netsah Yisrael*, 1, 6; *Gevurot HaShem*, 8,24; *Tiferet Yisrael*, 64; *Netivot Olam*, I, *Netiv HaAvodah*, 5, 18; *Derekh Hayyim*, p. 189; *Perushim LeAggadot*, I, p. 59; IV, p. 103; *Gur Aryeh*, Shelah Lekha. Shelah, I, p. 168b. *Kedushat Levi*, pp. 21, 74. *Kitvei Rabbi Nahman*

DeBratslav, p. 192. *Sefat Emet*, III, p. 148; IV, pp. 174, 198-99. Rabbi S.R. Hirsch on Lev. 18:24; Deut. 4:5, 27:9, 32:9; *Iggrot Tsafon*, pp. 50-53; *Gesammelte Schriften*, II, Frankfurt a. Main: 1904, p. 322. Rav Kook, *Orot*, pp. 9, 33, 50-51, 165; *Hazon HaGeulah*, pp. 98-99; *Olat Reiyah*, I, pp. 203-4; II, p. 83; *Shabbat HaArets*, p. 8. *Mei Meirom*, VI, pp. 265, 280. Rabbi D.T. Hoffmann, *Bereshit*, I, p. 210; *Ha'amek Davar* on Gen. 15:7. R. Y.Y.L. Bloch, *Shiurei Da'at*, II, pp. 122-23. Rabbi B.Z. Safran, *Doresh LeTsion*, p. 12.

131. Cf. Exod. 23:30; Isa. 51:16. Sifrei 38 (Deut. 11:11). TY Hallah II, 1. TB. Ta'anit 10a. Gen. R. 1:1, 1:3, 1:5. Tanhuma Yashan, Bereshit 1. Rashi on Gen. 1:1; Lev. 20:2. Be'er Avraham, p. 145. Yitshak Breuer, *Nahliel*, Tel Aviv: 5711 (1951), p. 232. See also Rashi, Ibn Ezra and Seforno on Deut. 32:8. Zohar I, 24a; 118b; II, 108b; 119a-b; III, 229b. Hakdamat Tikkunei HaZohar, 6a. *Kuzari*, II, 14.

132. Cf. Ezek. 40:2, 47:18. See also II Kings 5:2, 6:23; Ezek. 27:17 et al. Mishnah Demai VI, 11; Shekalim III, 4; Ketuvot XIII, 11; Gittin I, 3; Mikvaot VIII, 1 et al. Rambam, *Hilkhot Terumot*, I, 2. *Likkutei Moharan*, II, 40. R. Ya'akov Yitshak HaLevi of Lublin, *Divrei Emet, Lekh Lekha*. Be'er Avraham, p. 145. *Shem MiShemuel, Haggadah*, p. 46.

133. Cf. Exod. 6:6-8. Mekhilta 10 (Exod. 15:17). Num. R. 23:11. Pirkei DeRabbi Eliezer 18. Tana Devei Eliyahu Zuta 2. Tanhuma, Bemidbar 17; Re'eh 8.

134. Cf. Exod. R. 37:5; Num. R. 15:13, 23:7. Tanhuma, Beha'alotkha 11. Cf. Rashi and Radak on Jer. 3:19. Shelah, I, p. 168b. *Mei Meirom*, VI, p. 290.

135. Lev. R. 13:2. Cf. Ps. 135:4, 132:13. Sifrei 37 (Deut. 7:12), 297 (Deut. 26:1), 301 (Deut. 26:9), 310 (Deut. 32:8). TB Kiddushin 37b; Bava Kama 38a. Gen. R. 44:17. Lev. R. 13:2, 28:4, 28:6, 28:7 (Gen. 44:17). Tanhuma, Bemidbar 17; see also Num. R. 3:1. Yalkut Shim'oni, Habakkuk 3:563. *Kuzari*, I, 95; II, 50. Rambam, *Peirush HaMishnayot*, Zevahim XIV, 8. Rashi on Gen. 15:8. Ramban on Deut. 7:7. Seforno on Exod. 6:8. Maharal, *Tiferet Yisrael*, 1, 17; *Gevurot HaShem*, 8, 24; *Derashot*, pp. 32-35. *Sefat Emet*, III, p. 198.

136. Cf. Mekhilta 9 (Exod. 15:16). Rashi on Deut. 10:14-15. TY Yoma VII, 1. Tanhuma, Bo 5; Behar 1. Rashi on Gen. 1:1. Targumei Onkelos, Yonathan, Yerushalmi and Ibn Ezra, Ramban, Seforno and Rabbi S.R. Hirsch on Exod. 19:5-6 (Isa. 43:21, 54:5). Ramban on Gen. 12:2, 28:21. Gen. R. 44:24; Zohar I, 22a; II, 81a. See also Ramban on Gen. 24:3, 26:5; Lev. 18:25; *Derashah LeRosh HaShanah (Kitvei Ramban I)*, pp. 249-50. II Kings 17:26. Alshekh on Yitro. Zohar II, 135a. *Sefat Emet*, III, p. 196. *Meshekh Hokhmah*, pp. 66, 259.

137. Cf. Gen. R. 1:1, 1:3; Tanhuma Yashan, Bereshit 1:11.

138. Cf. Sifrei 38 (Deut. 11:10), 40 (Deut. 11:12). Rashi on Deut. 11:11-12. TB Ta'anit 3b; 10a; Yevamot 63a; Avodah Zarah 10b. See also TY Shevi'it IV, 3; TB Sukkah 55b. Gen. R. 66:2; Lev. R. 36:2; Num. R. 1:3; Shir HaShirim R. 7:1; Shoher Tov, 109:4. Zohar I, 84b; 86a; 114a; II, 5b; 22b; 121a; 152b; 157a; 187a; III, 221b; 265b. Ramban on Deut. 11:11-12. Recanati, Lekh Lekha, p. 21b. *Hafla'ah*, Kiddushin, pp. 158a-b. *Or HaHayyim* on Gen. 28:14. *Toldot Ya'akov Yossef, Hakdamah. Maggid Devarav LeYa'akov*, 20, 118, 198. *Likkutei Moharan*, I, 47. *Orot*, pp. 17, 33; *Olat Reiyah*, I, p. 96. *Likkutei HaGra*, p. 76, in *Sifra DiTseniuta Im Biur HaGra*.

139. Cf. Shelah, III, p. 171. *Orot*, p. 9; *Shabbat HaArets*, p. 12. *Mei Meirom*, VI, p. 278. *Olat Reiyah*, I, p. 211; *Hazon HaGeulah*, pp. 98-99. *Sefat Emet*, IV, p. 381. R. D.T. Hoffmann, *Bereshit*, I, p. 210; II, p. 432.

140. Cf. *Derekh Hayyim*, pp. 246-48. Cf. Gen. R. 39:14, 39:18; Num. R. 11:4. *Orot*, pp. 152, 157. Cf. Num. R. 3:1.

141. Cf. *Derekh Hayyim*, p. 211. Cf. Ps. 105:45; Sifrei 41 (Deut. 11:13); Exod. R. 15:11. Zohar III, 193a.

142. Cf. TB Bava Metsia 114b (Ezek. 34:31); Yevamot 61a. Exod. R. 40:1; Lev. R. 5:7; Num. R. 10:5, 12:7. Cf. TB Sanhedrin 38b; see also TB Bava Metsia 84a; Bava Batra 58a. Zohar I, 35b; II, 111a; III, 83b. Cf. Gen. R. 19:18. Zohar I, 20b; 27b; 28b; 130b; II, 25a-b; 86a; III, 125a; 238b. Tikkunei HaZohar, 47. Tikkunei Zohar Hadash, 98a. Recanati, Bereshit, p. 7b. Shelah, I, pp. 3a, 9a, 11b, 21a-b, 70a, 137b, 162a; III, pp. 49a, 170a. Maharal, *Tiferet Yisrael*, 1, 17, 19, 24, 33; *Gevurot HaShem*, 23, 24; *Perushim LeAggadot*, IV, p. 26; *Derekh Hayyim*, pp. 42-43. *Likkutei HaGra*, p. 76 (in *Sifra DiTseniuta*); *Aderet Eliyahu*, pp. 482-84. *Tanya*, 19. *Nefesh HaHayyim*, 1. *Or HaHayyim* on Deut. 32:8-9. *Orot HaKodesh*, II, p. 303; III, pp. 43, 74, 81, 357; *Orot*, pp. 151, 169, 170. *Mei Meirom*, II, p. 138. *Sefat Emet*, I, pp. 73, 229; V, p. 131. *Ha'amek Davar (Harhev Davar)* on Gen. 34:1. *Bet Avraham*, p. 102. *Od Yossef Hai*, p. 142; *Da'at UTevunah*, p. 60b. *She'eilot UTeshuvot Harbaz*, III, p. 38. See A. Safran, *La Cabale*, p. 342.

143. Cf. Shelah, I, pp. 21a, 168a. *Orot HaKodesh*, III, pp. 47, 68. Cf. Zohar III, 221b; *Kuzari*, II, 36. Cf. also Eihah R. 2. See TY Terumot VIII, 4; Zohar III, 161a. Cf. Recanati, Yitro, p. 9a; Ki Tissa, p. 15b. Maharal, *Netsah Yisrael*, 8; *Gevurot HaShem*, 44; *Perushim LeAggadot*, IV, p. 26; *Derekh Hayyim*, p. 207. *Nefesh HaHayyim*, 1, 6. *Orot HaKodesh*, III, p. 349; *Orot*, p. 146; *Hazon HaGeulah*, p. 121; *Iggerot HaReiyah*, II, pp. 65-66. *Bet Avraham*, p. 154.

144. Cf. Gen. R. 1:5. Zohar I, 118b. Tikkunei HaZohar, 6(23b). Zohar Hadash, Yitro 37a. Cf. Radak on Gen. 49:24; TB Ta'anit 3b; Zohar II, 5b; *Maggid Devarav LeYa'akov*, 118. Cf. *Orot*, pp. 17, 19-21, 30, 130, 138, 152, 155-56, 168-70. Cf. also Ramban on Gen. 24:1.

145. Cf. Gen. 12:1-3; Lev. 25:23; Yalkut Shim'oni, Tehillim 24:695; Rashi on Ps. 24:1; Rashi and Ibn Ezra on Deut. 32:22; Kohelet R. 1:9. Zohar I, 205b; III, 266a. Cf. Sifra, Lev. 19:23, 23:10, 25:2. Num. R. 23:11. Mishnah Terumot XI, 5; Bikkurim III, 11; Ta'anit II, 4; Avot V, 9 et al. TB Ta'anit 10a; Gittin 47a; 76b; Bava Batra 91a; Makot 7a. Zohar II, 33a. *Likkutei Moharan*, II, 78; 109. *Mei Meirom*, VI, p. 144.

146. Cf. Sifrei 37 (Deut. 11:10). TB Ta'anit 10a; Yoma 54b (Job 38:5; Ps. 50:2). Gen. R. 69:3. Tana Devei Eliyahu Rabba 2. Zohar I, 72a; 231a; II, 222a. Tikkunei HaZohar, 18 (36b); 69 (110a). Zohar Hadash, Bereshit 2. TB Hullin 91 (Gen. 28:13); Zohar I, 156a. See also TB Sanhedrin 38a. *Sefat Emet*, I, p. 229. Cf. TB Sanhedrin 37a; Shoher Tov, 68:7; Tossafot Rosh HaShanah 23b. Cf. Avot DeRabbi Nathan 34:10. Targum on Jer. 11:19; Ezek. 26:20. Zohar I, 115a; III, 84a. *Yessod HaAvodah*, II, p. 83. Cf. Zohar II, 191a; III, 161a-b. Tikkunei HaZohar, 13 (29a). Ibn Ezra on Exod 8:18. Shelah, I, p. 192a. *Sefat Emet*, I, p. 109. See A. Safran, *La Cabale*, p. 330.

147. Cf. Sifrei 37 (Deut. 11:10), 353 (Deut. 33:17). TB Hullin 60b. Gen. R. 1:2, 32:2. Num. R. 23:7. Tanhuma, Mishpatim 17; Ki Tissa 2; Kedoshim 10;

Mass'ei 6; Re'eh 8. Shoher Tov, 5:1. Yalkut Shim'oni, Jer. 3:271. Zohar I, 78a; 114a; 128b; 186a; 226a; 231a; 260b; II, 157a; 184b; 222a; III, 65b; 161b. Zohar Hadash, Bereshit 10a; Ruth 76a. Tikkunei HaZohar, 21 (56a); 37 (78b). *Kuzari*, I, 95; II, 10-12; 20. Rashi on Gen. 12:9; Isa. 24:16; Ezek. 5:5. Ibn Ezra on Deut. 32:13. Ramban on Lev. 18:25; Deut. 11:10; *Derashah Al Divrei Kohelet*, p. 200; Derashah LeRosh HaShanah, p. 250 (*Kitvei Ramban* I); *Perush LeShir HaShirim*, p. 512 (*Kitvei Ramban* II). Radak on Ezek. 38:12. Maharal, *Gevurot HaShem*, *Hakdamah*, III; *Netivot Olam*, I, *Netiv HaTorah*, 10; *Netiv HaEmet*, 3; *Be'er HaGolah*, 6; *Derekh Hayyim*, pp. 7-8, 188, 226; *Perushim LeAggadot*, II, pp. 55-56. *Tossafot Yom Tov*, Sanhedrin IV, 3. *Hafla'ah*, Kiddushin IV, pp. 158a-b. Maharsha on Kiddushin 69a. See TB Bava Batra 158b. HaGra, *Biur*, Isa. 6:12; *Divrei Eliyahu*, p. 49. *Kitvei R. Nahman DeBratslav*, p. 194. *Avnei Nezer*, p. 154. *Bet Avraham*, pp. 109, 115. *Orot*, p. 151. Rav Harlap, *Mei Meirom*, VI, pp. 254, 267. R. D.T. Hoffmann, *Bereshit*, I, p. 210. *Meshekh Hokhmah*, 10. See A. Safran, *La Cabale*, p. 354.

148. Cf. Ramban, *Derashah LeRosh HaShanah* (*Kitvei Ramban* I), pp. 249-51. *Or HaHayyim* on Gen. 12:1. *Siddur Bet Ya'akov* (Emden), *Sulam Bet El*, pp. 10b, 11b. *Orot*, pp. 17, 19, 21, 30, 155-56; *Orot HaTorah*, pp. 9, 64.

149. Cf. Zohar Hadash, 120b-121a. Shelah, III, p. 170a. *Sefat Emet*, V, p. 18. *Orot*, pp. 33, 35, 98-99, 130, 155, 169-70; *Iggerot HaReiyah*, I, p. 39. Cf. TY Megillah I, 9. Rashi on Deut. 32:8. Rambam, *Hilkhot Avodat Kokhavim*, I, 1. Cf. Zohar II, 59a; 187a; III, 103b. See also TB Sukkah 55b. Cf. Maharal, *Gevurot HaShem*, 9. *Maggid Devarav LeYa'akov*, 20, 196 (Num. 31:2). *Tanya*, 37. *Shem MiShemuel*, *Devarim*, p. 236 (Deut. 32:7). Rabbi Yoel Teitelbaum of Satmar, *Divrei Yoel*, I, New York: 5731 (1971), pp. 580-81.

150. Cf. *Kitvei Maharal MiPrag*, I, p. 35. Cf. *Maggid Devarav LeYa'akov*, 196. *Orot*, p. 138; *Orot HaKodesh*, II, p. 384. Cf. Sifrei 37 (Deut. 11:10) (Prov. 8:26, 8:32). Cf. Eihah R. 8; Avot DeRabbi Nathan 37. Tana Devei Eliyahu Rabba 2. Yalkut Shim'oni, Shelah 137:43; Mishlei 8:943. Ramban on Deut. 11:10. Deut. 8:9. Maharal, *Derekh Hayyim*, p. 252. See also TB Hullin 9b; Zohar I, 156a. The Gaon of Rogachov, *Tsafnat Pa'aneah*, Bereshit, pp. 58-59. See also Amos 9:7-8.

151. Cf. Isa. 2:3; Mic. 4:2; Deut. 4:5-8. Sifrei 354 (Deut. 33:19); Ramban on Gen. 12:2. Cf. *Maggid Devarav LeYa'akov*, 20.

152. Cf. Lev. 20:26 et al. Mekhilta 12 (Exod. 12:26). See also Mekhilta 12 (Exod. 12:25); Sifra 1 (Lev. 19:2); Sifrei 92 (Num. 11:16). Cf. Lev. R. 24:4. Zohar II, 121a; III, 81a; 126a. Rashi on Lev. 19:2; Kiddushin 53a. Cf. *Kuzari*, IV, 3. Rambam, *Hilkhot Shemittah VeYovel*, XIII, 13. Ran on Nedarim 20b. Maharal, *Netivot Olam*, I, *Netiv HaTorah*, 1, 2, 3; *Tiferet Yisrael*, 1, 2, 5, 10; *Gevurot HaShem*, 8, 16, 24, 47; *Derekh Hayyim*, pp. 188-89; *Derashot*, p. 5; *Perushim LeAggadot*, I, p. 97; IV, p. 103. *Tanya*, *Iggeret HaKodesh*, 7. *Nefesh HaHayyim*, 3, 5. Malbim on Lev. 19:2. *Sefat Emet*, III, p. 184. *Orot*, pp. 35, 39, 155. *Ha'amek Davar* on Exod. 15:11. *HaKtav VeHaKabbalah*, II, *Devarim*, p. 30. M.D. Cassuto, *Shemot*, p. 163. Cf. *Maggid Devarav LeYa'akov*, 94.

153. Cf. Deut. 4:14. Pesikta Zutarta, VaYeitsei (Gen. 28:21). Yalkut Shim'oni, Shelah 13:743. *Kuzari*, II, 20. Rabbi S.R. Hirsch, *Gesammelte Schriften*, II, p. 322.

154. Cf. Mal. 2:6; Neh. 9:13. Ps. 19:10, 119:142, 119:151. Cf. TY Rosh HaShanah III, 8; TB Berakhot 5b; Petihta DeEihah Rabbati 2; Tana Devei Eliyahu Zuta 21; Zohar III, 85b; 90b. Cf. Mic. 7:20; Shir HaShirim R. 3:5; Zohar I, 120a; 146b; Zohar Hadash, 26b; Ari HaKadosh, *Likkutei Torah*, p. 122; Maharal, *Tiferet Yisrael*, 20; *Netivot Olam* I, *Netiv HaEmet*, 3. Ramban on Gen. 1:1, 19:5, 48:22, 49:15. *Kitvei Rabbi Nahman DeBratslav*, p. 192; *Likkutei Moharan*, I, 47. *Degel Mahaneh Ephraim*, Mass'ei. *Orot*, pp. 10, 12-13, 70; *Orot HaTorah*, pp. 13, 77. Cf. Gen. R. 30:1; Exod. R. 36:2 (Ps. 48:3; Isa. 60:3). See Rashi on Deut. 48:19.

155. Cf. Exod. 12:25, 13:5, 13:11ff. Deut. 4:1, 4:5, 6:18, 8:1, 11:8, 26:1, 30:16. Mekhilta 6 (Exod. 20:6); Sifrei 43 (Deut. 11:7). TY Shekalim III, 3; Lev. R. 34:7. *Kuzari*, II, 18; II, 20 with the commentaries ad loc.; V, 23. Rambam, *Sefer HaMitzvot*, *Mitzvot Asseh*, *Mitzvah* 153; *Hilkhot Kiddush HaHodesh*, I, 8; V, 13; *Hilkhot Terumot*, I, 2. Rashi on Deut. 11:18. Ramban on Gen. 26:5; Lev. 18:25; Deut. 4:5, 11:18; *Derashah Al Divrei Kohelet (Kitvei Ramban* I), pp. 200-1. Maharal, *Gur Aryeh*, Bereshit. Shelah, I, pp. 169a, 188a; *Siddur Sha'ar HaShamayim*, p. 512. Hatam Sofer, *She'eilot UTeshuvot*, Yoreh Deyah, 234; *Hiddushim*, Sukkah 36a. Rav Harlap, *Mei Meirom*, VI, p. 252. *Hafets Hayyim*, p. 4. R. B.Z. Safran, *Doresh LeTsion*, p. 25.

156. Cf. Lev. 25:8-10 and Sifra 2 ad loc. Num. 35:13-14. Deut. 17:14-19, 31:12. Mekhilta 2 (Exod. 12:2), 4 (Exod. 21:24). Sifrei 6 (Deut. 1:7). Mishnah Sotah IX, 1; Sanhedrin I; Shevuot II, 2. TB Berakhot 63a; Ketuvot 25a; Sotah 44b; Gittin 8b and Rashi and Tossafot ad loc.; Kiddushin 38a; Bava Batra 4a; Sanhedrin 2a; 20b; 56b; Makot 7a; Shevuot 14b; Avodah Zarah 21a and Tossafot ad loc.; Arakhin 32b. Tossefta Sanhedrin IV, 10. Rambam, *Sefer HaMitzvot*, *Shoresh* 14; *Mitzvot Asseh*, *Mitzvah* 153; *Hilkhot Terumot*, I; *Hilkhot Kiddush HaHodesh*, I, 8; V, 1; *Hilkhot Rotseah UShmirat Nafesh*, VIII, 1; *Hilkhot Sanhedrin*, I, 1; *Hilkhot Shemittah VeYovel*, X, 8; *Hilkhot Melakhim*, I; V; VII; *Moreh Nevukhim*, III, 48. *Sefer HaHinukh*, *Mitzvah* 4. *Sefat Emet*, IV, p. 174. *Hiddushei Maran Riz HaLevi*, p. 21.

157. Cf. Exod. 23. Lev. 19, 25. Num. 15, 18. Deut. 18, 24, 26. Mishnah Kiddushin I, 9. TY Shevi'it VI, 5; Kiddushin I, 8. TB Kiddushin 36b-37b-38a. Rambam, *Hilkhot Matnot Aniyim*, I; *Hilkhot Shemittah VeYovel*, XI, 1. *Sefer HaHinukh*, *Mitzvah* 216. *Shulhan Arukh*, Yoreh Deyah, 293, 333. *Bet HaLevi*, Shemot, p. 39.

158. Cf. Deut. 29:9; I Chron. 17:21. Mishnah Sanhedrin IV, 5; Temurah I, 6. TB Ketuvot 75a (Ps. 87:5); Bava Batra 119a; 122a; Makot 23b; Avodah Zarah 21a; Temurah 13a. Gen. R. 39:10. Exod. R. 1:13, 48:2. Tana Devei Eliyahu Rabba 25. TY Ta'anit IV, 2. Megillah III, 6 (Isa. 51:16). Zohar III, 35a. See also Zohar I, 172b. See Rashi on Hullin 135a; Tossafot on Bava Batra 44b; see also Tossafot on Pessahim 3b; Rambam, *Hilkhot Terumot*, I, 2. Ran on Nedarim 28. Alshekh on Nitsavim. Maharal, *Gevurot HaShem*, 11. Shelah, I, p. 21a; III, pp. 201a-b. *Or HaHayyim* on Lev. 26:43. *Hiddushei UBiurei HaGra*, p. 82. *Kitvei R. Nahman DeBratslav*, pp. 192-93; *Likkutei Moharan*, II, 71. *Sefat Emet*, III, p. 196; IV, pp. 174, 176. *Avnei Nezer*, pp. 149-53. Rav Kook, *She'eilot UTeshuvot Mishpat Kohen*, 154; *Olat Reiyah* I, p. 203; *Orot*, p. 45. R.I. Schepanski, *Erets-Yisrael BeSifrut HaTeshuvot*, Jerusalem: 5727 (1966), I, p. 27. *Shem MiShemuel*, *Vayikra*, p. 287. *Tsafnat Pa'aneah*, *Devarim* II, p.

REFERENCES, SOURCES & NOTES • 299

247. *Hazon Ish,* Shevi'it, 21:5. Cf. Lev. 26:42-43; Isa. 56:8. TY Yoma I, 1. Cf. also TB Yevamot 64a. Cf. Rambam, *Sefer HaMitzvot, Mitzvot Asseh, Mitzvah* 4. See also *She'eilot UTeshuvot Avnei Nezer, Yoreh Deyah,* 453; *She'eilot UTeshuvot Yeshuot Malko, Yoreh Deyah,* 66. R. B.Z. Safran, *Doresh LeTsion,* pp. 9-10.

159. Cf. Lev. 18:25-26, 18:28, 19:29, 20:22 and Sifra ad loc., 25:2 and *Kli Yakar* ad loc., 25:2, 25:4, 25:6, 25:19, 25:24, 26:34, 26:42 and Sifra ad loc., 26:43, 36:4. Num. 13:32; 14; 35:33-34. Deut. 24:4, 29:21-28. Isa. 24:5. Jer. 3:1-2. Hos. 2:23-24. Sifra 13 (Lev. 18:28), 7 (Lev. 26:34). Sifrei 37-38 (Deut. 11:10), 333 (Deut. 32:43). Avot V, 9. TY Kilaim I, 7; IX, 3; Shekalim III, 3; Ta'anit III, 3. TB Rosh HaShanah 16b; Gittin 57a; Ketuvot 111-12; Bava Batra 25b; Avodah Zarah 15b. Pesikta Zutarta, Exod. 3:8. Exod. R. 32:2; Lev. R. 36:4. Deut. R. 3:7; Petihta DeEihah Rabbati 34. Yalkut Shim'oni, Jer. 41:328. Tanhuma, Mishpatim 10; Re'eh 8. Onkelos on Deut. 32:43. Rashi on Lev. 18:25; Deut. 32:43; Kiddushin 37a. Tossafot on Bava Batra 81a. Ramban on Gen 1:1; Lev. 18:25; Num. 35:33; Yevamot 64a. Radak on Ezek. 33:25. *Kuzari,* I, 109; II, 18. Rambam, *Sefer HaMitzvot, Mitzvot Asseh, Mitzvah* 135; *Hilkhot Shemittah VeYovel,* I, 1; *Hilkhot Melakhim,* V, 11. *Tur, Orah Hayyim,* 208. Alshekh, Noah. Maharshal on Bava Metsia 91. Maharal, *Derekh Hayyim,* p. 189; *Perushim LeAggadot,* I, p. 59. Shelah, III, p. 23a. *Or HaHayyim* on Lev. 26:43; Deut. 32:43. *Siddur Bet Ya'akov* (Emden), *Sulam Bet El,* pp. 11a-b. *Sefat Emet,* III, p. 191. Rav Kook, *Shabbat HaArets,* pp. 10, 12. *Mei Meirom,* V, pp. 205-6; VI, pp. 144, 186. Rav Epstein, Tossefet Berakhah, V, pp. 259, 316 (Gen. 3:17). Rav B.Z. Safran, *She'eilot UTeshuvot Harbaz,* I, p. 21.

160. Cf. Isa. 54:1, 54:4-5, 62:4-5. Rashi and Radak ad loc. Cf. Lev. 26:4; Deut. 11:14.

161. Cf. Gen. R. 5:7; Pesikta Zutarta, Gen. 1:1; Zohar Hadash, 20a; Onkelos and Rashi on Lev. 26:34; *Sefat Emet,* III, p. 190; *Shem MiShemuel, Haggadah,* pp. 39, 46; see also A. Safran, *La Cabale,* pp. 41, 288. Cf. TB Bava Batra 25b; Lev. 25:23.

162. Cf. Tikkunei HaZohar, 47; 83b. Cf. *Biurei HaGra Al Aggadot,* II, pp. 9, 80 Cf. *Perushei Maharal MiPrag LeAggadot HaShas,* I, pp. 83-84.

163. Cf. II Sam. 7:10. See *Biurei HaGra Al Aggadot,* I, p. 13.

164. Cf. Deut. 12:11, 12:14, 12:18, 12:21, 12:26, 14:23-25, 15:20, 16:2, 16:6-7, 16:11, 16:15, 17:8, 17:10, 23:17, 31:11; Josh. 9:27. Neh. 1:9. II Chron. 7:12. Ps. 132:13. I Kings 8:16, 8:44, 8:48, 11:32, 11:36, 14:21. II Chron. 6:5, 6:34, 6:38, 12:13. I Kings 11:13, 11:32, 14:21. II Kings 21:7, 23:27. II Chron. 6:6, 12:13, 33:7. Zech. 1:17, 2:16, 2:32. II Chron. 6:34, 6:38, 7:16. See also Zohar I, 85a; Rashi on Ta'anit 16a. TB Bava Batra 75b.

165. Cf. Gen. R. 68:10 (Exod. 33:21). Cf. Mekhilta 1 (Exod. 13:21); Sifrei 134 (Num. 27:12). TB Berakhot 13b. See also Gen. R. 4:3, 46:2; see also TB Sukkah 5a. Cf. Exod. R. 2:9, 28:4, 34:1; 46:6. Num. R. 12:3-4. Shir HaShirim R. 3:15. Pesikta Rabbati 21:10; Pesikta Zutarta, Deut. 33:27. Shoher Tov, 90:10. Tanhuma, Ki Tissa 27. Zohar II, 99b; III, 242a. Tikkunei HaZohar, 26; 70. *Kuzari,* IV, 3. See Rambam, *Moreh Nevukhim,* I, 8. Cf. R. Yossef Albo, *Ikkarim,* II, 17. Rashi on Exod. 33:21. *Perushei HaTorah Le Rabbi Yehuda HeHassid,* p. 126. *Siddur Rabbeinu Shelomo de Garmaise,* pp. 176-77.

Maharal, *Netivot Olam*, I, *Netiv HaAvodah*, 5; *Gevurot HaShem*, 23, 30, 70. Shelah, III, p. 40b. Rema, *Torat HaOlah*, I, 2. R. Dov Baer of Mezerich, *Maggid Devarav LeYa'akov*, 124, 146. R. Hayyim of Volozhin, *Nefesh HaHayyim*, 2:14, 3:1, 3:4; *Ruah Hayyim*, pp. 41, 90. *Tanya*, 36. *Kedushat Levi*, p. 54. R. Nahman of Bratslav, *Haggadah Shel Pessah*, pp. 44-45, 47. See Deut. 4:39; Jer. 23:24; Isa. 6:3; see also I Kings 8:27; Isa. 60:1-2. See R. I. Weinstock, *BeMa'aglei HaNigleh VeHaNistar*, Jerusalem: 5730 (1969), p. 212. R.Y. Rozin, Gaon of Rogachov, *Mefa'aneah Tsefunot*, p. 253. Esther Starobinski-Safran, *Philon d'Alexandrie, De Fuga Et Inventione*, p. 156.

166. Cf. Ps. 135:21; Joel 4, 17, 21; Shelah, *Siddur Sha'ar HaShamayim*, p. 381; *Kedushat Levi*, p. 54; *Sefat Emet*, I, p. 9; Rabbi S.R. Hirsch on Exod. 15:17.

167. Cf. Ramban on Deut. 31:16; Maharal, *Derekh Hayyim*, pp. 188-89. Cf. *Tanhuma, Bo* 5. Cf. Zohar II, 85b. See Deut. 14:1; Avot III, 14; TB Kiddushin 36a. Cf. TB Sanhedrin 14b.

168. Cf. Deut. 11:12. Cf. *Derashot Maharal*, pp. 22-23. Shelah, I, pp. 168b-169a. *Maggid Devarav LeYa'akov*, 118, 142. *Sefat Emet*, I, p. 9; II, p. 139.

169. Cf. Num. R. 7:8, 7:10; Num. 35:34. Cf. Gen. R. 64:3 (Gen. 26:2). Zohar I, 141b. *Or HaHayyim* on Gen. 12:1. *Kitvei R. Nahman DeBratslav*, p. 194. Cf. Sifra 6 (Lev. 25:38); Shoher Tov, 105; Sifra 24 (Gen. 28:11; see also Gen. 35:15). Pirkei DeRabbi Eliezer 35. Cf. TY Shekalim III, 3; Shabbat I, 3. TB Pessahim 113; Ketuvot 111 and Meiri ad loc. Cf. Zohar I, 120a; II, 4b; 238b; 268a. Rashi and Radak on I Kings 9:3; Rashi on I Kings 9:7. Rambam, *Hilkhot Shemittah VeYovel*, XIII, 13. *Sefer HaHinukh, Mitzvah* 95. Shelah, I, p. 1b.

170. Cf. Exod. 20:24, 25:8, 29:45. Lev. 26:11. Num. 5:3, 35:34. Ezek. 37:26-28. Hos. 11:9. Ps. 78:60. Sifrei 38 (Deut. 11:10). Mishnah Berakhot IX, 1; Avot III, 2:6; 14. TY Bikkurim III, 3; Kiddushin I, 7. TB Berakhot 6a; 54a. Shabbat 31b; 33a; 55a (Ezek. 9:6). Ta'anit 22a (Exod. 19:13, 34:3). Haggigah 16b; 46b. Yevamot 6a (Lev. 19:30); 64a (Gen. 17:8). Ketuvot 5a. Sotah 17a; 38a. Bava Batra 25b. Shevuot 16a. Avodah Zarah 4a. Menahot 110a. Hullin 92a. (See also TY Ta'anit III, 10; Yevamot I, 6. TB Berakhot 16b; Shabbat 12b. Sukkah 33a; 35b. Nedarim 66b. Kiddushin 30b; 31b. Sanhedrin 17a; 46a.) Cf. Gen. R. 19:13, 68:7. Exod. R. 1:5, 18:6, 24:1, 30:20, 33:4, 33:10, 34:4, 45:6, 46:2. Lev. R. 29:3. Num. R. 12:3. Deut. R. 7:2. Shir HaShirim R. 1:20, 5:1, 8:16. Eihah R. 1:39, 2:4. Pirkei DeRabbi Eliezer 35, 40. Shoher Tov, 68. Yalkut Shim'oni, VaYeitsei 28:119. (See also Lev. R. 5:4, 11:8.) Cf. Zohar I, 55b; 68a; 85a; 150a (Gen. 28:17); 205b; II, 146a; 163b; III, 79b; 82a; 106b; 179b. Tikkunei HaZohar, 22b; 132a. Rashi on Gen. 28:10, 33:20, 35:7; Exod. 17:15; Jer. 3:16; Ibn Ezra on Exod. 8:18. Ramban on Deut. 11:22. Seforno on Exod. 3:5-6. Alshekh on Exod. 3:1, 25:8; I Kings 6:11-13. *Or HaHayyim* on Gen. 35:7, 35:15, 46:4; Lev. 26:11. Malbim on Jer. 7:4, 7:7. *Ha'amek Davar* on Gen. 35:15. Tossafot on Beitsa 5b. *Derashot Ran*, 8. Maharal, *Tiferet Yisrael*, 10, 33; *Gevurot HaShem*, 70; *Derekh Hayyim*, p. 208; see also ibidem, pp. 11-12. Maharsha on Berakhot 8a. Shelah, I, p. 117a; III, pp. 11b, 165b; *Siddur Sha'ar HaShamayim*, pp. 515-16. R. Eliyahu of Vilna, *Biur HaGra*, Shir HaShirim 1:16; *Siddur Ishei Yisrael*, p. 333. *Tanya, Likkutei Amarim*, 36, 37; *Iggeret HaKodesh*, 23. *Nefesh HaHayyim*, 1, 4. *Kedushat Levi*, pp. 59a, 119b. *Likku-*

tei Moharan, 94. R. Shemuel Shmelke of Nikolsburg, *Divrei Shemuel*, pp. 26-27. R. Yisrael of Koznitz, *Avodat Yisrael*, I, p. 205. R. Avraham of Slonim, *Yessod HaAvodah*, II, p. 83; *Bet Avraham*, pp. 140-43; *Be'er Avraham*, pp. 128-29, 160, 166, 182, 185, 189, 209. *Avnei Nezer*, p. 40; *Sefat Emet*, II, p. 140. Rav Kook, *She'eilot UTeshuvot Mishpat Kohen*, 185; *Olat Reiyah*, II, pp. 274-75. *Meshekh Hokhmah*, p. 68. Hafets Hayyim, *Al Siddur HaTefillah*, pp. 53-54.

171. Cf. Lev. R. 19:5; Tanhuma, Behar 1; Rashi on Hullin 92a; Tossafot on Avodah Zarah 21a; Or *HaHayyim* on Lev. 25:29. See also Gen. 28:17, 28:19, 30:30.
172. Cf. Lev. 25:38 and Sifra ad loc. See Lev. 25:23 and Sifra and Rashi ad loc. See also Lev. 25:42 and Sifra ad loc. TB Kiddushin 22b. Cf. Mekhilta 2 (Exod. 19:6). TB Ketuvot 110b and *P'nei Yehoshua* ad loc. (I Sam. 26:19). See Gen. 17:8; Exod. 6:6-8; Num. 15:41; see also Lev. 22:33 and Sifra ad loc. Cf. Rambam, *Hilkhot Melakhim*, V, 12. Ramban on Gen. 28:21. Maharal, *Derekh Hayyim*, p. 188. *Kitvei R. Nahman DeBratslav*, p. 193. Rav Kook, *Orot*, p. 140. R. Y.Y. Bloch, *Shiurei Da'at*, II, p. 123. Cf. Zohar I, 85a. Shelah, I, p. 169a. Cf. Shir HaShirim R. 1; Eihah R. 2. Zohar I, 27b. Tikkunei HaZohar, 1b; 21. Cf. Exod. 19:6. Cf. Zohar III, 84a. Cf. Zohar II, 126a. Cf. Shir HaShirim R. 5:3. Tikkunei HaZohar, 62. Cf. Zohar I, 256b-257a; II, 101b; III, 90b. Hida, *Nitsotsei Orot*, Zohar III, 159b. *Likkutei Moharan*, 74.
173. Cf. Zohar II, 85b. See also Zohar II, 79b-80a; 85b. Cf. R. Yisrael of Koznitz, *Avodat Yisrael*, I, pp. 204-5.
174. Cf. Zohar III, 82b-83a.
175. Cf. Lev. 22:32 and Sifra ad loc. Cf. Isa. 29:23. TY Shevi'it IV, 3. TB Sanhedrin 74b. Rambam, *Sefer HaMitzvot, Mitzvot Asseh, Mitzvah* 9; *Hilkhot Yessodei HaTorah*, V, 1; *Iggeret Teiman*. Cf. Lev. 11:44 and Sifra ad loc. See Lev. 20:7, 22:33. Cf. Exod. R. 15:24; Lev. R. 24:1. Zohar I, 61a; II, 133a; III, 24b; 80a. Cf. Lev. 22:32. TB Sotah 14a. *Biurei HaGra Al Aggadot*, I, p. 12. See also Maharal, *Gevurot HaShem*, 47.
176. Cf. Zohar I, 174a; *Biurei HaGra Al Aggadot*, I, p. 29. Cf. Gen. 32:11; see Zohar I, 148b (Gen. 28:11).
177. Cf. Gen. 32:29, 33:31, 35:9 and Seforno ad loc., 35:10 and Ramban ad loc. Cf. Ramban on Gen. 46:2. Cf. TB Hullin 101b; Shelah, I, p. 21a. Cf. Zohar I, 194b; Isa. 49:3; Tanhuma, Kedoshim 2. Cf. also TB Bava Batra 75b; Zohar I, 93b. See also Gen. 33:20 and Ramban and Rabbeinu Bahya ad loc. TB Megillah 18a. Gen. R. 79:10; Zohar I, 138a. Tanhuma, Kedoshim 5; Ps. 82:6. See also Zohar I, 213b; II, 66b; III, 86a. See also Zohar II, 38a; 90b; 124b. Rabbeinu Bahya on Exod. 33:7. Targum Yerushalmi, Rashbam and *Ha'amek Davar* on Gen. 25:22. See also Rashi and Ibn Ezra on Gen. 25:23. Gen. R. 63:8. TY Eruvin V, 1.
178. Cf. Gen. 49:8; Gen. R. 98:11; TB Sotah 36b and Rashi ad loc. Zohar I, 89b. Cf. Gen. R. 63:3. Ari HaKadosh, *Likkutei Torah*, p. 86. Cf. Sotah 37a; Ps. 114:2. See also Esther R. 6:2.
179. Cf. TB Sotah 36b; Gen. R. 71:3; Jer. 31:14; Rashi on Ps. 80:2; Maharsha on Berakhot 55b. See also Maharal, *Netivot Olam*, II, *Netiv Ahavat HaShem*, 2; *Perushim LeAggadot*, I, p. 39.
180. Cf. Zohar I, 154b. See TB Eruvin 18b; Zohar II, 228b. Cf. Rashi on Exod.

17:16; TB Berakhot 58a; Yalkut Shim'oni, Beshalah 17:268. Cf. TB Sanhedrin 20b; Mekhilta 1 (Exod. 17:16); Sifrei 296 (Deut. 25:19); Pesikta Rabbati 12 (Deut. 25:17-19); Ps. 9:7-8. Cf. Tanhuma, Ki Teitsei 11. See also TB Pessahim 50a; Kiddushin 71a. Num. R. 11:7; Rashi on Exod. 3:15. Zohar III, 230a; 281a. Tikkunei HaZohar, 17; 57. Cf. Exod. R. 3:9. Cf. *Perushei HaTorah LeRabbi Yehuda HeHassid*, pp. 75-76. *Hiddushei Maran Riz HaLevi*, p. 12.
181. Cf. Gen. 2:4; Gen. R. 12:9-10. TB Menahot 29b. Zohar I, 3b; 25a; 46b; 86b; II, 123b; III, 29a; 34b; 122b-123a. See also Zohar III, 4b; *Sefat Emet*, I, p. 109.
182. Zech. 14:9.
183. Cf. Yalkut Reuveni, Shelah; Num. 14:21; Isa. 43:7. Cf. Zohar I, 9a; II, 90b. Cf. Lev. R. 11:3 (Ps. 82:6). Cf. also Zohar II, 96a; 124a. See also TB Nedarim 81a; Maharal, *Tiferet Yisrael, Hakdamah*, p. 2a-b.
184. Cf. TB Nedarim 81a (Jer. 9:11-12; cf. Jer. 32:23); cf. TB Bava Metsia 85a. Cf. Sifrei 38 (Deut. 11:11), 41 (Deut. 11:13; Isa. 5:24; Amos 2:4). Sifra 5 (Lev. 26:19). TY Rosh HaShanah III, 8; Haggigah I, 7. Massekhet Kallah 8. TB Shabbat 119b. Deut. R. 3:12. Petihta DeEihah Rabbati 2; Eihah R. 1:1. Tana Devei Eliyahu Rabba 18; Tana Devei Eliyahu Zuta 1. Shoher Tov, 119. Yalkut Shim'oni, Eikev 11:860. Zohar I, 185a; Zohar Hadash, Bereshit 8. Ramban, *Derashah LeRosh HaShanah* (*Kitvei Ramban* I), p. 289. Don Yitshak Abrabanel on Exod. 20 (II, p. 191). Maharal, *Netsah Yisrael*, 19. Shelah, III, p. 203a. *Or HaHayyim* on Lev. 36:43. *Sefat Emet*, V, p. 5. See also TB Sotah 14a; Rav Harlap, *Mei Meirom*, VI, p. 277. Hatam Sofer, *Haggadah Shel Pessah*, p. 71.
185. Cf. Deut. 11:13ff. 29:23-24. Sifra 1 (Lev. 26:3). See Sifrei 40 (Deut. 11:12). Cf. Tana Devei Eliyahu Rabba 11, 12, 14. Tanhuma, Re'eh 8. See also TB Yoma 38b. Cf. *Siddur Bet Ya'akov* (Emden), *Sulam Bet El*, pp. 11a-b. *Meshekh Hokhmah*, p. 63. Hafets Hayyim, *Al HaTorah*, p. 65; *Perushim al Siddur HaTefillah*, p. 18.
186. Cf. Lev. 18:25; Deut. 11:17, 29:21-28 et al. TY Peyah VII, 7 (Ps. 106:34); Kilaim IX, 3; Ta'anit IV, 5. Zohar III, 114a. Deut. R. 11:17. Gen. R. 19:18 (Gen. 3:17). Lev. R. 17:5. Zohar II, 262b; III, 122a. (Hos. 6:7). See also Avot V, 9; Avot DeRabbi Nathan 20. TB Shabbat 33a; Sanhedrin 39a. Tanhuma, Behar 1; Nitsavim 3 (Dan. 9:11). Rashi on Lev. 25:15. Shelah, III, pp. 168a, 169b, 170a. R. Yeruham HaLevi Levovitch, *Da'at Torah*, p. 160.
187. Cf. Num. R. 7:10 (Num. 5:2; Jer. 15:1). Rav Kook, *Shabbat HaArets*, p. 11.
188. Cf. Shelah, III, pp. 170a-b (Num. 33:2). *Likkutei Moharan*, p. 74. See also *Toldot Ya'akov Yossef, Noah; Bnei Issakhar*, I, p. 111a.
189. Cf. TY Peyah II, 5. TB Sukkah 30b and Tossafot ad loc.; Bava Batra 44b and Tossafot ad loc.; 119a. R. I. Schepanski, *Erets-Yisrael BeSifrut HaTeshuvot*, I, p. 27. N. Rakover, *HaShelihut VeHaHarsha'a BaMishpat HaIvri*, Jerusalem: 5732 (1972), pp. 257-58; R. Y. Rozin, Gaon of Rogachov, *Mefa'aneah Tsefunot*, p. 184; Hazon Ish, *Hoshen Mishpat*, 1, 27.
190. Cf. Gen. 15:13-16, 46:4; Lev. 26:34. Deut. 30:2-5. Isa. 65:8-9, 65:21-23. Jer. 3:14, 29:10, 30:10-11, 31:10, 31:15-16, 32. Ezek. 20:41-42, 28:25-26, 36:24-25, 37:21-22, 38:16, 39:28. Zech. 8:7-8. Cf. TY Kiddushin I, 8. Gen. R. 44:21, 46:4, 68:12. Exod. R. 3:4, 46:4. Lev. R. 29:2. Num. R. 23:14. Pesikta DeRav Kahana, II, 23, Rosh HaShanah 2, p. 336; *Likkutei Midrash*, p. 464. Ramban

on Gen. 46:1-2; Lev. 26:16. Or *HaHayyim* on Lev. 25:2. HaGra, *Siddur Ishei Yisrael*, p. 44 (*Siah Yitshak*). *Ha'amek Davar* on Lev. 26:42-43.

191. Cf. Gen. 13:15, 17:8 (see also Gen. 15:5, 22:16-17). Exod. 32:13. Jer. 7:7. Ezek. 37:25. I Chron. 16:15-18. Cf. Sifra 13 (Lev. 18:25, 18:28). TB Rosh HaShanah 12b. Gen. R. 17:8. Esther R. 1. Cf. Ramban on Gen. 15:18, 22:16; Deut. 9:4; see also Ramban on Lev. 26:16; Rambam, *Hilkhot Teshuvah*, VII, 5; *Hilkhot Melakhim*, XI, 1. Num. R. 7:10 (Isa. 30:15); TB Sanhedrin 97b. See Maharal, *Gevurot HaShem*, 8. *Bet HaLevi*, I, p. 22 (TB Megillah 31b). *Meshekh Hokhmah*, p. 63. Rabbi S.R. Hirsch on Exod. 32:13. *Olat Reiyah*, II, p. 83. *Mikhtav MeEliyahu*, II, p. 50.

192. Cf. Deut. 4:20 and Targum Yerushalmi ad loc.; I Kings 8:51; Jer. 11:14; Zech. 13:9. Cf. TB Berakhot 56a; Ta'anit 16a; Ketuvot 112b; Sanhedrin 37b. Cf. Gen. R. 44:1, 44:8. Zohar I, 83a; III, 216a. *Kuzari*, II, 44; III, 11-12; IV, 23. Abrabanel on Gen. 15:12. R. Moshe Cordovero, *Pardess Rimonim*, 13, 3. Maharal, *Netsah Yisrael*, 14; *Gevurot HaShem*, 3. Shelah, III, pp. 22b, 170a-b; *Siddur Sha'ar HaShamayim*, p. 517. Or *HaHayyim* on Lev. 25:26. *Kedushat Levi*, p. 36a. Rav Kook, *Hazon HaGeulah*, p. 96. *Shem MiShemuel*, *Haggadah Shel Pessah*, p. 46.

193. Cf. Tanhuma, Re'eh 8; *Kedushat Levi*, p. 74. Cf. also Shelah, III, p. 23a. Cf. Sifrei 8 (Deut. 1:8), 31 (Deut. 6:4). See *Or HaHayyim* on Deut. 11:26. Cf. Gen. 12:7, 12:15, 13:17, 15:18 and Ramban ad loc., 17:8, 26:3-4 and Ramban ad loc., 28:13, 35:12. Exod. 6:4-8; Josh. 1:3-4; Jer. 31:4-5; I Chron. 16:15. Cf. Mekhilta 17 (Exod. 13:5); Yalkut Shim'oni, Bo 13:222.

194. Cf. TB Bava Batra 117b; 119b; Avodah Zarah 53b; cf. also Bava Batra 119a. Cf. Ramban on Gen. 13:17; Abrabanel on Gen. 17:7-8; *Biurei HaGra Al Aggadot*, I, p. 63; *Ha'amek Davar* on Gen. 15:7. Cf. TB Bava Batra 49b. Maharal, *Gevurot HaShem*, 47. *Mei Meirom*, V. p. 235; VI, pp. 276-78. See also *Meshekh Hokhmah*, p. 328. Cf. also TY Bava Batra VIII, 2 (Exod. 6:8); TB Bava Batra 119b; Deut. 26:15; Zohar II, 79b. Ezek. 11:15, 33:24. Lev. R. 35:7. See Seforno on Deut. 26:5. See also A. Safran, *La Cabale*, pp. 177-78.

195. Cf. Ezek. 20:31-40. Sifrei 132 (Deut. 32:1); TY Ta'anit I, 1; TB Sanhedrin 97b; Exod. R. 3:7; Exod. 6:1, 11:1. Seforno on Lev. 26:15. *Akeidat Yitshak*, Nitsavim 99. Maharal, *Netsah Yisrael*, 11. *Gevurot HaShem*, 38. Hatam Sofer, *Derashot*, II, p. 312. Rav Kook, *Orot*, p. 63; *Olat Reiyah*, I, p. 203. Rav Harlap, *Mei Meirom*, V, p. 238. *Bet HaLevi*, II, p. 5. *Meshekh Hokhmah*, pp. 191-92. R. Elhanan Wasserman of Baranovic, *Ikveta DiMeshiha*, IV. Sifrei 32 (Deut. 6:5); Exod. R. 1:1; Tanhuma, Shemot 1; Shoher Tov, 94:2. TB Berakhot 5a. Maharal, *Derashot*, p. 5. *Siddur Bet Ya'akov* (Emden), *Sulam Bet El*, p. 11b. Shelah, I, p. 169b. *Kitvei R. Nahman DeBratslav*, p. 194. Rav Harlap, *Mei Meirom*, VI, p. 276. R. Yossef Hayyim of Baghdad, *Benayahu Ben Yehoyada*, I, p. 3a.

196. Cf. Lev. 20:24. Deut. 1:8, 15:4, 16:20, 17:14, 26:1, 30:5. Josh. 1:5. Ezek. 33:24. Cf. TB Bava Batra 117b; 119b; Avodah Zarah 53b and Rashi ad loc. Pesikta Zutarta, Shelah, Num. 15:2. See TY Shevi'it VI, 1. See Ramban on Gen. 15:7 (8). *Kedushat Levi*, p. 74b. *Sefat Emet*, III, p. 202. *Mei Meirom*, VI, p. 302. *Ha'amek Davar* on Gen. 15:7. Mekhilta 18 (Exod. 13:11). Deut. 26:3. *Sefat Emet*, III, p. 196.

197. Cf. Deut. 28:65; Eihah 1:3; Gen. R. 33:8; Shoher Tov, 146. *Sefat Emet*, V, p.

5; *Orot*, p. 11; *Mei Meirom*, VI, pp. 242, 277; Hatam Sofer, *Haggadah*, p. 120.
198. Ezek. 20:32. Cf. Sifra 6 (Lev. 26:30); Tanhuma, Nitsavim 3; Rashi on Num. 15:41; Rambam, *Iggeret Teiman*, p. 136; Shelah, I, pp. 68a-b-69a; *Sefat Emet*, III, p. 185. See also TB Hullin 16b; Rashi on Gen. 36:7; Rav Kook, *Mishpat Kohen*, 144. Cf. Hos. 11:4. *Kitvei R. Nahman DeBratslav*, Tel-Aviv: 5711, pp. 192-93, 343.
199. Cf. Lev. 25:23; Sifra 4 (Lev. 25:23), 7 (Lev. 26:34).
200. According to Rabbi Nahman of Bratslav, the prayers for Jerusalem and Erets-Yisrael which Jews recite daily are a "cry of protest" by Israel against those who have appropriated the Land of Israel by force. See *Kitvei R. Nahman DeBratslav*, pp. 192-94. Cf. TY Ma'asser Sheini V, 2. TB Berakhot 44a; 48b; 49a. Num. R. 23:7; Shir HaShirim R. 5:5. Shoher Tov, 121. Tanhuma, Noah 11; Mass'ei 6. Zohar I, 134a; II, 157b; 169a; III, 274a. Rambam, *Hilkhot Berakhot*, I, 1; II, 1, 3. *Tur* and *Shulhan Arukh, Orah Hayyim*, 187. Maharal, *Netivot Olam*, I, *Netiv HaAvodah*, 18; *Gevurot HaShem*, 24. Cf. also Targum Onkelos and Rashi on Gen. 48:22.
201. Cf. Exod. 32:2; Num. R. 9 *in fine* (Ezek. 37:21-26); Zohar Hadash, 69a. Cf. TY Ta'anit IV, 5; Sukkah IV, 6. TB Berakhot 32b; 58b; 59a; Shabbat 63a; 119b; Ta'anit 29a; Megillah 12b; Sotah 48a-b-49a; Bava Metsia 30b; Bava Batra 12b; 25b; 60b; Sanhedrin 75a; Avodah Zarah 3b; Arakhin 11b; Massekhet Sofrim XIX, 12. Exod. R. 31:9; Num. R. 16:12; Shir HaShirim R. 4:11; Eihah R. 1:32, 4:5; Tana Devei Eliyahu Rabba 21; Pirkei DeRabbi Eliezer 17; Tanhuma, Tetsaveh 13. Zohar II, 5b; 6a; 170a; III, 15b; 74b; 236a; 267a.
202. Cf. Alshekh, Behukotai; Shelah, I, pp. 168b-169a; *Bnei Issakhar*, I, p. 111a.
203. Cf. Eihah 1:1; TB Sanhedrin 104b. See also Zohar III, 277a; *Ha'amek Davar* on Lev. 26:32. Cf. also Rashi on Berakhot 58b.
204. Cf. Radak on Isa. 54:1, 54:6.
205. Cf. Lev. 26:32; Sifra (6:5), Rashi and *Or HaHayyim* ad loc. Cf. Ramban on Lev. 26:16; *Tefillah Al Horvot Yerushalayim* (*Kitvei Ramban* I, p. 428); *Sefer HaGeulah* (*Kitvei Ramban* I, p. 270. Recanati, Lev. 33:1). Cf. also Shelah, III, p. 26b; *Siddur Bet Ya'akov* (Emden), *Sulam Bet El*, pp. 11a-b. Cf. also TB Berakhot 58b. See TB Gittin 57a; Ketuvot 112a. TY Peyah VII, 3; Kilaim IX, 3; Ta'anit IV, 5. Petihta DeEihah Rabbati 34; Eihah R. 7. Pirkei DeRabbi Eliezer 34. Rashi and Maharsha on Sanhedrin 98a. Maharal, *Netsah Yisrael*, 6; *Perushim LeAggadot*, IV, p. 103. *Mei Meirom*, VI, p. 292. Cf. also Amos 9:14; Isa. 61:4.
206. See Isa. 54:4 (-8), 62:4 and Radak ad loc. See also Isa. 61:10-11, 62:5. See Hos. 2:18. Cf. TB Sanhedrin 104a (Eihah 1:1); see Radak on Isa. 54:1, 54:6.
207. Cf. *Sefat Emet*, IV, p. 199. Rav Kook, *Orot*, p. 9; *Olat Reiyah*, II, p. 265. *Mei Meirom*, VI, p. 59. Cf. Radak on Isa. 54:6; TB Sanhedrin 104b. Maharal, *Netsah Yisrael*, 56.
208. Cf. Ezra 9:9. Ps. 44:18, 44:23. TB Gittin 57b. Exod. R. 15:7, 42:9. Num. R. 11; 13:3. Shir HaShirim R. 1:63. Tanhuma, Tetsaveh 5. Shoher Tov, 9. Zohar II, 119b; III, 61a. Rashi on Deut. 32:43; Shir HaShirim 3:5, 5:8, 8:7. Ramban on Deut. 7:7, 32:26, 32:40. Rambam, *Iggeret Teiman*, pp. 134-35. Maharal, *Perushim LeAggadot*, II, p. 123. Rashi on Shir HaShirim 1:15. Ramban, *Sefer HaGeulah* (*Kitvei Ramban* I), p. 263. See also Lev. 26:42. TB Megillah 11a;

Pessahim 87a. Exod. R. 23:6. Zohar III, 112a; 256a. Tikkunei HaZohar, 40a. Ps. 94:14, 132:13, 135:4. Rambam, *Perush HaMishnayot*, Zevahim XIV, 8. Shelah, *Siddur Shaʿar HaShamayim*, p. 518. *Siddur HaGeonim VeHaMekubalim*, II, p. 502. *Mei Meirom*, VI, pp. 179-81, 205.

209. Cf. TB Gittin 57b; Sifrei 1 (Deut. 32:1); Deut. R. 2:6, 3:2; Rashi on Deut. 29:12; Ramban, *Sefer HaGeulah* (*Kitvei Ramban* I), p. 263. See also TB Pessahim 87a. Deut. R. 2:23. *Orot*, p. 142.

210. Cf. Ps. Lev. 26:44; 91:15; Tanhuma, Shemot 14; Zohar III, 298a; Rashi on Exod. 3:2; Maharal, *Gevurot HaShem*, 3.

211. Cf. Zohar I, 69a; *Meshekh Hokhmah*, p. 268. *Haʿamek Davar* on Exod. 6:6; Lev. 26:42. Cf. Deut. 11:12. See also Zohar III, 298a-b; Petihta DeEihah Rabbati 24. Eihah R. 1:33; Tanhuma (Buber ed.), Shemot 10. TB Rosh HaShanah 31a; Gittin 57b. *Sefer Yereim*, 249.

212. Cf. TB Megillah 29a; Mekhilta 14 (Exod. 12:41). Sifrei 84 (Num. 10:38), 161 (Num. 35:34). Exod. R. 15:17, 23:6, 30:21. Lev. R. 9:3. Num. R. 7:10, 11:19. Shir HaShirim R. 4:8. Petihta DeEihah Rabbati 20. Kohelet R. 4:3. See also Gen. R. 19:7; Num. R. 12:6. Cf. Tanhuma, VaYishlah 10; Shemot 14; Ahrei 12. Shoher Tov, 13, 20. Yalkut Shimʿoni, Shemot 27:376, Zekharia 9:577; Eihah 1:1009. Cf. Gen. 46:4; Lev. 26:44; Deut. 33:29. Isa. 45:17, 56:1, 63:9. Zech. 9:9; Ps. 3:9, 13:6, 50:23, 80:3-4, 80:8, 80:20, 91:15. I Chron. 17:21. TY Sukkah IV, 3. TB Berakhot 3a; Megillah 11a; Haggigah 5b; 15b; Sanhedrin 46a; Avodah Zarah 3b. Zohar I, 28a; 69a; 120b; 124a; 128a; 134a; 149a; 166a; 194a; 211a; 213b; II, 2b; 41b; 55a; 57b; 82a; 216b; III, 17a; 28a; 69a; 75a; 90b; 112a; 197b; 203b; 266b. Tikkunei HaZohar, 6 (23a). Rashi on Exod. 3:14; Deut. 30:3. Radak on Exod. 2:7, 2:23; II Sam. 7:23. Maharal, *Netsah Yisrael*, 62; *Gevurot HaShem*, 23; *Netivot Olam* I, *Netiv Gemilut Hassadim*, 1. *Sefer HaHinukh*, Mitzvah, 95. Maharsha on Taʿanit 16a. *Toldot Yaʿakov Yossef*, VaYera. *Tanya, Iggeret HaTeshuvah*, 6. *Benei Issakhar, Haggadah*, pp. 24, 25. HaGra, *Sefer HaEmunah VeHaHashgahah*, I, p. 15a. *Sefat Emet*, I, pp. 210-11; V, p. 5. *Orot*, pp. 77-78. *Mei Meirom, Missaviv LiShmonah Perakim LeHaRambam*, p. 216. *Bnei Yehoyada*, II, p. 1b. *Siddur HaGeonim VeHaMekubalim*, III, pp. 715-16.

213. Cf. Lev. 16:16 and Rashi ad loc. TB Yoma 56b-57a. Exod. R. 15:6, 15:19, 18:6. Num. R. 7:9. Pirkei DeRabbi Eliezer 39. Tanhuma, VaYishlah 10. Zohar III, 155a. Rashi on Num. 23:21, 36:34. Shelah, *Siddur Shaʿar HaShamayim*, p. 518. *Orot*, pp. 150-51.

214. Cf. Rambam, *Hilkhot Terumot*, I, 5; 10; *Hilkhot Bet HaBehirah*, VI, 16; Mishnah Eduyot VIII, 6 and Rambam ad loc. TY Sheviʿit VI, 1; Demai III, 4. TB Haggigah 3b; Shevuot 16a; Arakhin 32b. Ramban on Lev. 26:42. Hatam Sofer, *Sheʾeilot UTeshuvot, Yoreh Deyah*, 234.

215. Cf. Mishnah Megillah III, 3 (Lev. 26:31). Rambam, *Hilkhot Bet HaBehirah*, I, 2-3; VI, 14, 16; Mishnah Zevahim IV, 8 and Rambam ad loc. See also Ps. 132:14. II Chron. 7:16, 30:8. Pesikta Zutarta, VaYeitsei, Gen. 28:16. Exod. R. 2:2; Num. R. 11:3; Shir HaShirim R. 2:22. Tana Devei Eliyahu Rabba 21. Shoher Tov, 11:3. Tanhuma (Buber ed.), Shemot 51. Yalkut Shimʿoni, Mikhah 4:552. TB Megillah 28a; Zevahim 119a. Zohar II, 5b; 116a. Tossafot on Yoma 44a; Shevuot 14b. *Sefer Yereim*, 277. *Rashbats*, III, 201. *Hiddushei HaRashba* and HaRitva on Megillah 10a. *Hiddushei HaRamban* on Shevuot

16a; see also Ramban, *Milhamot*, Avodah Zarah 52b. *Sefer HaHinukh, Mitzvot* 184, 362, 363. *Semag, Mitzvat Asseh* 363. Maharsha on Ta'anit 29b. Tselah on Berakhot 48b. Hatam Sofer, *Yoreh Deyah*, 233, 234. Rav Kook, *Orot HaKodesh*, III, p. 288; *Hazon HaGeulah*, p. 161; *Mishpat Kohen*, 63, 96. See also *Shulhan Arukh, Orah Hayyim*, 151:10-11. But see also Rabad on Rambam, *Hilkhot Bet HaBehirah*, VI, 4; Meiri on Shevuot 16a. *She'eilot UTeshuvot HaRadbaz*, II, 591. But see also TY Ta'anit II, 1; TB Yoma 21b (but see also TB Yoma 9b); Shir HaShirim R. 8; Zohar I, 26a. See also Petihta DeEihah Rabbati 24. Cf. *Mei Meirom*, VI, p. 237. *Ha'amek Davar* on Lev. 26:31. Cf. Rabbi Yossef Rozin, Gaon of Rogachov, *Mefa'aneah Tsefunot*, Jerusalem: 5736 (1976), p. 141.

216. See also Yalkut Shim'oni, Eihah 3, 10, 38.
217. See above, p. 11. Ref. 198. (Pago to be cheked ˇ p. 22 in French edition).
218. Cf. Jer. 16:11; Petihta DeEihah Rabbati 2; TY Haggigah I, 7; Massekhet Kallah VIII.
219. Cf. Massekhet Kallah VIII, Mekhilta 1 (Exod. 12:1); TB Moed Katan 25a and Rashi ad loc.; Pesikta Rabbati 35; Zohar II, 79b; *Kuzari*, II, 14; Rashi on Jon. 1:3; Ramban on Lev. 13:47. See also TY Haggigah I, 7; TB Sanhedrin 14a. Cf. Maharal, *Tiferet Yisrael, Hakdamah*, pp. 2a-b.
220. TB Ketuvot 110b (Lev. 25:38; I Sam. 26:19). Cf. Sifra 5:4 (Lev. 25:38). Zohar II, 79b; III, 109b. The Rif and *Hafla'ah* on Ketuvot 110; *Meiri* on Ketuvot 111. Rashi on Gen. 17:8; Deut. 11:16. Ramban on Gen. 28:21; Lev. 18:25; Deut. 4:28. Rambam, *Perush HaMishnayot*, Avodah Zarah I, 4. *Teshuvot HaRashba*, I, 134. *Tashbatz Katan*, 562. Maharal, *Derekh Hayyim*, p. 188. See Tossefta on Avodah Zarah V; Gen. R. 25:3, 64. Avot DeRabbi Nathan 26. Rambam, *Hilkhot Melakhim*, V. See also TB Bava Batra 91a. Cf. Alshekh on Eikev, Deut. 11:12. Shelah, I, pp. 168a-b; III, pp. 22b, 23b. *Or HaHayyim* on Deut. 26:17. *Mikhtav MeEliyahu*, III, p. 194. *Benayahu Ben Yehoyada*, II-III, p. 74b.
221. Cf. Isa. 43:10; Sifrei 346 (Deut. 33:5); Lev. R. 6:1; Yalkut Shim'oni, Yeshayahu 63:507; Ba'al HaTurim on Deut. 6:4.
222. Cf. Gen. R. 46:7 (Gen. 17:8); Tossefta Avodah Zarah V; Zohar III, 4b; Rashi on Gen. 17:8; Lev. 25:38; Ketuvot 110b; Ramban on Gen. 28:21; Lev. 18:25. Maharal, *Derekh Hayyim*, p. 188. HaGra, *Sefer HaEmunah VeHaHashgahah*, p. 1 (Eruvin 18b).
223. Cf. Zohar I, 177b (Deut. 11:16); TB Avodah Zarah 8a; cf. also Zohar I, 225a; II, 9a; III, 226b. Tikkunei HaZohar, 69 (97b). Cf. Rashi and Ramban on Deut. 4:28; Ramban on Lev. 18:25; R. Moshe Cordovero, *Shiur Koma*, 110; Maharal, *Gevurot HaShem*, 8, 47. *Siddur Bet Ya'akov* (Emden), *Sulam Bet El*, p. 20; *Sefat Emet*, I, p. 188.
224. Cf. Shelah, *Siddur Sha'ar HaShamayim*, p. 512.
225. TB Bava Batra 8a and Rashi ad loc. Sanhedrin 99b. Zohar III, 270a; Zohar Hadash, Shir HaShirim 74; Exod. R. 30:5; Lev. R. 7:3; Targum on Isa. 35:4; Pesikta Rabbati 16, 17; Tana Devei Eliyahu Zuta 14; Yalkut Shim'oni, Hosea 8:525. See Eihah R. 3:19 (Ps. 119:92). See also TB Berakhot 8a; Zohar III, 202b. Cf. Shelah, I, p. 168a; *Sefat Emet*, V, p. 8; *Mei Meirom*, VI, p. 15. See also Rabbi Bezalel Ze'ev Safran, *Doresh LeTsion*, p. 12.
226. Cf. Sifrei 43 (Deut. 11:17); Rashi and Ramban on Deut. 11:18; Ramban on

Lev. 18:25; Deut. 4:5; *Derashah Al Divrei Kohelet* (*Kitvei Ramban* I), pp. 200-1. Cf. Zohar II, 11b.

227. See below, p. 43. Ref. 677 (Pages to be checked ˇ p. 49-50 in French edition).

228. Cf. Mishnah Demai VI, 2. TY Moed Katan II, 4. TB Sukkah 36a; Bava Kama 81b; Bava Metsia 101a; Sanhedrin 102b. Gen. R. 2:8, 39:10, 64:3. Hida, *Yossef Omets*, 19. Hatam Sofer on Sukkah 36a. Rav Kook, *Hazon HaGeulah*, pp. 221-22.

229. My father (blessed be his memory) in his *Doresh LeTsion* analyzed all the halakhic implications that arise from the *mitzvah* commanding the Jew to live in Erets-Yisrael. In it, he examined in depth the various (and indeed complementary) theses advanced in this regard by Ramban on the one hand and by Rashi, Rambam and the Tosafists on the other. He reconciled their points of view relating whether to the *mitzvah*, the duty of the Jew to act so that he may reside in Erets-Yisrael, or to the *havtahah*, the divine promise to help the Jew to stay there. See Sifrei 38 (Deut. 11:10), 80 (Deut. 12:29), 333 (Deut. 32:43). TB Ketuvot 110b and Tossafot ad loc. Cf. TY Shekalim III, 3; Shabbat I, 3. TB Ketuvot 110b-111a; Pessahim 113a. Tossefta Avodah Zarah V, 3. Zohar Hadash, 44a. Ramban on Num. 33:53; see also Rashi, *Or HaHayyim* and Malbim on Num. 33:53. But see also Rashi on Gittin 8b; 47a. Rambam, *Sefer HaMitzvot*, *Mitzvah* 4; *Hiddushim*, Shabbat 130b; *Derashah Al Divrei Kohelet* (*Kitvei Ramban* I), p. 204. *Sefer Hareidim*, 2 (*Halakhot HaTluyot BaArets*). Cf. *Tashbatz*, *She'eilot UTeshuvot* III, 288; *Mabit*, I, 245; *Maharit*, *Yoreh Deyah*, 28; *Noda BiYehuda*, II, *Yoreh Deyah*, 206; *Avnei Nezer*, *Yoreh Deyah*, 254; *Igrot Moshe* (R. Moshe Feinstein), *Even HaEzer*, 102. See Shelah, I, p. 169a. R. Ovadya Yossef, *Mitzvat Yishuv Erets-Yisrael Bazeman Hazeh*, in *Torah SheBe'Al Pe*, XI, Jerusalem: 5729 (1969), pp. 35ff. See also R. Yoel Teitelbaum of Satmar, *VaYoel Moshe*, New York: n.d., pp. 237-39, 254, 260, 294.

230. Cf. TB Gittin 8b; Bava Kama 80b; cf. also TB Sotah 44b. Yalkut Shim'oni, Eikev 11:860. Ramban, *Hiddushim*, Shabbat 130b. Rambam, *Hilkhot Shabbat*, VI, 11. *Tur* and *Shulhan Arukh*, *Orah Hayyim*, 248:4, 306:11. *Mishpat Kohen*, 146. *Doresh LeTsion*, p. 24. See *Noam Elimelekh*, Noah. Cf. also TY Shabbat I, 8; Moed Katan II, 4. TB Shabbat 19a; 129a. Gen. R. 47:12; Num. R. 14:5. Tanhuma, Mass'ei 5.

231. Cf. *Noam Elimelekh*, Noah; *Mei Meirom*, VI, p. 213. See TB Shabbat 118b.

232. Cf. TB Ta'anit 5a; Num. R. 12; Tanhuma, Pekkudei 1. Zohar I, 1b; 35a; 129a; 231a; II, 55b; 140b; 159a; 234b; 235b; III, 3b; 15b; 68b; 147b; 262b; 267a; 278a. Tikkunei HaZohar, 6 (21a); 26 (71a); 50 (86b). See also TB Sanhedrin 99b; Zohar II, 240a; Zohar Hadash, Noah 20; Terumah 42; Shir HaShirim 71. See *Sha'arei Zohar*, pp. 55, 151. *Hazon HaGeulah*, p. 127.

233. Cf. Exod. R. 23:11; Shir HaShirim R. 1:16; Zohar I, 171b; Tikkunei HaZohar, 6 (146a); Eihah 5:5.

234. Cf. TB Berakhot 43b; Pesikta DeRav Kahana, 1: 1.

235. Cf. TB Pessahim 87b; cf. Deut. 32:8; cf. TB Sukkah 55a; Zohar III, 117a. *Kuzari*, IV, 23. Recanati, Lekh Lekha, p. 21b. Maharal, *Gevurot HaShem*, 9. Shelah, III, p. 201. Ari HaKadosh, *Likkutei Torah*, pp. 208-9; *Ets Hayyim*, 1, 2. HaGra, *Siddur Ishei Yisrael* (*Siah Yitshak*), p. 45; *Sefer HaEmunah VeHaHashgahah*, II, p. 8b. *Or HaHayyim* on Lev. 25:39; Num. 10:35, 24:8. *Maggid*

Devarav LeYa'akov, 66, 70, 78. *Bnei Issakhar, Haggadah*, pp. 44-45, 99. *Kedushat Levi*, pp. 59a, 74b, 82. *Likkutei Moharan*, II, 76. *Be'er Mayim Hayyim* on Deut. 30:3-4. *Sefat Emet*, I, pp. 54-55, 109, 123, 211, 273; II, p. 80; V, p. 35. *Bet HaLevi*, I, p. 32; II, p. 33. *Orot HaKodesh*, II, p. 343; III, pp. 116, 367. Rav Harlap, *Mei Meirom*, VIII, pp. 80, 98, 106, 255. R. S.R. Hirsch, *Perush Tehillim*, pp. 415ff.; *Igrot Tsafon*, pp. 54-55. *VaYoel Moshe* (Satmar), p. 316. *Matan Torah* (Ashlag), pp. 36-37, 45.

236. Cf. Gen. R. 30:11, 47:8. Shelah, III, p. 170a. *Kedushat Levi*, p. 21a. *Orot*, pp. 98-99, 152, 156, 169, 170.

237. Cf. TB Ta'anit 3b and Rashi ad loc. Maharsha on Pessahim 87b; Avodah Zarah 10b. Shelah, III, pp. 169b-170a. *Tanya*, 37. *Sefat Emet*, II, p. 32; V, p. 5. *VaYoel Moshe*, p. 317.

238. Cf. Sifrei 37 (Deut. 11:10). Yalkut Shim'oni, Shelah 13:743. See TB Kiddushin 49b. See also Ramban on Gen. 26:5; Lev. 18:25; *Derashah Al Divrei Kohelet* (*Kitvei Ramban* I), p. 200.

239. Cf. Sifrei 37 (Deut. 11:10); Gen. R. 16:7. Lev. R. 13:4, 34:7. Esther R. 1. Avot DeRabbi Nathan 28. See also TB Bava Metsia 85a; Sanhedrin 24a. Cf. Maharal, *Netivot Olam*, I, *Netiv HaTorah*, 13; *Perushim LeAggadot*, I, p. 97. *Likkutei Moharan*, I, p. 246; II, p. 71; *Shivhei HaKan*, p. 52. *Orot HaKodesh*, I, p. 133.

240. Cf. Gen. R. 46:7; Shoher Tov, 105:1.

241. Cf. Ramban on Gen. 24:3; Lev. 18:25; Deut. 31:16; see II Kings 17:26; II Chron. 32:19. Cf. Maharal, *Derekh Hayyim*, pp. 8-9, 188.

242. Cf. Isa. 54:5; Zech. 14:9; Cf. Zohar I, 171a.

243. Cf. Gen. R. 47:8; cf. also Gen. R. 68, 78, 82; Yalkut Shim'oni, VaYishlah 35:136; Zohar III, 28b; 257b. Rambam, *Iggeret Teiman*, p. 162; Ramban on Deut. 11:22; R. Hayyim Vital, *Ets Hayyim*, 1. Shelah, III, pp. 23b, 161a, 201b; *Maggid Devarav LeYa'akov*, 65; *Tanya*, 18, 23; *Sefat Emet*, II, p. 3.

244. Cf. Num. R. 10:14; cf. also Maharal, *Derekh Hayyim*, pp. 8, 188; *Maggid Devarav LeYa'akov*, 90; see also ibidem, 67. *Orot*, p. 119. See also Rambam, *Moreh Nevukhim*, III, 24.

245. Cf. Gen. R. 17:4; cf. also Tanhuma (Buber ed.), Bereshit 30. Cf. Zohar Hadash, Ahrei 49a; Ruth 84a (Prov. 10:7), 89b. Philo, *Mos*. II, 38; idem, *Mutat*. 60-129. Rambam, *Moreh Nevukhim*, II, 30. Ramban on Gen. 2:20; cf. idem on Exod. 3:13. Radak on Ps. 24:4. Seforno on Exod. 1:1. *Teshuvot HaRashba*, IV, 30. Maharal, *Gevurot HaShem*, 43, 70; *Derekh Hayyim*, pp. 62, 129, 143-45; *Derashot*, p. 26; *Perushim LeAggadot*, I, p. 59. Shelah, I, p. 20b. R. Ya'akov Yossef of Polonnoye, *Tsafnat Pa'aneah*, 6; R. Dov Baer of Mezerich, *Maggid Devarav LeYa'akov*, 13, 188; R. Elimelech of Lyzhansk, *Noam Elimelekh, Shemot*; R. Simha Bunem of Przysucha, *Midrash Simhah*, I, p. 24; R. Levi Yitshak of Berdichev, *Kedushat Levi*, p. 50; R. Abraham Hayyim of Zloczow, *Orah LeHayyim, Bemidbar*; R. Shneur Zalman of Lyady, *Tanya, Sha'ar HaYihud VeHaEmunah*, 1; R. Nahman of Bratslav, *Likkutei Moharan*, 260 (Gen. 2:19); *Kitvei Rabbi Nahman DeBratslav*, p. 193. *Or HaHayyim* on Deut. 29:19, 31:1. R. Eliyahu of Vilna, *Biurei HaGra Al Aggadot*, I, pp. 19, 51. R. Abraham of Sochaczew, *Avnei Nezer*, pp. 27-28. R. Yossef Rozin, Gaon of Rogachov, *Mefa'aneah Tsefunot*, p. 237. R. Yeruham HaLevi Levovitch, *Da'at Torah*, I, pp. 17-18.

246. Cf. TY Megillah I, 11; Sanhedrin X, 2. TB Berakhot 7b; Shabbat 147b; Eruvin 13b; Rosh HaShanah 25a; Megillah 12b; 13a; Sotah 11b; 13b; Bava Batra 14b; 90a-b; Sanhedrin 44b; 82b; 94b; 102b; 105a; 109b; Avodah Zarah 3a; Temurah 16a. Gen. R. 6:6, 23:4, 37:10, 42:4, 61:4, 67:10, 70:17, 98:21. Exod. R. 1:7, 1:21, 1:39. Lev. R. 10:10, 11:7. Num. R. 10:14, 13:9, 21:4. Eihah R. 5:6. Kohelet R. 9:9. Tanhuma, Toldot 6; VaYeshev 6; VaYakhel 3; Ha'azinu 7. Pirkei DeRabbi Eliezer 32. Maharal, *Derekh Hayyim*, p. 128.
247. Cf. Gen. R. 1:5; Kohelet R. 7:3; Tanhuma, VaYakhel 1. Sefer HaBahir, 35. Cf. Gen. R. 78:7. Exod. R. 40:4, 48. Lev. R. 32:5. Num. R. 10:14, 10:18, 11:19-21. Shir HaShirim R. 4:24; Ruth 2:7. Cf. TY Berakhot I, 6. TB Berakhot 7b; 13b; 17a; 39b; 55a; Pessahim 54a; Megillah 14a; Yoma 38b; Sotah 12a. Tanhuma, Shemot 4; Ki Tissa 13; Ha'azinu 7. See Gen. 17:19, 21:3. Isa. 49:1. Cf. Zohar I, 6a; 58b; 157b; II, 179b; 223a; III, 75b. Zohar Hadash, Shir HaShirim 72:3. Tikkunei HaZohar, 57 (91b). Rashi on Gen. 15:5, 17:19, 21:9, 25:26; Mic. 6:9; Sanhedrin 44a. Ramban on Gen. 35:18. Radak on Isa. 40:26. R. Yehuda HeHassid, *Sefer Hassidim*, 246. Alshekh on Mikeits. Maharal, *Derekh Hayyim*, pp. 62, 143-45; *Netivot Olam*, II, *Netiv Ahavat HaShem*, 2. Shelah, *Siddur Sha'ar HaShamayim*, pp. 517-18. *Sefat Emet*, I, p. 48 (Gen. 12:2); II, pp. 3ff., 7; IV, p. 174. Rav Kook, *Orot HaKodesh*, III, pp. 137, 139. R. Yossef Yehuda Leib Bloch, *Shiurei Da'at*, II, p. 140. R. Yitshak Heinemann, *Darkei HaAggadah*, Jerusalem: 5710 (1949), pp. 111-12. R. A.H. Galitzenstein, *Rabbi Yisrael Ba'al Shem Tov*, New York-Kfar Chabad: 5720, p. 43. R. Yossef Hayyim of Baghdad, *She'eilot UTeshuvot Torah Sheleimah*, p. 375.
248. Cf. Exod. 2:10; TB Yoma 83b et al. Cf. Gen. R. 42:5, 42:8, 42:9, 85:5 et al. Cf. Rashi on Gen. 14:2. See *Siddur HaGeonim VeHaMekubalim*, III, pp. 565, 575-76.
249. Cf. TB Shabbat 89a; Yevamot 61a; Bava Metsia 114b. Shoher Tov, 9. Zohar I, 20b; II, 75b; 86a; III, 29a; 48a; 125a; 145b. Zohar Hadash, 16a. Recanati, Bereshit, p. 10a; Rashi and Radak on Gen. 1:26; Rashi and Malbim on Ps. 49:3. Rambam, *Hilkhot Yessodei HaTorah*, IV, 8. Rabbeinu Bahya on Gen. 5:1. Alshekh on Lev. 3:2. Maharal, *Gevurot HaShem*, 44; *Tiferet Yisrael*, 3; *Netivot Olam*, I, *Netiv HaTorah*, 14, 15; *Netiv HaEmet*, 3; *Derekh Hayyim*, pp. 109-10, 119, 126-27, 158. *Biur HaGra*, Isa. 2:9; Prov. 8:4, 14:28; I Chron. 1:1; *Aderet Eliyahu*, p. 383. *Toldot Ya'akov Yossef*, Tsav. Malbim on Lev. 1:2. *HaKtav VeHaKabbalah*, II, p. 46a. See also Gen. R. 17:4-5; Tanhuma, Tsav 14; Vezot HaBerakhah 6. Rashi on Gen. 2:7; Isa. 2:9. Radak on Gen. 2:20. *Moreh Nevukhim*, I, 14. Maharsha on Bava Batra 164b. Cf. Gen. R. 2:4; Rashi on Isa. 8:1; Rambam, *Hilkhot Avodat Kokhavim*, I, 1. Cf. Deut. 1:13; I Sam. 17:12. TY Sanhedrin X, 1. TB Yoma 71a (Prov. 8:4). Lev. R. 36:5; Deut. R. 11:4. Sefer HaBahir, 48. Tanhuma, Shemini 9. Yalkut Shim'oni, Mishlei 8:940. Zohar II, 128a. Rashi on Isa. 2:9; Avodah Zarah 19a. See Rambam, *Hilkhot Yessodei HaTorah*, VII, 1. Maharal, *Tiferet Yisrael*, 12; *Perushim LeAggadot*, I, p. 73. *Biur HaGra*, Prov. 12:14. *HaKtav VeHaKabbalah*, II, p. 35a.
250. Cf. Isa. 14:14; Shelah III, p. 201b; Rabbi S.R. Hirsch on Gen. 1:26; R. Abraham of Slonim, *Be'er Avraham*, p. 341 (TB Shabbat 133b).
251. Cf. TB Sotah 5a; Zohar III, 29b.

252. Cf. TB Sotah 42b; Eihah R. 1:2; Zohar I, 58a-b; II, 179b.
253. Cf. Gen. 2:19-20 and Rashi, Ramban, Radak, *Hizkuni* and Abrabanel ad loc. Gen. R. 17:5; Yalkut Shim'oni, Yeshaya 42:551; *Aderet Eliyahu*, p. 50; *Sefat Emet*, V, p. 152; R. D.T. Hoffmann, *Bereshit*, I, p. 55; M. D. Cassuto, *MeAdam Ad Noah*, Jerusalem: 5713 (1953), pp. 85-86.
254. Cf. Abrabanel, *Perush Al HaTorah*, I (Gen. 2), p. 96.
255. Cf. Exod. R. 1:3; Maharal, *Gur Aryeh*, VaYishlah.
256. Cf. Shedal (Shemuel David Luzzatto), *Perush Al Hamishah Humshei Torah* (Gen. 2:19), p. 26. See R. Hayyim Vital, *Ta'amei HaMitzvot*, in *Likkutei Torah DeAri HaKadosh*, Eikev, p. 97.
257. Cf. Seforno on Gen. 2:19.
258. Cf. TB Eruvin 13b.
259. Cf. TY Sanhedrin X, 1; Yalkut Shim'oni, Iyov 29:917. *Orot HaKodesh*, III, p. 139; *Sefat Emet*, IV, p. 93. R. Yossef Hayyim of Baghdad, *Da'at UTevunah*, p. 113a.
260. Cf. TB Sanhedrin 106b; cf. also TB Sotah 34b. Cf. Gen. R. 42:4, 71:4, 85:5. Lev. R. 11:7. Num. R. 10:14. Tanhuma, Shemot 2. Zohar I, 25b. Zohar Hadash, 32a. Rashi on Gen. 14:2; Exod. 35:27. *Sefat Emet*, II, p. 3. R. Hayyim of Volozhin, *Ruah Hayyim*, p. 21.
261. Cf. TB Megillah 14a; Tana Devei Eliyahu Zuta 22; Midrash Shemuel, 23. See Zohar II, 174a; III, 135b.
262. See Maharsha on Hullin 139b.
263. Cf. Gen. 12:2; Rashi and *Behor Shor* ad loc. Cf. Gen. R. 14:14, 43:2. Num. R. 13:6. Tanhuma, Lekh Lekha 16. Yalkut Shim'oni, Tehillim 45:747. Cf. Isa. 62:2, 65:15. *Hizkuni* on Lekh Lekha, Gen. 17:5, p. 24. Alshekh on I Sam. 19. Ramban on Num. 10:29 (cf. TB Yevamot 22a; Bekhorot 47a).
264. Cf. TY Berakhot I, 6. TB Bava Kama 66b; Rosh HaShanah 16b; Horayot 11b; Bava Metsia 75b. Cf. Gen. 17:5 and Rashi ad loc., 17:19, 32:29, 35:10. Cf. Isa. 65:15. Cf. Gen. R. 30:4, 39:17, 44:12, 44:15, 61:4, 64:4, 77:8. Exod. R. 2:12, 17:5. Pesikta Rabbati 44. Pesikta DeRav Kahana 22. Pirkei DeRabbi Eliezer 32. Tanhuma, Shoftim 11. Zohar I, 60a; 90b; 96a; 126a; 133b; 174a; III, 9a; 76b; 111b; 113a; 148a; 217b. Zohar Hadash, Shir HaShirim 72a-b; Ruth 79a; 85a. Philo, *Mutat.* 60-129. Rashi on Gen. 15:5, 25:26. Ramban on Num. 10:29. *Be'er Mayim Hayyim* on Gen. 2:19. Rambam, *Hilkhot Teshuvah*, II, 4. Rabbi Yehuda HeHassid, *Sefer Hassidim*, 244-46. Maharal, *Gevurot HaShem*, 43; see also ibidem, 7. R. D.T. Hoffmann, *Bereshit*, I, p. 55; II, p. 498. R. Eliyahu Lapian, *Lev Eliyahu*, p. 194. R. Yeruham HaLevi Levovitch, *Da'at Hokhmah UMussar*, p. 111. R. Barukh HaLevi Epstein, *Tossefet Berakhah*, I, p. 204.
265. Cf. TB Bava Batra 75b; Sotah 10a. Zohar II, 90b; 124a. Tikkunei HaZohar, 9a; 69 (111a). Maharal, *Derekh Hayyim*, p. 143; *Perushim LeAggadot*, I, pp. 39-40. Rabbi Eliyahu of Vilna, *Divrei Eliyahu*, p. 42.
266. Cf. Zohar II, 96a; 124a-b (Deut. 4:4, 32:9; Ps. 81:9). Maharal, *Netivot Olam*, II, *Netiv Ahavat HaShem*, 2; *Perushim LeAggadot*, I, p. 104; see also ibidem, p. 67. Cf. Exod. R. 3; Num. R. 10:14.
267. Cf. TB Sotah 36b; Shoher Tov, 20 (Isa. 43:7); see also Exod. R. 17:5; Zohar II, 36a.
268. Cf. Lev. R. 27:1; 35:6. See also Gen. R. 39:21. Cf. Tanhuma, Ki Tavo 1. TB

Sanhedrin 99b. Zohar II, 198a; III, 113a. Zohar Hadash, 11a. See A. Safran, *La Cabale*, p. 115.
269. Cf. Midrash Shemuel, 23.
270. Cf. Zohar I, 173b. Cf. Exod. 3:6; Zohar II, 42b. Cf. Zohar I, 174a. Cf. Gen. 35:10, 35:15. Cf. TB Berakhot 7b; Zohar I, 99b. See Gen. R. 17:5 (Isa. 42:8); Num. R. 16:3. Yalkut Shim'oni, Isa. 42:551. See also Maharal, *Tiferet Yisrael*, 33; see also Rashi on Gen. 4:26. Cf. *Kitvei Rabbi Nahman DeBratslav*, Steinman ed., Tel-Aviv: 5711, p. 193.
271. Cf. Lev. R. 27:1; Zohar III, 113a; 152a. Cf. Shelah, I, p. 22b; III, p. 136b.
272. Cf. TB Bava Batra 75b; Ta'anit 22b and Rashi ad loc. Zohar III, 149a. Maharal, *Tiferet Yisrael*, 17. R. Yeruham HaLevi Levovitch, *Da'at Hokhmah UMussar*, pp. 22-23. R. Yossef Hayyim of Baghdad, *Ben Ish Hai*, p. 175; *Od Yossef Hai*, p. 113; *She'eilot UTeshuvot Torah Sheleimah*, pp. 28-29.
273. Cf. TB Berakhot 55a; Zohar II, 152a; 222-24; 234a-b. Tikkunei HaZohar, 13a. Tanhuma, Pekkudei 3. *Od Yossef Hai*, p. 194.
274. Cf. Gen. R. 79:10; Zohar I, 138a; 213b; Ramban on Gen. 33:20. See Gen. R. 38:6.
275. Cf. Ramban on Gen. 12:8. Cf. TB Sotah 36b. Gen. R. 43:4. Num. R. 11:7. Yalkut Shim'oni, Isa. 43:552. Zohar III, 4b; 149a. Tikkunei HaZohar, 17b; 57 (91b). R. Yisrael of Koznitz, *Avodat Yisrael*, p. 204.
276. Cf. Zohar II, 87a; 124a; III, 13b; 73a; Ramban, *Hakdamah, Perush HaTorah*; Shelah, III, p. 9a. See A. Safran, *La Cabale*, p. 14.
277. Cf. Zohar III, 73a. Cf. Shelah, *Siddur Sha'ar HaShamayim*, p. 399. *Tanya*, 23; see ibidem, 4. *Nefesh HaHayyim*, 1:6; 1:17; 4:22. *Sefat Emet*, V, p. 53.
278. Cf. Zohar Hadash, 120b-121a.
279. Cf. Gen. 33:20; TY Ta'anit II, 6 and Korban HaEda ad loc. TB Megillah 18a. Cf. Zohar I, 138a; 213b; II, 66b; III, 86a. Tikkunei HaZohar, 21 (45a). Cf. Gen. R. 77:1; Kedushat Levi, pp. 20b-21a (II Sam. 23:3). TB Moed Katan 16b; Shabbat 63b. Zohar II, 15a; III, 15a. See TB Pessahim 111a; Zohar I, 94a. See also Tanhuma, Kedoshim 5.
280. Cf. Gen. 35:10; Isa. 49:3; Tanhuma, Kedoshim 2. Cf. Zohar II, 132b (Ps. 48:11).
281. Cf. Esther R. 6; see also TB Megillah 13a. Cf. TB Pessahim 118a.
282. Cf. Exod. R. 29:3. Cf. Sifrei 134 (Num. 27:12), 31 (Deut. 6:4), 319 (Deut. 32:18). See also TB Haggigah 3b. Tanhuma, Kedoshim 5.
283. Cf. TY Ta'anit II, 6; Yalkut Shim'oni, Yehoshua 7:17; see Rashi on Josh. 7:9; Jer. 14:9. Cf. Pirkei DeRabbi Eliezer 40. See Rabbi Nahman of Bratslav, *Likkutei Moharan*, II, 66, p. 30a.
284. Cf. Deut. 33:26 and Sifrei ad loc., 355; Gen. R. 77a. Cf. Tana Devei Eliyahu 21 (Isa. 44:2). Shoher Tov, 4; 25 (Ps. 25:8); 69. Zohar I, 177b. See TB Avodah Zarah 25a; see also TB Hullin 101b. Maharal, *Netivot Olam*, I, *Netiv HaAvodah*, 1; ibidem, II, *Netiv HaTemimut*, 2; *Derekh Hayyim*, p. 8; *Derashot*, pp. 33-34; *Perushim LeAggadot*, II, pp. 52, 55, 77, 95. See Gen. 17:1. Deut. 18:13, 33:4. Mic. 6:8. Prov. 11:3; see also Gen. 25:27; Job 1:1. See also Deut. 32:15. Cf. Rambam, *Hilkhot Shemittah VeYovel*, XIII, 13. See Zohar II, 150a (Eccl. 7:29). Cf. Ramban on Deut. 33:5. Shelah, III, p. 176b. *Biur HaGra*, Mishlei 2:7. *Kedushat Levi*, p. 20b. *Olat Reiyah*, II, p. 326. *Sefat Emet*, V, p. 90 (Deut. 32:9; Mal. 3:6). *Ha'amek Davar*, I, *Petihah, Bereshit*, p.

1. *Meshekh Hokhmah*, p. 318. *Avnei Nezer*, p. 37. See also A. Safran, *La Cabale*, p. 190.
285. TY Ta'anit II, 6. Cf. Tikkunei HaZohar, 11a.
286. TY Ta'anit II, 6. Cf. Maharal, *Netsah Yisrael*, 10. R. Hayyim of Volozhin, *Nefesh HaHayyim*, 1:19.
287. Cf. Zohar II, 79b-80a; III, 210b. Maharal, *Gevurot HaShem*, 23. HaGra, *Siddur Ishei Yisrael (Siah Yitshak)*, p. 44. Cf. Zohar I, 148b; 174a; III, 112; 210b; 306b. (Isa. 44:2; Exod. 4:22.) Maharal, *Gevurot HaShem*, 3, 44. Shelah, III, pp. 51a, 52a, 53a-b, 54a (Ps. 135:4), 176b. *Kedushat Levi*, p. 20b. *Or HaHayyim* on Gen. 35:10, 47:28; Num. 24:17. *Avnei Nezer*, p. 86. *Ha'amek Davar* on Gen. 35:10, 48:20. Rabbi Nahman of Bratslav, *Siddur Sha'arei Ratson*, p. 135; *Likkutei Moharan*, 47, p. 55b. R. S.R. Hirsch, *Perush Tehillim*, p. 416.
288. Cf. TY Berakhot I, 6; TB Berakhot 13a. Gen. R. 46:6, 78:5. Zohar I, 96a; 173b-174a; 177b. Zohar Hadash, Hukat 51. Ibn Ezra on Gen. 35:10; Exod. 6:3. Ramban and Rabbeinu Bahya on Gen. 35:10. Abrabanel on Gen. 17:4. *Biurei HaGra Al Aggadot*, I, p. 29.
289. Cf. Gen. 32:29. Zohar III, 73a. Shelah, I, p 4a, 28b; III, pp. 52-53. Cf. Gen. 28:12.
290. Cf. Gen. R. 63:3. Ari HaKadosh, *Likkutei Torah*, p. 86. Shelah, III, p. 164b.
291. Cf. Rashi on Gen. 32:5. Cf. Shelah, I, pp. 21a-b, 25b, 27a-b.
292. Cf. Prov. 16:15. Cf. Zohar I, 146b. *Biurei HaGra Al Aggadot*, II, p. 5.
293. Cf. Rabbi Nahman of Bratslav, *Likkutei Moharan*, II, 82, p. 38b.
294. Cf. Sifrei 36 (Deut. 6:9); TB Shabbat 14a; Targum on Eccl. 5:14; Tanhuma, Shemot 12. Zohar III, 110a; 175a; cf. also Avot VI, 1. Maharal, *Tiferet Yisrael*, 13. *Biur HaGra*, Mishlei 31:21. *Tanya*, 4, 8, 9, 10, 23. *Likkutei Moharan*, 33:4, 34:4. *Bnei Issakhar*, *Haggadah*, p. 31. *Sefat Emet*, I, p. 60; II, p. 62. Malbim on Exod. 28:2.
295. Cf. Zohar III, 110b; *Bnei Issakhar*, II, p. 21a; cf. also Rabbi Nahman of Bratslav, *Siddur Sha'arei Ratson*, p. 207.
296. Cf. Tanhuma, Behar 1; *Kuzari*, II, 12; V, 23. Cf. Exod. 19:6; Lev. 11:44, 20:7; Deut. 7:6; Isa. 6:13; Sifrei 104 (Deut. 14:21); TB Yevamot 20a; Rashi on Lev. 20:2; *Hatam Sofer, She'eilot UTeshuvot, Yoreh Deyah*, 234. Rav Kook, *Orot*, p. 160; *Mei Meirom*, VI, p. 233. Cf. Mishnah Kelim I, 6; Num. R. 7-8; Rambam, *Hilkhot Bet HaBehirah*, VII, 12.
297. Cf. Rabbi Nahman of Bratslav, *Likkutei Moharan*, II, 40, p. 26a (Isa. 49:3).
298. Mal. 3:12; cf. Zohar I, 3a.
299. Cf. Yalkut Shim'oni, Yitro 19:276.
300. Cf. Num. R. 23:11; Tanhuma, Mass'ei 10.
301. TB Yoma 86a.
302. Kohelet R. 1:9 (Mal. 3:12). Cf. Zohar I, 31b; III, 85b; 216b; 266b. Cf. Deut. 29:23-27; Joel 4:2; Rashi on Deut. 32:43; Kohelet 1:4. Rabbi Eliyahu, Gaon of Vilna, *Aderet Eliyahu*, pp. 483-84.
303. Isa. 51:16.
304. Zohar I, 5a; III, 35a. Cf. TY Ta'anit IV, 2; Megillah III, 6; cf. also TB Ketuvot 75a. Cf. Eihah R. 3:18; Yalkut Shim'oni, Eihah 3:1038. Tikkunei HaZohar, 69 (104a). Cf. HaGra, *Aderet Eliyahu*, p. 440. See also Zohar I, 117b. See Rambam, *Sefer HaMitzvot, Mitzvot Asseh, Mitzvah* 153. Cf.

Likkutei Moharan, 47, p. 55b. *Sefat Emet*, I, p. 5. See also M. M. Buber, *Darko shel Mikra*, Jerusalem: 5724 (1964), pp. 90, 93, 300. Rabbi Bezalel Ze'ev Safran, *Doresh LeTsion*, p. 4. Rabbi Barukh HaLevi Epstein, *Tossefet Berakhah*, I, p. 164.

305. Cf. Zohar II, 86a.
306. Cf. Gen. 49:1; Isa. 2:2; Hag. 2:9. Cf. Sifrei 37 (Deut. 7:12). TB Ta'anit 10a; Sanhedrin 38a. Gen. R. 1:5, 8:1-2, 14:1, 63:10-11, 78:11, Pesikta Zuṭarta and Rashi on Gen. 33:2. Lev. R. 14:1, 19:1; Deut. 5:6. Shir HaShirim R. 2:6. Kohelet R. 1:30. Tanhuma, Lekh Lekha 19. Zohar I, 177b; 266b; II, 28a; 108b; III, 159a; 221a. Tikkunei HaZohar, 6a. Rambam, *Moreh Nevukhim*, I, 34. Abrabanel, I, Bereshit 2, p. 77; II, Yitro, p. 73. R. Yitshak Arama, *Akeidat Yitshak*, Noah, 15, p. 109. Ari HaKadosh, *Likkutei Torah*, VaYishlah, p. 44. Maharal, *Tiferet Yisrael*, 12, 17; *Gevurot HaShem*, 70; *Derekh Hayyim*, pp. 9, 52; *Perushim LeAggadot*, I, pp. 94-95. Shelah, III, pp. 9a, 22a. Rabbi Eliyahu of Vilna, *Biurei HaGra Al Aggadot*, I, p. 79; *Sefer HaEmunah VeHaHashgahah*, I, p. 12; see also *Aderet Eliyahu*, p. 427. Rabbi Hayyim of Volozhin, *Nefesh HaHayyim*, 1:6. Rabbi Dov Baer of Mezerich, *Maggid Devarav LeYa'akov*, 30, 79. Rabbi Nahman of Bratslav, *Haggadah*, p. 47. Rabbi Yehuda Aryeh Leib of Gur, *Sefat Emet*, I, p. 244. Rabbi Yossef Dov Baer of Brisk, *Bet HaLevi*, I, p. 26. Rabbi Abraham of Slonim, *Be'er Avraham*, pp. 114-15, 267. Rabbi Abraham Yaffen, *HaMussar VeHaDa'at*, II, p. 83. Rabbi Yossef Hayyim of Baghdad, *Ben Ish Hai*, p. 98 (Job 8:7).
307. Cf. Shelah, III, p. 40a.
308. See Sifrei (85) and Rashi on Num. 11:1; Num. R. 20:5 (Mic. 6:3); Exod. 17:4; Isa. 1:4; Jer. 13:10. See also Isa. 19:25; Zech. 2:15. See also Hosea 1:9, 2:25; Pesikta Rabbati 44.
309. Cf. Lev. 19:15; TB Bava Metsia 59a. See also Tossefet Berakhah I, 164.
310. Cf. Exod. R. 31:12. Cf. also Shir HaShirim R. 3:21; Rashi on Lev. 5:21 and Sifra (22) ad loc.; Isa. 51:4; Shir HaShirim 3:11. See also Gen. R. 20:28. Cf. also TB Kiddushin 20a.
311. See Rambam, *Hilkhot Temurah*, IV, 13 (Isa. 25:1; Jer. 32:19; Prov. 22:20-21). Cf. Sifrei 322 (Deut. 32:28); TB Sanhedrin 26b; Num. R. 14:22. Zohar II, 82b; III, 53b. Maharal, *Tiferet Yisrael*, 13, pp. 16a-b.
312. Cf. Rashbam on Lev. 19:18. Prov. 3:29.
313. See Julius Fuerst, *Librorum Sacrorum ... Concordiantae*, Lipsiae: 1932, p. 842.
314. Cf. Zohar II, 86a-b; 160b.
315. Cf. Isa. 5:7; Ps. 80:9. Shir HaShirim 1:6, 2:15. Cf. TB Bava Metsia 83b; Hullin 92a. Gen. R. 42:4; Exod. R. 44:1; Lev. R. 36:2. Shir HaShirim R. 1:42, 8:12. Tana Devei Eliyahu Rabba 7. Pesikta DeRav Kahana, I, 14:4, p. 244.
316. Cf. Jer. 3:17. Pesikta Rabbati 12. Otiot DeRabbi Akiva, Dalet. See also I Chron. 29:23; TB Sanhedrin 20b. Rav Kook, *Orot HaKodesh*, III, p. 191; *Orot*, p. 160. See also Rambam, *Moreh Nevukhim*, I, 9 (Jer. 17:12).
317. Ps. 50:2. Cf. TB Yoma 54b; Ta'anit 16a. Tanhuma (Buber ed.), VaYera 45 (Isa. 2:3; cf. Mic. 4:2; Isa. 42:6, 60:3; Shir HaShirim R. 1, 21:65). Zohar Hadash, Hukat 50. See also Gen. R. 70:8.
318. Cf. TY Shevi'it IV, 3. Num. R. 21:22. Shoher Tov, 109 (Ps. 109:4-5). Lekah Tov, Shemot. Tanhuma, Beshalah 25. R. Dov Baer of Mezerich, *Maggid*

Devarav LeYa'akov, 198. Rav Kook, *Olat Reiyah*, I, p. 96; *Orot*, p. 33. *Mei Meirom*, VI, pp. 28-29. Cf. TB Yevamot 63a. Gen. R. 66:2; Lev. R. 1:11. Zohar II, 5b; III, 148b.

319. Cf. Isa. 2:3; Mic. 4:2; Isa. 55:4. Shoher Tov, 87. Zohar II, 218b.
320. Cf. Tana Devei Eliyahu Rabba 10; Rambam, *Hilkhot Shemittah VeYovel*, XIII, 13; R. Y.H. Ashlag, *Matan Torah*, p. 46.
321. Cf. Zech. 8:23; cf. also Num. R. 1:3.
322. Cf. Avot DeRabbi Nathan 36. Zohar II, 176b; III, 83a; 103b; 242b. Rambam, *Hilkhot Melakhim*, XII, 4; *Hilkhot Teshuvah*, IX, 1. Rabbi Nahman of Bratslav, *Likkutei Moharan*, 17; *Siddur Sha'arei Ratson*, p. 480 (Isa. 44:5). *Sefat Emet*, I, p. 5; III, p. 200. *Olat Reiyah*, I, p. 234. *VaYoel Moshe*, p. 317. R. Y.H. Ashlag, *Hakdamah, Ets Hayyim*, p. 2. See also A. Safran, *La Cabale*, pp. 342-43.
323. Cf. Sifrei 1 (Deut. 1:1); Yalkut Shim'oni, Yeshaya 60:503. Zohar II, 220a; III, 56a. *Sefat Emet*, I, p. 5. *Mei Meirom*, VI, pp. 254-55.
324. Cf. Zech. 2:15; see also Isa. 56:6-7. Cf. Rabbi S.R. Hirsch on Ps. 147:20 (German ed., p. 306; Hebrew ed., p. 548).
325. Exod. 19:6. See also Tanhuma (Buber ed.), Tetsaveh 9; Lev. R. 2:2; Num. R. 15:13; Yalkut Shim'oni, Terumah 25:364.
326. Cf. Isa. 66:21; Tana Devei Eliyahu Zuta 20. See also Exod. R. 19:4.
327. Cf. Isa. 61:6; Num. R. 8:2; Sifrei 119 (Num. 18:20). Zohar III, 234b. Rashi on Exod. 28:3, 29:30. Rabbeinu Bahya, Seforno and *Or HaHayyim* on Exod. 19:6 (Zeph. 3:9); Hirsch and Cassuto on Exod. 19:5-6.
328. Cf. Zech. 2:15.
329. Cf. Mic. 4:5.
330. Isa. 19:25; cf. Exod. R. 35:5. Cf. TB Pessahim 118b.
331. Cf. Zohar III, 111b; *Sefat Emet*, III, pp. 189, 192-98.
332. Cf. Gen. 32:29.
333. Cf. Gen. R. 39:18, 61:4. Exod. R. 19:5, 36:2-3. Num. R. 13:15. Deut. R. 1:11. Pesikta Zutarta, Hayei Sarah, Gen. 25:1. Tanhuma, Hayei Sarah 7. TB Shabbat 122a; Ta'anit 8b; Sotah 38b. Zohar I, 199b; II, 3a; 86b; III, 63b; 147b; 220a; 242b; 272b. Zohar Hadash, Bereshit 8. Tikkunei Zohar Hadash, 94a. Rashi on Sotah 10a. Ibn Ezra on Deut. 11:27. Recanati, Yitro, p. 9. Maharal, *Netivot Olam*, I, *Netiv Gemilut Hassadim*, 1; *Perushim LeAggadot*, I, p. 116. Shelah, III, pp. 24b, 202a, 204a. *Hafla'ah*, II, p. 158a. *Biurei HaGra Al Aggadot*, II, p. 30. *Tanya*, 36. See *Nefesh HaHayyim*, 3:5. Cf. Rabbi Avraham HaMalakh, *Hessed LeAvraham*, p. 114. *Avnei Nezer*, p. 160. *Orot*, pp. 39, 156. *Mei Meirom*, VI, pp. 182-83; VIII, p. 94. See also Isa. 40:5, 49:26. Prov. 22:9.
334. Cf. Gen. 12:2-3.
335. Cf. Lev. R. 2:2; Num. R. 15:13. Yalkut Shim'oni, Terumah 25:364; Maharal, *Derashot*, p. 41. See Shelah, III, p. 202a.
336. See Mishnah Sanhedrin X, 1 and Rambam ad loc.; TB Sanhedrin 90a. Cf. Pirkei DeRabbi Eliezer 37. Zohar I, 33a; 59b; 93a; 216a; II, 23a; 82b. Shir HaShirim R. 6:8. Rashi on Kiddushin 39b. Rambam, *Hilkhot Teshuvah*, III, 5; see also ibidem VIII, 7-8. Maharal, *Derekh Hayyim*, pp. 6-8. Shelah, III, p. 171b. *Da'at Torah*, I, p. 147.
337. See Lev. 20:26. Cf. Sifra 12:3 (Lev. 11:44). *Kuzari*, II, 14. Rambam, *Hilkhot*

REFERENCES, SOURCES & NOTES • 315

Avodat Kokhavim, XI, 1. Maharal, *Tiferet Yisrael*, 44; *Gevurot HaShem*, 8, 16, 23, 29, 44; *Derekh Hayyim*, p. 132, 175, 188; *Perushim LeAggadot*, I, pp. 85-86; II, pp. 8, 80; IV, pp. 15, 103. HaGra, *Siddur Ishei Yisrael*, p. 46. *Tanya*, *Iggeret HaKodesh*, 17. R. Abraham of Sochaczew, *Neot HaDesheh*, p. 202.

338. Cf. Maharal, *Netsah Yisrael*, 11; *Be'er HaGolah*, 3. Shelah, III, p. 175a; *Sefat Emet*, I, p. 11; III, p. 191; IV, p. 17.

339. Cf. Avot VI, 7. TB Kiddushin 30b; Shabbat 30b; 88a; Eruvin 54a; Yoma 72b; Ta'anit 7a; Avodah Zarah 5a. Tana Devei Eliyahu Rabba 18. Deut. R. 7:3; Shir HaShirim R. 1:19. Zohar III, 135a; 177b. Zohar Hadash, 49b. Tikkunei HaZohar, 21 (49a); 70 (137a). Maharal, *Tiferet Yisrael*, 15; *Derekh Hayyim*, pp. 34-35, 62. *Biurei HaGra Al Aggadot*, I, p. 51. R. Hayyim of Volozhin, *Nefesh HaHayyim*, 4:32. *Tanya*, 36. *Be'er Avraham*, p. 309.

340. Cf. TB Avodah Zarah 5a; Avot DeRabbi Nathan 34 (Deut. 4:4); Exod. R. 32:1; Zohar I, 13a; III, 218a (Isa. 65:22). Maharal, *Derekh Hayyim*, p. 2. Shelah, III, p. 175a. *Biurei HaGra Al Aggadot*, I, p. 51.

341. Cf. Ps. 116:9; Ezek. 26:20; Mekhilta 1 (Exod. 18:9) (Gen. 33:19). TY Kilaim IX, 3; Shekalim III, 3. TB Ketuvot 111a; Pessahim 113a. Avot DeRabbi Nathan 34. Gen. R. 74:1; Deut. R. 11:4. Shoher Tov 56. Yalkut Shim'oni, Mishlei 17:956. Zohar I, 1b; 114a; 115a; 131a; 177b; 193a; 205b; 216a; 219b; II, 152a; 184b; III, 84a; 284b. Rashi on Kiddushin 39b; Ibn Ezra on Gen. 13:19. Rambam, *Hilkhot Teshuvah*, III, 5. Maharal, *Netivot Olam*, I, *Netiv HaAvodah*, 55; *Derekh Hayyim*, pp. 7-8, 188, 252. Alshekh on Lekh Lekha. Shelah, III, p. 171b. *Sefat Emet*, III, p. 201. *Orot*, p. 13; *Mei Meirom*, VIII, pp. 19, 21; *Ben Ish Hai*, p. 234.

342. Cf. Zohar I, 63b; III, 25a; 113a; 152b; 176a. *Perushei Maharal MiPrag LeAggadot HaShas*, IV, p. 103. *Nefesh HaHayyim*, 4:32. *Sefat Emet*, V, pp. 90, 130.

343. Cf. TB Shabbat 88b; Ketuvot 111b. Sifra DiTseniuta 5, p. 66 (I Sam. 25:29; Ps. 116:9). *Nefesh HaHayyim*, 4:17.

344. Cf. Prov. 3:18 and Ibn Ezra ad loc. Avot VI, 7. Sifrei 47 (Deut. 11:21). TB Arakhin 15b. Gen. R. 12:5, 32:2. Lev. R. 9:3, 35:5; Num. R. 13:11. Avot DeRabbi Nathan 34. Yalkut Shim'oni, Mishlei 3:934. Zohar I, 193a; II, 60b; 121a; 134b; III, 53b; 83a; 153a; 159b; 176a; 218a. Tikkunei HaZohar, 21 (60a). Maharal, *Derekh Hayyim*, pp. 3, 113. R. Hayyim of Volozhin, *Nefesh HaHayyim*, 4, 26, 33.

345. Cf. Isa. 65:22; Sifrei 47 (Deut. 11:21); TB Ta'anit 7a; Avot DeRabbi Nathan 34; Gen. R. 12:5; Zohar I, 178a; II, 48b; 84b; 121a; III, 66b, 82b. Tikkunei HaZohar, 43 (82b).

346. Cf. Zohar III, 159b; Maharal, *Derashot*, p. 41.

347. Cf. *Sefat Emet*, I, p. 11; *Mei Meirom*, VI, p. 51.

348. Cf. Zohar I, 61a (Ps. 68:35); II, 32b.

349. Cf. Isa. 60:3; Prov. 6:23; TB Bava Batra 4a; Lev. R. 31:6; Maharal, *Tiferet Yisrael*, 15.

350. Cf. TB Berakhot 5a; Mekhilta 1 (Exod. 18:9); Maharal, *Tiferet Yisrael*, 13; *Derekh Hayyim*, pp. 9, 96, 236. *Ben Ish Hai*, pp. 132-33.

351. Cf. TB Berakhot 17a; Ketuvot 111a. Zohar I, 177b; Zohar Hadash, 49b. Shoher Tov, 56. Rambam, *Hilkhot Teshuvah*, VIII, 7; *Hilkhot Melakhim*, V, 11. *Sefat Emet*, III, p. 197. R. Yisrael of Koznitz, *Avodat Yisrael*, p. 204.

352. Cf. TB Shabbat 152a; Maharal, *Derashot*, p. 17.
353. Cf. Zohar III, 113a.
354. Cf. Maharal, *Gevurot HaShem*, 23; *Sefat Emet*, III, pp. 196-97.
355. Cf. TB Berakhot 17a; Bava Batra 16b-17a; Hullin 44b. Shoher Tov, 1. Zohar II, 86b; III, 301b. Maharal, *Tiferet Yisrael*, 15; *Netivot Olam*, I, *Netiv HaTorah*, 1; *Perushim LeAggadot*, III, p. 80; *Derekh Hayyim*, pp. 62, 236. *Mei Meirom*, VI, p. 279.
356. Cf. Zohar II, 85b. *Tanya, Likkutei Amarim*, 4, 35; *Iggeret HaKodesh*, 23.
357. Cf. TB Sanhedrin 99b; Ps. 51:16.
358. Cf. TB Bava Metsia 59b; Deut. 30:12. Maharal, *Perushim LeAggadot*, I, pp. 146-47; II, p. 121; *Derashot, Hesped*, p. 15.
359. Cf. TB Ta'anit 5a; Shoher Tov, 122. Zohar I, 1a; II, 55b.
360. Cf. Avot II, 7; TB Pessahim 113a; Shabbat 63a. Exod. R. 2:6. Zohar I, 88a; 168a; 175b; 190a; II, 86b; III, 301b. R. Yossef Hayyim of Baghdad, *Ben Ish Hai*, 133.
361. Cf. Zohar I, 171b; 177b; 179a; 205b; III, 82b. *Perushei Maharal LeAggadot HaShas*, I, pp. 85-86.
362. Cf. TY Shekalim III, 3. TB Ketuvot 111a; Pessahim 113a; Bava Batra 158b. Shoher Tov, 56. Yalkut Shim'oni, Mishlei 17.556. Zohar I, 177b; III, 245b. Tikkunei HaZohar, 5 (141b). *Shirei Yehuda HaLevi (Tsion halo tishali)*, p. 233. Rambam, *Hilkhot Teshuvah*, III, 5. Ibn Ezra on Gen. 33:19; Ramban on Gen. 33:18. Maharal, *Derekh Hayyim*, pp. 7, 252. Shelah, III, pp. 23a, 171b. *Sefat Emet*, III, pp. 197, 201. *Mei Meirom, Missaviv LiShmonah Perakim LeHaRambam*, p. 212. *Ben Ish Hai*, p. 133.
363. Cf. Mekhilta 4 (Exod. 16:25), 1 (Exod. 18:9). TB Berakhot 5a. Maharal, *Derashot*, pp. 5, 41; *Derekh Hayyim*, pp. 251-52. *Sefat Emet*, III, pp. 201-2.
364. Cf. TY Rosh HaShanah I, 3. TB Kiddushin 32b and Rashi ad loc.; Avodah Zarah 19a and Rashi ad loc. Exod. R. 47:13; Tanhuma, Shoftim 5. Rashi on Ps. 1:2. Rabbi Bezalel Ze'ev Safran, *She'eilot UTeshuvot Harbaz*, I, p. 30.
365. Cf. Exod. 3:7 et al.; Num. 11:29, 17:6. II Sam. 14:13; Ezek. 36:20; Ps. 50:7; I Chron. 28:2 et al. TB Hullin 101b. Petihta DeRuth Rabba. Zohar II, 160b.
366. Cf. Joel 4:2. Rambam, *Hilkhot Terumot*, I, 2. Ramban, *Derashah LeRosh HaShanah (Kitvei Ramban* I), pp. 249-51; Ramban on Deut. 31:16. Maharal, *Derekh Hayyim*, p. 188.
367. Cf. Mekhilta 18 (Exod. 13:5). TB Eruvin 13b; 54a; Rosh HaShanah 17b; Ta'anit 7a; Megillah 29a; Nedarim 55a; Sotah 5a; 21b; Avodah Zarah 5b; Hullin 89a. Cf. Num. 12:13. Avot I, 1; IV, 9. Num. R. 1:6; Shir HaShirim R. 1:19. Zohar I, 256a; 260b; II, 54a. Rashi on Shabbat 104a; Sotah 5a; Zevahim 54b. Shelah, III, p. 22b. Hida, *Nitsotsei Orot*; Zohar III, 159b. *Toldot Ya'akov Yossef*, VaYakhel. Rabbi Shneur Zalman of Lyady, *Likkutei Torah, Bemidbar*. Rabbi Ya'akov Yitshak of Lublin, *Divrei Emet*, Shelah. *Sefat Emet*, V, pp. 24, 26. *Bet Avraham*, p. 78; *Be'er Avraham*, pp. 171, 206. *Shem MiShemuel, Bereshit*, II, p. 321.
368. Cf. Maharal, *Tiferet Yisrael*, 10. R. Shemuel of Sochaczew, *Shem MiShemuel, Haggadah*, pp. 43-44. See also A. Safran, *La Cabale*, p. 288.
369. Cf. TB Hullin 89a (Deut. 7:7); cf. also TB Shabbat 88b; Avot V, 19. Cf. Num. R. 13:5; Tanhuma, Eikev 3. Lekah Tov, Shemot 5. *Sefat Emet*, I, p.

REFERENCES, SOURCES & NOTES • 317

201; III, p. 190. Rabbi Bezalel Ze'ev Safran, *She'eilot UTeshuvot Harbaz*, I, p. 27.
370. Cf. Isa. 41:16, 55:5. Cf. Deut. 10:21. Ps. 89:18, 105:3 and Rashi ad loc.
371. Cf. II Sam. 22:33; Ps. 43:2.
372. Cf. Exod. 7:4 and *Or HaHayyim* ad loc., 12:41. Cf. Isa. 5:7. Cf. also TB Shevuot 35b; Berakhot 31b. Ramban on Num. 11:16; *Or HaHayyim* on Exod. 19:6. See also Tikkunei HaZohar, 86a.
373. Cf. Ps. 20:6.
374. Cf. Ezek. 34. TB Yevamot 61a; Bava Metsia 114b. Zohar II, 21a; 25b; 119b. See Exod. R. 24:3.
375. Cf. Ezek. 36:38. Ps. 36:7, 73:22-24; Shir HaShirim 1:4. TB Hullin 5b and Rashi ad loc.; Kiddushin 22b and Rashi ad loc.; Avodah Zarah 5b; Bekhorot 44b and Tossafot ad loc. Exod. R. 24:3, 34:4. Lev. R. 27:1; Num. R. 23:2. Kohelet R. 1:31, 1:39. Tana Devei Eliyahu Rabba 2, 22. Zohar II, 87a; III, 108a; 147a. Maharal, *Netivot Olam*, II. *Netiv HaTemimut*, 2. *Sefat Emet*, III, pp. 192, 205; V, pp. 9, 136. *Orot*, pp. 74, 167; *Mei Meirom*, VI, p. 311. *Avnei Nezer*, p. 118. *Da'at Torah*, p. 194.
376. Cf. TB Yevamot 62a; Niddah 17a. Lev. R. 20:2. Tanhuma, VaYera 23; Pirkei DeRabbi Eliezer 31; Maharal, *Gevurot HaShem*, 54.
377. Cf. Maharal, *Derashot*, p. 90; Alshekh on Lekh Lekha; cf. also Alshekh on Noah.
378. Cf. Isa. 30:7 and Rashi ad loc. TB Megillah 6a; Bava Batra 10b. Num. R. 11. Maharal, *Gevurot HaShem*, 44.
379. Cf. TB Hullin 89a; cf. Rabbi S.R. Hirsch on Exod. 19:5-6.
380. Cf. Maharal, *Netsah Yisrael*, 14; *Gur Aryeh* on Lekh Lekha and Matot.
381. Cf. Zohar I, 158a; II, 23a; 240a-b; III, 71b; 73a-b; 98b. Recanati, Bereshit, p. 7b. Shelah, III, p. 199b; *Siddur Sha'ar HaShamayim*, pp. 515-16. *Nefesh HaHayyim*, 1:6; *Kedushat Levi*, p. 57b; *Bnei Issakhar, Haggadah*, p. 63. *Likkutei Moharan*, II, 39. *Sefat Emet*, I, pp. 42, 60, 76, 202; III, pp. 200-2; IV, p. 68. *Orot*, p. 156. *Mei Meirom*, VI, p. 312; VIII, pp. 91, 94; *Missaviv LiShmonah Perakim LeHaRambam*, pp. 7-8, 209-12. R. Y.L.H. Ashlag, *Hakdamah, Sefer HaZohar Im Perush HaSulam*, I.
382. **Torah:** Cf. TB Pessahim 119a; Sukkah 49b; Haggigah 13a. Gen. R. 1:1. Deut. R. 1:17, 7:10. Tanhuma, Ki Tissa 34. Zohar II, 111b; III, 3a; 73a; 91b; 98b. Tikkunei HaZohar, 28 (72:2). Tikkunei Zohar Hadash, 107. Recanati, Yitro, p. 9a. R. Moshe Cordovero, *Sefer HaPardess*, 27. Maharal, *Perushim LeAggadot HaShas*, I, pp. 63-64; 97; *Derekh Hayyim*, p. 226. *Nefesh HaHayyim*, 4:28. *Sefat Emet*, III, p. 206; IV, pp. 64, 150-51. *Avnei Nezer*, pp. 133, 154, 160.
Israel: Cf. TB Sukkah 29a; Ketuvot 111a; Bava Batra 10b. Gen. R. 6:5; Exod. R. 19:7. Num. R. 10:3; 20:21. Shir HaShirim R. 6:4. Tana Devei Eliyahu Rabba 7, 8. Shoher Tov, 18, 114. Pesikta Zutarta, Exod. 12:3. Zohar I, 230b. Tikkunei HaZohar, 22. Zohar Hadash, 44b. Recanati, Yitro, p. 9a. Maharal, *Netivot Olam*, I, *Netiv HaAvodah*, 13; *Gevurot HaShem*, 18, 23, 43, 63, 67; *Perushim LeAggadot*, IV, 27; *Derashot*, pp. 35-36. Shelah, I, pp. 4a, 21a, 22a; III, pp. 24b, 26a, 34a, 171a, 183b; *Siddur Sha'ar HaShamayim*, p. 517. *Toldot Ya'akov Yossef, Hakdamah. Kedushat Levi*, p. 97. Hatam Sofer, *Derashot*, II,

p. 244. Rav Kook, *Orot*, pp. 94, 192; *Orot HaKodesh*, I, pp. 86-87; III, pp. 33, 180, 181; *Mishpat Kohen*, 124. *Mei Meirom*, VI, p. 312; VIII, pp. 91, 94, 118. *Sefat Emet*, IV, pp. 158, 202. R. Abraham of Slonim, *Be'er Avraham*, pp. 115, 257-58. R. Abraham of Sochaczew, *Avnei Nezer*, p. 42; *Neot HaDesheh*, pp. 138, 173. R. Samuel of Sochaczew, *Shem MiShemuel, Haggadah*, pp. 42-43. R. Y.L.H. Ashlag, *Hakdamah, Sefer HaZohar Im Perush HaSulam*, I, p. 18. **Erets-Yisrael:** Cf. Mishnah Berakhot IV, 5-6; TB Berakhot 28b; TY Berakhot IV, 4. Mishnah Kelim I, 6. TB Berakhot 30a; 31a; 34b; Ta'anit 10a; Hullin 91b; 92a and Rashi ad loc. Ps. 84:11. Gen. R. 4:5; Deut. R. 4:10. Derekh Erets Zuta 9. Tana Devei Eliyahu Zuta 2. Shoher Tov, 68. Tanhuma, Kedoshim 10; Re'eh 8. Zohar I, 55a; 72a; 84a; 128b; II, 157a; III, 84a; 161a-b. Zohar Hadash, 69a. Tikkunei HaZohar, 37 (78b). Maharal, *Gur Aryeh*, Shemot. Shelah, III, pp. 23b, 24a-b, 172b-173a. *Hafla'ah*, II, p. 158b. *Likkutei Moharan*, II, 40. *Nefesh HaHayyim*, 1, 4. *Orot*, p. 9. *Mei Meirom*, VI, pp. 233, 235, 254, 293-94, 312; VIII, pp. 19, 21; *Missaviv LiShmonah Perakim LeHaRambam*, p. 212. *Sefat Emet*, I, p. 60; III, pp. 189, 200, 202, 206; IV, pp. 96, 102, 109; V, p. 26. Be'er Avraham, p. 324.

383. Cf. Maharal, *Derashot*, pp. 88-89.
384. Cf. Maharal, *Derekh Hayyim*, pp. 21, 96. R. Eliyahu of Vilna, *Siddur Ishei Yisrael*, p. 287.
385. Cf. Maharal, *Derashot*, p. 88.
386. Cf. Rav Kook, *Orot*, pp. 33, 155-56; *Orot HaKodesh*, I, pp. 86-87.
387. Cf. Tanhuma, Ki Tissa 34. See A. Safran, *La Cabale*, p. 57.
388. Cf. Tanhuma, Noah 3.
389. Cf. TY Peyah II, 4. TB Gittin 60b and Tossafot ad loc. Exod. R. 47:1, 47:4; Num. R. 14:22. Tanhuma, VaYera 5; Ki Tissa 34. *Bet HaLevi*, II, pp. 41, 45, 48.
390. Cf. TB Sotah 38a; Rambam, *Moreh Nevukhim*, III, 8; Ramban on Exod. 30:13. Maharal, *Netivot Olam*, II, *Netiv HaTseniut*, 3; *Gevurot HaShem*, 43. *Likkutei Moharan*, 19. *Sefat Emet*, III, p. 191; IV, p. 157. Franz Rosenzweig, *Kokhav HaGeulah*, Jerusalem: 5730 (1970), p. 326. Rav Kook, *Orot*, p. 164. Rabbi Bezalel Ze'ev Safran, *She'eilot UTeshuvot Harbaz*, I, p. 21.
391. Cf. TY Megillah I, 9; TB Berakhot 55a; Shir HaShirim R. 1. Tanhuma, Noah 19. Zeph. 3:9; Rashi on Gen. 11:1. Zohar I, 204a; 205b; II, 265a. Shelah, I, p. 25a; *Siddur Sha'ar HaShamayim*, p. 512. *Sefat Emet*, III, pp. 191, 200; IV, p. 20; V, p. 17. *Siddur HaGeonim VeHaMekubalim*, III, p. 724.
392. Cf. Sifrei 46 (Deut. 11:19). TY Shekalim III, 3; Shabbat 1, 3.
393. Cf. Gen. R. 18:6, 31:8; see also ibidem 1:1; 1:12. Tanhuma, Lekh Lekha 9. Rashi on Gen. 2:23; Ramban on Exod. 30:13. Shelah, I, p. 17a. *Sefat Emet*, V, pp. 4, 14.
394. Cf. TB Berakhot 5a; Sukkah 42a; Nedarim 22b; Gittin 60b; Kiddushin 37a and Rashi ad loc. Exod. R. 47:1; Num. R. 14:22; Deut. R. 7:10. Zohar I, 247b; II, 129b (Lev. 22:32); 166a; III, 4b. Rambam, *Perush HaMishnah*, Avot II; *Hakdamah, Mishneh Torah. Tur, Orah Hayyim*, 139; *Bah, Tur, Orah Hayyim*, 47. Recanati, Yitro, p. 8a. Shelah, III, pp. 21b, 202a, 204a; *Siddur Sha'ar HaShamayim*, p. 512. Maharsha, *Hiddushei Aggadot*, Sotah 37a. *Kedushat Levi*, p. 75. *Aderet Eliyahu*, pp. 429-30. *Likkutei Moharan*, 19. *Sefat Emet*, I, p. 5; III, pp. 189, 191; IV, pp. 103, 174-75, 202; V, p. 5. *Orot*

REFERENCES, SOURCES & NOTES · 319

   HaKodesh, III, p. 356; *Orot*, pp. 26, 86-87; *Orot HaTorah*, pp. 7-9, 69, 75. *Mei Meirom*, VI, pp. 254, 302. *Hiddushei HaRiz*, p. 86; *Ben Ish Hai*, pp. 182, 253. R. B.Z. Safran, *She'eilot UTeshuvot Harbaz*, I, p. 21; *Doresh LeTsion*, p. 25.

395. Cf. Lev. 20:22-26; Sifra and Rashi ad loc. Num. 23:9; Ibn Ezra, Ramban and Malbim ad loc. Deut. 32:12. Exod. R. 15:8, 36:1; Num. R. 10:3, 23:9. Deut. R. 7:3. Shir HaShirim R. 1:21, 6:4. See also TB Shabbat 156a; Bava Batra 8a; Sanhedrin 39a. Maharal, *Tiferet Yisrael*, 1; *Gevurot HaShem* 11, 12.

396. See above, p. 11. Ref. 205.

398. Cf. Gen. R. 1:5; cf. Zohar I, 24a; 118b; II, 108b; 119a-b; III, 229b. Zohar Hadash, Yitro 37a. Tikkunei HaZohar, 6a; 6(23b).

399. Cf. Gen. 1:5-6, 8:2. Exod. R. 30:6. Lev. R. 19:1. Shoher Tov, 90. Zohar I, 2b; II, 49a; 84b; III, 91b. Zohar Hadash, Bereshit 5a.

400. Cf. Sifrei 37 (Deut. 11:10).

401. Cf. Mishnah Peyah I, 1; Kohelet R. 1:9; Tana Devei Eliyahu Zuta 1; Tanhuma, Beshalah 20; Rambam, *Hilkhot Talmud Torah*, III, 3.

402. Tana Devei Eliyahu Rabba 14. Cf. Rabbeinu Sa'adya Gaon, *Emunot VeDeot*, III, 7; *Kuzari*, II, 56. Maharal, *Derekh Hayyim*, pp. 8-9; Shelah, III, p. 11a.

403. Cf. TB Avodah Zarah 13a and Tossafot ad loc. Exod. R. 47:4; Num. R. 14:23. Maharal, *Derashot, Hesped*, pp. 14-15; *Derekh Hayyim*, p. 99; *Perushim LeAggadot*, I, p. 81; *Gevurot HaShem*, 8, 47. Shelah, I, p. 11a. *Biurei HaGra Al Aggadot*, I, p. 37. R. Hayyim of Volozhin, *Nefesh HaHayyim*, 1:16, 4:11; *Ruah Hayyim*, p. 12. Rav Kook, *Orot HaTorah*, p. 8; *Sefat Emet*, III, p. 184.

404. Cf. Exod. R. 47:4; Shelah, I, p. 4a; R. Ya'akov Emden, *Siddur Bet Ya'akov, Sulam Bet El*, p. 11b; Rav Kook, *Mishpat Kohen*, 144.

405. Cf. Exod. R. 40:1; Shir HaShirim R. 2:6; Esther R. Petihta; Pesikta Zutarta, Bereshit 30:4. Zohar III, 11a; 221b. R. Hayyim of Volozhin, *Nefesh HaHayyim*, 4:25; *Ruah Hayyim*, pp. 88-90. Rabbi Samson Raphael Hirsch on Deut. 4:5.

406. Cf. TB Pessahim 118a; Berakhot 6b; 17b; Eruvin 18b; Bava Metsia 58b and Tossafot ad loc. TY Orlah I, 3. See R. Ovadya Bartenora, Avot III, 11; Tossafot Yom Tov, Orlah I, 5. Cf. Gen. R. 91:5; Num. R. 12:14. Alshekh on Lekh Lekha. R. Moshe Hayyim Luzzatto, the "Ramhal," *Derekh HaShem*, 1:2. HaGra, *Siddur Ishei Yisrael*, p. 98; R. Hayyim of Volozhin, *Ruah Hayyim*, p. 93. R. Ya'akov Yitshak, the "Hozeh of Lublin," *Divrei Emet*, Hayei Sarah. *Sefat Emet*, I, pp. 28, 48-49, 64-65; 121; IV, p. 27. *Meshekh Hokhmah*, p. 189. R. Abraham of Slonim, *Yessod HaAvodah*, p. 233; *Be'er Avraham*, pp. 145, 273, 285; *Bet Avraham*, p. 151. R. Abraham of Sochaczew, *Avnei Nezer*, p. 91. *Shem MiShemuel, Shemot*, II, p. 175. R. Eliyahu Lapian, *Lev Eliyahu*, p. 149.

407. Cf. Rashi on Gen. 27:28. Rashi, Seforno and *Ha'amek Davar* on Deut. 11:12-13. Malbim on Gen. 48:15. Hatam Sofer, *Haggadah Shel Pessah*, p. 139. *Sefat Emet*, I, pp. 54-56. Rav Kook, *Olat Reiyah*, II, p. 154. R. Simha Zissel Ziv, *Hokhmah UMussar*, I, p. 245. R. Yitshak Hutner, *Pahad Yitshak, Yerah HaEitanim*, pp. 46-47, 54; *Yarha Telitaei*, New York: 5731 (1971), pp. 64-65; 98-99. R. Y.H. Ashlag, *Matan Torah*, pp. 23-26.

408. Cf. Sifrei 307 (Deut. 32:4).

409. Cf. Gen. 2:16-17. Cf. Exod. R. 30:6, 30:18. Cf. TB Avodah Zarah 3a; Tanhuma, Shoftim 9; Zohar III, 122a. Rambam, *Mishneh Torah, Hilkhot Melakhim*, IX. Maharal, *Tiferet Yisrael*, 4, 7, 17.
410. Cf. Sifrei 322 (Deut. 32:28). TB Avodah Zarah 17b. Num. R. 10:9. Zohar II, 82b; 96b; III, 77a. Rambam, *Hilkhot Temurah*, IV, 13. Rabbeinu Bahya Ibn Pakuda, *Hovot HaLevavot, Sha'ar HaPerishut*, 7.
411. Cf. Gen. R. 95:2. Ramban on Gen. 6:2, 6:13; *Torat HaShem Temimah* (*Kitvei Ramban* I), p. 173. Abrabanel on Yitro, Exod. 19 (II, p. 161ff.). Maharal, *Tiferet Yisrael*, 25; *Derekh Hayyim*, pp. 111, 212, 220. *Likkutei Moharan*, II, 78. *Be'er Avraham*, p. 49.
412. Cf. Num. R. 11:4; Zohar II, 32a. R. D.T. Hoffmann, *Bereshit*, I, p. 206.
413. Cf. Gen. R. 39:12; Rashi on Gen. 22:2. Ramban on Gen. 12:1; idem, *Derashah Al Divrei Kohelet* (*Kitvei Ramban* I), p. 202. *Or HaHayyim* on Gen. 12:1. See also Zohar I, 78a. Cf. Ari HaKadosh, *Likkutei Torah*, p. 42. Shelah, III, pp. 23b-24a; *Kitvei Rabbi Nahman DeBratslav*, p. 287. *Sefat Emet*, I, pp. 46, 48; III, p. 200. *Mei Meirom*, V, p. 237; VI, pp. 293, 312; VII, pp. 62-64; *Missaviv LiShmonah Perakim LeHaRambam*, p. 212. R. D.T. Hoffmann, *Bereshit*, I, pp. 209-10.
414. Cf. TB Kiddushin 31a; Zohar Hadash, 44a. Ramban on Gen. 26:5; Lev. 18:25.
415. Cf. TB Makot 23b; Exod. R. 30:6; Zohar II, 82b; Tanhuma, Mass'ei 6; Maharal, *Tiferet Yisrael*, 7.
416. Cf. Gen. 6:6 and Ramban ad loc., Gen. R. 27:6-7.
417. Cf. Massekhet Sofrim XVI, 10; Gen. R. 14:6; Exod. R. 28:1; cf. also TB Avodah Zarah 19a.
418. See also Rambam, *Moreh Nevukhim*, I, 63; II, 39; Abrabanel, Yitro 19 (II, p. 161ff.).
419. Cf. Maharal, *Tiferet Yisrael*, 20.
420. Cf. Gen. R. 39:24, 49:20. See Zohar I, 105b. Cf. R. Yitshak Arama, *Akeidat Yitshak*, I, Lekh Lekha 18.
421. Cf. Gen. 18:18-19 and Seforno ad loc. I. Chron. 16:16-19. TY Sanhedrin X, 1; see also TB Shabbat 55a. Cf. Gen. R. 44:6, 63:2-3. Lev. R. 36:3-5. Tanhuma, Shemot 4. Zohar I, 86a; 154b. Rambam, *Hilkhot Avodat Kokhavim*, I, 2. Radak on Gen. 12:7. Rashi on Gen. 18:19. Rambam on Gen. 24:1. Rabbeinu Bahya on Gen. 46:8. Maharal, *Netsah Yisrael*, 11. Shelah, I, pp. 21b, 142b. *Mikhtav MeEliyahu*, III, pp. 200-1. *Bet HaLevi*, II, p. 9.
422. Cf. Exod. 3:8, 3:12, 3:17, 6:6, 6:8. Exod. R. 3:4; Num. R. 11:4. Zohar III, 221a.
423. Cf. Maharal, *Tiferet Yisrael*, 17.
424. Cf. TB Avodah Zarah 2b; Zohar I, 25a; II, 3a; III, 91b; 192a-193a; 227b. Cf. Tossefta Demai II, 4; Sifrei 343 (Deut. 33:2); TB Bekhorot 30b; Rambam, *Hilkhot Issurei Bi'a*, XIV, 5; Maharal, *Tiferet Yisrael*, 1.
425. Cf. TB Avodah Zarah 2b. Tanhuma, Vezot HaBerakhah 4; see also Eihah R. 3:3. Cf. Ramban on Deut. 26:17-18.
426. Cf. Exod. 6:7-8.
427. Cf. TB Shabbat 89a; Pirkei DeRabbi Eliezer 41. Rambam, *Iggeret Teiman*. Maharal, *Be'er HaGolah*, 7; *Derekh Hayyim*, p. 219. Hatam Sofer, *Haggadah*

Shel Pessah, p. 5; R. Abraham of Slonim, *Be'er Avraham*, p. 145; R. Abraham of Sochaczew, *Avnei Nezer*, pp. 97, 148; Rav Kook, *Orot*, pp. 38-39, 49-50, 52-53, 88-89, 112, 138, 155, 157.

428. Cf. Isa. 42:1. Cf. Lev. R. 13:14. Maharal, *Gevurot HaShem*, 54; Alshekh on Noah.
429. Cf. Mekhilta 3 (Exod. 14:15).
430. Cf. Num. 10:35 and Rashi ad loc.; Exod. R. 13:2. Sifrei 84 (Num. 10:35) (Exod. 15:7; Ps. 74:23, 83:4; Zech. 2:12). Lekah Tov, Shemot. Deut. 32:10; Rashi and Ramban on Deut. 32:7. Rashi on Deut. 32:11. Ramban on Deut. 32:40. Jer. 2:3; TB Haggigah 5b; Exod. R. 24:13; Num. R. 2:12, 10:5. Mekhilta 6 (Exod. 15:7). Eihah R. 1; Esther R. 7; Tana Devei Eliyahu Rabba 30; Zohar III, 122a; *Sefer HaHinukh, Mitzvah* 603. See also TB Sanhedrin 58b, Isa. 63:9; Yalkut Shim'oni, Matot 31:785. *Bet HaLevi*, II, p. 11.
431. Cf. Kohelet R. 1:9. Cf. Exod. 4:22; Avot III, 14; TB Shabbat 31a. Isa. 41:8-9, 42:1, 42:19, 44:2 (Zohar I, 145b), 44:21, 45:4, 49:3 (Zohar III, 112a), 49:6, 52:13. Jer. 30:10, 46:27-28. Lev. 25:55. TB Kiddushin 22b; Bava Kama 116b. Shir HaShirim R. 1:39. Maharal, *Gevurot HaShem*, 44. *Sefat Emet*, III, p. 193.
432. Cf. Gen. 15:1, 28:15. Isa. 41:9; Zohar I, 145b; 177b. Ps. 121:4. Tanhuma, Nitsavim 3. Tanhuma Yashan, Lekh Lekha 14. Yalkut Shim'oni, Yitro 19:276.
433. Cf. Rashi on Num. 23:9.
434. Cf. TB Avodah Zarah 18a. Rabbeinu Sa'adya Gaon, *Emunot VeDeot*, III, 7.
435. Cf. Tanhuma, Eikev 2.
436. Cf. Gen. 18:19; Deut. 10:15. See Lev. R. 36.
437. Cf. Gen. 6:12.
438. Cf. Lev. R. 9:3, 35:5. Tana Devei Eliyahu Rabba 1. Tanhuma, Lekh Lekha 11. *Kuzari*, I, 47. Rambam, *Hilkhot Avodat Kokhavim*, I, 1-3. Rabbeinu Bahya Ibn Pakuda, *Hovot HaLevavot, Sha'ar HaPerishut*, 2:7. Maharal, *Netivot Olam*, II, *Netiv Derekh Erets*, 1; *Derekh Hayyim*, pp. 3, 8. Shelah, I, p. 101b. *Likkutei Moharan*, II, 78. *Sefat Emet*, I, p. 55. *Mikhtav MeEliyahu*, III, p. 201. *Da'at Torah*, I, p. 10.
439. Cf. Gen. R. 14; TB Haggigah 12a; Zohar I, 53b; 142b; III, 83b; 117a.
440. Cf. Targum Yonathan Ben Uziel on Gen. 22:19; Targum Yerushalmi and Rashi on Gen. 25:22. TB Megillah 16b; Yoma 28b; Avodah Zarah 36b; Makot 23b. Gen. R. 36:9, 37:10, 56:20, 63:7, 63:14, 63:15, 67:8; Tanhuma, Shemot 1. Zohar I, 137b; 138b; 139a; 255b. Tikkunei HaZohar, 69 (113a). *Kuzari*, I, 47; 63; 95; 103; II, 68. Rambam, *Hilkhot Avodat Kokhavim*, I, 2; *Moreh Nevukhim*, II, 39. Rashi on Gen. 21:8, 25:16, 25:27, 28:9, 28:11. Ramban on Gen. 37:3. Rabbi S.R. Hirsch on Gen. 10:21. Hatam Sofer, *She'eilot UTeshuvot, Yoreh Deyah*, 356.
441. Cf. Gen. 12:6-7 and Rashi ad loc. Gen. 14:18 and Rashi ad loc. Gen. 9:18, 9:22, 10:6, 24:31. Mic. 1:15 and Rashi ad loc. Gen. R. 1:3, 42:13, 59:12. Lev. R. 17:5. Cf. Mekhilta 1 (Exod. 13:17); Gen. 21:23. Ramban on Gen. 15:11. See also Mekhilta 9 (Exod. 15:15-16); Sifrei 38 (Deut. 11:10). Cf. TB Sanhedrin 97a; Tikkunei HaZohar, 36 (77b). Cf. Pirkei DeRabbi Eliezer 31; Tanhuma, Shelah 8. Cf. Gen. 15:13, 15:15-16 and Rashi ad loc. Lev. 18:28; 20:23-24. Isa.

27:8. Zohar I, 113b. Cf. Mekhilta 18 (Exod. 13:5); Ramban on Gen. 10:15; see Gen. R. 59:12; Lev. R. 17:5. Cf. TB Sanhedrin 91a; 94a. TY Shevi'it VI, 1; see also Zohar I, 83a.

442. Cf. TB Yoma 28b; Zohar I, 264b.
443. Cf. Avot V, 1; Exod. 34:28. Exod. R. 24:4, 29:7. Lev. R. 35:4; Num. R. 14:24. Pesikta Rabbati 21. Zohar I, 63b; III, 11b; 117a. Shelah, I, pp. 56b, 176b. *Likkutei Moharan*, II, 78. See A.Safran, *La Cabale*, p. 50.
444. Cf. Gen. 15:16 and Rashi and Ramban ad loc. Deut. 9:4-5 and Ramban ad loc. Exod. R. 30:1; Shir HaShirim 2:12. Yalkut Shim'oni, Shelah 13:742. Mekhilta 18 (Exod. 13:5), 1 (Exod. 13:17). See also TB Arakhin 15a. Cf. Zohar I, 61b; 73b; 113b; 121b. Recanati, Noah, p. 20b.
445. Cf. Sifra 9 (Lev. 18:4); TB Yoma 67b; Eruvin 100b; Sanhedrin 56a; 108a; Bava Kama 87a. Gen. R. 61:1, 95:2. Lev. R. 2:9, 9:3, 13:2. Shir HaShirim R. 1:16. Tanhuma, Lekh Lekha 11. Rabbeinu Sa'adya Gaon, *Emunot VeDeot*, III, 1; 2. Ibn Ezra on Gen. 26:5; Exod. 20:2. *Kuzari*, II, 48. Rambam, *Shemonah Perakim*, VI; *Hilkhot Genevah*, VII, 12; *Hilkhot Rotseah Ushmirat Nafesh*, IV, 9; *Hilkhot Melakhim*, VIII, 11. Rashi on Gen. 26:5; Kiddushin 40a. Ramban on Gen. 6:2, 6:13, 15:25, 26:5; Lev. 19:2; Deut. 6:18; *Torat HaShem Temimah* (*Kitvei Ramban* I), p. 173. Rabbeinu Bahya on Gen. 13:17. Maharal, *Gevurot HaShem*, 29; *Tiferet Yisrael*, 19, 20; *Derekh Hayyim*, pp. 3, 48, 52. *Likkutei Moharan*, II, 78. *Sefat Emet*, I, pp. 24, 55; II, pp. 31, 33; III, pp. 32-33. *Olat Reiyah*, I, p. 215; *Orot HaKodesh*, III, pp. 21, 32-33; *Orot HaTorah*, pp. 64-65. *Mei Meirom*, VIII, p. 18. *Meshekh Hokhmah*, p. 328. *Mikhtav MeEliyahu*, III, p. 51. *Ben Ish Hai*, p. 180.
446. Cf. Sifrei 343 (Deut. 33:2). TB Shabbat 88b; Sotah 36b. Exod. R. 28:4; Num. R. 14:22. Tanhuma, Lekh Lekha 19. Yalkut Shim'oni, Yeshaya 60:503. Zohar II, 146a; 220a. Tikkunei HaZohar, 22 (64a). Maharal, *Tiferet Yisrael*, 1, 17; *Derashot*, pp. 26-28.
447. Cf. TB Bava Kama 38a; Avodah Zarah 2b. Lev. R. 13:2; Shir HaShirim R. 19:11; Eihah R. 3:3; Yalkut Shim'oni, Yeshaya 43:454. Zohar I, 25a; II, 3a; III, 91b; 192a. Ramban on Deut. 32:26. Maharal, *Perushim Al Aggadot*, I, p. 63; *Derekh Hayyim*, p. 212. Rav Kook, *Olat Reiyah*, I, pp. 363, 386.
448. Cf. Sifrei 312 (Deut. 32:9). TB Arakhin 10b. Gen. R. 39:13. Lev. R. 1:12, 36:4. Num. R. 3:8, 14:22. Shir HaShirim R. 2:12, 3:5. Tanhuma, Bo 5; Terumah 9. Tana Devei Eliyahu Zuta 2; Shoher Tov, 132; Yalkut Shim'oni, Yehezkel 1:336. Zohar I, 86a. *Kuzari*, I, 95; II, 44. R. Moshe Cordovero, *Pardess Rimonim*, 13:3; Alshekh on Toldot. Maharal, *Gevurot HaShem*, 9; *Netivot Olam*, II, *Netiv HaTemimut*, 2. *Sefat Emet*, I, p. 25. *Be'er Avraham*, p. 145; *Shem MiShemuel, Haggadah*, p. 76. *Meshekh Hokhmah*, pp. 18-19. Cf. Gen. 21:12; Rashbam and Radak ad loc. Gen. 28:4 and Rashi ad loc. Mishnah Nedarim III, 11 and Rambam ad loc. TY Nedarim IX, 8. TB Nedarim 31a; Rashi and Ran ad loc. Zohar I, 120a. Rambam, *Hilkhot Nedarim*, IX, 21; *Hilkhot Melakhim*, X, 7; *Iggeret Teiman*, pp. 140-41. TB Sanhedrin 59b. Gen. R. 53:12, 63:11. Tanhuma, Vezot HaBerakhah 1. Ramban on Gen. 17:6, 26:3. Ramban and Seforno on Gen. 25:19. Radak on Gen. 17:7. *Or HaHayyim* on Gen. 16:5, 28:12. Maharal, *Gevurot HaShem*, 54. *Tossefet Berakhah*, V, p. 34. Mekhilta 1 (Exod. 12:1). Mishnah Zevahim XIV; TB Zevahim 112b; 115a.

Rambam, *Hilkhot Bet HaBehirah*, I, 3; Shelah, III, 204a; HaGra, *Siddur Ishei Yisrael*, p. 287; Rav Harlap, *Mei Meirom*, VI, p. 254.
449. Cf. Lev. 20:26; Num. R. 10:3; Ramban on Deut. 32:26; *Sefat Emet*, I, p. 11; *Orot HaKodesh*, III, pp. 439-41.
450. Cf. TB Avodah Zarah 2b; Yalkut Shim'oni, Yeshaya 43:454; Recanati, Noah, p. 20b; *Or HaHayyim* on Deut. 32:9; *Mikhtav MeEliyahu*, III, pp. 200-1.
451. Cf. Isa. 44:5 and Rashi ad loc.; cf. Isa. 40:5. See Isa. 2:3; Mic. 4:2. Cf. Sifrei 1 (Deut. 1:1); Exod. R. 23:11; Shir HaShirim R. 7:10; Avot DeRabbi Nathan 35; Yalkut Shim'oni, Yeshaya 60:503; *Likkutei Moharan*, 47.
452. Cf. Maharal, *Derekh Hayyim*, p. 111; Rav Kook, *Orot*, p. 33; *Olat Reiyah* I, p. 363. R. Y.H. Ashlag, *Matan Torah*, pp. 36-37, 41.
453. Cf. TY Hallah II, 1.
454. Cf. TB Sanhedrin 98a; Zohar I, 177b; Rabbeinu Sa'adya Gaon, *Emunot VeDeot*, VIII, 2; Ramban on Exod. 12:42; *Sefer HaGeulah (Kitvei Ramban I)*, p. 277. R. Y.H. Ashlag, *Matan Torah*, pp. 64-65. See also Ramban on Exod. 2:25; *Sefer HaGeulah*, p. 287. *Or HaHayyim* on Lev. 25:27. Cf. R. Moshe Hayyim Luzzatto, the "Ramhal," *Pithei Hokhmah*, p. 8b.
455. Cf. Exod. R. 34:1; Pesikta Rabbati 16:8; Tanhuma, Ki Tissa 10; Yalkut Shim'oni, Yitro 43:454.
456. Cf. Mekhilta 1 (Exod. 19:2); Tanhuma, VaYakhel 8; Yalkut Shim'oni, Yitro 19:275. See Tossafot on Sotah 35b.
457. Cf. Mekhilta 5 (Exod. 20:2); TB Avodah Zarah 2b; Lev. R. 2:8; Num. R. 2:16; Tana Devei Eliyahu Zuta 7; Yalkut Shim'oni, Yeshaya 43:454. See Rashi on Num. 22:5; *Sefat Emet*, IV, pp. 151-53, 156.
458. Cf. Sifrei 357 (Deut. 34:10); TB Bava Batra 15b; Gen. R. 52:7, 65:16. Num. R. 14:34. Zohar II, 22a. Num. 23:4, 23:16. Rashi on Lev. 1:1; Num. 23:4. Maharal, *Derekh Hayyim*, p. 11. Rav Kook, *Orot*, p. 35; *Mei Meirom*, VIII, p. 74.
459. Cf. Num. R. 20:1. Rambam, *Moreh Nevukhim*, II, 45; see *Hilkhot Yessodei HaTorah*, VII, 1. Shelah, III, p. 164b (Jer. 4:22). See Massekhet Sofrim XIII, 9. Rabbi Samson Raphael Hirsch on Num. 22:8; *The Hirsch Siddur*, pp. 340-41. R. Yossef Hayyim of Baghdad, *Od Yossef Hai*, p. 48.
460. Cf. TB Sanhedrin 105b; Tanhuma, Balak 12; Pesikta Zutarta 24:6. Tossafot on Avodah Zarah 4b. Maharal, *Derekh Hayyim*, p. 204. *Ben Ish Hai*, p. 252. R. Y.Y.L. Bloch, *Shiurei Da'at*, I, pp. 72ff., 250ff.
461. Cf. Maharal, *Tiferet Yisrael*, 1. *Likkutei Moharan*, 17.
462. Cf. Exod. 1:5; TB Sukkah 55b; Sotah 36b. Num. R. 13:15, 21:21. Pesikta DeRav Kahana 30. Tanhuma (Buber ed.), VaYishlah 30. Zohar II, 58b-59a; 187a; III, 24b; 103b. Rashi on Deut. 32:8; Recanati, Lekh Lekha, p. 21b. *Ba'al HaTurim* on Num. 11:16. Maharal, *Gevurot HaShem*, 9, 11. Shelah, III, pp. 171a, 201. *Maggid Devarav LeYa'akov*, 78, 107. *Or HaHayyim* on Gen. 28:14; Deut. 32:8. *Likkutei Moharan*, 136a. *Avnei Nezer*, p. 74.
463. Cf. TY Shevi'it VI, 1. Sifra 9 (Lev. 18:3). Gen. R. 44:27; Shir HaShirim R. 1:37. Ramban on Deut. 19:8. Ari HaKadosh, *Likkutei Torah*, Lekh Lekha, p. 50. Maharal, *Gevurot HaShem*, 4. R. Dov Baer of Mezerich, *Maggid Devarav LeYa'akov*, 78. *Ha'amek Davar* on Deut. 9:4-5; *Avnei Nezer*, pp. 13, 76, 78; *Ben Ish Hai*, p. 174. Cf. Gen. 15:19, 15:21; Deut. 7:1. Lev. R. 17:5. See TB

Bava Batra 56a. Cf. Rashi on Exod. 13:5; Rashi and Ramban on Deut. 18:2.
464. Cf. Zohar III, 193a; Ramban on Deut. 11:10. See Rabbi D.T. Hoffmann, *Bereshit*, I, pp. 210-11.
465. Cf. Sifra 13 (Lev. 20:22). See Num. 35:33; Deut. 24:3-4, 24:14, 25:15. Cf. Ramban on Gen. 1:1, 19:5; Lev. 18:25; Num. 35:33. Radak on Ezek. 33:25. Alshekh on Eikev. Maharal, *Derekh Hayyim*, p. 188. *Mei Meirom*, VI, p. 237. *Mikhtav MeEliyahu*, III, pp. 194-96.
466. Cf. Lev. 18:25; Amos 3:2. TB Avodah Zarah 4a and Rashi ad loc. Exod. R. 3:11; Lev. R. 27:1. Ramban on Gen. 19:5; Lev. 18:25; *Derashah Al Divrei Kohelet (Kitvei Ramban* I), p. 200-2; *Derashah LeRosh HaShanah* (ibidem), pp. 249-50; *Iggeret* 7 (ibidem), p. 368. R. Hayyim Vital, *Peri Ets Hayyim*, p. 20. Alshekh on Deut. 11:12. Maharal, *Gevurot HaShem*, 9; *Derekh Hayyim*, p. 162. Shelah, III, p. 136b. *Sefat Emet*, III, p. 148; IV, p. 103. Rav Kook, *Shabbat HaArets*, p. 11; *Olat Reiyah*, II, pp. 156-57. *Mei Meirom*, VI, pp. 148-49; *Missaviv LiShmonah Perakim LeHaRambam*, pp. 7-8. R. S.R. Hirsch, *Iggerot Tsafon*, XI, p. 54. *Ha'amek Davar*, Deut. 7:6. *Od Yossef Hai*, p. 47. *Lev Eliyahu*, p. 162. *Avnei Nezer*, pp. 69-70.
467. Cf. Lev. 18 and Ramban ad loc. Lev. 19:12 and Sifra and Rashi ad loc. Lev. R. 24:6. Maharal, *Derekh Hayyim*, p. 188. Shelah, I, p. 169a. *Likkutei Moharan*, 36b.
468. Cf. Sifra 9 (Lev. 18:3). Ramban on Deut. 9:4, 32:35. Maharal, *Gevurot HaShem*, 4.
469. Cf. Lev. 18:28 and Sifra (13) ad loc. Rashi on Sotah 35b; Ramban on Gen. 15:7. See Rambam, *Hilkhot Teshuvah*, VI, 3.
470. Cf. Midrash Shemuel, VaYeshev. *Sefat Emet*, III, pp. 197-98. R. Menahem M. Kasher, *HaTekufah HaGedolah*, Jerusalem: 5729, p. 478.
471. Cf. Rashi on Exod. 19:4; Num. R. 10:5.
472. Cf. Gen. 15:16; Num. 32:22; Ps. 105:44-45. Sifrei 41 (Deut. 11:13), 50 (Deut. 11:23). Mishnah Berakhot IX, 1. TY Hallah II, 1. TB Avodah Zarah 45b; Temurah 16a and Rashi ad loc. Josh. 15:15-17; see *Arvei Nahal*, Shelah. Kohelet R. 11:10; Tanhuma, Kedoshim 11; Yalkut Shim'oni, Eikev 11:860; see also Pirkei DeRabbi Eliezer 34. Zohar I, 151b; III, 177a. Rambam, *Hilkhot Avodat Kokhavim*, VII, 1. Rashi on Deut. 12:10; Bava Metsia 89a. Ramban on Lev. 18:25. *Shulhan Arukh, Orah Hayyim*, 224:2. *Sefer HaHinukh*, Mitzvah 436. Malbim on Deut. 26:1. *Kedushat Levi*, p. 82. *Midrash Simhah* (Psishkhe), II, p. 221. *Sefat Emet*, III, pp. 197-200; IV, pp. 102, 175, 194, 199; V, p. 8. *Ben Ish Hai*, pp. 37, 171. *Shem MiShemuel, VaYikra*, p. 319; *Devarim*, p. 251. *Neot HaDesheh*, p. 84; *Mei Meirom*, VI, p. 310.
473. Cf. Ps. 42:6; Lev. R. 13:5; Gen. R. 16:7. Lev. 25:23. *Sefat Emet*, III, p. 190.
474. Cf. Gen. 6:11.
475. Cf. TB Sanhedrin 108a; Pesikta Zutarta, Bereshit 6:5; Tanhuma (Buber ed.), Bereshit 21. Zohar I, 66b-67a; Zohar Hadash, Noah 21. Gen. R. 19:18.
476. Cf. TY Sanhedrin XI, 5. Tanhuma, Shemini 9. See Num. R. 10:3. Cf. Maharal, *Perushim LeAggadot*, IV, p. 15. Rav Kook, *Orot HaKodesh*, I, p. 151; ibidem, II, pp. 376, 544-45; *Olat Reiyah*, I, p. 13; *Orot HaTeshuvah*, pp. 38-39. *Sefat Emet*, V, p. 18.
477. See Maharal, *Gevurot HaShem*, 44.
478. Cf. Isa. 11:9.

479. See Avot V; see also supra p. 7.
480. Cf. Lev. R. 23:3; Shir HaShirim R. 2:6.
481. Cf. Gen. R. 83:4; Num. R. 10:3, 17:7. Shir HaShirim R. 6:4, 7:7. See Zohar III, 193a. Cf. Rabbi S.R. Hirsch on Exod. 19:5-6; Lev. 25:7; Ps. 81 (German ed., II, pp. 53-56; Hebrew ed., pp. 337-40). Rav Kook, *Orot*, p. 155.
482. Cf. Exod. 4:22. Maharal, *Gevurot HaShem*, 29.
483. Cf. Isa. 44:5; Avot DeRabbi Nathan 36.
484. Cf. Num. 16:22, 27:16. Jer. 1:7. Exod. R. 29:3, 29:7. Isa. 40:5; Tana Devei Eliyahu Zuta 2.
485. Cf. Mekhilta 2 (Exod. 19:6), 19 (Exod. 22:30); Sifra (I) and Malbim on Lev. 19:2. See TB Pessahim 104a. Cf. Exod. R. 31:8; Num. R. 10:3; Shir HaShirim R. 6:4. Zohar III, 126a. Rashi on Lev. 20:26; Ramban on Exod. 22:30. See Ibn Ezra on Lev. 20:24.
486. Cf. Lev. 20:24, 20:26; Sifra (11) and Rashi ad loc. Deut. 4:20, 4:34. TY Berakhot V, 2. Gen. R. 14:1; Lev. R. 20:2. Num. R. 3:8, 10:3, 14:22. Tanhuma, Noah 1, Ahrei 2; Bemidbar 17. Tana Devei Eliyahu Zuta 2. Shoher Tov, 107, 114. Zohar II, 135a; III, 90b; 125a. Onkelos and Rashi on Exod. 8:19; Rashi on Deut. 26:17. Rambam, *Iggeret Teiman*, p. 140. Ramban on Exod. 20:3; Deut. 7:7. Ran on Nedarim 20b. Maharal, *Gevurot HaShem*, 3. *Sefat Emet*, I, p. 11; III, p. 197. *Shem MiShemuel*, Haggadah, p. 78. *Bet Avraham*, p. 153.
487. Exod. 24:7.
488. Lev. R. 23:3; Shir HaShirim 2:2; Cf. Shir HaShirim R. 2:6, 6:6, 7:7; Exod. R. 42:6; Zohar III, 61b. See Gen. R. 83:4. Zohar I, 1a; II, 189b; III, 286b-287a.
489. Cf. Isa. 54:5. Ramban, *Derashah LeRosh HaShanah* (*Kitvei Ramban* I), p. 250; Ramban on Lev. 18:25. Tanhuma, Mishpatim 17; Kedoshim 12.
490. Cf. Gen. 6:11.
491. Cf. TB Zevahim 113a. Cf. Gen. R. 33; Lev. R. 31:8; Shir HaShirim R. 1:68; Pirkei DeRabbi Eliezer 23; Zohar I, 61a.
492. Cf. Tanhuma, Re'eh 8; Deut. 32:9. Tanhuma, Bemidbar 17; Joel 4:2. See Yalkut Shim'oni, Eikev 11:860.
493. Cf. Deut. 11:12 and Alshekh ad loc.; cf. Exod. 33:14-15; Deut. 32:9, 32:12. Cf. Mekhilta 2 (Exod. 19:6); Sifrei 42 (Deut. 11:14). TY Shevi'it IV, 3; see also TB Shabbat 156a. TB Ta'anit 3a; 10a; see also TB Sukkah 29a; Yevamot 63a. Gen. R. 39:2, 39:19; Exod. R. 32:7-8; Num. R. 2:12; Shir HaShirim R. 7:7; Pesikta DeRav Kahana 32. Shoher Tov, 82. Pirkei DeRabbi Eliezer 24. Tanhuma, Mishpatim 17; Re'eh 8; Ha'azinu 4, 6. Yalkut Shim'oni, Yitro 19:276; Eikev 11:860. Zohar I, 10a; 61a; 69a; 108b; 177a-b; 195a; II, 152b; III, 12a; 260b. *Kuzari*, II, 14:44. Ibn Ezra on Deut. 4:19. Ramban on Gen. 12:2, 15:18, 28:12; Lev. 18:25; Deut. 4:16, 7:6, 10:21, 11:12, 32:12; *Derashah LeRosh HaShanah* (*Kitvei Ramban* I), pp. 249-50. Rabbeinu Bahya on Exod. 19:5. Recanati, Yitro, p. 7b. Abrabanel on Gen. 12, 17, 48. Maharal, *Derekh Hayyim*, p. 188. Shelah, III, p. 136b; *Siddur Sha'ar HaShamayim*, p. 354. *Maggid Devarav LeYa'akov*, 198. R. Eliyahu of Vilna, *Sifra DiTseniuta Im Biur HaGra, Likkutei HaGra*, p. 76; *Aderet Eliyahu*, pp. 85, 388; *Siddur Ishei Yisrael*, pp. 47, 329. *Or HaHayyim* on Deut. 26:17, 32:8; Malbim on I Kings 18:31. *Likkutei Moharan*, II, 8, 10, 40. Rabbi S.R. Hirsch on Ps. 105 (Hebrew ed. p. 415). *Sefat Emet*, III, pp. 190, 198, Rav Kook, *Orot*, pp. 16, 17. *Mei*

Meirom, VIII, p. 66. *Meshekh Hokhmah*, p. 315. *Ha'amek Davar* on Deut. 6:4; *Bet Avraham*, pp. 103-4; *Avnei Nezer*, pp. 102, 148; *Shem MiShemuel, Haggadah*, p. 85. *Mikhtav MeEliyahu*, II, p. 50.

494. Cf. Maharal, *Gevurot HaShem*, 23. *Sefat Emet*, IV, p. 35.
495. Cf. Zohar I, 205b; Isa. 45:12. Shir HaShirim R. 7:7. Shelah, III, p. 22a.
496. Cf. TB Sanhedrin 97a; Avodah Zarah 9a; Rosh HaShanah 31b. Tikkunei HaZohar, 36 (77b).
497. Cf. Gen. R. 2:4; Onkelos on Gen. 12:5. See TB Avodah Zarah 9a. Cf. Zohar I, 4a; 24b; II, 83b; 147b; Tikkunei HaZohar, 70 (137a). Maharal, *Gevurot HaShem*, 5; *Perushim LeAggadot*, I, p. 24. Shelah, III, pp. 23a, 25b. Malbim on Gen. 17:2.
498. Cf. Exod. R. 30:2 (Gen. 2:4; Ruth 4:18). *Tanya*, 36.
499. Cf. TB Shabbat 146a; 156a; Nedarim 32a; see also TB Moed Katan 28a. Cf. TY Rosh HaShanah III, 8. Gen. R. 44:14; Exod. R. 38:7; Num. R. 20:11. Deut. R. 8:6. Isa. 40:26; Jer. 10:2. Pesikta Rabbati 44:1; Pesikta Zutarta, Lekh Lekha, Gen. 15:5. Tanhuma, Shoftim 11. Zohar I, 90b; II, 78b; III, 148a; 216b; 235a. Zohar Hadash, Yitro 32. Tikkunei HaZohar, 50 (86b); 69 (100a). *Kuzari*, IV, 17; 27. *Iggeret Teiman*, pp. 157-59. Rashi on Gen. 1:14. Ibn Ezra on Exod. 6:3, 20:1, 33:21; Deut. 4:19. Abrabanel on Gen 12, R. Yehuda HeHassid, *Perushei HaTorah*, p. 122. Maharal, *Gevurot HaShem*, 7. Alshekh on Lekh Lekha, Bo. Shelah, III, pp. 23a-b-24a; *Siddur Sha'arei HaShamayim*, pp. 351-55. HaGra, *Siddur Ishei Yisrael*, pp. 44, 46. R. Hayyim of Volozhin, *Ruah Hayyim*, p. 36. *Maggid Devarav LeYa'akov*, p. 100; *Kedushat Levi*, p. 77a; *Bnei Issakhar*, II, p. 94. *Kli Yakar* on Exod. 19:4; *Sefat Emet*, I, pp. 53, 55; II, p. 58. *Shem MiShemuel, Bereshit*, II, p. 349; *Da'at Hokhmah UMussar*, pp. 146-47; *Mikhtav MeEliyahu*, I, pp. 185-86; III, pp. 169-70.
500. Cf. TB Shabbat 146a; Avodah Zarah 22b. Shir HaShirim R. 4, 7:1. Tana Devei Eliyahu Rabba 17. Zohar I, 36b; 52b; 63b; 70b; 126b; 228a; II, 94a; 168a; 193b; 236b; 242b; III, 14b; 97b; 117a. *Sha'arei Zohar*, p. 35. Maharal, *Perushim LeAggadot*, I, p. 25; *Derashot, Hesped*, p. 15. Shelah, III, pp. 22a-b, 137b. HaGra, *Siddur Ishei Yisrael*, pp. 43, 46, 47. *Sefat Emet*, I, p. 8; II, pp. 40, 84, 86, 93, 109; III, pp. 190, 200.
501. Cf. Gen. 2:4 and Radak ad loc. Gen. R. 12. Zohar II, 223a. Cf. R. D.T. Hoffmann, *Bereshit*, I, pp. 54ff., 117. See A. Safran, *La Cabale*, p. 366.
502. Cf. Zohar I, 55b (Gen. 2:4, 5:1); cf. Zohar I, 60b.
503. Cf. Gen. R. 13:3. Zohar I, 4a; 48b; II, 88a; III, 113b; 264a. Ibn Ezra on Gen. 2:12; Radak on Gen. 2:4; R. D.T. Hoffmann, *Bereshit*, I, p. 59; M.D. Cassuto, *MeAdam Ad Noah*, pp. 55-56. Shelah, III, p. 26a; HaGra, *Sefer HaEmunah VeHaHashgahah*, II, p. 6b; *Sefat Emet*, V, p. 165; *Be'er Avraham*, pp. 50-51.
504. Cf. TB Avodah Zarah 9a. Num. R. 13:5. Isa. 51:2; Ezek. 33:24. Zohar I, 85b. Alshekh on Toldot. Maharal, *Gevurot HaShem*, 5, 6, 36; *Derekh Hayyim*, p. 172.
505. See Avot V, 2; VI, 9. Massekhet Sofrim XVI, 10; XXI, 9. TB Rosh HaShanah 11a; Bava Batra 15a; 91a-b. Gen. R. 2:4, 14:6, 15:5, 39:13. Num. R. 13:5. Pesikta DeRav Kahana, II, 23, p. 341. Zohar I, 86a. Rambam, *Hilkhot*

Avodat Kokhavim, I, 2. Maharal, *Derekh Hayyim*, pp. 167-68, 244. *Sefat Emet*, I, p. 18.
506. Cf. Maharal, *Tiferet Yisrael*, 19; *Sefat Emet*, II, pp. 31-33.
507. Gen. 17:4-5. TY Bikkurim I, 4. TB Berakhot 13a; Shabbat 105a; Pessahim 88a; Sukkah 49b. Isa. 2:3. Zohar I, 96a; 105b; II, 89b-90a. Rambam, *Hilkhot Bikkurim*, IV, 3; *Hilkhot Avodat Kokhavim*, I, 2; *Iggeret Teiman*, pp. 161-62. Maharal, *Derekh Hayyim*, p. 200. Shelah, III, p. 26a. *Sefat Emet*, I, p. 66. *Mikhtav MeEliyahu*, II, p. 82.
508. Cf. Isa. 51:1-2. TB Berakhot 16b. Gen. R. 1:5. Zohar I, 1b. Maharal, *Netsah Yisrael*, 11; *Gevurot HaShem* 5, 6, 7, 9, 36; *Derekh Hayyim*, p. 169. Rav Kook, *Iggrot HaReiyah*, I, p. 320. *Mei Meirom*, VIII, p. 65. *Da'at Torah*, I, pp. 81,85.
509. Cf. Avot V, 2. Zohar III, 111b. HaGra, *Siddur Ishei Yisrael (Siah Yitshak)*, p. 43. *Sefat Emet*, I, p. 53.
510. Gen. 2:4. Cf. Gen. R. 12:8-9; see TB Menahot 29b. Zohar I, 3b; 4a; 25a; 86b; 91b; 93a; 105b; 128b; 154b; 230b; 247a; II, 31a; 48b; 79a; 220b; III, 31a; 38a; 298a. Zohar Hadash, 44a. *Sha'arei Zohar*, p. 256. *Ba'al HaTurim* on Gen. 12:3. Maharal, *Gevurot HaShem*, 5; *Perushim LeAggadot*, I, p. 24. Shelah, III, pp. 22a, 25b, 46a.
511. Cf. TB Nedarim 32a; Berakhot 7b and Maharsha ad loc. Gen. R. 64:4. Num. R. 14:7, 18:17. Tanhuma, Lekh Lekha 3; VaYigash 12; Behar 1. Rambam, *Hilkhot Avodat Kokhavim*, I, 3; *Iggeret Teiman*, p. 162. Maharal, *Netivot Olam*, I, *Netiv Gemilut Hassadim*, 1; *Perushim LeAggadot*, I, p. 24.
512. Cf. Gen. R. 61:1, 95:2. Tanhuma, VaYigash 11. Avot DeRabbi Nathan 33:1. Ramban and Or HaHayyim on Gen. 12:1. Rambam, *Hilkhot Avodat Kokhavim*, I, 3. Maharal, *Gevurot HaShem*, 29. Shelah, III, p. 23b. *Kedushat Levi*, pp. 142b-143a.
513. Cf. Mishnah Kiddushin IV, 14; TB Yoma 28b. Gen. R. 49:6, 64:4, 95:2. Lev. R. 2:9. Shoher Tov, 41, 112. Tanhuma, Lekh Lekha 11; Behar 1. Zohar III, 276b.
514. Cf. Ezek. 33:24. See also Radak on Gen. 12:7.
515. Cf. Gen. R. 40:8, 63:3, 76:6. Num. R. 14:22. Tanhuma, Lekh Lekha 9, 19. Zohar I, 83a. Rashi on Gen. 12:6-7. Ramban on Gen. 11:28, 12:6, 12:10; Lev. 24:10. Recanati, Shelah, p. 37b. Abrabanel on Gen. 15 (I, p. 214). Maharal, *Derekh Hayyim*, p. 172. Shelah, I, p. 142b; III, pp. 24b-25a. Rabbi S.R. Hirsch on Gen. 15:7; ibid. on Ps. 105 (Hebrew ed., p. 417). *Sefat Emet*, I, pp. 52-54,69. *Ben Ish Hai*, p. 18. *Meshekh Hokhmah*, p. 10.
516. Cf. TB Nedarim 32b. See Tanhuma, Lekh Lekha 11; Korah 12. Cf. Zohar I, 83a; Zohar Hadash, 44b. Ramban on Gen. 26:5.
517. Cf. TB Shabbat 146a; 156a. Zohar I, 78a; 90b; III, 148b. *Sefat Emet*, I, pp. 54-55.
518. Cf. Gen. R. 2, 35:2, 42:13, 44:22. Targum Yonathan Ben Uziel on Num. 23:21. Ramban on Gen. 22:16. Maharal, *Gevurot HaShem*, 29. Shelah, III, p. 29b. *Mikhtav MeEliyahu*, I, p. 158. R. M.M. Kasher, *HaTekufah HaGedolah*, p. 478.
519. Cf. Isa. 65:17, 66:22. Gen. 2:4.
520. Cf. Isa. 41:8.

521. Cf. Rambam, *Perush HaMishnah*, Hullin VI, 6.
522. Cf. TB Shabbat 137b; Kiddushin 72b; Menahot 43b. Exod. R. 19:6. Zohar III, 73b; Tikkunei HaZohar, 22 (65b). Rambam, *Hilkhot Milah*, III, 3. *Tur, Yoreh Deyah*, 260. *Sefer HaHinukh, Mitzvah* 2. Shelah, III, p. 21b.
523. Cf. Gen. 17:9-13. Mishnah Shabbat XIX, 6; Tossefta Shabbat XVI, 8; TB Shabbat 108a; 137a. TY Yevamot VIII, 1. Gen. R. 46:4, 48:2. Num. R. 10:5. Esther R. Petihta 10 (Job 19:26; cf. Jer. 11:5). Pirkei DeRabbi Eliezer 29. Tanhuma, Lekh Lekha 20. Zohar I, 94a; 95a; 214b; II, 86a; III, 29a. Rambam, *Hilkhot Milah*, II, 4; III, 1; *Moreh Nevukhim*, III, 49; Isa. 41:8 (Ps. 105:6). Rashi on Gen. 17:3, 17:14; Lev. 19:23. (See also Ramban on Deut. 19:8, 30:6. Cf. Deut. 10:16 and Pesikta Zutarta ad loc.; Lev. 26:4; Jer. 4:4, 9:25; Ezek. 44:7, 44:9.) Cf. Radak on Gen. 17:1-2; R. Yitshak Arama, *Akeidat Yitshak*, Lekh Lekha XVIII; Malbim on Gen. 17:2, 17:5. Maharal, *Tiferet Yisrael*, 19; *Derashot*, p. 40. Shelah, I, pp. 2b, 164b, 187a-b; III, pp. 9a, 169b. R. Nahman of Bratslav, *Likkutei Moharan*, II, 19; *Likkutei Halakhot, Hilkhot Milah*, 2. Rav Kook, *Orot*, p. 170; *Olat Reiyah*, I, pp. 397-98. *Sefat Emet*, I, pp. 45, 51, 61. *Bet HaLevi*, I, pp. 18-20.
524. Cf. Gen. 17:8. Tanhuma (Buber ed.), Beshalah 12. Tana Devei Eliyahu Zuta 25. Pirkei DeRabbi Eliezer 29. Ramban on Gen. 15:18.
525. Cf. Gen. 17:1. Ramban on Gen. 17:4. Abrabanel, Lekh Lekha, 17, 4-9 (I, pp. 222-23). *Sefat Emet*, I, p. 46.
526. Cf. Gen. 17:8-11. Gen. R. 46:7; Zohar I, 93b; II, 26a. Zohar Hadash, Bereshit 32. Pirkei DeRabbi Eliezer 29; Josh. 5:2. Ramban on Gen. 15:18. Shelah, III, pp. 21b-22a.
527. Cf. *Shem MiShemuel, Haggadah*, p. 76.
528. Cf. TB Bava Batra 91b.
529. Cf. Exod. R. 31:1; Lev. R. 9:3; Tanhuma, Lekh Lekha 11. Cf. Num. R. 10:1.
530. Cf. Mishnah Nedarim III, 11; TB Nedarim 31b (Jer. 33:25).
531. Cf. TB Shabbat 137b; Nedarim 32a. Zohar I, 32a; 56a; 59b; 66b; 89a; 91b; 93b. See Rabbi S.R. Hirsch on Gen. 17:2.
532. Cf. Gen. 17:1. TB Nedarim 31b; Tanhuma, Tazria 5; Zohar III, 14a; Tikkunei HaZohar, 37. *Moreh Nevukhim*, III, 49. Abrabanel on Gen. 17:1. Maharal, *Tiferet Yisrael*, 2, 19; *Derashot, Derush LeShabbat Teshuvah*, p. 29. *Sefat Emet*, I, pp. 44-45; III, p. 136. *Shem MiShemuel, Haggadah*, p. 26.
533. Cf. Exod. 19:5, 34:27. Deut. 4:13. TB Shabbat 33a; Avodah Zarah 3a. Lev. R. 21:6. Zohar III, 14a; 73b. Maharal, *Gevurot HaShem*, 8, 47.
534. Cf. TB Hullin 101b. Zohar I, 25a; 63b; II, 94a; III, 117a. *Sefat Emet*, II, pp. 52, 55, 85-86, 93; III, p. 190.
535. Cf. TB Shabbat 88a; Avodah Zarah 3a. Deut. R. 8:6; Tanhuma, Bereshit 1. Zohar I, 77a; 89a; 134b; 185a; II, 94a; 200a; III, 11b; 193a. Rashi on Gen. 1:31. Maharal, *Netivot Olam*, I, *Netiv HaTorah*, p. 3a; *Derashot, Hesped*, p. 15a; *Perushim LeAggadot*, I, pp. 24-25.
536. Cf. Lev. R. 35:4. Pesikta Rabbati 21 (Lev. 26:3; Jer. 33:25). Zohar III, 11b; 73b. Maharal, *Derekh Hayyim*, pp. 164-65. *Tanya*, 36.
537. Cf. Exod. R. 19:5; Tanhuma, Tsav 14; Tazria 5. Rambam, *Hilkhot Milah*, III, 8. *Siddur Rabbeinu Shelomo de Garmaise*, pp. 246, 306. *Shem MiShemuel, VaYikra*, p. 319. Gen. 15, 17. Exod. 19:5, 24:8. Ezek. 16:6. Lev. R. 6:5. Num. R. 9. Pirkei DeRabbi Eliezer 29. Zohar I, 93a. Sefer Yetsirah I, 3. Maharal,

Perushim LeAggadot HaShas, II, pp. 124-25. *Sefat Emet*, V, pp. 95-96. Rav Kook, *Orot*, p. 38. Zohar III, 73b. Maharal, *Perushim LeAggadot HaShas*, I, p. 6; *Derashot*, p. 39. *Sefat Emet*, I, p. 53. Zohar II, 92a. *Yessod HaAvodah*, p. 282; *Hessed LeAvraham*, p. 114; *Neot HaDesheh*, p. 208. *Avnei Nezer*, p. 8. Gen. R. 19:18. Zohar II, 168b; *Sefat Emet*, IV, p. 178.

Cf. Sifrei 36 (Deut. 6:9). TB Menahot 43b. *Shulhan Arukh, Yoreh Deyah*, 260. Tossafot Yom Tov, Mishnah Nedarim III, 11; TY Nedarim III, 9; TB Nedarim 32a. Zohar I, 197a; II, 61a; III, 13b. Tikkunei HaZohar, 47 (84a).

539. Cf. Mishnah Nedarim III, 11; TB Nedarim 31b. Rambam, *Hilkhot Milah*, III, 9. Shelah, III, p. 26a. *Ben Ish Hai*, p. 142.

540. Cf. Zohar I, 24b; III, 73b. Maharal, *Perushim LeAggadot*, II, pp. 8-9 (see TB Eruvin 40b). TB Berakhot 48b and Tossafot ad loc. Num. R. 23:7. Zohar II, 168b. Rambam, *Hilkhot Berakhot*, II, 3; *Tur* and *Shulhan Arukh, Orah Hayyim*, 187:3. Maharal, *Netivot Olam*, I, *Netiv HaAvodah*, p. 18.

541. Mishnah PeYah I, 1. Cf. Rambam, *Hilkhot Talmud Torah*, III, 3-4. *Tur* and *Shulhan Arukh, Yoreh Deyah*, 246:18.

542. Cf. Mishnah Nedarim III, 11. TB Nedarim 31b; Shabbat 137b; Rosh HaShanah 19a. Gen. R. 46:7; Exod. R. 36:9; Yalkut Shim'oni, Tehillim 147:888. Zohar II, 86a; III, 13b. Maharal, *Netsah Yisrael*, 6; *Gevurot HaShem*, 23. Bnei Issakhar, Haggadah, p. 63. *Olat Reiyah*, I, pp. 397-98. *Bet HaLevi*, I, pp. 19-20.

543. Cf. TB Nedarim 32a. Lev. R. 36. Pirkei DeRabbi Eliezer 29. Tanhuma, Lekh Lekha 20. *Siddur Rabbeinu Shelomo de Garmaise*, pp. 285, 289. *Ben Ish Hai*, p. 7.

544. Cf. Isa. 51:16. Zohar III, 35a. Alshekh on Lekh Lekha, Gen. 12:1. See also TB Niddah 30b.

545. Cf. Gen. R. 1:5; see also Zohar I, 24a; II, 108b; III, 229b.

546. Cf. Sifrei 37 (Deut. 11:10). See Rashi on Gen. 1:1.

547. Cf. Rabbi Eliyahu of Vilna, *Aderet Eliyahu*, p. 9.

548. Cf. TB Shabbat 88b; Pessahim 54a; Zevahim 116a. Gen. R. 8:2. Exod. R. 30:6. Lev. R. 19:1, 19:3 (Prov. 8:22). Shoher Tov, 90. Tanhuma, VaYeshev 4; Yitro 14. Sefer HaBahir 55. Zohar I, 5a; 24b; 47a; 90a; 134b; II, 161a; 200a; III, 34b; 35a; 69b. Tikkunei HaZohar, 4b; 11b; 28 (70a); 69 (98b); 70 (120a). Zohar Hadash, Bereshit 5a; VaYeshev 29b; Ahrei 49a. Sha'arei Zohar, p. 80. Maharal, *Netsah Yisrael*, 3.

549. Cf. TB Ta'anit 10a; Yoma 53b; Shabbat 32a and Rashi ad loc. Lev. R. 36:4 (Jer. 2:3). Zohar I, 1b. R. Yisrael of Koznitz, *Avodat Yisrael*, p. 211.

550. Cf. Gen. R. 1:5, 63:10; Zohar III, 34a.

551. Cf. Isa. 51:16. Cf. TB Pessahim 87b; *Aderet Eliyahu*, p. 13. *Kitvei Maharal MiPrag*, Kariv ed., Jerusalem: 5720 (1960), I, pp. 17-18, 375. Maharal, *Gevurot HaShem*, 29. *Sefat Emet*, I, pp. 11, 15; V, pp. 104, 110, 155.

552. Cf. Maharal, *Gevurot HaShem*, 38, 57; *Derekh Hayyim*, p. 7; *Derashot, Derashah LeShabbat HaGadol*, p. 88. See *Kuzari*, II, 20. Shelah, III, p. 199a-b. *Sefat Emet*, II, p. 140.

553. Cf. Exod. 23:19, 34:26. Num. 18:12; Deut. 26:2. Gen. R. 1:6. Zohar II, 79b; 121a-122b. *Sefer Hassidim*, 155. *Sefat Emet*, I, p. 15.

554. Cf. Lev. 25:23 and Sifra (4) ad loc. TB Sanhedrin 39a. Lev. 25:42 and Sifra (6) ad loc. (Gen. 15:13; Eihah 5:8). (See Gen. 23:4, 26:3, 37:1. Exod. 6:4. Ps.

39:13, 119:19. I Chron. 29:15.) Rambam, *Sefer HaMitzvot, Mitzvot Lo Ta'asseh, Mitzvah* 227; *Hilkhot Shemittah VeYovel,* XI, 1. *Sefer HaHinukh, Mitzvah* 339. Maharal, *Derekh Hayyim,* pp. 149-50. Shelah, I, p. 101a-b; III, pp. 22b-23a. Or *HaHayyim* on Lev. 25:2. *Sefat Emet,* V, p. 154. *Mei Meirom,* VI, pp. 282-83.

555. Cf. I Chron. 29:14. Avot III, 8. Exod. R. 31. TB Berakhot 35a; Gittin 47a. Maharal, *Derekh Hayyim,* pp. 96-97.
556. Cf. TB Menahot 62b. Gen. R. 1:6, 12:8. Exod. R. 48:2. Ezek. 44:30. Ps. 8:4. Prov. 1:7. Tanhuma (Buber ed.), Bereshit 3. Pesikta Zutarta, Bereshit 1:1. Zohar II, 79b (Deut. 26:3). *Sefat Emet,* I, p. 5.
557. Cf. Gen. R. 1; Lev. R. 36:4; Yalkut Shim'oni, Yeshaya 43:452; Otiot De Rabbi Akiva, A. Rashi on Isa. 45:11. R. Yehuda HeHassid, *Perushei HaTorah,* p. 2. Shelah, III, p. 201b. Maggid of Mezerich, *Maggid Devarav LeYa'akov,* 65.
558. Cf. Exod. R. 38:5. Maharal, *Gevurot HaShem,* 54. *Sefat Emet,* I, pp. 15-16.
559. Cf. Exod. R. 5:4, 21:6. Lev. R. 35:4. Zohar I, 47a; II, 49a; 56a; 170b. Rambam, *Perush HaMishnah,* Avot V, 5. Maharal, *Derekh Hayyim,* pp. 177-78.
560. Cf. TB Shabbat 88a; Avodah Zarah 3a (Jer. 33:25). Num. R. 19:3; Shir HaShirim R. 7, 8. Petihta Ruth R. 1. Tanhuma, Bereshit 1. Zohar I, 185a; II, 94a.
561. Cf. Lev. 26:3; see also Rashi on Avodah Zarah 5a. Deut. 11:13, 28:1 (see also Deut. 28:47-48). Isa. 1:19-20; Lev. R. 13:4. TB Shabbat 88a; Ketuvot 111a; Kiddushin 61b; Bava Metsia 66b. Tanhuma, Devarim 4. Rambam, *Hilkhot Mekhirah,* XI, 8. *Shulhan Arukh,* Hoshen Mishpat, 207:13.
562. Cf. Tanhuma, Re'eh 8 (Deut. 12:29). See also TY Ta'anit I, 1; Exod. R. 32:3; Eihah R. 12:8.
563. Cf. Mishnah Kiddushin IV, 3; TB Kiddushin 61a; Bava Metsia 94a; Bava Batra 137b.
564. Cf. Mekhilta 2 (Exod. 18:27), 1 (Exod. 19:2). Mishnah Kiddushin I, 9. TB Kiddushin 36b; 38a. TY Kiddushin I, 8. Shoher Tov 132. Yalkut Shim'oni, Tehillim 132:881; Melakhim I, 2:170. Ramban on Gen. 12:2.
565. Cf. Exod. 19:5. Deut. 28:9. Cf. Sifra on Lev. 20:26, 22:33, 25:42. Sifrei 96 (Deut. 14:1), 346 (Deut. 33:5). TB Shabbat 88b; Ketuvot 66b; Kiddushin 36a; Sanhedrin 98a. Exod. R. 25:13, 31:9. Lev. R. 35:1-2. Num. R. 12:5, 15:1, 15:3, 15:5. Deut. R. 3:2, 4:1, 4:4, 4:7, 4:10, 8:6. Tanhuma, Kedoshim 6; Nasso 22; Nitsavim 3. Pesikta Rabbati 5, 7. Zohar III, 112b; 125a. Zohar Hadash, Yitro 38a. Rambam, *Sefer HaMitzvot, Mitzvot Asseh, Mitzvah* 2, *Mitzvah* 9. Rashi on Gen. 27:40; Lev. 6:5, 11:45, 18:30, 20:24, 20:26, 22:33; Num. 15:41; Deut. 24:18. Rashi, Ibn Ezra and Ramban on Exod. 29:46. Ramban on Exod. 2:25, 12:42, 25:1, 29:46; *Sefer HaGeulah (Kitvei Ramban* I), p. 277 (TB Sanhedrin 94a). Abrabanel on Deut. 7:12. Maharal, *Netsah Yisrael,* 11; *Gevurot HaShem,* 8. Malbim on Ps. 132:12. *Ha'amek Davar* on Exod. 19:5; Deut. 26:18; *Tsafnat Pa'aneah, Devarim,* II, p. 300. *Bet Avraham,* p. 107.
566. Cf. Deut. 11:13ff., 11:22. Ps. 105:45. Mekhilta 5 (Exod. 15:25), 2 (Exod. 18:27). Sifrei 38 (Deut. 11:11), 40 (Deut. 11:12), 41 (Deut. 11:13). See TB Bava Batra 25b. Cf. Gen. R. 19:18, 46:7, 67:6. Exod. R. 15:11, 15:23, 31:9. Lev. R. 13:4, 28:6. Tana Devei Eliyahu Rabba 11. Tanhuma, Mass'ei 9; Re'eh

8. Tanhuma (Buber ed.), VaYishlah 10. Yalkut Shim'oni, Tehillim 132:881. Rashi on Gen. 27:40; Lev. 18:30, 26:3-4. Num. 15:41; I Kings 9:3 and Radak ad loc., 9:7. Radak on Ps. 105:44-45. Ibn Ezra on Lev. 25:1. Ramban on Gen. 1:1; Lev. 2:14; Deut. 19:8. Rashbam on Deut. 7:9; Bava Batra 117a. Maharal, *Derekh Hayyim*, p. 189. *Or HaHayyim* on Lev. 25:1-2. *Kedushat Levi*, p. 113b. *Ha'amek Davar* on Deut. 9:4. *Hiddushei Maran Riz HaLevi*, p. 5.

567. Cf. Sifrei 309 (Deut. 32:6), 310 (Deut. 32:7). Massekhet Sofrim XIII, 11. Exod. R. 15:18, 15:23. Deut. R. 3:3; Esther R. 7. Rashi on Exod. 6:6. Maharal, *Gevurot HaShem*, 7. Cf. Deut. 28:1-2, 28:8-9. Cf. *Olat Reiyah*, I, pp. 202-3.

568. Cf. TB Berakhot 7a; 32a; Megillah 11a (Lev. 26:44). See also TY Sanhedrin X, 2 (Deut. 31:18). Cf. Deut. R. 3:2; Tanhuma, Nitsavim 3. Rashi on Deut. 29:12. Ibn Ezra, Ramban, Abrabanel, Alshekh and Shedal on Gen. 15:6-8. Ramban on Deut. 7:7. Radak and Rabbi S.R. Hirsch on Gen. 22:16. Maharal, *Gevurot HaShem*, 8. Shelah, I, p. 69a.

569. Cf. Num. R. 4:6. Zohar III, 285b. Rashi on Exod. 6:6; Num. 15:41; Shabbat 119b. Ramban on Deut. 7:9.

570. Cf. TB Bava Metsia 85a; Sanhedrin 101a. Pesikta Zutarta, Eikev, Deut. 8:5; Tanhuma, Ki Teitsei 2; Shoher Tov, 94.

571. Cf. Ramban on Gen. 26:3; Deut. 32:40; *Sefer HaGeulah (Kitvei Ramban I)*, p. 277. Maharsha on Yoma 35b. HaGra, *Siddur Ishei Yisrael (Siah Yitshak)*, p. 48. *Siddur HaGeonim VeHaMekubalim*, III, p. 528. *Sefat Emet*, V, p. 130.

572. Cf. Sifrei 303 (Deut. 26:15). Ramban on Deut. 9:4.

573. Cf. Jer. 18:4, 18:6.

574. Cf. Exod. 19:5. Deut. 7:6, 14:2, 26:18. Ps. 135:4. Lev. R. 2:1; Yalkut Shim'oni, Yitro 19:276.

575. Cf. Mekhilta 2 (Exod. 19:5). Sifrei 309 (Deut. 32:6). TB Hullin 56b. Rashi on Gen. 14:19.

576. Cf. Mekhilta 9 (Exod. 15:16). Avot VI, 9. TB Pessahim 87b and Rashi ad loc. Massekhet Kallah Rabbati 8. Tana Devei Eliyahu Zuta 7; 9. Tanhuma, Ha'azinu 6. Maharal, *Derekh Hayyim*, pp. 241-46. *Sefat Emet*, I, p. 57. M.D. Cassuto, *Perush Al Sefer Shemot*, Jerusalem: 5719 (1959), p. 156.

577. Cf. Ps. 24:1, 104:24.

578. Cf. Ps. 84. Cf. Sifrei 298 (Deut. 26:2), 301 (Deut. 26:9). Mishnah Kelim I, 6. Rambam, *Perush HaMishnayot*, Sukkah III, 12; ibid., Rosh HaShanah IV, 1. TY Berakhot IV, 3; Ma'asser Sheini III, 6. TB Ketuvot 8a; Zevahim 119a (Deut. 12:9); see also TB Bava Kama 100b; Hullin 133b, as well as Rambam, *Hilkhot Nessiat Kapaim*, XIV, 39. Gen. R. 13:2. Exod. R. 15:9, 32:2. Shir HaShirim R. 7:10. Eihah R., Petihta 8. Tana Devei Eliyahu Zuta 2. Zohar II, 157a; III, 114b; 161b. Zohar Hadash, 69a. Tikkunei HaZohar, 6 (23a). Rashi on Deut. 12:9; Ta'anit 16a. Tossafot, Zevahim 60b. Ramban, *Sefer HaGeulah (Kitvei Ramban I)*, p. 283. R. Eliyahu of Vilna, *Hiddushei UBiurei HaGra*, p. 132; *Aderet Eliyahu*, p. 427; *Siddur Ishei Yisrael*, pp. 356-57; see also *Biurei HaGra Al Aggadot*, I, p. 69. *Orot HaKodesh*, III, p. 288. Rav Harlap, *Mei Meirom*, V, p. 235; *Missaviv LiShmonah Perakim LeHaRambam*, p. 211. *Da'at Torah*, p. 159.

579. Cf. Lev. R. 2:2. See Maharal, *Derekh Hayyim*, Avot VI, 9, pp. 245-46.

580. Isa. 60:21.
581. See R. Yitshak Arama, *Akeidat Yitshak*, Lekh Lekha, XVIII; *The Hirsch Siddur*, pp. 526-28.
582. Cf. Mekhilta 9 (Exod. 15:16). Cf. Gen. R. 13:4-5. *Sefat Emet*, I, p. 5.
583. Cf. Deut. 11:13-14ff. Avot V, 9. Sifra 1 (Lev. 26:4). TY Ta'anit III, 5. TB Ta'anit 7a; Shabbat 32b. Avot DeRabbi Nathan 38:1. Pirkei DeRabbi Eliezer 17. Gen. R. 13:5; Num. R. 8:4; Ruth R. 4:7. Tanhuma, Bereshit 12; Behar 1; Behukotai 1-2. Yalkut Shim'oni, Eikev 11:857. Zohar I, 27b. Rashi on Gen. 27:28; Lev. 25:18. Num. R. 9.
584. Cf. Exod. R. 33:1.
585. See Maharal, *Gevurot HaShem*, 23.
586. Cf. Sifrei 323 (Deut. 32:29). TB Bava Kama 17a; Pessahim 87a; Beitsa 25b; Sotah 21a. Tana Devei Eliyahu Rabba 2:18. Tana Devei Eliyahu Zuta, 1, 13. Zohar I, 132a; II, 134b; 167a. Maharal, *Gevurot HaShem*, 47; *Derashot, Hesped*, p. 15. R. Hayyim of Volozhin, *Nefesh HaHayyim*, 4:33.
587. Cf. TB Berakhot 61b; Avodah Zarah 3b. Zohar III, 278b; Shelah, I, pp. 43-44. *Nefesh HaHayyim*, 4:29.
588. Cf. TY Nedarim VI, 8. Rambam, *Sefer HaMitzvot, Mitzvot Asseh, Mitzvah* 153; *Hilkhot Kiddush HaHodesh*, V, 13; see also ibid., V, 2 and *Hilkhot Sanhedrin*, IV. R. Meir Simha Kohen of Dvinsk, *Or Sameah*, on Rambam's *Hilkhot Kiddush HaHodesh*, II, 8. R. Abraham of Sochaczew, *She'eilot UTeshuvot Avnei Nezer, Orah Hayyim*, pp. 310-11. *Sefat Emet*, V, p. 5. See also Lev. 26:44. TB Shabbat 55a and Tossafot ad loc. Megillah 11a; 12a; Sotah 41b; Bava Batra 115b; see also Ta'anit 7b. Lev. R. 36. Ramban on Exod. 3:15; Deut. 28:42. *Hiddushei Maran Riz HaLevi*, p. 20.
589. Cf. TY Horayot I, 2. TB Berakhot 58a; Horayot 3a; Arakhin 32b (Lev. 25:10). Yalkut Shim'oni, Behar (Lev.) 25:659. I Chron. 17:21. Rambam, *Perush HaMishnayot*, Horayot I, 1 and Bekhorot IV, 3; *Hilkhot Berakhot*, X, 11; *Hilkhot Shegagot*, XIII, 2. Maharal, *Netiv Olam*, I, *Netiv Gemilut Hassadim*, 1. *Sefat Emet*, III, pp. 191, 198. Rav Kook, *Orot*, pp. 163, 166; *Olat Reiyah*, I, pp. 387-88; *Hazon HaGeulah*, pp. 98-99. *Mei Meirom*, VI, pp. 302, 310. *Tsafnat Pa'aneah*, Bereshit, p. 60. R.J. Schepanski, *Erets-Yisrael BeSifrut HaTeshuvot*, II, Jerusalem: 5728 (1968), p. 79.
590. Cf. TB: Berakhot 58a; Sanhedrin 111a. Zohar I, 2b; 25a.
591. See *She'eilot UTeshuvot Hatam Sofer, Yoreh Deyah*, 234, p. 97.
592. Cf. Rambam, *Iggeret Teiman*, pp. 117, 127-28. Se TB Yoma 69b. Cf. *Kitvei Rabbi Nahman MiBratslav*, p. 193.
593. Cf. TB Pessahim 87b and Rashi ad loc.; cf. TB Gittin 88a; Sanhedrin 38a; Avodah Zarah 10b. Gen. R. 76:3. Tana Devei Eliyahu Zuta 10. Ramban on Gen. 32:9. Shelah, III, p. 170a. Hida, *Nahal Kedumim*, Deut. 4:26. *Bet HaLevi*, II, p. 6.
594. Cf. Jer. 46:28. Cf. Exod. R. 2:9-10, 15:27 (Exod. 3:2). Shir HaShirim R. 2:9.
595. Cf. Mal. 3:6. Deut. R. 3:9. Rambam, *Iggeret Teiman*, p. 129. *Likkutei Moharan*, 251. *Sefat Emet*, IV, p. 52.
596. Cf. Gen. 28:13; Isa. 59:21; Ps. 82:6. Gen. R. 41:12. Exod. R. 32:17, 47:9. Lev. R. 18:3; Kohelet R. 1:9. See also TB Eruvin 54a. Cf. Zohar I, 152b; II, 45b; 113b; 134b; 183a; III, 6b; 176. Rabbeinu Sa'adya Gaon, *Emunot VeDeot*, III, 7. Rambam, *Moreh Nevukhim*, II, 29. Maharal, *Gevurot HaShem*, 42; *Derekh*

Hayyim, p. 220. Alshekh on Ki Tissa. Cf. R. Yossef Rozin, Gaon of Rogachov, *Mefa'aneah Tsefunot*, p. 222. R. Abraham of Slonim, *Be'er Avraham*, p. 215.

597. Cf. Maharal, *Gevurot HaShem*, 47. Rav Kook, *Orot*, p. 64.
598. Cf. Maharal, *Gevurot HaShem*, 24. *Be'er Avraham*, pp. 214-15, 334. *Shem MiShemuel*, *Shemot*, I, p. 287; *Devarim*, p. 214; *Moadim*, p. 130 (TB Sanhedrin 92a); *Haggadah*, pp. 28, 42.
599. Cf. Shir HaShirim R. 6:10 (Deut. 4:4).
600. Cf. TB Megillah 29a; Menahot 53b. Gen. R. 6:5. Zohar I, 177b. Rabbeinu Bahya on Exod. 19:6. Maharal, *Netsah Yisrael*, 10; *Derashot*, p. 41. R. Menahem Nahum of Tchernobil, *Likkutim*, p. 243.
601. Cf. Zohar I, 60a; *Kitvei Rabbi Nahman MiBratslav*, p. 193. See TB Yoma 38b (Prov. 10:7).
602. Cf. Maharal, *Tiferet Yisrael*, 17; *Perushim LeAggadot*, I, pp. 146-47. Rav Kook, *Orot*, p. 157. See Lev. R. 18:3. Cf. Deut. 28:10. Num. R. 5:6 (Isa. 48:9). Maharal, *Netsah Yisrael*, 62.
603. Cf. TB Berakhot 12a; 32a. Exod. R. 17:5; 44:2. Zohar II, 36a; 96a. Rashi on Exod. 32:13. Rabbi S.R. Hirsch on Ps. 135:13 (Hebrew ed., p. 508).
604. Cf. II Kings 14:27. Isa. 54:10; 66:22; Cf. R. Yossef Albo, *Ikkarim*, IV, 42. Jer. 31:35-36, 33:20-21. Deut. 11:21. Mekhilta 3 (Exod. 14:15). Exod. R. 31:9. Num. R. 2:12. Esther R. 7. TB Berakhot 32a. Rambam, *Iggeret Teiman*, pp. 129, 130. Rashi on Exod. 32:13; Deut. 1:10, 30:9; Sanhedrin 44a. Ramban on Deut. 32:1. Maharal, *Gevurot Hashem*, 24. Hatam Sofer, *Haggadah*, p. 120. Malbim on Isa. 51:16. R. Hayyim of Volozhin, *Ruah Hayyim*, p. 94. *Mei Meirom*, V, p. 241; VI, p. 16. Rabbi B.Z. Safran, *Doresh LeTsion*, p. 17.
605. Cf. Kohelet R. 1:9. Gen. R. 41:12 (Gen. 13:16), 68, 100:10. Exod. R. 32:7. Lev. R. 29:2. Num. R. 2:12. Tanhuma, VaYeitsei 2. Pirkei DeRabbi Eliezer 35. Shoher Tov 36. *Iggeret Teiman*, p. 128. Ramban on Gen. 28:12. Rav Kook, *Hazon HaGeulah*, p. 97.
606. Cf. Exod. 1:12. Deut. 32:23. Isa. 6:13, 54:10, 65:8, 65:17, 66:22. Jer. 30:11, 31:35-36, 46:28. Ps. 83:5, 94:14, 129:1-2. Sifrei 47 (Deut. 11:21). TB Berakhot 32a; Sotah 9a; Menahot 53b; Ketuvot 111a. Gen. R. 41:1; Exod. R. 31:9. Lev. R. 29:2. Num. R. 2:12, 5:6, 10:5. Deut. R. 3:2. Esther R. 1. Tanhuma, Nitsavim 1, 3. Pesikta DeRav Kahana, II, 23, p. 336. Zohar I, 140b; 180b; 205a; II, 21b. *Kuzari*, II, 44. Rashi on Gen. 15:10; Num. 23:9; Deut. 29:12, 32:1. Rambam, *Hilkhot Issurei Bi'a*, XIV, 5; *Iggeret Teiman*, pp. 117, 126-29. Ramban on Gen. 22:16, 28:12; Num. 23:10; Deut. 32:2, 32:43. Radak on Gen. 15:11. Maharal, *Gevurot HaShem*, 8; *Perushim LeAggadot*, I, p. 32 (Sotah 9a). *Siddur Rabbeinu Shelomo de Garmaise*, p. 28. Shelah, I, p. 22a. HaGra, *Siddur Ishei Yisrael*, pp. 45, 543. R. S.R. Hirsch on Gen. 15:8-9. *Meshekh Hokhmah*, p. 192. *Mei Meirom*, VI, pp. 152-53; VIII, p. 67. *Yessod HaAvodah*, p. 235; *Be'er Avraham*, pp. 214, 334. *Shem MiShemuel*, *Haggadah*, p. 40. *Tossefet Berakhah*, V, pp. 247-48. *Mikhtav MeEliyahu*, III, p. 201.
607. Deut. 4:4; cf. Zohar I, 207b. Num. R. 12:23; Shir HaShirim R. 6:10. Avot DeRabbi Nathan 34. Tanhuma, Nitsavim 1. Maharal, *Perushim LeAggadot HaShas*, I, p. 32; II, pp. 124-25. *Tanya*, 50.
608. Cf. Isa. 4:10, 55:3, 61:8. Jer. 32:40; Ezek. 16:60, 37:26. Ps. 105:10 et al. TB Shabbat 55a and Tossafot ad loc.

609. Cf. Lev. 2:13; Num. 18:19. Cf. TB Berakhot 5a; Lev. R. 29b.
610. Cf. Sifrei 118 (Num. 18:19). See TB Bekhorot 8b; Rashi, Ibn Ezra and R. S.R. Hirsch on Lev. 2:13. *Kedushat Levi*, p. 113.
611. Cf. Tanhuma, Nitsavim 1 (Deut. 29:9). Cf. Yalkut Shim'oni, Re'eh 13:890. See also TB Sotah 9a; Kohelet R. 1:9. Cf. Zohar II, 216b. *Akeidat Yitshak*, Nitsavim.
612. Cf. Ps. 94:14.
613. Cf. Gen. R. 41:12, 69:3. Num. R. 2:11-12. (Gen. 13:6.) Maharal, *Netsah Yisrael*, 14.
614. Isa. 54:17.
615. See supra, p. 7.
616. Cf. Rabbi Dov Baer of Mezerich, *Maggid Devarav LeYa'akov*, 71. See Esther R. 7.
617. Cf. Gen. R. 66b; Exod. R. 37:4; Num. R. 1:3; Deut. R. 8:6; Shir HaShirim R. 7:1. Shoher Tov, 20, 109. Zohar III, 11a. See Ramban on Deut. 32:26.
618. Cf. TB Sanhedrin 96a; Avodah Zarah 9a; Tana Devei Eliyahu Rabba 2.
619. Cf. Gen. 9:11. Isa. 54:9. TB Sotah 11a; Zevahim 116a. Tossefta Ta'anit I, 11.
620. Cf. Exod. R. 40:1.
621. Cf. TB Shabbat 88a; Avodah Zarah 2b-3a. Gen. R. 1; Lev. R. 36. Tanhuma, Bereshit 1; Shemini 9. Shoher Tov, 20. TY Sanhedrin X, 2. Avot III, 14. Zohar III, 11b; 125a. Zohar Hadash, Yitro 38a. Maharal, *Netsah Yisrael*, 11; *Tiferet Yisrael*, 32; *Gur Aryeh*, Yitro; *Derashot, Hesped*, p. 15; *Perushim LeAggadot*, II, pp. 75, 121. R. Hayyim of Volozhin, *Nefesh HaHayyim*, 1, 16; *Ruah Hayyim*, p. 89. *Avnei Nezer*, pp. 80-81.
622. Cf. TB Ta'anit 3b; Yevamot 63a. Pesikta Zutarta, VaYeitsei, Gen. 28:14. Gen. R. 66:2; Exod. R. 38. Shoher Tov, 2, 109. Gen. 9:12. Jer. 33:25. Zohar I, 24b-25a; 121b; II, 5b. Zohar Hadash, VaYeitsei 28. Maharal, *Netivot Olam*, I, *Netiv HaTorah*, 1; *Derekh Hayyim*, p. 166. *Tanya*, 37. *Nefesh HaHayyim*, 1:6, 1:16, 2:6, 4:11, 4:25. *Sefat Emet*, II, 93. Rav Kook, *Orot*, pp. 139, 142-43.
623. Cf. TB Pessahim 68b; Esther R. 7:17; Tanhuma, Ha'azinu 3; Tana Devei Eliyahu Rabba 14, 18. Zohar I, 24b.
624. Cf. TB Avodah Zarah 3a; Exod. R. 7:5, 37:4. Deut. R. 8:6. Tanhuma, Bereshit 1. Zohar 1, 77a; 89a; 134b; 185a; II, 94a; 200a; III, 11b; 193a.
625. Cf. TB Sanhedrin 97a; Avodah Zarah 9a.
626. Cf. R. Hayyim Vital, *Ets Hayyim, Sha'ar HaKelim*, 1. See Ramban on Deut. 10:12. Cf. R. Dov Baer, Maggid of Mezerich, *Maggid Devarav LeYa'akov*, 125. R. Levi Yitshak of Berdichev, *Kedushat Levi*, p. 56b. R. Nahman of Bratslav, *Likkutei Moharan*, 64. R. Moshe Hayyim Luzzatto, *Pithei Hokhmah*, p. 10b. R. Yisrael, Maggid of Koznitz, *Avodat Yisrael*, p. 1.
627. Ps. 8:4, 104:31.
628. Cf. Ezek. 18:32. Cf. TB Berakhot 18b; Yoma 71a. Gen. R. 39:7. Tanhuma, Yitro 1; Vezot HaBerakhah 7. Tikkunei HaZohar, 66b. Ezek. 33:11.
629. Cf. TB Sanhedrin 99b. See Tanhuma (Buber ed.), Bereshit 3. Pesikta Zutarta, Bereshit I, 1. Cf. Ramban on Deut. 32:26. Maharal, *Derekh Hayyim*, pp. 215-16; *Derashot, Hesped*, pp. 14-15. *Ha'amek Davar* on Deut. 26:18.
630. Cf. Isa. 43:10; Lev. R. 6:1. See Rav Kook, *Orot*, p. 143.
631. Cf. TB Avodah Zarah 4b; Pesikta Zutarta, VaEthanan, Deut. 5:26. Maharal, *Netivot Olam*, II, *Netiv HaTeshuvah*, 4. See also Mekhilta 1 (Exod. 12:1);

Pirkei DeRabbi Eliezer 10.
632. Cf. Shir HaShirim R. 7:6. Cf. Rav Kook, *Orot*, pp. 26, 42, 141; *Orot HaTeshuvah*, pp. 37, 122; see also ibidem, pp. 33-34.
633. Cf. Gen. R. 1:5, 2:4-5; Lev. R. 36:4. See TB Pessahim 54a; Zohar I, 113a. See also TB Shabbat 119b.
634. Cf. Isa. 59:2. Zohar II, 262b; III, 122a. See Rambam, *Hilkhot Teshuvah*, VII, 7.
635. Cf. *Sefat Emet*, I, p. 211; *Orot HaTeshuvah*, p. 72.
636. Cf. TY Rosh HaShanah IV, 8. Lev. R. 30:3. Shoher Tov, 102. Yalkut Shim'oni, Pinhas 29:782 (Isa. 66:22). Rambam, *Hilkhot Teshuvah*, VII, 6. HaGra, *Divrei Eliyahu*, p. 39. Rav Kook, *Olat Reiyah*, II, p. 338.
637. Cf. TB Shevuot 39a; Shabbat 146a. Exod. R. 28:4. Tikkunei HaZohar, 86a. See Zohar I, 91a; Pirkei DeRabbi Eliezer 41.
638. Cf. TB Yoma 86b; Berakhot 34b; Sanhedrin 99a et al. Cf. Zohar Hadash, Noah 23. Cf. R. Abraham of Slonim, *Be'er Avraham*, p. 91.
639. Cf. *Orot HaKodesh*, III, pp. 175-78. *Da'at Hokhmah UMussar*, pp. 105-6, 113.
640. Cf. Isa. 27:13 et al. Cf. Lev. R. 27:4.
641. Cf. Exod. R. 23:11; Yalkut Shim'oni, Yonah 550; see also Tanhuma, Shemini 9; Ha'azinu 4. Zohar III, 122b. Maharal, *Netsah Yisrael*, 14; *Gevurot HaShem*, 44; *Netivot Olam*, II, *Netiv HaTeshuvah*, 4. *Tanya*, 19. *Bnei Issakhar*, II, p. 24. R. Nahman of Bratslav, *Haggadah*, p. 84. Ramhal, *Derekh HaShem*, II, 4. Rav Kook, *Orot*, p. 97; *Orot HaTeshuvah*, pp. 37, 122; *Olat Reiyah*, II, p. 2. Rav Harlap, *Mei Meirom*, VII, pp. 253ff.; *Missaviv LiShemonah Perakim LeHaRambam*, p. 199. *Hiddushei Maran Riz HaLevi*, p. 43. *HaMussar VeHaDa'at*, II, p. 280. *Ben Ish Hai*, p. 132. *Shem MiShemuel, Bereshit*, II, p. 244.
642. Cf. TB Pessahim 54a. Zohar I, 90a; 134b; III, 69b. Zohar Hadash, Ruth 85a. Cf. Gen. R. 1:5. *Orot HaKodesh*, III, p. 81. *Shem MiShemuel, Devarim*, p. 221.
643. Cf. Rambam, *Sefer HaMitzvot*, Mitzvot Asseh, Mitzvah 73; *Hilkhot Teshuvah*, I, 1. Ramban on Deut. 30:11.
644. Cf. TY Ta'anit I, 1; II, 2. TB Sanhedrin 97b-98a; Yoma 86b (Isa. 56:1). Num. R. 7:10; Shir HaShirim R. 5:3. Tanhuma, Behukotai 3. Zohar II, 188b; III, 122a; 270a; 278a. Zohar Hadash, Bereshit 8a; 23b. Tikkunei HaZohar, 6 (22b). Rashi and Maharsha on Sanhedrin 97b. Ramban on Lev. 26:16; *Sefer HaGeulah (Kitvei Ramban* I), pp. 267, 277. Maharsha on Megillah 31b. *Siddur Rabbeinu Shelomo de Garmaise*, p. 230.
645. Cf. Zohar Hadash, 59b. Rambam, *Hilkhot Teshuvah*, VII, 5 (Deut. 30:1-3); *Hilkhot Melakhim*, XI, 1. Ramban on Exod. 2:25, 12:42; Deut. 30:6, 30:11, 32:40. Maharal, *Netsah Yisrael*, 31. *Or HaHayyim* on Deut. 4:29. *Be'er Mayim Hayyim* on Deut. 30:3-4. Rav Kook, *Orot HaTeshuvah*, p. 123. See also Ezek. 36. Exod. R. 15:5. Maharal, *Netsah Yisrael*, 13, 62. Malbim on Isa. 12:2. *Mikhtav MeEliyahu*, II, p. 50. *Bet Avraham*, p. 93.
646. Cf. Gen. 22:16. Ezek. 36. Isa. 48:11. Ps. 106:8. Dan. 12:7. Exod. R. 1:41-42, 3:3. Shir HaShirim R. 2:6; 2, II, 19, 8:16. Shoher Tov, 94. Tanhuma, Shemot 12. Pesikta Zutarta, Tetsaveh 27:20. Yalkut Shim'oni, Malachi 3:595. See also TY Sanhedrin X, 1; TB Berakhot 32a; Shabbat 55a. Lev. R. 36:5. Cf. Zohar I,

117b; 119a; II, 6a; 10a; III, 66b. Tikkunei HaZohar 21 (55a); Tikkunei Zohar Hadash, 8b. Rambam, *Hilkhot Teshuvah*, VII, 5. Ramban on Lev. 26:45; Deut. 9:4, 32:26, 32:40, 32:43; *Sefer HaGeulah (Kitvei Ramban* I), pp. 277, 287, 290. Maharal, *Gevurot HaShem*, 21, 24. *Siddur Rabbeinu Shelomo de Garmaise*, p. 229. Shelah, III, pp. 24b, 165b. Or *HaHayyim* on Lev. 25:27; Num. 24:17. Rav Kook, *Orot HaTeshuvah*, pp. 33-34; *Iggerot HaReiyah*, II, pp. 186-87. *Mei Meirom*, VI, p. 16; *Missaviv LiShemonah Perakim LeHa-Rambam*, p. 192. R. M.M. Kasher, *HaTekufah HaGedolah*, pp. 471, 475; *Milhemet Yom HaKippurim*, Jerusalem: 5734, pp. 12-14, 32-33, 41, 62, 74. R. B.Z. Safran, *Doresh LeTsion*, pp. 5, 13.

647. Cf. Maharal, *Netsah Yisrael*, 62. Rav Kook, *Orot*, pp. 136-37.
648. Cf. TB Sotah 4b; Gen. 14:22. Avot VI, 10. TB Pessahim 87b. Gen. R. 13:5, 30:8, 43:8. Num. R. 12:13; Shir HaShirim R. 2:2. Tanhuma, Behar 1. Rashi on Sanhedrin 81b. *Akeidat Yitshak*, Lekh Lekha, XVIII. *Perushei Maharal LeAggadot HaShas*, I, p. 24. *Orot HaKodesh*, II, pp. 572-74; *Orot*, p. 22. A. Safran, *La Cabale*, p. 343.
649. Cf. Pesikta Rabbati 28. *Sefer Yereim HaShalem*, 413. Shelah, I, *Toldot Adam*. *Maggid Devarav LeYa'akov*, 66, 127. *Be'er Mayim Hayyim* on Gen. 1:1, 1:6. *Sefat Emet*, I, p. 16; III, pp. 189, 191, 195, 197, 200. *Orot HaKodesh*, I, p. 151.
650. Cf. TB Sanhedrin 38b. Zohar I, 23b; 24b; 34b; 130b; 205b; II, 23b; III, 83a. Rashi on Gen. 2:7.
651. Cf. Gen. 28:17. Pirkei DeRabbi Eliezer 35. Shoher Tov, 91. Zohar I, 147b; II, 190b. *Sefat Emet*, III, pp. 197-98. *Shem MiShemuel, Bemidbar*, 347-48.
652. Ramban, *Torat HaAdam(Kitvei Ramban* II), p. 296. See Gen. R. 19:18.
653. Cf. Gen. R. 14:9. Targum Yonathan on Hos. 6:7. Zohar I, 80a; 147b; II, 262b. Shelah, I, p. 70a.
654. Cf. Maharal, *Derekh Hayyim*, pp. 210-11, 220. Rav Kook, *Orot HaKodesh*, I, p. 151.
655. Cf. Gen. R. 13:5. Shelah, I, pp. 24b, 26a. *Sefat Emet*, I, pp. 5, 16; II, p. 49; III, pp. 190, 196-97, 200; V, p. 164. Rav Kook, *Orot HaKodesh*, II, p. 573; *Orot HaTeshuvah*, p. 30.
656. Cf. Gen. R. 43. Maharal, *Derekh Hayyim*, p. 245. *Sefat Emet*, III, p. 197. *Avnei Nezer*, pp. 1-2. See TB Rosh HaShanah 31a; Ramban on Gen. 14:18-19.
657. Cf. Shelah, *Siddur, Sha'arei HaShamayim*, p. 576. HaGra, *Siddur Ishei Yisrael*, p. 395. *Sefat Emet*, III, p. 191. *Mei Meirom*, VI, p. 311; VIII, p. 64.
658. Cf. TB Pessahim 118b; Avodah Zarah 24a; Sanhedrin 92b; Shevuot 39a. Gen. R. 6, 8, 54. Exod. R. 29. Tanhuma, Ahrei 9. *Sefat Emet*, II, pp. 65, 68; III, pp. 189, 190, 198-200. *Mei Meirom*, VI, p. 257.
659. Cf. R. Abraham of Slonim, *Be'er Avraham*, p. 143.
660. Cf. Maharal, *Gevurot HaShem*, 57; cf. also TB Eruvin 41a.
661. Cf. Pirkei DeRabbi Eliezer 8; Yalkut Shim'oni, Pinhas 29:782. Zohar III, 100b; Zohar Hadash, Bereshit 14. Shelah, I, p. 11a.
662. Cf. *Tanya, Iggeret HaKodesh*, 14. *Sefat Emet*, I, p. 56 et al.; III, p. 196. *Be'er Avraham*, p. 123.
663. Cf. *Sefat Emet*, V, pp. 78, 154-56.
664. Cf. Lev. 16:30. TB Rosh HaShanah 18a. Rambam, *Hilkhot Teshuvah*, II, 6-7.

REFERENCES, SOURCES & NOTES • 337

Shelah, I, pp. 11a, 26a. Rav Kook, *Olat Reiyah*, II, 342; *Orot HaTeshuvah*, p. 57.

665. Cf. TB Rosh HaShanah 16a; 34b. *Siddur Rabbeinu Shelomo de Garmaise*, pp. 210-14.
666. Cf. Isa. 44:6 et al.
667. Ps. 103:19. See Shelah, *Siddur Sha'ar HaShamayim*, p. 576.
668. Cf. R. Eliyahu of Vilna, *Biur HaGra*, Mishlei 27:27, pp. 81a-b; *Aderet Eliyahu*, p. 10; *Siddur Ishei Yisrael*, p. 69. R. Nahman of Bratslav, *Likkutei Moharan*, 17. See also Rashi on Deut. 6:4.
669. Zech. 14:9; cf. also Ps. 47:8.
670. Prayers for Rosh HaShanah and Yom Kippur. Cf. Maharal, *Gevurot Hashem*, 24.
671. Cf. Ps. 145:17. Num. R. 11:1; Shir HaShirim R. 5:2. Zohar I, 93a (Prov. 3:33; Isa. 60:21); 216a (Isa. 26:2); II, 23a; III, 61a; 125a; 266b. See also Rambam, *Hilkhot Melakhim*, III, 6. Cf. Rashi on Ps. 72:7; Rabbeinu Bahya on Exod. 19:6; Maharal, *Derashot, Hesped*, pp. 10-11; *Maggid Devarav LeYa'akov*, 191; *Nefesh HaHayyim*, 116.
672. Prov. 10:25. Cf. TB Haggigah 12b. Zohar I, 31a; 45b; 59b; 105b; 195a; 208a; II, 116a. Tikkunei HaZohar, 1a; 2b; 21 (50b). Zohar Hadash, Bereshit 7. See TB Sanhedrin 97b; 103b; Yoma 38b. Gen. R. 35b. Tanhuma, Nitsavim 2. *Orot HaKodesh*, III, pp. 156-57.
673. Cf. TB Berakhot 16b.
674. Cf. TB Sanhedrin 27b; Shevuot 39a. Lev. R. 30. Rashi on Rosh HaShanah 29a. Rambam, *Perush HaMishnah*, Makot III, 16. R. Yossef Albo, *Sefer HaIkkarim*, 29. Ari HaKadosh and R. Hayyim Vital, *Likkutei Torah* and *Ta'amei HaMitzvot*, Kedoshim, p. 77. R. Moshe Cordovero, *Tomer Devorah* 1. Shelah, III, p. 2a. R. Ya'akov Yossef of Polonnoye, *Toldot Ya'akov Yossef*, Hakdamah II, Bereshit, Lekh Lekha. R. Elimelech of Lyzhansk, *Noam Elimelekh*, Devarim. R. Shneur Zalman of Lyady, *Tanya*, 41. *Or HaHayyim* on Exod. 39:32.
675. Cf. *Kuzari*, II, 24. *Sefat Emet*, III, pp. 195-97, 189, 200. *Orot HaKodesh*, I, p. 134; *Hazon HaGeulah*, pp. 98-99, 118; *Orot*, pp. 12, 166. *Mei Meirom*, VI, pp. 244, 282-83.
676. Cf. TY Shekalim III, 3. TB Rosh HaShanah 9b; Moed Katan 2b; Gittin 36-37; Kiddushin 36b-37a; 38b; Arakhin 32b. Lev. R. 34:7; Num. R. 17:7. Rambam, *Hilkhot Shemittah VeYovel*, X, 8. Ramban on Deut. 11:18. Hatam Sofer, *Yoreh DeYah*, 234. *Olat Reiyah*, I, pp. 387-88; *Orot*, p. 13; *Orot HaTorah*, pp. 68, 78.
677. Cf. TB Berakhot 17a; Shabbat 14b; Pessahim 34b; Yoma 57a; Megillah 12b; 14a; Ketuvot 110b; Nedarim 22a (Deut. 28:65); Sanhedrin 24a; Avodah Zarah 5a; Zevahim 60b; Menahot 52a; 110a. Cf. *Meiri* on Ketuvot 111a. Yalkut Shim'oni, Beshalah 14:234; Mishlei 17:956. Zohar I, 28a; 141b; II, 40a; III, 82b; 238b. Tikkunei HaZohar, 69 (97b). Rambam, *Hilkhot Shofar*, III, 2; *Moreh Nevukhim*, II, 36. Ramban on Lev. 18:25. Alshekh on Lekh Lekha, Gen. 12:1; Ki Tavo, Deut. 26:6. Shir HaShirim 5:2. Maharal, *Gevurot HaShem*, 8; *Derashot, Derush LeShabbat Teshuvah*, pp. 32-33. Shelah, *Siddur Sha'ar HaShamayim*, p. 521. R. Eliyahu of Vilna, *Hiddushei UBiurei HaGra*,

p. 58; *Sefer HaEmunah VeHaHashgahah*, I, p. 1. *Likkutei Moharan*, I, 19; II, 17. *Sefat Emet*, III, p. 198. Hatam Sofer, *Haggadah*, p. 27. Rav Kook, *Orot*, pp. 10, 42, 77-78, 86, 90, 94, 142, 158; *Orot HaKodesh*, I, p. 134; III, pp. 116, 288; *Hazon HaGeulah*, pp. 89, 103, 114; *Orot HaTorah*, p. 9; *Iggrot HaReiyah*, I, p. 110. *Mei Meirom*, V, pp. 243-44; VI, pp. 26, 63-64, 85, 244, 256, 309; VIII, pp. 53, 67, 69; *Missaviv LiShmonah Perakim LeHaRambam*, p. 200. *Mikhtav MeEliyahu*, III, p. 192. *Pahad Yitshak, Yerah HaEitanim*, pp. 45-46. *Ben Ish Hai*, p. 104. *Tossefet Berakhah*, V, p. 88. *Shem MiShemuel, Haggadah*, p. 46.

678. Cf. Sifrei 37 (Deut. 11:10). TB Sanhedrin 24a; Berakhot 6b. Gen. R. 16:7, 70:8. Lev. R. 13:4. Avot DeRabbi Nathan 28, 34. Shoher Tov, 147. Zohar III, 118a. Recanati, Yitro, p. 8b. Shelah, I, p. 169b. *Or HaHayyim* on Deut. 26:1. *Kedushat Levi*, p. 25b. *Sefat Emet*, I, p. 216; V, p. 5. Rav Kook, *Orot HaTorah*, p. 80; *Iggrot HaReiyah*, I, pp. 123ff.; *Shabbat HaArets*, p. 12; *Orot*, pp. 12, 77-78; *Mussar Avikha*, p. 85; *Orot HaKodesh*, III, pp. 138, 288. *Mei Meirom*, II, p. 79; VI, pp. 253, 258, 265, 310; VIII, pp. 20, 69, 106. *Haʻamek Davar* on Gen. 16:7. *Beʼer Avraham*, p. 145; *Daʻat Torah*, p. 160.

679. Cf. Deut. 26:13; cf. also Lev. 26:42; Deut. 25:19. Cf. Zohar I, 170b. Rabbeinu Yonah Gerondi, *Perushim*, Avot III, 1, p. 39. Ramban on Deut. 8:11. Maharal, *Derekh Hayyim*, p. 161. HaGra, *Siddur Ishei Yisrael*, p. 98. *Toldot Yaʻakov Yossef*, Mikeits; *Maggid Devarav LeYaʻakov*, 110; *Kedushat Levi*, pp. 142ff. Moharan, *Sefer HaMiddot*, pp. 229-30; *Kitvei R. Nahman DeBratslav*, p. 193. *Orot HaKodesh*, III, p. 187. *Mei Meirom*, VI, pp. 66, 254. *Avnei Nezer*, p. 29; *Neot HaKodesh*, pp. 108-9. *Shem MiShemuel, Bereshit*, II, pp. 254, 322; *Haggadah*, p. 22. *VaYoel Moshe*, pp. 162-63. See also Deut. 8:14, 32:15. Hos. 13:6. *Haʻamek Davar* on Deut. 8:11-12. TB Sukkah 20a. *Tossefet Berakhah*, V, p. 244.

680. Cf. Maharsha on Megillah 13b.

681. Cf. Sifrei 92 (Num. 11:16). Lev. R. 2:2. Tanhuma, Terumah 3. Rashi on Lev. 26:12. Maharal, *Derashot*, p. 41. *Kedushat Levi*, p. 87b. *Sefat Emet*, II, p. 149.

682. Cf. Deut. 12:9; Ps. 95:11, 132:14. TB Zevahim 119a; Horayot 10b. Shir HaShirim R. 1:66. Zohar II, 221b; 240a. Maharal, *Derekh Hayyim*, pp. 7, 188. *Kedushat Levi*, p. 59a. *Biurei HaGra Al Aggadot*, II, 71. Rav Kook, *Mussar Avikha*, p. 80. *Mei Meirom*, VI, pp. 278, 281-82. *Sefat Emet*, III, pp. 189, 198. *Neot HaDesheh*, p. 123. See Avot IV, 15; Rashi on Gen. 37:1. See also Zohar II, 174a; Jer. 46:27.

683. Cf. Midrash HaGadol, VaYeshev, Gen. 37:1. Yalkut Shimʻoni, Behukotai 26:672. Lev. 26:5 and Sifra ad loc. Deut. 8:12, 12:9. TY Moed Katan III, 1; Tossafot on Avodah Zarah 21a. See TB Menahot 44a; Rambam, *Hilkhot Tefillin*, V, 10; *Tur* and *Shulhan Arukh, Yoreh Deyah*, 286:22. *Bet Yossef, Orah Hayyim*, 228. Deut. 8:12. See TY Sotah VIII, 4. See also Gen. R. 39:10, 74:1.

684. Cf. Gen. 13:7. Ps. 84:8. TB Berakhot 4a; Zohar I, 151a; II, 143a; III, 61a; 218b. TB Berakhot 64a and Maharsha ad loc. See also TB Berakhot 17a; Avot DeRabbi Nathan 1:5. Shoher Tov, 48. Rambam, *Hilkhot Teshuvah*, VIII, 2. See also R. Hayyim Vital, *Peri Ets Hayyim*, p. 20. Maharal, *Netivot Olam*, I, *Netiv HaTorah*, 9; *Derekh Hayyim*, p. 188. Cf. Gen. R. 37:2, 84:1. Exod. R. 31:4. Pesikta Zutarta, VaYeshev, Gen. 37:1. Tanhuma, Behukotai 2. Lev.

26:3. Amos 9:15. Yalkut Shim'oni, Tehillim 84:833. See also Isa. 57:20; Avot IV, 15. See also *Moreh Nevukhim*, III, 24. Cf. Shelah, I, pp. 25a-b; II, p. 23a. Maharsha on Makot 24b. HaGra, *Siddur Ishei Yisrael*, p. 235. R. Hayyim of Volozhin, *Ruah Hayyim*, p. 92. *Kedushat Levi*, p. 59a. *Sefat Emet*, I, pp. 42, 211. *Olat Reiyah*, II, p. 181; *Orot*, p. 84. *Mei Meirom*, VI, pp. 247, 282. *Da'at Torah*, pp. 144, 222.

685. Cf. Mishnah Berakhot I, 5. TB Berakhot 12b; Avodah Zarah 3b; Zevahim 118b. Gen. R. 91:13; Zohar I, 126a. Num. R. 21:20; Isa. 60:1. See also TB Shabbat 63a; Zohar I, 88a.
686. Cf. Prov. 3:6. Deut. 32:43 and Sifrei (333) ad loc. TY Berakhot IX, 5; Shekalim III, 3; Shabbat I, 3. TB Berakhot 63a; Pessahim 113a; Ketuvot 111a; Bava Batra 158b. Pesikta Zutarta, VaYeitsei, Gen. 28:21. Gen. R. 26:11; Shoher Tov, 56, 84. Yalkut Shim'oni, Yeshaya 1:390; Mishlei 17:956. Zohar I, 177b; III, 70b. Shelah, I, *Toldot Adam*, I, p. 169b. *Tanya*, 37. *Kitvei Rabbi Nahman DeBratslav*, p. 354. *Sefat Emet*, III, pp. 189, 195, 200. *Orot*, pp. 22, 28-29, 171. *Bet Avraham*, p. 153.
687. Cf. Deut. 8:11, 8:14. Sifrei 43 (Deut. 11:16), 319 (Deut. 32:15). TB Berakhot 32a. Rashi on Sotah 5a.
688. Cf. Lev. 25:18-19, 26:5 and Sifra ad loc.
689. Cf. TB Kiddushin 81b (Lev. 5:17).
690. Cf. *Sefat Emet*, III, p. 198.
691. Cf. Ps. 48:3; see also Isa. 24. Cf. Shir HaShirim R. 7:10. Zohar III, 118a. R. Abraham of Slonim, *Yessod HaAvodah*, II, pp. 83-84.
692. Cf. Ps. 2:11. Deut. 26:3-5.
693. Cf. TB Berakhot 9b; Shabbat 67a; 128a. Bava Metsia 113b; Horayot 13a. Zohar II, 26b; III, 255a; 276a. Tikkunei HaZohar, 1b; 21 (60a). Zohar Hadash, Yitro 33.
694. Cf. Rabbi B.Z. Safran, *Doresh LeTsion*, p. 25.
695. Cf. Sifrei 188 (Deut. 19:14). TY Berakhot VIII, 5. TB Sanhedrin 99b. Rashi on Hullin 92a. Ramban on Gen. 19:5; *Derashah LeRosh HaShanah* (*Kitvei Ramban* I), pp. 249-51. Alshekh on Deut. 11:12. Hafets Hayyim, *Perush, Seder HaTefillah*, pp. 169-70. *Doresh LeTsion*, p. 12.
696. Cf. TB Eruvin 19a. Avot DeRabbi Natan 34. Shoher Tov, 56. Zohar II, 184b; III, 84a. Shelah, I, p. 168a; III, pp. 22a, 169b-170a. *Mei Meirom*, VI, pp. 233-34; VIII, pp. 20-21.
697. Gen. 2:15. See Lev. R. 25:3 (Lev. 19:23); Gen. R. 64:3. Cf. Zohar I, 27a. Sifrei 41 (Deut. 11:13). Pirkei DeRabbi Eliezer 12. Shelah, III, pp. 169b-170a.
698. Cf. Gen. R. 19:18. Ramban, *Derashah LeRosh HaShanah* (*Kitvei Ramban* I), pp. 200-1, 251. Ari HaKadosh, *Likkutei Torah*, Lekh Lekha, p. 48.
699. See above, p. 13.
700. Cf. TB Berakhot 63b; Shabbat 138b.
701. Cf. Ps. 137:5-6. Cf. Lev. 26:42. TY Berakhot V, 3. Tana Devei Eliyahu Rabba 30. Tanhuma, Noah 11; VaYikra 2. Talkut Shim'oni, Tehillim 137:885. *Tur, Orah Hayyim*, 126. Tossafot on Avodah Zarah 3b. Cf. Zohar I, 114a; III, 213b; 221a; 298a-b.
702. Cf. *Bet HaLevi*, I, p. 21.
703. Cf. Deut. 4:39. Jer. 2:3, 3:12, 31:2, 31:8. Hos. 7:1, 14:2, 14:5. Shir HaShirim 4:3, 6:7. TB Berakhot 17a; 57a; Eruvin 19a; 21b; see also Rosh HaShanah 17a;

Haggigah 27a; Yevamot 7b; Kiddushin 53a; Bava Batra 47b; Sanhedrin 37a; 44a and Rashi ad loc.; 102b; Bekhorot 30b; Keritot 6a. Gen. R. 32:16, 41:1, 65. Exod. R. 24:3, 42:9. Lev. R. 30:11. Num. R. 3:1, 7:10, 13; Deut. R. 2. Shir HaShirim R. 4:5, 4:7, 5:7, 6:17. Tana Devei Eliyahu Rabba 18. Pirkei De Rabbi Eliezer 43. Yalkut Shim'oni, Shir HaShirim 4:988. Zohar II, 100a; 119b; 121a; III, 25a-b; 27a; 112a. Tikkunei HaZohar, 6 (44a); 22 (68b). Zohar Hadash, 44b; 120b-121a. Zohar Hadash, Ruth 83. Rambam, *Perush HaMishnah*, Sanhedrin X, XII; *Hilkhot Gerushin*, II, 20; *Hilkhot Ishut*, IV, 15; *Hilkhot Teshuvah*, III, 5; VII, 5; *Iggeret Teiman*. *Tur, Orah Hayyim*, 619. *Shulhan Arukh, Even HaEzer*, 157:5; *Hoshen Mishpat*, 253. Rashi on Shabbat 105b; Kiddushin 70b. Tossafot on Shabbat 55a. *Tomer Devorah* 2. Maharal, *Gevurot HaShem*, 23, 42; *Perushim LeAggadot*, II, p. 123; *Derekh Hayyim*, pp. 200, 251-52; *Tiferet Yisrael*, 5; *Netsah Yisrael*, 11; *Be'er HaGolah*, 3. Shelah, I, p. 69a; II, p. 44b; III, p. 200b. HaGra on Isa. 1:25; *Siddur Ishei Yisrael*, p. 543. B. Landau, *HaGaon HeHassid MiVilna*, Jerusalem: 5728, pp. 104, 187, 192. *Tanya*, 14, 18, 19, 25, 32, 41, 44. *Noam Elimelekh, Devarim*. *Me'or Einaim, Likkutim*, Nitsavim. *Moharan, Siddur Sha'arei Ratson*, p. 206. *Sefat Emet*, I, pp. 103, 202; III, p. 197; V, pp. 9, 102. *Bet HaLevi*, II, p. 12. Rav Kook, *Orot*, pp. 12-13, 74, 76, 84, 144-47, 150-51, 171; *Hazon HaGeulah*, p. 275. *Mei Meirom, Missaviv LiShmonah Perakim LeHaRambam*, pp. 198-99. *Avnei Nezer*, p. 57. *Be'er Avraham*, p. 314. *Mikhtav MeEliyahu*, II, p. 278. *HaMussar VeHaDa'at*, II, pp. 79-80. *Siddur HaGeonim VeHaMekubalim*, III, p. 528. Alexandre Safran, *Mussar VeHevrah BeIdan HaModerni*, in *Hagut Ivrit BeAiropa*, Tel-Aviv: 5729 (1969), pp. 216ff.
704. Cf. TB Sanhedrin 105b. Lev. R. 35:1. Zohar III, 143b. Zohar Hadash, 59b. Shoher Tov, 22. Rav Harlap, *Mei Meirom*, V, pp. 243-44.
705. Cf. Exod. 4:22; Deut. 14:1; Jer. 31:19; Ps. 2:7. Avot III, 14. TB Shabbat 31a; 89a; Yoma 85b. Massekhet Gerim I, 5. Num. R. 10:5. Deut. R. 2; see also Exod. R. 29:4. Cf. Avot DeRabbi Nathan 3. Zohar I, 47a; 154b; 205b; 213b; II, 2a; 43b; III, 111b; 237b; 238a; 277b; 278b; 298a. Maharal, *Netsah Yisrael*, 11; *Be'er HaGolah*, 3.
706. Cf. Isa. 1:2, 1:4; 30:1, 30:9. Jer. 3:14, 3:22. TB Berakhot 3a; 32b; Shabbat 89a; Pessahim 87b; Yoma 85b (Mishnah Yoma VIII, 9); Ta'anit 23a; 25b. Deut. R. 2:16. Tana Devei Eliyahu Rabba 18. Zohar I, 47a; II, 43b; III, 4b; 99b; 143b; 257a; R. Hayyim Vital, *Peri Ets Hayyim, Sha'ar HaShofar*, I, p. 23a. *Toldot Ya'akov Yossef*, Noah.
707. Cf. TB Kiddushin 36a. Rashi on Shabbat 89b. *Teshuvot HaRashba*, II, 194; 242. *Iggerot HaReiyah*, II, p. 194. *Sefat Emet*, III, p. 198. *Shem MiShemuel, Haggadah*, p. 46.
708. Cf. TB Avodah Zarah 3; Num. R. 13:15. See also Num. R. 8:2; Ps. 146:8. Cf. Zohar Hadash, Ruth 78. Rambam, *Hilkhot Teshuvah*, III, 5; *Hilkhot Melakhim*, VIII, 11. Rabbi Yehuda HeHassid, *Sefer Hassidim*, 358. Cf. *Teshuvot HaRashba*, 194; 242. Cf. Rabbi B.Z. Safran, *Doresh LeTsion*, p. 21.
709. Cf. Isa. 63:8. Jer. 31:2. Hos. 1:9, 2:1, 2:21, 2:25. Sifrei 96 (Deut. 14:1), 308 (Deut. 32:5). TY Kiddushin I, 7; Sanhedrin X, 1. TB Berakhot 3a; 32b; Shabbat 55a; Kiddushin 36a; Bava Batra 10a; Sanhedrin 44a; 105a. Pesikta Rabbati 44; Targum Yonathan on Hos. 2:1. Gen. R. 20:16. Exod. R. 24:1, 24:3, 30:5, 42:6-7, 49:1; see also Exod. R. 25:13. Lev. R. 36:5. Num. R. 2:16,

9:4, 10:2. Deut. R. 2:16, 3:2, 7:10. Shir HaShirim R. 7:16, 8:7. Eihah R. Petihta 31, Tana Devei Eliyahu Rabba 18; Shoher Tov, 100:3. Tanhuma, Mass'ei 7; Eikev 3. See also Pirkei DeRabbi Eliezer 45; Ezek. 36:20. Zohar I, 95b; 213b; II, 20a; 205b; III, 11b; 81a; 111b; 112b; 256a; 286b; 298a. Rambam, *Perush HaMishnah*, Avot V, 15; *Iggeret Teiman*, pp. 128-29. Rashi on Num. 23:21; Deut. 7:8, 29:12, 32:6, 32:9, Isa. 63:8; Shabbat 89b; Sanhedrin 44a. Ramban on Deut. 7:7, 9:4. Tossafot on Yevamot 22b. *Siddur Rabbeinu Shelomo of Garmaise*, p. 28. Maharal, *Netsah Yisrael*, 11; *Perushim LeAggadot*, I, p. 32; *Derashot, Derush LeShabbat Teshuvah*, p. 32. Shelah, *Siddur Sha'ar HaShamayim*, p. 516. Maharsha on Bava Batra 10a. R. Nahman of Bratslav, *Haggadah*, p. 39. *Bet HaLevi*, II, p. 60. *Sefat Emet*, III, p. 198. Rav Kook, *Orot*, pp. 150-51; *Iggrot HaReiyah*, II, pp. 184-98; *Mishpat Kohen*, 124. *Ha'amek Davar* on Deut. 7:8. R. Abraham of Slonim, *Be'er Avraham*, p. 314. R. B.Z. Safran, *Doresh LeTsion*, p. 21.

710. Isa. 60:21. Cf. Num. 23:13, 23:21. Isa. 44:5. Jer. 2:21, 31:36. (Prov. 10:25; Eccl. 7:20.) Shir HaShirim 4:7. TB Pessahim 87a; Sukkah 45b; Sanhedrin 97b; Avodah Zarah 4b; Menahot 53b. Gen. R. 35:2. Exod. 7:4, 32:7; Exod. R. 41:12, 42:6 (Hos. 1:9, 2:1). Num. 2:16, 13. Zohar I, 95b; 105b; 216a; II, 106a; 190a; III, 234b. Rambam, *Hilkhot Teshuvah*, III, 5; *Iggeret Teiman*, pp. 128-29. Rashi on Ps. 72:8; Sanhedrin 44a; Avodah Zarah 22b. Ramban on Gen. 22:16; Deut. 9:4. Radak on Gen. 22:16. Alshekh on Gen. 15:7-8. Maharal, *Tiferet Yisrael*, 5; *Netsah Yisrael*, 11; *Derekh Hayyim*, p. 55; *Gevurot HaShem*, 3. R. Eliyahu of Vilna, *Aderet Eliyahu*, p. 483. *Or HaHayyim* on Lev. 26:11. *Noam Elimelekh, Devarim. Sefat Emet*, III, p. 13. Rav Kook, *Orot*, pp. 12, 63-64, 74, 144, 149, 183; *Hazon HaGeulah*, p. 104; *Orot HaKodesh*, III, p. 319; *Olat Reiyah*, II, p. 490; *Iggerot HaReiyah*, I, p. 369. *Mei Meirom*, V, p. 212; VI, pp. 12, 327, 329; VIII, pp. 79, 91, 94; *Missaviv LiShmonah Perakim LeHaRambam*, pp. 199-200. R. S.R. Hirsch on Exod. 32:13. *Meshekh Hokhmah*, p. 324. *Bet Avraham*, pp. 137, 235. *Lev Eliyahu*, p. 143. *Pahad Yitshak, Hanukah*, New York: 5724, p. 72. R. Yossef Rozin, Gaon of Rogachov, *Mefa'aneah Tsefunot*, pp. 180, 189, 239.

711. Cf. *Bet HaLevi*, I, p. 21 (Gen. 17:7); *Mei Meirom*, V, p. 241.

712. Cf. TB Berakhot 17a; Avodah Zarah 4b. Gen. R. 65:10. Shir HaShirim 1:5-6, 1:41. Yalkut Shim'oni, Shir HaShirim 4:988. Pesikta Zutarta, VaEthanan, Deut. 5:26. Zohar II, 107b. *Biur HaGra*, Zohar II, 119b; cf. B. Landau, *HaGaon HeHassid MiVilna*, pp. 187, 192. Cf. Rashi on Num. 23:21. Maharal, *Netsah Yisrael*, 11, 25; *Gevurot HaShem*, 8; *Netivot Olam*, II, *Netiv HaTeshuvah* 4; *Perushim LeAggadot*, II, p. 79; *Derashot, Derush LeShabbat Teshuvah*, pp. 30, 32. Isa. 1:18; Ps. 130:4; Eihah 1:17. *Or HaHayyim* on Lev. 13:2. *Bnei Issakhar*, I, p. 112a; II, p. 24a. R. Tsadok HaKohen of Lublin, *Dover Tsedek*, 19. *Sefat Emet*, V, p. 87. Rav Kook, *Orot*, pp. 74-76, 149, 154-55. *Mei Meirom*, V, p. 243; VI, pp. 11, 162-63; VII, p. 253. R. Abraham of Slonim, *Yessod HaAvodah*, p. 248; *Be'er Avraham*, pp. 214, 297. *Avnei Nezer*, p. 121. R. B.Z. Safran, *Doresh LeTsion*, p. 21.

713. Cf. Deut. 4:4. TB Gittin 57b; Pessahim 87a. Lev. R. 24:2. Deut. R. 2:23; Ps. 73:25. Eihah R. 3:19; Ps. 44:18. Tanhuma, Tetsaveh 1. Zohar I, 95b; 178a; III, 61a; 80b; 112a; 260b. Rashi on Yevamot 49b; Isa. 1:18. Ramban on Lev. 1:14. Maharal, *Derekh Hayyim*, p. 9; *Gevurot HaShem*, 8, 42; *Netivot Olam*, II,

Netiv Koah HaYetser, 4. Shelah, I, p. 21a; II, p. 44b; III, p. 200b. Moharan, *Siddur Sha'arei Ratson*, p. 206. Rav Kook, *Orot*, pp. 63-64, 142; *Shabbat HaArets*, p. 7; *Olat Reiyah*, I, p. 236. *Mei Meirom*, V, p. 212; VI, pp. 12, 329; VIII, p. 91; *Missaviv LiShmonah Perakim LeHaRambam*, p. 216. R. Abraham of Slonim, *Be'er Avraham*, p. 49; *Bet Avraham*, p. 163. R. B.Z. Safran, *Doresh LeTsion*, p. 35.

714. Cf. Zohar Hadash, 44b. Rambam, *Hilkhot Gerushin*, II, 20. HaGra, *Siddur Ishei Yisrael*, p. 21. *Tanya, Iggeret HaKodesh*, 18. *Kedushat Levi*, p. 47a. *Likkutei Moharan*, II, 78; *Moharan, Haggadah*, pp. 39, 53. *Sefat Emet*, I, pp. 62, 88, 103, 202, 210-11; III, pp. 13, 153, 157; V, pp. 9, 62, 88, 175. *Olat Reiyah*, II, pp. 254-55. *Mei Meirom*, V, p. 243; VIII, pp. 19, 118. *Avnei Nezer*, pp. 34, 125, 127. *Yessod HaAvodah*, pp. 164, 253; *Be'er Avraham*, p. 297. *Shem MiShemuel, Haggadah*, pp. 42-43. *Lev Eliyahu*, p. 145.

715. Cf. *Perushei Maharal LeAggadot HaShas*, IV, p. 27. Ramban on Deut. 32:32. *Tanya*, 32. R. Hayyim of Volozhin, *Nefesh HaHayyim*, 1:5.

716. Cf. S.A. Horodezki, *Religiöse Strömungen im Judentum*, Bern, Leipzig: 1920, p. 64.

717. Cf. Ps. 102:13-15. Isa. 66:13. TB Ketuvot 112a-b. *Shirei Yehuda HaLevi*, p. 194. Shelah, I, p. 168b. *Or HaHayyim* on Lev. 19:23. *Mei Meirom*, VI, p. 14.

718. Cf. TB Bava Kama 38a. See Rabbeinu Yona Gerondi on Avot IV, 17. See also Tossafot on Avodah Zarah 3a.

719. Cf. TY Nedarim IX, 4. Rav Kook, *Orot*, p. 149. Lev. 19:18; Deut. 6:5.

720. See above, pp. 30, 40.

721. See above, p. 13.

722. See above, p. 21.

723. Cf. TB Berakhot 6a (Deut. 6:4; I Chron. 17:21; II Sam. 7:23); Pessahim 118a. Gen. R. 38:6, 46:3, 77:1 (Gen. 32:25; Isa. 2:17). Zohar I, 164a. Maharal, *Gevurot HaShem*, 23; *Derekh Hayyim*, pp. 9, 245-46.

724. Cf. Esther R. 6; see TB Sanhedrin 106a.

725. Cf. Lev. 20:26 and Rashi ad loc. Yonathan Ben Uziel on Num. 23:9. See Tanhuma, Ki Teitsei 9. Maharal, *Gevurot HaShem*, 42. Bet HaLevi, II, pp. 3-6.

726. Cf. Num. 23:9; Isa. 49:6. Maharal, *Gevurot HaShem*, 23. Rav Kook, *Orot*, p. 152.

727. Cf. *Mei Meirom*, VI, pp. 28-29. See above, p. 35.

728. Cf. Maharal, *Derekh Hayyim*, pp. 172, 242ff. See also Rambam, *Moreh Nevukhim*, III, 24.

729. Cf. Gen. 14:13; Gen. R. 42:13. Pesikta Rabbati 33. See Rav Kook, *Orot*, p. 169.

730. Cf. Num. 23:9, Targum and Rashi ad loc. Deut. 32:12. See Jer. 30:11, 46:28. Sifrei 356 (Deut. 33:8). Gen. R. 42:13, 46:3, 77:1. Zohar III, 210b. Shelah, III, 201a; *Siddur Sha'ar HaShamayim*, p. 518. R. Dov Baer of Mezerich, *Maggid Devarav LeYa'akov*, 198. R. Yeruham HaLevi Levovitch, *Da'at Torah*, pp. 205-6.

731. Cf. Gen. R. 59:12; Hos. 12:8. Lev. R. 17:5. Num. R. 23:10. Tanhuma, Mass'ei 9. Targum Yonathan on Zech. 14:21.

732. Cf. Isa. 40:5.

733. Cf. Isa. 2:3; Mic. 4:2.

734. Cf. Deut. 11:12.
735. See below p. 48.
736. Cf. Jer. 42:2, 43:5 et al. Zohar II, 54a. Rav Harlap, *Mei Meirom*, VIII, p. 20. *Shem MiShemuel, Haggadah*, p. 43.
737. Cf. Gen. R. 2:7, 85:2; Jer. 29:11; Hag. 2:9. Cf. Maharal, *Be'er HaGolah*, 5. Shelah, III, p. 166a. *Tanya, Likkutei Amarim*, 36; *Iggeret HaKodesh*, 20. See *Tur, Orah Hayyim*, 292. *Mikhtav MeEliyahu*, I, p. 158. *Da'at Torah*, p. 5.
738. Cf. Gen. R. 1:8, 2:4, 2:5, 2:9, 85:2. Lev. R. 14:1. Pesikta Rabbati 35-37. Yalkut Shim'oni, Yeshaya 60:499. TB Pessahim 54a. Zohar I, 113a; 130b-131a; 192b; 203b; 240a; III, 34b. Zohar Hadash, Bereshit 5a; Ruth 88a. Tikkunei HaZohar, 26 (71b); 30 (73b). Cf. Rav Kook, *Orot*, pp. 27-30.
739. Cf. TB Haggigah 12a; Ta'anit 7b. Gen. R. 3:6, 11:2, 12:5. Num. R. 13:7. Tana Devei Eliyahu Zuta 21. Zohar I, 1a; 31b; II, 148b; III, 231b. Zohar Hadash, Ruth 85a. Meor Einaim, Tsav. *Degel Mahaneh Ephraim*, Bereshit.
740. Cf. Hida, *Nahal Kedumim*, Bereshit. Cf. Mic. 4:7; Zeph. 3:13. Lev. R. 35:4.
741. Cf. Gen. R. 3:6, 11:2, 12:5. Num. R. 13:7.
742. Cf. Gen. R. 63:10; Isa. 41:27. Cf. *Be'er Avraham*, pp. 299-300. See TY Berakhot II, 4.
743. Cf. TB Berakhot 12b; Shabbat 30b; Bava Batra 16b; 17a; Sanhedrin 97b. Maharal, *Derekh Hayyim*, p. 236; *Perushim LeAggadot*, III, p. 80. Shelah, III, p. 23a. *Orot HaKodesh*, III, p. 74; *Olat Reiyah*, II, p. 157. *Mei Meirom*, VI, pp. 14, 240. See Rambam, *Hilkhot Teshuvah*, VIII, 8.
744. Cf. TY Berakhot I, 1; Zohar I, 170a.
745. Sabbath Hymn: *Lekha Dodi*, by Rabbi Shelomo Alkabets (16th century). See R. Dov Baer of Mezerich, *Maggid Devarav LeYa'akov*, 79.
746. Cf. Zohar I, 86a; Isa. 41:4.
747. Isa. 46:9-10.
748. Cf. TB Sanhedrin 98a; Isa. 60:22. Cf. TY Ta'anit I, 1; Shir HaShirim R. *in fine*. Zohar I, 117b; 119a; II, 10a; III, 66b; 252a. Tikkunei HaZohar, 21 (55a). Tikkunei Zohar Hadash, 98b.
749. Isa. 41:4.
750. Cf. Lev. R. 36:4; Jer. 2:3. See Shelah, III, p. 9a.
751. Cf. Rashi on Gen. 1:1; Ps. 111:6. See *Mei Meirom*, VI, pp. 292-94.
752. Cf. Maharal, *Netsah Yisrael*, 39.
753. Maharal, *Gevurot HaShem*, 70. Shelah, III, pp. 26a, 29b, 166a. *Biurei HaGra Al Aggadot*, I, p. 59. *Be'er Mayim Hayyim* on Deut. 33:10.
754. Cf. Deut. 11:26, 26:16, 27:9. Mekhilta 18 (Exod. 13:11). Sifrei 33 (Deut. 6:6). Pesikta DeRav Kahana, 12. Pesikta Zutarta, VaEthanan, Deut. 6:6. TY Peyah II, 4. TB Berakhot 63b; Eruvin 54b; Kiddushin 30a. Gen. R. 97:5; Shir HaShirim R. 1:52. Tanhuma (Buber ed.), Yitro 13:10; Tanhuma, Ki Tavo 1. Lekah Tov, Ki Tavo. Zohar I, 4b; II, 79b; III, 179b; 216b. Rashi on Deut. 6:6, 26:16, 27:9. *Tur* and *Shulhan Arukh, Orah Hayyim*, 61. Shelah, III, 200b. *Kedushat Levi*, VaEthanan, p. 85b; Re'eh, pp. 88b-89a; Ki Tavo, p. 90b. *Moharan, Haggadah*, p. 42. *Degel Mahaneh Ephraim*, Eikev. *Bnei Issakhar*, I, p. 106a. *Sefat Emet*, III, p. 10; V, p. 20.
755. Cf. Avot VI, 2. Onkelos on Deut. 5:19. TB Sanhedrin 17a and Rashi ad loc. Zohar I, 224a; II, 5a; III, 52b; 127b. *Kedushat Levi*, Hayei Sarah, p. 12b; VaEthanan, p. 85b; Ki Tavo, p. 90b. *Degel Mahaneh Ephraim*, VaYikra. *Sefat*

Emet, V, pp. 20, 27, 35-37. *Neot HaDesheh*, p. 153. A. Safran, *La Cabale*, pp. 11ff., 110ff., 118ff.
756. Cf. Isa. 26:2. Lev. R. 5:7; Num. R. 11:1. Zohar I, 216a. Rashi on Ps. 72:7. Rambam, *Hilkhot Issurei Bi'a*, XIV, 4. *Noam Elimelekh, Devarim*. See Shir HaShirim R. 5:2.
757. See below, pp. 48, 54.
758. Cf. Gen. 44:26; Jer. 32. TY, Hallah II, 1. TB Berakhot 5b and Tossafot ad loc.; 8a; 17a; Ta'anit 30b; Bava Batra 60b; Horayot 10b. Gen. R. 77:1. Shoher Tov, 105. Sefer HaBahir, 5, p. 2. Zohar I, 10a; 114b; III, 301b. Zohar Hadash, 49b. Ramban on Deut. 11:22. R. Hayyim Vital, *Ets Hayyim, Hakdamah*, p. 1b. Maharal, *Gevurot HaShem*, 7; *Netsah Yisrael*, 10; *Derekh Hayyim*, pp. 93, 216; *Gur Aryeh*, Balak; *Netivot Olam*, I, *Netiv Gemilut Hassadim*, 1. Shelah, III, pp. 171b-172a; 174a; *Siddur Sha'ar HaShamayim*, p. 530. R. Hayyim of Volozhin, *Ruah Hayyim*, p. 1. *Meor Einaim*, Tsav. Rav Kook, *Mussar Avikha*, p. 101. Rav Harlap, *Mei Meirom*, VI, p. 14. R. Moshe Grossberg, *Tsefunot HaRogatchovi*, Jerusalem: 5736, p. 22. *Tossefet Berakhah*, I, p. 225.
759. Cf. Gen. 14:19. Isa. 42:5, 44:24, 45:7, 45:18. Ps. 115:15, 121:2, 124:8, 134:3. Eihah 3:23 and Targum ad loc. TB Berakhot 11b. Gen. R. 44:26, 49:6, 64:4. Zohar III, 216b. *Tanya, Sha'ar HaYihud VeHaEmunah*, 1, 2. *Kedushat Levi*, Bereshit, p. 1a; Re'eh, p. 88b. *Sefat Emet*, II, p. 87; III, p. 190; IV, p. 28. A. Safran, *La Cabale*, pp. 117-118.
760. Cf. Ps. 33:9, 119:89; Isa. 40:8. Shoher Tov, 119. *Tanya, Sha'ar HaYihud VeHaEmunah*, 1.
761. Cf. TY Rosh HaShanah IV, 8. Shoher Tov, 102. Yalkut Shim'oni, Pinhas 29:782. *Degel Mahaneh Ephraim*, Eikev.
762. Cf. Deut. 31:19. TB Berakhot 63b. Rambam, *Hilkhot Haggigah*, III, 6. Rashi on Deut. 26:16. Tossafot on Megillah 3a. *Shulhan Arukh, Orah Hayyim*, 61. Lekah Tov, Ki Tavo. *Sefat Emet*, IV, p. 175. *Avnei Nezer*, p. 99. *Shem MiShemuel, Shemot*, I, p. 242.
763. Cf. Prov. 3:17. Cf. *Sefat Emet*, IV, p. 175.
764. Cf. Deut. 4:2, 4:8. TB Berakhot 11b.
765. Cf. Deut. 26:17, 27:9 and Rashi ad loc. TY Yoma VIII, 1. TB Berakhot 6a; 63b and Maharsha ad loc.; Kiddushin 30a; see also TB Hullin 101b. Cf. Zohar III, 179b.
766. Cf. Lev. 14:34, 23:10. Num. 13:2, 15:2, 15:18. Deut. 4:1, 11:17, 16:20, 26:1, 27:3, 28:8, 32:49, 32:52. Ps. 147:2. Mekhilta 18 (Exod. 13:11). Sifrei 297 (Deut. 26:1). Zohar I, 172b; II, 79b. Maharsha on Menahot 87a. HaGra, *Siddur Ishei Yisrael*, p. 133. *Or HaHayyim* on Lev. 25:2. *Tanya, Iggeret HaKodesh*, 14. *Kedushat Levi*, Shelah, p. 74b. *Sefat Emet*, III, pp. 196, 202. *Mei Meirom*, VI, pp. 276, 282. A. Safran, *Orah Shel Yerushalayim*, in *Shanah BeShanah*, Jerusalem: 5738, pp. 192ff.
767. Cf. *Sefat Emet*, V, p. 178.
768. Cf. R. Abraham of Slonim, *Bet Avraham*, p. 274.
769. Cf. Exod. 15:2, 33:20. Lev. 26:12. Isa. 25:9, 30:20, 40:5, 52:8. Ps. 48:15, 102:17. Mekhilta 3 (Exod. 15:2), 9 (Exod. 20:18). TB Ta'anit 31a and Rashi ad loc.; Sanhedrin 102a. Exod. R. 21:3, 23:15. Num. R. 14:36, 20:19. Shir HaShirim R. 1:23. Kohelet R. 1:30. Tanhuma, Tsav 12; Bemidbar 17; Devarim 1. Shoher Tov, 13, 105. Zohar I, 115a; II, 5; 55b; 60a; 82a; 94a; III, 84a.

Kuzari, V, 23. Rashi on Exod. 15:2; Lev. 26:12; Num. 23:23. Ramban on Lev. 26:12. Maharal, *Derekh Hayyim*, p. 149. Shelah, III, pp. 11b, 118b. *Kedushat Levi*, p. 87b. *Likkutei Moharan*, 33:5.

770. Cf. Tikkunei Zohar Hadash, 95b.
771. Cf. Ps. 102:13-14. See also *Mei Meirom, Missaviv LiShemonah Perakim LeHaRambam*, p. 153.
772. Cf. Gen. R. 95:2; Exod. R. 21:3. Lev. R. 11:3; Isa. 58:4. Num. R. 19:4, 20:19. Kohelet R. 11:12. Tana Devei Eliyahu Zuta 20. Tanhuma, Ki Tavo 4. Yalkut Shim'oni, Yeshaya 54:479. Shoher Tov, 21 (Isa. 54:13). Zohar I, 118a; III, 23a. Rashi on Num. 23:23. Shelah, I, p. 96a; *Siddur Sha'ar HaShamayim*, p. 530. HaGra, *Aderet Eliyahu*, p. 483; B. Landau, *HaGaon HeHassid MiVilna*, p. 143. R. Hayyim of Volozhin, *Nefesh HaHayyim*, 4:21. R. Dov Baer of Mezerich, *Maggid Devarav LeYa'akov*, 5. *Likkutei Moharan*, 33:5. R. Moshe Hayyim Ephraim of Sudylkow, *Degel Mahaneh Ephraim*, Bereshit. Rav Kook, *Orot*, pp. 30, 84, 89, 90-91, 93, 96; *Hazon HaGeulah*, pp. 89, 115; *Orot HaKodesh*, III, pp. 116, 138. *Mei Meirom, Missaviv LiShmonah Perakim LeHaRambam*, pp. 214, 218-19. R. M.M. Kasher, *HaTekufah HaGedolah*, pp. 473, 486, 496, 506, 515. R. Y.H. Ashlag, *Matan Torah*, pp. 10-11, 133-35, 200. R. Yossef Hayyim of Baghdad, *Da'at UTevunah*, p. 72a.
773. Shelah, III, p. 26a. *Mei Meirom*, VI, pp. 234, 282; VIII, p. 68.
774. Cf. R. Abraham Hanokh Galitzenstein, *Rabbi Yisrael Ba'al Shem Tov*, p. 151.
775. Isa. 40:5. Cf. Massekhet Sofrim XIV, 2. Zohar I, 118a. Shelah, *Siddur Sha'ar HaShamayim*, p. 576.
776. Cf. Ps. 107:42. Or HaHayyim on Deut. 32:43.
777. Cf. Exod. 15:14. Cf. Isa. 52:15; Ps. 99:1. Mekhilta 9 (Exod. 15:14). Yalkut Shim'oni, Tehillim 99:852. Rambam, *Iggeret Teiman*, pp. 159-60, 181-82. Rashi on Num. 23:9. Ibn Ezra on Ps. 118:22. *Mei Meirom*, VI, pp. 186, 266-67.
778. Cf. TB Sanhedrin 91a.
779. Cf. Ps. 2:1-2, 83:3-8, 83:19. TB Avodah Zarah 3b. Tanhuma, Noah 18. Rashi on Num. 11:35. Ramban on Deut. 32:40. R. Hayyim Vital, *Hagahot*, Zohar II, 65b. Maharal, *Netsah Yisrael*, 38. *Be'er Avraham*, p. 223.
780. Cf. TB Bava Batra 74a. TY Rosh HaShanah III, 8. Tanhuma, Korah 11. Zohar III, 82b. *Sefer HaHinukh, Mitzvah* 603. *Likkutei Moharan*, 251.
781. Cf. Zech. 2:14.
782. Cf. Isa. 52:8. See *Mei Meirom*, VI, p. 275.
783. Cf. Isa. 62:4, Rashi and Radak ad loc.; see also Radak on Isa. 54:5. Cf. TB Berakhot 58b and Rashi ad loc.
784. Cf. TB Sanhedrin 97a; Isa. 59:15. See Maharal, *Netivot Olam*, I, *Netiv HaEmet*, 2.
786. Cf. Ps. 98:2. Num. R. 13:5. Rashi on Deut. 25:18; 32:43.
787. Cf. Exod. 17:8-16; Num. 24:20; Deut. 25:17-19. Jer. 2:3. TB Hullin 89a. Onkelos, Yonathan Ben Uziel, Rashi, Ramban and Ba'al HaTurim on Num. 24:20. Rashi on Exod. 17:14; Num. 21:1; Deut. 25:17. Ramban on Exod. 17:9. Exod. R. 3:17, 26:4. Num. R. 13:5. Tana Devei Eliyahu Rabba 24. Shoher Tov, 9. Tanhuma, Yitro 3; Ki Teitsei 9. Zohar I, 25a; 29a; II, 64-67;

194b; III, 160a; 199b; 240a. Zohar Hadash, 121a. Tikkunei HaZohar, 69a. *Sefer HaHinukh, Mitzvah* 603. Maharal, *Netsah Yisrael*, 10; 60; *Gevurot HaShem*, 42, 54. *Kedushat Levi*, Ki Tissa p. 56b. *Likkutei Moharan*, II, 19. Malbim on Deut. 25:18. *Sefat Emet*, V, pp. 6, 114. *She'eilot UTeshuvot Avnei Nezer, Orah Hayyim*, 508. *Orot,* pp. 74, 85. *Be'er Moshe, Shemot* I, Tel Aviv: 5726, pp. 489ff.; *Devarim*, II, Tel Aviv: 5730, pp. 816ff. *Dalyot Yehezkel*, pp. 274-75, 277-78.

788. Isa. 62:1.
789. Cf. Galatia.
790. Cf. Ta'anit 5a; Ps. 122:3. Cf. Rav Kook, *Orot*, pp. 22-24, 45-46, 168-71; *Orot HaKodesh*, II, pp. 391-92, 411.
791. Cf. Exod. R. 8:3; Ezek. 29:3. Zohar II, 67b.
792. Cf. TB Megillah 6a and Rashi ad loc. Rashi on Num. 20:1. *Sefer Hareidim*, 2 (*Mitzvot Lo Ta'asseh HaTeluyot BeErets-Yisrael*). Shelah, I, p. 169a.
793. Cf. Jer. 2:21, 10:10.
794. Mic. 7:20.
795. Cf. Isa. 40, 49:13, 51, 52:9-10 et al. Zech. 1:17. Ps. 102:14, 102:22. Tana Devei Eliyahu 20.
796. See above, p. 48.
797. See above, p. 27.
798. Cf. Jer. 31:1; Ps. 85:2. TB Makot 24a. Gen. R. 92:3. *Iggeret Teiman*, pp. 169-70. Rashi on Exod. 38:1; Deut. 32:40-43.
799. Cf. Exod. 19:2, Mekhilta (1) and Rashi ad loc. Pesikta DeRav Kahana, 12. Lev. R. 9:9. Tanhuma, Yitro 13. Zohar III, 84b; 176b. Ibn Ezra on Exod. 19:8. *Neot HaDesheh*, p. 67. *Avnei Nezer*, pp. 35, 39, 107, 115. *Be'er Avraham*, p. 176. *Mei Meirom*, VI, p. 237-38, 319. S.Y. Agnon, *Atem Reitem*, Jerusalem: 5718-19 (1959), p. 36.
800. Cf. Gen. R. 38:6, 65:16, 98:2. Exod. R. 1:35. Lev. R. 32:5. Num. R. 11:20. Deut. R. 5:10, 5:14. Tanhuma, Shoftim 18; Nitsavim 1. Tana Devei Eliyahu 24. Shoher Tov, 114. Massekhet Derekh Erets Zuta IX. Mishnah Uktsin III, 12. TB Keritot 6b; Yoma 9b. Zohar I, 76b; 171a; 200b; II, 58b. Maharal, *Netsah Yisrael*, 1; 10; 25; 53; *Gur Aryeh*, VaYehi. *Or HaHayyim* on Deut. 33:5. *Noam Elimelekh, Bereshit*. Rav Kook, *Orot*, p. 77; *Hazon HaGeulah*, p. 143. Rav B.Z. Safran, *Doresh LeTsion*, p. 5.
801. Cf. Deut. 6:4; I. Chron. 17:21; II Sam. 7:23. Cf. Jer. 31:19 and Rashi ad loc.; Hos. 4:17. Cf. Ps. 133. Cf. also Esther 3:8. Sifrei 42 (Num. 6:26), 346 (Deut. 33:5). Sifra, Shemini, Lev. 9:6, p. 43b. Avot III, 2-4. TY Megillah I, 9; Sanhedrin IV, 9; X, 1; TB Berakhot 6a; 8a; Pessahim 56a; Haggigah 3a; Sanhedrin 37a; 39a; 106a. Gen. R. 21:1, 21:5, 38:6, 77:1, 98:4. Lev. R. 4, 30:11; Num. R. 10, 11:16-17, 14, 15:14, 18:7, 23:6. Deut. R. 2:22-23, 2:25-26. Esther R. 6:2. Tana Devei Eliyahu Rabba 10. Pirkei DeRabbi Eliezer 48. Pesikta Zutarta, Eikev 11:9. Tanhuma, Mishpatim 17; Beha'alotkha 11; Korah 5; Shoftim 18. Yalkut Shim'oni, Shemini 9:521; Nasso 6:711; Zohar I, 13a; 48a; 76b; 164a; 200b; II, 16b; 116a; 119a; 126a; 160b; 216a; III, 7b; 81a; 93b; 96a; 128a; 262b-263a. Tikkunei HaZohar, 62b. Rambam, *Sefer HaMitzvot, Mitzvot Asseh, Mitzvah* 2; *Perush HaMishnah*, Sanhedrin X, XII; *Hilkhot Teshuvah*, III, 11; *Hilkhot Eivel*, I, 10. Rashi on Gen. 46:27; Num. 16:6; Jer. 31:19; Zeph. 3:9; Rosh HaShanah 29a; Menahot 27a. *Da'at Zekeinim*

MiBa'alei HaTossafot on Deut. 33:5. Ramban on Deut. 32:22, 33:5. *Siddur Rabbeinu Shelomo de Garmaise*, p. 226. R. Hayyim Vital, *Ta'amei HaMitzvot*, in *Likkutei Torah*, of Ari HaKadosh, Kedoshim, p. 77; *Sha'arei Kedushah*, 2:4. Alshekh on Nitsavim, Deut. 29:9. Maharal, *Netsah Yisrael*, 10, 38, 44; *Gevurot HaShem* 3, 23; *Gur Aryeh*, Balak; *Be'er HaGolah*, 3; *Netivot Olam*, I, *Netiv HaAvodah*, 1; *Netiv Gemilut Hassadim*, 1; *Netiv HaTsedakah*, 6; *Derekh Hayyim*, pp. 8-9, 42-43, 93, 140, 216. Shelah, I, pp. 21a-b-22a, 93a, 99a; III, pp. 201a, 205a; R. Eliyahu of Vilna, *Biurei HaGra Al Aggadot*, II, p. 61; *Siddur Ishei Yisrael*, p. 287. *Tanya*, 32, 41. *Kedushat Levi*, pp. 119b, 141b, 143. *Toldot Ya'akov Yossef*, Hayei Sarah. *Sefat Emet*, III, pp. 186, 188-89, 200; IV, pp. 44, 52; V, pp. 31, 33, 35-36, 66. *Meshekh Hokhmah*, pp. 178, 217, 255-56. *Orot*, pp. 55, 146. *Bet Avraham*, pp. 143, 150-51, 235, 261; *Be'er Avraham*, p. 259. *Hessed LeAvraham*, p. 120. *Siddur HaGeonim VeHaMekubalim*, III, p. 654. *HaMussar VeHaDa'at*, II, p. 134. Hafets Hayyim, *Shemirat HaLashon*, pp. 43-44. A. Safran, *Mussar VeHevrah BeIdan HaModerni*, p. 206ff.

802. Cf. II Sam. 7:23; Ps. 133:3. Zohar I, 205b; III, 93b. Maharal, *Netivot Olam*, I, *Netiv HaTsedakah*, 6; *Derashot*, p. 34. *Likkutei Moharan*, II, 40; *Kitvei Rabbi Nahman MiBratslav*, p. 287. *Sefat Emet*, III, pp. 191-92; IV, pp. 198-99. R. S.R. Hirsch on Ps. 133:1 (German ed., p. 256; Hebrew ed., p. 505). Rav Kook, *Orot*, pp. 10, 12, 44-45, 75, 163; *Orot HaKodesh*, I, p. 134; *Hazon HaGeulah*, pp. 98-99. *Mei Meirom*, VI, pp. 237-38, 302, 310. *Tsafnat Pa'aneah*, Makot 24a; Sanhedrin 43b. *Be'er Avraham*, p. 145. *Shem MiShemuel*, Bemidbar, p. 339. *She'eilot UTeshuvot Avnei Nezer*, *Orah Hayyim*, II, 314; *Yoreh Deyah*, I, 126.

803. Cf. TB Horayot 3a; Arakhin 29a; 32b; Berakhot 58a; Ta'anit 11b. Rambam, *Hilkhot Shemittah VeYovel*, X, 9; *Hilkhot Bikkurim*, V, 5; *Issurei Bi'a*, XX, 3. Ramban on Lev. 1:2. *Hatam Sofer*, Sukkah 36. Rabbi Nahman of Bratslav, *Likkutei Tefillot*, I, 84; II, 29. *Sefat Emet*, V, p. 12. Rav Kook, *Orot*, p. 166; *Olat Reiyah*, I, pp. 387-88; *Mishpat Kohen*, 124; 144. Rabbi Yossef Rozin, Gaon of Rogachov, *Pa'aneah Tsefunot*, p. 179.

804. Cf. Rav Kook, *Orot*, p. 45 See above, p. 50.

805. Cf. TY Sanhedrin X, 2. TB Shevuot 39a. Maharal, *Gevurot HaShem*, 61. *Kuzari*, III, 17. *Orot*, pp. 146, 157; *Iggerot HaReiyah*, I, p. 369; II, pp. 186-87. *Shiurei Da'at*, II, p. 242. *Ben Ish Hai*, pp. 153-55.

806. Cf. Lev. 25:23 and Sifra ad loc. Tanhuma, Bemidbar 17 (Joel 4:2). Zohar I, 145a. Ramban on Lev. 18:25. *Sefat Emet*, III, p. 196. *Bet Avraham*, p. 261.

807. Cf. I Sam. 8:20; Ezek. 20:32, 25:8.

808. See above, p. 000.

809. Cf. Lev. 20:24; Deut. 11:10, Sifrei (35) and Ramban ad loc., 11:13-14.

810. Cf. I Sam. 26:19. Ezek. 38:15-16; Joel 4:2; cf. also Jer. 21:7; Ezek. 36:5; Joel 1:6. Mekhilta 10 (Exod. 15:17).

811. Cf. Lev. 20:22, 20:24. Cf. Lev. 19:23, 23:10, 25:2, and Sifra ad loc. Maharal, *Perushim LeAggadot HaShas*, IV, p. 103. *Netivot Olam* I, *Netiv HaAvodah*, 18; *Tiferet Yisrael*, 64; *Gevurot HaShem*, 8. HaGra, *Siddur Ishei Yisrael*, p. 287.

812. Cf. Deut. 27:2-3, 27:8. TB Sotah 32a; Sanhedrin 91a and Maharsha ad loc. TY Shevi'it VI, 1. Tana Devei Eliyahu Rabba 14. *Kedushat Levi*, Mass'ei, p. 82a;

KiTavo, p. 90b. *Sefat Emet*, V, p. 8. *Mei Meirom*, VI, pp. 292-93.
813. Cf. Gen. R. 1:3, 61:6. Tanhuma Yashan, Bereshit 1, 11. Rashi on Gen. 1:1. See Mekhilta 18 (Exod. 13:11).
814. Cf. Yalkut Shim'oni, Kedoshim 19:615. See also Sifra 11 (Lev. 20:24). Rashi on Gen. 12:6 (Gen. 12:7, 14:18). Ramban on Gen. 10:5, 11:28. Rashbam on Bava Batra 119a. See Ezek. 28:25, 33:24. Jer. 7:7. TB Bava Kama 119a; Avodah Zarah 53b; Bava Batra 100a. Tossafot on Yevamot 82b.
815. See Num. 13:31, 14:11. Deut. 1:28-32, 9:23. Ps. 37:3, 37:34, 106:24. Isa. 57:13. TB Shabbat 119b; Ketuvot 110b. Exod. R. 23. Num. R. 16:3, 16:6, 16:9, 16:12, 23:5. Maharal, *Netivot Olam*, I, *Netiv HaEmunah*, 2. Rabbi Nahman of Bratslav, *Likkutei Moharan*, 7, 129, 155; *Likkutei Tefillot*, I, 84. Rav Kook, *Orot*, p. 163; *Hazon HaGeulah*, pp. 36, 47, 294, 302.
816. Cf. Isa. 51:16. Ps. 24:1, 134:3. TB Yoma 54b. Zohar I, 186a; II, 39b; III, 103b. Ramban on Gen. 10:15. Maharal, *Netivot Olam*, I, *Netiv HaAvodah*, 5; *Gevurot HaShem*, 8. HaGra, *Siddur Ishei Yisrael* (*Siah Yitshak*), p. 44. *Likkutei Moharan*, II, 8. Rav Kook, *Orot*, pp. 24, 165; *Olat Reiyah*, I, pp. 203-4.
817. Cf. Mekhilta 18 (Exod. 13:11). Sifra 11 (Lev. 20:24). Sifrei 311 (Deut. 32:8). TY Shevi'it VI, 1. TB Sanhedrin 91a; 94a; Tamid 32a. Lev. R. 17:6. Tanhuma, Kedoshim 12; Re'eh 8. Yalkut Shim'oni, Bo 13:222; Beshalah 17:268; Kedoshim 19:615 (Shir HaShirim 6:8-9); Yirmiah 3:270; Tehillim 32:719. Zohar I, 177a. *Kuzari*, II, 16. Ramban on Gen. 10:5, 10:15, 14:18; Num. 20:19; *Perush LeShir HaShirim* (*Kitvei Ramban* II), p. 512. Recanati, Noah, p. 20b; VaYeitsei, p. 29a. Maharal, *Netsah Yisrael*, 1. Hatam Sofer, Va'era. *Da'at Torah*, p. 159. *Mikhtav MeEliyahu*, III, p. 200.
818. Cf. Ramban on Num. 25:18, 33:53; Deut. 2:10, 2:23, 23:7. See also Ramban on Gen. 26:20; Deut. 12:20, 19:8; *Sefer HaGeulah* (*Kitvei Ramban* I), pp. 264, 277. Rambam, *Hilkhot Rotseah UShemirat Nafesh*, VIII, 4 (Deut. 12:20, 19:8, 30:5); *Hilkhot Melakhim*, XI, 2.
819. Cf. Sifrei 51 (Deut. 11:24). TB Gittin 8a-b (Rashi and Tossafot ad loc.); 47a. Tossafot on Avodah Zarah 21a. Rambam, *Hilkhot Terumot*, I, 2-3; *Perush HaMishnah*, Demai VI, 11. See TY Hallah II, 1. Rambam, *Hilkhot Melakhim*, V, 6. Ramban on Deut. 11:24. Tanhuma, Matot 5. See Gen. 15:18. Num. 34. II Kings 14:25. TY Shevi'it III, 1; VI, 1; Hallah II, 1; IV; Megillah I, 1; Kiddushin I, 8. TB Gittin 44b; Bava Batra 56a; Sanhedrin 5a; Bekhorot 55. Lev. R. 5:3. Tossefta, Ma'asser Sheini II; Gittin I; Bava Kama VIII. Rambam, *Hilkhot Sanhedrin*, IV, 6; *Hilkhot Terumot*, I, 5. Cf. Rabbi Yossef Rozin, Gaon of Rogachov, *Tsafnat Pa'aneah*, Bereshit, pp. 58, 62.
820. See Sifrei 51 (Deut. 11:24); Ramban on Deut. 11:24. See Mishnah Ohalot XVIII, 7; TB Ta'anit 10a; Targum and Ibn Ezra on Job 5:10.
821. Cf. Gen. 15:18, 15:21. Deut. 7:1. Rashi on Deut. 18:2. TB Bava Batra 56a and Rashbam ad loc. Ramban on Exod. 13:5; Deut. 18:1. Mekhilta 75 (Exod. 12:25), 184 (Deut. 19:8). TY Shevi'it VI, 1; Kiddushin I, 8. Gen. R. 44:27; Deut. R. 4:8. Rashi on Gen. 15:19. Ramban on Gen. 26:20; Deut. 2:23, 12:20, 19:8-9. Rambam, *Hilkhot Melakhim*, XI, 2; *Rotseah UShemirat Nafesh*, VIII, 4. Zohar I, 141b. Malbim on Deut. 1:7.
822. Cf. TB Pessahim 50a; Bava Batra 75a-b. Exod. R. 23; Shir HaShirim R. 7:10. Avot DeRabbi Nathan 35. Tanhuma, Tsav 12. Yalkut Shim'oni, Yeshaya

49:472, 60:503; Zekharya 9:575. Zohar I, 84b; III, 56a; 220a. Rabbeinu Sa'adya Gaon, *Emunot VeDe'ot*, VIII. Rambam, *Iggeret Teiman*, p. 181 (Isa. 18:2, 18:7). Rabbi Nahman of Bratslav, *Likkutei Moharan*, I, 47; II, 8, 10; *Likkutei Tefillot*, I, 84; II, 29. Rabbi Y.H. Ashlag, *Hakdamat Ets Hayyim*, p. 2. A. Safran, *La Cabale*, pp. 342-43.

823. Cf. Mic. 4:1-2. Isa. 2:2-3, 60:3. Sifrei 23 (Deut. 1:25), 37 (Deut. 11:10), 152 (Deut. 17:8). TY Berakhot IV, 4. TB Kiddushin 69b; Sanhedrin 87a; Zevahim 54b. Shir HaShirim R. 1:21. Avot DeRabbi Nathan 35:9. Yalkut Shim'oni, Mishlei 8:943. Zohar III, 10a. Rashi on Gen. 45:9; Exod. 33:1. Ramban, *Torat HaAdam* (*Kitvei Ramban* II), p. 296. Radak on Ezek. 38:12. Maharal, *Tiferet Yisrael*, 64. Maharsha and *Hafla'ah* (II, p. 158a) on Kiddushin 69a. *Mei Meirom*, VI, 254. See also Deut. 4:7, 26:19. *Sefat Emet*, V, p. 90.

824. Cf. Deut. 1:21, 9:23, 11:31, 12:29. Ramban on Num. 35:53; Deut. 11:24; *Kitvei Ramban* I, *Derashah Al Divrei Kohelet*, p. 204; *Derashah LeRosh HaShanah*, p. 251; *Hassagot LeSefer HaMitzvot, Essin, Mitzvah* 4, *Hossafot*. See also R. Yitshak de Leon, *Sefer Megillat Esther* ad loc. Cf. Sifra on Lev. 25. Sifrei 80 (Deut. 12:29). TY Bikkurim III, 3. TB Ketuvot 110-11; Gittin 76b; Yevamot 64a and Rashi, Ramban and Rashba ad loc.; Bava Batra 91a-b and Rashbam ad loc.; Avodah Zarah 13a. Tossefta, Avodah Zarah V. Tossafot on Nazir 54b. Rambam, *Hilkhot Ishut*, XIII, 19-20; *Hilkhot Melakhim*, V, 9; 11. *Shulhan Arukh, Even HaEzer*, 75. *She'eilot UTeshuvot Maharit*, II, *Yoreh Deyah*, 28. Zohar I, 205b. Zohar Hadash, 44a. See also TY Berakhot III, 1. TB Eruvin 47a; Ketuvot 111a. Tossafot on Ketuvot 110b; Avodah Zarah 13a; Nazir 54b. Cf. *Or HaHayyim* on Deut. 30:20; see also *Or HaHayyim* on Num. 33:53. Cf. R. Eliyahu of Vilna, *Aderet Eliyahu*, p. 426. *She'eilot UTeshuvot Avnei Nezer, Yoreh Deyah*, 454. Cf. Sifrei 8 (Deut. 1:8). TY Sotah VIII, 4; Bava Kama IXa. TB Bava Metsia 101a; Bava Batra 14a; Sanhedrin 102b; Menahot 44a. Gen. R. 38:8, 64:3, 79:7. Lev. R. 25:3. Tanhuma, Re'eh 11. Rambam, *Hilkhot Tefillin*, V, 10. *Shulhan Arukh, Yoreh Deyah*, 286:22. Hatam Sofer on Sukkah 36. Cf. Sifrei 51 (Deut. 11:24). Mishnah Shevi'it VI, 1; Kelim I, 6. TY Demai VII, 2. TB Shevuot 16a; Gittin 47a; Sotah 44b; Bava Batra 100a; 119a; Avodah Zarah 53b; Arakhin 32b. Gen. R. 41:6. Rambam, *Hilkhot Terumot*, I, 2; 5-6; *Hilkhot Bet HaBehirah*, VI, 16; *Hilkhot Melakhim*, V, 1; 6. Rashi on Lev. 20:2; Sanhedrin 2a; Niddah 46b. Ramban on Lev. 18:25; Num. 33:53; Bava Batra 56a. *Hazon Ish*, Shevi'it 3:1. R. B.Z. Safran, *Doresh LeTsion*, 6.

825. Cf. TB Makot 23b. *Aderet Eliyahu*, pp. 393, 428. *Orot*, pp. 76, 144; *Olat Reiyah*, II, p. 157. *Pahad Yitshak, Hanukah*, pp. 71-72; *Pessah*, New York: 5730, pp. 68-69. See Gen. R. 70:8; Deut. R. 7:9. Zohar I, 2b.

826. Cf. Lev. 25:23 and Rashi ad loc. Ps. 44:4. Onkelos on Gen. 48:22. Mekhilta 3 (Exod. 15:2). Sifrei 89 (Num. 11:9). TB Pessahim 8b; Zevahim 116a. Gen. R. 39:10, 79:7 (Gen. 23:16, 33:19; I Chron. 21:25); Lev. R. 35:7. Num. R. 22:6. Tanhuma, Kedoshim 12; Re'eh 8. Zohar II, 58a; 94a. Ramban on Deut. 20:1. Tossafot on Shabbat 63a. Ibn Ezra on Gen. 33:19. Maharal, *Gevurot HaShem*, 47. Maharsha on Bava Batra 123a. See also TB Haggigah 5b; Sanhedrin 99a. Rambam, *Hakdamah LePerek Helek; Hilkhot Melakhim*, XII, 3, 4. Rashi on Sanhedrin 91b. Cf. Rambam, *Hilkhot Teshuvah*, IX, 1; Shelah, III, p. 171b. HaGra, *Siddur Ishei Yisrael*, pp. 48, 331. *Kedushat Levi, Mass'ei*, p.

82. *Sefat Emet*, III, p. 196. Rav Kook, *Orot*, pp. 9, 14, 52, 58-60. R. Yehoshua of Kutna, *She'eilot UTeshuvot Yeshuot Malko*, 66.
827. Cf. Gen. 13:17, Targum Yonathan Ben Uziel and Rabbeinu Bahya ad loc. See Gen. 13:15. Cf. Ps. 48:13. TY Kiddushin I, 3. TB Ketuvot 11a; Bava Batra 100a; 119a and Rashbam ad loc.; 158b. See Ramban on Gen. 13:17, 15:18. *Or HaHayyim* on Gen. 13:15, 13:17.
828. Cf. Gen. 13:14; Deut. 34:1, 34:4. Cf. Sifrei 134 (Num. 27:12). Num. R. 23:4. See also Num. 27:12-13. Deut. 3:27, 32:49. Cf. *Sefat Emet*, V, p. 26.
829. See above, p. 11.
830. See above, p. 30.
831. Cf. Deut. 2:26, 20:10. Sifrei 157 (Num. 31:7). TY Shevi'it VI, 1. Lev. R. 17:6. See Deut. R. 5:14; TB Gittin 45a. Rambam, *Hilkhot Melakhim*, VI, 1; 5; 7. Ramban on Deut. 2:34, 20:10. Rashi and Ramban on Num. 21:21; see also Ramban on Deut. 23:7; Rambam, *Hilkhot Melakhim*, VI, 4. See also Sifrei 202 (Num. 20:18); TB Sotah 35b; Rashi on Deut. 20:18. See Tossefta Sotah VIII, 7.
832. Cf. Gen. 15:13-16; Gen. R. 1:3; Tanhuma Yashan, Bereshit 1,11. Ramban on Gen. 1:1, 9:26, 10:5, 12:6, 15:16; Exod. 3:8; Deut. 2:23, 9:4, 12:20, 19:8. *Perushei HaTorah LeRabbi Yehuda HeHassid*, p. 18. *Ha'amek Davar* on Deut. 9:5.
833. Cf. TY Hallah II, 1. TB Yoma 54a; Rosh HaShanah 16b and Rashi ad loc.; Moed Katan 25a and Rashi ad loc. Tanhuma, Bemidbar 17; Re'eh 8 (Deut. 11:12). Pirkei DeRabbi Eliezer 18. Zohar I, 186a; II, 157a. Rashi on Jon. 1:3. *Kuzari*, II, 14. Rambam, *Hilkhot Terumot*, I, 2; Rashi on Lev. 20:2. Ramban on Gen. 33:20; *Hashmatot*, Gittin 2. *Kaftor VaFerah*, 10. *She'eilot UTeshuvot Tashbatz*, III, 60; *She'eilot UTeshuvot Maharit*, Yoreh Deyah, 28. Maharal, *Derekh Hayyim*, pp. 188-89, 207, 252. *She'eilot UTeshuvot Hatam Sofer*, Yoreh Deyah, 234. *Bnei Issakhar*, I, p. 22a. *Likkutei Moharan*, II, 40. Rav Kook, *Orot*, pp. 12-13, 62, 77, 171; *Orot HaKodesh*, I, p. 134; II, p. 303. *Mei Meirom*, V, p. 207; VI, p. 290. *She'eilot UTeshuvot Yeshuot Malko*, Yoreh Deyah, 67. R. Abraham of Slonim, *Bet Avraham*, p. 146. Hazon Ish on Zeraim 3, 19; but see also Tossafot on Gittin 2a. R. B.Z. Safran, *Doresh LeTsion*.
834. Cf. Lev. 18, 19:2 and Sifra ad loc., 19:25. Deut. 24:4. Sifrei 110 (Deut. 14:29); 188 (Deut. 19:14). Mishnah Eduyot VIII, 6 and Rambam ad loc.; Kelim I, 6. TB Shabbat 33a; Rosh HaShanah 8b-9b; 13a; Haggigah 3b; Yevamot 6b and Tossafot ad loc. (I Sam. 2:2); 82b and Tossafot Yashanim ad loc.; Kiddushin 30b; Shevuot 16a. Num. R. 7:8. *Kuzari*, II, 9; 14; III, 19. Rashi on Bava Metsia 89a; Arakhin 32b. Rambam, *Hilkhot Terumot*, 1, 5; *Hilkhot Bet HaBehirah*, VI, 16; VII, 12. Ramban, *Hakdamah* to Leviticus; Lev. 18:25, 26:42; *Derashah LeRosh HaShanah* (*Kitvei Ramban* I), pp. 250-51. Maharal, *Netsah Yisrael*, 6; *Gevurot HaShem*, 8; *Netivot Olam*, I, *Netiv HaTorah*, 10; *Netiv HaAvodah* 17; *Derekh Hayyim*, pp. 188-90, 206-7; *Perushim LeAggadot*, IV, p. 103-4. *Sefat Emet*, IV, p. 119. *Orot*, p. 160; *Olat Reiyah*, I, pp. 105, 236; *Iggrot HaReiyah*, II, p. 186. *Mei Meirom*, VI, p. 314; VIII, p. 74. *Mikhtav MeEliyahu*, III, p. 194.
835. Cf. Deut. 11:9, 11:21, 32:43. Mic. 4:2. Isa. 2:3, 26:19. Ps. 102. Mekhilta 1 (Exod. 12:1). Sifrei 37 (Deut. 11:10). Avot V, 5. Avot DeRabbi Nathan 26:2,

35:8. TY Shekalim III *in fine*; Nedarim VI, 8; Ketuvot XII, 3; see also Kilaim IX, 4. TB Berakhot 8a; 44a; 63b; Shabbat 138b; Yoma 21a; Rosh HaShanah 16b; Moed Katan 25a and Rashi ad loc.; Yevamot 64a and Rashi, Ramban and Rashba ad loc.; Ketuvot 110-12 and *Meiri in fine*; Gittin 57a; Bava Batra 158b and Rashbam ad loc.; Sanhedrin 14a; 98a; Makot 7a; Arakhin 32b. Targum and Tanhuma, VaYehi 3. Pirkei DeRabbi Eliezer 8, 33. Shoher Tov, 91. Yalkut Shim'oni, Yeshaya 1:390, 42:451; Yehezkel 20:358; Yonah 1:549; Tehillim 85:833. Zohar I, 79b; 141a; 166a; 205b; II, 4a; 141a; 151b-152a; III, 4b; 72b; 84a; 245b; 266b. Tikkunei HaZohar, 22 (64a). Zohar Hadash, VaYeitsei 28:4. *Kuzari*, II, 14; *Shirei Rabbi Yehuda HaLevi*, p. 233. Rashi on Jon. 1:3; Bava Batra 15a; Sanhedrin 90b. Rambam, *Perush HaMishnah*, Sanhedrin I; *Sefer HaMitzvot, Mitzvot Asseh, Mitzvah* 153; *Hilkhot Kiddush HaHodesh*, I, 5:1; 8 et al.; *Hilkhot Sanhedrin*, IV, 11; *Hilkhot Melakhim*, V, 10-11. Ramban on Gen. 28:21; Deut. 4:28; *Derashah LeRosh HaShanah* (*Kitvei Ramban* I), pp. 249-51. Radak on Jon. 1:2. *Bah, Tur, Orah Hayyim*, 208. *Shulhan Arukh, Yoreh Deyah*, 363, 1-2. Maharal, *Gevurot HaShem*, 8, 24; *Perushim LeAggadot*, I, p. 97; IV, p. 103; *Derekh Hayyim*, pp. 207-8; *Netivot Olam*, I, *Netiv HaTorah*, 10; *Netiv HaAvodah*, 18. Shelah, I, pp. 168a-b; III, pp. 23a; 171b. *She'eilot UTeshuvot Hatam Sofer, Yoreh Deyah*, 233-34. *Likkutei Moharan*, I, 7a; 152; II, 11; 40. *Kitvei Rabbi Nahman MiBratslav*, pp. 192-94; 287. Rav Kook, *Orot*, pp. 9, 171; *Orot HaKodesh*, I, pp. 133, 236; III, p. 200; *Iggrot HaReiyah*, I, pp. 112-13. *Mei Meirom*, VI, pp. 233-36, 281; VIII, pp. 67-68. *Yessod HaAvodah*, II, p. 101. *Avnei Nezer*, p. 113. *Mikhtav MeEliyahu*, III, pp. 191-96.

836. Cf. Lev. 18:25, 18:30. Num. 35:33-34. Deut. 21:23, 24:4. Sifrei 38 (Deut. 11:10). TY Shekalim IV, 1. Tanhuma, Kedoshim 9; Behar 1. Rashi and Ramban on Gen. 1:1. Rambam, *Hilkhot Terumot*, I, 5; *Hilkhot Bet HaBehirah*, VII, 12. Ramban on Gen. 19:5; Lev. 18:25. *Sefer Yereim*, 249. HaGra on Kelim I, 6. *Kedushat Levi*, VaYigash, p. 25b. *Bnei Issakhar*, I, p. 11b. *Avodat Yisrael*, p. 205. *Mei Meirom*, VI, p. 314. R. J. Schepanski, *Erets-Yisrael BeSifrut HaTeshuvot*, II, pp. 87, 101.

837. Cf. TB Ta'anit 29a. Avot DeRabbi Nathan 4, 8. Zohar I, 202b. See Tanhuma, Pekkudei 1.

838. Cf. Mishnah Shekalim VI, 1-2. TB Yoma 53b; Ta'anit 5a. Tanhuma (Buber ed.), Shemot 10. Zohar I, 1b; II, 240b. *Shirei Rabbi Yehuda HaLevi*, p. 233. II Macc. 2:4-7.

839. Cf. Isa. 30:18; Zeph. 2:1. Mishnah Ta'anit IV, 8; Tamid VII, 3; see also Avot V, 20; 23. TB Shabbat 31a; Sukkah 41a; Ta'anit 17a and Rashi ad loc.; 30b; Megillah 15b; 29a; Ketuvot 75a; Bava Batra 60b; Sanhedrin 97b; 98a; Hullin 91b. Eihah R. 3:19. Targum Yonathan Ben Uziel on Gen. 49:18. Tana Devei Eliyahu Rabba 4; Tana Devei Eliyahu Zuta 17. Pesikta DeRav Kahana, Beshalah 87:2. Pirkei DeRabbi Eliezer 26. Zohar I, 99b-100a (Megillah 19a); 130b; 211b; II, 225a; III, 278b (Gen. 47:1, 47:27). *Emunot VeDeot* V, 3. *Kuzari*, V, 27. Rambam, *Hilkhot Melakhim*, XI, 1; see also *Moreh Nevukhim*, III, 47. Rashi on Gen. 28:17; Hullin 91b; see also *Sefer HaHinukh, Mitzvah* 184. Meiri on Ketuvot 111a. Maharal, *Tiferet Yisrael*, 5; *Netsah Yisrael*, 8, 29; *Netivot Olam*, I, *Netiv Gemilut Hassadim*, 1. Shelah, I, pp. 168b-169a; 175b; *Siddur Sha'ar HaShamayim*, p. 520. Maharsha on Berakhot 8a; Sotah 14a. *Or*

HaHayyim on Lev. 25:22. *Maggid Devarav LeYa'akov,* 77, 85, 132. *Degel Mahaneh Ephraim,* Bereshit. *Bnei Issakhar,* I, p. 111. R. Nahman of Bratslav, *Likkutei Moharan,* I, 55b; II, 5; 15; 40; 76; *Likkutei Tefillot,* I, 84; II, 29; *Siddur Sha'arei Ratson,* p. 480; *Shivhei Moharan,* II, p. 6. Rabbi Zadok HaKohen of Lublin, *Tsidkat HaTsaddik,* p. 144; *Sefat Emet,* V, p. 5. Rav Kook, *Orot,* pp. 9-13, 57-60, 62; *Shabbat HaArets,* p. 12; *Mussar Avikha,* p. 19; *Olat Reiyah,* I, pp. 279, 381; *Orot HaKodesh,* I, p. 133; III, p. 295. *Mei Meirom,* V, pp. 84-85; VI, pp. 11, 59, 87, 187, 240-41, 253-54, 276-77, 301, 313. *Kol Kitvei H. N. Bialik,* Tel-Aviv: 5709 (1949), pp. 1-2. R. A. H. Galitzenstein, *Rabbi Yisrael Ba'al Shem Tov,* p. 159. *Meshekh Hokhmah,* p. 317. *Siddur HaGeonim VeHaMekubalim,* III, p. 609. R. Abraham of Sochaczew, *Avnei Nezer,* pp. 21, 88 (Mishnah Eruvin IV, 7; TB Eruvin 49b); *Neot HaDesheh,* pp. 105, 124. *Shem MiShemuel, Haggadah,* p. 41. R. Yossef Hayyim of Baghdad, *Ben Ish Hai,* pp. 59, 63; *Od Yossef Hai,* pp. 112-13. *VaYoel Moshe,* pp. 340-41. *Mefa'aneah Tsefunot,* p. 121.

840. Cf. Lev. 26:42. Deut. 8:10-11, 25:19, 32:18-21. Ps. 102:13-14, 137:4-6. Eihah 1:7. Mekhilta 6 (Exod. 20:3); Sifrei 43 (Deut. 11:16-17), 320 (Deut. 32:21). Mishnah Rosh HaShanah IV, 1-4; Sukkah III, 12; Sotah IX, 15. TY Kiddushin IV, 1. TB Pessahim 114b-115a; Sukkah 41a-b; Rosh HaShanah 30a-b; 31b; Gittin 7a; Sotah 49a-b; Menahot 43b; 66a; Bava Batra 60b. Tossefta Sotah *in fine*; Bava Batra II. Massekhet Sofrim XIX. Num. R. 17:7; Eihah R. 1:54. Tanhuma, Shelah 15. Pesikta Rabbati 30; Pesikta Zutarta, Beshalah 16; Shelah 155. Pirkei DeRabbi Eliezer 17. Yalkut Shim'oni, Tehillim 137:885. Zohar II, 157b. *Kuzari,* V, 27. Rambam, *Hilkhot Ta'anit,* V, 1; 12-15 (Deut. 11:7; Jer. 31:20; cf. Eihah 3:38-39). Rashi on Deut. 11:18; Ramban on Lev. 18:25. *Shulhan Arukh, Orah Hayyim,* 560; *Yoreh Deyah,* 65:3. *Kitvei Rabbi Nahman MiBratslav,* p. 193. *Sefat Emet,* V, p. 5. Rav Kook, *Orot,* pp. 9, 11, 57; *Hazon HaGeulah,* p. 101. *Mei Meirom,* VI, p. 277. Rav S. Goren, *Sefer HaMoadim,* Tel-Aviv: 5724, pp. 443-47. R. Yossef Hayyim of Baghdad, *Ben Yehoyada,* II, p. 78b; *Ben Ish Hai,* p. 63.

841. Cf. Shoher Tov, 121 (Ps. 137:5-6). See Mishnah Ta'anit IV, 8; Avot V, 20; Tamid VII, 3. TB Ta'anit 27b. Exod. R. 30:21; Num. R. 18:21. Tanhuma, Ahrei 12. Shoher Tov, 13. Zohar I, 210b; 266b; II, 557b; III, 203b. *Kitvei Ramban* II, p. 324-25. *Kitvei Rabbi Nahman MiBratslav,* pp. 194, 287 (Ps. 37:34). *Moharan, Likkutei Tefillot,* I, 84; II, 29. *Mei Meirom,* VI, p. 301. *Siddur HaGeonim VeHaMekubalim,* III, pp. 510, 778.

842. Cf. Rashi on Ketuvot 8a; cf. Ps. 137:6. Cf. Isa. 33:10-11; 54:1; cf. also Jer. 7:34; see Rambam, *Hilkhot Berakhot,* II, 11. Cf. TB Berakhot 6b; Ta'anit 30b; Bava Batra 60b. Pesikta Rabbati 29:3. Zohar II, 55b. Cf. Isa. 61:2-3; *Shulhan Arukh, Even HaEzer,* 65:3; see Tossafot on Berakhot 31a. Ish Shuv (initials of Avraham Yitshak Shperling. Shohet U'Vodek), *Ta'amei Ha-Minhagim,* Jerusalem: n.d., p. 412.

843. Cf. Isa. 61:3, 66:10-13. Jer. 13:17. Ps. 79, 119:62, 137. Sifrei 80 (Deut. 12). TY Kilaim IX, 4; Berakhot IV, 3; Ta'anit II, 2; Ketuvot V *in fine*. TB Berakhot 3b; 58b; Ta'anit 26b; 30a-b; Haggigah 16b; Moed Katan 26a; Ketuvot 67a; Gittin 57a; Bava Kama 59a; Bava Batra 60b; Sanhedrin 37b; 104b; Makot 5b; 24b. Tossefta Sotah XV. Eihah R. Petihta 7; Eihah R. 1:25, 1:50, 4:11. Shoher Tov, 22. Zohar I, 38b; 85b; 210b; 215a; III, 118a. Rambam, *Hilkhot Ta'anit,*

V, 9; 14; 16. *Or Zarua*, II, 419. *Bet Yossef, Tur, Shulhan Arukh, Orah Hayyim*, 554, 557, 559, 561, 580. *Shulhan Arukh, Orah Hayyim*, 1:3; *Yoreh Deyah* 363:1 and *Rema* ad loc., 379:2. R. Hayyim Vital, *Peri Ets Hayyim*, pp. 55-58. Shelah, I, pp. 209a-b, 210a; *Siddur Sha'ar HaShamayim*, p. 7. Maharsha on Berakhot 5b. R. Nahman of Bratslav, *Siddur Sha'arei Ratson*, pp. 48, 54. *Siddur HaGeonim VeHaMekubalim*, III, p. 606.

844. Cf. Zohar III, 11b.
845. Cf. Deut. 32:43, Rashi and *Or HaHayyim* ad loc. Isa. 60:3, 61:5-9, 62:2ff. TB Avodah Zarah 3a. Gen. R. 62:6; Exod. R. 35:5. Pesikta Zutarta, VaYehi 49:10. Shoher Tov, 87, 98. Zohar III, 103b. Rashi on Gen. 25:9; Num. 23:23. Seforno and Ibn Ezra on Gen. 16:12. Maharal, *Netsah Yisrael*, 43, 55. *Or HaHayyim* on Gen. 25:6; Lev. 26:5. *Likkutei Moharan*, 14:2 (Zeph. 3:9). *Orot*, pp. 15-17, 33, 35, 88, 90-91, 151, 155. *Mei Meirom*, VI, pp. 28-29, 83, 207, 292-94; VIII, pp. 77, 80, 86, 110-11. R. David Cohen, *Kol HaNevuah*, Jerusalem: 5730 (1970), p. 256.
846. See Sifrei 69 (Num. 9:10); Pirkei DeRabbi Eliezer 44; Pesikta Zutarta 25:18; Rashi on Gen. 33:4; *Iggeret Teiman*, p. 147; *Avnei Nezer*, p. 38.
847. See above, p. 20.
848. Cf. *Likkutei Moharan*, I, 17:6; II, 78. *Sefat Emet*, III, p. 200; V, p. 5. *Tsidkat HaTsaddik*, p. 256. *Orot*, pp. 68, 91, 138, 169; *Orot HaKodesh*, II, p. 303. *Be'er Avraham*, p. 296.
849. Cf. Ps. 83:4-5, 83:13. Tanhuma, Ki Tissa 34. Rashi on Gen. 1:1. Ramban on Deut. 32:26. Maharal, *Tiferet Yisrael*, 68. *Mei Meirom*, VI pp. 292-93. R. Y.H. Ashlag, *Hakdamah*, Sefer HaZohar (*Im Perush HaSulam*), I, p. 19.
850. See TB Sanhedrin 99a.
851. Cf. Deut. 30:12; TB Bava Metsia 59b.
852. Cf. Prov. 3:6; TB Berakhot 63a; *Likkutei Moharan*, II, 116; *Orot*, pp. 26-29, 86.
853. Cf. Exod. 19:6; Rabbeinu Bahya (II, p. 169), *Ha'amek Davar* (II, p. 81a), M.D. Cassuto (p. 156) ad loc. TB Bava Batra 10a. Pesikta DeRav Kahana, II, 12:2. Rashi on Isa. 1:4. *Bet Avraham*, p. 153.
854. Cf. Shir HaShirim R. 2:6. Maharal, *Netivot Olam*, I, *Netiv HaTsedakah*, 6, p. 70b. HaGra, *Biur, Mishlei*, Prov. 3:26, p. 12; *Siddur Ishei Yisrael (Siah Yitshak)*, p. 45. *Ha'amek Davar* on Gen. 48:4 (I, p. 179). See J. Heinemann, *Darkei HaAggadah*, pp. 113-14; M.M. Buber, *Darko Shel Mikra*, p. 300.
855. Cf. Deut. 4:7; II Sam. 7:23. Mekhilta 2 (Exod. 9:6). Rabbeinu Bahya on Exod. 19:6. Maharal, *Netivot Olam*, I, *Netiv HaTorah*, 10; *Derashot*, p. 5. *Bnei Issakhar*, II, p. 21. *Sefat Emet*, I, p. 61. Rav Kook, *Orot*, pp. 32, 170-71; *Orot HaKodesh*, II, p. 423; III, p. 295; *Olat Reiyah*, II, pp. 401-3.
856. Cf. Gen. 35:11; II Sam. 7:23; Ps. 106:5. TB Berakhot 57b; Shabbat 88b; Yevamot 20a. Shelah, I, p. 21a.
857. Cf. Zohar II, 121a.
858. Cf. Deut. 4:6-8, 26:18-19. TB Sotah 39a. Zohar II, 121-22. Rashi on Num. 11:11; Isa. 1:4. Ramban on Gen. 17:6. Maharal, *Tiferet Yisrael*, 1; *Gevurot HaShem*, 3, 14, 18, 44; *Gur Aryeh* on Num. 13:18; *Perush LeAggadot*, II, p. 80. Shelah, I, p. 21a; III, p. 164b. HaGra, *Biur, Mishlei*, Prov. 14:28, p. 45b; *Siddur Ishei Yisrael*, p. 21. Rav Kook, *Orot*, pp. 24, 53-54, 62, 64, 67-69, 72-74, 80, 83, 89-90, 98, 133, 141, 159; *Orot HaKodesh*, I, pp. 59-60; II, p. 311;

Hazon HaGeulah, pp. 184-86; *Olat Reiyah*, I, p. 96. *Mei Meirom*, VI, pp. 14, 265. *Avnei Nezer*, p. 29.

859. See above, p. 24.
860. Cf. Sifrei 43 (Deut. 11:18), 301 (Deut. 26:5). Num. R. 10, 11:4. Rashi on Deut. 11:18. HaGra on Isa. 1:4, 2:3. *Hiddushei Maran Riz HaLevi*, p. 20.
861. Cf. Exod. 3:8. Lev. 20:24. Deut. 7:12-15, 8:7-10, 11:10-17. Jer. 3:19. Mekhilta 1 (Exod. 18:9). Sifra 1 (Lev. 26:4). Sifrei 8 (Deut. 1:8), 28 (Deut. 3:25), 37 (Deut. 11:10), 47 (Deut. 11:21), 114 (Deut. 15:4), 303 (Deut. 26:15), 333 (Deut. 32:43), 355 (Deut. 33:24). Mishnah Bikkurim I, 3; Sanhedrin X, 1 (Isa. 60:21). TY Bikkurim I, 8; Peyah VII, 3; Bava Batra IX, 5. TB Berakhot 36b-37a; 41a and Rashi ad loc.; Shabbat 30b; 63a; Pessahim 113a; Yoma 81b; Sukkah 35a; Megillah 6a and Rashi ad loc.; Ketuvot 111-12; Bava Batra 146a; Sanhedrin 90a; Menahot 53b; 85b. Gen. R. 16:3, 39:10, 64:3, 65:16-17. Exod. R. 3:4. Lev. R. 3:1, 25:3. Num. R. 9:24. Eihah R. 2:17. Kohelet R. 2:5. Yalkut Shim'oni, Eikev 11:864; Yeshaya 54:478; Kohelet 2:968. Zohar I, 95b; 177b; III, 65b; 72b; 84a; 284b. Rashi on Gen. 12:1. Ibn Ezra on Gen. 33:19. Ramban on Exod. 3:8; *Torat HaAdam (Kitvei Ramban* II), p. 296. Rambam, *Hilkhot Teshuvah*, III, 5. Maharal, *Gevurot HaShem*, 24; *Perushim LeAggadot*, I, p. 103; *Derekh Hayyim*, pp. 188, 251-52; *Netivot Olam*, I, *Netiv HaTorah*, 10; *Netiv HaAvodah*, 18. Shelah, III, pp. 23a-b, 171b, 172b. Maharsha on Sanhedrin 98. *Biurei HaGra Al Aggadot*, I, pp. 100-1; II, pp. 5; 55; 58. *Likkutei Moharan*, I, 20; II, 116; *Kitvei Rabbi Nahman MiBratslav*, pp. 193, 354. Yemei Maharnat, II, pp. 83b-84a. Rav Kook, *Orot*, p. 79; *Orot HaKodesh*, III, p. 295. *Mei Meirom*, II, p. 41; VI, pp. 259; 270; 327. Rabbi Yossef Hayyim of Baghdad, *Ben Yehoyada*, II, p. 81a. R. B.Z. Safran, *Doresh LeTsion*, p. 24.
862. Cf. TY Berakhot IV, 5. TB Sanhedrin 90a; 99b. Shir HaShirim R. 4:4. Tanhuma, Pekkudei 1. Zohar I, 29a; 31b; 80b; 128b; 205b; II, 85b; III, 4b; 12a; 13a; 45b; 84a; 85b; 93a-b; 96a; 235a; 268a. *Tikkunei HaZohar*, 86a. Ari HaKadosh, *Likkutei Torah*, Eikev, p. 193. Alshekh on Lekh Lekha, Gen. 12:1. Shelah, III, pp. 21b, 23a, 26a, 45b, 171b, 172b, 173a, 202b, 204a; *Siddur Sha'ar HaShamayim*, p. 525. *Biurei HaGra Al Aggadot*, I, p. 69. *Sefat Emet*, III, p. 202; V, p. 5. *Shem MiShemuel, Bemidbar*, p. 128. R. Yossef Hayyim of Baghdad, *Ben Yehoyada*, II, p. 80b.
863. Cf. Esther 3:8. TB Moed Katan 16b. Maharal, *Tiferet Yisrael*, 1; *Gevurot HaShem*, 12, 23, 24. *Likkutei Moharan*, 7:1. *Orot*, p. 9. *Mei Meirom*, VI, pp. 237-38, 327-28; VIII, p. 111.
864. Cf. Mekhilta on Exod. 12:2. TB Sukkah 29a; Gittin 57b; Bava Batra 10b; Sanhedrin 42a; Avodah Zarah 2b. Yonathan Ben Uziel on Gen. 25:25. Gen. R. 6:5, 65:16, 63-67. Exod. R. 15:27, 15:30, 21. Num. R. 10, 21. Shir HaShirim R. 1:21, 6:4. Tanhuma, Toldot 7; Tanhuma (Buber ed.), Terumah 7. Shoher Tov, 18. Pesikta Rabbati 15-16. Pesikta Zutarta, Bo 12:3. Pirkei DeRabbi Eliezer 37, 38, 51. Tana Devei Eliyahu Zuta 14. Yalkut Shim'oni, Beshalah 17:268. Zohar I, 230b. Tikkunei HaZohar, 6 (22a). *Kuzari*, II, 13. Rashi on Gen. 25:31. Rambam, *Hilkhot Shemittah VeYovel*, XIII, 12-13. *Siddur Rabbeinu Shelomo de Garmaise*, p. 196. Maharal, *Netsah Yisrael*, 14, 46; *Tiferet Yisrael*, 1, 2; *Gevurot HaShem*, 11, 12, 18, 24, 44, 54, 67, 68; *Perushim LeAggadot*, I, p. 135; IV, p. 15; *Derekh Hayyim*, p. 13; *Netivot*

REFERENCES, SOURCES & NOTES · 355

Olam, I, Netiv HaAvodah, 13. Shelah, III, p. 183b. HaGra, Sefer HaEmunah VeHaHashgahah, p. 12; Siddur Ishei Yisrael, p. 335. Hatam Sofer, Derashot, II, p. 244; Haggadah, Bnei-Brak: 5736, p. 26. Bet HaLevi, I, p. 33. Sefat Emet, III, p. 197. Rav Kook, Orot, pp. 9, 14, 49-50, 54, 64, 139, 150, 158-59, 168-69; Olat Reiyah, I, pp. 386-87; Orot HaKodesh, III, pp. 33-34. Mei Meirom, VI, p. 323; Missaviv LiShmonah Perakim LeHaRambam, p. 141. Be'er Avraham, pp. 223-24, 257, 258. R. Yossef Hayyim of Baghdad, Od Yossef Hai, pp. 209-10.

865. Cf. Zohar II, 54a.
866. See above, p. 26.
867. See above, p. 51.
868. Cf. Gen. R. 2:4; Exod. R. 15:8; Shir HaShirim R. 7:1. See Shelah, II, p. 44b.
869. Cf. Shelah, Siddur Sha'ar HaShamayim, p. 520. Bet HaLevi, I, p. 33; II, pp. 5-6. Pahad Yitshak, Hanukah, pp. 13-14, 113.
870. Cf. Sifrei 343 (Deut. 33:2). Hatam Sofer, Haggadah, p. 27-28.
871. Cf. TB Hullin 91a; Yalkut Shim'oni, Beshalah 17:268; Iggeret Teiman, pp. 116-17, 126-27, 132-33.
872. Cf. TB Rosh HaShanah 19a; Bava Batra 60b; Meilah 17a. Rashi on Shir HaShirim 3:5, 5:8, 8:7. Ramban on Deut. 32:40. Maharal, Be'er HaGolah, 7.
873. Cf. Tossafot on Berakhot 12a.
874. Cf. Gen. R. 64:4. Lev. R. 36. Shir HaShirim R. 1:21, 2:9. Tanhuma, Eikev 5; Nitsavim 1. Zohar I, 17b. Maharal, Derashot, Hesped, 12.
875. Cf. TB Shabbat 31a. Gen. R. 83:3; Shir HaShirim R. 7:7. Semak, Mitzvat Asseh, 1.
876. Cf. R. Y.H. Ashlag, Hakdamah, Sefer Hazohar Im Perush HaSulam, I, p. 18; Hakdamah, Sefer Ets HaHayyim, p. 2. See A. Safran, La Cabale, p. 342.
877. Cf. TB Berakhot 17a; Shabbat 10a; Bava Batra 16b. Zohar I, 92a; III, 301b. Shelah, III, p. 204a. Rav Kook, Orot, p. 26; Olat Reiyah, II, p. 157. See also Rambam, Hilkhot Teshuvah, VIII, 8.
878. Cf. Sifrei 310 (Deut. 32:7). Tanhuma, VaYikra 7:8. Zohar Hadash, Behar 49.
879. Cf. Rav Kook, Hazon HaGeulah, p. 143.
880. Cf. Mekhilta 2 (Exod. 19:6). TY Nedarim IX, 4. TB Ta'anit 11a. Lev. R. 4:6 (Jer. 50:17). Shir HaShirim R. 6:17. Eihah R. 1. Tana Devei Eliyahu Rabba 23. Tana Devei Eliyahu Zuta 1, 15. Pesikta Rabbati 11. Pesikta Zutarta, Beshalah 17:2. Yalkut Shim'oni, Yitro 19:276. Zohar III, 126a. Rambam, Hilkhot Matnot Aniyim, X, 12. Ari HaKadosh, Likkutei Torah and Rabbi Hayyim Vital, Ta'amei HaMitzvot, Kedoshim, p. 77 (Lev. 19:18). Rabbi Moshe Cordovero, Tomer Devorah 1. Alshekh on Nitsavim (Deut. 29:9). Maharal, Netivot Olam, I, Netiv HaTorah, 2; Netiv HaTsedakah, 6. Rabbi Levi Yitshak of Berdichev, Kedushat Levi, p. 141. Tanya, 32. Likkutei HaGra, p. 38 (in Sifra DiTseniuta Im Biur HaGra). Rabbi Yossef Hayyim of Baghdad, She'eilot UTeshuvot, Torah Sheleimah, 325. Hafets Hayyim, Shemirat HaLashon, pp. 43-44.
881. Cf. TB Shevuot 39a; Sanhedrin 27b; 43b; Rashi ad loc.; Shabbat 119b; Rosh HaShanah 29a-b and Rashi ad loc.; Makot 23b and Rashi ad loc.; Hullin 135a and Rashi ad loc. Lev. R. 4:6. Tanhuma, Nitsavim 1, 3. R. Hayyim Vital, Ta'amei HaMitzvot, p. 77. Tomer Devorah, 1. Maharal, Gevurot HaShem, 6; Netivot Olam, I, Netiv HaTorah, 5 and Netiv HaTsedakah, 6; see also

Perushei Maharal LeAggadot, IV, p. 49. HaGra, *Aderet Eliyahu*, p. 483. *Meshekh Hokhmah*, p. 217. *Tsafnat Pa'aneah, Devarim*, II, p. 247; Makot 24a. *Tossefet Berakhah*, III, pp. 151-52. R. Y.H. Ashlag, *Matan Torah*, pp. 44ff. Hafets Hayyim, *Perush Al Siddur HaTefillah*, p. 74.

882. Cf. TB Ketuvot 75a.
883. Cf. Deut. 4:13-14. Mekhilta 5 (Exod. 20:2). TY Sotah VII, 5. TB Sanhedrin 43b. Tanhuma, Yitro 13. Zohar III, 93b. Rashi on Deut. 29:28. Maharsha on Bava Batra 88b. *She'eilot UTeshuvot Avnei Nezer, Orah Hayyim*, 314; *Yoreh Deyah*, I, 126. *Tsafnat Pa'aneah*, Sanhedrin 43b. *Pahad Yitshak, Sha'ar Hodesh HaAviv*, p. 172.
884. Cf. TB Sukkah 45b; Zohar I, 219a; Tanhuma, Nitsavim 2.
885. Cf. Zohar I, 154b.
886. Cf. Mekhilta 6 (Exod. 20:8). See Zech. 10:3. Cf. Rambam, *Hilkhot Melakhim*, V, 1.
887. Cf. Lev. 22:32; Deut. 6:4; Shir HaShirim 8:6. TY Shevi'it IV, 2. TB Berakhot 61b; Gittin 57b and Rashi ad loc.; Sanhedrin 44a and Rashi ad loc.; 74a. (See also TB Keritot 6b; Menahot 27a; *Tur, Shulhan Arukh, Orah Hayyim*, 619.) Shir HaShirim R. 1. Shoher Tov, 9. Zohar I, 93a; 124a; II, 119a; III, 195b; 281a. Tikkunei HaZohar, 60. Rambam, *Hakdamah LePerek Helek; Hilkhot Yessodei HaTorah*, V, 1. Ramban, *Petihta, Sefer Devarim*. Rashba, *Teshuvot*, I, 55. Maharal, *Netivot Olam*, II, *Netiv Ahavat HaShem*, 1; *Netsah Yisrael*, 13; *Derekh Hayyim*, pp. 6ff. *Tanya*, 14, 18, 19, 25, 32, 41. *Kedushat Levi*, p. 47a. *Likkutei Moharan*, I, 14; 3; II, 82. *Sefat Emet*, I, p. 176; V, p. 182. Rav Kook, *Orot*, pp. 12-13, 74, 76, 84-85, 95-96, 144, 146, 148-51, 153, 155-56, 166, 167; *Hazon HaGeulah*, pp. 36, 139, 148-50, 210, 275; *Orot HaKodesh*, I, pp. 17-18; III, pp. 324, 326-28, 330-33; *Iggrot HaReiyah*, I, pp. 263, 369; II, pp. 194, 281, 320. *Mei Meirom*, VI, pp. 11, 18, 274. *Meshekh Hokhmah*, p. 324. *Shem MiShemuel, Haggadah*, pp. 44, 46-47. R. B.Z. Safran, *Doresh LeTsion*, pp. 12, 21.
888. Cf. Lev. 19:18; Deut. 6:5, 8:10; Jer. 16:11. See TY Haggigah I, 7. Exod. R. 32. Zohar III, 73a. *Sefer HaHinukh*, Mitzvah 243. TB Ketuvot 112a. Tana Devei Eliyahu Rabba 22. Rav Kook, *Orot*, pp. 44-45, 75, 79, 85-86, 96, 134, 146, 148-49, 151, 155-56, 158-59, 166; *Hazon HaGeulah*, pp. 148-50; *Olat Reiyah*, II, p. 3-4; *Orot HaTeshuvah*, pp. 32-33, 111-12, 122-23, 137-38. *Mei Meirom*, VI, p. 150. R. B.Z. Safran, *Doresh LeTsion*, p. 8.
890. Cf. *Olat Reiyah*, I, pp. 386-87.
891. Cf. Isa. 1:27. Sifrei 116 (Deut. 15:6). Avot V, 19. TY Sanhedrin XI. TB Beitsa 32b; Sotah 14a; Yevamot 79a; Bava Batra 9a. Gen. 41:1. Num. R. 3:1. Tanhuma (Buber ed.), VaYera 4. *Shulhan Arukh, Yoreh Deyah*, 251. Maharal, *Netivot Olam*, I, *Netiv HaTsedakah*, 5. *Likkutei Moharan*, I, 37; 4; II, 71. *Tanya, Iggeret HaKodesh*, 6. Rav Kook, *Orot*, pp. 148-49. Rabbi Abraham of Slonim, *Bet Avraham*, pp. 121, 129, 134, 274. *Bet HaLevi*, II, p. 39. *Ben Ish Hai*, p. 245. R. B.Z. Safran, *Doresh LeTsion*, p. 24.
892. Cf. Mishnah Peyah I, 1; Rambam, *Hilkhot Talmud Torah*, III, 3. TB Bava Batra 9a. Sifrei 80 (Deut. 12:29). TY Peyah I, 1-2. Ramban on Shabbat 130. See Rambam, *Sefer HaMitzvot, Shoresh* IV. See also *Kuzari*, II, 96; III, 17. Cf. Maharsha on Makot 23b. *Or HaHayyim* on Deut. 30:20. R. Eliyahu of

Vilna, *Aderet Eliyahu*, pp. 366-67. Rav Kook, *Orot*, p. 163. R. Y.H. Ashlag, *Matan Torah*, p. 19ff.
893. Cf. Isa. 51:11ff.
894. Cf. Jer. 3:17, 17:12; Mic. 4:7. Obad. 1:21. Ps. 48. Dan. 7:27, 9:24-25. TB Shabbat 63a; Ta'anit 5a; Sanhedrin 98a. Exod. R. 21. Num. R. 11 (I Sam. 2:8); Esther R. 1; Kohelet R. 1. Shir HaShirim Zuta 3. Zohar I, 1b; 231a; II, 55b; III, 83a; 234b (Ps. 126); 266b. Tikkunei HaZohar, 62a. *Kuzari*, II, 16. Rashi on Sanhedrin 91b. *Da'at Zekeinim MiBa'alei HaTossafot*, Exod. 17:16. Rambam, *Hakdamah LePerek Helek*; *Hilkhot Teshuvah*, IX, 2. Maharal, *Netsah Yisrael*, 43; *Gevurot HaShem*, 47, 70. *Likkutei Moharan*, 4, 2. *Or HaHayyim* on Lev. 26:6. Rav Kook, *Orot*, pp. 26, 52-53, 155-57, 160; *Hazon HaGeulah*, pp. 29, 47, 127, 129-30, 143; *Olat Reiyah*, I, pp. 233, 386-87.
895. CF. TB Berakhot 58a. Jer. 17:12. Isa. 2:3; Mic. 4:2. Isa. 52:9. Tanhuma, Kedoshim 10; Zohar I, 114a; 128b; III, 161b. Yalkut Shim'oni, Isa. 60:503; Maharal, *Gur Aryeh*, VaYeitsei.
896. Cf. Rashi on TB Berakhot 48b-49a.
897. Ps. 117:1-2.
898. See TB Yoma 54b; Exod. R. 23:11; Avot DeRabbi Nathan 35; Pesikta Rabbati 10:2. Zohar I, 226a; II, 184b; III, 65b. Tikkunei HaZohar, 37 (78b). *Likkutei Moharan*, II, 8; 10.
899. Cf. Gen. R. 82:3.
900. Isa. 2:3; Mic. 4:2.

Chapter Two

1. Cf. Gen. 28:15; Deut. 30:1-5; Jer. 32. Mishnah Shekalim II,4; Nazir V,4; Middot III, 1. Gen. R. 44:21, 75:8. Exod. R. 3:4; Num. R. 7:10. Zohar I, 214b. Rabbi Tsevi Yehuda Berlin of Volozhin, the "Netsiv", *Ha'amek Davar*, III, Lev. 26:42, p. 121.
2. Cf. *Midrash Shemuel*, 8:35.
3. Cf. Elihah Rabbati, 5:19; TB Makot 24b. See also TB Berakhot 18b. Cf. Zohar II, 188-189. Cf. Ramban on Deut. 32:40 *in fine*; *Sefer HaGeulah* (*Kitvei Ramban* I), p. 280.
4. Cf. Gen. R. 44:20-22, 56:3, 69:4. Exod. R. 15:18. Shir HaShirim R. 7. Rashi on Sanhedrin 92b. Ramban on Gen. 28:12.
5. Cf. Lev. R. 29:2. Ramban, *Iggeret Teiman*, pp. 117, 128. Ramban on Gen. 15:7, 15:18, 22:16; Lev. 26:45; Deut. 28:42. See also Rashi, Ibn Ezra, Ramban and Rabbeinu Bahya on Num. 23:19. Cf. Maharal, *Netsah Yisrael*, *Hakdamah*.
6. See Ibn Ezra and Ramban on Num. 23:21.
7. See Gen. 22:17, 26:3. Exod. 33:1. Num. 14:23-24, 32:11-12. Deut. 1:35-36, 10:11, 31:20-21, 31:23, 34:4. Josh. 1:6. Judg. 2:1. Jer. 11:5 et al.
8. Cf. Maharal, *Netsah Yisrael*, 40. Hatam Sofer, *Derashot*, p. 316. Rav Kook, *Orot*, pp. 63-64.
9. Cf. Eikhah R.1:29. Exod.R.15:8. TB Megillah 12a. Dan. 1:6. Yalkut Shim'oni, Balak 768. Zohar III, 221b; Zohar Hadash, Yitro 40. Ramban on Deut. 32:26. *Mishnah Berurah on Shulhan Arukh*, Orah Hayyim, 560.

10. Cf. Deut. 28:65; Eihah 1:3. Gen. R. 33:8, 63:18. Zohar II, 15a. R. Yitshak Arama, *Akeidat Yitshak*, Behukotai. *Bet HaLevi, Shemot*, pp. 3, 5-6. *Meshekh Hokhmah*, p. 191.
11. Exod. R. 36:1; cf. Shir HaShirim R. 1:21.
12. Cf. Ibn Ezra and Ramban on Num. 23:9; cf. Esther 3:8.
13. Cf. Ba'al HaTurim and Seforno on Num. 23:9. See Rashi on Berakhot 48b.
14. Cf. Lev. 26:33. Deut. 4:27, 28:64. Ezek. 5:10. Amos 9:9 et al. Gen. R. 44:20-21, 68, 69. Lev. R. 29:2. Num. R. 7:10. Maharal, *Gevurot HaShem*, 8, p. 30; 23, p. 63: *Netivot Olam*, I, *Netiv Gemilut Hassadim*, 1, p. 57. Ari HaKadosh, *Likkutei Torah*, Ki Teitsei, pp. 208-210.
15. Cf. Maharal, *Gevurot HaShem*, 8, p. 30.
16. Cf. Zohar III, 11b; 252a. Ramban on Gen. 28:12; Rabbeinu Bahya, *Kad HaKemah*, Geulah. Shelah, III, p. 74b; *Or HaHayyim*, on Exod. 6:6.
17. Cf. *Shem MiShemuel, Bemidbar*, p. 348.
18. Cf. TB Megillah 29a; Berakhot 8a; 9b. TY Sukkah IV, 3; Ta'anit I, 1. Mekhilta Bo (Exod. 12:41), Messikhta DePissha, 14, pp. 20a-b. Sifrei Beha'alotkha 84, p. 22b; Mass'ei 161, p. 62b. Exod. R. 3:7, 15:13. Lev. R. 9:3. Num. R. 7:10. Deut. R. 4:1. Tanhuma, Ahrei 12. Shoher Tov, 13. Yalkut Shim'oni, Zekhariah 19:577; Eihah, 1038. Zohar I, 28a; 69a; 120b; 124a; 134a; 149a; 159b; 166a; 182b; 189a; 210a; 211a; 212b; II, 2b; 41b; 55b; 82a; 196a; 216b; III, 4b; 23b; 57b; 66a; 69a; 75a; 90b; 114b; 115a-b; 197b; 203b; 242a; 266b; 281a; 297b. Tikkunei HaZohar, 9a; 12a; 6 (21b); 13 (28a); 21 (51a, 53b); 70 (124b). Zohar Hadash, A'hrei 47-48; Hukat 51; Ruth 84, 94. Sha'arei Zohar, 118. Rashi on Exod. 3:2; Deut. 30:3. Maharal, *Gevurot Hashem*, 23, p. 61b; *Netsah Yisrael*, 10, 62. *Sefat Emet*, II, pp. 6-7.
19. Cf. *Toldot Ya'akov Yossef*, VaYakhel; *Sefat Emet*, I, p. 211; II. p. 25.
20. Cf. Maharal, *Netsah Yisrael*, 1, 24. *Gur Aryeh*, Deut. 30:3; *Bnei Issakhar*, I, p. 22a.
21. Cf. *Kuzari*, II, 34s, 44. Maharal, *Netsah Yisrael*, 1, 24; *Gevurot HaShem*, 8, pp. 29, 54, 148; *Gur Aryeh*, Deut. 30:3. See Ps. 24:1; Esther R. 10:11; Tanhuma, Toldot 5.
22. Cf. Rabbeinu Sa'adya Gaon, *Emunot VeDeot*, VIII, 1; Abrabanel, I, Gen. 15, p. 203; Maharal, *Gevurot HaShem*, 9, p. 33.
23. Cf. Zohar II, 215b; Ari HaKadosh, *Likkutei Torah*, KiTeitsei, pp. 208-10; Rabbi Hayyim Vital, *Peri Ets Hayyim*, p. 28b; *Bet HaLevi, Shemot*, p. 19; *Sefat Emet*, II, p. 5.
24. Exod. 14:13. TY Sukkah V, 1; Sanhedrin X, 9. Deut. 17:16. Rambam, *Hilkhot Melakhim*, V, 8.
25. Cf. Exod. 12:36; TB Berakhot 9b. See TB Pessahim 119a; *Kuzari*, II, 44. Cf. Maharal, *Gevurot HaShem*, 8, p. 33. Shelah, III, p. 74b. See also Rav Kook, *Orot*, p. 115.
26. Gen. R. 16:7. But see also Mekhilta Bo (Exod. 13:1); Messikhta DePissha, 16, p. 24a. See *Sefat Emet*, II, p. 7.
27. Exod. 1:16. Cf. Exod. R. 1:22, 1:41.
28. Cf. Lev. 26:32-33. Deut. 4:25-27, 28:36, 28:64. Ezek. 12, 20, 22:15, 36:19. I Kings 14, 15. Gen. R. 36:7. Exod. R. 1:35, 31:9, 51:3. Num. R. 7:10, 23:14 *in fine*. Deut. R. 2:13. Petihta DeEihah Rabbati. Eihah R. 1:37. Tanhuma, Nitsavim 3. Yalkut Shim'oni, Tsefanya 567. Avot I, 11; V, 9. Avot DeRabbi

Nathan 20, 38. TB Shabbat 33a; Yoma 9b; Sanhedrin 39a; Menahot 53b. Pesikta Rabbati 25:3. Pesikta DeRav Kahana (Mandelbaum ed.), II, 5, p. 464. Zohar II, 175b; III, 69b. See also Rabbeinu Sa'adya Gaon, *Emunot VeDeot*, VIII, 1. *Kitvei Ramban* I. *Sefer HaGeulah*, pp. 279-80. *Shem MiShemuel, Haggadah Shel Pessah*, pp. 23-25.

29. Cf. R. Mordehai Gifter, *Pirkei Emunah*, Jerusalem: 5729, pp. 180-81. Cf. Lev. 4:22; TB Horayot 10b.
30. Cf. Shelah, III, p. 136b. Cf. Rabbi Ya'akov, "Ha Maggid Midubna," *Ohel Ya'akov, VaYikra*, pp. 156-57; Rabbi Yossef Hayyim of Baghdad, *Od Yossef Hai*, p. 47; Rabbi Abraham of Slonim, *Bet Avraham, BeSha'ar HaSefer*.
31. Cf. Eihah R. 1:37. Cf. Rabbi Avraham Yaffen, *HaMussar VeHaDa'at*, II, p. 274.
32. See also Ramban on Deut. 32:28.
33. Amos 3:2. See *Kuzari*, II, 44.
34. Tanhuma, Yitro 16.
35. Maharal, *Derekh Hayyim*, Avot IV, p. 162.
36. Cf. TB Yevamot 121b. See also TB Ta'anit 11a; Bava Batra 33b; Sanhedrin 104a. Massekhet Semahot VIII. Lev. R. 27:1; Num. R. 20:25. Tanhuma, Emor 5; Balak 20. Pesikta Zutarta, Shemot 4:26. Zohar I, 140a; 185b; II, 247b. Rambam, *Hilkhot Yessodei Hatorah*, V, 11; *Hilkhot Deot*, V. Ralbag on I Kings 17, 18. Rabbi Hayyim Vital, *Peri Ets Hayyim*, p. 20. Maharal, *Gevurot HaShem*, 9; *Derekh Hayyim*, Avot IV *in fine*, p. 162; *Derashot, Hesped*, pp. 12-13. Rabbi Samson Raphael Hirsch, *Iggrot Tsafon*, 9, 15. Rabbi Nathan Tsevi Finkel, "HaSaba MiSlobodka," *Or HaTsafun*, II, p. 57; Rabbi Eliyahu Lapian, *Lev Eliyahu*, p. 162; Rabbi Eliyahu Eliezer Dessler, *Mikhtav MeEliyahu*, III, pp. 194-96. Rabbi Abraham of Sochaczew, *Avnei Nezer*, pp. 70, 76; *Shem MiShemuel, Vayikra*, p. 139. *Mei Meirom*, VI, p. 148; VIII, p. 148. *Tossefet Berakhah*, I, p. 202.
37. Tana Devei Eliyahu Rabba 2.
38. Is. 60:21.
39. Cf. *Avnei Nezer*, p. 76.
40. Exod. 2:25, 4:22; Deut. 7:8. Cf. Exod. R. 32:2. Shir HaShirim R. 1:19, 1:44, 5:13. Zohar III, 197b; 219b.
41. Deut. 8:5. Cf. Ari HaKadosh, *Likkutei Torah, Shemot*, p. 95a.
42. Prov. 3:12. Cf. TB Berakhot 5a. Tanhuma, Yitro 16; Nitsavim 3.
43. TB Berakhot 3a. See Petihta De Eihah Rabbati 24.
44. Yalkut Shim'oni, Yirmiah 9:283; Eihah 3:1038; TB Sukkah 52b.
45. Cf. Rabbi Levi Yitshak of Berditchev, *Kedushat Levi*, VaYigash, p. 25b; Pekkudei, p. 59b. *Sefat Emet*, II, p. 7; *Avnei Nezer*, p. 76.
46. Deut. 14:1.
47. Cf. Deut. 28:69. Cf. *Sefat Emet*, III, p. 45.
48. Cf. TB Pessahim 87b; Tana Devei Eliyahu Rabba 10; Ramban on Gen. 32:9 and on Deut. 32:26; Exod. R. 30:5.
49. Jer. 23:3, 31:6-9. See Is. 46:3; Mic. 2:12, 5:6-7. Cf. Rabbi Abraham of Slonim, *Yessod HaAvodah*, pp. 234-35.
50. See also *Ohel Ya'akov, Sefer VaYikra*; Behukotai, p. 159s. *Bet HaLevi, Sefer Bereshit*; VaYeitsei, p. 32.
51. Cf. Ezek. 18:23.

52. Cf. TB Megillah 11a. Exod. R. 3, 23:6. Petihta De Esther Rabba p. 464. Pesikta De Rav Kahana (Mandelbaum ed.), II, 5. Rashi on Sanhedrin 92b; Ramban on Deut. 28:42.
53. Cf. Exod. R. 23:6. Deut. R. 3:2. TB Megillah 11a. Zohar III, 112a. Tikkunei HaZohar, 40a.
54. Lev. 26:44. Cf. Rambam, *Iggeret Teiman*, pp. 169-70.
55. Exod. 3:14 and Rashi ad loc. Cf. TB Berakhot 9b. Zohar Hadash, Ahrei 48a. See TB Megillah 29a; Zohar I, 28a.
56. Mal. 3:6. See also Tikkunei HaZohar, *Tikkun* 26.
57. Gen. 15:5.
58. Cf. TB Shabbat 156a. Zohar I, 78a; 90b; III, 148a; 216b. Abrabanel, I, Gen. 15, p. 207. *Shem MiShemuel, Haggadah*, p. 86.
59. Cf. Tikkunei HaZohar, 50 (86b). Maharal, *Gevurot HaShem*, 8, p. 31.
60. Rashi on Gen. 15:5.
61. Cf. TB Pessahim 87b; Yoma 69b. Tana Devei Eliyahu Rabba 10. Gen. R. 78:1; Esther R. 10:11. Tanhuma, Toldot 5. *Kuzari*, II, 32. Ramban on Gen. 32:9. Rabbi Abraham of Slonim, *Be'er Avraham*, p. 334.
62. Cf. Mishnah Yadaim IV, 4. TB Yoma 54a. Shoher Tov, 36. Tanhuma, Mass'ei 13 *in fine*. Rabbi Yossef Albo, *Ikkarim*, 42.
63. Cf. Gen. R. 44. See also Gen. R. 69:3. Cf. Pesikta DeRav Kahana, I, 5, p. 80. Rashi on Gen. 15:10. Maharal, *Gevurot HaShem*, 54, p. 146.
64. Cf. Exod. 1:12. Tanhuma, Toldot 5; Nitsavim 1. *Kuzari*, II, 44. Maharal, *Netsah Yisrael*, 14. Rabbi Hayyim Yossef David Azulay, The "Hida", *Midbar Kedemot*, p. 30.
65. Cf. TB Beitsa 25b; Exod. R. 42:9; *Avnei Nezer*, p. 110.
66. Cf. Mal. 3:6; Tanhuma, Nitsavim 1.
67. Cf. *Ba'al HaTurim* and Seforno on Num. 23:9.
68. Jer. 30:11, 46:28. Cf. Pesikta DeRav Kahana, I, 5. p. 80. Rambam, *Iggeret Teiman*, pp. 116-17; 128-29.
69. Cf. Gen. 15:16 and Rashi ad loc. *Kuzari*, II, 44. See TB Sotah 9a. Cf. *Yessod HaAvodah*, pp. 234-35.
70. Cf. TB Sotah 9a. Lev. R. 29:2; Gen. 28:12. Tanhuma, Nitsavim 1; Deut. 29:12 and Rashi ad loc. *Kuzari*, II, 44. Rambam, *Hilkhot Issurei Bi'a*, XIV, 5. Maharal, *Netsah Yisrael*, 14. *Meshekh Hokhmah*, p. 192.
71. Cf. Gen. 15:16; Gen. R. 44:21. See Deut. 30:3-5.
72. Cf. Rashi, Ramban and Seforno on Gen. 15:6-8. Maharal, *Gevurot HaShem*, 8, p. 30. Rabbi Yeruham HaLevi Levovitch, *Da'at Torah*, p. 249s.
73. Cf. Maharal, *Netsah Yisrael*, Hakdamah; *Gevurot HaShem*, 8, pp. 32-33. Rabbi Eliyahu of Vilna, *Biurei HaGra Al Aggadot*, I, p. 25.
74. Cf. Gen. R. 44:24. Pesikta DeRav Kahana, I, 5, p. 80.
75. Cf. Exod. R. 3, 23:6. TB Megillah 11a. Rashi on Sanhedrin 92b. Ramban on Gen. 15:7, 22:16. See also Pesikta DeRav Kahana, II, 5, p. 464.
76. Gen. R. 69:3.
77. Rashi on Deut. 29:12.
78. Deut. 4:4. Cf. Maharal, *Netsah Yisrael*, 10.
79. Deut. 29:24-26.
80. TB Shabbat 55a.
81. Cf. Shelah, III, pp. 161-62. Tana Devei Eliyahu Zuta 11. Abrabanel, I, Gen.

REFERENCES, SOURCES & NOTES • 361

15, pp. 203, 214. *Kedushat Levi*, Pekkudei, p. 59b. *Noam Elimelekh*, Mikeits, p. 128. *Sefat Emet*, I, pp. 134, 199; II, p. 7. See also TB Berakhot 60b; Zohar I, 181a.
82. Prov. 6:23. Lev. R. 30:2. Rabbi Nahman of Bratslav, *Likkutei Moharan*, II, 77, p. 35a; Kohelet 1:18.
83. Cf. Tanhuma, Noah 13; Gen. R. 65:4; Rashi on Gen. 37:2. Cf. Gen. 47:9.
84. Cf. Rashi on Gen. 37:2, 43:14, 47:9. Maharal, *Derekh Hayyim*, Avot V, 5, p. 172. *Sefat Emet*, VaYeshev.
85. Cf Lev. 18:5.
86. Cf. Sifrei VaEthanan 32 (Exod. 6:5), pp. 73a-b. Shoher Tov, 94:2; TB Sanhedrin 101a. TB Berakhot 62a; Shabbat 13b; Bava Metsia 85a. Shoher Tov, 118. Tanhuma, Yitro 16. See TB Shabbat 12b; Zohar III, 234b. See also Tanhuma, Nitsavim 1.
87. Cf. TB Shabbat 88b; *Kuzari*, III, 11-12. *Iggeret Teiman*, p. 134.
88. Cf. Ps. 31:20. TB Berakhot 5a; Gen. R. 92:1; Zohar I, 181. See TB Shabbat 88b; Zohar III, 57b; 199b. Pesikta Zutarta, Eikev 8:5. Rambam, *Hilkhot Issurei Bi'a*, XIV, 3. Abrabanel, I, Gen. 15, p. 203. Maharal, *Gevurot HaShem*, 9, p. 33. Hermann Cohen, *Die Religion der Vernunft aus den Quellen des Judentums*, Leipzig: 1919, p. 511.
89. Cf. TB Megillah 29a; TY Ta'anit I, 1. Sifrei Mass'ei 161 (Num. 35:34), p. 62b; Num. R. 7. Zohar I, 28a; 211a; II, 2b; 41b; III, 4b; 197b. Tikkunei HaZohar, 6 (21b).
90. Cf. Eihah R. 1. See Shoher Tov, 146.
91. Cf. Gen. R. 70:1; Exod. R. 21:7; Eihah R. 1:23. Ramban on Exod. 2:25, 12:42. Maharal, *Gevurot HaShem*, 24. *Noam Elimelekh*, VaYakhel. See also TB Rosh HaShanah 17b; Tana Devei Eliyahu Zuta 23.
92. Ps. 22:2; Cf. Zohar III, 25b. (Cf. Math 27,46). Cf. Exod. 32:12. Ps. 79:10, 115:2. Cf. TB Berakhot 5a. Num. R. 13:3; Shir HaShirim R. 7:2. Pesikta Rabbati 15, 21. Zohar II, 47a; Is. 26:16. Ps. 44:23; Tanhuma, Nitsavim 1; Rambam, *Iggeret Teiman*, pp. 134-35; Ramban on Deut. 32:40; *Sefer HaGeulah* (*Kitvei Ramban* I), pp. 279-80. Rashi on Deut. 32:43. See also Maharsha on Yoma 54b.
93. Cf. Rabbeinu Bahya Ibn Pakuda, *Hovot HaLevavot*, *Sha'ar Ahavat HaShem*, 1. Abrabanel, I, Gen. lt, p. 203. Maharal, *Gevurot HaShem*, 9, p. 34s. *Sefat Emet*, I, p. 266; II, pp. 6, 24; V, p. 4. Job 13:15.
94. Cf. TB Berakhot 3a; Shabbat 88b. Eihah R. wl. Tanhuma, Ki Teitsei 2; Nitsavim 3. Tikkunei HaZohar, 26. Maharal, *Gevurot HaShem*, 9, pp. 34-35. *Ohel Ya'akov*, Behukotai. *Sefat Emet*, V, p. 5. *Bet Avraham*, pp. 91-94; *Be'er Avraham*, p. 315.
95. Rabbi Kalonymos Shapira, *Aish HaKodesh*, Jerusalem: 5730 (1960), p. 139. Cf. Eihah R. 1:53; HaGra, *Siddur Ishei Yisrael*, p. 543.
96. Quoted by Mordehai Eliav in *Ani Ma'amin*, Jerusalem: 5729 (1959), p. 246.
97. Quoted by Mordehai Eliav, in *Ani Ma'amin*, p. 66.
98. TB Berakhot 61b.
99. Shim'on Bernfeld, *Sefer HaDemaot*, I, Berlin: 5684 (1923), pp. 182 et al. See also Hayyim Nahman Bialik, *Im Yesh Et Nafshekha Lada'at* (*Kol Kitvei H.N. Bialik*, Tel-Aviv: 5709 (1949), p. 17).
100. Deut. 14:1; Mishnah Avot III, 14; Yoma VIII, 9.

101. Rabbi Eliyahu, of Vilna, *Siddur Ishei Yisrael*, p. 543. See Maharal, *Gevurot HaShem*, 9, p. 33.
102. Cf. TB Ta'anit 16a; Sanhedrin 37b; Berakhot 56a; Ketuvot 112b. Gen. R. 44:1, 44:8. Zohar I, 83a; III, 124a, 216a. Rabbi Moshe Cordovero, *Pardess Rimonim*, 13:3.
103. Cf. Deut. 4:20 and Targum Yerushalmi ad loc. I Kings 8:51; Jer. 11:4; Zech. 13:9. *Kuzari*, II, 44; III, 11-12; IV, 23. Maharal, *Derekh Hayyim*, Avot III, 4, p. 172; *Netsah Yisrael*, 14. Shelah, III, pp. 170a-b; *Siddur Sha'ar HaShamayim*, pp. 517-18. Or *HaHayyim* on Lev. 25:26; *Torah Or*, p. 45a; *Kedushat Levi*, Bo, p. 36a; *Likkutei Moharan*, II, 76, p. 35a; *Bnei Issakhar, Haggadah Shel Pessah*, pp. 44-45; *Sefat Emet*, II, pp. 16, 80; *Be'er Avraham*, p. 315. See also Gen. R. 44:1, 44:8.
104. Cf. TY Rosh HaShanah III, 5. Rabbeinu Sa'adya Gaon, *Emunot VeDeot*, VIII, 1. *Kuzari*, IV, 23. Shelah, III, p. 22b. Rav Kook, *Orot*, p. 115. *Ha'amek Davar* on Deut. 8:2, 8:16.
105. Cf. Zech. 13:9. Maharal, *Netsah Yisrael*, 14; *Gevurot HaShem*, 5, pp. 17-18; 9, p. 33; *Derashot, Hakdamah*, p. 5. *Bnei Issakhar, Haggadah*, p. 37. See also Rabbi Moshe Cordovero, *Pardess Rimonim*, 13:3.
106. Cf. Dan. 9:24 and Rashi ad loc. HaGra, *Siddur Ishei Yisrael*, p. 45. Rav Kook, *Hazon HaGeulah*, pp. 90, 96. Cf. Ps. 104:35; TB Berakhot 10a. See Amos 9:10.
107. Cf. Maharal, *Gevurot HaShem*, 8, p. 33.
108. Cf. Rabbeinu Sa'adya Gaon, *Emunot VeDeot*, VIII, 1. Cf. Ari HaKadosh, *Likkutei Torah*, VaYehi, pp. 50b-51a.
109. Cf. Ezek. 18:23. Cf. Deut. 30:1-5; TY Kiddushin 1, 8.
110. Deut. R. w,2. See Rabbi Elimelech of Lyzhansk, *Noam Elimelekh*, I, MiKeits, p. 128.
111. Cf. Deut. 4:20; Jer. 11:4; Is. 48:10-11; Ezek 22:15-16. Eihah R. 1:53; Deut. 26:17-18. Maharal, *Derekh Hayyim*, Avot III, 4, p. 172; *Derashot, Hakdamah*, p. 5. *Sefat Emet*, II, p. 25.
112. Exod. 14:10; cf. Exod. R. 21:5; Shir HaShirim R. 2:30. Zohar I, 81a; II, 47a. Isa. 26:16. *Avnei Nezer*, pp. 16, 101, 159.
113. Cf. TB Sanhedrin 97b; Esther 3:8-10; TB Megillah 14a; Eihah R. 4:27. Deut. 4:30. Ramban on Deut. 32:32. *Sefat Emet*, V, p. 34; *Avnei Nezer*, pp. 111, 159. *Bet HaLevi, Shemot*, pp. 3-6, 12; *Meshekh Hokhmah*, p. 191.
114. TB Menahot 53b; Shir HaShirim R. 1:21.
115. Cf. Avot VI, 2; TB Eruvin 54a; Deut. R. 2:6; Shir HaShirim R. 8:3; Pirkei DeRabbi Eliezer 46; Tana Devei Eliyahu Zuta 4. Zohar I, 152b; II, 113b-114a; III, 6b; 176a; 276a. Tikkunei HaZohar, 55 (88b).
116. Cf. Isa. 10:5; TB Pessahim 68b; Tana Devei Eliyahu Rabba 18. Gen. R. 66:2; Exod. R. 37:4; Num. R. 1:3. Shoher Tov, 109:4. Zohar II, 152b. See also TB Menahot 53b; Shir HaShirim R. 1:21; Deut. R. 3:2.
117. See also Rashi on Num. 22:21; TB Sanhedrin 105b; Ibn Ezra, Ramban and *Ha'amek Davar* on Num. 22:19-20. *Derashot Ben Ish Hai*, p. 187. Cf. Zohar III, 207a. Cf. HaGra, *HaEmunah VeHaHashgahah*, p. 10b; *Perush al Kama Aggadot*, p. 12a.
118. Cf. Isa. 55:8.
119. Cf. TB Berahot 33b; Zohar I, 59a; Tikkunei Zohar Hadash, 121a. TB

Shabbat 104a; Zohar I, 54a. TB Makot 10b; Zohar I, 198b; II, 50a; III, 47a; 207a. Zohar Hadash, Ruth 85a.
120. See TB Sanhedrin 56a.
121. Cf. Exod. R. 15:18; Num. R. 10:5.
122. See Rashi on Gen. 15:13. (See also Rashi on Gen. 12:1; 22:2).
123. Cf. Zohar I, 198b; II, 50a. Ramban on Deut. 32:26. *Bet HaLevi, Shemot*, p. 12. See also *Meiri* on Shabbat 87b.
124. Cf. Rambam, *Hilkhot Teshuvah*, VI, 1:3.
125. Cf. Rashi on Gen. 15:14; cf. Gen. R. 44:22.
126. Cf. Isa. 66:6. Num. R. 10:5.
127. Cf. Exod. R. 15:27, 22:1; Midrash HaGadol, VaYeitsei, 29, 31.
128. Cf. Exod. 1:8. See Ramban, Abrabanel, *Or HaHayyim, HaKtav VeHaKabbalah* and *Meshekh Hokhmah* on Gen. 15.
129. Cf. Exod. R. 30; TB Sanhedrin 91a.
130. Deut. 32:41; Ramban on Deut. 32:40, Cf. Ps. 44:23; Shir HaShirim R. 1:63.
131. Ps. 79:6-10, 83:2-19.
132. Zech. 1:14-16.
133. Cf. TB Ketuvot 111a; Tanhuma, Devarim 4. See also Shir HaShirim R. 2:18.
134. Cf. Deut. 32:41-43; Eihah 1:22, 3:64-65.
135. Cf. Num. 25:16-18, 31:2.
136. Ps. 104:35; TB Berakhot 10a. See also Ps. 145:20; Eihah 3:66.
137. Cf. Deut. 32:43.
138. Deut. 1:17.
139. Ramban on Deut. 1:17.
140. Cf. TB Sanhedrin 72a.
141. Cf. Isa. 50:6.
142. Cf. Shir HaShirim R. 1:63.
143. Cf. TB Shabbat 88b; Yoma 23a; Gittin 36b. See Rabbi Bezalel Ze'ev Safran, *She'elot UTeshuvot Harbaz*, I, p. 27.
144. Cf. Mal. 2:10.
145. Cf. Rashi on Deut. 6:4; Zech. 14:9.
146. Exod. 20:2; Deut. 5:6.
147. Cf. TB Berakhot 63b.
148. TB Bava Kama 92b.
149. Exod. R. 1:41.
150. Rashi on Yevamot 78b.
151. Mishnah Pessahim X, 5; TB Pessahim 116b; Exod. 13:8; Pesikta Zutarta, Bo 12:27.
152. Cf. Exod. 3:12; Shelah HaKadosh, III, p. 22; Rabbi Hayyim Yossef David Azulay, The "Hida", *Kisse Rahamim*, p. 10a.
153. Cf. Exod. 12-13.
154. Cf. TY Rosh HaShanah III, 5; Jer. 34:13-17.
155. TY Nedarim IX, 4; cf. TB Shabbat 31a; Pesikta Zutarta, Kedoshim 19:18.
156. Cf. Isa. 57:19; cf. Exod. 11:2.
157. Lev. 19:18.
158. Deut. 10:19; see also Lev. 19:34.
159. Deut. 6:5, 10:20.
160. Cf. Ps. 119:19.

161. Cf. TB Shabbat 127a; Shevuot 35b; Bava Metsia 86b; Tikkunei HaZohar, 6 (23b).
162. Cf. Jon. 4:11.
163. Deut. 32:41.
164. Cf. Rambam, *Mishneh Torah, Hilkhot Shabbat*, II, 3.
165. Ps. 94:1.
166. TB Berakhot 33a; Sanhedrin 92b.
167. Cf. Ps. 79:7.
168. Cf. Gen. R. 26:14; Lev. R. 28:1; Kohelet R. 1:4.
169. Exod. R. 23:1.
170. TB Megillah 10b; Sanhedrin 39b. Cf. Zohar I, 57b; 121b; II, 170b.
171. Isa. 19:25. Cf. TB Pessahim 118b.
172. Cf. Zohar I, 61b; 121b; III, 297b.
173. Mishnah Pessahim X, 5; TB Pessahim 116b.
174. Cf. Lev. 23:40; Deut. 16:11, 16:14-15; Yalkut Shim'oni, Emor 23:654; see also Pesikta DeRav Kahana, 29; Rabbeinu Bahya on Deut. 16:14 (III, p. 345).
175. Cf. TB Berakhot 10a.
176. Cf. TB Megillah 10b.
177. Cf. *Derekh Hayyim*, Avot IV, 19, p. 53.
178. Cf. Prov. 24:17-18; Avot IV, 19.
179. Cf. TB Berakhot 54b; Shoher Tov, 107; Zohar I, 173b.
180. Cf. TB Megillah 10b.
181. Cf. TB Berakhot 56a and Rashi ad loc; Pessahim 118a.
182. Cf. TB Pessahim 117b; Arakhin 10b.
183. See Mishnah Pessahim X, 5-8; TB Pessahim 116b.
184. See *Shulhan Arukh, Orah Hayyim*, 488, 490.
185. See *Shulhan Arukh, Orah Hayyim* 494, 644. Cf. Yalkut Shim'oni, Emor 23:654.
186. Cf. TB Shabbat 21b.
187. See Massekhet Sofrim XX, 8; Rambam, *Hilkhot Hanukah*, III, 1.
188. See *Meshekh Hokhmah*, pp. 50-51.
189. Cf. Ps. 15:3. See also Rambam, *Sefer HaMitzvot, Mitzvot Assei*, 206 *Hilkhot Deot*, VI, 3 and *Hikhot Evel*, XIV, 1.
190. Cf. Exod. 2:13, 11:2, 21:14, 21:18. Deut. 4:42, 19:11, 27:24 et al. See also Gen. 38:7. AR = RA (Ayin Resh = Resh Ayin).
191. Cf. Isa. 19:25; see also TB Pessahim 118b.
192. Cf. Tikkunei HaZohar, 70 (129a-b).
193. See Exod. 23:4-5 and Mekhilta ad loc.
194. See Lev. 19:18 and Rashi ad loc. TY Nedarim IX, 4. See also TB Shabbat 31a.
195. Exod. 23:4-5 and Mekhilta and Ibn Ezra ad loc. Cf. TB Pessahim 113b; Bava Kama 54b; Bava Metsia 31a; 32a-b. See also TB Bava Kama 38a; Rambam, *Perush HaMishnah*, IV, 3 (Kafa trans., Jerusalem: 5724, II, p. 16); see also idem, *Hakdamah LeMishnah* (Jerusalem: 5725), I, p. 22.
196. Cf. TB Bava Metsia 31a; 32b.
197. Cf. TB Sanhedrin 39a; Menahot 53b.
198. Cf. *Kuzari*, X, 5; Abrabanel, I, p. 214; Maharal, *Gevurot HaShem*, 9.
199. Rashi on Gen. 42:2; *Ba'al HaTurim* on Gen. 15:8, 15:13. Cf. TB Gittin 88b; Rashi and Ramban on Deut. 4:25; See also Ramban on Deut. 32:40 *in fine*.

Rambam, *Iggeret Teiman*, pp. 172-73. See Gen. R. 78:8. See also Gen. R. 44; TY Hallah II, 1; Tana Devei Eliyahu Rabba 18.
200. Cf. Maharal, *Gevurot HaShem*, 54, p. 148.
201. Cf. Rav Kook, *Orot*, pp. 84-85.
202. Cf. *Sefat Emet*, I, pp. 276-77; II, p. 7. See also Rambam, *Iggeret Teiman*, p. 168; *Hilkhot Ta'anit*, I, 3.
203. Cf. Maharal, *Gevurot HaShem*, 8, p. 29; *Netivot Olam*, II, *Netiv HaTeshuvah*, 4, p. 146b.
204. TB Sukkah 52b.
205. TB Pessahim 88a; cf. Rashi on Deut. 30:3. See also TB Berakhot 59a.
206. Maharal, *Gevurot HaShem*, 54, p. 148.
207. Cf. *Kuzari*, IV, 23. See *Sefat Emet*, VaYeshev.
208. Gen. 1:1.
209. Gen. R. 1:5. Cf. TB Pessahim 54a.
210. Gen. 1:2.
211. Gen. R. 2:5. See Zohar III, 279a; Zohar Hadash, Noah 23.
212. Cf. Pirkei DeRabbi Eliezer 35; cf. also Gen. 28:12.
213. Cf. Maharal, *Gevurot HaShem*, 8, pp. 31-32.
214. Gen. 1:2.
215. Gen. R. 2:5. Cf. Zohar I, 192b; 240a. See Ezek. 11:19; Isa. 57:16; Eihah 4:20; Tossafot on Avodah Zarah 5a.
216. Gen. 1:3.
217. Isa. 41:2; cf. TB Bava Batra 15a; Zohar I, 86a.
218. Gen. R. 2:4. Cf. Zohar I, 252b; II, 147b. Tikkunei Zohar Hadash, 116a. See also Gen. R. 30:10 *in fine*; Zohar I, 45b. *Shem MiShemuel, Bemidbar*, p. 189.
219. Cf. Isa. 11:5.
220. Cf. Mic. 7:20. Zohar I, 45b; III, 238a. Zohar Hadash, Toldot 27a. TB Ketuvot 8b.
221. Cf. Eihah R. 1.
222. Cf. TB Bava Batra 16b.
223. Cf. Gen. 15:12-14; Gen. R. 44:20-21. See also Lev. R. 29:2.
224. Cf. *Kuzari*, IV, 23.
225. Cf. Ramban on Deut. 32:26. *Sefat Emet*, I, pp. 123, 126; II, p. 7; III, p. 26. *Mei Meirom*, VIII, p. 98.
226. Cf. TB Pessahim 87b; *Bet HaLevi*, I, p. 32; II, p. 33. Rav Kook, *Orot*, p. 115.
227. Cf. Ramban on Gen. 24:3 and Lev. 18:25; *Derashah Al Divrei Kohelet (Kitvei Ramban* I), p. 200.
228. Zech. 14:9.
229. Cf. Ari HaKadosh, *Likkutei Torah*, Ki Teitsei, pp. 208-10. Rabbi Hayyim Vital, *Peri Ets Hayyim*, p. 28b.
230. Cf. Rabbi Hayyim Yossef David Azulay, the "Hida", *Midbar Kdemot*, p. 30; Rabbi Yehuda HaLevi Ashlag, *Hakdamat Sefer HaZohar Im Perushei HaSulam*, I, p. 156; Rabbi Yoel Teitelbaum of Satmar, *Divrei Yoel*, I, pp. 580-81.
231. Cf. *Or HaHayyim* on Gen. 47:27; Exod. 3:8; *Toldot Ya'akov Yossef*, VaYakhel; *Maggid Devarav LeYa'akov*, 70, p. 119; *Bnei Issakhar, Haggadah*, p. 37: *Likkutei Moharan*, II, 76, p. 35a; *Sefat Emet*, II, p. 80. Alexandre Safran, *La Cabale*, pp. 338-39.
232. Cf. Zohar III, 221b; *Kuzari*, II, 35; Rabbeinu Bahya, *Kad HaKemah, Geulah*.

Sefat Emet, I, p. 123; II, p. 80. *Bet Avraham,* p. 54.
233. Cf. Abrabanel, I, Gen. 15, p. 203.
234. Cf. Gen. R. 1:4-6.
235. Cf. Exod. 19:5-6; cf. TB Berakhot 11b.
236. Cf. Exod. 6:7-8.
237. Cf. Maharal, *Gevurot HaShem,* 54, p. 146.
238. Cf. Maharal, *Gevurot HaShem,* 4, p. 18; *Avnei Nezer,* p. 10.
239. Cf. Gen. R. 1:4-6.
240. See A. Safran, *La Cabale,* p. 117s.
241. Cf. Exod. R. 51:5.
242. Cf. Gen. 18:19 and Rashi and Ramban ad loc.
243. Cf. Amos 3:2 and Targum and Rashi ad loc. Cf. Maharal, *Gevurot HaShem,* 9.
244. Cf. Deut. 26:5; Sifrei Ki Tavo 301 (Deut. 26:5), p. 128a and *Meir Ayin* ad loc. Maharal, *Gevurot HaShem,* 54, pp. 146, 148. Shelah, *Siddur Sha'ar HaShamayim,* p. 520. *Avnei Nezer,* p. 113. See also TB Shabbat 89a; *Shoher Tov,* 105; Gen. R. 86:1; Tanhuma, VaYeshev 3; Pesikta Zutarta, VaYeshev 39:1; Zohar I, 194b.
245. Deut. 26:5-6.
246. Cf. *Noam Elimelekh,* I, VaYeitsei, p. 79; *Sefat Emet,* I, p. 123.
247. Cf. Maharal, *Gevurot HaShem,* 54, p. 148; Rabbi Abraham of Sochaczew, *Neot HaDesheh,* p. 193. See also Num. R. 1:1.
248. Jer. 30:11, 46:28.
249. Cf. Ps. 31:20; Isa. 64:3. TB Berakhot 34b; Kiddushin 39b; Sanhedrin 99a. Num. R. 10:5, 13:3. Zohar I, 59a; II, 156b; 163a; 210b; 211a. Tikkunei HaZohar, 12a. Rashi on Deut. 32:43. Rambam, *Hilkhot Issurei Bi'a,* XIV, 4-5. Ramban on Deut. 32:40.
250. Cf. Ps. 66:5; Tanhuma, VaYeshev 4; see also Tanhuma, Emor 9. Cf. Zohar III, 159b; Zohar Hadash, Bereshit 18. Ari HaKadosh, *Likkutei Torah,* Bereshit. See also Deut. 22:17; I Sam. 2:3; Jer. 32:19; Rashi on Num. 11:2. See also TB Avodah Zarah 3a.
251. Cf. Abrabanel, I, Gen. 15:12, p. 214.
252. Within the general human scope, according to Bible and Talmud judicial rules, Galut may be a consequence of an intentional or even an unintentional transgression. Cf. Gen. 3:23-24, 4:12-14, 11:8. Gen. R. 19:18, 30:8. Num. 11:13. TB Sotah 49a; Sanhedrin 37b; Makot 10a; Menahot 37a. Mishnah Shevi'it X, 8; Makot I; II; III, 14. Tossefta Sanhedrin VII.
253. Cf. Rashi on Josh. 14, 15.
254. Cf. Maharal, *Gevurot HaShem,* 9, p. 33.
255. Kohelet 7:20. See TB Arakhin 17a.
256. Cf. Avot V, 2-3; Avot DeRabbi Nathan 32, 33.
257. Cf. Shir HaShirim R. 4:15.
258. Cf. TB Shabbat 97a; Gen. 15:6.
259. Cf. Maharal, *Gevurot HaShem,* 9, p. 34.
260. Cf. Gen. R. 59:9. Cf. TB Berakhot 13b.
261. Cf. Gen. 18, 19; TB Yevamot 79a; Maharal, *Gevurot HaShem,* 9, pp. 33-37.
262. Cf. Tossafot on Shabbat 10b.
263. Cf. Maharal, *Gevurot HaShem,* 9, p. 33: "Man is judged according to his

present acts and not according to his future behavior." Cf. TY Rosh HaShanah I, 3; TB Rosh HaShanah 16b; Gen. R. 53:19; Exod. R. 3:3; Rashi on Gen. 21:17.
264. Cf. Gen. 15:12 and Rashi ad loc. Cf. Gen. R. 44:20-21; Exod. R. 51:5. Maharal, *Gevurot HaShem*, 8, pp. 30, 54, 146. See Gen. R. 68:20-21; Tanhuma, VaYeitsei 2; Lev. R. 29:2; Ramban on Gen. 28:12. See Pirkei DeRabbi Eliezer 35. See TB Berakhot 9b; Exod. R. 3:7, 3:14. See also Deut. 2:14.
265. TB Nedarim 32a.
266. Cf. Isa. 41:8.
267. Gen. 15:6.
268. Gen. 15:13.
269. Cf. TB Nedarim 32a. See *Ba'al HaTurim* on Gen. 15:8.
270. Cf. Abrabanel, I, Gen. 15, p. 202s.
271. Ramban, *Perushei Iyov (Kitvei Ramban* I), pp. 28, 96.
272. Cf. Gen. 17:1 and commentaries ad loc. Cf. TB Nedarim 32a.
273. Cf. TB Sanhedrin 104a.
274. *Perushei Shedal Al Hamishah Humshei Torah*, Lekh Lekha, Gen. 15:8, p. 69.
275. Cf. TB Nedarim 32a (but see also TB Nedarim 32a-b); Gen. R. 18. Cf. TB Hullin 89a; Gen. 18:27 and Rashi ad loc.; Gen. R. 49:23. See also Rashi on Gen. 32:8; TB Berakhot 4a.
276. *Likkutei Moharan*, 7a, p. 8b.
277. *Mikhtav MeEliyahu*, II, pp. 173-77.
278. Maharal, *Gevurot Hashem*, 9, pp. 31-37.
279. Cf. Maharal, *Netivot Olam*, I, *Netiv HaEmunah*, I, p. 79b.
280. *Likkutei Moharan*, 7a, p. 8b.
281. Cf. Rashi on Gen. 15:15; Ramban on Exod. 12:42.
282. Cf. Abrabanel, I, p. 203. See also Maharal, *Gevurot Hashem*, 9, p. 33.
283. Maharal, *Gevurot HaShem*, 9, p. 31.
284. Cf. Ramban on Deut. 29:17.
285. Maharal, *Gevurot HaShem*, 9, p. 37.
286. Shelah, III, p. 24b. Cf. Rashi on Num. 16:5.
287. Cf. Abrabanel, I, Gen. 15, p. 203.
288. See Ramban on Gen. 12:10, 16:6. *Ba'al HaTurim* on Gen. 21:10. See also Maharal, *Gevurot HaShem*, 9, p. 33.
289. Cf. TB Yoma 38b; Sanhedrin 104a; Sotah 46b. See also Gen. R. 36.
290. Cf. Num. 14:11; Num. R. 16:6.
291. Cf. Num. 13; TB Sanhedrin 104a-b; Ta'anit 29a. Eihah R. 1:23. See also TB Sotah 46b.
292. TB Ta'anit 29a; Num. R. 16:12.
293. Cf. TB Yoma 38b.
294. Cf. TB Yoma 9b.
295. Exod. 20:5, 34:7. Num. 14:18. Deut. 5:9. TB Berakhot 7a. See Ezek. 18:20; TB Makot 24a. Deut. 24:16; Sifrei Ki Teitsei 280 (Deut. 24:16), p. 124. Jer. 31:29-30. See also Deut. 32:19; TB Ketuvot 8b. Num. R. 8:4. "The verse saying, 'God visits the iniquity of the fathers upon the children' (Exod. 20:5); is it not counterpoised by the following one (Deut. 24:16): 'the children shall not be put to death for the fathers'? How can one explain this contradiction? The given reply is that there is none, for the first verse applies to those who

follow the fathers' bad example, and the second to those who do not" (TB Berakhot 7a).
296. Cf. Exod. R. 30:5.
297. Shelah, III, p. 56a. See Gen. R. 85:2, 86:1. Tanhuma, VaYeshev 4.
298. TB Shabbat 10b.
299. *Perushei Maharal LeAggadot HaShas*, II, Shabbat 10b, p. 2.
300. Maharal, *Be'er HaGolah*, Be'er 7, p. 147.
301. Ps. 105:17, 105:19 and Rashi ad loc. See Shoher Tov, 105. Zohar III, 55a.
302. Cf. TB Sotah 11a.
303. Gen. 37:14.
304. Rabbi Yossef Rozin, the Gaon of Rogachov, *Mefa'aneah Tsefunot*, p. 170.
305. See Gen. R. 85:2, 86a. Tanhuma, VaYeshev 4.
306. Gen. R. 91:13.
307. Cf. TB Sanhedrin 102a; Sotah 13b. Rashi, Ibn Ezra and Seforno on Gen. 38:1.
308. Cf. Rashi, *Da'at Zekeinim MiBa'alei HaTossafot* and Seforno on Gen. 39:1. See Rambam, *Hilkhot Melakhim*, XI, 1.
309. Cf. Gen. R. 85:4. TB Sotah 13b; Sanhedrin 102a. But see also Gen. R. 85:6.
310. Cf. TB Nazir 23b and Tossafot ad loc. Gen. R. 85:8. Pesikta Zutarta, VaYeshev 38:14. See also Rashi on Gen. 39:10.
311. Cf. Gen. R. 85:9.
312. Cf. TB Sotah 10a-b; TY Sota I, 4. Gen. R. 85:8. Rashi on Gen. 39:1. Ari HaKadosh, *Likkutei Torah*, VaYeshev, p. 47b. Alshekh on Ruth, 3:2.
313. Gen. R. 85:2.
314. Cf. Gen. 38:29; Ruth 4:18-22.
315. Cf. Maharal, *Netivot Olam*, II, *Netiv HaTeshuvah*, 4, pp. 146-47.
316. Cf. TB Berakhot 34b; Sanhedrin 99a. Zohar I, 39a; 129b; II, 106a; 113b; III, 16b; 202b.
317. Cf. Targum Yonathan Ben Uziel on Num. 16:32. TB Shabbat 96b. Zohar III, 156b; 157a; 205b. Cf. TB Berakhot 47b; Sukkah 30a. Tossafot on Yevamot 103a. Maharik, *Shoresh* 165.
318. Cf. Ari HaKadosh, *Likkutei Torah*, VaYeshev, pp. 47b, 48a; Alshekh on Ruth 3:2.
319. Cf. TB Shabbat 55b-56a; Ta'anit 22a; Avodah Zarah 4b. Pesikta Zutarta, VaEthanan 5:26. Zohar I, 176a; II, 107a-b; III, 114a.
320. Cf. Tanhuma, Tetsaveh 6.
321. See Rashi on Deut. 29:12.
322. See TB Shabbat 30a; Zohar I, 218a.
323. Cf. Tana Devei Eliyahu Rabba 18; Exod. R. 29:8; Lev. R. 23:2; Rashi on Deut. 29:12.
324. Gen. 15:18.
325. Gen. R. 44. See TY Hallah II, 1.
326. Cf. Tanhuma, Tetsaveh 6. TB Rosh HaShanah 18a; Yevamot 105a. Maharal, *Netivot Olam*, I, *Netiv Gemilut Hassadim*, 1, p. 57a.
327. See Gen. 17, 32.
328. Cf. Job 28:23. TB Gittin 17a; Pessahim 87b. See also TB Avodah Zarah 3a; Exod. R. 34a; Tanhuma, Ki Tissa 10; Pesikta Rabbati, 16:8.
329. Cf. Ps. 33:15. Avot III, 15. HaGra, *Siddur Ishei Yisrael*, p. 48.

330. Cf. Gen. 3:22.
331. Cf. Deut. 11:26s.
332. Rambam, *Hilkhot Teshuvah*, V, 1-2. See also Meiri, Massekhet Shabbat, p. 87b.
333. *Toldot Ya'akov Yossef*, VaYakhel. See also Maharal, *Derekh Hayyim*, Avot II, 1, p. 50.
334. Cf. Deut. 34:10. TB Rosh HaShanah 21b. Rambam, *Hilkhot Yessodei HaTorah*, VII, 6; *Moreh Nevukhim*, II, 33; *Iggeret Teiman*, p. 177.
335. Lev. 19:1 and Alshekh ad loc.
336. TB Berakhot 33b. Cf. Zohar I, 59a; Tikkunei Zohar Hadash, 121a. Cf. TB Makot 10b; Num. R. 20:11; Tanhuma, Balak 8. Pesikta Zutarta, Shelah 13; Balak 22. Zohar I, 198b; II, 50a; III, 47a; Rav Kook, *Mishpat Kohen*, 144.
337. Cf. Rambam, *Hilkhot Deot*, IV; V; VI.
338. Cf. TB Rosh HaShanah 18a; Yevamot 105a. See Maharal, *Netivot Olam*, I, *Netiv Gemilut Hassadim*, 1, p. 57a.
339. Cf. Jer. 9:11, 16:10-11; I Kings 9:8. TB Bava Metsia 85a; Petihta De Eihah Rabbati 2; Sifrei and Rashi on Num. 15:41. Shoher Tov, 18. TB Shabbat 33a-b; Berakhot 61b; Avodah Zarah 17b. Cf. Deut. 29:23.
340. Cf. Mekhilta Yitro 6 (Exod. 20:5), p. 76a; Lev. R. 32:1; Shoher Tov, 12.
341. Cf. TB Ketuvot 111a; Shir HaShirim R. 2:18; Tanhuma, Noah 10; Devarim 4. See Maharal, *Netsah Yisrael*, 24; *Be'er HaGolah*, *Be'er* 7, p. 147. Rambam, *Iggeret Teiman*, p. 189.
342. Cf. TB Avodah Zarah 18a; Hatam Sofer, *Derashot*, II, p. 312.
343. TB Rosh HaShanah 18a.
344. Cf. TB Berakhot 8a; Ta'anit 8a and Rashi ad loc. Zohar I, 105b; 234a. *Hiddushei HaGra* on Berakhot 8a. See *Derashot HaRa*, *Derush* I.
345. Cf. TB Megillah 23b. Tikkunei HaZohar, 16b; 10(25a); 18(35b); 19(41b); 21(57a); 24(69a); 39(79b); 70(132a); Sha'arei Zohar, 118. Zohar Hadash, Yitro 34.
346. Cf. TB Shevuot 39a; Shabbat 146a. Exod. R. 28:4. Zohar I, 91a.
347. Cf. TY Ta'anit I, 4; II, 1. TB Yoma 86a; Rosh HaShanah 16b; 17b; Sanhedrin 10b. Gen. R. 44:15; Lev. R. 10:5; Kohelet R. 5:4, 9:7. Yalkut Shim'oni, Kohelet 11:1389. Pesikta Rabbati, 45:9; Pesikta Zutarta, Lekh Lekha 15:5. Zohar III, 218a. Maharal, *Netivot Olam*, II, *Netiv HaTeshuvah*, 6, p. 148.
348. Prayer Ritual for the High Holidays. See also TB Berakhot 10b. Lev. R. 35:1. TB Sanhedrin 108a. Maharal, *Perushim LeAggadot HaShas*, I, Bava Metsia 85a, p. 145.
349. Cf. Maharal, *Gevurot HaShem*, 7, p. 25.
350. Cf. Lev. R. 35:1.
351. Cf. Mishnah Yoma VIII, 9.
352. See Num. 13-14; Exod. 32-33. See also TB Sanhedrin 108a.
353. Cf. Tana Devei Eliyahu Rabba 14, See Maharal, *Netsah Yisrael*, 13.
354. Cf. Zohar III, 279a; Zohar Hadash, Noah 30. See Gen. R. 2:5. See also Maharal, *Netsah Yisrael*, 19.
355. Cf. TB Yoma 1b. Rabbi Eliyahu of Vilna, *Sefer HaEmunah VeHaHashgahah*, p. 5a.
356. Cf. TY Sanhedrin X, 2; TB Berakhot 10b; Gen. R. 65:4; Kohelet R. 9:27. Isa. 38.

357. Cf. Ezek. 18, 24. Eihah R. 1:22. Rashi on Gen. 6:14. See TB Rosh HaShanah 31a.
358. Cf. TB Rosh HaShanah 16b.
359. Cf. Dan. 9:13. Eihah R. 1:23. See also Ps. 127:1; Zohar III, 221a.
360. Cf. TB Gittin 88b; Rashi on Deut. 4:25. Gen. 15:13 and commentaries ad loc. Gen. R. 91:2; Zohar I, 198a. See also Lev. R. 10:5. TY Ta'anit I, 1; TB Sanhedrin 98a; Is. 60:22; Shir HaShirim R. 8 *in fine*; Zohar I, 117b; 119a; II, 10a; 188-189; III, 66b; 178b; 252a. Tikkunei HaZohar, 21(55a); Zohar Hadash, Ahrei 59. Tikkunei Zohar Hadash, 98b. Sha'arei Zohar, 101. Ramban on Exod. 12:42. See also Rabbi Moshe Hayyim Luzzatto, the "Ramhal," *Pithei Hokhmah*, pp. 8a-b.
361. Ps. 95:7; TB Sanhedrin 98a.
362. Cf. Gen. R. 33:4; Exod. R. 28:16. TB Shabbat 119b.
363. TB Shabbat 63a; cf. TB Shabbat 59b; Moed Katan 16b. See also Zohar II, 15a; III, 15a. 2 Sam. 23:3.
364. Rabbi Levi Yitshak of Berditchev, *Kedushat Levi*, VaYishlah, pp. 20b-21a.
365. Cf. TB Ta'anit 16a; Rashi on Jon. 3:8.
366. Cf. TB Pessahim 87b.
367. Cf. *Sefat Emet*, IV, pp. 45, 47.
368. Cf. Isa. 2:2-3; Mic. 4:1-2.
369. Avot V, 23.
370. Cf. Num. R. 19:1; Kohelet R. 8:5; Tanhuma, Hukat 8; Rashi on Num. 19:2. TB Yoma 67b; Shoher Tov, 9.
371. See infra, note 351.
372. Cf. TB Pessahim 54a; 68b; Avodah Zarah 3a. Gen. R. 1:1-2. Shoher Tov, 90. Zohar I, 5a; 24b; 47a; 90a; 134b; II, 161a; 200a; III, 35a; 69b. Tikkunei HaZohar, 4b; 11b; 28(70a); 69(98b); 70(120a). Zohar Hadash, Bereshit 5a; VaYeshev 29b; Ahrei 49a. Sha'arei Zohar, 40, 41.
373. Num. 19:2. Cf. *Kedushat Levi*, Hukat, p. 77a. Cf. TY Kilaim I, 7; Lev. 19:19.
374. Cf. Gen. R. 1:5, 44:27; Zohar I, 131b.
375. Isa. 55:9.
376. Cf. Deut. 32:7 and Rashi ad loc.
377. Cf. TB Haggigah 13a; Gen. R. 8:2; Zohar II, 270b; Tikkunei Zohar Hadash, 99.
378. Cf. Sifra and Rashi on Lev. 20:26.
379. Cf. Rambam, *Hilkhot Meilah*, III, 8 *in fine; Hilkhot Mikvaot*, XI, 12 *in fine; Moreh Nevukhim*, I, 32; III, 25.
380. See supra, note 347.
381. See also Job 15:7-8.
382. Ps. 148:6.
383. Cf. TB Shabbat 88a; Avodah Zarah 2b. Shir HaShirim R. 8:2. Zohar III, 125a. See also Tanhuma, Yitro 13.
384. Cf. Rambam, *Hilkhot Yessodei HaTorah*, IX, 1; *Hilkhot Melakhim*, XI, 3.
385. TB Berakhot 7a. Cf. Zohar II, 117b; III, 168a; 231a; 276b. Tikkunei HaZohar, 45(83a); 56(90b); 60(93b). See also Maharal, *Netsah Yisrael*, 19.
386. TB Menahot 29b. Cf. TB Berakhot 61b. Zohar I, 131b; III, 27b. Zohar Hadash, Ki Tissa 46a; Tikkunei Zohar Hadash, 99. Tikkunei HaZohar, 19 (39b, 40b). See also TY Haggigah II, 1.

387. Exod. R. 29:9 *in fine*.
388. Rambam, *Hilkhot Yessodei HaTorah*, I, 1.
389. Cf. TB Zevahim 115b; Rashi on Lev. 10:3.
390. Cf. Sifrei Ha'azinu 307 (Deut. 32:4), pp. 132b-133a; TB Avodah Zarah 18a; Massekhet Semahot VIII; Massekhet Derekh Erets Zuta III. *Kuzari*, III, 11.
391. Sifrei Ha'azinu 307 (Deut. 32:4), p. 132b.
392. Cf. Gen. 1:31; Gen. R. 9.
393. See Jer. 13:17. TB Haggigah 5b and Rashi ad loc. Zohar II, 17b; III, 15b.
394. Cf. *Toldot Ya'akov Yossef*, Terumah; VaYakhel *Maggid Devarav LeYa'akov*, 12, p. 25. *Biurei HaGra* on Tikkunei HaZohar, 48b. *Shem MiShemuel, Shemot*, I, p. 19.
395. See supra, notes 18, 90.
396. Cf. *Sefat Emet*, I, pp. 211, 257; II, p. 7.
397. "'In the morning, the Lord will show who is His' (Num. 16:5). 'In the morning': Moses told them: The Lord, blessed be He, defined in His world the different areas. Can you make morning out of evening? Neither can you cancel this (situation of Aaron), for it is said (Gen. 1:5-4): 'there was evening, and there was morning... and God separated (the light from the darkness).' In the same way (1 Chron. 23:13): 'Aaron was set apart to consecrate'" (Le commentaire de Rashi sur le Pentateuque, T. II, Paris, p. 63).
398. Cf. Pesikta DeRav Kahana, II, p. 463; see infra, note 379. Cf. Maharal, *Netsah Yisrael*, 62, 63. See A. Safran, *La Cabale*, p. 339s.
399. Cf. Esther 3:8. Tikkunei Zohar Hadash, 139.
400. Isa. 60:21.
401. Cf. Mekhilta Yitro, Messikhta DeAmalek 2 (Exod. 18:13), p. 67b; TB Shabbat 10a; 119b.
402. Gen. 2:3.
403. Cf. TB Pessahim 88a; see supra, note 375.
404. Cf. Deut. 30:1-5.
405. Cf. Isa. 35:10; TB Shabbat 88a. See Maharal, *Netsah Yisrael*, 63.
406. Cf. Zohar I, 116-119. *Kitvei Ramban* I, *Sefer HaGeulah*, p. 280. Maharal, *Tiferet Yisrael*, 52, p. 67. *Bet HaLevi*, II, p. 18.
407. Cf. Zohar II, 215b. Cf. TB Berakhot 12b; Maharal, *Tiferet Yisrael*, 52, pp. 65-66; *Netsah Yisrael, Hakdamah*.
408. Cf. *Sefat Emet*, II, p. 5; III, p. 45; IV, p. 195. Cf. Maharal, *Netsah Yisrael*, 53, 54; *Gevurot HaShem*, 3, 18: Rabbi Hayyim Yossef David Azulay, the "Hida," *Lehem Min HaShamayim*, p. 76b.
409. Num. 33:1; Ramban, Seforno and *Or HaHayyim* ad loc. See Rav Kook, *Olat Reiyah*, I, p. 363.
410. Cf. Ezek. 20:35.
411. Cf. *Sefat Emet*, IV, pp. 142, 197.
412. Gen. R. 44:20-21. See Rashi on Sanhedrin 92b.
413. Exod. R. 15:18.
414. Mic. 7:15; cf. Exod. R. 15:12.
415. TB Rosh HaShanah 11b; cf. Exod. R. 15:12; Zohar II, 120a; III, 249a. Cf. Maharal, *Gevurot HaShem*, 35, p. 81. Cf. Ari HaKadosh, Shemot p. 54a.
416. Cf. TY Pessahim X, 1; Gen. R. 88:4; Zohar II, 25a; Ramban on Gen. 28:12.
417. Mekhilta Bo, Messikhta DePissha 16 (Exod. 13:1), p. 24a. But see also Deut.

16:3; Mishnah Berakhot I, 5; TB Berakhot 12b; Rambam, *Mishneh Torah, Sefer Zemanim, Nossah HaHaggadah* (after *Hilkhot Hamets UMatsah*).
418. Cf. Mekhilta BeShalah, Messikhta DeShira I (Exod. 15:1), p. 42a; Exod. R. 23. Yalkut Shim'oni, Zekhariah 9:577; Zohar I, 114a; Zohar Hadash, Ahrei 59; Maharal, *Netsah Yisrael*, 46, 47, 63.
419. Cf. Hos. 2:18, 3:5; Zohar I, 225a; III, 6a; 52a; 178b; 239-40; 270a. Maharal, *Netsah Yisrael*, 47.
420. Cf. Ezek. 20:6-10; Exod. R. 17:3; Ramban on Exod. 2:25, 12:42. Maharal, *Netsah Yisrael*, 13, 31, 42; *Gevurot HaShem*, 35, pp. 81-82. *Sefat Emet*, III, p. 46. See also Exod. R. 1:16; Lev. R. 32:5; Num. R. 13:17, 20:21; Shir HaShirim R. 4:24. Pesikta Zutarta, Shemot 6:6; Bo 12:6. Pirkei DeRabbi Eliezer 48; Tana Devei Eliyahu Rabba 17; Tanhuma, Balak 16; Shoher Tov, 114; Yalkut Shim'oni, Emor 24:657; Balak 23:768. Zohar II, 7a.
421. Cf. Exod. 12:11; Deut. 16:3. Mekhilta Bo, Messikhta DePissha 7 (Exod. 12:11), p. 10a; TB Berakhot 9a; Zohar II, 4b; 94b. Maharal, *Netsah Yisrael*, 47; *Gevurot HaShem*, 36, p. 83.
422. Cf. Yalkut Shim'oni, Zekhariah 9:577. Maharal, *Netsah Yisrael*, 31, 62.
423. Even when God "sends ahead of" Israel "Moses, Aaron and Miriam" (to be Israel's guides), He Himself and none other "brings Israel up from the land of Egypt and redeems them from the house of bondage" (cf. Mic. 6:4). In fact, the Torah says clearly that "the Lord brought us out of Egypt" (Deut. 6:21, 26:8). The Pessah Haggadah insists that "the Lord brought us out of Egypt: not through an angel, neither through any other intermediary; but the Lord, blessed be His name, in all His glory, redeemed us himself." See Maharal, *Netsah Yisrael*, 13; Shelah, *Siddur Sha'ar HaShamayim*, pp. 517-18. See also Exod. R. 1:22, 1:25, 32:3.
424. See also Ps. 147:2.
425. Cf. Maharal, *Netsah Yisrael*, 1; *Kedushat Levi*, VaYigash, p. 25b.
426. Cf. Maharal, *Netsah Yisrael*, 13, 31; *Shem MiShemuel, Haggadah*, p. 86.
427. Cf. TY Berakhot II, 4. See also Gen. R. 5:2; Isa. 66:7. Cf. *Kitvei Ramban* I, *Vikuah*, p. 306. Petihta De Esther R. *in fine*.
428. Cf. Exod. R. 1:31. Maharal, *Netsah Yisrael*, 26, 28; *Gevurot HaShem*, 18, pp. 51-52.
429. Cf. *Mei Meirom*, VI, p. 242.
430. Cf. *Sefat Emet*, II, p. 24; V, p. 5. See TB Pessahim 118b. Cf. *Or HaHayyim* on Lev. 25:25.
431. Cf. *Kedushat Levi*, Bo, p. 36b.
432. Cf. Hatam Sofer, *Haggadah Shel Pessah*, p. 120.
433. Gen. 47:4.
434. See *Kli Yakar* on Lev. 18:3.
435. Cf. Exod. 12:49 et al.
436. Cf. Ps. 137:5.
437. Cf. *Avnei Nezer*, p. 21; *Shem MiShemuel, Haggadah*, p. 41.
438. Cf. Pesikta DeRav Kahana, I, 21, p. 328. See also *Moreh Nevukhim*, III, 47; *Sefer HaHinukh*, Mitzvah 184. See also *El HaTsipor* by H. N. Bialik (*Kol Kitvei H. N. Bialik*, Tel Aviv: 5709 (1949), p. 1).
439. Cf. Shelah, III, p. 24a; *Toldot Ya'akov Yossef*, Noah; *Bnei Issakhar*, I, p. 111a; *Sefat Emet*, V, p. 5; *Shem MiShemuel, Devarim*, p. 34.

440. Cf. *Sefat Emet*, II, p. 25(13); cf. *Torah Or*, p. 45a. See *Studies in the History of Jewish Education* (Jerusalem: 5743 (1983)), by my brother, Rabbi Dr. Joseph Safran. Chapter dedicated to the *Shoah*, the Holocaust, pp. 510-55.
441. Cf. TB Shabbat 146a; Zohar III, 14b; Lev. R. 18:4; Kohelet R. 8:3; Pesikta Rabbati, 7:7, 26:6; Maharal, *Gevurot HaShem*, 9, p. 33.
442. *Neot HaDesheh*, p. 193; *Sefat Emet*, I, p. 56.
443. Cf. TB Kiddushin 22b; see also TY Rosh HaShanah III, 5; Maharal, *Gevurot HaShem*, 9, p. 33; *Sefat Emet*, II, p. 25; III, pp. 190, 196; *Meshekh Hokhmah*, p. 59. See also Mekhilta Yitro, Messikhta DeAmalek 2 (Exod. 19:1), p. 69b; Avot III, 5.
444. Ps. 105:45.
445. Cf. Rambam, *Hilkhot Melakhim*, XI; *Iggeret Teiman*, p. 181.
446. Cf. Maharal, *Netsah Yisrael*, 26; *Gevurot HaShem*, 4, 5, 18, p. 51. *Sefat Emet*, V, p. 5. *Shem MiShemuel, Bemidbar*, p. 335; Rabbi Yehuda HaLevi Ashlag, *Matan Torah*, pp. 147-48. See Mishnah Pessahim X, 4.
447. Cf. Gen. 1:2-3; TB Shabbat 77a and Maharsha ad loc. Lev. R. 31:7. Ramban on Gen. 2:3 *in fine; Kitvei Ramban* I, *Torat HaShem Temimah*, p. 169. Rabbi S.R. Hirsch on Gen. 1:4, I, p. 9.
448. Cf. Mishnah Berakhot I, 5. TB Pessahim 2b. Gen. R. 1:8, 2:5, 91:13. Shir HaShirim R. 3. Pesikta Zutarta, VaYishlah 32:25. Maharal, *Gevurot HaShem*, 8, p. 32. See TB Sanhedrin 24a. See 2 Sam. 23:4; Zech. 14:7. See also Zohar III, 238b. Cf. *Biur HaGra* on Zohar II, 119b.
449. Cf. Zohar II, 7b.
450. Cf. Mekhilta Yitro, Messikhta DeAmalek 2 (Exod. 19:1), p. 69b; Exod. R. 15:10, 45:2. Hatam Sofer, *Derashot*, p. 315.
451. Gen. 12:10, 13:1.
452. Cf. Shelah, III, p 24b.
453. Cf. Gen. R. 86:1; TB Shabbat 89b; Zohar I, 194b.
454. Cf. TB Berakhot 26b; Zohar I, 163a; cf. Ps. 92:3.
455. Cf. *Biur HaGra* on Zohar II, 119b.
456. Jer. 30:7; cf. Deut. R. 2:6; Ezek. 29:20-21; Zohar III, 212b. Rambam, *Iggeret Teiman*, p. 176. Rabbi Yehonathan Eibeschutz, *Tiferet Yehonathan*, Va'era. *Sefat Emet*, V, p. 34.
457. Esther 9:1. See Seforno on Gen. 41:14.
458. Cf. TY Ta'anit II, 5; Exod. 14:13.
459. Cf. Ps. 113:7.
460. "For our soul is bowed down to the dust, our body cleaves to the ground. Rise up, come to our help: Deliver us for the sake of Thy steadfast love" (Ps. 44:25-26). See TB Rosh HaShanah 31b; Isa. 52:2. Se also Rambam, *Iggeret Teiman*, pp. 158-59.
461. Cf. Pesikta Rabbati, 15; Tanhuma, Shemot 6. *Sefat Emet*, I, p. 210.
462. See Rambam, *Hilkhot Melakhim*, XI; *Iggeret Teiman*, pp. 177-82.
463. Cf. Rambam, *Hilkhot Melakhim*, XII, 2; Ramban, *Sefer HaGeulah* (*Kitvei Ramban* I), pp. 279-80; Maharal, *Netsah Yisrael*, 24, 44, 45. See also TB Pessahim 54b; Sanhedrin 99a. Kohelet R. 12:10. Rambam, *Iggeret Teiman*, pp. 152-55, 172.
464. See Rabbi Menahem M. Kasher, *HaTekufah HaGedolah*, Jerusalem: 5729 (1969); idem, *Milhemet Yom HaKippurim*, Jerusalem: 5734 (1974). Rabbi

Tsevi Yehuda Kook, *LeNetivot Israel*, Jerusalem: 5727 (1967). Rabbi Shelomo Goren, *Torat HaMoadim*, Tel-Aviv: 5724 (1964). Rabbi Yoel Teitelbaum of Satmar, *VaYoel Moshe*, New York: n.d.; idem, *Kunterass Al HaGeulah VeAl HaTemurah*, New York: 5727 (1967). Yeshayahu Leibovitz, *Yahadut: Am Yehudi UMedinat Yisrael*, Tel-Aviv: 5736 (1975). Cf. A. Neher, *L'Existence Juive*, Paris: 1962.

465. Cf. TB Sanhedrin 98-99; Deut. R. 2:6. See TB Berakhot 6b. *Siddur HaGeonim VeHaMekubalim*, III, p. 714. *Neot HaDesheh*, p. 139.
466. Cf. Gen. R. 85:2.
467. Cf. Gen. R. 56:13; Num. R. 11:1; Shir HaShirim R. 1:21. *Kuzari*, IV, 23; Abrabanel, I, Gen. 15:12, p. 214. Maharal, *Netsah Yisrael*, 1; *Derekh Hayyim*, Avot V, 5, p. 172; *Derashot, Hesped*, pp. 12-13. Shelah, III, pp. 161-62. Rabbi Eliyahu of Vilna, *Aderet Eliyahu*, p. 394. *Kedushat Levi*, pp. 25b. 59b. *Sefat Emet*, I, pp. 134, 199, 257. Rav Kook, *Orot HaKodesh*, II, p. 479.
468. Cf. Num. R. 7:10. Rambam, *Hilkhot Teshuvah*, VII, 5; *Hilkhot Melakhim*, XI, 1; Ramban on Lev. 26:16; Deut. 30:6. *Mikhtav MeEliyahu*, II, p. 50. See also TB Shabbat 104a; Shir HaShirim R. 5:3; Pesikta Rabbati, 15:6. See Deut. 30:1-5.
469. Cf. Hab. 2:3; *Kuzari*, III, 11-12; Rambam, *Hilkhot Melakhim*, XII, 2; *Iggeret Teiman*, p. 169. Rav Kook, *Orot*, p. 9.
470. Cf. Num. R. 13:3.
471. Cf. Rambam, *Hilkhot Teshuvah*, IX, 2; *Hilkhot Melakhim*, XII, 4.
472. Cf. *Sefat Emet*, I, p. 200.
473. Mic. 7:8.
474. Shoher Tov, 22.
475. Cf. Exod. R. 15:17.
476. Cf. TY Yoma III, 2; Zohar I, 170a; Tanhuma, Devarim 1.
477. Cf. *Sefat Emet*, I, p. 7.
478. *Mei Meirom*, VI, p. 52; see ibidem, pp. 60, 242.
479. Cf. Maharal, *Netsah Yisrael*, 1; *Kedushat Levi*, p. 25b.
480. See Gen. R. 78:1. Cf. Ramban, *Sefer HaGeulah* (*Kitvei Ramban* I), p. 280; Maharal, *Netsah Yisrael*, 1.
481. Cf. TB Makot 24b.
482. Cf. Lev. R. 35:1.
483. Cf. Zohar III, 143b; Zohar Hadash, 59b.
484. Ps. 98:3.
485. Prov. 29:4.
486. Rashi on Gen. 1:1.
487. See Gen. R. 8:4, 12:15, 14:1. Zohar I, 2b; 58b; 114b; 180b; 230b; II, 113b; 212b; III, 32a; 38a. Tikkunei HaZohar, 16a. Zohar Hadash, Shir HaShirim 63; Ruth 88. Rabbi Hayyim Yossef David Azulai, the "Hida", *Midbar Kedemot*, p. 31. Isa. 11:5.
488. Prayer Ritual for the High Holidays.
489. Cf. *Mei Meirom*, VI, p. 158.
490. Cf. Gen. R. 85,z; Exod. R. 45:2. *Sefat Emet*, II, p. 7. Isa. 66:7. Pesikta Zutarta, Shemot 3:1. TB Megillah 13b. Shir HaShirim R. 4:12.
491. Cf. Deut. R. 2:14. See TY Ta'anit I, 1.
492. Cf. *Kedushat Levi*, Pekkudei, p. 59b.

493. See Ramban on Exod. 2:25.
494. Zohar III, 143b.
495. Rabbi Hayyim Vital, *Peri Ets Hayyim, Sha'ar HaShofar*, 1, p. 23. See *Toldot Ya'akov Yossef*, Noah; *Noam Elimelekh*, VaYigash.
496. *Toldot Ya'akov Yossef*, Bereshit.
497. HaGra, *Sefer HaEmunah VeHaHashgahah*, pp. 12b-13a.
498. *Toldot Ya'akov Yossef*, Bereshit.
499. Cf. Amos 5:4, 5:6.
500. Tikkunei HaZohar, *Tikkun* 26.
501. Cf. Rabbi Abraham of Slonim, *Bet Avraham*, pp. 91, 94.
502. *Sefat Emet*, II, pp. 3, 25.
503. *Sefat Emet*, II, p. 7.
504. *Sefat Emet*, I, pp. 211, 257.
505. Cf. *Sefat Emet*, II, pp. 3, 25, 27.
506. Cf. *Sefat Emet*, II, p. 23.
507. Rav Kook, *Olat Reiyah*, I, pp. 307-8.
508. Cf. Gen. 1:31; Gen. R. 9:8-12; see also Exod. R. 31. Zohar I, 14a; 47a; 144b; II, 68b; 149b; 163a; 249a; 264b; III, 63a; 185a. Tikkunei HaZohar, 21 (49a). Sha'arei Zohar, 128. See also Mishnah Berakhot I, 5.
509. Isa. 40:5; see also Isa. 52:8; see also Num. 14:14. Cf. Maharal, *Gevurot Hashem*, 47, pp. 116-17. See also Zohar I, 216a.
510. Cf. Exod. 33:20; TB Megillah 19b and Maharsha ad loc. See TB Yevamot 49b.
511. Cf. Ps. 31:20.
512. Cf. Yalkut Shim'oni, Hos. 14. Cf. *Sefat Emet*, I, pp. 134, 199.
513. Cf. Num. R. 10:5, 13:3. See Ramban on Deut. 32:40; Rashi on Deut. 32:43.
514. Cf. Rambam, *Hilkhot Teshuvah*, VIII, 1; Ramban, *Sefer HaGeulah (Kitvei Ramban* I), pp. 279-80.
515. Ps. 118:21.
516. Isa. 12:1; cf. TB Niddah 31a; Shoher Tov, 118, 119.
517. *Avnei Nezer*, p. 113.
518. TB Pessahim 50a.
519. Cf. Rashi on Exod. 6:2; Lev. 18:5, 19:16 et al.
520. Cf. Gen. R. 78:1.
521. *Sefat Emet*, I, p. 267. *Be'er Avraham*, pp. 94-95. Cf. Lev. R. 32:7; Shir HaShirim R. 4:16; Pesikta Rabbati, 8; Zech. 4:2. Cf. Maharal, *Netsah Yisrael*, 1.
522. Cf. Rabbi Yehoshua D'ostrova, *Toldot Adam, Shabbat HaGadol*.
523. See *Sefat Emet*, I, p. 266.
524. Cf. Ramban on Deut. 30:6.
525. Cf. Maharal, *Netsah Yisrael*, 1; *Gevurot HaShem*, 23, p. 63.

Chapter Three

1. It is upon the *even shetiyya*, the "founding stone," that *shat Ya*, "God set" the universe. Cf. Mishnah Yoma V, 2; Tossefta Yoma II; TB Yoma 54b. Zohar I, 71b-72a; 78a; 231a; II, 157a-b; 222a. Tikkunei HaZohar, 18 (36b); 69

(110a); 70 (126b). Zohar Hadash, Bereshit 2:4; VaYeitsei 28a. Shir HaShirim R. 3:18. Tanhuma, Kedoshim 10; Ahrei 3. Yalkut Shim'oni, VaYeitsei 28:120. Ramban on Gen. 1:1. Jerusalem "is the pre-eminent place, for the life of the world starts there; its potential develops therein, its climates and the species of all orders appear in it." "This place is therefore the root of all other places." "Erets-Yisrael — The Land of Israel — is the soul of the universe, and Jerusalem is its spirit." Cf. TB Ta'anit 10a. Zohar II, 23b. Ramban, *Perushei HaTorah, Hakdamat HaRamban*, Shavell ed., vol. I, p. 6; *Kitvei Ramban*, Shavell ed., vol II, Shir HaShirim 8, p. 518. *She'elot UTeshuvot HaRadbaz*, I, No. 591, p. 18; No. 539, p. 9. Maharal, *Gur Aryeh*, Gen. 2:7; idem, *Perushei Maharal LeAggadot HaShas*, IV, on TB Ketuvot 110-111; idem, *Netsah Yisrael*, 8; *Netivot Olam*, I, *Netiv HaTorah*, 10, p. 18b. Rabbi Moshe Alshekh, *Torat Moshe*, VaYeitsei, Gen. 28:13. Rabbi Shelomo Ephraim Lunschitz, *Kli Yakar*, VaYeitsei, Gen. 28:13. Rabbi Dov Baer of Mezerich, *Maggid Devarav LeYa'akov*, 15, p. 29; 20, pp. 32-33. Rabbi Eliyahu of Vilna, *Biurei HaGra Al Aggadot*, II, pp. 36a-b; idem, *Divrei Eliyahu*, p. 49. Rabbi Hayyim of Volozhin, *Nefesh HaHayyim*, 1, 4-5. Rabbi Yehuda Aryeh Leib of Gur, *Sefat Emet*, I, p. 229. Rabbi Abraham of Slonim, *Yessod HaAvodah*, II, p. 83.

2. Jerusalem is *Sha'ar HaShamayim*, "the entry to Heaven." Through this entry, prayers from all over the world rise and enter. Cf. Gen. R. 69:5-6; Rashi on Gen. 28:17. Cf. TB Pessahim 88a. Zohar II, 69b. Shoher Tov, 81. Likkutim MeRav Hai Gaon, 9b, quoted in *Siddur HaGeonim VeHaMekubalim*, I, pp. 10-11. Rabbi Yehuda HaLevi, *Kuzari*, II, 23. Ramban, *Tefillah Al Horvot Yerushalayim* (*Kitvei Ramban* I, p. 424). Rabbi Eliyahu of Vilna, quoted in *HaGaon HeHassid MiVilna*, by R. Betsalel Landau, p. 241. See infra, notes 9, 33.

3. Cf. TB Rosh HaShanah 23b and Tossafot ad loc. TB Sanhedrin 37a and Rashi ad locum. Rashi on TB Sotah 48b. Zohar I, 226b. Zohar Hadash, Bereshit 2, 9.

4. *Kav emtsai*, "the medium line," "is the inner, spiritual bolt, which contains all, which connects all parts of the world among themselves and to their original point." Furthermore, "through this line, God causes His Grace to descend and spread throughout the world." Cf. Recanati, Bereshit, p. 8a; VaYeitsei, pp. 28, 29a. Shelah, *Siddur Sha'ar HaShamayim*, pp. 192, 478. Rabbi Eliyahu of Vilna, *Siddur Ishei Yisrael*, p. 332. Rabbi Shemuel Shmelke of Nikolsburg, *Divrei Shemuel*, pp. 94, 119; Rabbi Abraham of Sochaczew, *Neot HaDesheh*, pp. 106, 136-37, 141. Cf. also *Sefer HaZohar Im Perushei HaSulam*, IV, Yitro, p. 140 (545).

5. "The Jerusalem on high corresponds to the Jerusalem below; the Jerusalem below corresponds to the Jerusalem on high": There exists a relationship and even an interdependence between the heavenly Jerusalem and the earthly one. Thanks to this relationship, their joint role can be accomplished, a creative, beneficent role, constructive and messianic. Cf. Mekhilta on Beshalah, Exod. 15:17; Messikhta DeShira, 10, pp. 51b-52a. TY Berakhot IV, 5. TB Ta'anit 5a. Gen. R. 55:9, 69:6. Exod. R. 33:4. Shir HaShirim R. 4:11. Midrash Tanhuma, Mishpatim 18; VaYakhel 7; Pekkudei 1-3. Shoher Tov, 30. Avot DeRabbi Nathan 26:2. Zohar I, 2a; 80b; 128b; 159a; 183b; II, 5a;

108a. Zohar Hadash, Terumah 42. Rashi on Gen. 28:17. Ramban on Gen. 14:18. Rabbi Yitshak Aizik of Sovalk, in his commentary *Be'er Yitshak*, on *Aderet Eliyahu*, by Rabbi Eliyahu of Vilna, pp. 371, 373.
6. *Melo kol HaArets Kevodo.* "The whole world is full of His glory" (Isa. 6:3): this glory is shown through His acts. However, God reveals His *Shekhinah* — His presence — in a special place: *Barukh Kevod HaShem MiMekomo*: "Blessed be the Lord's Glory (which comes) from His place" (Ezek. 3:12)." (Maharsha on TB Haggigah 13b). "Behold, there is a place by Me": *Makom iti* (Exod. 33:21). He carries this place of revelation everywhere in the world, for "it is He who is the place of the world" (Gen. R. 60:10). "No place is devoid of Him." His Presence is everywhere. Cf. Alsheikh on Ki Tissa, Exod. 34:22. Rabbi Eliyahu of Vilna, *Biurei HaGra al Aggadot*, I, p. 13. Rabbi Hayyim, *Be'er Mayim Hayyim*, on Gen. 42:7-12. Yossef Dan, *Iyunim BeSifrut Hassidut Ashkenaz*, Ramat-Gan: Massada, 1975, p. 83. But see also TB Bava Batra 25a; see infra, notes 22 and 29.
7. Cf. Gen. R. 68:10. Shir HaShirim R. 3:9. Pesikta DeRav Kahana, *Pisska VeYehi BeYom Kalot Moshe* (Num. 7:1). Philon of Alexandria, *Confus.*, 136.
8. "Shout, and sing for joy, O inhabitant of Zion, for great in your midst is the Holy One of Israel!" (Isa. 12:6). Cf. Rabbi Eliyahu of Vilna, *Siddur Ishei Yisrael*, p. 332.
9. "The entry to the Heavens" (see supra, note 2), Jerusalem is the place which connects the earth to the Heavens (cf. Rabbi Eliyahu of Vilna, *Sefer Ha Emunah VeHaHashgahah*, p. 10b. HaGra on Isa. 8:11. *Be'er Mayim Hayyim* on Gen. 28:17. *Sefat Emet*, III, pp. 198, 200. *Avnei Nezer*, p. 113). Jerusalem is the place which Jacob saw in his dream (Gen. 28:12-17) and where he received the "good news" regarding the Land promised to him and to his children. The ladder Jacob saw in his dream "hung over the site of *Bet HaMikdash*," the future sanctuary of Jerusalem (Rashi on Gen. 28:17; Gen. R. 69:5). This ladder connects Heaven and earth, it joins their boundaries and therefore makes them one upon earth (cf. Zohar I, 149a; Keli Yakar on Gen. 28:12).
10. Cf. TB Bava Batra 74a. Cf. *Be'er Mayim Hayyim* on Gen. 1:1 (V); see Rabbi Ya'akov Moshe Harlap, *Mei Meirom, Missaviv LiShmonah Perakim LeHa-Rambam*, p. 218. See also Targum and Rashi on Eihah 2:1; see also Isa. 66:1; TB Sanhedrin 7a.
11. Cf. Gen. R. 3:12; ibid. 4. Midrash Tanhuma, Behukotai 3. Zohar I, 57b; 61a; II, 32b; 65b; III, 44a. Maharal, *Derekh Hayyim*, Avot V, 1, p. 166; Avot III, 6, p. 95. Shelah, I, p. 3a. *Or HaHayyim* on Gen. 1:1 (22). Rabbi Hayyim of Volozhin, *Nefesh HaHayyim*, 1:3-4. Rav Kook, *Orot*, p. 169; *Orot HaKodesh*, II, pp. 427-29, 433-34, 444; *Olat Reiyah*, I, p. 13. In the Jerusalem Sanctuary, the Heavenly Father, "God, wishes to cooperate" with man, and the work man does in Jerusalem must be a "heavenly work" (cf. Tossafot on TB Bava Batra 21a). See also Esther Starobinski-Safran, "*De Fuga et Inventione*" by *Philon of Alexandria*, Paris: éditions du Cerf, 1970, pp. 307-8.
12. Cf. TB Yevamot 61a; Bava Metsia 114b. Zohar I, 20b; II, 25a-b; 86a; III, 238b. Hakdamat Tikkunei HaZohar, 6a. Zohar Hadash, Yitro 37a. See also Zohar III, 173b; Tossafot on TB Yevamot 61a; Avodah Zarah 3a; Bava Kama 38a; Sanhedrin 59a. TY Shekalim I, 4. Cf. also Gen. R. 68:18. Zohar I, 24a; 72a;

97a; II, 241-42. Tikkunei HaZohar, 22 (65b). Zohar Hadash, Bereshit 14. Sha'arei Zohar, p. 89. Ramban on Gen. 33:20. Pirkei DeRabbi Eliezer 35. *Kuzari*, I, 95, 103; II, 44; III, 73. Recanati, Bereshit, pp. 9a, 10a. Shelah, I, p. 21a. Rav Kook, *Orot*, p. 170; *Orot HaKodesh*, III, pp. 43, 68, 435, 444-45. Avraham Kariv, *Kitvei Maharal MiPrag* (Jerusalem: 5720 (1960)), I, pp. 35, 37, 42. *Perushei Maharal MiPrag LeAggadot HaShas*, IV, on TB Ketuvot 66b, p. 68.

13. Cf. Zohar I, 2; 157a; 222a; 231a. See also Ramban on Gen. 1:1.
14. Cf. Ramban on Gen. 14:18.
15. Cf. *Kuzari*, IV, 11.
16. Cf. Ibn Ezra on Gen. 2:12. See also *Kli Yakar* on Gen. 3:23; M.D. Cassuto, *MeAdam Ad Noah*, pp. 101-3; Rabbi Ya'akov Moshe Harlap, *Mei Meirom*, V, on Gen. 2:15, pp. 11-12. See also *Kuzari*, II, 20. Cf. TB Sanhedrin 38b; Pirkei DeRabbi Eliezer 20.
17. "And they heard the sound of the Lord God walking in the garden in the cool of the day, and the man and his wife hid themselves from the presence of the Lord God among the trees of the garden. But the Lord God called to the man, and said to him: where are you? *Ayeka*? And he said, I heard the sound of thee in the garden, and I was afraid, because I was naked, and I hid myself" (Gen. 3:8-10).
18. The sacrifices and the prayer are called *minhah*. They form an "offering." Netsiv, Cf. Ramban on Num. 16:15; Netsiv, *Ha'amek Davar*, I, on Gen. 4:3-5. Cf. also TB Hullin 60a; Zohar II, 34a; Ramban on Gen. 4:3.
19. Israel is called "Man." Cf. TB Yevamot 61a; TB Bava Metsia 114b; *Kuzari*, II, 14. See supra, note 12.
20. "In the future, Jerusalem will become the metropolis of all lands" (Exod. R. 23:11; Shir HaShirim R. 1:37. Cf. also Avot DeRabbi Nathan 38; Zohar II, 220a.
21. Cf. Gen. R. 47:8. See Rabbi Shneur Zalman of Lyady, *Tanya, Likkutei Amarim*, 23, p. 28b.
22. Isa. 6:3. Cf. Gen. R. 4:3; Exod. R. 2:9; Zohar III, 225a; Tikkunei HaZohar, 57; Rabbi Nahman of Bratslav, *Likkutei Moharan*, I, 33, p. 46b. Cf. Philon, *Confus.*, 136; *Somn.*, II, 211. See supra, note 6.
23. Cf. Zohar I, 80a; 147b.
24. "'The Lord God formed man of the dust of the earth' (Gn. 2:7). God picked up dust from all over the earth, from the four cardinal points. Wherever man will die, the earth accepts his grave. A different explanation: it was dust taken from the place of which it was said: 'an altar of earth you shall make for me' (Exod. 20:24). God said to Himself: may it be his atonement, so that he can continue to live" (Rashi ad loc.; cf. TB Sanhedrin 38a). TY Nazir VII, 2. Gen. R. 14:9. Tanhuma, Pekkudei 3. Zohar I, 34b; 80a; 130b; 205b; II, 23b; 24b; III, 46b; 83a; 161b. Zohar Hadash, Yitro 31. Tikkunei Zohar Hadash, 98a. *Kuzari*, II, 14. Ramban, *Torat HaAdam, Sha'ar HaGemul* (*Kitvei Ramban* II, p. 296). Maharal, *Perushei Maharal MiPrag LeAggadot HaShas*, IV, p. 93; Idem, *Gur Aryeh* Gen. 2:7.
25. From the summit of Mount Moriah, the great and divine Teaching for man comes down into the world; from its heights the Torah is heard for Israel. At that place, *Moriah* personifies *Yerushalayim* (cf. Rashi on Gen. 22:2); from

afar, Moriah personifies Sinai (cf. Tossafot on TB Ta'anit 16a). This is why, all over the world, Zion is with the Torah's Sages (cf. TB Sotah 49a and Maharsha ad loc). This is why "from out of Zion shall go forth the Torah and the word of the Lord from Jerusalem" (Isa. 2:3). See TY Berakhot IV, 5. TB Berakhot 8a; Ta'anit 16a; Bava Batra 21a; Makot 10a. Sifrei on Deut. 17:8. Gen. R. 55:9. Yalkut Shim'oni, VaYehi 49:9, 160. Yalkut Reuveni, Vezot HaBerakhah. Zohar I, 15a; 151a; III, 20a. Zohar Hadash, Hukat 50a. Rashi and Ramban on Gen. 22:2. *Sefer HaHinukh, Mitzvah* 360, p. 210. Shelah, I, p. 26b s., *Derush Har HaMoriah*. Cf. Rabbi Eliyahu of Vilna, *Hidushei UBiurei HaGra* on Avot V, 22, p. 132; idem, *Biurei HaGra Al Aggadot*, I, pp. 83, 85, 90, 113; The Torah comes out of Zion and the word of the Lord (both in the generosity of Prophecy and in the precision of the Law) out of Jerusalem (but see also idem, *Biurei HaGra Al Aggadot*, II, p. 64). See Rabbi Yehuda HaLevi, *Kuzari*, III, 39; Rambam, *Moreh Nevukhim*, III, 45; Rabbi Yehuda Aryeh Leib of Gur, *Sefat Emet*, IV, p. 85; Rabbi Abraham of Slonim, *Be'er Avraham*, p. 33; Rabbi Meir Simha Kohen of Dvinsk, *Meshekh Hokhmah*, pp. 20, 321.

26. Cf. Maharal, *Netsah Yisrael*, 5.
27. "If you come to My house, I shall come to yours; if you do not come to My house, I shall not come to your house, for it is said (Exod. 20:24) 'In every place where I cause my name to be remembered, I will come to you and bless you ' " (TB Sukkah 53a; see Tossafot ad loc). See also Rashi and Tossafot on TB Sotah 38a; Ramban on Exod. 20:24. Cf. Rabbi Eliyahu of Vilna, *Aderet Eliyahu*, p. 56; idem, *Biurei HaGra Al Aggadot*, I, p. 12; idem, *Siddur Ishei Yisrael*, pp. 333-34. Cf. Rabbi Abraham of Slonim, *Be'er Avraham*, p. 189.
28. God is everywhere. Cf. Sifrei Eikev 40 (Deut. 11:12), p. 786; Pesikta DeRav Kahana, Ki Tissa; Exod. R. 34:1; Num. R. 12:4.
29. "God is called 'the Place of the world" (Gen. R. 68:10), because He creates all places and makes them exist in the world," says the Maharal. *Mekomo shel olam*, "the Place of the world," comes towards man (see supra, note 17), whom the holy word calls upon in these words: *MeEize Makom Ata?* "From what place do you come?" What is your relation with Him who is the Place of the world? Which is for you the main place? Do you wish to find your place near Him? (Cf. Rabbi Ya'akov Moshe Harlap, *Mei Meirom*, II, on Avot VI, 9, p. 249; cf. also idem, *Mei Meirom*, V, on Gen. 28:11, p. 83. See also Tikkunei HaZohar, 26 (71b).)
30. *HaMakom asher yivhar HaShem*: "It is here, to the place chosen by the Lord your God to make His name dwell there, that you shall bring all that I command you" (Deut. 12:11; cf. ibidem, 16:11). The *makom*, the place *par excellence*, is *Yerushalayim* (cf. Rabbi Shelomo of Radomsk, *Tiferet Shelomo*, Mass'ei). See TB Sotah 38a; Num R. 11:9; Shelah, III, p. 99s.; Rabbi Eliyahu of Vilna, *Aderet Eliyahu*, p. 399.
31. God "has chosen the City," "He will choose Jerusalem," "He has chosen Zion, He wished for it to be His dwelling," "He has chosen Jacob for Himself, Israel as his own possession" (1 Kings 8:48; Zech. 1:17, 2:16; Ps. 132:13, 135:4). "God chose Jerusalem to become the heritage of His Shekhinah (the residence of His presence), He chose Israel to be His jewel" (Rambam, *Perush HaMishnayot*, on Zevahim XIV, 8). Cf. Ralbag on Gen.

28:10; Abrabanel on Gen. 28:12; Alshekh on Exod. 23:20.
32. The Jew says his prayers in the direction of Jerusalem. Cf. 1 Kings 8:30; Dan. 6:11; TY Berakhot IV, 5; TB Berakhot 30a; Shir HaShirim R. 4:11; Zohar I, 209b.
33. Cf. TB Berakhot 30a.
34. "And let them make Me a sanctuary: *Mikdash*" (Exod. 25:8). Rashi (ad loc.): "and they will make for My Name a holy house: *Bet Kedushah*." Cf. Rabbi Eliyahu of Vilna, *Biurei HaGra Al Aggadot*, I, p. 83.
35. Cf. TB Berakhot 30a.
36. The value of an offering lies in the eagerness and the generosity which man displays when he chooses it. His gift is accepted by God when it combines the finest expression with the purest and the best of a man's possessions, honestly acquired: expression in prayer; possessions in the act of charity. See traditional commentaries on Gen. 4:3-4; Rashi on Deut. 12:11; Tossefta Menahot VIII; Tossafot on Menahot 10; TB Yoma 34b; Gen. R. 1:6, 22:8-9; Sifrei and Pesikta Zutarta, Deut. 12:11; Rambam, *Mishneh Torah, Hilkhot Issurei Mizbeah*, IV, 11; Rabbi Eliyahu of Vilna, *Aderet Eliyahu*, p. 399. See also TB Menahot 64b.
37. Cf. Ps. 48:2-3.
38. *Tsedakah*, charity, is widely practiced by those who "go up" to the Holy Place, to the *Bet HaMikdash*; it contributes to the joy both of those who give and of those who receive it. Cf. Sifrei Re'eh 143 (Deut. 16:16), p. 102b. See also Mishnah Shekalim V.
39. Cf. Ps. 78:60.
40. Offerings and prayers of thanks will not be abolished in times to come, for they express man's gratitude towards his holy Benefactor forever. Cf. Pesikta Zutarta, Tsav 7. Tanhuma, Tsav 7; Emor 19. Lev. R. 9:7. Shoher Tov, 56:4, 100:4. Yalkut Shim'oni, Tehillim 56:774. Ramban on Lev. 23:17; on Num. 16:15.
41. "Jerusalem is the choicest site in the midst of the inhabited world" Ramban on Gen. 14:18). Cf. Tanhuma, Kedoshim 10. Zohar II, 157a; III, 161b; 221b.
42. "The sanctuary on high corresponds to the sanctuary below; the sanctuary below corresponds to the sanctuary on high." Cf. Mekhilta Beshalah, Messikhta DeShira 10 (Exod. 15:17), pp. 51b-52a. TY Berakhot IV, 5. TB Ta'anit 5a. Gen. R. 55:9. Exod. R. 33:4. Shir HaShirim R. 3:19, 4:11. Tanhuma, Mishpatim 18; VaYakhel 7; Pekkudei 1. Shoher Tov, 26. Zohar I, 80b; 87a; 128b; 159a; 183; II, 143a-b; 150a; 241; III, 66a; 84a. Zohar Hadash, Bereshit 20:4. Rashi on Gen. 28:17; on Exod. 15:17. Ramban on Gen. 3:22, 14:18; idem, *Torat HaAdam, Sha'ar HaGemul (Kitvei Ramban* II, p. 296). Recanati, VaYeitsei 29a. Alshekh on Terumah, Exod. 25:8. Rabbi Moshe Cordovero, *Pardess Rimonim, Sha'ar* 23.
43. "You shall be called (Jerusalem!) city of righteousness, the faithful city. Zion shall be redeemed by justice" (Isa. 1:26-27). See supra, p. 000.
44. Cf. Midrash HaGadol, Bereshit; Gen. R. 43:6; Shir HaShirim R. 7:10; Tanhuma, Shoftim 1; Zohar III, 56a; 291b. Ramban, Radak (p. 87) and Recanati (p. 22a) on Gen. 14:18. Shelah, *Siddur Sha'ar HaShamayim*, p. 197.
45. Cf. Exod. R. 33:1; Zohar II, 241a.

46. Cf. Rabbi Yehuda HaLevi, *Kuzari*, V, 27.
47. Jerusalem is the light of the world. Cf. Gen. R. 59:8; Pesikta DeRav Kahana, 21; *Sefat Emet*, IV, p. 85.
48. Cf. Tana Devei Eliyahu Rabba 2.
49. God desires to have His residence among men. He desires to be present in this world. However, by their wickedness, the wicked prompt the *Shekhinah* (God's presence) to rise back to heaven; they "expel" it into another world. The sinner "excludes" the *Shekhinah* from this world because he does not wish to be troubled by it; he wants to act alone. On the other hand, the righteous man, who wishes to live at God's side, "in His light," invites God to "come down" into this world, to join mankind. Cf. Gen. R. 19:13, 54:5. Exod. R. 2:2. Num. R. 13:4. Shir HaShirim R. 5:1. Petihta DeEihah Rabbati 24. Midrash Tanhuma, Behukotai 3. Yalkut Shim'oni, Melakhim (I, 8) 195. TB Berakhot 43b; Haggigah 16a; Sotah 5a; Bava Kama 83a. Zohar I, 84. Rabbi Eliyahu of Vilna, *Aderet Eliyahu*, p. 59. Netsiv, *Ha'amek Davar*, on Deut. 33:27, V, p. 153.
50. "The Holy One, blessed be He, said: I will not return to the Jerusalem above before I have returned to Jerusalem below," "before Israel has returned to the Jerusalem below!" (TB Ta'anit 5a; Zohar I, 1b; III, 15b). See supra, p. 218.
51. "Unless the Lord builds the house, those who build it labor in vain; unless the Lord watches a city, the watchman stays awake in vain" (Ps. 127:1).
52. "Man joined Eve, his wife. She conceived and bore Cain, saying, 'I have gotten — *kaniti* — a man with the help of the Lord!' " (Gen. 4:1). Eve would have wanted Cain to understand that there are "three helpers" who supervise man's coming into the world: God, the father and the mother (cf. TB Kidushin 30b; Kohelet R. 5:13; Pesikta Zutarta, Tazria 12:3; Zohar II, 83a; 93a; 219b). Man should therefore respect his Creator and serve Him (Cf. 1 Sam. 1:20, 1:28), for He is the first Creator, of the parents as well as that of the children; therefore He is the genuine Creator. However, Cain ignores the teaching in the word *kaniti* presented by his mother; he considers himself as a *kinyan*, as an "acquisition" of which he himself is both the "creator" and the "owner" (cf. Rashi on Gen. 14:19), the *koneh* and the *kayin*: a *Kayin* created by himself, existing by himself, who is real and the only reality. Pharaoh as well will say: "I have made myself!" (Ezek. 29:3). The consequences of this kind of false and arrogant reasoning will be fatal: man exists when he knows that God made him; he does not exist if he does not know it. The Hebrew *Massorah* expressed this fundamental idea in an effective "reading" of a verse in the Book of Psalms (100:3): *Hu assanu veLo anahnu*: "Know that the Lord is God, it is He who made us, and we are his: *Lo*. The text brings the word *lo* with the better *vav*, which means "his." But the *Massorah* reads this word with an *alef*, meaning "not." It wants us to discern that man (mankind) "does not" exist when it does not recognize the fact that God created it and therefore it belongs to Him.
53. "Beware lest you say in your heart: my power and the might of my hand have gotten me this wealth." (Deut. 8:17).
54. Cf. Rambam, *Mishneh Torah, Hilkhot Yom Tov*, VI, 16-20.

55. Sin "separates man from his God." "But your iniquities have erected a barrier between you and your God" (Isa. 59:2); cf. Rambam, *Mishneh Torah, Hilkhot Teshuvah*, VII, 7.
56. Cf. TB Sanhedrin 38b. The man who, because of his sin, "drives himself away from God," is "a fugitive and a wanderer on earth." Cf. Gen. 3:24, 4:12.
57. See supra, p. 219.
58. Ibid.
59. Deut. 12:11.
60. *Erets-Yisrael*, particularly *Yerushalayim*, represents "the interior" "House" of the world, towards which lead "the ways of other lands": these ways "surround" *Erets-Yisrael* and particularly *Yerushalayim*. Cf. Shoher Tov, 68:4; TB Ta'anit 10a; Rabbi David Shelomo Eibeschutz, *Arvei Nahal*, Balak.
61. From the Temple in Jerusalem the blessing spreads all over the world. In the *Bet HaMikdash*, the Sanctuary of *Yerushalayim*, the Jews say prayers and bring offerings for the well-being and the salvation of all nations of the world. Cf. Sifrei *ad Eikev* 40 (Deut. 11:12). TB Ta'anit 10a; Sukkah 55a. Lev. R. 35:8. Shir HaShirim R. 4:11. Zohar I, 108b; 209b; II, 59a; 157a; 187a; III, 24b; 36a; 54b; 103b; 123b; 157a; 161b; 256a; 259a. Tikkunei HaZohar, 6 (145-146). Shelah, III, p. 99b. See *Ha'amek Davar*, V, on Deut. 28:8, p. 224.
62. The Diaspora calls for the regathering of salvation. Cf. Maharal, *Gevurot HaShem*, p. 63. Cf. Ramban on Lev. 26:41. "I will scatter them, but I will also gather them again!" (Gen. R. 44:21).
63. Cf. Maharal, *Netsah Yisrael*, I. See also Ramban, *Vikuah, Milhamot HaShem* (*Kitvei Ramban* I, p. 306). Cf. also TB Rosh HaShanah 18b; Rabbi Yossef Karo, *Shulhan Arukh, Orah Hayyim*, 580:2.
64. Sin itself contains the seed of repentance. Cf. Rav Kook, *Orot HaTeshuvah*, p. 22.
65. "When you are in tribulation, in the latter days you will return to the Lord your God" (Deut. 4:30; cf. Ps. 139). Cf. TY Ta'anit I, 1. TB Megillah 14a; Sanhedrin 97b. Eihah R. 4:27; Tanhuma, Behukotai 3. Cf. Ramban, *Derashah Al Divrei Kohelet* (*Kitvei Ramban* I, pp. 201-2). Being remote (from God) brings about the return to God (cf. Maharal, *Netivot Olam*, II, *Netiv HaTeshuvah*, 3-4, pp. 145a-146b), because "the remoteness itself is the beginning of coming together" (Rabbi Nahman of Bratslav, *Likkutei Moharan*, I, 74, p. 89b).
66. *Evrah MiMekha Elekha*: "I flee from Thee towards Thee!" cries out Rabbi Shelomo Ibn Gevirol (1021-1058) in his great liturgical poem *Keter Malkhut* ("The Crown of Royalty"). Cf. Esther Starobinski-Safran, "De Fuga et Inventione" by *Philon of Alexandria*, p. 141.
67. "In the *Galut*, in exile, where they will have to live (temporarily), they will pray 'by way of Jerusalem.' Thus they will make their *teshuvah*, their 'return,' to God." See Radak and Ralbag on 1 Kings 8:46, 8:52.
68. See supra, note 24.
69. *MiMekom kaparato nivra*: "Adam (was) created with dust from the Place (*Bet HaMikdash*), where (he will receive) his atonement." Cf. Gen. R. 14:9. TY Nazir VII, 2. Zohar I, 34b; 80a; 130b; 147b; 205b; II, 23b; 24b; 55a; III, 46b; 83a. Zohar Hadash, Yitro 31:3; Shir HaShirim 67:3; Ruth 79:4. Alshekh on Terumah, Exod. 25:8. *Kli Yakar* on Lekh Lekha, Gen. 12:1.

70. Cf. Avot DeRabbi Nathan 35.
71. *UMalki-Tseddek Melekh Shalem*: "And Melchizedek King of Salem" (Gen. 14:18). These words are translated as follows in Targum Onkelos (ad locum.): *UMalki-Tseddek Malka DiYerushlem* ("and Melchizedek, King of Jerusalem"). Ramban (ad locum.) writes: "Malki-Tseddek went from his country to Jerusalem to serve God there." See Gen. 14:18-20, 14:22; Joshua 10:1, 10:3. Cf. also Ps. 66:3, 110:4. See supra, notes 43 and 44.
72. Cf. Ibn Ezra, Ramban and Seforno on Gen. 14:18.
73. *Malki-Tseddek hu Shem ben Noah*: "Melchizedek is Shem, Noah's son." (Cf. TB Nedarim 32b; Zohar I, 87a; Ibn Ezra and Ramban on Gen. 14:18.) Rashi (on Gen. 12:6) writes: "The Canaanites were in the land"; they were conquering Erets-Yisrael which belonged at that time to the descendants of Shem. This land was allotted to Shem when Noah distributed the land among his sons, as it is said: 'And Melchizedek king of Salem' (Gen. 14:18). This is why God said to Abraham: 'To your descendants I shall give this land' (verse 7). I shall give it back to your children who are Shem's descendants."
74. Shem and Ever had the responsibility of transmitting pure faith. Cf. Gen. R. 62:6, 63:7, 68:5. Midrash HaGadol, Toldot; Midrash Tanhuma Yashan, VaYishlah. Cf. Rashi on Gen. 25:16, 25:22; Ramban on Gen. 14:18.
75. Cf. Gen. R. 43:7-8. Cf. Josephus Flavius, *Antiquitiés, I, 10:2*. Cf. Targum Onkelos, Targum Yonathan Ben Uziel, Rashi, Ibn Ezra, Radak, Ramban, *Or HaHayyim* and Rabbi S.R. Hirsch on Gen. 14:18. Cf. Recanati, Lekh Lekha, pp. 21b-22a. Cf. TB Nedarim 32b; Zohar III, 291b. Cf. Rashi and *Kli Yakar* on Gen. 14:19. Cf. Rabbi D.T. Hoffmann on Gen. 14:18-20. *Sefer Bereshit*, I, pp. 232-33. Cf. Rabbi Meir Simha Kohen of Dvinsk, *Meshekh Hokhmah*, p. 20; but see also Malbim on Gen. 14:19.
76. Cf. TB Berakhot 7b; Zohar I, 99b; 110a.
77. Cf. TB Sotah 4b; Nedarim 32b. Cf. Gen. R. 43:8; Num. R. 14:7. Midrash Tanhuma, Shemini 2; Ahrei 9; Behar 1.
78. Gen. 17:4. Abraham, "Father of all men," intended to "unite all those born" in one "fraternity" acknowledging God's paternity. Cf. TB Berakhot 13a; Gen. R. 39:3; Midrash Aggadah, Bereshit 17; Rambam, *Mishneh Torah, Hilkhot Bikkurim*, IV, 3.
79. Cf. Gen. R. 39:24; Rashi on Gen. 12:9.
80. Cf. Ibn Ezra on Gen. 11:29, 12:1. Radak on Gen. 11:29. Ramban, *Mavo LiDerashah Al Divrei Kohelet (Kitvei Ramban* I, p. 177). Rabbeinu Bahya on Gen. 11:30 (I, p. 132; cf. TB Yevamot 64b). *Ha'amek Davar* on Gen. 11:31 (I, p. 40).
81. Cf. *Be'er Mayim Hayyim* on Gen. 11:31.
82. See supra, note 60.
83. See supra, notes 14 and 15.
84. Cf. Ramban on Gen. 12:1; cf. also Ibn Ezra and Radak on Gen. 11:29.
85. See Alshekh on Gen. 12:1; on Lev. 25:2; *Kli Yakar* on Gen. 12:1. *Noam Elimelekh*, I, p. 25 (Gen. 12:1).
86. "The Lord said to Abram 'Go to the land which I will show you.' " (Gen. 12:1; see Rashi on Gen. 12:2).
87. Cf. Ramban on Gen. 12:1.
88. "Go to the land which I *show you: Areka*" (Gen. 12:1).

89. Cf. Gen. 21:12 et al.
90. Cf. Rashi on Gen. 22:2; Gen. R. 39:12; Rashi on Gen. 12:1.
91. *VaYissa Avraham Et Eynav VaYar Et HaMakom MeRahok*: "Abraham lifted up his eyes and saw the place — *HaMakom* — from far off" (Gen. 22:4).
92. Cf. TB Avodah Zarah 8a. Gen. R. 34:8; Lev. R. 2:6; Num. R. 4:6. Pirkei DeRabbi Eliezer 31. Rambam, *Mishneh Torah, Hilkhot Bet HaBehirah*, II, 1-2. Ramban on Gen. 22:2; cf. also Ibn Ezra on Gen. 8:20.
93. Cf. Gen. 8:20. TB Zevahim 116a. Gen. R. 22:9, 34:9. Lev. R. 7:4. Ramban on Gen. 46:1.
94. *VaYavo'u el HaMakom asher amar lo Elokim*: "They came to the place of which God had told him" (Gen. 22:9). See infra, notes 115-116.
95. *VaYiven Sham Avraham Et HaMizbeah*: "And Abraham built an altar there" (Gen. 22:9). Cf. Pirkei DeRabbi Eliezer 31; Ramban on Gen. 22:2; Rabbeinu Bahya on Gen. 22:9 (I, p. 196).
96. Cf. Lev. R. 7:2. Cf. Midrash Tanhuma, Tsav 13, 14. Cf. Ramban, *Derashat Torat HaShem Temimah* (*Kitvei Ramban* I, p. 165).
97. Moriah really is Jerusalem. Cf. 2 Chron. 31:1. Cf. Rashi, Radak and Rabbeinu Bahya on Gen. 22:2. Cf. Rambam, *Mishneh Torah, Hilkhot Bet HaBehirah*, I, 3-4; II, 1-2; V, 1. Rabbi Yitshak ben Rabbi Yehuda HaLevi, one of the last Tossafists (13th cent.) remarks in *Pa'aneah Razah* that the numerical value of the letters composing the words *El Erets HaMoriah* ("towards the land of Moriah," Gen. 22:2) equals the value of the letters composing the word *BiYerushalayim* (in Jerusalem) (= 588).
98. Cf. Tossafot on TB Zevahim 60b.
99. Cf. Mekhilta BeShalah, Messikhta DeVaYehi 3 (Exod. 14:15). See supra, p. 204.
100. Gen. R. 56:16.
101. Cf. TB Pessahim 54a; TB Nedarim 39b; Gen. R. 1:5; Pirkei DeRabbi Eliezer 2. Zohar I, 113a; III, 34b. Zohar Hadash, Bereshit 5a. *Kuzari*, III, 73. *Or HaHayyim* on Gen. 28:17. *Bnei Issakhar*, II, p. 20b. Rabbi Moshe Sofer, *She'elot UTeshuvot Hatam Sofer, Yoreh DeYah*, 234.
102. See supra, p. 214.
103. "And God said to him (Jacob): 'Your name is Jacob; no longer shall your name be Jacob, but Israel shall be your name'" (Gen. 35:10; see Seforno ad loc.). God confers upon Jacob the name of Israel, a name he deserves (cf. Gen. 22:29). God gives to the city which "deserves" to shelter the *Bet HaMikdash*, the House of Sanctity, the name of *Yerushalayim* (cf. Massekhet Semahot, VIII; see Ramban on Gen. 33:20; on Lev. 18:25).
104. Cf. Zohar III, 93b.
105. Cf. Sifrei Re'eh 67 (Deut. 12:10), p. 88b; TB Sanhedrin 20b; cf. also TB Bava Batra 4a. See Rambam, *Moreh Nevukhim*, III, 45.
106. Cf. TB Zevahim 119a; Rashi on Gen. 12:9.
107. See Malbim on Ps. 132:13.
108. Cf. TB Bava Kama 97b.
109. Cf. TB Zevahim 24a and Tossafot ad locum.
110. Cf. Ps. 132:17; TB Megillah 17b-18a (but see also Maharsha on TB Megillah 18a); Num. R. 13:13; Midrash Lekah Tov, Bereshit 32:20; Rabbi Yehuda

HaLevi, *Kuzari*, III, 73; Rambam, *Mishneh Torah, Hilkhot Melakhim*, XI, 1; Rabbi Eliyahu of Vilna, *Siddur Ishei Yisrael*, p. 133; see also idem, *Biurei HaGra Al Aggadot*, I, p. 46.

111. See supra, p. 207.
112. "God will see" (Gen. 22:14). In these words, Abraham means God's *Hashgahah*. "The Lord, blessed be He, watches (everything) in His world; His reign is present everywhere." Cf. Ramban on Gen. 22:2; Rabbi Eliyahu of Vilna, *Biurei HaGra Al Aggadot*, II, p. 18 (Rabbi Avraham's commentary). See supra, note 99.
113. Cf. 1 Kings 8:29; cf. also Deut. 11:12.
114. "The Lord your God will choose the place of His dwelling" Deut. 12:11).
115. Cf. 1 Kings 8:52.
116. "But you shall seek — *tidreshu* — the place which the Lord your God will choose... thither you shall go" (Deut. 12:5).
117. Cf. Rashi on Gen. 22:14; on Deut. 6:6.
118. *HaShem Yireh*: "The Lord will see to it." Cf. Gen. 22:14; cf. also Targum Onkelos, Rashi and *Kli Yakar* ad locum. Cf. Exod. 23:17, 34:23; Deut. 16:16. Cf. TB Berakhot 62b; Pessahim 88a. Cf. Rambam, *Moreh Nevukhim*, III, 45. Cf. Rabbi Eliyahu of Vilna, *Aderet Eliyahu*, p. 59; idem, *Kol Eliyahu*, pp. 9-10.
119. Cf. Exod. 33:20. See also Rambam, *Mishneh Torah, Hilkhot Yessodei HaTorah*, I, 10; idem, *Moreh Nevukhim*, I, 4-5.
120. Cf. 1 Kings 8:61.
121. Cf. Deut. 23:17 et al.
122. God, always present, for He was, is and will be, calls the city *Yerushalayim* (cf. Gen. R. 56:16; Pesikta Zutarta, VaYera 22:14; Yalkut Shim'oni, Tehillim 76, 814). David, who introduces the city into the present history and prepares its messianic future, calls it *Yerushalayim* (cf. Rabbi Asher Ben Yehiel (13th-14th cent.), *Rosh Al HaTorah* on Gen. 22:14)). *Yeru-shalayim*, city of Wholeness, will be *Yeru-shalom*, city of Peace (cf. Ibn Ezra on Gen. 14:18; Deut. R. 5:14; Num. R. 11:20; Tanhuma, Tsav 7; Rabbi Shelomo Ephraim Lunschitz, *Siftei Da'at, Ha'azinu*; Rabbi S.R. Hirsch, *Sefer Tehillim*, Ps. 76:3, p. 309; cf. Ps. 122:6).
123. The name *Yerushalayim* is in the plural (cf. Rabbi Meir Simha Kohen of Dvinsk, *Meshekh Hokhmah*, p. 20; see also p. 148); but this name is also found in the singular (cf. Tossafot on TB Ta'anit 16a).
124. Cf. Gen. 22:12 et al.
125. Cf. *Meshekh Hokhmah*, p. 20.
126. Man "brings" God "down" towards himself. Cf. Avot DeRabbi Nathan 34; Gen. R. 19:13; Rabbi Eliyahu of Vilna, *Aderet Eliyahu*, p. 59; idem, *Siddur Ishei Yisrael*, p. 19. Cf. Exod. 19:20; cf. also TB Sukkah 5a; Sifra VaYikra, I, p. 3. Zohar II, 86a; 270b. Rashi on Exod. 9.22. See also Rabbi Eliyahu of Vilna, *Aderet Eliyahu*, p. 345.
127. God "brings" man "up" towards Him. Cf. Gen. 22:2 et al; Exod. 19:3. (See also Gen. 5:22, 5:24; 1 Kings 2:1, 2:11).
128. See supra, p. 213.
129. Cf. TB Bava Batra 75b.

130. Cf. Derekh Erets Zuta, 67.
131. Cf. Tossafot on TB Bava Batra 21a.
132. See supra, note 49 and infra, page 147.
133. Rabbi Shim'on Bar Yohai: "Come and see how much Israel is loved by the Holy One blessed be He: wherever Israel is in exile, the Shekhinah is with him in exile; the Presence of God follows him 'to protect him' " (TB Megillah 29a; Zohar III, 75a. Cf. also Zohar I, 28a; 69a; 120b; 134a; 149a; 159b; 182a; 189a; 210a; 211a; 212b; 213b; II, 2b; 41b; 82a; 196a; 216b; III, 4b; 66a; 90b; 114a; 197b; 242a. Hakdamat Tikkunei HaZohar, 9a. Tikkunei HaZohar, 6(21b); 13(28a); 21(51a); 70(124b). Zohar Hadash, Ahrei 47-48; Hukat 51. Sha'arei Zohar, 118. *Shem MiShemuel, Devarim* 53.
134. Cf. Exod. R. 37:5.
135. Cf. TB Berakhot 3a; Tikkunei HaZohar, 10 (23a). Rabbi Eliyahu of Vilna, *Biurei HaGra Al Aggadot*, I, p. 3. See also Zohar I, 166a.
136. Cf. Yalkut Shim'oni, Tehillim 132, 881; Radak on 1 Kings 9:3.
137. Cf. Exod. 19:5-6 and Mekhilta ad locum. Cf. *Or HaHayyim* on Hukat, Num. 19:1.
138. Cf. Exod. R. 2:2
139. *VaHashimoti Et Mikdasheihem — Kedushatan Af KeSheHem Shomemim:* "I shall devastate your sanctuaries; nevertheless they will remain holy, though they may be in ruins" (Lev. 26:31). Mishnah Megillah III, 3; TB Megillah 28a). The *Bet HaMikdash* is in ruins; however, its "sanctity still stands." Cf. Rambam, *Mishneh Torah, Hilkhot Bet HaBehirah*, I, 3; VI, 14-16; VII, 7. Tossafot on TB Yevamot 82b; Yoma 44a; Shevuot 14b. Rabbi Eliezer of Metz (12th cent.), *Sefer Yereim*, 277. Rabbi Moshe de Coucy (13th cent.), *Semag, Sefer Mitzvot Gadol, Mitzvat assei* 163. Rabbi Shim'on Ben Tsemah Duran (15th cent.), *Tashbatz*, III, 5; 201. See Sifra on Lev. 19:30. Sifrei on Deut. 33:12. TB Megillah 10a; 25a; Shevuot 16a; Arakhin 32b and Hazon Ish ad locum. (Bnei Brak ed., 5626, p. 330). Shir HaShirim R. 4:7; Exod. R. 2:2. Shoher Tov, 11; Yalkut Shim'oni, Melakhim I 8:195. But see also TB Zevahim 107b; Yoma 54a-b. TY Shekalim VI, 1. Ramban, *Milhamot*, on TB Avodah Zarah 52b; idem, *Hiddushei HaRamban*, on TB Makot 19. Rabbi Avraham Ben David De Posquières (12th cent.), the "Rabad," on Rambam's *Mishneh Torah, Hilkhot Bet HaBehirah*, VI, 14; however, see also Perush HaRabad al Sifra, Kedoshim VIII, 8, p. 90b. Rabbi Meir Simha Kohen of Dvinsk, *Or Sameah*, on Rambam's *Mishneh Torah, Hilkhot Bet HaBehirah*, VI, 16 (cf. 2 Chron. 7:16, 30:8). Rabbi David Ibn Zimra (15th cent.), *She'elot UTeshuvot HaRadbaz*, II, 648. Rabbi Menahem Ben Shelomo (13th cent.), *Meiri*, on TB Makot 19a; Shevuot 16a. Rabbi Yitshak Abrabanel (15th-16th cent.) on Ki Tavo; Rabbi David Shelomo Eibschutz (17th cent.), *Arvei Nahal, Behukotai*. See also Maharsha, *Hiddushei Aggadot*, on TB Ta'anit 16a.
140. Cf. Eihah 5:19; TB Makot 24b.
141. *Kol HaMekudash MeHavero, Harev Yoter MeHavero: Yerushalayim Yoter Hareva Min HaKol:* All that is holy is particularly liable to suffer. Jerusalem, a holy place, has suffered more than other places. (Israel, a holy people, has suffered more than other peoples.) Ramban, epistle from Jerusalem to his son Nahman (*Kitvei Ramban* I, p. 368). Cf. Rabbi Eliyahu of Vilna on Isa. 6:12 (quoted by R. Betsalel Landau, *HaGaon HeHassid MiVilna*, p. 248). Cf.

also Shir HaShirim R. 4:7; Rabbi Yaakov Moshe Harlap, *Mei Meirom* (on the "Eight Chapters" by Rambam), pp. 7-8.

142. Israel's being chosen implies a special responsibility on its part towards God. "You only have I known of all the families of the earth; therefore I will punish you for all your iniquities" (Amos 2:2). "The Holy One, blessed be He, is extremely exacting towards those who surround Him," "towards the just" (TB Yevamot 121b). Cf. Avot DeRabbi Nathan 4. Lev. R. 27:1; Num. R. 20:25; Eihah R. 1. Petihta DeEihah Rabbati 1. Midrash Tanhuma, Emor 5; Balak 20. Zohar I, 140a; 185b. Tikkunei HaZohar, 18 (38a). Zohar Hadash, Yitro 34. *Perushei Maharal MiPrag LeAggadot HaShas*, IV, on TB Yevamot 121b, p. 52; on TB Ketuvot 66b, pp. 67-69.
143. Exod. 19:6; Deut. 7:6.
144. Israel is the *sensitive* heart of the nations. Cf. Zohar III, 221b; *Kuzari*, II, 36; Ramban, *Perush LeShir HaShirim, Kitvei Ramban* II, p. 503. Recanati, Bereshit 10a; Yitro 9a. Cf. also Sefer HaBahir, 96; Lev. R. 30:13; TB Ta'anit 3b; 10a. Cf. *Perushei Maharal MiPrag LeAggadot HaShas*, IV, on TB Ketuvot 111a, p. 95.
145. Cf. Ramban on Num. 35:33. Cf. also Lev. 18:28, 20:22. TB Shabbat 33a; Tikkunei HaZohar, 56 (90a). Cf. also Seforno on Deut. 11:30.
146. Zion is the *delicate* center of the world. Cf. Zohar III, 161b; cf. also Zohar II, 157a; 193a. See Pesikta Rabbati, 10:2; Recanati, Bereshit 10a; Yitro 9a; Rabbi Yitshak Aizik of Sovalk, *Be'er Yitshak* on *Aderet Eliyahu*, pp. 38, 530; Rabbi D.T. Hoffmann *Bereshit*, I, pp. 210, 211. See infra, note 202.
147. Isa. 1:26. See supra, note 43.
148. *Erets-Yisrael*, and especially *Yerushalayim*, "city of justice," "cannot abide injustice," "cannot tolerate sinners." Jerusalem has its own moral personality, its own ethical demands. It is harsh for those who offend its moral sensitivity, who transgress its ethical laws. Cf. Ramban on Gen. 1:1, 19:5; Sifra and Ramban on Lev. 18:25; Rashi on Lev. 18:28.
149. The place which the King-Messiah chooses to dwell in is Mount Zion (Midrash Shemuel, 19), in Jerusalem, where the exiled will gather (Rambam, *Iggeret Teiman*, pp. 180-81), in the Lord's Temple (Mal. 3:1). Cf. Yalkut Shim'oni, Yeshaya 49:472.
150. The messianic process includes the reconstruction of the Temple in Jerusalem and the gathering of the exiled in Erets-Yisrael. See Ps. 147:2. TY Ma'asser Sheini V, 2. TB Berakhot 49a and Rashi ad locum.; Megillah 17b-18a and Rashi ad locum. Tanhuma, Noah 11. Rambam, *Mishneh Torah, Hilkhot Melakhim*, XI, 1. Rabbi Ya'akov Ben Asher, *Tur, Orah Hayyim*, 118. Rabbi Eliyahu of Vilna, *Siddur Ishei Yisrael*, p. 132. *Siddur HaGeonim VeHaMekubalim VeHaHassidim*, II, pp. 607, 623. Cf. also Zohar I, 114a; 134a. Cf. also Jer. 32:11; TB Berakhot 6b. See also Isa. 60:8, 60:14; TB Sanhedrin 20b; Rambam, *Iggeret Teiman*, p. 180.
151. See supra, p. 220.
152. Ibid.
153. Cf. Shelah, *Siddur Sha'ar HaShamayim*, p. 484.
154. See supra, p. 226.
155. Cf. Esther 2:5-6 et al. See supra, p. 222.
156. Cf. Ps. 84:3-5.

157. "As I live! says the Lord God. With a mighty hand and an outstretched arm I will be king over you. For on My holy mountain, the mountain height of Israel, there all the house of Israel shall serve Me, all of Israel" (Ezek. 20).
158. See supra, p. 222.
159. Mal. 3:6; see Rashi and Radak ad locum.; TB Megillah 11a; Sotah 9a; Lev. 26:44.
160. TB Berakhot 58a.
161. Cf. Eihah R. 1:32.
162. Cf. TB Berakhot 32a; Gittin 57b. Tana Devei Eliyahu Rabba 24; Tana Devei Eliyahu Zuta 10; cf. also TB Sotah 9a; Pirkei DeRabbi Eliezer 25; Tanhuma, Nitsavim 1; cf. also Exod. R. 2:10. See supra, note 159.
163. Eihah R. 1:32; Shir HaShirim R. 2:22. Cf. Num. R. 11:3; Yalkut Shim'oni, Shir HaShirim 2; cf. also Zohar I, 114a; cf. also TB Sotah 9a.
164. Cf. TB Bava Batra 25a and Tossafot ad locum.
165. Cf. TB Megillah 29a; Sifrei and Rashi on Num. 35:34; Zohar III, 179b. See also supra, note 132.
166. Cf. Exod. R. 2:2. Tanhuma (Buber ed.), Shemot 51; Yalkut Shim'oni, Melakhim 195 (I, 8); Shir HaShirim 2. Cf. Zohar II, 5b; 116a. Cf. also Zohar II, 143a. Cf. Ramban, *Perush LeShir HaShirim, Kitvei Ramban* II, p. 491. See also Rabbi David Ibn Zimra, *She'elot UTeshuvot HaRadbaz*, II, 648. See supra, note 139.
167. Shir HaShirim 2:9.
168. See supra, p. 229.
169. Isa. 25:9. Midrash Tanhuma, Tsav 12. Cf. Exod. 15:2 and Rashi ad locum.; Mekhilta, Beshalah, Messikhta DeShira 3, p. 44b; Exod. R. 23:15; Shir HaShirim R. 4:3; Zohar I, 55b; 114a.
170. Shir HaShirim 2:9; cf. Shir HaShirim R. 2:22. Cf. Rav Kook, *Hazon HaGeulah*, pp. 42, 43.
171. Cf. Isa. 52:8; cf. also *Kuzari*, II, 23. Cf. *Kli Yakar* on Deut. 3:26-27.
172. See Ramban, *Perush LeShir HaShirim, Kitvei Ramban* II, p. 491.
173. See supra, p. 229.
174. Cf. 1 Kings 9:3: "My eyes and my heart will be there for all time."
175. Shir HaShirim 2:8: "It is the voice of my beloved!"
176. Cf. Rabbi Menahem Mendel Kasher, *HaTekufah HaGedolah*, p. 404. Cf. Ramban, *Tefillah Al Horvot Yerushalayim, Kitvei Ramban* I, p. 425. Cf. Tikkunei HaZohar, 11 (26b). Cf. also TB Berakhot 32b; Bava Batra 59a. See *Siah Lohamim*, "Fighters' Talk," "Chapters of listening and thoughts" (thoughts of the soldiers of the Six-day War and conversations in the kibbutzim), chapter on "Jerusalem," 3rd ed., Tel-Aviv: 1968, pp. 223-44.
177. Cf. Isa. 66:8, 66:13. Cf. Ps. 87:5-6.
178. "As one man, with one heart" (Rashi on Exod. 19:2). Cf. Mekhilta, Yitro, Messikhta DeBaHodesh 1 (Exod. 19:2), p. 70; Pesikta DeRav Kahana, 12; cf. Gen. R. 98:2, 98:4; Lev. R. 9:9; Deut. R. 5.
179. See Zohar II, 116a.
180. See Obad. 1:8.
181. Cf. Rabbi D.S. Eibeschutz, *Arvei Nahal*, Balak.
182. The Sages of Israel reproach the Jewish people for a certain lack of eagerness for *aliyah* to Zion and for the rebuilding of Jerusalem. This shortcoming

results in the absence of the *Shekhinah*, of God's Presence, from that Place. Cf. TB Yoma 9b and Rashi ad loc.; Shir HaShirim R. 8:11; cf. Zohar II, 9b. Cf. *Kuzari*, II, 23-24; V, 27; Rabbi Ya'akov Emden, *Siddur Bet Ya'akov*, I, *Sulam Bet El*, p. 20; Rabbi Hayyim Attar, *Or HaHayyim*, on Lev. 25:22.

183. Cf. Recanati, Yitro 9a.
184. Cf. Rabbi Abraham of Slonim, *Be'er Avraham*, pp. 102, 109, 215.
185. See supra, p. 230.
186. TY Bava Kama VII, 7, Ps. 122:3.
187. TY Haggigah III, 6; cf. Mishnah Bikkurim III, 3.
188. Jerusalem personifies Israel's unity. Cf. Rabbi Hayyim of Volozhin, *Nefesh HaHayyim*, 2:17, p. 54; cf. Jer. 2:2.
189. Cf. TB Megillah 26a.
190. In Jerusalem all the generations of Israel meet: "The coin of Jerusalem has on one face the names of David and Solomon, and on the other — the name of Jerusalem, the holy city" (TB Bava Kama 97b).
191. The preliminary condition of Israel's *deliverance*, of which Jerusalem is the symbol, is the unity of Israel, the union of all Jews (cf. Gen. R. 98:2 et al. See *Nefesh HaHayyim*, 2:17, p. 54).
192. *Kelr SheHubrah LaYahdav*: "Jerusalem is united within itself: its center is within itself" (Rabbi S.R. Hirsch, *Die Psalmen*, on Ps. 122:3, II, p. 235).
193. *Yerushalayim HaBenuyah*: The "Jerusalem which is built" (Ps. 122:3), the Jerusalem which is rebuilt, reunified, contributes to the joining of the Jerusalem above and the Jerusalem below (cf. Rabbi M.M. Kasher, *HaTekufah HaGedolah*, p. 494, according to the Gaon of Vilna's school).
194. In Jerusalem, Israel is called one: "one people" (Zohar III, 93b; 2 Sam. 7:23).
195. "The children of Israel will return to the *Bet HaMikdash* (the Temple of Jerusalem) and will seek the Holy One, blessed be He" (Rashi on TB Megillah 18a).
196. Jerusalem and Israel deserve each other. Cf. Lev. R. 13:2; Num. R. 23:7; *Kuzari*, III, 73; Maharal, *Derekh Hayyim*, on Avot V, p. 189.
197. Cf. Rav Kook, *Hazon HaGeulah*, p. 35.
198. In Messianic times, "Jerusalem will become the spiritual Capital of all States" (Shir HaShirim R. 1:37; Exod.R. 23:11; Rashi on Shir HaShirim 1:5).
199. See supra, note 1.
200. Cf. Ps. 48:2; Zohar II, 235a; III, 5a.
201. Jer. 3:17. Cf. Zohar I, 84b.
202. "Jerusalem, the heart of the world." Cf. Zohar II, 193a.
203. "At that time Jerusalem shall be called the throne of the Lord. All nations shall gather to it, to the presence of the Lord in Jerusalem" (Jer. 3:17).

Chapter Four

1. Cf. Pesikta DeRav Kahana, 15.
2. Cf. Gen. R. 3:8; cf. also Gen. R. 1:2. See Rashi on Gen. 1:1, 1:14; Mishnah

Berakhot I, 1. Cf. Shelah, I, pp. 7b-8a; *Sefat Emet,* I, *Bereshit; Shem MiShemuel, Moadim,* p. 116.

3. Cf. Maharal, *Derekh Hayyim,* Avot V, 22, pp. 210-11. See TB Sanhedrin 101a; Prov. 15:23; *Perushei Rabbeinu Yonah MeGerondi,* Avot II, 1, p. 18. Cf. *Sifra DiTseniuta Im Biur HaGra, Likkutei HaGra,* p. 78. *Shem MiShemuel, Devarim,* p. 212. *Tossefet Berakhah,* V, p. 329; Kohelet 3:11.

4. Cf. TB Eruvin 27a; cf. also TB Shabbat 129a; Pessahim 105b; Kiddushin 33a; Sanhedrin 101a. Tanhuma, VaYehi 15; Ki Teitsei 2. See *Siddur Sha'arei Ratson* by Rabbi Nahman of Bratslav, pp. 206, 345.

5. Cf. TB Makot 23b. Midrash Mishlei, 31. Zohar III, 110b. Sefer HaBahir, 35, 36, p. 9. Rambam, *Sefer HaMitzvot, Shoresh* 13. Recanati, *Bereshit,* p. 8b. Maharal, *Tiferet Yisrael,* 4, p. 7a. Shelah, I, p. 210a; III, p. 3a. Ramhal, *Messilat Yesharim,* 2, p. 19. *Biur HaGra, Mishlei* 31:21, p. 180. *Maggid Devarav LeYa'akov,* 86, p. 149. *Od Yossef Hai,* p. 234.

6. Cf. TY Rosh HaShanah I, 3. TB Berakhot 26a and Tossafot ad loc.; 49a; Shabbat 32b; Pessahim 68b; Beitsa 17a; Rosh HaShanah 24a; Sanhedrin 42a; 99b; 101a. Massekhet Kallah, I, Exod. R. 16; Shir HaShirim R. 15. Mekhilta, Pesikta Zutarta and Rashi on Exod. 12:17; Rashi on Temurah 14a. *Sefer HaHinukh, Hakdamah,* p. 11. Shelah, I, pp. 176a-b-177a. *Divrei Shemuel* (of Nikolsburg), p. 155. *Likkutei Moharan,* 33, 3-4, p. 47a. *Sefat Emet,* I, p. 229; III, pp. 186, 197-98; V, p. 64. Rav Kook, *Orot,* p. 55. R. Y. Hutner, *Pahad Yitshak, Yerah HaEitanim,* pp. 171, 174, 176, 222. R. Moshe Grossberg, *Tsefunot HaRogachovi,* pp. 1-24. The Gaon of Rogachov, *Mefa'aneah Tsefunot,* chapters 3, 5. *Mikhtav MeEliyahu,* II, pp. 151-53.

7. Cf. *Emet VeEmunah,* p. 54.

8. Ps. 90:12. Cf. Rambam, *Hilkhot Shemittah VeYovel,* X, 1; Lev. 25:8. *Sefer HaHinukh, Mitzvah* 84. *Perushei Maharal MiPrag LeAggadot HaShas,* II, on Shabbat 137b, p. 124.

9. Cf. TB Kiddushin 40b; Rambam, *Hilkhot Teshuvah,* III, 4. Cf. TB Yoma 86a; Sanhedrin 37a; Avodah Zarah 10b. Gen. R. 65:18. Rabbeinu Yonah Gerondi, *Sha'arei HaAvodah,* p. 22.

10. Exod. 20:8.

11. Mekhilta Messikhta DeBaHodesh VII (Exod. 20:8), p. 77a. Ramban on Exod. 20:8 writes: "The non-Jews count the weekdays for themselves and name them after those (divinities) who protect them, while the Jews count the weekdays as regarding the Sabbath: "first day of the Shabbath, second day of the Shabbath..." because [God] commanded us to remember the Shabbath through a *mitzvah,* forever, every single day." Cf. Zohar II, 204a.

12. Cf. *Ben Ish Hai,* p. 98. But see also Mishnah Tamid VII, 4. TB Shabbat 69b; *Neot HaDesheh,* pp. 136-37; *Shem MiShemuel, Shemot,* I, p. 169; R. Mordekhai Yossef Leiner, *Mei HaShiloah,* VaYelekh.

13. Cf. Gen. R. 10. Zohar I, 17a; 47b; II, 222b. Kuzari, V, 10. Rabbi Yitshak Arama, *Akeidat Yitshak, Sha'ar Revi'i;* Abrabanel on Gen. 2. Maharal, *Derekh Hayyim,* Avot V, 9, pp. 187-88.

14. Cf. Seforno on Exod. 20:11. Maharal, *Derekh Hayyim,* p. 9. *Kedushat Levi,* p. 69a. *Likkutei Moharan,* II, 39, pp. 25a-b. *Be'er Mayim Hayyim* on Gen. 2:1. *Sefat Emet,* I, p. 15. *Shem MiShemuel, Bereshit,* I, pp. 25-27.

15. Compare Exod. 20:11 with Exod. 23:12; Gen. 2:2 with Exod. 23:12; Gen. 2:3

with Exod. 20:11; Exod. 31:17 with Exod. 23:12.
16. Cf. Rabbi S.R. Hirsch, *Iggrot Tsafon*, pp. 70-71.
17. "God exerted no effort in creating the world. 'God's word' was enough for 'the Heavens to be made' " (Ps. 33:5; Gen. R. 3:2, 10:12, 12:9-10. Mekhilta Yitro, Messikhta DeBahodesh VII (Exod. 20:11), p. 77b). "And He rested on the seventh day" (Exod. 20:11). "If one can say so, God speaks of rest for Himself. It stands to reason then that all the more so, man, for whom work means hardship and tiredness, must rest on the Sabbath" (Rashi ad loc.). "The One of Whom it is said: 'He does not faint or grow weary' (Isa. 40:28), and whose work was done by the Word, has nevertheless written in the Torah the word 'rest' with reference to Himself! This is to make it understandable by the human ear" (Rashi on Exod. 31:17). Cf. Ibn Ezra on Exod. 31:17.
18. Cf. Gen. 1:31.
19. Cf. Gen. 2:3; cf. Gen. R. 11:2. Cf. Malbim on Gen. 2:3. Cf. B. Jacob, *Das erste Buch der Tora, Genesis*, Berlin: 1934, pp. 67-68. Cf. M. D. Cassuto, *MeAdam Ad Noah*, p. 40.
20. Cf. Isa. 58:13-14. Tana Devei Eliyahu Rabba 1. Cf. Tikkunei HaZohar, 6 (37). *Perushei Maharal MiPrag LeAggadot HaShas*, II, on Shabbat 118b, pp. 98-99; *Derashot Maharal MiPrag, Derush Al HaTorah*, p. 39. *Neot HaDesheh*, p. 128.
21. Lev. 19:2-3. Cf. *Sefer HaZohar Im Perush HaSulam*, IV, 528, pp. 134-35; V, VaYakhel, 205, p. 68. Cf. Shelah, *Siddur Shaʿar HaShamayim*, p. 385.
22. Some commentators prefer to have the masculine of the verb *LeKadesho* agree with the masculine noun *Yom* preceding the word *HaShabbat*. But cf. Isa. 56:2, 56:6; *Shomer Shabbat MeHalelo*, and Isa. 66:23: *UMidei Shabbat BeShabbato!* In the mystical literature the commandment of *Zakhor*, "Remember the day of the Shabbath" (Exod. 20:8) means the Shabbath in the masculine; and the commandment of *Shamor*, "Keep the day of the Shabbath" (Deut. 5:12) means the Shabbath in the feminine. Cf. Zohar I, 48b; II, 88b; 92a-b; 165b. Tikkunei HaZohar, 55. Tikkunei Zohar Hadash, 120a. Cf. Ramban on Exod. 20:8 and commentary ad loc. by R.C.B. Shavell (*Perushei HaRamban Al HaTorah*, I, pp. 398-99). Recanati, Yitro p. 9a. Rabbi Yaʿakov Yossef of Polonnoye, *Toldot Yaʿakov Yossef, Hakdamah; VeYeitsei; Kedushat Levi*, p. 55a. Rabbi Avraham Yehoshua Heshel of Apta, *Ohev Yisrael*, VaEthanan. Rabbi Eliyahu of Vilna, *Biurei HaGra Al Aggadot*, II, p. 71. *Ben Ish Hai*, p. 142. Cf. TB Bava Kama 32b. Cf. also TB Menahot 43b; TY Berakhot I, 5; Num. 15:39: *UReitem Oto*.
23. Cf. Rabbi Shelomo Ephraim Lunschitz, *Kli Yakar*, on Exod. 20:8. Exod. R. 25:16.
24. Cf. Zohar II, 88a-b; 128a. Cf. Tikkunei HaZohar, 2a. *Sefer HaZohar Im Perushei HaSulam*, IV, Yitro, p. 141; V, VaYakhel, p. 68. Cf. Zohar Hadash, Bereshit 22a. *Bnei Issakhar*, I, p. 1.
25. Cf. Zohar I, 15b.
26. Cf. *Sefat Emet*, II, p. 209.
27. Cf. Exod. 20:9.
28. Cf. Gen. 2:3; Exod. 23:12. See *HaKetav VeHaKabbalah*, II, p. 49a.
29. Cf. Philon of Alexandria, *De specialibus legibus*, II, 15, 64. Maimonides, *Moreh Nevukhim*, II, 31. Cf. *Shem MiShemuel, Bereshit*, I, pp. 290, 359.

30. Cf. Philon of Alexandria, *De Decalogo*, 20, 100-1; *De specialibus legibus*, II, 15; 64.
31. Cf. *Sefer HaHinukh, Mitzvah* 84; cf. *Sefat Emet*, I, p. 234.
32. Cf. Shelah, I, pp. 193b-194a; *Siddur Sha'ar HaShamayim*, p. 309.
33. Rav Kook, *Olat Reiyah*, II, pp. 1-2; *Orot HaTeshuvah*, 14:33, p. 101; *Orot HaTorah*, p. 24. Cf. TB Eruvin 40b. Cf. *Kuzari*, III, 5. Cf. Rabbi Nahman of Bratslav, *Siddur Sha'arei Ratson*, p. 511. *Sefat Emet*, V, p. 190. *Shem MiShemuel, Bereshit*, II, pp. 351, 353; *Shemot*, p. 240; *Bemidbar*, p. 141. Rabbi Yossef Hayyim of Baghdad, *Da'at UTevunah*, p. 65a. Rabbi Shneur Zalman of Lyady writes in the *Tanya* (*Iggeret HaTeshuvah*, 10, p. 198): "The *Shabbat* has the meaning of *Teshuvah* (of 'returning,' repenting). The letters in the word *Shabbat* are the same as those of the word *Tashev*: 'Thou causest man to return' (Ps. 90:3). For on the *Shabbat*, [man, and with him] the worlds rise toward their source." Cf. *Kedushat Levi*, Bereshit, p. 2a; Bo, p. 36b. *Bnei Issakhar*, II, p. 19a. *Likkutei Moharan*, I, 6:3, p. 6b; 79, p. 93a; *Siddur Sha'arei Ratson*, pp. 478, 608. Rabbi Shemuel Shmelke of Nikolsburg, *Divrei Shemuel*, p. 4. *Sefat Emet*, I, pp. 5-7; II, p. 91; V, pp. 164, 166, 168, 190. *Avnei Nezer*, p. 125. *Shem MiShemuel, Bereshit*, I, pp. 28, 295, 335; *VaYikra*, p. 170; *Devarim*, pp. 5, 49; *Moadim*, pp. 93, 98-99. *Be'er Avraham*, p. 109. *Da'at UTevunah*, p. 74a.
34. Cf. *Sefat Emet*, II, p. 228; *Shem MiShemuel, Devarim*, pp. 226-27.
35. *Sheiltot* (8th cent.), quoted in Tanhuma, Bereshit 2. Cf. *Sifrei Beha'alotkha* 77 (Num. 10:10), p. 19b. Cf. TY Megillah I, 4; Gen. R. 9. Cf. Ibn Ezra and *Ba'al HaTurim* on Num. 10:10. Cf. Zohar II, 165b. *Sefer HaZohar Im Perush HaSulam*, V, VaYakhel, 204, p. 68. Cf. *Kuzari*, V, 10. Cf. TB Pessahim 68b. See Rabbi Dov Baer of Mezerich, *Maggid Devarav LeYa'akov*, 31, p. 50. *Kedushat Levi*, Bereshit, p. 2a. *Siddur Sha'arei Ratson*, p. 530. R. S. R. Hirsch, *Iggrot Tsafon*, p. 81. *Sefat Emet*, I, p. 54; II, p. 111; V, p. 182. *Shem MiShemuel, Bereshit*, I, pp. 10-11; *Shemot*, I, p. 240. *Ben Ish Hai*, p. 102.
36. Exod. 20:8; Deut. 5:13.
37. Mekhilta Yitro, Messikhta DeBaHodesh 7 (Exod. 20:8), p. 277a.
38. Cf. Gen. R. 5:7, 10:5, 10:12, 46:2. TB Haggigah 12a. Tanhuma, Mikeits 10. Zohar III, 119b. See *Sefat Emet*, II, p. 37; III, p. 28. *Be'er Avraham*, p. 213.
39. See supra, p. 268.
40. TB Beitsa 15b. Cf. Zohar II, 255a. See *Perushei HaTorah LeRabbi Yehuda HeHassid*, p. 6.
41. Cf. *Kuzari*, III, 5.
42. Cf. Maharal, *Derekh Hayyim*, pp. 7, 188; cf. also *Perushei Maharal MiPrag LeAggadot HaShas* on Shabbat 113b (II, p. 88).
43. Cf. Exod. R. 20:12. Cf. Maharsha on Shabbat 10b. The gift of Shabbat, rest, which God has made to man, eases the curse that befell him after he committed his first crime: "By the sweat of your brow shall you eat bread" (Gen. 3:19). However, the Mekhilta (Beshalah, Messikhta DeVayassa V, p. 58b, on Exod. 16:21) writes: " 'Morning by morning they gathered it [the manna].' [We learn] by this verse that even as regarding the [harvesting of the] manna, the sentence of 'by the sweat of your brow shall you eat bread' still remains." And the manna has been given to the Jews to prove to them the special character of the Shabbat!

44. See supra, p. 257.
45. Cf. Seforno on Exod. 20:9. Cf. Avot IV, 1; Prov. 13:25; Zohar II, 153b. See also TB Shabbat 119a.
46. Cf. TB Kiddushin 22b; Bava Metsia 10a; Bava Batra 116b. TY Kiddushin I, 2; Tossefta Bava Kama VII, 2. Zohar II, 192a. Rabbeinu Yonah Gerondi, *Sha'arei HaAvodah*, pp. 16-17. Abrabanel, II, Yitro 20, p. 190. Lev. 25:55.
47. Cf. *Shirei Rabbi Yehuda HaLevi*, p. 7. Ibn Ezra on Num. 6:7.
48. Cf. TY Pessahim V, 5. Rashi on Deut. 5:15. *Meshekh Hokhmah*, p. 258. Cf. Zohar III, 223a.
49. Cf. TB Shabbat 118b; Zohar Hadash, 48a. *Shirei Rabbi Yehuda HaLevi*, p. 335. Rabbi Yossef Karo, *Bet Yossef, Tur, Orah Hayyim*, 242. Rabbeinu Yonah Gerondi, *Sha'arei HaAvodah*, p. 50. Rabbi Abraham of Slonim, *Be'er Avraham*, p. 184.
50. Cf. Philon of Alexandria, *De specialibus legibus*, II, 15; 61-63; idem, *De vita Mosis*, II, 39; 215. Cf. Zohar II, 47a. Cf. TB Bava Batra 8b; Zohar I, 23b.
51. Cf. TB Yoma 74b.
52. Cf. TY Shabbat XV, 3; Pesikta Rabbati, 23:9. Cf. Radak on Gen. 2:3 (Kamelhar ed., p. 24). Cf. Seforno on Deut. 5:12.
53. Exod. 23:12.
54. Cf. Rabbi Meir Simha of Dvinsk, *Meshekh Hokhmah*, p. 51; cf. also Rashi on Exod. 23:13. *Shem MiShemuel, Moadim*, p. 90. Rabbi Yossef Rozin, *Mefa'aneah Tsefunot*, p. 147.
55. Cf. Exod. 20:10.
56. Cf. TB Beitsa 13b; Keritot 19b. Rabbi S. R. Hirsch on Gen. 2:2 (I, p. 39); *Iggrot Tsafon*, pp. 70-71. See also Abrabanel, II, Yitro, Exod. 20, p. 190.
57. Cf. Rambam, *Hilkhot Shabbat*, I, 1; XXI, 1. Cf. also Rabbi Hayyim Attar, *Or HaHayyim*, on Exod. 31:16, 35:1.
58. Cf. *Aggadat HaGeonim VeHaMekubalim*, Weinstock ed., Jerusalem: 5734 (1974), p. 213. See also Abrabanel, II, Yitro, Exod. 20, p. 190.
59. Exod. 31:17.
60. *Or HaHayyim* on Gen. 2:2 and on Exod. 35:2; cf. Recanati, Ki Tissa, p. 15b; Alshekh on Gen. 2; *Toldot Ya'akov Yossef, Hakdamah; Sefat Emet*, I, p. 246.
61. Cf. Rabbi Tsevi Elimelekh of Dynow, *Bnei Issakhar*, I, 9a; 38a; *Haggadah Shel Pessah*, p. 75.
62. Cf. *Sefat Emet*, I, pp. 9-10, 246-47; II, pp. 88, 210; III, pp. 153, 196. See also *Shem MiShemuel, Moadim*, p. 209; Rabbi Nahman of Bratslav, *Siddur Sha'arei Ratson*, p. 511.
63. Cf. Gen. R. 10:10. Rashi (on Gen. 2:2) writes: "God finished His work on the seventh day." What was the world lacking? Rest: *menuhah*. The Shabbat came and so rest came! Only then was the work of creation achieved and terminated." Cf. Rashi on TB Megillah 9a; cf. Zohar II, 222b. Cf. Rabbeinu Bahya on Gen. 2:2 (I, p. 53). Cf. also Seforno ad loc.
64. Cf. Num. R. 10:1. Recanati, Bereshit, p. 8b; Shelah, I, p. 11b; *Or HaHayyim* on Gen. 2:2-3; *Sefat Emet*, I, p. 211; *Shem MiShemuel, Bereshit*, I, p. 276; Rav Kook, *Olat Reiyah*, II, p. 47.
65. Cf. Gen. R. 10:10, 10:12; Pirkei DeRabbi Eliezer 18; Recanati, Bereshit, p. 8b; *Arvei Nahal*, Bereshit; Malbim on Gen. 2:2-3; *Shem MiShemuel, Moadim*, p. 120.

66. Cf. Zohar I, 47b; *Shem MiShemuel, Bereshit*, I, pp. 5, 32. *Sefat Emet*, II, p. 210.
67. Cf. *Shem MiShemuel, Bemidbar*, p. 129.
68. Cf. Zohar I, 247a; II, 89b; III, 94b; 103b; Tossafot on TB Sanhedrin 38a. Cf. TB Megillah 9a. See Rashi on Gen. 2:3; R. Shemuel David Luzzatto on Gen. 2:2, pp. 19-20.
69. Gen. 2:2.
70. See supra, p. 267.
71. Cf. Zohar II, 88b; 207a; III, 238b. Zohar Hadash, Bereshit 22. Tikkunei HaZohar, 6; 24; 48. Rabbi Levi Yitshak of Berditchev, *Kedushat Levi*, p. 2a.
72. Cf. *Kuzari*, III, 5. Cf. also Franz Rosenzweig, *Kokhav HaGeulah*, p. 338.
73. *Maggid Devarav LeYa'akov*, 90, p. 156.
74. Cf. Zohar II, Terumah.
75. Cf. Gen. R. 1:2; Zohar I, 5a.
76. Cf. *Sefat Emet*, I, p. 80.
77. Cf. Zohar II, 206b. Cf. *Sefat Emet*, I, p. 15; F. Rosenzweig, *Kokhav HaGeulah*, pp. 334-35.
78. Cf. *Sefat Emet*, III, p. 203.
79. Cf. Ramban on Lev. 26:1-2; Tikkunei HaZohar, 21 (86b); cf. Zohar II, 92a.
80. Cf. Zohar III, 173b-174a. Cf. also Zohar I, 4-5. Cf. Ari HaKadosh, *Likkutei Torah*, p. 126; *Bnei Issakhar*, I, p. 10a; *Sefat Emet*, I, p. 80.
81. Gen. 2:13.
82. TB Shabbat 119b.
84. Cf. TB Shabbat 88a; Avot DeRabbi Nathan 31. Or *HaHayyim* on Gen. 2:3; *Toldot Ya'akov Yossef, Hakdamah; Kedushat Levi*, p. 69a; *Likkutei Moharan*, II, 39, p. 25a; *Be'er Mayim Hayyim* on Gen. 2:1; *Sefat Emet*, I, pp. 15, 244.
85. Cf. Zohar I, 3b; 15b.
86. Cf. Maharsha on TB Shabbat 119b; Rabbi Hayyim of Volozhin, *Nefesh HaHayyim*, pp. 28-32.
87. Cf. Rabbi Yossef Gikatilla (1248-1305), *Ginat Egoz*, p. 36.
88. Cf. Philon of Alexandria, *De vita contemplativa; De Decalogo*, 20, 100-1. Cf. Esther Starobinski-Safran, *"De Fuga et Inventione,"* by Philon of Alexandria, p. 82s.
89. Cf. Zohar II, 205a. See *Be'er Avraham*, p. 184.
90. Cf. Maharal, *Derekh Hayyim* on Avot V, 15, pp. 194-95; 21, p. 210. Cf. Gen. R. 30:8 and *Matnot Kehuna* ad loc. Pesikta DeRav Kahana on Lev. 23:24; Num. 29:1 (*UVaHodesh HaShevi'i*, "in the seventh month" of the year, Tishri; the first month of the year being Nissan; cf. Exod. 12:2), there is a "surfeit" of *mitzvot*, given rise to by several holidays celebrated during of the same month. Cf. TB Rosh HaShanah 11a; Zohar II, 184a. Cf. *Sefat Emet*, V, p. 227; *Shem MiShemuel, Moadim*, p. 147. Cf. also Rabbi Yossef Hayyim, *Od Yossef Hai*, Beshalah, p. 149. This Gaon and Tsaddik of Baghdad sets up a relationship between *shiva*, "seven," and *sevia*, "satiety." The Sages of Israel set up a relationship between *sova*, "satiety," and *sheva*, "seven": *Al tikrei sova ela sheva*: "do not read (in Ps. 16:11) '*sova*' but rather '*sheva*'!" Cf. TB Arakhin 13b. Lev. R. 29:7, 30:2. Num. R. 15:8. Shoher Tov, 16. Tanhuma,

Beha'alotkha 7. Yalkut Shim'oni, Emor 645; Pinhas 782. Cf. TB Megillah 15b.
91. "The Shabbat day is the fruit of the week," says Rabbi Yehuda HaLevi, *Kuzari*, III, 5.
92. Cf. Tana Devei Eliyahu Rabba 1; Lev. R. 3:1; cf. also Gen. R. 11:2; Shir HaShirim R. 1:36. Cf. Zohar II, 89a; Isa. 14:3. Cf. Philon of Alexandria, *Fug.* 173-74; Esther Starobinski-Safran, "*De Fuga et Inventione*," by Philon of Alexandria, p. 83.
93. Cf. Mekhilta DeRabbi Shim'on Bar Yohai on Exod. 20:9. Cf. also Rabbi Tsevi Ashkenazi, *She'elot UTeshuvot Hakham Tsevi*, 83. Generally speaking, the commandments of the Torah pertaining to the Shabbat are preceded by the reference to the six days of work. Cf. Gen. 2:15; Gen. R. 16:8. See TB Shabbat 88b. Cf. Shelah, I, p. 177b; *Sefat Emet*, II, pp. 88-89; *Shem MiShemuel, Shemot*, I, p. 260. See also Shelah, I, p. 25a; Rabbi Eliyahu of Vilna, *Divrei Eliyahu*, p. 4.
94. Cf. *Sefer HaZohar Im Perush HaSulam*, V, VaYakhel, p. 60; Zohar III, 125a. Rabbi Hayyim Vital, *Peri Ets Hayyim, Sha'ar HaShabbat*, p. 63a. *Likkutei Moharan*, 94, p. 96a. Rabbi Shemuel Shmelke of Nikolsburg, *Divrei Shemuel*, pp. 95-96. Rabbi Avraham Yehoshua Heshel of Apta, *Ohev Yisrael*, VaEthanan; *Sefat Emet*, I, p. 16; II, pp. 66, 88, 202; V, pp. 16, 57, 70, 167, 182. *Shem MiShemuel, Bereshit*, I, pp. 20, 92-93, 276, 295, 329, *Bemidbar*, p. 418; *Moadim*, p. 204. Rabbi Avraham of Sochaczew, *Neot HaDesheh*, p. 89. Rabbi Ya'akov Moshe Harlap, *Mei Meirom*, VIII, p. 60.
95. Cf. TB Berakhot 8a; Shabbat 117a; 119; Beitsa 16a; Bava Kama 82a. Yalkut Shim'oni, Tehillim 92:843. Rambam, *Hilkhot Shabbat*, XXX, 3, 6. Rabbi Yossef Karo, *Bet Yossef, Tur, Orah Hayyim*, 285; *Shulhan Arukh, Orah Hayyim*, 1, 250. Cf. Num. R. 14:9; Shir HaShirim R. 1. Cf. Rabbi Nahman of Bratslav, *Siddur Sha'arei Ratson*, pp. 296, 331s. *Be'er Avraham*, p. 145.
96. Cf. *Kedushat Levi*, p. 55; *Bet Avraham*, p. 162.
97. Cf. The "Netsiv," Rabbi Naftali Tsevi Yehuda Berlin of Volozhin, *Ha'amek Davar*, on Exod. 16:5 (II, p. 134), and on Deut. 5:16k (V, p. 60).
98. Cf. Ibn Ezra on Exod. 31:16. Rabbi Hayyim Vital, *Peri Ets Hayyim, Sha'ar HaShabbat*, pp. 63a-b.
99. Cf. TB Avodah Zarah 3a; Ruth Rabba 3:3; Petihta DeEihah Rabbati 18; Kohelet R. 1:36. *Peri Ets Hayyim, Sha'ar HaShabbat*, pp. 62b-63a. See also Abrabanel, II, Yitro, Exod. 20, pp. 180, 190. Cf. Maharal, *Derekh Hayyim*, p. 9. *Ohev Yisrael*, Ki Tissa; *Sefat Emet*, I, pp. 16, 190; II, pp. 105, 208, 226, 227; V, p. 176.
100. Cf. TB Ketuvot 62b; Zohar I, 14a; II, 89a; III, 82a. *Sefat Emet*, II, p. 86.
101. Cf. Mekhilta Yitro, Messikhta DeBaHodesh VII (Exod. 20:8), p. 77a. TB Beitsa 16a; Shabbat 118b; 119a; Rashi and Ramban on Exod. 20:8; Rabbeinu Bahya on Exod. 31:16 (II, p. 324). See Rashi on Num. 25:17; Rabbi Barukh HaLevi Epstein, *Tossefet Berakhah*, V, pp. 36-37.
102. Cf. Shelah HaKadosh, III, p. 129b.
103. Cf. *Sefat Emet*, II, pp. 67, 88.
104. Cf. Rabbi Eliyahu of Vilna, *Siddur Ishei Yisrael*, p. 254; *Sefat Emet*, I, p. 102; II, p. 208.
105. Cf. Rashi on TB Gittin 77a; cf. TB Pessahim 106a. Cf. Sefer HaBahir, 51, p.

15. Rabbi Hayyim Vital, *Peri Ets Hayyim*, II, *Sha'ar HaShabbat*, p. 63a; *Perushei Maharal MiPrag LeAggadot HaShas* on TB Shabbat 118b (II, p. 97); Rav Kook, *Olat Reiyah*, II, pp. 1-2.

106. Cf. Zohar III, 82a; *Sefat Emet*, I, p. 247; II, pp. 204, 208-9.
107. See *Shulhan Arukh*, *Orah Hayyim*, 299:6.
108. Cf. Shelah, I, p. 190a. *Bnei Issakhar*, *Haggadah Shel Pessah*, pp. 76-77. *Divrei Shemuel* (of Nikolsburg), pp. 24, 134. Rabbi Eliyahu of Vilna, *Aderet Eliyahu*, p. 216. Rabbi Avraham Danzig, *Hayei Adam*, *Hilkhot Shabbat*, *Klal* 1. *Arvei Nahal*, Bereshit. *Likkutei Moharan*, 1, 5:2, p. 5b; II, 39, p. 25b. *Ohev Yisrael*, VaEthanan. Rabbi Avraham of Sochaczew, *Avnei Nezer*, p. 8; *Neot HaDesheh*, pp. 136-37. *Shem MiShemuel*, *Bereshit*, I, pp. 86-87, 225, 295; *Bereshit*, II, p. 243; *Bemidbar*, p. 206; *Devarim*, pp. 172, 203-4. *Sefat Emet*, I, pp. 16, 123; II, pp. 88-89, 227; IV, pp. 168, 194. *Ben Ish Hai*, p. 99. Rav Kook, *Olat Reiyah*, II, pp. 45-47. HaRav David Kohen (HaRav HaNazir), *Kol HaNevua*, p. 243. Philon of Alexandria, *Fug*. 174; Esther Starobinski-Safran, "*De Fuga et Inventione*," *by Philon of Alexandria*, p. 84.
109. Cf. Zohar II, 63b; 88a. TB Pessahim 103a; 106a. Ramban on Gen. 2:3. *Likkutei Moharan*, I, 5, p. 5b. *Sefat Emet*, I, pp. 5, 51, 119. *Neot HaDesheh*, pp. 145, 190-91. *Shem MiShemuel*, *Bereshit*, I, p. 276. Rabbi David Kohen (HaRav HaNazir), *Kol HaNevua*, p. 243.
110. This is the way to understand the Talmudic proverb: "If the children of Israel kept two *Shabbatot* according to their *halakhah* (laws), they will be delivered immediately" (TB Shabbat 118b; see Maharsha, *Hiddushei Aggadot* ad loc.). In fact, in order to keep one Shabbat properly, one has to go back to the preceding Shabbat which influences the days separating it from the next Shabbat. But see also *Toldot Ya'akov Yossef*, VaYeitsei. Cf. *Perushei Maharal MiPrag LeAggadot HaShas*, II, on TB Shabbat 118b, (II, pp. 97-100). *Kedushat Levi*, pp. 17, 36, 69. *Divrei Shemuel* (of Nikolsburg), pp. 96, 125. *Sefat Emet*, II, p. 66. *Neot HaDesheh*, pp. 107, 191; *Avnei Nezer*, p. 88. *Be'er Avraham*, p. 118. *Ben Ish Hai*, p. 142. *Mefa'aneah Tsefunot*, p. 100. However, another Talmudic proverb says: "If Israel had kept only one Shabbat appropriately, the Messiah would already have come" (cf. Mekhilta Ki Tissa, Messikhta DeShabta I (Exod. 31:16), p. 110b; TY Ta'anit I, 1; TB Shabbat 118b; Exod. R. 25:16; Shoher Tov, 95; Tikkunei HaZohar, 21 (57a); cf. also TB Shabbat 18b; Zohar Hadash, Beshalah 30a). My father has given thought to the apparent difficulty raised by the contradiction between the two Talmudic proverbs (ideal observation of one or two Shabbatot as a condition to the arrival of the Messiah). See Rabbi B. Z. Safran, *She'elot UTeshuvot Harbaz*, I, p. 19.
111. Cf. Ramban (I, p. 400-1) and Abrabanel (II, p. 189) on Exod. 20:8. Cf. also Ramban on Exod. 12:2; Rabbi Yehuda HaLevi, *Kuzari*, II, 20. See also Mishnah Tamid VII, 4; TY Rosh HaShanah III, 1; TB Rosh HaShanah 3a; Lev. R. 1:1; Kohelet R. 11:5. *Tossefet Berakhah*, II, p. 185-86.
112. The daily psalm which the religious Jew recites at the end of his morning prayers is preceded by the statement: "Today is the first (second...) day *in* the Shabbat." The days of the week are thus included in the Shabbat. Cf. Shelah, I, pp. 176a, 188a, 189a, 190a, 192a, 193b, 194a; II, p. 11a, 16a; III, p. 45a. *Likkutei Moharan*, I, 63a, p. 77a. *Aderet Eliyahu* (*Be'er Yitshak*), p. 429. *Sefat*

Emet I, pp. 5-6, 51, 102. *Shem MiShemuel, Devarim,* pp. 226-27. *Bet HaLevi,* p. 9.
113. Cf. Rabbi Moshe Hayyim Luzzatto, *Sheloshah Sefarim Niftahim, Pithei Hokhmah,* p. 10b; *Shem MiShemuel, Bereshit,* I, p. 25.
114. Cf. *Sefat Emet,* I, p. 13; *Shem MiShemuel, Bereshit,* I, p. 11; II, p. 218. See also Gen. R. 10:2. Cf. Rabbi Yossef Horowitz of Novhardok, *Madregat HaAdam* (Jerusalem: 5730); Rabbi Yehezkel Sarna, *Dalyot Yehezke'el* (I, Jerusalem: 5735; II, Jerusalem: 5736).
115. The relationship between the Shabbat and the sabbatical year, itself called Shabbat, was often dwelt on. Rav Kook (cf. *Shabbat HaArets,* p. 8) writes that the Shabbat has a special influence on the Jewish nation. Rabbi Shmuel of Sochatzew (cf. *Shem MiShemuel, VaYikra,* p. 318) also shows, based upon the Zohar, the essential rapport between the *Shemittah* and *Knesset Yisrael,* between the sabbatical year and the Jewish community. Cf. Sifra, Rashi, Ramban, Recanati, *Akeidat Yitshak,* Abrabanel, Malbim and *Meshekh Hokhmah* (p. 185) on Lev. 25. Mishnah Shevi'it I, 4. Mekhilta 20 (Exod. 23:12), p. 107a. Exod. R. 30:12. Zohar III, 208a; 210b. *Sefer HaHinukh, Mitzvah* 84. Maharal, *Derekh Hayyim,* on Avot V, 9, pp. 188-89. Rabbi Avraham HaMalakh, *Hessed LeAvraham,* p. 26. *Sefat Emet,* III, p. 196. Y. Breuer, *Nahliel,* Tel-Aviv: 5711 (1951), pp. 236-37. *Tossefet Berakhah,* I, p. 7. Rabbi Yehezkel Abramski, *Tossefta Im Perushei Hazon Yehezke'el,* Kodashim II, pp. I-II.
116. Sifra Behar 4 (Lev. 25:23), p. 108; see also Sifra Behukotai 7 (Lev. 26:34), p. 112; cf. Rashi on Lev. 25:23; *Kli Yakar* on Lev. 25:3.
117. Cf. *Sefat Emet,* I, p. 247; II, p. 209; III, p. 207. Cf. *Be'er Avraham,* p. 184; *Shem MiShemuel, Shemot,* II, p. 277.
118. Cf. Tanhuma, Shemini 2. *Sefat Emet,* II, p. 111; *Iggrot Tsafon,* pp. 70-71.
119. The radiance of the human, Jewish face on the Shabbat day is not the same as on the weekdays (cf. Gen. R. 11:2). The credibility inspired by the Jew on the Shabbat is greater than that of the weekdays (cf. Mishnah Demai IV, 1 and *Perush HaRambam* ad loc.; TY Demai IV, 1; Rambam, *Hilkhot Ma'asser,* XII, 1; Tossafot on TB Ketuvot 55b; cf. also Mishnah Haggigah III, 6; Rambam, *Hilkhot Metamei Mishkav UMoshav,* XI, 9). See also *Sefat Emet,* I, p. 51; II, pp. 75, 203; *Shem MiShemuel, Bereshit,* I, pp. 180, 349; *Moadim,* p. 100; Rabbi Nahman of Bratslav, *Siddur Sha'arei Ratson,* p. 608.
120. See supra, p. 255.
121. Cf. TY Shabbat XV, 3; Sotah I, 4. Zohar III, 173b; Exod. R. 5:22; Tana Devei Eliyahu Rabba I; Shoher Tov, 19; cf. Yalkut Shim'oni, I, VaYakhel 408; II, Mishlei 864. Philon of Alexandria, *De vita Mosis,* II, 39, 215-16; idem, *De specialibus legibus,* II, 15, 61-62; idem, *De Fuga,* 176. Josephus, *Contra Apionem,* II, 17. Rashi on TB Sotah 49a; Ramban on Exod. 20:7; Rabbeinu Bahya on Exod. 20:8, II, p. 195; cf. 2 Kings 4:23; TB Rosh HaShanah 16b. Cf. Rabbi Ya'akov Ben Asher, *Tur, Orah Hayyim,* 290; Rabbi Yossef Karo, *Bet Yossef, Tur, Orah Hayyim,* 290. Cf. Esther Starobinski-Safran, "De Fuga et Inventione," by Philon of Alexandria, p. 83.
122. Cf. Peskita Rabbati, Aseret HaDibbrot 3.
123. Cf. *Kuzari,* III, 10.
124. Cf. Rambam, *Moreh Nevukhim,* III, 43; Rabbeinu Bahya on Exod. 20:8 (II,

p. 197); R. Shemuel David Luzzatto, the "Shedal," *Perush Al Hamishah Humshei Torah*, Yitro, Exod. 20:11, p. 331.

125. Cf. TB Berakhot 57b. Zohar I, 1b; 48a; II, 10a; III, 95a. Zohar Hadash, Bereshit 16. Tikkunei HaZohar, 77. Shelah, *Siddur Sha'ar HaShamayim*, p. 385. Cf. Mishnah Tamid VII, 4. TB Sanhedrin 97a; Rosh HaShanah 31a. Zohar II, 10a. Cf. Ramban on Gen. 2:3. Rabbeinu Bahya on Gen. 2:3 (I, pp. 53-54); on Exod. 20:8, II (p. 197-98); on Num. 10:35 (III, pp. 56-58). *Be'er Mayim Hayyim* on Gen. 2:1.

126. Cf. Mekhilta Ki Tissa, Messikhta DeShabta I (Exod. 31:14), p. 110a; Isa. 43:12. Cf. Zohar II, 90a.

127. Cf. Mekhilta Yitro, Messikhta DeBaHodesh 8 (Exod. 20:16), p. 78b; ibidem Ki Tissa, Messikhta DeShabta I (Exod. 31:14), p. 110a; Isa. 43:12. Cf. Rambam, *Moreh Nevukhim*, II, 31. Ramban on Exod. 20:8; on Deut. 5:15; cf. also Ramban on Deut. 6:20.

128. Cf. Deut. 4:32; Isa. 40:26, 40:28. Cf. *Moreh Nevukhim*, II, 30; III, 10; cf. Ibn Ezra and *Aderet Eliyahu* (p. 10) on Gen. 1:1. Cf. also M.D. Cassuto, *Me-Adam Ad Noah*, pp. 43-44. See Rabbi Yossef Rozin, the Gaon of Rogachov, *Mefa'aneah Tsefunot*, pp. 142-43.

129. Cf. Rambam, *Moreh Nevukhim*, I, 71; cf. also idem, *Mishneh Torah, Hilkhot Yessodei HaTorah*, I, 1-3. Cf. *Kuzari*, V, 18; II, 50.

130. Rav Kook, *Olat Reiyah*, II, p. 69.

131. Cf. Rambam, *Moreh Nevukhim*, II, 25; cf. also idem, ibidem, II, 31.

132. Cf. Ramban on Gen. 1:1; on Lev. 29:30. Cf. Rambam, *Moreh Nevukhim*, II, 25. See also Rabbi Yitshak Arama, *Akeidat Yitshak*, VaYakhel 55; Rabbi Yossef Albo, *Sefer HaIkkarim*, III, 26.

133. Cf. Rabbi Yisrael Meir HaKohen, *Hafets Hayyim Al HaTorah*, pp. 13-14, 88-89.

134. See supra, p. 271.

135. Cf. TY Berakhot I, 5; Nedarim III, 9. Exod. R. 25:16. Zohar II, 47a; 89a; 91a; 92a. Tikkunei HaZohar, 12a; 19 (40b); 21 (57a-b). Zohar Hadash, Bereshit 17a, 22a; Yitro 33b; Ki Tissa 45a. Rambam, *Hilkhot Shabbat*, XXX, 15. Ramban on Lev. 26:1. Rabbi Yisrael Meir HaKohen (the "Hafets Hayyim"), *Mishnah Berurah Shulhan Arukh, Orah Hayyim*, III, 1.

136. Cf. Ramban on Lev. 19:30.

137. Cf. Rambam, *Mishneh Torah, Hilkhot Shabbat*, XXX, 15 and *Hilkhot Ma'asei HaKorbanot*, III, 4.

138. Cf. TB Eruvin 69b; Hullin 5a. See Tossafot on TB Hullin 14a.

139. Cf. Rashi on TB Hullin 5a; cf. also Rashi on TB Yevamot 48b; on Num. 15:41. Cf. TB Horayot 8a. Rambam, *Perush HaMishnah*, Hullin I, 1; *Mishneh Torah, Hilkhot Shabbat*, XXX, 15; *Hilkhot Gerushin*, III, 15; *Ma'asei HaKorbanot*, III, 4; *Shegagot*, III, 7. *Tur, Even HaEzer*, 44. *Shulhan Arukh, Yoreh Deyah*, 2:5. *Mishnah Berurah, Hakdamah, Hilkhot Shabbat*.

140. Cf. TB Shabbat 118b; Bava Batra 10a. *Bet Yossef, Tur, Orah Hayyim*, 242. Tossafot on TB Sanhedrin 78b; on TB Bava Batra 119a. Cf. Rashi on TB Hullin 5a. Meiri on TB Kiddushin 50; see TB Yevamot 47b. See Rabbi D.T. Hoffmann, *She'elot UTeshuvot Melamed LeHoil, Orah Hayyim*, 29; *Yoreh Deyah*, 52. *Hazon Ish, Yoreh Deyah*, 2:28. Cf. Rabbi B.Z. Safran, *She'elot UTeshuvot Harbaz*, I, p. 19. The Bible presents the prescriptions regarding

REFERENCES, SOURCES & NOTES • 399

the Shabbat together with the interdictions regarding idolatry. Cf. Lev. 19:3-4; Exod. 23:12-13, 34:12-21; Neh. 9:13-14. See TY Nedarim III, 9; Rambam, *Hilkhot Shabbat*, XXX, 15. Cf. also *Ba'al HaTurim* on Lev. 26:1-2.

141. Cf. Ramban on Exod. 20:2, 20:8 idem, *Derashah Al Divrei Kohelet* (*Kitvei Ramban* I, p. 189). Rabbeinu Bahya on Exod. 20:8 (II, p. 195). Cf. also TB Pessahim 117b; *Sefer HaHinukh, Mitzvah* 31. See also Zohar III, 115b. Cf. Shelah, II, p. 10b; III, pp. 88b, 118b.
142. Rabbi Yossef Karo, *Bet Yossef, Tur, Orah Hayyim*, 242.
143. Rabbi Ya'akov Ben Asher, *Tur, Orah Hayyim*, 292, Cf. Zohar II, 205b. The morning and evening prayers framing the reciting of the *Shema* (Deut. 6:4), the Jewish profession of faith, are addressed to God who creates and supports the world, who gives Israel the Torah and who delivers Israel. Cf. Maharal, *Derekh Hayyim*, pp. 8-9. Cf. Franz Rosenzweig, *Kokhav HaGeulah*, pp. 335-36. But cf. also *Sefer HaZohar Im Perush HaSulam*, IV, Yitro, 530, p. 135; V, VaYakhel, 207, p. 68.
144. Cf. Maharal, *Derekh Hayyim*, pp. 8-9; *Sefat Emet*, I, p. 13.
145. Cf. *Biurei HaGra Al Aggadot*, I, pp. 98-99; *Siddur Ishei Yisrael*, p. 251.
146. Cf. Rashi on Gen. 1:31: "*Yom HaShishi*: 'Day the Sixth.' The letter *Heh* (of the definite article *Ha*, which did not appear in the wording of the preceding days) indicates the end of Creation, as if to tell us: it is on the condition that Israel accepts to keep the five books of the Torah that the world was created. (The Hebrew letter *Heh* has the numerical value of five.) Another explanation: 'The sixth day': everything was done with The Sixth Day in view, the one in the month of Sivan intended for the revelation of the Torah on Sinai." Cf. Shelah, III, p. 23a; *Sefat Emet*, I, p. 8. Cf. TB Shabbat 88a; Zohar I, 47a; Tikkunei HaZohar, 22 (67a); 47 (83a); cf. Zohar Hadash, Yitro 38a.
147. Cf. Gen. R. 1:5; Zohar I, 24a; 118b; II, 108b; 119a-b. Hakdamat Tikkunei HaZohar, 6a; Tikkunei HaZohar, 6 (23b); 40 (80a). Zohar Hadash, Yitro 37a. Cf. TB Shabbat 88a; Zohar III, 125a; Zohar Hadash, Yitro 38a. Cf. *Sefat Emet*, I, p. 244. Cf. TB Pessahim 68b; Zohar I, 24b. Cf. TB Rosh HaShanah 32a. Cf. *Akeidat Yitshak*, VaYakhel.
148. Cf. TB Sanhedrin 97-98; Exod. R. 25:16; Zohar II, 130b.
149. Cf. TB Shabbat 86b; Zohar III, 73a. Cf. Hakdamat Tikkunei HaZohar, 11b.
150. Cf. *Shem MiShemuel, Shemot*, II, p. 274.
151. Cf. Mekhilta Ki Tissa, Messikhta DeShabta 1 (Exod. 31:16), p. 110b.
152. Cf. Gen. R. 44:26. Zohar I, 117a; III, 32a; 54a. Rashi on Gen. 15:18; Ramban on Gen. 1:4. *Likkutei Moharan*, I, 64:4, p. 79a. See also TB Temurah 3b; *Shem MiShemuel, Moadim*, p. 90.
153. Cf. Zohar I, 232b; 87b. Ibn Ezra on Gen. 2:12.
154. See supra, p. 260.
155. "I made the earth, and created man upon it" (Isa. 45:12). "I made the earth," certainly! But why did I make the earth? Because I "created man upon it!" (Zohar I, 205b; cf. Isa. 44:24).
156. When "the Lord God called man and asked him: 'Where are you?' Adam did not answer clearly. His answer was evasive, quibbling" (Gen. 3:9-11).
157. Cf. TB Sanhedrin 38b; Lev. R. 29:1; Pirkei DeRabbi Eliezer 20; cf. Yalkut Shim'oni, Pinhas 29:582. Cf. Pesikta Rabbati, 47; Pesikta DeRav Kahana, Rosh HaShanah I, p. 23; II, p. 334.

158. Cf. TB Sanhedrin 38a; cf. *Sefat Emet*, V, p. 167.
159. Cf. Zohar II, 134a; Shoher Tov, 92.
160. Cf. Pirkei DeRabbi Eliezer 19; Tanhuma, Bereshit 10; Kohelet R. 1:3; Gen. R. 22:28; Yalkut Shim'oni, Tehillim 92:843. According to tradition, Adam, after having been defended before God by the Shabbat and exonerated by the Supreme Judge thanks to his repentance — the *teshuvah* he had made — was the first to exclaim: *Mizmor Shir LeYom HaShabbat*, and to sing the "Song for the day of the Shabbat" (Ps. 92:1). But the Shabbat reacted and cried out: "You (O Man!) and I, we must praise God and sing a song in His honor!" (See supra, note 2).
161. Cf. TB Yoma 28b; Zohar III, 276b; cf. Gen. R. 11:8, 79:7, 92:4, 95:2; cf. Tanhuma, Lekh Lekha 11, cf. Rabbi Yossef Karo, *Bet Yossef, Tur, Orah Hayyim*, 292.
162. Cf. Zohar Hadash, Bereshit 12a, 13a. See Gen. R. 13:3; Ibn Ezra on Gen. 2:12; *Sefat Emet*, V, p. 165; *Shem MiShemuel, Shemot*, I, p. 106.
163. The numerical value of the word *Elohim* (God, Creator of Nature) is the same as that of the word *HaTeva* ("the Nature"): 86 (cf. Shelah, *Sha'ar HaOtiot*, 89).
164. Gen. 2:31. Cf. Rashbam on Exod. 20:8; Maharal, *Tiferet Yisrael*, 44, p. 55.
165. B. Jacob, *Das erste Buch der Torah, Genesis*, p. 66; M. D. Cassuto, *MeAdam Ad Noah*, p. 39.
166. Cf. Rabbi S. R. Hirsch on Exod. 31:13, p. 455.
167. Cf. Gen. 2:3; Exod. 31:13; TB Beitsa 17a; Zohar III, 95a.
168. Cf. Rashbam on TB Pessahim 101a; Joel 2:16; Zohar II, 47a. *Neot HaDesheh*, pp. 110, 133, 141; *Avnei Nezer*, p. 103. See also TB Beitsa 17a. Cf. also *The Hirsch Siddur*, p. 591.
169. Cf. *Likkutei Moharan*, I, 91, p. 41a.
170. Cf. Gen. R. 1:5; Tikkunei HaZohar, 6a; Zohar Hadash, Yitro 37a. Cf. also Pirkei DeRabbi Eliezer 18; Recanati, Bereshit, p. 8a.
171. Cf. TB Yevamot 61a and Tossafot ad loc. Cf. TB Bava Metsia 114a; Tossafot on TB Sanhedrin 59a. Cf. Zohar I, 20b; II, 25a-b; III, 125a; 238b. Cf. Tikkunei HaZohar, 47. But see also Zohar III, 173b. Cf. Rabbi Reuven Margaliot, *Sha'arei Zohar*, Jerusalem: 5716 (1956), pp. 134, 178, 194. Cf. *Kuzari*, II, 44. Cf. *Perushei Maharal MiPrag LeAggadot HaShas*, IV, p. 68, on Ketuvot 66b.
172. See supra, p. 259.
173. Cf. TY Nedarim III, 9.
174. Gen. 2:1.
175. Cf. Mekhilta Ki Tissa, Messikhta DeShabta 1 (Exod. 31:17), p. 111a; cf. *Or HaHayyim* on Gen. 2:3.
176. Maharal, *Gur Aryeh*, Shelah Lekha (Num. 15:32; see Rashi ad loc.); see also Maharal, *Tiferet Yisrael*, 44, pp. 55a-b.
177. See supra, p. 260.
178. Cf. Exod. 16:29; TB Shabbat 10b; Beitsa 16a; Tossefta Berakhot III, 7. Zohar III, 122b.
179. Cf. TB Shabbat 86b.
180. See supra, p. 265.

181. Cf. TB Shabbat 118a; cf. also Gen. R. 11:9; Yalkut Shim'oni, Beshalah 16:261.
182. Cf. Deut. 5:15.
183. Cf. Isa. 58:13; Exod. R. 25:16; TB Shabbat 118b.
184. Cf. Isa. 56:2; TB Shabbat 118a.
185. Cf. Mekhilta Ki Tissa, Messikhta DeShabta 1 (Exod. 31:16), p. 110b; TB Shabbat 118b.
186. The holy name *Elohim* indicates the "quality of severity," the attribute of force, justice, concentration. The Tetragrammaton, *Shem Havaya*, indicates the "quality of mercy," the attribute of love, goodness, openness. Cf. Esther Starobinski-Safran, "Signification des noms divins d'après Exod. 3," in *Revue de théologie et de philosophie*, Vol. VI (1973), pp. 426-35. Cf. Ramban and Rabbeinu Bahya on Exod. 20:2. Cf. *Shem MiShemuel*, I, p. 106.
187. Cf. Mishnah Makot III, 16; Avot VI, 11.
188. At the end of the creation story in the book of Genesis (1:31-2:1), the Tetragrammaton, *Shem Havaya*, is only mentioned symbolically, in the first letters of the words *Y*om *H*aShishi *V*aYekhulu *H*aShamayim: "the sixth day, the heavens were finished." These four words — part of two different but successive verses — begin the *Kiddush* (the prayer of "sanctification" of the Shabbat recited aloud over wine). Cf. *Shulhan Arukh, Orah Hayyim*, 271, *Levush*.
189. Cf. Tikkunei HaZohar 9 (24b); 24 (136b); cf. Zohar III, 128a; cf. TB Yevamot 6a-b; 93a. Cf. Midrash HaGadol, Leviticus (E.N. Rabinowitz ed.), Lev. 19:30, p. 497.
190. Cf. *Tanya, Likkutei Amarim*, 43, p. 61b; *Divrei Shemuel* (of Nikolsburg), pp. 42-43, 121, 135; *Likkutei Moharan*, II, 17, p. 21b. *Shem MiShemuel, Bereshit*, I, p. 224.
191. Cf. Exod. 31:17; Zohar II, 89a; TB Beitsa 16a.
192. Cf. Mekhilta Ki Tissa Messikhta DeShabta 1 (Exod. 31:16-17), p. 110b; TB Beitsa 16a; Exod. R. 25:15; Zohar II, 63b; 88b; 204b; Recanati, Ki Tissa, p. 15b; Ramban on Deut. 5:15; cf. also TB Shabbat 119a.
193. See supra, p. 265.
194. Exod. 31:16-17.
195. Cf. Exod. 35:1-3; Lev. 19:2-3.
196. Cf. Gen. 9:12-13.
197. Exod. 31:17. Cf. Shelah, I, p. 178a.
198. Cf. *Kuzari*, II, 34; Mekhilta Yitro, Messikhta DeBaHodesh 2 (Exod. 19:5), p. 71a; Zohar II, 92a; III, 29a; Tikkunei HaZohar, 73a; Yalkut Shim'oni, VaYakhel 35:408; Rabbi Yossef Karo, *Bet Yossef, Tur Orah Hayyim*, 290; *Shem MiShemuel, Bereshit*, I, p. 223.
199. Cf. *Ben Ish Hai*, p. 142. See supra, note 136.
200. Cf. Exod. 31:16 and Mekhilta ad loc. (Ki Tissa, Messikhta DeShabta 1, p. 110b).
201. Cf. Mekhilta Ki Tissa, Messikhta DeShabta 1 (Exod. 31:17), p. 110b; Esther R. 7; *Kuzari*, III, 10.
202. Cf. Rabbi Ya'akov Ben Asher, *Tur, Orah Hayyim*, 292; Tossafot on TB Haggigah 3b. Zohar II, 90a; Yalkut Shim'oni, Yeshaya 43:454; Rabbi Elime-

lekh of Lyzhansk, *Noam Elimelekh, Bereshit.* Cf. also *Perushei Maharal MiPrag LeAggadot HaShas* on TB Shabbat 118b (II, pp. 98-99). Maharal, *Tiferet Yisrael,* 40, p. 50b; 44, p. 55; idem, *Derekh Hayyim,* p. 9. Cf. also Pirkei DeRabbi Eliezer 20. Tana Devei Eliyahu Rabba 26.
203. Cf. TB Shabbat 118b; Beitsa 16a.
204. Cf. Gen. R. 11:9; Zohar II, 63b; cf. also Zohar II, 94b. Cf. Maharal, *Tiferet Yisrael,* 40, p. 50b; *Perushim LeAggadot HaShas* on TB Shabbat 118b (II, p. 99); *Derekh Hayyim,* pp. 8-9.
205. *Shabbat* (usually in the feminine gender, cf. supra, note 23) is called *malkah,* "queen," *kalah* "bride," by the Jews (cf. TB Shabbat 119a; Tikkunei HaZohar, 24, 69a). See Rabbi Hayyim Vital, *Peri Ets Hayyim, Sha'ar HaShabbat,* p. 68b; Maharal, *Derekh Hayyim,* pp. 8-9; Rabbi Eliyahu of Vilna, *Biurei HaGra Al Aggadot,* I, pp. 98-99.
206. See supra, p. 265.
207. Maharal, *Derekh Hayyim,* on Avot I, 15, p. 35; on Avot III, 18, p. 120. Cf. TB Megillah 28b; Niddah 73a. The *halakhah* is neither rigid nor static; it moves along the path of life, on the highways of the world. Cf. Rambam, *Mishneh Torah, Hilkhot Temurah,* IV, 13. See also *Divrei Shemuel,* p. 82.
208. Cf. TB Shabbat 12a; Mekhilta BeShalah, Messikhta DeVaYassa 1 (Exod. 15:25), p. 54a.
209. Cf. Pesikta Rabbati, Aseret HaDibbrot; Philon of Alexandria, *Migr.* 89-93.
210. Cf. Mekhilta BeShalah, Messikhta DeVaYassa 5 (Exod. 16:29), p. 59b; Zohar II, 123b.
211. See supra, p. 244.
212. Exod. 31:16.
213. Zohar III, 238b; 243b-244a. The Zohar allows itself to read *BeDiratam* instead of *BeDorotam,* for the two *vav* (= o) are missing in this last word. Cf. Yalkut Reuveni, Ki Tissa. See Rabbi Yisrael of Koznitz, *Avodat Yisrael,* p. 210.
214. See supra, p. 244.
215. Cf. Rabbi Moshe Alshekh (16th cent.), *Torat Moshe,* VaYakhel. See also Zohar III, 244a; Tikkunei HaZohar, 6; 48. Pirkei DeRabbi Eliezer 18. Ari HaKadosh, *Likkutei Torah*; Rabbi Hayyim Vital, *Ta'amei HaMitzvot,* pp. 60-61. Shelah, *Siddur Sha'ar HaShamayim,* p. 385. *Biurei HaGra Al Aggadot,* II, p. 36a-b. Rabbi Nahman of Bratslav, *Siddur Sha'arei Ratson,* p. 205. Rabbi Abraham of Slonim, *Yessod HaAvodah,* II, pp. 83-84; idem, *Bet Avraham,* p. 150. Rabbi Avraham of Sochaczew, *Avnei Nezer,* pp. 88, 96, 105; idem, *Neot HaDesheh,* pp. 113, 118. *Shem MiShemuel, Bereshit,* II, pp. 350, 359; *Bemidbar,* p. 47; *Devarim,* p. 53. Cf. *Sefer HaZohar Im Perush HaSulam,* V, VaYakhel, p. 60. Cf. TB Shabbat 113b; Maharal, *Perushim LeAggadot HaShas* on TB Shabbat 113b, II, p. 88. See Rav Kook, *Orot HaTeshuvah,* 12:5, pp. 72-73. Rabbi Yossef Hayyim of Baghdad, *Da'at UTevunah,* p. 65a.
216. Cf. Abrabanel (II, pp. 190-91) and Malbim on Yitro, Exod. 20:12. See also Mekhilta BeShalah, Messikhta DeVaYassa 1 (Exod. 15:25), p. 54a.
217. Exod. 20:8, 20:12; Deut. 5:12-16; Lev. 19:3. Cf. TB Sanhedrin 56a.
218. See Supra, p. 244.

219. Cf. TB Shabbat 23b; Zohar I, 48b.
220. See supra, p. 240.
221. Cf. Yalkut Shim'oni, Tehillim 139:888; Tana Devei Eliyahu 1; cf. Rabbi Yehuda HeHassid, *Sefer Hassidim* (Margaliot ed.), p. 487.
222. Cf. Hermann Cohen, *Die Religion der Vernunft aus den Quellen des Judentums*, Leipzig: 1919, pp. 183-84.
223. Cf. Franz Rosenzweig, *Kokhav HaGeulah*, Jerusalem: 5730 (1970), pp. 338-39.
224. Cf. Zohar I, 48a; II, 135b. Tikkunei HaZohar, 6 (21a). Tossafot on TB Ketuvot 7a; the Shabbat brings the one who keeps it a "new soul," it gives him a "new face."
225. Cf. Mishnah Shabbat I; Eruvin X; Sotah V, 3; TY Eruvin III, 4; TB Shabbat 2; Eruvin 17b; 88b-89a. Rambam, *Mishneh Torah, Hilkhot Shabbat*, XII, 15; XXVIII, 1. *Shulhan Arukh, Orah Hayyim*, 345.
226. See supra, p. 244.
227. Cf. TB Sukkah 44b; Rambam, *Mishneh Torah, Hilkhot Shabbat*, XXX, 11; *Tur, Shulhan Arukh, Orah Hayyim*, 249. See Num. R. 16:1; *She'elot UTeshuvot Tsemah Tsedek, Yoreh Deyah*, 92. See also TB Shabbat 19a; 113b; Berakhot 6b. *Tossefet Berakhah*, V, p. 100; Isa. 58:13.
228. Cf. Exod. 16:29. TB Eruvin 48a; 51a. Rambam, *Mishneh Torah, Hilkhot Shabbat*, XXVIII. See also *Shulhan Arukh, Orah Hayyim*, 273, 1. Cf. Rabbi Nahman of Bratslav, *Siddur Sha'arei Ratson*, p. 205; Rabbi Tsadok HaKohen of Lublin, *Ressissei Lailah*, p. 52.
229. Gen. R. 11:8, 79:7.
230. Cf. Maharal, *Tiferet Yisrael*, 20, p. 22a.
231. Cf. *Sefer HaHinukh, Mitzvah* 24.
232. See TY Moed Katan II, 3.
233. See supra, p. 224.
234. Cf. TY Nedarim III, 2; TB Shevuot 20b; Berakhot 20b; Rosh HaShanah 27a. Cf. Zohar III, 92b; 180b. But see also *Ha'amek Davar* on Deut. 10:4, 10·5 (V, p. 96).
235. Cf. TB Berakhot 20b; Shevuot 20b. The Talmud wishes to teach us in its remark: *Kol SheYeshno BiShmirah, Yeshno BiZkhirah*, that women who have to observe the negative mitzvot of *lo ta'asseh — shmirah* — which include the Shabbat, must also observe the positive *mitzvat asseh — zekhirah —* of *Kiddush HaYom*, the "sanctification of the day" of the Shabbat over the wine. Cf. also Ramban on Exod. 20:8; *Sefat Emet*, I, p. 54; *Shem MiShemuel, VaYikra*, p. 315; *Devarim*, p. 34; *Tossefet Berakhah*, II, pp. 183-84.
236. Cf. TB Pessahim 106a.
237. Cf. *Shulhan Arukh, Orah Hayyim*, 271; *Tossefet Berakhah*, II, p. 285.
238. Cf. TB Megillah 27b.
239. "*Sight* leads to *remembering; remembering* leads to *action*"; cf. TB Menahot 43b; Num. 15:39. Cf. TY Berakhot I, 5. Cf. also Yalkut Shim oni, Shelah Lekha 15:703. Cf. also Tana Devei Eliyahu Rabba 26. See *Biur HaGra Al Sefer Rayah Mehemnah*, Jerusalem: 5735 (1975), p. 11.
240. Cf. Shelah, I, p. 26b.
241. Cf. Rambam, *Sefer HaMitzvot, Mitzvot Asseh*, 9; *Mitzvot Lo Ta'asseh*, 63;

Mishneh Torah, Hilkhot Yessodei HaTorah, V. Cf. also *Kuzari,* II, 54. But see also TB Sanhedrin 74a-b. Cf. TY Shevi'it IV, 3; Sanhedrin III, 6. TB Sanhedrin 75a and *Hiddushei HaRan* on Sanhedrin 75. See also Maharsha on TB Yevamot 47b; cf. Tossafot on TB Bekhorot 2b; but see also Rabbi Yehezkel Landau (18th cent.), *Noda BiYehuda, Mahadura Tinyana, Helek Yoreh Deyah,* 148.

242. Cf. Rabbi Yossef Karo, *Bet Yossef, Tur, Orah Hayyim,* 290. See Rambam, *Moreh Nevukhim,* III, 24; Maharal, *Tiferet Yisrael,* 44, p. 55; Rabbi Meir Simha Kohen of Dvinsk, *Meshekh Hokhmah,* pp. 179, 258-59.
243. Cf. Pesikta Rabbatai, Aseret HaDibbrot 23. See also Exod. R. 25:15. Ramban on Deut. 5:5. Rabbeinu Bahya on Exod. 20:1 (II, p. 181); on Exod. 20:17 (II, p. 203).
244. Cf. Rambam, *Moreh Nevukhim,* III, 43; *Kuzari,* III, 10.
245. On the "Shabbat rest" for animals and objects (*Shevitat Behemah VeKelim*), see Exod. 20:10, 23:12; Deut. 5:14; Mishnah Shabbat I, 5 (and commentaries ad loc.); V, 4. TY Shabbat V, 2. TB Shabbat 18a; Bava Kama 54a-b; Avodah Zarah 15a-b. Rambam, *Hilkhot Shabbat,* VI, 16; XX.
246. Cf. supra, notes 40, 41.
247. Cf. Zohar III, 223a.
248. See supra, p. 266.
249. Cf. Ramban on Gen. 2:3; on Exod. 31:13; cf. Rabbeinu Bahya on Exod. 20:8 (II, p. 198). Cf. Recanati, Bereshit, p. 8b. Cf. also *Sefer HaZohar Im Perush HaSulam,* IV, Yitro, pp. 134, 527; Tikkunei HaZohar, 10 (21b).
250. Cf. TY Ta'anit I, 1; TB Shabbat 118b. Exod. R. 25:16; Lev. R. 3:1; Kohelet R. 4:10; cf. also Lev. R. 23:6. Cf. also Ibn Ezra on Exod. 20:10.
251. Cf. Zohar I, 14b; Pirkei DeRabbi Eliezer 20.
252. Cf. *Sefat Emet,* V, pp. 163, 167; IV, p. 29; III, *Parashat Behar;* I, p. 11, II, pp. 89, 198. Cf. Hermann Cohen, *Die Religion der Vernunft aus den Quellen des Judentums,* p. 184; cf. also ibidem, p. 423; cf. also *The Hirsch Siddur,* pp. 543, 595.
253. Deut. 5:12.
254. Cf. Rabbi Yossef Karo, *Bet Yossef, Tur, Orah Hayyim,* 290. See Zohar II, 209a.
255. Cf. Isa. 43:12; Yalkut Shim'oni, Ezek. 43:454. Mekhilta Ki Tissa, Messikhta DeShabta 1 (Exod. 31:14, 31:16), pp. 110a-b. Lev. R. 3:1; Kohelet R. 4:10. Zohar II, 90a. *Be'er Mayim Hayyim* on Gen. 2:1. See Rabbi B.Z. Safran, *She'elot UTeshuvot Harbaz,* I, p. 19.
256. Cf. Zohar II, 88b; 156a. Maharal, *Derekh Hayyim,* p. 9; *Gevurot HaShem,* 36, p. 83; *Shem MiShemuel, Bemidbar,* p. 408.
257. Cf. Ps. 139:16. Zohar I, 219b; II, 135a-b. Pirkei DeRabbi Eliezer 18. See Maharal, *Derekh Hayyim,* p. 9; *Tiferet Yisrael,* 40, p. 50b.
258. Israel is one, because its unity, uniqueness, is based on God's unity, uniqueness: Israel reflects it in the world (cf. TB Berakhot 6a). The "Shabbat," which is "God's name" (cf. Zohar II, 88b; 128a), strengthens Israel's unity (and every Jew's personal unity as well). See Maharal, *Derekh Hayyim,* p. 9. Shelah, I, p. 21a; Rav Kook, *Olat Reiyah,* II, p. 47.
259. Cf. Isa. 45:17.
260. See supra, p. 269.

261. See supra, p. 271.
262. Cf. Zohar II, VaYakhel.
263. Mishnah Tamid *in fine.*
264. Ps. 92. Cf. Mishnah Tamid VII, 4. TB Rosh HaShanah 31a; Sanhedrin 97a. Avot DeRabbi Nathan 1; Yalkut Shim'oni, Tehillim 139:888; Shoher Tov, 92; Pirkei DeRabbi Eliezer 18. Ramban on Gen. 2:3; on Lev. 25:2; *Perush LeShir HaShirim* (*Kitvei Ramban* II, p. 518). Rabbeinu Bahya on Lev. 25:2 (II, p. 564). *Peri Ets Hayyim, Sha'ar HaShabbat,* p. 66a. Shelah, I, pp. 55b, 177b; III, pp. 114b, 118b.
265. Ps. 92:2.

Chapter Five

1. Deut. 30:9; see TB Niddah 30b; Zohar I, 76; 233b; II, 161b; III, 13a-b. Zohar Hadash Ahrei 47a; 49a.
2. Cf. Tanhuma, Ki Tavo 1. See Rashi on Gen. 25:25. See also *Or HaHayyim* on Gen. 47:29.
3. Cf. Exod. R. 15:24.
4. Cf. Jean-Paul Sartre, *Refléxions sur la question Juive,* Paris, 1954.
5. See Num. 22-24.
6. Cf. TB Yoma 86a.
7. Deut. 28:10.
8. Exod. 15:2; cf. Mekhilta (3) and Rashi ad loc. Cf. TB Shabbat 133b; Sukkah 50a; Sotah 14a.
9. Cf. Gen. R. 11:7; Petihta DeEsther Rabba.
10. Cf. Rambam, *Hilkhot Tefillah,* VII, 6; *Shulhan Arukh, Orah Hayyim,* 46:4 and *Turei Zahav* ad loc.; see also *Magen Avraham* ad loc. See TB Menahot 43b. *Bet Yossef, Tur, Orah Hayyim,* 46. Cf. Shelah, I, p. 206b. R. B. Landau, *HaGaon HeHassid MiVilna,* p. 152. Rav Kook, *Olat Reiyah,* II, p. 401. R. Abraham of Slonim, *Be'er Avraham,* p. 215. R. Barukh HaLevi Epstein, *Tossefet Berakhah,* II, p. 176. R. Yoel Teitelbaum of Satmar, *VaYoel Moshe,* p. 500. R. Yossef Rozin, the Gaon of Rogachov, *Mefa'aneah Tsefunot,* pp. 149-50.
11. Cf. TB Berakhot 63b; Pesikta Zutarta, Deut. 6:6; Tanhuma (Buber ed.), Exod. 13:10. Rashi on Deut. 6:6, 26:16, 27:9.
12. Cf. R. Yehuda Aryeh Leib of Gur, *Sefat Emet,* IV, p. 7. R. Avraham of Sochatczew, *Avnei Nezer,* p. 14. R. Shemuel of Sochaczew, *Shem MiShemuel, Bereshit,* I, p. 92.
13. Cf. TB Shabbat 105b.
14. Cf. Jer. 11:20, 17:10; Ps. 7.10; Prov. 17:3; 1 Chron. 29:17.
15. Cf. TB Sanhedrin 44a; Yevamot 47b; Menahot 99b; Bekhorot 30b; see also *Shulhan Arukh, Orah Hayyim,* 55:1; *Tur* and *Shulhan Arukh, Yoreh Deyah,* 345; Rif and Rosh, *Moed Katan,* in fine; Mishnah Berurah, Orah Hayyim, 55:46. See TB Shabbat 96a; Rosh HaShanah 28a; Sotah 42a. See also Rambam, *Hilkhot Ishut,* IV, 15; *Hilkhot Gerushin,* II, 20. Cf. Zohar I, 191b. Ramban on Lev. 26:15. Maharal, *Gevurot HaShem,* 42. R. Tsevi Elimelekh of Dynow, *Bnei Issakhar,* I, p. 112a. R. Hayyim Attar, *Or HaHayyim,* on Num.

16:15. R. Dov Baer of Mezerich, *Maggid Devarav LeYa'akov*, 132. R. Elimelekh of Lyzhansk, *Noam Elimelekh, Devarim*. R. Shneur Zalman of Lyady, *Tanya*, 31. R. Nahman of Bratslav, *Likkutei Moharan*, I, 14, 3, p. 19a; 17, p. 22a; II, p. 38b; 125, p. 44a. R. Yossef Dov Baer of Brisk, *Bet HaLevi*, II, p. 60. R. Abraham of Slonim, *Avodat Yisrael*, p. 267; *Be'er Avraham*, pp. 214, 289, 297. R. Avraham of Sochaczew, *Neot HaDesheh*, pp. 96, 127-28; *Avnei Nezer*, pp. 10, 23. *Shem MiShemuel, Bereshit*, I, p. 286; *Moadim*, pp. 206, 259. Rav Kook, *Orot*, pp. 12, 63-64, 94, 138, 142, 147. R. Yitshak Hutner, *Pahad Yitshak, Sha'ar Hodesh HaAviv*, pp. 228-36. R. Barukh HaLevi Epstein, *Barukh SheAmar*, Avot, Tel-Aviv: 5725 (1965), pp. 14-15. R. Eliyahu Eliezer Dessler, *Mikhtav MeEliyahu*, II, p. 21. R. Bezalel Ze'ev Safran, *Doresh LeTsion*, p. 21.

16. Cf. R. Yehuda HaLevi, *Kuzari*, I, 95; Ramban on Deut. 7:9; Tossafot on Yevamot 24b. See TB Gittin 57b; Tanhuma, VaYakhel 8; Shoher Tov, 1:16; R. B. Z. Safran, *She'elot UTeshuvot Harbaz*, I, p. 39.
17. Cf. TY Haggigah I, 7. TB Pessahim 50b; see also TB Berakhot 17a. Cf. Massekhet Kallah VIII; Petihta DeEihah Rabba 2; Zohar I, 184b; III, 85b. R. Hayyim of Volozhin, *Nefesh HaHayyim*, 4:3.
18. Cf. TB Shabbat 118b; 130a; Ta'anit 21b; Ketuvot 17a; Sanhedrin 111a; Moed Katan 28b. See also TB Sotah 3b; Kiddushin 39b. TY Kiddushin I, 9. Avot DeRabbi Nathan 31:2. Tanhuma, Ki Tavo 1. Cf. Rabbeinu Sa'adya Gaon, *Emunot VeDeot*, V, 4. Alexandre Safran, *Mussar VeHevrah BaIdan HaModerni*, pp. 216-17.
19. Cf. Maharal, *Netivot Olam*, I, *Netiv HaTorah*, 3. *Likkutei Moharan*, 34, p. 48a. *Be'er Mayim Hayyim*, Beshalah (Humash, II, Lemberg: 1869), p. 86. R.B. Landau, *HaGaon HeHassid MiVilna*, p. 171. R. H. Y. Lipkin, in *Messilat Yesharim* of R. Moshe Hayyim Luzzatto, pp. 226-27. *Be'er Avraham*, pp. 116, 343. *Neot HaDesheh*, pp. 27, 141-42, 197. *Shem MiShemuel, Bemidbar*, pp. 337, 359; see also *Shem MiShemuel, Moadim*, p. 31. *Sefat Emet*, IV, p. 7. R. Naftali Tsevi Yehuda Berlin, the "Netsiv of Volozhin," *Ha'amek Davar*, V, *Devarim*, on Deut. 10:12, p. 51. R. Meir Simha Kohen of Dvinsk, *Meshekh Hokhmah*, pp. 320, 328.
20. Cf. *Tanya*, 14; 18.
21. Cf. Avot V, 20. TY Sanhedrin I, 2. TB Shabbat 118b; Sanhedrin 111a; Moed Katan 28b. Tanhuma, Ki Tavo 1. See also TY Haggigah II, 2. Gen. R. 2:5, 44:20. Lev. R. 15:9. Tanhuma, Tazria 11. Zohar, *HaSulam*, V, 208, p. 68; see also Rambam, *Hilkhot Kiddush HaHodesh*, I, 8. Cf. Rabad of Sefer Yetsirah III, 1. *Or HaHayyim* on Num. 16:1. *Tanya*, 40. R. Avraham HaMalakh, *Hessed LeAvraham*, p. 110. R. Eliyahu of Vilna, *Kol Eliyahu*, II, pp. 89, 95. *Sefat Emet*, III, pp. 202, 206; IV, pp. 6-7, 134, 174. R. Ya'akov Moshe Harlap, *Mei Meirom, Missaviv LiShmonah Perakim LeHaRambam*, p. 186. *Avnei Nezer*, pp. 37-38. *Shem MiShemuel, Bereshit*, I, pp. 285-86.
22. Cf. Maharal, *Derashot*, p. 39.
23. Avot IV, 2. Cf. Avot DeRabbi Nathan XXV, 4. Tanhuma, Ki Teitsei 1. Zohar III, 124a; 228b. *Sefat Emet*, IV, pp. 47, 78.
24. Mishnah Makot III, 16.
25. Cf. Rambam, *Perush HaMishnah*, Makot III, 16. Cf. Rashi on Makot 24a. See also TB Shabbat 55a; Ramban on Lev. 26:11-12.

26. R. Yossef Albo, *Ikkarim*, 29.
27. The people of Israel consists of three hereditary categories: the *kohanim*, priests; the *leviim*, levites; and the *isra'elim*, "simple" Jews.
28. *Or HaHayyim* on Exod. 39:32. Cf. Lev. R. 30; Num. R. 13. See TB Keritot 6b; Rashi on Menahot 27a; *Tur, Orah Hayyim*, 619. Cf. Zohar II, 174a. *Kuzari*, III, 19. R. Aharon HaLevi of Barcelona, *Sefer HaHinukh, Iggeret HaMehaber*, pp. 7, 11. Ari HaKadosh, *Likkutei Torah*, p. 77. R. Ya'akov Yossef of Polonnoye, *Toldot Ya'akov Yossef*, Bereshit; Lekh Lekha. *Tanya, Likkutei Amarim*, 32, 37. Rabbi Shemuel Shmelke of Nikolsburg, *Divrei Shemuel*, p. 95. R. B. Landau, *HaGaon HeHassid MiVilna*, p. 151. Hatam Sofer, *Haggadah*, p. 148. *Avnei Nezer*, pp. 70, 146; *Neot HaDesheh*, pp. 65-66, 128, 243, 297. *Shem MiShemuel, Bereshit*, I, pp. 285-86; *VaYikra*, pp. 286-87; *Bemidbar*, pp. 50-51, 128; *Devarim*, pp. 55, 200, 209-10; *Moadim*, pp. 136, 199, 200-1, 204, 207. *Sefat Emet*, III, pp. 207-9; IV, p. 7. *Meshekh Hokhmah*, p. 217. See also TB Sotah 3b; Yevamot 64a; Bekhorot 30b. Gen. R. 70:8; Exod. R. 28:4; Deut. R. 7:9. Avot DeRabbi Nathan XXX, 20; XXXI, 2. Zohar I, 2b. Cf. Ish Shuv, *Ta'amei HaMinhagim*, p. 106; *Shem MiShemuel, Bemidbar*, pp. 5, 7, 8. See *Tanya, Iggeret HaTeshuvah*, 5; *Iggeret HaKodesh*, 7. R. Hayyim of Volozhin, *Ruah Hayyim*, Avot VI, 3, p. 97.
29. Cf. TB Shevuot 39a; Sanhedrin 27b; Hullin 91b. Mekhilta 5 (Exod. 20:2); Tana Devei Eliyahu Rabba 11; Lev. R. 30:11; Tanhuma, Nitsavim 2; Yalkut Shim'oni, Kohelet 7:976; Rashi on Rosh HaShanah 29a-b; Ritva, Rosh HaShanah 29a. Rambam, *Hilkhot Berakhot*, I, 13. Rabbi Nahman of Bratslav, *Kitsur Likkutei Halakhot*, 186. *Hafets Hayyim Al HaTorah*, p. 237.
30. Cf. Avot II, 4 and Maharal, *Derekh Hayyim*, ad loc.; I, 14; III, 7. TB Ta'anit 11a; Sanhedrin 37a; Menahot 27a; Makot 23b and Rashi ad loc. Lev. R. 4; Tana Devei Eliyahu Rabba 25. Rashi on Shabbat 105a; Hullin 135a. Cf. TB Berakhot 57a; Eruvin 19a; Sanhedrin 37a. Gen. R. 32; Shir HaShirim R. 4. Zohar II, 100a. Cf. Lev. R. 4. *Kuzari*, III, 10-19. Maharal, *Gevurot HaShem*, 60; *Netivot Olam*, I, *Netiv HaTorah*, 2. R. Moshe Cordovero, *Tomer Devorah* 1. Shelah, I, p. 21a; III, p. 201a. R. Eliyahu of Vilna, *Aderet Eliyahu*, pp. 483, 514; *Kol Eliyahu*, II, p. 94. R. B. Landau, *HaGaon HeHassid MiVilna*, p. 145. *Toldot Ya'akov Yossef*, Hayei Sarah. *Likkutei Moharan*, 36:1, p. 50a. *Sefat Emet*, III, p. 207. Rav Kook, *Orot*, pp. 12-13, 74, 77, 94, 142, 144, 146-49, 171; *Orot HaKodesh*, III, pp. 138, 319-20; *Orot HaTeshuvah*, p. 81 (XIII, 3); *Shabbat HaArets*, p. 7; *Hazon HaGeulah*, p. 275; *Mishpat Kohen*, 124; *Olat Reiyah*, I, p. 279; II, pp. 2, 157, 254-55. *Mei Meirom*, VI, pp. 11-12. *The Hirsch Siddur*, pp. 414, 435-36. *Neot HaDesheh*, p. 119; *Avnei Nezer*, pp. 34-35, 37-38. *Shem MiShemuel, Bereshit*, I, pp. 224, 266, 285-86; *Bereshit*, II, p. 58; *Shemot*, II, pp. 74-77; *Bemidbar*, pp. 58-59, 94, 359; *Devarim*, pp. 55, 210, 254. *Meshekh Hokhmah*, p. 156. *Sefat Emet*, IV, p. 7. *Pahad Yitshak, Hanukah*, pp. 71-72; *Sha'ar Hodesh HaAviv*, pp. 29, 68-69. *Mefa'aneah Tsefunot*, pp. 182, 189, 239.
31. Cf. TB Sanhedrin 47a; Yevamot 22b; Rosh HaShanah 17a; Berakhot 30a. Massekhet Semahot II, 10; TY Sanhedrin I, 2. Avot DeRabbi Nathan XVI, 5. Rambam, *Hakdamah LePerek Helek, Yessod* 13; *Hilkhot Teshuvah*, III, 11; *Hilkhot Evel*, I, 10; *Tur and Shulhan Arukh, Yoreh Deyah*, 345. Rashi on Sanhedrin 47a. Cf. *Sefer Yereim*, 221. Cf. Rav Kook, *Orot HaTorah*, p. 13.

Shem MiShemuel, Bemidbar, p. 372; *Devarim*, p. 210. *Pahad Yitshak, Sha'ar Hodesh HaAviv*, pp. 172-73. R. Avraham Yaffen, *HaMussar VeHaDa'at*, I, p. 96. R. B. Z. Safran, *She'elot UTeshuvot Harbaz*, I, p. 267.

32. Cf. TB Pessahim 113b; Rambam, *Hilkhot Rotseah UShemirat Nafesh*, XIII, 14; *Sefer HaHinukh, mitzvah* 238.
33. Cf. *Tanya*, 32. See Tikkunei Hazohar, 60.
34. Cf. *Tanya*, 14. *Hessed LeAvraham*, p. 42. *Avnei Nezer*, p. 23.
35. Cf. Zohar I, 108b; III, 7b; 295b.
36. Cf. *Be'er Avraham*, pp. 102, 109, 159, 214-15, 297, 334. *Neot HaDesheh*, p. 128. R. M. Grossberg, *Tsefunot HaRogachovi*, p. 126. *Mefa'aneah Tsefunot*, pp. 182, 189, 239.
37. Cf. TB Berakhot 6a; Pessahim 56a.

PART II
Chapter One

1. See Num. 11:21; Avot VI, 3; Mekhilta 3 (Exod. 19:1). TY Shekalim VI, 1. TB Berakhot 13b; 57b; 58a. Rashi and Maharsha ad loc. *Shulhan Arukh, Orah Hayyim*, 224:5. TB Shabbat 146a; Eruvin 54a; Rosh HaShanah 31a; Haggigah 15a; Ketuvot 17a; Kiddushin 30a; Bava Metsia 85b; Bava Batra 15a; Avodah Zarah 9a; Sanhedrin 93a; 97a; 111a; Shevuot 39a; Menahot 29b-30b. Gen. R. 70:8. Exod. R. 28:4. Lev. R. 1:3, 7. Num. R. 14, 18. Deut. R. 7:9. Shir HaShirim R. 1:64, 4:6, 6:14, 7:2. Tanhuma, Bereshit 1; Beshalah 10. Pesikta Zutarta, VaEthanan, Deut. 8:3. Tana Devei Eliyahu Zuta 4. Pirkei DeRabbi Eliezer 46. Yalkut Shim'oni, Hoshea 2:518. Zohar I, 2b; 12a; 18b; 158a; 253a; II, 4b; 14b; 66b; 126b; 191b; III, 145a; 148b; 216a; 273a; 276a; 282b. Zohar Hadash, 74b; 108a. Tikkunei HaZohar, 29b; 77b; 86a; 100a; 112a; 114a; 144b; 147b. Onkelos on Deut. 33:21. Rashi on Shabbat 105b. Tossafot on Bava Metsia 107b. Ramban, *Hakdamah, Bereshit*, Gen. 2:3. *Perushei HaTorah LeRabbi Yehuda HeHassid*, pp. 133-34. Abrabanel, II, p. 161. Maharal, *Gevurot HaShem*, 3, 12; *Tiferet Yisrael*, 17, 41; *Be'er HaGolah*, 5. Ari HaKadosh, *Likkutei Torah*, p. 47, 158; *Perush HaAri al Sefer Yetsirah*, p. 29a. Shelah, I, pp. 27a, 70a; II, p. 32b; III, pp. 9a, 11a, 153a. R. Hayyim Yossef David Azulay, "The HIDA," *Midbar Kedemot*, 10:6. Rabbi Hayyim Attar, *Or HaHayyim*, on Num. 16:1. R. Dov Baer of Mezerich, *Maggid Devarav LeYa'akov*, 192, 196. R. Levi Yitshak of Berditchev, *Kedushat Levi*, p. 70a. R. Tsevi Elimelekh of Dynow, *Bnei Issakhar, Haggadah*, pp. 40, 44. Rabbi Nahman of Bratslav, *Likkutei Moharan*, I, 14:3. R. Shneur Zalman of Lyady, *Tanya, Likkutei Amarim*, 4, 37; *Torah Or*, pp. 32a, 49a, 66b. R. Eliyahu of Vilna, *Aderet Eliyahu*, p. 483; *HaEmunah VeHaHashgahah*, I, p. 3a; *Biurei HaGra Al Aggadot*, I, p. 18. R. Hayyim of Volozhin, *Nefesh HaHayyim*, 4:11; *Ruah Hayyim*, p. 6. R. Menahem Nahum of Tchernobil, *Me'or Einaim*, Hukat; VaEthanan. R. Yehuda Aryeh Leib of Gur, *Sefat Emet*, II, pp. 63-65; IV, pp. 6, 7, 64; V, pp. 30, 132. Rabbi Shalom Mordechai Shvadron, *Tkhelet Mordekhai*, BeHa'alotkha. Rabbi Abraham of Slonim, *Bet Avraham*, p. 224; *Yessod HaAvodah*, p. 273. Rav Kook, *Orot HaKodesh*, III, pp. 138-39; *Orot*,

p. 12; *Orot HaTorah*, pp. 19-22, 60; *Olat Reiyah*, I, pp. 387-88. R. Meir Simha Kohen of Dvinsk, *Meshekh Hokhmah*, pp. 28, 48. R. Bezalel Landau, *HaGaon HeHassid MiVilna* (HaGra), p. 35. Rabbi Yitshak Hutner, *Pahad Yitshak*, Shavuot, p. 137. R. Menahem M. Kasher, *HaTekufah HaGedolah*, pp. 41, 442-43; idem, *Milhemet Yom HaKippurim*, pp. 30-31. Rabbi Simha Bunim of Przysucha, *Midrash Simhah*, I, p. 135. Rabbi Yossef Hayyim of Baghdad, *Od Yossef Hai*, p. 27; idem, *Da'at UTevunah*, pp. 72a-b. Rabbi Avraham of Sochachew, *Avnei Nezer*, pp. 68, 70.

Chapter Two

1. Cf. Abrabanel, *Perush Al HaTorah*, I, pp. 261, 362.
2. See also *Or HaHayyim* on Exod. 6:4.
3. See *Hovot HaLevavot, Sha'ar Heshbon HaNefesh*, III, 30.
4. Cf. *Kli Yakar* on Lev. 18:3.
5. See also *Ha'amek Davar* on Gen. 12:10, I, *hossafot*, p. 5.
6. Cf. Hermann Cohen, *Die Religion der Vernunft aus den Quellen des Judentums* (Berlin, 1919), p. 148; ibid., p. 179; cf. idem, *Jüdische Schriften* (Berlin, 1924), I, p. 179.
7. Cf. TB Sukkah 28b; *Shulhan Arukh, Orah Hayyim*, 639:1.
8. Cf. TB Sukkah 28b; *Shulhan Arukh, Orah Hayyim*, 643; Zohar III, 103b.
9. Cf. Mishnah Sukkah II, 9; Rambam, *Hilkhot Sukkah*, VI, 5; see *Moreh Nevukhim*, III, 43.
10. Cf. TB Sukkah 23a.
11. See Ibn Ezra and Ramban on Lev. 23:43; Rabbi S.R. Hirsch on Lev. 23:39.
12. Lev. 23:43.
13. Cf. also Isa. 4:6.
14. Cf. TB Sukkah 46a; Rambam, *Hilkhot Sukkah*, VI, 12.
15. Cf. *Tur, Orah Hayyim*, 625; see *Bet Yossef* ad loc.
16. Cf. Exod. R. 32:5; Yalkut Shim'oni, Beshalah 13:228; Exod. 13:21; see *Be'er Avraham*, p. 213.
17. Cf. TB Sukkah 11b; Yalkut Shim'oni, Emor 23:655; see also Mekhilta Beshalah, Messikhta DeVaYehi 1 (Exod. 13:20), p. 30a. See *Shulhan Arukh, Orah Hayyim*, 625:1.
18. Cf. Ezek. 20:35-36.
19. Cf. Ps. 27:5, 140:8. See also *HaGra, Siddur Ishei Yisrael*, p. 182; Rabbi Nathan of Bratslav (disciple of Rabbi Nahman of Bratslav), *Sefer Tehillim Im Perush Noam VeRatson* (Bnei Brak, 5739), p. 64.
20. Cf. Rabbi Alexander Susskind of Horodna, *Yessod VeShoresh HaAvodah* (Jerusalem, 5738), p. 221. See also Zohar I, 48a.
21. Cf. Rabbi Abraham of Slonim, *Be'er Avraham*, p. 209; *Shem MiShemuel, Moadim*, pp. 146, 148.
22. Cf. *She'elot UTeshuvot Avnei Nezer, Orah Hayyim*, 459:10; *Ha'amek She'elah al Sheiltot, Sheilta* 169; see also Hatan Sofer, *Yoreh Deyah*, 271.
23. Cf. *Shulhan Arukh, Orah Hayyim*, 634; see also Mishnah Sukkah III, 7.
24. Cf. Rabbi Avraham Mordechai of Gur, *Imrei Emet* (Jerusalem/Tel-Aviv,

5738), p. 85 about the *Mikvah*, the ritual bath that totally contains the human body.
25. Cf. R.B. Landau, *HaGaon HeHassid MiVilna* (HaGra) (Jerusalem, 5728), pp. 246-47.
26. Cf. *Shulhan Arukh, Orah Hayyim*, 631:3. See also Mishnah Sukkah II, 2; TB Sukkah 22a-b.
27. See TB Shabbat 33a; Rashi on Gen. 33:18.
28. Cf. Deut. 16:13; TB Sukkah 11b; 15a; 27b.
29. Cf. Zohar III, 103a-b; Shir HaShirim 2:3.
30. Deut. 8:17.
31. Cf. Rabbeinu Bahya on Deut. 16:14 (III, p. 346).
32. Cf. Ps. 18:12, 27:5, 31:21.
33. Cf. Zohar III, 103b.
34. Cf. Mishnah Sukkah I, 1; TB Sukkah 2a; Yalkut Shim'oni, Emor 23:654; *Shulhan Arukh, Orah Hayyim* 633.
35. Cf. Mishnah Sukkah II, 2; TB Sukkah 22a-b; *Shulhan Arukh, Orah Hayyim*, 626, 631.
36. Cf. *Shulhan Arukh, Orah Hayyim*, 629:1.
37. See also Zohar III, 103a.
38. Cf. Yalkut Shim'oni, Emor 23:655.
39. Gen. 33:17; cf. Rabbeinu Bahya on Deut. 16:14 (III, p. 346); see TB Megillah 17a. Cf. *Menorat HaMaor, Hilkhot Rosh Hodesh*.
40. Cf. Zohar III, 110a; see also Zohar III, 100b.
40a. See R. Nathan of Bratslav, *Torat Natan* (Bnei Brak, 5739), p. 190: "The ideal home — *Bayit* — can be found in the *Sukkah*."
41. See Gen. 33:17-18; Rabbeinu Bahya, ad loc. and on Deut. 16:14 (III, p. 346).
42. See Rabbi Elazar of Worms, *Rokeah, Hilkhot Sukkah*.
43. Cf. I Kings 8:2; 2 Chron. 7:8. But see also Rabbeinu Bahya on Exod. 10:9 (II, p. 74).
44. Cf. TB Sanhedrin 20b; Tanhuma, Ki Teitsei 11; *Torat Natan*, I, p. 61.
45. Cf. TB Berakhot 6b.
46. Cf. Zohar I, 48a.
47. Cf. Ezra 3:4; Neh. 8:16-17; See TB Arakhin 32b; see also Malbim on Neh. 8:14.
48. See *Sefat Emet*, VaYeitsei.
49. Gen. 28:21.
50. Cf. Sifra and Rashi on Lev. 23:42-43.
51. Kohelet 5:7.
52. Exod. 20:10; Deut. 5:14.
53. Cf. Deut. 16:3.
54. Cf. Mekhilta Bo, Messikhta DePissha 15 (Exod. 12:49), p. 22b; see also Tanhuma, Bo 10; Exod. 12:19-20; Rashi on Exod. 12:49.
55. God "loves the stranger, giving him food and clothing" (Deut. 10:18), and Rashi (ad loc.) notes: "This is important, because this is what our ancestor Jacob asked for with all his might in his prayer" (Gen. 28:20).
56. *Hizkuni* on Emor, p. 65; see also Rashbam on Lev. 23:39, 23:42.
57. Amos 9:11 and Malbim ad loc. Cf. Rambam, *Sefer HaMitzvot* (Jerusalem, 5718), p. 53.

REFERENCES, SOURCES & NOTES • 411

58. R. Nathan of Bratslav, *Tehillim Im Perush Noam VeRatson*, p. 8.
59. Cf. Zohar III, 103a-b; see TB Sukkah 11b.
60. Cf. *Be'er Avraham*, p. 218.
61. Cf. Zohar I, 48a.
62. Cf. TB Shabbat 55a; Yoma 69b. Gen. R. 81:2; Deut. 1:7. Zohar I, 2b; 162a; II, 220b; III, 54b; 162a; 297a.
63. Cf. Zohar I, 48a.
64. See TB Sukkah V.
65. Cf. Shoher Tov, 76:3.
66. Cf. Isa. 40:15.
67. Cf. TB Avodah Zarah 3a.
68. Cf. Amos 7:2; *Be'er Avraham*, p. 212.
69. Cf. Deut. 7:7.
70. TB Hullin 89a; *Be'er Avraham*, pp. 212, 218.
71. Cf. Zech. 14:16-19; *Bnei Issakhar*, II, p. 30a.
72. Cf. TB Sukkah 47a; 48a; 55b; see TB Yoma 3a; Tikunei HaZohar, 13 (29b); Tikunei Zohar Hadash, 93b; see also Rabbi S.R. Hirsch on Lev. 23:9 (III, p. 528).
73. Zech. 14:9.
74. Isa. 2:17.
75. Isa. 11:6.
76. Isa. 11:9.
77. Cf. Gen. 28:20; Rabbeinu Bahya, Ralbag and *Kli Yakar* ad loc. See also Prov. 30:8; Gen. R. 70:5. Cf. also Deut. 8:3-4.
78. Cf. Exod. 16:4-5; also 1 Kings 8:59; Ps. 68:20.
79. Cf. Avot IV, 1; Maharal, *Derekh Hayyim*, Avot IV, 1, pp. 122-24; idem, *Netivot Olam*, II, *Netiv HaOsher*, 1, p. 169. Cf. Ps. 136:25, 145:15-16. TB Pessahim 118a; Sotah 48b; Tanhuma, Beshalah 20.
80. Cf. TB Hullin 91a.
81. Cf. Gen. 33:11 and *Kli Yakar* ad loc. Ps. 34:10. See also TB Berakhot 48b.
82. See Ibn Ezra, Rashbam and *Ba'al HaTurim* on Gen. 28:22.
83. Cf. Rashi on Gen. 29:30; Rambam, *Hilkhot Skhirut*, XIII, 7.
84. Deut. 31:10, 31:13.
85. Cf. Lev. 25; Deut. 15.
86. Lev. 23:39.
87. Cf. Ps. 121:1.
88. Cf. Gen. R. 68:2; Ps. 121:1.
89. See infra, note 117.
90. Cf. Exod. 23:16, 34:22.
91. See infra, note 99.
92. Cf. Lev. 23:36; Num. 29:35; see also Neh. 8:18.
93. Cf. Num. R. 21:22; Rashi on Lev. 23:36 and on Num. 29:35; TB Sukkah 55b; Zohar I, 64b; III, 104b; 256b.
94. See Rabbeinu Bahya on Deut. 16:14-15 (III, p. 345).
95. Cf. Lev. 23:29-40; Deut. 16:13-15. See TB Haggigah 18a. Yalkut Shim'oni, Emor 23:654.
96. Cf. TB Shabbat 30b; Pesikta Zutarta, VaYigash 45:27.
97. See Rashi and Ibn Ezra on Deut. 16:15. See TB Sukkah 48a.

98. See also *Yalkut Shim'oni, Emor* 23:654; *Mahzor Vitry*, 384.
99. Cf. Deut. 16:15; TB Sukkah 48a.
100. See *Shulhan Arukh, Orah Hayyim,* 666, 667, 668; Rambam, *Hilkhot Sukkah,* VI, 13; Rashi on Sukkah 47a; also TB Sukkah 55b.
101. During the days of Sukkot, the Jew "takes" ... "four kinds" of plants in his hand and says a blessing over them, a prayer. These ... "four kinds" are: an *Etrog* — a citron; a *Lulav*, a palm branch; *Hadassim*, three myrtle sprigs and *Aravot*, two willow branches.
102. Cf. Deut. 16:15; see Rashi and Ibn Ezra ad loc.
103. Cf. TB Berakhot 11b.
104. Cf. Mishnah Makot III, 16; Avot DeRabbi Nathan 41:17.
105. Cf. Rambam, *Hilkhot Yom Tov,* VI, 20.
106. Cf. Rabbeinu Bahya on Deut. 16:14, III, p. 346.
107. Cf. idem, ibidem.
108. Cf. Lev. 23:40; Deut. 16:14-15. See Rabbeinu Bahya on Deut. 16:14 (III, p. 345).
109. Kohelet 1:1.
110. Cf. Kohelet R. 3.
111. Kohelet 1:2.
112. Kohelet 12:13-14.
113. Cf. TB Shabbat 30b; Lev. R. 28:1; Kohelet R. 1:4. Pesikta DeRav Kahana, 8.
114. Cf. *Torat Natan,* VI, p. 8.
115. Cf. TB Berakhot 30b-31a.
116. See Gen. 1:28.
117. Cf. TB Berakhot 6b; Kolbo, 75; *Tashbets Katan*, 160. *Maharam Minz*, 109; *Ta'amei HaMinhagim*, 407. See also *Hagahot Maimoniyot* on Rambam, *Hilkhot Shabbat*, XXX, 2.
118. Cf. TB Sukkah 28b.
119. Cf. Lev. 23:40; TB Berakhot 57a; Lev. R. 30:11, 30:13; Rabbeinu Bahya on Lev. 23:40 (II, pp. 552-53); *Shulhan Arukh, Orah Hayyim,* 638, 639. See TB Sukkah 28b; Shabbat 133b. See also Rabbi S.R. Hirsch on Lev. 23:40.
120. Cf. Lev. 23:43. See Bach on *Tur, Orah Hayyim,* 628.
121. Cf. Rabbeinu Bahya on Deut. 16:14 (III, p. 346).
122. Cf. Avot IV, 16; Pesikta Zutarta, Gen. 1:1.
123. Cf. TB Berakhot 17a.
124. Cf. Zohar III, 103b-104a; Isa. 58:14; Rabbeinu Bahya on Deut. 16:15 (III, p. 346).
125. Cf. Zohar III, 100b; see also Mekhilta Beshalah, Messikhta DeVaYehi 1 (Exod. 13:20), p. 30a.
126. Cf. *Shem MiShemuel, Moadim,* p. 146. See also *Bnei Issakhar,* II, p. 30a.
127. Cf. Isa. 4:5-6, 25:8.

Chapter Three

1. Cf. Zohar II, 193a; III, 161b; 221b. Petihta DeEihah Rabbati 16; Lev. R. 1. Rabbi Yehuda HaLevi, *Kuzari*, II, 32; Recanati, Yitro, p. 9a. Maharal,

Netsah Yisrael, 8; Rabbi Shemuel of Sochaczew, *Shem MiShemuel, Moadim*, p. 208.
2. Cf. *Kuzari*, II, 20, 36. Recanati, Yitro, p. 9a. *Kitvei Rabbi Nahman MiBratslav* (Steinmann ed.), p. 192.
3. Cf. Pesikta Rabbati, 10:2. Derekh Erets Zuta (with commentaries by the Gaon of Vilna, Tel-Aviv ed., 5731) IX, 34, p. 58. Tanhuma, Kedoshim 10. Pirkei DeRabbi Eliezer 3. Zohar I, 78; 186a; 226a; 231a; II, 157b; III, 65b; 161b; 221b. *Lettre d'Aristée*, 83. Philon, *Legatio ad Gaium*, 294. *Kuzari*, II, 20. Rashi on TB Yoma 54b; Sanhedrin 37a. Ibn Ezra on Gen. 1:2. Ramban on Gen. 14:18. Recanati, Bereshit, p. 8a, Yitro, p. 9a. See Maharal, *Perushei Maharal MiPrag LeAggadot HaShas*, IV, on TB Ketuvot 111a, pp. 93, 95; *Netivot Olam*, I, *Netiv HaEmet*, 1, pp. 78-79; *Netivot Olam*, II, *Netiv HaTseddek*, 3, pp. 141a-b; *Gevurot HaShem, Hakdamah Shelishit*, pp. 12-13. *Gur Aryeh* on Gen. 2:7; *Be'er HaGolah*, 6, p. 121; *Derekh Hayyim* on Avot, *Hakdamah*, p. 3; V, 8, p. 188; VI, pp. 226, 252. Cf. Rabbi Eliyahu of Vilna, *Biur HaGra Al Aggadot*, II, p. 36b. Rabbi Abraham of Slonim, *Be'er Avraham*, pp. 102, 109; *Bet Avraham*, pp. 215, 217. Rabbi Avraham of Sochaczew, *Avnei Nezer*, p. 113; *Neot HaDesheh*, p. 120. Cf. also TB Hullin 91b. Zohar I, 72a; 156a; III, 84a. Zohar Hadash, VaYeitsei 28:4. Recanati, VaYeitsei, p. 28b. Alshekh, VaYeitsei, on Gen. 28:13.
4. Cf. *Kuzari*, IV, 11; Ramban on Gen. 14:18.
5. Cf. TB Hullin 60b. Pesikta Zutarta, Deut. 3:9. Sifrei VaEthanan 31 (Deut. 6:4), p. 72; Eikev 37 (Deut. 11:10), p. 76b. Exod. R. 32:2. Num. R. 23:7. Tanhuma, Mishpatim 17; Mass'ei 6; Re'eh 8. Yalkut Shim'oni, Jer. 3:271. Zohar I, 209b; III, 161b. Tikkunei HaZohar, 6 (146a). *Kuzari*, II, 20. Rashi on Deut. 33:17. Seforno on Gen. 11:31, 12:5. Tossafot on TB Rosh HaShanah 23b.
6. Cf. Lev. R. 30:5. Shoher Tov, 118; Tossafot on TB Ta'anit 16a et al.
7. See supra, note 2.
8. Cf. R. Eliyahu of Vilna, *Sefer HaEmunah VeHaHashgahah*, p. 10b; HaGra on Isa. 8:11; *Be'er Mayim Hayyim* on Gen. 28:17. *Sefat Emet*, III, pp. 198, 200. *Avnei Nezer*, p. 13.
9. Rashi on Gen. 28:17; Gen. R. 69:5.
10. Cf. Zohar I, 149a; *Kli Yakar* on Gen. 28:12.
11. Cf. Alshekh, VaYeitsei, on Gen. 28:13.
12. Cf. Gen. R. 47:8. Zohar I, 97a; II, 241. Ramban on Gen. 17:22; 35:13; idem, *Hakdamah LeSefer Shemot*; idem, *Sefer HaEmunah VeHaBitahon* (*Kitvei Ramban* II), 15. Rabbi Shneur Zalman of Lyady, *Tanya, Likkutei Amarim*, 29, p. 37.
13. Cf. Mekhilta Beshalah, Messikhta DeVaYehi 3 (Exod. 14:15). Sifrei Vezot HaBerakhah 352 (Deut. 33:12). TB Zevahim 118b. Messekhet Semahot, VIII. Targum Onkelos on Gen. 22:14. Targum Yonathan Ben Uziel on Deut. 3:25. Gen. R. 62:2, 69:6. Shoher Tov, 81. Rashi on Gen. 22:14. Rambam, *Moreh Nevukhim*, III, 45. Ramban on Gen. 22:2. Maharsha, *Hiddushei Aggadot*, on TB Ta'anit 16a. Rabbi Eliyahu of Vilna, *Biurei HaGra Al Aggadot*, I, 83.
14. Ramban, *Sefer HaGeulah* (*Kitvei Ramban* I), p. 283.
15. Rabbi Eliyahu of Vilna, *Aderet Eliyahu*, p. 426.

16. Tossafot on TB Zevahim 60b.
17. Zohar Hadash, 49a.
18. R. Shemuel of Sochaczew, *Shem MiShemuel, Bemidbar*, p. 375. Cf. Philon, *De spec. leg.*, II, 148; Mekhilta DeRabbi Shimeon Ben Yohai, Beshalah 15:18. Sifrei Ki Tavo, Pisska 298. Mishnah Bikkurim III, 2; Rosh HaShanah IV, 1; Zevahim V, 6-8. TY Sukkah III, 11; see also Rashi on TB Rosh HaShanah 29b; Avot V, 5. TB Yoma 21a; Sukkah 41a; Bava Batra 75b and Maharsha ad loc. Sanhedrin 20b. Exod. R. 15:9, 32:2. Lev. R. 12:5, 13:2. Petihta DeEihah Rabbati 8; Eihah R. I, 62. Yalkut Shim'oni, Jer. 320. Rashi on TB Megillah 17b; and on TB Ketuvot 62b; see also Maharsha on TB Megillah 18a. Rambam, *Perush HaMishnayot*, on Shekalim I, 3; on Sukkah III, 12; on Rosh HaShanah IV, 1. Rambam, *Mishneh Torah, Hilkhot Bikkurim*, I; *Hilkhot Shofar*, II, 8; *Hilkhot Bet HaBehirah*, VI, 16; *Hilkhot Klei HaMikdash*, V, 7. Ramban, *Derashah LeRosh HaShanah* (*Kitvei Ramban* I, p. 252). *Meiri* on TB Sanhedrin 42. Rabbi Eliyahu of Vilna, *Siddur Ishei Yisrael*, pp. 356-57. Rabbi S.R. Hirsch, *Siddur Tefillot Yisrael*, p. 607. Rav Kook, *Olat Reiyah*, I, p. 185.
19. Cf. 1 Kings 8:30; Dan. 6:11; TY Berakhot IV, 5; TB Berakhot 30a; Shir HaShirim R. 4:11; Zohar I, 209b. Rambam, *Mishneh Torah, Hilkhot Tefillah*, V, 6.
20. 1 Kings 8:48; 2 Chron. 6:21.
21. TB Berakhot 30a. Cf. Mishnah Berakhot IV, 5-6; Tossefta Berakhot III, 16; Shir HaShirim R. 4:11. Zohar I, 209b; II, 116a; III, 109a. Rambam, *Mishneh Torah, Hilkhot Tefillah*, V, 3. R. Yossef Karo, *Shulhan Arukh, Orah Hayyim*, 94:2. Rashi and Ramban on Gen. 28:17. Radak on 1 Kings 8:46, 8:52. Rabbi Eliyahu of Vilna, *Aderet Eliyahu*, p. 377. See also TY Berakhot IV, 4.
22. Cf. TB Berakhot 30a et al.
23. Cf. TB Sanhedrin 106b; Zohar II, 162b; Rabbi Abraham of Slonim, *Be'er Avraham*, p. 201.
24. Cf. Isa. 40:2.
25. Cf. Rabbi Shemuel of Sochaczew, *Shem MiShemuel, Devarim*, pp. 55-56.
26. Cf. Rabbi Shemuel Shmelke of Nikolsburg, *Divrei Shemuel*, p. 141.
27. Cf. Rashi on Exod. 25:8; Rabbi Aharon HaLevi, *Sefer HaHinukh, Mitzvah* 95; Rabbi Eliyahu of Vilna, *Biurei HaGra Al Aggadot*, I, p. 83 (commentary by Rabbi Avraham).
28. Cf. TB Berakhot 30a.
29. See Mishnah Kelim I, 6; 8; 9; Zevahim XIV, 4; Ketuvot XIII, 11. TY Bikkurim III, 2; Bava Batra X, 2. TB Megillah 10b and Rashi ad locum; Moed Katan 26a; Ketuvot 110b; Menahot 98b and Tossafot ad locum; Sanhedrin 11b; Zevahim 119a. Exod. R. 32:2, 37:5; Num. R. 7:8; Eihah R. 1:59. Tanhuma, Bo 5; Terumah 9. Zohar I, 84b; II, 157a; III, 161b. Rambam, *Mishneh Torah, Hilkhot Kiddush HaHodesh*, IV, 12; *Hilkhot Bet HaBehirah*, VI, 14-16; VII, 15; *Hilkhot Bet HaMikdash*, III, 8. Ramban, *Derashah LeRosh HaShanah* (*Kitvei Ramban* II, p. 252). Rabbi Yossef Karo, *Shulhan Arukh, Orah Hayyim*, 561:2-3; *Even HaEzer*, 75:3-5. Abrabanel on Deut. 32:8. Alshekh on Gen. 28:13. R. Aharon HaLevi, *Sefer HaHinukh, Hakdamah*, p. 9. Rabbi Moshe Sofer, *She'elot UTeshuvot Hatam Sofer, Yoreh Deyah*, 234; Rabbi Avraham Yitshak HaKohen Kook, *She'elot UTeshuvot Mishpat Kohen*, 96. Shelah, *Siddur Sha'ar HaShamayim*, p. 471. R. Shemuel Shmelke

of Nikolsburg, *Divrei Shemuel*, pp. 85, 103. R. Avraham of Sochaczew, *Neot HaDesheh*, pp. 136-37; Rabbi Shemuel of Sochaczew, *Shem MiShemuel, Bereshit*, II, p. 252; *Moadim*, p. 135. Rabbi Abraham of Slonim, *Be'er Avraham*, pp. 102, 108-9, 115, 215, 297. Rabbi Eliyahu of Vilna, *Aderet Eliyahu*, p. 352.
30. Zohar II, 193a.
31. Cf. Rabbi Shemuel of Sochaczew, *Shem MiShemuel, Shemot*, II, p. 246.
32. Ps. 84:3.
33. Ps. 132:14.
34. Cf. Rabbi Ya'akov Tsevi Meklenburg, *HaKtav VaHaKabbalah*, I, on Exod. 20:24, p. 42.
35. Derekh Erets Zuta, 67; see also TB Yoma 54a; Zohar II, 152b; *Be'er Mayim Hayyim*, Mikeits, on Gen. 42:7, 42:12.
36. Cf. Exod. 19:20. See Exod. R. 12:4; Tanhuma, Va'era 15.
37. Cf. Gen. 22:2.
38. Cf. Ramban on Exod. 3:5. Cf. Exod. 3:5; Exod. R. 46:2; Rabbi Baruch HaLevi Epstein, *Tossefet Berakhah*, II, p. 65; Esther Starobinski-Safran, *Le rôle des signes dans l'épisode du buisson ardent*. See also Yalkut Shim'oni, Tehillim 53:785.
39. Cf. Exod. 19:12-13; Rashi on Exod. 19:13; TB Beitsa 5a-b; Rabbi Pinhas HaLevi Ish Horovitz, *Sefer Hafla'ah* II, *Sefer HaMakneh*, p. 7.
40. Exod. 19; cf. Rashi on Exod. 19:12.
41. Gen. 22.
42. Cf. Isa. 11:9; Jer. 31:22 et al.
43. Cf. Rambam, *Mishneh Torah, Hilkhot Bet HaBehirah*, VI, 14-16.
44. Cf. TB Zevahim 61b.
45. Exod. 20:21.
46. Cf. TB Sotah 38a.
47. Cf. TY Berakhot IV, 4.
48. Cf. *Sefer HaHinukh, Mitzvah* 95.
49. Cf. Rashi on Gen. 28:17; TB Hullin 91b.
50. Cf. Num. R. 11:3.
51. Tossafot on TB Ta'anit 16a.
52. Exod. 19:10-19.
53. See Rabbi Eliyahu of Vilna, *Aderet Eliyahu*, p. 345; Rabbi B. Landau, *HaGaon HeHassid MiVilna*, pp. 243-44.
54. On the relationship between Sinai and Jerusalem, Sinai and Moriah, see Gen. R. 68:16; Exod. R. 52:4; Shir HaShirim R. 3:21.
55. Cf. Ibn Ezra on Gen. 22:4.
56. Cf. Gen. 22:1; Avot V, 3.
57. TB Ta'anit 4a. Cf. also Rav Kook, *Iggrot HaReiyah*, II, p. 43.
58. See also Malbim on Gen. 22:2.
59. Cf. Gen. R. 56:2; Tanhuma, VaYera 23; cf. also Abrabanel on Gen. 22:5; cf. TB Moed Katan 18a; see also Ibn Ezra on Gen. 22:4; Rabbeinu Bahya on Gen. 22:5 (I, p. 195).
60. Cf. TB Nedarim 32b; Makot 23b.
61. Cf. Rabbi Shemuel of Sochaczew (grandson of the Rabbi of Kotsk), *Shem MiShemuel, Bemidbar*, p. 105.

62. Cf. Rambam, *Moreh Nevukhim*, III, 24; Ramban (I, p. 125), Abrabanel (I, p. 268) and *HaKtav VeHaKabbalah* (I, pp. 39-40) on Gen. 22:1; R. Yossef Albo, *Ikkarim*, V, 13.
63. Cf. TB Haggigah 2a.
64. Cf. Gen. 22:12; Deut. 14:23.
65. Cf. *Sefat Emet*, IV, p. 47.
66. Cf. TB Zevahim 62a.
67. Exod. 23:17, 34:23-24; Deut. 16:16, 31:11; cf. also Ps. 84:8.
68. Lev. 19:30; Deut. 14:23 and Sifrei ad loc.; see Tossafot on TB Bava Batra 21a.
69. Exod. 25:8.
70. Cf. Rambam, *Mishneh Torah, Hilkhot Bet HaBehirah*, I, 1; ibidem, *Hilkhot Melakhim*, I, 1; *Sefer HaHinukh*, *Mitzvah* 95; see also Tanhuma, Ki Tissa 10; Eruvin 2b; Shevuot 15b.
71. TB Yevamot 6a; cf. also Deut. 14:23; Gen. R. 58:9.
72. Cf. Deut. 14:23.
73. Cf. Isa. 41:8; Num. R. 16:3; Tanhuma, Shelah Lekha 3.
74. Gen. 22:12. See *Sefat Emet*, I, p. 64.
75. Cf Ramban on Gen. 22:2.
76. Deut. 34:5; cf. Jos. 1:15 et al.; Mal. 3:22.
77. Cf. Avot I, 3.
78. Cf. Kohelet 3:14.
79. Cf. Ps. 111:10; cf. also Prov. 1:7; Kohelet 12:13.
80. Cf. Deut. 10:12; TB Shabbat 31b; Rabbi Bahya Ibn Pakuda, *Hovot HaLevavot, Sha'ar Ahavat HaShem*, I; Ramban on Exod. 20:8; R. Shneur Zalman of Lyady, *Tanya, Likkutei Amarim*, 41, pp. 56-59a-b; *Sefat Emet*, V, p. 113.
81. Cf. TB Sotah 27b.
82. Cf. Rabbi Pinhas HaLevi Ish Horovitz of Frankfurt on Main, *Sefer Hafla'ah* II, *Sefer HaMakneh*, p. 62.
83. See Rambam, *Hilkhot Yessodei HaTorah*, II, 2; IV, 12; *Hilkhot Teshuvah*, X, 6; cf. also *Sefat Emet*, I, p. 108.
84. Cf. Ps. 34:10; cf. also Ps. 23.
85. Cf. Rashi, Rashbam and *Kli Yakar* on Gen. 22:12; Ramban on Deut. 11:1; Rambam and Rabbi Ya'akov Moshe Harlap on Avot I, 3 (*Mei Merom*, II, pp. 21-23); TB Berakhot 6b; Sotah 31a. Rambam, *Mishneh Torah, Hilkhot Yessodei HaTorah*, II, 1-2; Maharal, *Derekh Hayyim*, on Avot I, 3, p. 23; *Tanya, Likkutei Amarim*, 43, p. 61b; *Aderet Eliyahu*, p. 500, with commentary *Be'er Yitshak* ad locum; idem, *Siddur Ishei Yisrael*, p. 97; Rabbi Ya'akov Yossef HaKohen of Polonnoye, *Tsafnat Pa'aneah* (Pietrkow, 5644, p. 19a); Rabbi Avraham HaMalakh, *Hessed LeAvraham*, p. 108; Rabbi Shemuel Shmelke Horovitz, *Divrei Shemuel*, pp. 24, 50, 57, 103, 121, 141; *Sefat Emet*, V, p. 240; R. Meir Simha Kohen of Dvinsk, *Meshekh Hokhmah*, p. 15; Rav Kook, *Olat Reiyah*, I, p. 93.
86. Cf. Sifrei Devarim 1 (Deut. 1:1), p. 65a; Sifrei Re'eh 66 (Deut. 12:9), p. 88b. TB Zevahim 119a; Megillah 10a. Yalkut Shim'oni, Yeshaya 49:472; Tehillim 132:882. Isa. 33:20. Rashi on Zech. 9:1; on Deut. 12:9; see also Rashi on Ps. 122:3. Zohar II, 240. Maharal, *Derekh Hayyim* on Avot V, 1, p. 188. Cf. Ps. 76:9.
87. Rashi on Gen. 12:2; cf. Rashi on Gen. 22:2. Cf. Ramban on Gen. 12:1. Cf.

Gen. R. 39:12, 55:8. See also Rambam, *Moreh Nevukhim*, III, 45. *Be'er Mayim Hayyim* on Gen. 12:1; cf. also *Sefat Emet*, I, pp. 46, 48.
88. Cf. Ramban on Gen. 12:1; idem, *Mavo LiDerashah Al Divrei Kohelet* (*Kitvei Ramban* I, p. 132). See also Alshekh on Gen. 12:1 and *Be'er Mayim Hayyim* on Gen. 12:5.
89. Midrash Tanhuma, VaYera 23.
90. Cf. Maharsha on TB Taʻanit 16a.
91. Cf. 2 Chron. 3:1. TB Zevahim 62a; Sotah 48b. Rambam, *Mishneh Torah, Hilkhot Bet HaBehirah*, II.
92. Cf. Ezek. 40; Yalkut Shimʻoni, Yehezke'el 382; TB Zevahim 62.
93. Cf. Rambam, *Mishneh Torah, Hilkhot Bet HaBehirah*, I, 4; *Hilkhot Melakhim*, XI, 1; see also Rashi on TB Rosh HaShanah 30a.
94. Cf. 2 Sam. 24:16 and Malbim ad loc.; 2 Sam. 24:18-19, 24:25; 1 Chron. 21:18-19, 21:26, 22:1; 1 Chron. 21:25 and Malbim ad loc.; Ezek. 28:19, 43:10s. TB Zevahim 62a; Yalkut Shimʻoni, Shemuel Bet 24:165. See also *Or HaHayyim* on Gen. 12:1.
95. Maharal, *Netivot Olam*, I, *Netiv HaTorah*, 10, p. 19a. See also Sifra, Mekhilta DeMiluim, parashat Shemini, 7; Yalkut Shimʻoni, Ki Tissa 32:391; Pekkudei 39:417. See also Rashi on 2 Chron. 5:1; Midrash Tanhuma, Nasso 14; Yalkut Shimʻoni, Yirmiah 320; Lev. R. 12:4.
96. See Zohar I, 127b-128a. Cf. Maharal, *Gur Aryeh*, on Rashi, Gen. 12:2. Cf. *Meshekh Hokhmah*, p. 9. Cf. *Shem MiShemuel, Bereshit*, p. 340. Cf. *Mei Merom*, V, p. 36; VIII, p. 62.
97. Cf. Gen. 15:13; Lev. 25; TB Berakhot 5a et al. Cf. Gen. 18:19, 22:18, 26:4-5.
98. See Gen. 12:7, 13:15, 15:18, 17:7-8, 17:19, 17:21, 21:12, 26:3, 28:4, 28:13, 31:42. Cf. Abrabanel on Gen. 28:12, 35:1. Alshekh on Gen. 35:12. *Or HaHayyim* on Gen. 16:5, 25:5. *Haʻamek Davar* on Gen. 25:5, 28:13. Cf. Rashi on Gen. 28:4, 36:7; on Deut. 32:9. Ramban on Gen. 17:6, 25:19, 26:3. Radak on Gen. 17:7; Seforno on Gen. 25:19. Cf. Mishnah Nedarim III, 11. TY Nedarim III, 8. TB Nedarim 31a; Rashi and Ran ad loc. TB Sanhedrin 59b. Gen. R. 53:12, 63:11. Exod. R. 5:26. Zohar I, 120a. Rambam, *Perush HaMishnah*, Nedarim III, 11; *Hilkhot Nedarim*, IX, 21; *Hilkhot Melakhim*, X, 7; *Iggeret Teiman* (Jerusalem ed., 5720), pp. 140-41. R. Yossef Karo, *Shulhan Arukh, Orah Hayyim*, 591:7. Maharal, *Gevurot HaShem*, 54, p. 146b. Rav Kook, *Olat Reiyah*, I, pp. 202-3. *Meshekh Hokhmah*, pp. 18-19, 25. R. Barukh HaLevi Epstein, *Tossefet Berakhah*, I, pp. 157-58; II, pp. 135-36; V, pp. 34, 77.
99. Cf. Sifrei Re'eh 62 (Deut. 12:5), p. 87b; see also *Mei Merom*, V, pp. 235-37.
100. Cf. Ramban and Rabbeinu Bahya on Deut. 12:5.
101. Cf. Sifrei Eikev 40 (Deut. 11:12), p. 78b; Mekhilta, Messikhta DeAmalek 2 (Exod. 18:27), p. 69.
102. Cf. Zohar II, 116a; cf. also Zohar I, 209b.
103. TB Rosh HaShanah 30a.
104. Cf. Ibn Ezra on Ps. 122:6.
105. Ramban on Deut. 12:5; cf. Jer. 50:5; cf. Pesikta DeRav Kahana, 3.
106. Cf. Yalkut Shimʻoni, Shemuel Beit 24:165; see *Sefat Emet*, I, pp. 198, 211; IV, p. 102; V, p. 29.
107. Cf. Gen. 12:1; Gen. R. 39:12; Rashi on Gen. 12:2.

108. Cf. Gen. 22:2.
109. Cf. TB Sanhedrin 89b.
110. Cf. Gen. 11:31-12:1.
111. Cf. Gen. 22:3-4.
112. See *Ha'amek Davar* on Gen. 34:14-15 (I, p. 131).
113. Cf. Deut. 12:11 and Rashi ad locum; cf. also Sifrei Re'eh 67 (Deut. 12:10); TB Sanhedrin 20b; Tanhuma Kì Teitsei 11; Shoher Tov, 7:7.
114. Cf. Rashi on Deut. 12:11; Pirkei DeRabbi Eliezer 31; Rambam, *Mishneh Torah, Hilkhot Bet HaBehirah*, I, 3; II, 1, 2; Ramban on Gen. 22:2; Rabbeinu Bahya on Gen. 22:9; on Deut. 12:5.
115. Cf. 1 Kings 8:16; 2 Chron. 6:6.
116. Cf. Ps. 30:1, 132:1-5. TB Zevahim 62a; Radak on 1 Kings 8:13, 8:16; Zohar II, 198a.
117. Cf. TB Zevahim 24a.
118. Cf. Ps. 132:13-14; cf. *Kuzari*, II, 50.
119. Cf. Ps. 132:12. Cf. *Aderet Eliyahu*, p. 397; *Mei Merom*, VIII, p. 62.
120. Cf. TB Haggigah 3b; Shevuot 16a; Zevahim 24a; see also Rambam, *Mishneh Torah, Hilkhot Terumot*, I, 5 and *Hilkhot Bet HaBehirah*, VI, 16.
121. See also Mishnah Shevuot II, 2; Sanhedrin I, 5. TB Shevuot 14a-15a-b-16a; Sanhedrin 16a. Rambam, *Mishneh Torah, Hilkhot Bet HaBehirah*, VI, 11; see also TB Bava Batra 73b.
122. Cf. Gen. R. 68:13.
123. See also *Sefer HaHinukh, Mitzvah* 95.
124. Cf. Zohar I, 72a; cf. also Zohar I, 231a; Zohar Hadash, VaYeitsei; Yalkut Shim'oni, VaYeitsei 28:120; see supra, note 1.
125. Cf. Yalkut Shim'oni, Va Yeitsei 28:119.
126. Cf. Pirkei DeRabbi Eliezer 35; Rambam, *Mishneh Torah, Hilkhot Bet HaBehirah*, II, 2; See Gen. R. 68:16; see also Yossef Heinemann, *Aggadot VeToldoteihen* (Jerusalem, 1974), pp. 192, 245. Cf. Ralbag on Gen. 28:10 and on Deut. 3:25; R. Yitshak Arama, *Akeidat Yitshak*, Sha'ar XXV; Abrabanel on Gen. 28:12; Alshekh on Exod. 23:20, 25:8; R. Yossef Hayyim of Baghdad, *Ben Ish Hai*, p. 31.
127. See *Shem MiShemuel, Bereshit*, I, p. 341.
128. Cf. Zohar I, 214b. See TB Hullin 91b; cf. TB Pessahim 88a; Gen. R. 70:8; Zohar I, 247b.
129. Cf. Gen. 13:14 and Rabbi Eliyahu of Vilna ad loc. *Aderet Eliyahu*, p. 56; cf. TB Berakhot 6b; Zohar II, 39b.
130. Zohar II, 39b; cf. TB Berakhot 6b, Menahot 29a; see also Ramban and Seforno on Gen. 24:62, regarding the choice by Isaac of a place for prayer, a place already sanctified by a very sincere prayer. See also Maharal's thoughts (*Netivot Olam*, I, *Netivot HaAvodah*, p. 34) as to the Talmudic adage (TB Berakhot 6b): "One who assigns a place for his prayer receives the help of the God of Abraham."
131. R. Abraham of Slonim, *Yessod HaAvodah*, II, p. 94.
132. Cf. Deut. 12:11, 12:14, 12:18, 12:21, 12:26, 16:11, 17:8. Mekhilta Yitro 2, Messikhta DeBaHodesh (Exod. 19:4), p. 71a. Mishnah Ma'asser Sheini V, 12. Tossefta Sanhedrin IV, 5; Menahot VII, 8. Num. R. 11:9. Cf. also 1 Kings 8:16, 8:48. Cf. also Zech. 1:17, 2:16.

133. Rav Kook, *She'elot UTeshuvot Mishpat Kohen*, p. 185.
134. Maharal, *Gevurot HaShem*, 70, pp. 197-98; cf. *Kli Yakar* on Gen. 13:17.
135. Zohar II, 116a; cf. TB Berakhot 30a.
136. Cf. TB Bava Batra 25a and Tossafot ad locum. TB Shabbat 22b; Megillah 21b; Menahot 98b: Zohar II, 5b. Rambam, *Mishneh Torah, Hilkhot Bet HaBehirah*, IV, 1; VII, 9; idem, *Moreh Nevukhim*, III, 45. Rabbi David Ibn Zimra, *She'elot UTeshuvot Haradbaz* I, 219; II, 648. Maharal, *Gevurot HaShem*, 5, p. 198. Rabbi Yomtov Lippmann Heller, *Tossfot Yomtov*, on Mishnah Yoma V; *Biurei HaGra Al Aggadot*, I, p. 105; *Tanya, Likkutei Amarim*, 42, p. 61, *Hagahah*. *Sefat Emet*, I, pp. 198, 234, 243. Rabbi Avraham of Sochaczew, *Neot HaDesheh*, pp. 165, 167-68. Rabbi B.Z. Safran, *She'elot UTeshuvot Harbaz*, I, p. 219.
137. 1 Kings 8:27.
138. Maharal, *Gevurot HaShem*, 70, pp. 197-98; cf. also idem, *Netivot Olam*, I, *Netiv HaAvodah*, 4, p. 34; cf. also Targum and Rashi, on 1 Kings 9:3; Rambam, *Moreh Nevukhim*, I, 25. Cf. Jos. 18:28; Sifrei on Deut. 33:12; TB Zevahim 54b; TB Menahot 53a-b.
139. Cf. Sifrei Re'eh 143 (Deut. 16:16), p. 102b. Mishnah Gittin IX, 8; Avot V, 5. TB Megillah 26a; Yevamot 93a; Gittin 87b; Bava Kama 82b; Bava Batra 93b; Sanhedrin 23a. Messekhet Sofrim XIV, 14. *Kuzari*, III, 21. Rambam, *Mishneh Torah, Hilkhot Ma'asser Sheini*, III, 1. Rashbam on Deut. 14:23. R. Abraham of Slonim, *Yessod HaAvodah*, II, p. 83.
140. Maharal, *Netivot Olam*, II, *Netiv HaTeshuvah*, 3, p. 145a.
141. R. Shemuel Shmelke of Nikolsburg, *Divrei Shemuel*, p. 138.
142. Cf. TB Bava Batra 75b; Rashi on TB Sukkah 53a; Radak on 1 Kings 8:16; *Or HaHayyim* on Gen. 28:17; R. Yitshak Ze'ev HaLevi of Brisk, *Hiddushei Maran Riz HaLevi*, p. 94. See also Shir HaShirim R. 4:11.
143. Tossafot on TB Bava Batra 21a.
144. Rashi on Shir HaShirim 3:10. See also Rambam, *Mishneh Torah, Hilkhot Ma'akhalot Assurot*, XI, 25 and *Hilkhot Mikvaot*, X, 5.
145. See supra, p. 217.
146. Cf. Deut. 14:23-26; Sifrei and Rashbam on Deut. 14:23. Mishnah Haggigah III, 6; Sanhedrin VIII, 2. TB Haggigah 26a; Kiddushin 76b; Bava Kama 82b; Sanhedrin 70a; Niddah 34a. Pesikta Rabbati, 15:24. Gen. R. 28:9; Exod. R. 52:4; Num. R. 21:19. Midrash Tanhuma, Pinhas 13. *Kuzari*, III, 21. Rambam, *Mishneh Torah, Hilkhot Metamei Mishkav UMoshav*, XI, 9; *Hilkhot Tum'at Okhlin*, XVI, 10. Rabbi Aharon HaLevi, *Sefer HaHinukh, Mitzvah* 360. Rabbi Hayyim of Volozhin, *Ruah Hayyim* on Avot V, 5, pp. 78-79. *Ha'amek Davar* on Deut. 14:23, p. 68; idem on Gen. 34:25. *Harhev Davar*, p. 128. *Sefat Emet*, V, p. 234; Rabbi Abraham of Slonim, *Be'er Avraham*, p. 109; Rav Kook, *Orot HaTeshuvah*, p. 113.
147. Cf. 1 Kings 8:27.
148. Cf. R. Nahman of Bratslav, *Likkutei Moharan*, II, 56, p. 28; cf. Ps. 73:26; Gen. R. 68:10.
149. Exod. 25:8; cf. Alshekh ad loc. Cf. Lev. 26:11; 1 Kings 6:13; Jer. 7.4; Ezek. 11:16, 37:29; Exod. R. 33:4. See *Kuzari*, III, 23.
150. Ramban on Deut. 11:22; cf. Recanati, Eikev, p. 49a. Cf. Rabbi Menahem

Nahum of Tchernobil, *Me'or Einaim*, Shemot.
151. Maharal, *Netivot Olam*, II, *Netiv HaTeshuvah*, 1, p. 143a.
152. *Divrei Shemuel*, p. 27; see also ibidem, p. 26. Cf. *Kuzari*, III, 73; *Yessod HaAvodah*, II, p. 83; idem, *Bet Avraham*, p. 131; idem, *Be'er Avraham*, p. 166. Rabbi S.R. Hirsch, *Sefer Tehillim Im Perush*, on Ps. 27:4, pp. 131-32. See *Biurei HaGra Al Aggadot*, I, p. 46.
153. Rabbi Hayyim of Volozhin, *Nefesh HaHayyim*, 1:4, p. 8. Jer. 7:4. See Exod. R. 33:4; Rabbi Barukh HaLevi Epstein, *Tossefet Berakhah*, II, p. 243.
154. TB Ta'anit 5a; Zohar I, 1b; III, 15b.
155. Zohar II, 55b.
156. Hakdamat HaZohar, Zohar I, 1b.
157. Zohar I, 128b.
158. Cf. *Ruah Hayyim* on Avot V, 1 (Jerusalem), p. 75. Rabbi Yoel Teitelbaum of Satmar, *VaYoel Moshe*, p. 9. Cf. TB Sukkah 53a; Rashi and Tossafot ad locum. Tana Devei Eliyahu Zuta 21. Midrash Tanhuma, Pekkudei 1. Yalkut Shim'oni, Yeshaya 60:499. Zohar I, 1b; 231a; II, 240b; III, 15b; 68b; 93b; 147b; 262b; 267a. Hakdamat Tikkunei HaZohar, 17b. Tikkunei HaZohar, 6 (21a); 26 (71a); Zohar Hadash, Noah 20:4. Rabbi Eliyahu of Vilna, *Siddur Ishei Yisrael*, pp. 333-34. *Meshekh Hokhmah*, pp. 148, 188. Rabbi Reuven Margaliot, *Sha'arei Zohar*, p. 55. Rabbi Menahem M. Kasher, *HaTekufah HaGedolah*, p. 494.
159. Zohar III, 4b-5a.
160. Rabbi Hayyim Attar, *Or HaHayyim*, Bereshit, 1:1(22).
161. Cf. Rabbi Eliyahu of Vilna, *Aderet Eliyahu*, p. 51. Rabbi Menahem Mendel Schneerson, of Lubavitch, *Likkutei Sihot*, VaYishlah (Kfar Habad, 5736/1975), p. 7. Cf. TB Sanhedrin 38b; Messekhet Derekh Erets Rabba V; Otiot DeRabbi Akiva Yod; Rashi on Gen. 3:9; Rabbi S.R. Hirsch, *Die Genesis*, p. 67.
162. Cf. Gen. 3:24, 4:12, 4:14, 4:16 and Targum ad locum. Cf. also Targum on 2 Kings 17:18. Cf. TB Sanhedrin 107b; Jon. 1:3. Cf. Gen. R. 19:18; *Kuzari*, II, 14; Ramban on Gen. 1:1.
163. Cf. TB Sanhedrin 38a.
164. Cf. Gen. R. 19:18; Petihta DeEihah Rabbati 4; Eihah R. 1:1.
165. Cf. TB Menahot 37a.
166. Cf. Zohar I, 29a.
167. Rabbi Avraham of Sochaczew, *She'elot UTeshuvot Avnei Nezer*, Yoreh Deyah, I, 126:4.
168. See *Da'at Zekeinim MiBa'alei HaTossafot*, on Deut. 25:18.
169. See Mishnah Ta'anit IV, 6. TY Ta'anit IV, 8. TB Rosh HaShanah 18b; Ta'anit 26b; 28b. Rambam, *Mishneh Torah*, Hilkhot Berakhot, II, 4 and Hilkhot Ta'anit, V. Cf. Jer. 39:2; Ezek. 24:1-2. Zech. 8:19.
170. Cf. TY Berakhot IV, 3. *Siddur Rav Sa'adya Gaon*, p. 318; *Seder Rav Amram Gaon*, II, p. 132a.
171. Cf. TY Sukkah IV, 6. TB Sotah 48b; Eihah R. 4. Shoher Tov, 137.
172. Cf. Tossafot on Berakhot 31a. See also *Shulhan Arukh, Orah Hayyim*, 560; *Even HaEzer*, 62 and commentaries.
173. See Tossefta Bava Batra II; TB Bava Batra 60b; Yalkut Shim'oni, Tehillim 137:885. Cf. *Shulhan Arukh, Orah Hayyim*, 560.

174. Cf. Jos. 12:10, 15:63; cf. 2 Sam. 5.
175. Malbim on Ps. 132:13; see also 1 Kings 8:16; 2 Chron. 6:6. Cf. 1 Kings 8:15-16, 15:4. Ps. 122:3-5, 132:10-11. 2 Chron. 6:6. TY Berakhot II, 4; IV, 3. TB Berakhot 48b-49a; Bava Kama 97b. Rambam, *Mishneh Torah, Hilkhot Berakhot*, II, 4; *Hilkhot Melakhim*, I, 10; XI, 1. Zohar I, 209b. Rabbi Israel Schepanski, *Erets Yisrael BeSifrut HaTeshuvot*, II, pp. 248-49. Rabbi Yitshak Ze'ev HaLevi of Brisk, *Hiddushei Maran Riz HaLevi*, p. 54.
176. Rabbi Shelomo of Radomsk, *Tiferet Shelomo*, Re'eh.
177. Cf. Shir HaShirim R. 4:11; Shoher Tov, 146; cf. Isa. 52:9; TB Berakhot 49a.
178. Cf. Isa. 52:9; Mic. 1:9; Dan. 9:16; Num. R. 14:24; Petihta DeEihah Rabbati 16; Jer. 4:18. Zohar I, 5a; III, 35a. TY Ta'anit IV, 2. Isa. 51:16. Rashi on Gen. 49:11; *Be'er Avraham*, pp. 102, 109, 215.
179. Cf. Isa. 40:1; TB Berakhot 30a; Midrash Eihah Rabbati, Petihta 16; Zohar I, 84b; II, 142b; III, 221b; *Kuzari*, II, 32; *Aderet Eliyahu*, p. 491.
180. Cf. Recanati, Yitro, 9a; *Aderet Eliyahu*, pp. 340-41; cf. also ibidem, pp. 102, 109, 115, 297. *Be'er Avraham*, p. 215.
181. Cf. Ps. 132:13, 135:4; Rambam, *Perush HaMishnayot*, on Zevahim XIV, 6-8; cf. Ps. 94:14; TB Zevahim 119a; Rabbeinu Bahya on Deut. 12:9 (III, p. 324).
182. See supra, p. 222.
183. Cf. Petihta DeEihah Rabbati 16; cf. Zohar I, 84b.
184. Cf. Gen. R. 70:8; Ramban on Gen. 29:2.
185. Cf. Shir HaShirim R. 4:11; see also *Biurei HaGra Al Aggadot*, I, 46.
186. Cf. Exod. 34:23-24.
187. See also 1 Kings 12:27-28; TY Ta'anit IV, 7; TB Ta'anit 28a. Cf. *Nefesh HaHayyim*, 2:17, p. 27b.
188. Cf. Jer. 17:12-14; Rabbi S.R. Hirsch, *Sefer Tehillim*, on Ps. 78:4, p. 303.
189. R. David Shelomo Eibeschutz, *Arvei Nahal*, Balak.
190. Cf. Isa. 2:3; Mic. 4:2. Mishnah Sanhedrin XI, 2.
191. Isa. 51:16; TY Ta'anit IV, 2; Zohar I, 5a; cf. Zohar III, 35a; cf. also Ps. 122:2, 125:2.
192. Cf. Gen. R. 1:5; Midrash Tanhuma, Nasso 11; cf. also Pirkei DeRabbi Eliezer 3.
193. Cf. Ps. 74:2.
194. Cf. Jer. 33:11; TY Berakhot IV, 3; TB Berakhot 6b; 32b; 49a.
195. Cf. Recanati, Yitro, 9a.
196. Cf. Shir HaShirim R. 4:11.
197. Zohar I, 113b; 128b; cf. Rashi on Gen. 28:13; TB Hullin 91b; Gen. R. 69:3; Zohar I, 72a; 156a; cf. also Zohar III, 84a; Zohar Hadash, VaYeitsei 28; Ramban, *Derashah LeRosh HaShanah* (*Kitvei Ramban* I, p. 252); Recanati, VaYeitsei 28b; Alshekh, VaYeitsei, Gen. 28:13; *Aderet Eliyahu*, p. 491; *Sefat Emet*, IV, p. 105; *Shem MiShemuel, Bereshit*, p. 336; Rav Kook, *Iggrot HaReiyah*, I, p. 34; *Mei Merom*, VI, p. 290.
198. *Kuzari*, V, 27; see Ps. 102:15; TB Ketuvot 112a-b; cf. *Kuzari*, II, 23. See TY Shevi'it IV, 7; Midrash Tanhuma, Shelah Lekha; Rambam, *Mishneh Torah, Hilkhot Melakhim*, V, 10; Tossafot on TB Ketuvot 112a; Rav Kook, *Orot HaTeshuvah*, p. 135. Cf. also TB Berakhot 48b; Num. R. 23:7; Zohar I, 172b.
199. 2 Chron. 36:23.
200. Cf. Tanhuma, Lekh Lekha 9. Ramban on Gen. 12:6, 14:1, 26:1, 32:4, 32:17,

32:26, 33:18, 43:14, 48:6-7, 48:22; Ramban on Exod., *Hakdamah*.
201. 2 Chron. 36:23.
202. Cf. Gen. 12:10, 46:4; Exod. 3:8, 3:17, et al. Exod. R. 34 et al.
203. Cf. Sifrei Devarim, on Deut. 1:25; Sifrei Shoftim, on Deut. 17:8; Sifrei Ha'azinu, on Deut. 32:13; Sifrei Vezot HaBerakhah, on Deut. 33:12. TB Kiddushin 69a-b; Sanhedrin 87a; Zevahim 54b. Shir HaShirim R. 4:11. Rashi on Gen. 45:9, on Exod. 33:1. See also TB Bava Batra 75b. Cf. also Mishnah Sotah I, 4-5; Kiddushin VI, 1; Sanhedrin XI, 4. Cf. also Num. 13:130; Jer. 23:8; Ps. 122:4. See Maharal, *Tiferet Yisrael*, 64, p. 82a. See also *Sefer HaHinukh*, *Mitzvah* 88.
204. TB Yoma 21; Shir HaShirim R. 1, 4, 8.
205. Deut. 26:2.
206. Cf. Mishnah Bikkurim III, 2; Tanhuma, Ki Tavo 4; Rambam, *Mishneh Torah*, *Hilkhot Bikkurim*, II, 21.
207. Cf. Rabbi Yitshak Shemuel Reggio, "Yashar," on Exod. 33:1 (*Lekh Ale MiZeh*...). Cf. Rabbi Moshe Sofer, *She'elot UTeshuvot Hatam Sofer*, *Yoreh Deyah*, 234, p. 97.
208. Cf. Mishnah Ketuvot XIII, 11; TB Ketuvot 110b; *Shulhan Arukh*, *Even HaEzer*, 75:3-5; Zohar I, 79a; *Kuzari*, II, 22.
209. Cf. Rambam, *Sefer HaMitzvot*, *Mitzvat Asseh* 4.
210. Cf. R. Wolf Kranz, the Maggid ("Preacher") of Dubno, *Ohel Ya'akov*, Shelah Lekha, on Num. 13:30 (*alo na'ale*...).
211. Cf. Isa. 2:3; Mic. 4:2. Gen. R. 16:7. *Kuzari*, II, 23.
212. Cf. Deut. 32:49, 34:1; cf. also Rashi on Deut. 3:25; Zohar III, 279b-280a.
213. Cf. Deut. 26:19; Tanhuma, Ki Tavo 2; Yalkut Shim'oni, Ki Tavo 26.
214. Cf. Exod. R. 52:4; Shir HaShirim. R. 7:10; cf. also Isa. 66:10. Cf. also Rav Kook, *Olat Reiyah*, I, p. 63. See also *Or HaHayyim* on Deut. 21:1.
215. Cf. TB Shabbat 30b; Zohar I, 180b.
216. Cf. Ps. 100:2 but also ibidem, 2:11; Deut. 28:47; Zohar I, 216b.
217. Cf. TB Arakhin 11a.
218. Cf. Tossafot on TB Sukkah 50b; see also TY Sukkah V, 1; cf. also *Sefat Emet*, V, p. 12.
219. Cf. Ps. 2:11.
220. Cf. Rashbam on Deut. 14:23; Rav Kook, *Olat Reiyah*, I, p. 185; *Sefat Emet*, V, p. 34.
221. Zohar Hadash, VaYeitsei 36.
222. Cf. Rambam, *Mishneh Torah*, *Hilkhot Bet HaMikdash*, II, 11; See TB Haggigah 4a and Rashi ad loc.
223. Regarding God's service in joy in Jerusalem, see also: Deut. 14:26, 16:11, 26:11; Deut. 16:17, 27:7, and Sifrei ad loc. Tossefta Pessahim V, 3. TY Haggigah I, 2. TB Haggigah 8a; Pessahim 70a; 109a. Zohar Hadash, Bereshit 28:4. Shoher Tov, 118. Yalkut Shim'oni, Tehillim 48:775. *Sefer HaHinukh*, *Mitzvah* 489. Shelah, *Siddur Sha'ar HaShamayim*, p. 486. *Aderet Eliyahu*, p. 427; *Biurei HaGra Al Aggadot*, II, p. 25. *Shem MiShemuel*, *Devarim*, p. 183; idem, *Bemidbar*, p. 196. Cf. Yalkut Shim'oni, Eihah 1009. Rav Kook, *Orot HaTeshuvah*, p. 113.
224. See Targum and Ibn Ezra on Ps. 76:3; Tossefta Berakhot I; cf. also Zohar I, 86b; 172b.

225. Cf. Ramban on Gen. 22:2.
226. See also *Likkutei Moharan*, 154, p. 105. Cf. Tossafot on TB Ta'anit 16a. Cf. Pirkei DeRabbi Eliezer 28. Cf. *Meshekh Hokhmah*, p. 20.
227. Cf. Exod. 23:17 et al; Cf. *Biurei HaGra Al Aggadot*, I, p. 83; *Kol Eliyahu*, p. 89.
228. Cf. Exod. 23:17; Deut. 16:16. TB Haggigah 2a; 3a. TY Haggigah I, 1. *Avnei Nezer*, p. 89.
229. Cf. TB Pessahim 54a.
230. See supra, p. 211.
231. Cf. Isa. 1:21; Jer. 31:22; Ps. 118:19.
232. Shelah, *Siddur Sha'ar HaShamayim*, pp. 197-98. Cf. Exod. R. 30:12, 30:15; Tanhuma, Tsav 14; Ahrei 10. Midrsh Lekah Tov, Eikev; Yalkut Reuveni, Shoftim. Cf. also Ps. 122:5. Mishnah Sanhedrin XI, 2; Middot V, 4. TB Sanhedrin 86b; 88b. See also Zohar III, 13a.
233. Rabbi Menahem Mendel Kasher, *HaTekufah HaGedolah* (Jerusalem, 5729/1969), p. 519.
234. *Shem MiShemuel, Bereshit*, I, p. 304.
235. Maharal, *Netivot Olam*, I, *Netiv HaEmet*, 3, p. 78b.
236. Cf. Ps. 31:6.
237. Shoher Tov, 9:12.
238. Pessikta DeRav Kahana, 21. Cf. Shir HaShirim R. 1:31; Deut. R. 4:11; *Tur, Orah Hayyim*, 112; Zohar III, 6a-b. Cf. also Ezek. 36:22-27; Zech. 9:9.
239. Cf. Zohar III, 35a; TY Ta'anit IV, 2; Megillah III, 6; Isa. 1:28; 51:16; TB Bava Batra 75b; Zohar I, 93b; see also TY Berakhot IV, 3. Cf. *Nefesh HaHayyim*, 2:17, p. 27b; Rabbi B.Z. Safran, *Doresh LeTsion*, p. 4.
240. See TB Zevahim 119a.
241. *Mei Merom*, V, p. 235.
242. Cf. TY Sotah VII, 35; TB Sotah 37b; TB Sanhedrin 43b.
243. *She'elot UTeshuvot Avnei Nezer, Yoreh Deyah*, I, 126:4; cf. Rabbi Shemuel of Sochaczew (son of the author of Responsa *Avnei Nezer*), *Shem MiShemuel, Devarim*, pp. 210, 254; *Moadim*, pp. 144-45; cf. also Maharal, *Netsah Yisrael*, 5.
244. Ran on TB Nedarim 28a. See also Sifra BeHar 2:3:2 (Lev. 25:10), p. 106b. TB Arakhin 32b; Rambam, *Mishneh Torah, Hilkhot Shemittah VeYovel*, X, 8.
245. TY Bava Kama VII, 7.
246. Cf. Ibn Ezra on Exod. 19:8. See also Gen. 13:6.
247. Zohar III, 93b.
248. Cf. Mishnah Haggigah III, 6; TB Haggigah 26a; Rambam, *Mishneh Torah, Hilkhot Metamei Mishkav UMoshav*, XI, 9; Judg. 20:11; Maharal, *Perushei Maharal MiPrag LeAggadot HaShas*, on Gittin 55b (IV, p. 140); *Netsah Yisrael*, 5. Malbim on 1 Kings 8.16. Cf. also Ps. 42:5; Eihah R. 1:59.
249. Rashi on TB Berakhot 48b; 49a; cf. Zohar I, 1b; Yalkut Shim'oni, VaYehi 50:162. Cf. R. Menahem M. Kasher (of the school of the Gaon of Vilna), *HaTekufah HaGedolah*, p. 494.
250. Rabbi S.R. Hirsch, *Die Psalmen*, on Ps. 122:3 (II, p. 235).
251. TY Haggigah III, 6; cf. Mishnah Bikkurim III, 3.
252. Cf. *Nefesh HaHayyim*, p. 54; cf. Jer. 2:2.
253. Zohar III, 93b; 2 Sam. 7:23.

254. Cf. TB Yoma 12a; Rashi, Tossafot and Ritva (R. Yomtov Ben Avraham) ad loc.; TB Megillah 26a; TB Bava Kama 82b and Tossafot ad loc. TB Zevahim 54b; 116b; TB Menahot 53a-b; Tossefta Negaim VI; Sifrei on Deut. 33:12; Avot DeRabbi Nathan 35; Gen. R. 99:1; Rambam, *Perush HaMishnayot*, Nedarim V, 4-5; idem, *Moreh Nevukhim*, III, 45; Rashi on Deut. 12:14 (cf. 2 Sam. 24; 1 Chron. 21); Rabbeinu Yonah of Gerona, *Sha'arei HaAvodah*, p. 51; *Kli Yakar* on Gen. 28:11; *Sefat Emet*, V, p. 80. See also Zohar II, 251a and *Bet Yossef, Orah Hayyim*, 90.
255. Cf. Tossefta Ma'asser Sheini I; Sukkah II. TY Ma'asser Sheini III; Orlah I; Sotah IX. TB Yoma 12a; Megillah 26a. Philon, *De spec. leg.*, I, 70; Josephus, *Antiq.*, IV, 8:7. Shemuel Safrai, *HaAliyah LaRegel BiYemei HaBayit HaSheini* (Tel Aviv, 1965), pp. 133, 163-64. Shaul Lieberman, *Tossefta Ki-Fshutah, Seder Zeraim* (New York, 5715/1955), p. 724.
256. Cf. Gen. R. 98:2; Num. R. 11:16-17; Sifrei Vezot HaBerakhah 346 (Deut. 33:5), p. 144; Mishnah Uktsin III, 12; cf. also Mishnah Eduyot VIII, 7.
257. Cf. Rashi on TB Berakhot 49a. Cf. Bava Batra 93b.
258. Maharal, *Netsah Yisrael*, 1.
259. *Shem MiShemuel, Bemidbar*, p. 91.
260. Num. R. 15:14.
261. Rashi on Deut. 33:5.
262. Cf. TB Menahot 27a; Ramban on Gen. 26:20-22.
263. Cf. Gen. 49:1; cf. TB Pessahim 56a; cf. Zohar I, 54b; II, 43b; cf. also TB Berakhot 6a.
264. Cf. Zohar II, 235a; III, 5a; cf. Zohar Hadash, Ki Tissa 44a; Hukat 51b; Shir HaShirim 71a and Rashi et al. Ps. 48:2.
265. See TB Yoma 9b; cf. TB Gittin 55b; Zohar Hadash, VaYeshev 29.
266. See *Or HaHayyim* on Gen. 47:27 et al.
267. Rav Kook, *Orot HaKodesh*, III, p. 324. Cf. also *Tanya, Iggeret HaKodesh*, p. 304.
268. Shir HaShirim R. 1:37; Exod. R. 23:11; Rashi on Shir HaShirim 1:5; Rambam, *Iggeret Teiman*, p. 181. See Avot DeRabbi Nathan 35. Cf. Maharal, *Gevurot HaShem*, 5, p. 199.
269. Cf. Isa. 2:3; Jer. 3:17; Mic. 4:2 et al.; Zech. 2:14-17, 8:22 et al. Shir HaShirim R. 4:11.
270. Num. R. 14:24. Cf. TB Sukkah 55a and Rashi ad locum; Num. R. 21:21; Pesikta DeRav Kahana, 30; cf. Zohar II, 59a; 187a; III, 24b; 54b.
271. Num. R. 1:3; cf. 1 Kings 8:41-43; 2 Chron. 6:32-33; Tanhuma, Tetsaveh 13. *Or HaHayyim* on Gen. 28:14.
272. Cf. Sifrei Devarim 1 (Deut. 1:1), p. 65; TB Pessahim 50a; Lev. R. 10:9; Shir HaShirim R. 7.1; Esther R. 1; Tanhuma, Tsav 12; Pesikta Rabbati, BeShabbat VeRosh Hodesh, 2; Avot DeRabbi Nathan 35; Yalkut Shim'oni, Isa. 49:472, 60:499, 60:503; Yalkut Shim'oni, Zech. 9:575; Rashi on Zech. 9:1; cf. also Jer. 31:37; cf. Zohar I, 114a; 128b; II, 220a; 234a; III, 56a; cf. Rabbi Eliyahu of Vilna, *Biur Sefer Mishlei* (on Prov. 15:25), p. 48; cf. also TB Bava Batra 75b; but see also Mishnah Shevuot II, 2; TB Shevuot 14-15; Rambam, *Mishneh Torah, Hilkhot Bet HaBehirah*, VI, 11; R. Yossef Rozin, the Gaon of Rogachov, *Tsafnat Pa'aneah, Devarim*, I, p. 2. See also *Sefat Emet*, V, pp. 28-29; *Neot HaDesheh*, pp. 69-70.

273. Shir HaShirim 4:4.
274. Shir HaShirim R. 4:11; Tikkunei HaZohar, 6 (145-146); cf. Zohar I, 209b.
275. Jer. 3:17; see Lev. R. 10:9; Pesikta Rabbati, 12. Cf. *Da'at Zekeinim MiBa'alei HaTossafot* on Exod. 17:16. See also Rambam, *Moreh Nevukhim*, I, 9; Maharal, *Gevurot HaShem*, 5, p. 199.
276. Cf. Mekhilta and Rashi on Exod. 15:17; Tanhuma, Ki Teitsei 11; Ramban, *Derashat Torat HaShem Temimah* (*Kitvei Ramban* I, p. 165); Rav Kook, *Orot HaKodesh*, III, p. 191; idem, *Olat Reiyah*, I, p. 185. R. Yehuda HaLevi, *Shirim* (Bernstein ed.), p. 232 (in *Tsion HaLo Tish'ali*).
277. Cf. Zohar I, 128b; II, 55b; III, 66a; 93b; 161b.
278. Cf. Zohar II, 240a.
279. Isa. 60:3.
280. Isa. 60:19.
281. Gen. R. 59:8; Yalkut Shim'oni, Isa. 60:499.
282. Pesikta DeRav Kahana, 21.
283. Cf. TB Zevahim 119a; Rashi on Deut. 12:9; Alshekh on Exod. 22:4; *Mei Merom*, V (Deut. 12:9), p. 235.
284. Zech. 2:16.
285. Cf. Isa. 52:1.
286. Cf. Petihta DeEihah Rabbati 1:8.
287. Rav. Kook, *Orot HaKodesh*, III, p. 191.
288. Zohar III, 56a.
289. Jer. 3:17.
290. Zech. 14:9.
291. Cf. Shir HaShirim R. 8.
292. Cf. Maharsha on TB Sotah 49a.
293. Cf. Isa. 4:5, 8:18, 10:12, 10:24, 10:32, 16:1, 18:7, 24:23, 29:8. Joel 3:5. Obad. 1:17, 1:21. Mic. 4:7. Zech. 8:3. Ps. 43:12. 2 Chron. 33:15. Cf. also 1 Kings 81. Isa. 60:14. Gen. R. 48:2.
294. Cf. Jer. 26:18. Mic. 3:12. Midrash Tanhuma, Ki Tavo 4.
295. Cf. Gen. R. 70:8; cf. also Pirkei DeRabbi Eliezer 35 and *Be'er Mayim Hayyim* on Gen. 26:32.
296. Cf. Ps. 122:3. TY Berakhot IV, 3. TB Shabbat 59a; Ta'anit 5a; Ketuvot 111b; Sanhedrin 2a and Rashi ad locum. Tanhuma, Ki Tavo 4. Tikkunei Zohar Hadash, 113a et al.; see also 1 Kings 8:1; Isa. 66:20; Zohar II, 218a.
297. Cf. Ps. 102:14, 133:3, 143:3.
298. Cf. Zohar I, 186a; III, 31a; 262b; cf. also Isa. 1:27.
299. Cf. Zohar III, 36a.
300. Cf. Zohar III, 36a; 65b; cf. Ps. 128:5.
301. Cf. *Aderet Eliyahu*, pp. 500-4.
302. *Be'er Yitshak* ad locum.
303. TB Berakhot 8a.
304. Cf. Zohar I, 5a.
305. Cf. Rav Kook, *Hazon HaGeulah*, pp. 35-41.
306. Idem, ibidem, p. 282.
307. Cf. Shelah, *Siddur Sha'ar HaShamayim*, p. 471.
308. Cf. *Divrei Shemuel*, p. 141; cf. Jer. 31:20.
309. Cf. *Biurei HaGra Al Aggadot*, II, p. 64.

310. Rashi on TB Taʻanit 16a.
311. Cf. Rabbeinu Yonah of Gerona, *Shaʻarei HaAvodah*, p. 51.

Chapter Four

1. Cf. *Reshit Hokhmah, Shaʻar HaKedushah*, 2.
2. Cf. TB Ketuvot 62b; Zohar II, 63b; Recanati on Gen. 2:3, p. 8a.
3. Cf. Zohar Hadash, 33b; Zohar III, 94a.
4. R.S.R. Hirsch on Gen. 2:3 (I, p. 41). Cf. R. Abraham of Slonim, *Be'er Avraham*, 117b.
5. Cf. TB Pessahim 117b.
6. Mekhilta Ki Tissa, Messikhta DeShabta I (Exod. 31:16), p. 110b; cf. Rabbeinu Bahya on Exod. 31:16 (II, p. 324); *Or HaHayim* on Exod. 35:1; *Sefat Emet*, IV, p. 29; R. Yossef Hayyim of Baghdad, *Ben Yehoyada*, II, p. 25b.
7. Zohar II, 88b; 128a.
8. Zohar II, 63b; 205b.
9. Cf. TB Berakhot 6a.
10. Cf. Rambam, *Mishneh Torah, Hilkhot Shabbat*, V, 3; R. Yossef Karo, *Shulhan Arukh*, 263:3, 263:6 and R. Yisrael Meir HaKohen (The "Hafets Hayyim"), *Mishnah Berurah*, ad loc.
11. Eve "extinguished" the first man's soul. "Man's soul is God's candle" (Prov. 20:27).
12. Cf. Gen. R. 17:13; TY Shabbat II, 6; cf. Mishnah Shabbat II, 6; TB Shabbat 31b-32a; cf. Tanhuma, Noah 1; Zohar I, 48b. See also Rashi on TB Shabbat 32a.
13. Cf. TB Shabbat 23b. See Mishnah Shabbat II, 7.
14. Cf. TB Shabbat 118b; Mishnah Yoma I, 1. TB Yoma 13a; Yevamot 62b; Gittin 52b; Sotah 44a. Zohar II, 4a; III, 178b. Tikkunei HaZohar, 55 (89a).
15. Cf. Gen. R. 60:15; Zohar I, 133a.
16. Cf. R. Avraham of Sochaczew, *Avnei Nezer*, p. 104.
17. Cf. Zohar III, 94a; R. Avraham of Sochaczew, *Neot HaDesheh*, p. 89.
18. Gen. 2:17. Cf. Zohar II, 135a-b; *Be'er Avraham*, pp. 109, 323; *Neot HaDesheh*, pp. 1, 5.
19. Cf. *Be'er Avraham*, p. 184; *Neot HaDesheh*, p. 5; Ps. 92:2.
20. R.S.R. Hirsch, *The Hirsch Siddur*, p. 281.
21. Cf. Zohar I, 48a; III, 176b.
22. Cf. TB Shabbat 23b. *Shulhan Arukh, Orah Hayyim*, 263:3, 271:2-3. See also Rambam, *Mishneh Torah, Hilkhot Shabbat*, V, 1; *Hilkhot Hanukah*, IV, 4.
23. Isa. 49:3; Zohar Hadash, Ahrei 60a; cf. Zohar III, 179b. See also Zohar II, 209a.
24. TB Sotah 17a and *Perushei Maharal* ad loc. (I, p. 48). Cf. Pesikta Zutarta, Bereshit 2:23; Pirkei DeRabbi Eliezer 12.
25. Cf. Zohar I, 55b-122a; 228b. Hakdamat Tikkunei HaZohar, 10b; Tikkunei HaZohar, 22 (68a). Ramban, *Iggeret HaKodesh* (*Kitvei Ramban* II, pp. 324, 326). Shelah, I, p. 164a.
26. Cf. TB Pessahim 54a; Zohar II, 207b-208a; R. Yossef Gikatilla, *Ginat Egoz*,

28; *Shulhan Arukh, Orah Hayyim,* 296.
27. Exod. 35:3; cf. Mekhilta VaYakhel, Messikhta DeShabta I (Exod. 35:3), pp. 111b-112; TB Shabbat 70a.
28. Cf. Zohar I, 48a; II, 203b; cf. Tikkunei HaZohar, 24; 28. Cf. TB Sanhedrin 35a-b; TY Sanhedrin IV, 6. Rambam, *Sefer HaMitzvot, Mitzvah* 322; *Mishneh Torah, Hilkhot Shabbat,* XXIV, 7. *Sefer HaHinukh, Mitzvah* 114. Shelah, *Siddur Sha'ar HaShamayim,* p. 310.
29. Cf. Zohar I, 48a; cf. TB Sanhedrin 65b; Tanhuma, Ki Tissa 33; Peskita Rabbati, 23; Zohar Hadash, Ruth 79b; Zohar II, 130a; 135b; III, 105a.
30. Cf. *Shem MiShemuel, VaYikra,* pp. 140, 353.
31. *Zakhor:* "Think of the day of Shabbat (remember the day of Shabbat in order to sanctify it" (Exod. 20:8). *Zekhirah BeMohah:* "The thought (the memory) is in the brain" (Zohar III, 224a).
Zakhor BaPeh, VeShamor BaLev: "Remember, by (the) mouth; keep, by heart!" (express your thought by mouth, keep its value in your heart: carry it out!) (cf. Midrash Tanaim, VaEthanan 5, 12; cf. Sifra on Lev. 26:3; cf. Zohar III, 224a; cf. also TB Megillah 18a; see infra, note 33).
32. Cf. Zohar III, 95a.
33. R. Aharon HaLevi of Barcelona, *Sefer HaHinukh, Mitzvah* 31: "We shall arouse ourselves through this act (the Kiddush) to remember the day's (the Shabbat's) greatness.... We do it over wine, for man's nature is to wake through food and joy.... By waking, by acting, man is affected by things (by important subjects of thought)." Cf. *Ha'amek Davar* on Deut. 11:31 (V, p. 58): "Any concrete act awakens the soul's memory." See supra, note 31.
34. Cf. Rambam, *Moreh Nevukhim,* II, 31.
35. See supra, p. 261.
36. TB Pessahim 106a.
37. Exod. 20:8; Deut. 16:3; cf. TB Pessahim 117b; Exod. R. 19:8.
38. The very recital of the Shabbat Kiddush, because it testifies to the ceasing of physical, human work, and links the speaker to the One who endowed him with speech, becomes an *act* (cf. Zohar III, 92b), resembling the first Act of God, which was Speech (cf. Ps. 33:6); cf. TB Shabbat 119b. Cf. *Tossefet Berakhah,* II, p. 285. See Rambam, *Mishneh Torah, Hilkhot Shabbat,* XXIX, 1.
39. See supra, notes 31 and 38.
40. Deut. 5:12.
41. *Tanya, Kuntress Aharon,* p. 163.
42. Cf. Zohar II, 89a.
43. Cf. Ramban on Exod. 20:8 (Source: Zohar II, 118b).
44. Cf. TB Eruvin 96a; Shevuot 36a.
45. Cf. Ramban on Exod. 20:8.
46. Zohar II, 89a; *Or HaHayim* on Exod. 31:16. Cf. also R. Ya'akov Emden, *Siddur Bet Ya'akov,* I, p. 332.
47. Gen. 37:11.
48. Cf. TB Shabbat 137b; *Meshamer Et HaYayin,* "purifies the wine," "distills the wine."
49. Cf. *Be'er Avraham,* pp. 61, 114, 164; *Neot HaDesheh,* pp. 110, 111, 121, 125,

140; *Shem MiShemuel, Shemot,* I, p. 99. *Sefat Emet,* II, p. 208.
50. Cf. Zohar III, 180b; cf. also ibidem, 92b. See also Part I, p. 152 (note 235). See also TB Shevuot 20b.
51. Cf. Zohar I, 27a; 199b; Rabbeinu Bahya on Exod. 20:8 (II, p. 198).
52. Cf. Zohar II, 91a; Rabbeinu Bahya on Exod. 20:8 (II, p. 198); *Neot HaDesheh,* pp. 55, 104; *Sefat Emet,* II, p. 64.
53. Cf. Yalkut Shim'oni, Beshalah 16:261.
54. Cf. TB Yoma 63b.
55. Cf. Shelah, III, p. 6a; cf. *Sefat Emet,* I, p. 74; V, p. 164. See also *Shulhan Arukh, Orah Hayyim,* 263:1.
56. Cf. TB Berakhot 39b; Shabbat 33b; 117b. Zohar III, 98a; 272b-273a. Tikkunei HaZohar, 21 (57); cf. also *Shulhan Arukh, Orah Hayyim,* 263:1, 273:7, 274:1; and commentaries ad loc.
57. Cf. Zohar II, 206a; III, 273a; cf. also TB Pessahim 109b; Zohar III, 245a; Tikkunei HaZohar, 47.
58. Cf. TB Shabbat 119b. Zohar I, 144b; 165b; II, 106b. Tikkunei HaZohar, 24 (69b).
59. Zohar II, 207a, cf. also TB Eruvin 17b; 51a. Zohar I, 5b; II, 64a. Tikkunei HaZohar, 23 (69a). Cf. R. Nahman of Bratslav, *Likkutei Moharan,* II, 83, p. 38b.
60. Cf. Tossafot on Pessahim 101a. See *Shulhan Arukh, Orah Hayyim,* 273.
61. Cf. Sifra Behukotai 1:3 (Lev. 26:4); Sifrei Eikev 42 (Deut. 11:14); TB Ta'anit 22b; Rashi on Deut. 11:14.
62. Cf. TB Ketuvot 62b and Rashi ad loc. TB Bava Kama 82a. Zohar I, 14a; 50a; 112a; 257a; II, 63b; 89a; 136a-b; 204b; III, 49b; 71a; 78a; 81a; 143a. Tikkunei HaZohar, 6 (21a); 19 (38b); 21 (57a, 61a); 36 (78a); 56 (90a-b). *Sha'arei Zohar,* p. 70. Rambam, *Perush HaMishnah, Nedarim,* VIII, 6; *Mishneh Torah, Hilkhot Shabbat,* XXX, 14; *Hilkhot Ishut,* XIV, 1. Ramban, *Iggeret HaKodesh (Kitvei Ramban* II, pp. 326-27). Recanati, Bereshit, p. 8a. R. Yitshak Aboab, *Menorat HaMaor,* 3:6. R. Hayyim Vital, *Peri Ets Hayyim,* II; *Sha'ar HaShabbat,* pp. 58a-b, 62b. Shelah, II, pp. 6a, 9a; III, p. 118b; *Siddur Sha'ar HaShamayim,* p. 385. R. Shemuel Shmelke of Nikolsburg, *Divrei Shemuel,* p. 31. *Likkutei Moharan,* II, 5-6-7, p. 15a. *Siddur Bet Ya'akov,* pp. 162, 332-33. *Shem MiShemuel, Bereshit,* I, p. 5; II, p. 350. R. Yossef Hayyim of Baghdad, *Od Yossef Hai,* p. 193.
63. Zohar III, 81b.
64. Cf. Ibn Ezra and Rashbam on Lev. 19:3; Rabbeinu Bahya on Exod. 20:12 (II, p. 199).
65. TB Kiddushin 30b.
66. Cf. TB Ta'anit 2a.
67. TB Kiddushin 30b; cf. TY Peyah I, 1. Cf. Kohelet R. 5:13. Zohar II, 93a; III, 83a; 219b. Zohar Hadash, Bereshit 16a. Rambam, *Mishneh Torah, Hilkhot Mamrim,* VI, 1. Ramban on Exod. 20:12. Cf. also Kiddushin 32a; *Meshekh Hokhmah,* p. 159.
68. Gen. 1:26; Ramban, *Iggeret HaKodesh,* p. 325.
69. Cf. TB Yevamot 5b-6a; Zohar III, 81b; Rashi on Lev. 19:3; Rambam, *Mishneh Torah, Hilkhot Mamrim,* VI, 12; *Shulhan Arukh, Yoreh Deyah,* 240:15; Cf. also TB Bava Metsia 32a; cf. Yitshak Breuer, *Nahliel,* p. 57s.

70. Cf. R. Yossef Karo, *Bet Yossef, Tur, Orah Hayyim,* 292.
71. See TB Shabbat 118b.
72. See TB Pessahim 68b.
73. Cf. TB Shabbat 113a; 118b.
74. Cf. Zohar I,47a; Rashbam on Pessahim 101a.
75. Cf. Rambam, *Mishneh Torah, Hilkhot Shabbat,* XXXI, 1. Also Mishnah Ta'anit IV, 3; *Shulhan Arukh, Orah Hayyim,* 242.
76. Cf. Tana Devei Eliyahu Rabba 1; Yalkut Shim'oni, Tehillim 139:888.
77. Cf. *Be'er Avraham,* p. 333.
78. Cf. TB Berakhot 8a; Shabbat 25b; 33b; 113a; 118; 119; Pessahim 101a; Beitsa 15b-16a; Ketuvot 62b; Gittin 38b; Bava Kama 32b; 82a. TY Peyah VIII, 7; Shabbat XV, 2. Gen. R. 10:10, 11:2. Num. R. 10:3. Tanhuma, Bereshit 2-3; Metsora 9. Rambam, *Mishneh Torah, Hilkhot Tefillah,* XIII, 25; *Hilkhot Shabbat,* XXX. *Shulhan Arukh, Orah Hayyim,* 242, 249, 250, 260, 262, 263, 271, 281, 288. *Sefer HaHinukh, Mitzvah* 31. R. Yehuda HeHassid, *Sefer Hassidim* (Jerusalem ed., 5724/1964), p. 487. Sefer Yetsirah 2, 4. Zohar I, 14a; 24b; 32a; 48b; 50a; 144b; II, 47b; 63b; 88b; 89a; 136a-b; 165b; 204a-b; 205a; 207a; III, 49b; 71a; 94a-b; 243b; 272b; 273. Zohar Hadash, Ahrei 60a; Ruth 103b. Hakdamat Tikkunei HaZohar, 11a. Tikkunei HaZohar, 6; 21 (57a, 86a); 24 (69a-b); 48 (85a); 56. Rabbeinu Bahya on Exod. 20:8 (II, p. 195). Recanati, Bereshit, p. 8a. *Perushei Maharal MiPrag LeAggadot HaShas* on TB Shabbat 117b (II, p. 94). Shelah, I, p. 142a; II, p. 7b; *Siddur Sha'ar HaShamayim,* p. 385. *Biurei HaGra Al Aggadot,* II, p. 72. R. Ya'akov Yossef of Polonnoye, *Toldot Ya'akov Yossef,* Kedoshim. R. Dov Baer of Mezerich, *Maggid Devarav Le Ya'akov,* 87, p. 151. *Likkutei Moharan,* I, 11:7, p. 15a; 31:1, p. 43; II, 72, p. 33a; 83, p. 38b; *Siddur Sha'arei Ratson,* p. 541. *Sefat Emet,* III, p. 26. *Neot HaDesheh,* p. 53. *Shem MiShemuel, Bereshit,* I, pp. 221, 359; II, p. 350; *Shemot,* I, pp. 263-64; *Bemidbar,* p. 93; *Devarim,* pp. 51, 99, 180; *Moadim,* pp. 93, 135. R. Avraham of Slonim, *Yessod HaAvodah,* p. 215; *Be'er Avraham,* p. 110. R. Yossef Hayyim of Baghdad, *Ben Ish Hai,* p. 103. *Tossefet Berakhah,* II, pp. 181, 285, 287. R.B.Z. Safran, *She'elot UTeshuvot Harbaz,* I, pp. 27-28.
79. Cf. Exod. R. 19:8; cf. R. Yossef Dov Baer of Volozhin, *Bet HaLevi,* p. 10; R. Levi Yitshak of Berditchev, *Kedushat Levi,* pp. 68-69. *Sefat Emet,* III, p. 75. *Shem MiShemuel, Shemot,* I, p. 188.
80. Cf. *Meshekh Hokhmah,* p. 51; cf. Rashi on Exod. 23:13; cf. Rabbi S.R. Hirsch on Exod. 31:13 (II, p. 454). Cf. Ibn Ezra on Exod. 20:2.
81. Cf. TB Eruvin 96a; Shevuot 7a.
82. Cf. TB Shabbat 49b. See TY Shabbat VII, 9. See Mishnah Shabbat VII, 2.
83. Cf. TB Bava Kama 2a. See also Tossafot on TB Pessahim 114b.
84. Cf. TB Yevamot 6a.
85. Cf. TB Shabbat 119b. See TB Ta'anit 29a; Esther R. 1; Midrash Eihah Rabbati 1:36. See also R. Tsevi Elimelech of Dynow, *Bnei Issakhar,* I, p. 22a.
86. Cf. TB Shabbat 88b and Rashi ad loc.
87. Cf. TB Shabbat 118b.
88. Cf. TB Haggigah 10a.
89. See Mekhilta Yitro 1 (Exod. 20:18), p. 79; see also Zohar I, 130b; III, 128b; 292b; Isa. 26:19. Cf. TB Shabbat 88b; TY Berakhot V, 2; Pirkei DeRabbi

Eliezer 33, 34; Zohar I, 130b; Cf. *Or HaHayyim* on Exod. 35:1.
90. Cf. Tossafot on Haggiga 3b.
91. Cf. Sifra and Rashi on Lev. 19:30; Mekhilta VaYakhel, Messikhta DeShabta 1 (Exod. 35:1), p. 111; Rashi on Exod. 35:2. Cf. TB Shabbat 119b. Regarding Shabbat worship in the *Bet HaMikdash*, see also Sifrei Pinhas 142 (Num. 28:2), p. 53a; Tossefta Shabbat XVI; Yalkut Shim'oni, Pinhas 782.
92. Mekhilta Ki Tissa, Messikhta DeShabta 1 (Exod. 31:14), pp. 110a-b.
93. Cf. TY Yoma VIII, 5; Tanhuma, Yitro 8.
94. Cf. Zohar III, 122b.
95. Exod. 25:8; cf. Exod. 29:45-46; Ezek. 37:27. Cf. Tikkunei HaZohar, 22b; Alshekh on Exod. 25:8; Shelah, I, p. 117a; R. Hayyim of Volozhin, *Nefesh HaHayyim*, 1:4, p. 8. R. Ze'ev Wolf of Zhitomir, *Or HaMeir, Devarim*. See *Reshit Hokhmah, Sha'ar HaAhavah*, 6; *Or HaHayyim* on Lev. 26:11.
96. Cf. TB Shabbat 132a; Yoma 82a; 83a; 84b; 85a. Tanhuma, Mass'ei 1. See TB Shabbat 151b; Num. R. 23:1.
97. Cf. Mishnah Yoma VIII, 6; TB Yoma 83a; TY Yoma VIII, 5; Tanhuma, Yitro 8; cf. Tossefta Shabbat XVI. Cf. Ramban on Exod. 31:13. See *Shulhan Arukh, Yoreh Deyah*, 263:1-3. Cf. Avinoam Bezalel Safran, *Medicine and Judaism* (Forum for Jewish Thought, Tel-Aviv, 1971).
98. See Rambam, *Mishneh Torah, Hilkhot Shabbat*, II; *Shulhan Arukh, Orah Hayyim*, 328 and the commentators ad loc. Cf. TY Yoma VIII, 5. See R. Tsevi Elimelech of Dynow, *Bnei Issakhar*, I, p. 104a-b. See also TB Yoma 83-84; Ketuvot 15b. Cf. Avinoam Bezalel Safran, "Médicine et Halakhah: Les transplantations" (*Revue Juive*, Zurich, 14 and 21 January 1972).
99. Cf. Zohar III, 29a-b; 124b; 152b. TB Hullin 111a; Shabbat 119. Cf. Rabbi B.Z. Safran, *She'elot UTeshuvot Harbaz*, I, p. 19.
100. Lev. 18:5; cf. TB Yoma 85b. See Ezek. 20:11-12. Rambam, *Mishneh Torah, Hilkhot Yessodei HaTorah*, V, 1. *Shulhan Arukh, Yoreh Deyah*, 157. See also Lev. 22:32. TB Sanhedrin 74a; Avodah Zarah 54a. Rambam, *Hilkhot Yessodei HaTorah*, V, 2s.
101. Cf. Sifra (Ahrei 12, p. 85b) and Rashi on Lev. 18:5; cf. Exod. R. 25:16. Cf. Rambam, *Mishneh Torah, Hilkhot Shabbat*, XXX, 15.
102. Cf. Zohar Hadash, Bereshit 22a; Tikkunei HaZohar, 6; 19. *Perushei Maharal MiPrag LeAggadot HaShas* on TB Shabbat 118a (II, pp. 96-97). Abrabanel on Exod. 31:12. *Sefat Emet*, II, p. 91. Cf. also Yalkut Shim'oni, Beshalah 16:261.
103. Cf. Mekhilta Beshalah, Messikhta DeVaYassa 1 (Exod. 15:25), p. 54a; cf. Zohar III, 113a.
104. Cf. *Kuzari*, III, 10.
105. See Rambam, *Moreh Nevukhim* II, 31; *Tanya, Kuntress Aharon*, p. 163; *Mishnah Berurah*, III, *Hakdamah, Hilkhot Shabbat*.
106. Cf. Mekhilta Yitro, Messikhta DeBaHodesh 7 (Exod. 20:8), p. 77a; *Kuzari*, III, 9; *Perushei HaTorah LeRabbi Yehuda HeHassid*, Yitro 20:11, p. 99; *Perushei Maharal MiPrag LeAggadot HaShas* on TB Sotah 35b (I, pp. 63-64); *Or HaHayyim* on Exod. 31:16; R. Levi Yitshak of Berditchev, *Kedushat Levi*, p. 47; Hermann Cohen, *Die Religion der Vernunft aus den Quellen des Judentums*, p. 181. See TB Sanhedrin 58b; Deut. R. 1:18.
107. Cf. R. Hayyim Vital, *Ets Hayyim*, 1; Philon of Alexandria, *De opificio*

mundi, 5:21; Rashi on TB Sanhedrin 81b.
108. Cf. M.D. Cassuto, *MeAdam Ad Noah*, pp. 40-43; idem, *Perush Al Sefer Shemot*, p. 169.
109. Cf. TB Shabbat 156a-b; Tikkunei HaZohar, 70 (124b); cf. Zohar III, 227b. See also Pirkei DeRabbi Eliezer 6; Maharsha on TB Shabbat 156a; R. Yonathan Ebeschutz, *Ya'arot Devash*, 2.
110. Tanhuma, VaYera 1. See TB Moed Katan 24a; Gen. R. 100:7; Zohar I, 48a-b; *Sefer HaHinukh, Mitzvah* 114. Shelah, II, p. 7a; III, p. 114b. See also TB Ta'anit 29b; *Shulhan Arukh, Orah Hayyim*, 552:10.
111. Cf. *Sefer HaZohar Im Perush HaSulam*, IV, Yitro, p. 135 (529); Zohar Hadash, 44a; Rabbeinu Bahya on Exod. 20:8 (II, p. 198). Cf. *Shem MiShemuel, Bereshit*, I, p. 291; *Shemot*, II, p. 277; *Devarim*, p. 180. Cf. *Sefat Emet*, V, p. 164. *Be'er Avraham*, p. 184.
112. Cf. TY Shabbat XV, 3; Lev. R. 34:15; Tanhuma, VaYera 2; Zohar II, 169a; Shelah, *Siddur Sha'ar HaShamayim*, p. 385; cf. also Zohar II, 205a; TB Pessahim 112b. Cf. R. Eliyahu of Vilna, *Siddur Ishei Yisrael*, p. 217; R. Yossef Hayyim of Baghdad, *She'elot UTeshuvot Torah Shelemah*, pp. 85-86.
113. Cf. Zohar II, 88b; 204a; III, 95a; 105a. TB Shabbat 65b; Tanhuma, Ki Tissa 33; Pesikta Rabbati, 23; Zohar II, 130a; 135b; III, 243b; Zohar Hadash, Ruth 79, 97.
114. Cf. TB Shabbat 14a; Moed Katan 24a; Ta'anit 29b. Zohar III, 135a; 176b. Yalkut Shim'oni, Mishlei 31:564; *Shulhan Arukh, Orah Hayyim*, 287, 288, 652; Shelah, II, p. 7a; *Or HaHayim* on Gen. 47:28.
115. Cf. TB Shabbat 10b; cf. also Zohar Hadash, Yitro 41a.
116. Cf. Zech. 14:9.
117. 2 Sam. 7:23; cf. TB Berakhot 6a; Num. R. 14:11.
118. Cf. Zohar III, 176b.
119. Cf. *Sefat Emet*, I, p. 13; II, p. 79.
120. Cf. TB Shabbat 117b-118a; TB Pessahim 68b; 105a. Zohar I, 48b; II, 88a-b; 204b; III, 273a.
121. Cf. Zohar II, 204a. Cf. *Sefat Emet*, I, p. 80; *Neot HaDesheh*, pp. 136-37; *Shem MiShemuel, Bemidbar*, pp. 114, 144.
122. Cf. Mekhilta Beshalah, Messikhta DiVaYassa V (Exod. 16:25), p. 59a; TB Shabbat 117b; cf. *Shulhan Arukh, Orah Hayyim*, 291 and Rema ad loc., 291:1.
123. Cf. Gen. 2:4.
124. Cf. Deut. 27:9; TB Berakhot 63b.
125. Cf. Joel 3:4.
126. See R. Yitshak Luria (the Ari HaKadosh), *Likkutei Torah*, p. 13.
127. Cf. Zohar II, 88a-b.
128. Cf. TB Shabbat 117-119. Zohar II, 204b; III, 273a.
129. See *Shem MiShemuel, Bemidbar*, p. 341.
130. Cf. Maharsha, *Hiddushei Aggadot*, on Berakhot 64a. Shelah, I, p. 25a. Rabbi J.Z. Meklenburg, *HaKetav VeHaKabbalah*, I, p. 41a; II, p. 49a. *Sefat Emet*, I, p. 211; *Shem MiShemuel, Moadim*, p. 90. Rabbi Baruch HaLevi Epstein, *Tossefet Berakhah*, V, pp. 38-39. Philon of Alexandria, *Spec.* II, 64; *Fug.* 176. Esther Starobinski-Safran, *"De Fuga et Inventione," by Philon d'Alexandria*, pp. 83-84.

131. Cf. Exod. 31:13; TB Shabbat 10b. *Likkutei Moharan*, I, 83, p. 38b; 111, p. 101a; II, 17, p. 21b; *Siddur Sha'arei Ratson*, pp. 608, 610; *Haggada Shel Pessah*, p. 17. *Sefat Emet*, II, pp. 75, 203. R. Abraham of Slonim, *Be'er Avraham*, p. 118; *Bet Avraham*, p. 197.
132. Cf. TY Berakhot V, 2. See Zohar II, 25a; 141b.
133. Cf. Zohar III, 12a; *Sefat Emet*, V, pp. 163, 165. See Gen. 4:1.
134. Cf. Exod. 31:13. Rabbi S.R. Hirsch on Exod. 31:13 (II, p. 455). *Sefat Emet*, II, p. 203.
135. Cf. TB Shabbat 10b; cf. Zohar II, 25a; 221a; III, 122b. Tikkunei HaZohar, 18 (37a). Shelah, I, p. 11a. R. Abraham of Slonim, *Yessod HaAvodah*, p. 89.
136. Cf. Isa. 11:9 (cf. also Isa. 5:13). Cf. Zohar Hadash, Yitro 41a; Zohar II, 221a.
137. Cf. R. Ya'akov Ben Asher, *Tur, Orah Hayyim*, 268; R. Yossef Karo, *Shulhan Arukh, Orah Hayyim*, 268; R. David HaLevi Segal, *Turei Zahav* on *Shulhan Arukh, Orah Hayyim*, 268:5. Cf. also Rabbi S.R. Hirsch, *The Hirsch Siddur*, pp. 277-79. Cf. *Sefat Emet*, II, p. 6. Cf. Zohar II, 90a. See TB Shevuot 30b. Cf. Rabbi B.Z. Safran, *She'elot UTeshuvot Harbaz*, I, pp. 20-21.
138. Cf. R. Moshe Isserles ("the Rema") on *Shulhan Arukh, Orah Hayyim*, 271:10.
139. Cf. Ps. 33:9. See Rambam, *Moreh Nevukhim*, I, 67.
140. Cf. Gen. 2:7 and Targum Onkelos ad loc.
141. Ps. 33:6; TB Shabbat 119b. Cf. TB Rosh HaShanah 32a. Cf. *Neot HaDesheh*, p. 55. See Gen. R. 44:26.
142. Avot V, 1.
143. Cf. Exod. 34:28; TB Bava Kama 54b-55a.
144. *Avnei Nezer*, p. 95.
145. Idem, ibidem, p. 65. Cf. *Likkutei Moharan*, 91, p. 41a. See TB Shabbat 63a; see also TB Makot 11a.
146. Cf. Ibn Ezra and *Ha'amek Davar* on Deut. 26:17; *Sefat Emet*, IV, p. 62; *Bnei Issakhar*, II, p. 20b; *Shem MiShemuel, Moadim*, p. 110. See also Ramban and *Or HaHayim* on Lev. 21:1. See Mekhilta and Rashi on Exod. 19:3; Zohar II, 79b; Ari HaKadosh, *Likkutei Torah*, Yitro, p. 122; Shelah, *Siddur Sha'ar HaShamayim*, II, p. 11.
147. Cf. Mishnah Yevamot II, 1, et al. See Zohar III, 17b; *Divrei Shemuel*, pp. 96-98. About the rather irrelational character of the Holy word of creation, of the holy Act of creation, see Zohar I, 232b. See also Rambam, *Moreh Nevukhim*, I, 65, 66, 67. About *Amirah* and *Dibbur*, see also Sifrei Beha'alotkha 99 (Num. 12:1), p. 26b; Pesikta Zutarta, Va'era 6:2; Exod. R. 42:1-2; Tanhuma, Tsav 13; TB Makot 11a; Rashi on Num. 12:1.
148. Cf. Zohar I, 67; III, 185a. See Sifra DiTseniuta II, 11, with the commentary *Netivot Yair* of R. BenZion Moshe Yair Weinstock (Jerusalem, 5735), pp. 145-46.
149. Cf. Zohar II, 90a.
150. Cf. Zohar I, 158b; cf. also Gen. R. 1:4.
151. See supra, p. 260.
152. Rashi on Exod. 31:13.
153. Cf. Pirkei DeRabbi Eliezer 18; TB Beitsa 15b; 16a; Zohar II, 63b. Cf. Exod. 4:22.
154. Cf. R. Ya'akov Yossef of Polonnoye, *Toldot Ya'akov Yossef*, Beshalah; *Biurei*

HaGra Al Aggadot, II, *Likkutei HaGra*, p. 72; *Divrei Shemuel*, p. 15; R. Nahman of Bratslav, *Haggadah*, p. 31; *Sefat Emet*, I, pp. 13, 54, 102; II, p. 145; III, pp. 189, 192; IV, p. 194; V, pp. 30, 31, 99, 167. *Avnei Nezer*, pp. 103-4. *Shem MiShemuel, Bereshit,* I, p. 223; *Shemot*, II, pp. 266, 279. Cf. also *Kuzari*, III, 5.

155. Cf. TB Shabbat 33b.
156. Cf. Tikkunei HaZohar, 19 (38a). Shelah, I, p. 142a; *Toldot Ya'akov Yossef*, VaYehi; *Divrei Shemuel*, p. 2; *Likkutei Moharan*, II, 72, p. 33a. *Shem MiShemuel, Bereshit*, I, pp. 203, 270; II, p. 335; *Bemidbar*, p. 398; *Devarim*, p. 199. See also TB Beitsa 16a; *Sefat Emet*, II, p. 208. Cf. Sefer Yetsirah II, 4; *Shem MiShemuel, Devarim*, p. 99. Cf. R. Yossef Hayyim of Baghdad, *Ben Ish Hai*, p. 102.
157. Cf. TB Beitsa 16a. Zohar I, 48a; II, 88b; 204a; III, 95a; 173a; 242b. Tikkunei HaZohar, Hakdamah, 13b.
158. Cf. Prov. 1:7; Ps. 111:10. Zohar III, 122b; cf. also Rambam, *Mishneh Torah, Hilkhot Yessodei HaTorah*, II, 2. *Shem MiShemuel, Moadim*, p. 180.
159. Cf. TY Demai IV, 1; Ramban on Exod. 20:8; Tikkunei HaZohar, 73a.
160. Cf. TB Yevamot 6b; *Sefat Emet*, I, p. 14; V, p. 240; *Be'er Avraham*, pp. 111, 194; cf. Zohar I, 11b. See also Ramban on Exod. 20:8; Recanati, Yitro, p. 9a.
161. *Kuzari*, I, 25; Ibn Ezra on Exod. 20:2; Ramban on Exod. 20:2 (*Kitvei Ramban* I, pp. 388-89); Rabbeinu Bahya on Exod. 20:2 (II, p. 186-87). *Kedushat Levi*, pp. 45b-46a, 68b-69a; Lev. 23:15; TB Menahot 65b.
162. Cf. Exod. 19:4. Rashi on Deut. 11:7. Ramban on Exod. 6:3, 20:2; Deut. 5:12, 5:15. Rabbeinu Bahya on Exod. 20:2. *Or HaHayim* on Exod. 10:1. *Kli Yakar* on Exod. 6:3. *Kuzari*, II, 54. *Ikkarim*, III, 26; *Sefer HaHinukh*, 31:306. Maharal, *Tiferet Yisrael*, 12, 44. Shelah, *Siddur Sha'ar HaShamayim*, p. 514. R. Dov Baer of Mezerich, *Maggid Devarav LeYa'akov*, 62:133. *Likkutei Moharan*, I, 64:6, p. 79b. *Sefat Emet*, II, p. 88; V, p. 165. *Shem MiShemuel, Bemidbar*, pp. 42-45. R. Simha Bunem of Przysucha, *Midrash Simhah*, I, p. 108. *Tossefet Berakhah*, II, p. 176. See also TB Pessahim 116b.
163. See Tanhuma and Rashi on Deut. 26:16; cf. Rashi on Deut. 6:6.
164. Cf. Ramban on Deut. 4:9.
165. Regarding the Shabbat preceding Pessah which is traditionally called *Shabbat HaGadol*, see *Tur* and *Shulhan Arukh, Orah Hayyim*, 430.
166. Cf. *Kuzari*, I, 25.
167. Cf. Zohar I, 87b; 205b. Pesikta Rabbati, 34; See Gen. R. 1:4; Isa. 44:25, 45:12. Shir HaShirim R. 7:1; Ps. 75:4. Exod. R. 3:6.
168. Ramban on Deut. 5:15. Cf. Zohar II, 38a.
169. *Kedushat Levi*, pp. 68b-69a.
170. Cf. Ramban on Gen. 26:5; cf. also TB Yevamot 46a and Rashi ad loc.; cf. also Rambam, *Mishneh Torah, Hilkhot Issurei Bi'ah*, XIII. See supra, p. 000.
171. Cf. *Sefer HaZohar Im Perush HaSulam*, V, VaYakhel, p. 61; cf. also Num. R. 14:17; Zohar Hadash, Toldot 34a; cf. also Exod. R. 1:32.
172. Cf. *Kuzari*, I, 86-87; Malbim on Gen. 2:1-3.
173. Cf. *Kli Yakar* on Exod. 16:15-18; idem on Lev. 25:20.
174. Cf. TB Beitsa 16a; Abrabanel on Exod. 15; *Kedushat Levi*, pp. 37, 55.
175. Cf. Exod. R. 25:15; cf. *Sefat Emet*, II, p. 74; cf. Rabbi S.R. Hirsch on Exod. 16:23, p. 174; cf. M.D. Cassuto, *Perush Al Sefer Shemot*, pp. 131-32.

176. See Exod. 16:16-20; cf. Zohar III, 105b.
177. Cf. TB Yoma 76a; Rashi, Rashbam, Ibn Ezra, Seforno and *Or HaHayyim* on Exod. 16:4.
178. See also TB Haggigah 12b; Shelah, *Siddur Sha'ar HaShamayim*, p. 525.
179. Cf. Zohar II, 88. Cf. TB Yoma 74b; Zohar III, 105b; Rashi on Exod. 16:22; Ramban, *Sefer HaEmunah VeHaBitahon*, (*Kitvei Ramban* II), p. 353; *Meshekh Hokhmah*, p. 64; *Be'er Avraham*, p. 50.
180. Cf. Gen. R. 11:2.
181. Cf. Maharal, *Tiferet Yisrael*, 26, p. 55b.
182. Cf. TB Beitsa 16a; Zohar III, 242b; Hakdamat Tikkunei HaZohar, 13b; Tikkunei HaZohar, 19:21. See Ibn Ezra on Exod. 20:8.
183. Cf. Exod. R. 25:3.
184. See Tanhuma, Beshalah 20. TB Yoma 75a.
185. Cf. TB Shabbat 119a.
186. Cf. Mekhilta Beshalah, Messikhta DeVaYassa V (Exod. 16:22), p. 58b; Rashi on Exod. 16:22.
187. See TB Yoma 75b; Num. R. 7:4; R. Hayyim of Volozhin, *Ruah Hayyim*, on Avot III, 3 (pp. 48-49).
188. Cf. Mekhilta Beshalah, Messikhta DeVaYassa IV, V. TB Yoma 74b; 75b. Zohar II, 62a-63b; 88b; 156b.
189. Exod. 16:29; Exod. R. 25:15. Cf. TB Shabbat 87b and Tossafot ad loc.; Sanhedrin 56b. Yalkut Shim'oni, Beshalah 16:261; Rashi on Deut. 5:12.
190. Cf. Abrabanel and Rashbam ad loc.
191. Cf. Seforno on Deut. 5:12.
192. *Sefat Emet*, III, p. 209.
193. Rashi on Exod. 16:29.
194. Cf. *Kuzari*, I, 86-87.
195. Cf. Exod. 15:25; TB Sanhedrin 96b. Cf. *Sefat Emet*, II, p. 74; IV, p. 21; cf. Mekhilta Beshalah, Messikhta DeVaYassa I (Exod. 15:25), p. 54a; see also Ramban on Exod. 15:25.
196. Cf. Pirkei DeRabbi Eliezer 18; *Be'er Avraham*, p. 285; *Shem MiShemuel*, *Bemidbar*, p. 10.
197. Cf. Exod. 19:5; cf. also Exod. 24:7-8. Cf. *Sefat Emet*, IV, p. 21.
198. Cf. Lev. R. 27:10. *Perush Maharal MiPrag LeAggadot HaShas* on TB Nedarim 31b (I, p. 7); *Turei Zahav* and *Biurei HaGra* on *Shulhan Arukh*, *Yoreh Deyah*, 265; *Kli Yakar* on Lev. 9:1; R. Israel of Koznitz, *Avodat Yisrael*, p. 74.
199. Cf. also Rabbeinu Bahya on Exod. 20:8 (II, pp. 197-98); *Shem MiShemuel*, *Bereshit*, I, p. 93.
200. TB Shabbat 86b; cf. Zohar III, 273a.
201. Maharal, *Derekh Hayyim*, p. 9; cf. idem, *Tiferet Yisrael*, 40, p. 50b.
202. Mekhilta Beshalah, Messikhta DeVaYassa V (Exod. 16:29), p. 59b. Cf. Yalkut Shim'oni, Beshalah 16:261. Cf. Zohar Hadash, Yitro 42b. Cf. *Sefer HaZohar Im Perush HaSulam*, V, VaYakhel, pp. 62, 66-67. Cf. *Kuzari*, III, 10. Cf. *Tur* and *Shulhan Arukh*, *Orah Hayyim*, 267. Cf. *Neot HaDesheh*, p. 109. See also Esther R. 7; *Or HaHayyim* on Gen. 2:3.
203. Zohar II, 123b.

204. Hermann Cohen, *Die Religion der Vernunft aus den Quellen des Judentums* (Leipzig, 1919), p. 184.
205. Cf. TB Shabbat 86b.
206. Cf. Tana Devei Eliyahu 1; Yalkut Shim'oni, Tehillim 139:888; cf. also *Sefat Emet*, II, p. 77.
207. Cf. Shelah, II, p. 10b s.; R. Yoel Teitelbaum of Satmar, *Haggadah Shel Pessah Im Perush MaHaRi TaB* (New York, 5729/1959), p. 11.
208. Rashi on Exod. 31:13.
209. Cf. Mekhilta Ki Tissa, Messikhta DeShabta 1 (Exod. 31:14), p. 110a.
210. It is interesting to mention here a remark made by a great halakhic authority, R. Meir Simha Kohen of Dvinsk (the author of *Or Sameah*, an important commentary on the halakhic work of the Rambam), who writes: "Let us not wonder that the observance of Shabbat is set aside in the case of *pikkuah nefesh*, when even one soul in [the people of] Israel is in danger or even there is only a risk of danger menacing a man's life. In fact, the holiness of the Shabbat cannot be weighed against the soul of a Jew (in the case of a Jew's life being endangered). For if Israel is not alive in the world, there will be no Shabbat in the world any more. And who will then testify [as to the origin of the world and its Creator]? Moreover, if a Jew does not respect the Shabbat, he should be thought of as one who excludes his soul from the powerful bond tying the community of Israel to God and His Torah." (*Meshekh Hokhmah*, pp. 92-93).
211. R. Shemuel of Sochaczew sees both aspects of the Shabbat revealed in the *Zakhor* (Exod. 20:8) and in the *Shamor* (Deut. 5:12). The *mitzvah* of *Zakhor*, "think of the Shabbat day," calls on all Jews, individually, to *think* of the Shabbat, each according to his *personal* ability. The *mitzvah* of *Shamor*, calling to "keep the Shabbat day," compels the whole *community* of Israel, including all its members, to observe the Shabbat *in practice* (cf. *Shem MiShemuel, VaYikra*, p. 318; *Bemidbar*, p. 8). R. Avraham of Sochaczew (father of Rabbi Shemuel of Sochaczew) sees both aspects of the Shabbat revealed historically: the communal Shabbat in Mara (Exod. 15-16; cf. TB Shabbat 87b); the individual Shabbat in Sinai (Exod. 20). (*Avnei Nezer*, p. 75.)
212. Exod. 31:16.
213. Cf. Lev. 19:3; cf. TB Beitsa 16a.
214. Cf. Exod. 35:1-2.
215. Cf. TB Shabbat 118b.
216. Isa. 56:4-7.
217. Israel is the Shabbat's guardian. This is why the Talmud and the codifiers of Jewish Law severely chastize any Jew who "desecrates the Shabbat *in public.*" Such a Jew is considered "as idolatrous," strengthening idolatry in the world. The Jew must therefore avoid transgressing laws regarding the Shabbat, mostly *Mipnei Mar'it HaAyin*, "so that the eye cannot see," so that the bad example given by the one who "desecrates" the Shabbat, which heralds God, does not prompt others to do the same (cf. TB Beitsa 9a). The Jew who "sanctifies" the Shabbat "sanctifies God's name;" the Jew who "desecrates" the Shabbat "desecrates the name of God."

218. See also Recanati, Bereshit, p. 8a; Abrabanel, Yitro 11, p. 190; HaGra, *Siddur Ishei Yisrael*, p. 222.
219. See also Sefer HaBahir, 52, p. 30. Sifra DiTseniuta (Vilna ed., 1882), I, with *Biur HaGra*, pp. 14-16; V, with *Biur HaGra*, p. 66. Maharal, *Tiferet Yisrael*, 40. *Be'er Avraham*, p. 51; R. Yossef Hayyim of Baghdad, *Ben Ish Hai*, pp. 98, 100; *Tossefet Berakhah*, I, p. 75; R.M. Grossberg, *Tsefunot HaRogachovi*, p. 3.
220. Cf. TB Menahot 65b; *Shulhan Arukh, Orah Hayyim*, 489:7-8; *Sefer HaHinukh, Mitzvah* 306. See also TB Berakhot 63b.
221. Avot I, 14.
222. Cf. R. Nahman of Bratslav, *Siddur Sha'arei Ratson*, pp. 206, 345, 843-45; *Sefat Emet*, III, p. 207. See also Zohar I, 224a; *Or HaHayyim* on Gen. 47:29.
223. Cf. Shelah, II, pp. 11a, 16a; II, p. 45a. Cf. *Sefat Emet*, I, pp. 5-6. Cf. R. Yossef Dov Baer of Volozhin, *Bet HaLevi*, p. 9.
224. Cf. Gen. R. 11:2; Kohelet R. 11:5; Pesikta Rabbati, *Asseret HaDibrot*, 3; cf. Zohar II, 290a; *Sefer HaZohar Im Perush HaSulam*, V, VaYakhel, p. 60. See Rashi on TB Bava Metsia 58a; Rambam, *Hilkhot Ishut*, XIV, 6; 9.
225. Cf. Lev. 23:15. Cf. Shelah, III, p. 129b.
226. Cf. Lev. 23:15; cf. Sifra, Rashi and other biblical commentaries on Lev. 23:2-3; cf. TB Yevamot 93a. Cf. Abrabanel, Yitro, Exod. 20:8 (II, pp. 180, 190). Cf. Shelah, I, pp. 176a, 195b-196a; cf. Maharsha, *Hiddushei Aggadot*, on TB Yoma 2a; cf. Gen. R. 60:15; Zohar I, 133a. R. Eliyahu of Vilna, *Divrei Eliyahu*, p. 29. *Shem MiShemuel, Bereshit*, I, p. 123. Cf. Yitshak Breuer, *Nahliel* (Tel-Aviv, 5711/1951), p. 65. *Ben Ish Hai*, p. 133.
227. Cf. Shelah, I, p. 188a; *Avnei Nezer*, p. 103; cf. Lev. 23:2. Cf. Zohar I, 5a-b; III, 94-95. *Reshit Hokhmah, Sha'ar HaKedushah*, 2. Shelah, I, p. 188a. *Shem MiShemuel, Shemot*, I, p. 318. TY Rosh HaShanah I, 3. TB Beitsa 17a; Exod. R. 16:3. Cf. *Ben Ish Hai*, p. 99.
228. Cf. R. Levi Yitshak of Berditchev, *Kedushat Levi*, p. 37a. See also TB Rosh HaShanah 24a; TY Sanhedrin I, 2. Lev. 23:2, 23:4.
229. See Zohar III, 81b; 94a. (See also Zohar II, 47a.) Cf. Rabbi B.Z. Safran, *She'elot UTeshuvot Harbaz*, I, p. 19.
230. Cf. *Sefat Emet*, I, pp. 9, 87; *Neot HaDesheh*, p. 92. Cf. Rashi on Exod. 31:15. Cf. also Maharal, *Gevurot HaShem*, p. 159; *Perushei Maharal MiPrag LeAggadot HaShas* on Shabbat 118a (II, pp. 96-97).
231. Cf. TB Berakhot 57b; Zohar I, 1b; 5b; 48a; III, 95a. Otiyot DeRabbi Akiva, A. *Kuzari*, V, 10. *Kedushat Levi*, p. 51. R. Nahman of Bratslav, *Likkutei Moharan*, II, 72, p. 33a. R. Aharon of Karlin, *Bet Aharon*, p. 144a. *Sefat Emet*, I, pp. 6, 17, 247; II, p. 153; V, pp. 57, 198. *Shem MiShemuel, Bereshit*, I, p. 265; *Moadim*, p. 101.
232. Cf. TB Shabbat 118a and Rashi ad loc.; TB Pessahim 113a. Pirkei DeRabbi Eliezer 18; Rashi on Exod. 31:15; *Tanya*, p. 13. See *Perushei Maharal MiPrag LeAggadot HaShas* on Shabbat 118a, (II, pp. 95-96). See also R. Yossef Hayyim of Baghdad, *Ben Yehoyada*, II, pp. 19-20.
233. Cf. Gen. R. 11:8.
234. Cf. Exod. 15:25; Mekhilta and Maharal (*Gur Aryeh*) ad loc.
235. Cf. TB Haggigah 12. See Ari HaKadosh, *Likkutei Torah* and R. Hayyim Vital, *Ta'amei HaMitzvot*, Beshalah, p. 60.

236. Isa. 40:28.
237. Cf. Zohar III, 119b; II, 257a; Philon of Alexandria, *De Decalogo*, 20, 100-101; cf. also Mekhilta on Exod. 20:11. Cf. *Sefat Emet*, I, p. 159. *Shem MiShemuel, Bereshit*, I, pp. 20, 25, 28; II, pp. 57-58.
238. Cf. Gen. R. 11:8. TB Shabbat 118a. Cf. *Shem MiShemuel, Bereshit*, I, pp. 28-29; II, pp. 57-59.
239. Cf. Shelah, III, p. 129b.
240. Cf. *Kedushat Levi*, p. 57b; *Tanya, Kuntress Aharon*, p. 163. Cf. *Sefat Emet*, I, pp. 9, 13; II, pp. 198, 208, 210; III, p. 153; IV, p. 68. Cf. *Shem MiShemuel, Bereshit*, II, p. 359; *Devarim*, pp. 53, 183; *Moadim*, p. 135. Cf. R. Yossef Hayyim of Baghdad, *She'elot UTeshuvot Torah Sheleimah*, p. 329. See TB Beitsa 16a; Zohar II, 205a.
241. Cf. *Be'er Avraham*, pp. 50, 146. Cf. Zohar Hadash, Yitro 47b; Tikkunei HaZohar, 19. Cf. *Sefat Emet*, I, pp. 198, 247; II, pp. 84-85; *Shem MiShemuel, Devarim*, p. 6. Cf. TB Berakhot 57b. Zohar I, 2; 48a; III, 95a. Zohar Hadash, Bereshit 16. Cf. Shoher Tov, 13. Cf. Exod. 33:13; TB Berakhot 7a. Isa. 55:8-9. Mishnah Berakhot IX, 2. TB Berakhot 54a; 58b; 59b; Pessahim 50a. Zohar II, 174a.
242. Cf. Isa. 60:2-19. Gen. R. 11:2, 91:13. (Exod. R. 18:9; Isa. 30:26.) Lev. R. 30:2. Deut. R. 1:13. Yalkut Shim'oni, Bereshit 6:47. TB Ta'anit 8b. Zohar I, 21a; 203b; II, 135b. *Perushei HaTorah LeRabbi Yehuda HeHassid* on Gen. 2:3 (p. 6). *Sefat Emet*, II, p. 81; III, p. 26. R. Yossef Hayyim of Baghdad, *Ben Ish Hai*, p. 83.
243. TY Berakhot VIII, 5.
244. Zech. 14:7; cf. Zohar I, 113a; II, 17a; Pirkei DeRabbi Eliezer 18; *Biurei HaGra Al Aggadot*, II, *Likkutei HaGra*, p. 73.
245. Cf. Zohar II, 63b; 204a.
246. Cf. Zohar II, 63b; R. Yossef Dov Baer of Volozhin, *Bet HaLevi*, p. 9. *Sefat Emet*, I, p. 5; III, pp. 188-89; IV, p. 67.
247. Cf. Zohar III, 92b; Rabbeinu Bahya on Exod. 20:8 (p. 198); Maharal, *Derashot, Derush Al HaTorah*, p. 39; R. Ya'akov Yossef of Polonnoye, *Hakdamah*; R. Avraham Yehuda Heshel of Apta, *Ohev Yisrael*, VaEthanan; *Sefat Emet*, IV, p. 21; *Shem MiShemuel, VaYikra*, p. 325.
248. Cf. Zohar I, 5b; II, 97b; R. Ya'akov Yossef of Polonnoye, *Toldot Ya'akov Yossef*, VaYeitsei; *Kedushat Levi*, p. 69a; *Divrei Shemuel*, p. 77; *Sefat Emet*, I, pp. 14, 17, 102; *Shem MiShemuel, Devarim*, p. 178; *Be'er Avraham*, p. 110.
249. Cf. Zohar III, 176b; Shelah, *Siddur Sha'ar Hashamayim*, p. 385; *Sefat Emet*, I, p. 74.
250. Ari HaKadosh, *Likkutei Torah*, p. 13.
251. Cf. Maharal, *Gevurot HaShem*, pp. 159-60; *Kedushat Levi*, p. 55; *Neot HaDesheh*, p. 105; *Shem MiShemuel, VaYikra*, pp. 140, 352-53.
252. Cf. also Zohar I, 9a. See also R. Eliyahu of Vilna, *Divrei Eliyahu*, p. 4.
253. Cf. R. Ya'akov Ben Asher, *Ba'al HaTurim*, on Gen. 1:1; R. Eliyahu of Vilna on Gen. 1:1. *Aderet Eliyahu*, p. 17; M.D. Cassuto, *MeAdam Ad Noah*, p. 6; Esther Starobinski-Safran, "Sabbats, années sabbatiques et jubilés" (in *Mélanges*, E. Bréguet, Geneva, 1975).
254. Cf. TB Berakhot 29a; cf. Zohar I, 24a; II, 206a. Cf. Shelah, *Siddur Sha'ar HaShamayim*, p. 372. Cf. Exod. R. 28:4; Ramban on Exod. 19:20; Rabbeinu

Bahya on Exod. 20:1 (p. 184); idem on Deut. 5:19 (p. 272). See also Recanati, Bereshit, pp. 8-9.
255. Cf. *Ba'al HaTurim* on Gen. 1:1.
256. *Ba'al HaTurim* on Exod. 20:8.
257. Ps. 68:5.
258. Ps. 96:10.
259. Gen. 5:22.
260. Exod. 19:3.
261. 1 Chron. 2:15.
262. Exod. 23:11.
263. Lev. 25:10.
264. Gen. 2:3.
265. Lev. 23:24.
266. Lev. R. 29:9; cf. Zohar III, 108b. Cf. Zohar I, 253b. Zohar Hadash, Bereshit 9a, 12a. Pirkei DeRabbi Eliezer 19. Cf. R. Yossef Gikatilla, *Ginat Egoz*, p. 40; Rabbeinu Bahya on Lev. 25:2 (II, pp. 563-64).
267. Cf. Zohar II, 222b; Tikkunei HaZohar, 22 (67b); Recanati, Yitro, p. 9a; Rabbeinu Bahya on Exod. 20:8 (II, pp. 198-99); Maharal, *Gevurot HaShem*, Hakdamah Shelishit, p. 13.
268. Cf. Tikkunei HaZohar, 22 (67a); 48 (88a).
269. Cf. Zohar Hadash, Bereshit 3.
270. Cf. Tanhuma, Nasso 16; Pirkei DeRabbi Eliezer 12, 18; Shoher Tov, 92:2; Yalkut Shim'oni, Tehillim 139:888.
271. Cf. Shelah, *Siddur Sha'ar HaShamayim*, p. 385.
272. Cf. Rabbeinu Bahya on Exod. 20:1 (II, p. 184); on Exod. 20:8 (II, p. 197). Cf. Rambam, *Moreh Nevukhim*, III, 43. Cf. Maharal, *Tiferet Yisrael*, 40, pp. 49a-b. Cf. *Be'er Avraham*, p. 108; *Neot HaDesheh*, p. 120.
273. Cf. TB Haggigah 12b; Avot DeRabbi Nathan 37:9; Pirkei DeRabbi Eliezer 18; Shoher Tov, 92:2, 114:2. Cf. Tanhuma, Nasso 16. Cf. Zohar I, 32b; II, 30b; 164b.
274. Cf. Num. R. 15:7; Pirkei DeRabbi Eliezer 6; Zohar I, 34a; II, 103a.
275. Cf. TB Bava Batra 74b; Zohar I, 52a; 260b; II, 23a; III, 9b. Cf. Tikkunei HaZohar, 21 (43b); Zohar Hadash, 76a.
276. Cf. Avot DeRabbi Nathan 37:9. Cf. Zohar I, 9b; 24b; 39b. Cf. Tikkunei HaZohar, 32 (76b); 65 (95b). Cf. Lev. R. 29:9.
277. Cf. Exod. R. 28:4. Tikkunei HaZohar, 21 (45b; 47b).
278. Cf. TB Berakhot 29a; Zohar I, 24a; II, 206a; Rashi on Deut. 4:35; Ramban on Exod. 19:20; Rabbeinu Bahya on Exod. 20:1 (II, p. 184). Cf. also TB Pessahim 112a; David celebrated the "seven voices" of God's power in nature (cf. Ps. 29).
279. Cf. Num. R. 15:5; cf. also Exod. R. 15:28.
280. Cf. Zohar II, 23a.
281. Cf. Zohar I, 24b; Tikkunei HaZohar, 11 (26b); Cf. Zohar I, 24a.
282. Cf. TB Pessahim 54b; Pirkei DeRabbi Eliezer 3; Tana Devei Eliyahu Rabba 31; Tanhuma, Nasso 11; Zohar III, 34b.
283. Cf. Prov. 9:9; TB Sanhedrin 38a; Rabbeinu Bahya on Lev. 25:8 (II, pp. 564-65); R. Nahman of Bratslav, *Likkutei Moharan*, II, p. 22. — *Septem artes liberales*.

284. Cf. TB Pessahim 54b; Gen. R. 68:7; Lev. R. 36:4.
285. Cf. Sifrei Devarim 10 (Deut. 1:10), p. 67a; TB Bava Batra 17a; Massekhet Kallah III; Avot DeRabbi Nathan 37; Gen. R. 30:2; Exod. R. 44:6; Lev. R. 30:2; Tanhuma, Balak 11; Shoher Tov, 11:6; Zohar I, 82a; 247a.
286. Cf. Mic. 5:4; TB Sukkah 52b; Massekhet Kallah VII; Massekhet Derekh Erets Zuta I; Shir HaShirim R. 8:11. Cf. Zohar III, 103a-b; 301b. Cf. Zohar Hadash, Toldot 26.
287. Cf. TB Bava Batra 17a; Massekhet Kallah III; VII; Massekhet Derekh Erets Zuta I; Exod. R. 44:6; Tanhuma, Balak 11; Zohar III, 302a.
288. Cf. also TB Yoma 47a; Lev. R. 20:7; Tanhuma, Ahrei 7.
289. Cf. TB Megillah 14a; 15a; Bava Batra 15b. Tana Devei Eliyahu Rabba 28.
290. Cf. Pirkei DeRabbi Eliezer 52; Yalkut Shim'oni, Lekh Lekha 15, 77. Cf. Sifrei Beha'alotkha 83 (Num. 10:34), p. 22a; TB Sukkah 11b; Num. R. 1:2; Tanhuma, Beshalah 3; Zohar III, 103a; Tikkunei HaZohar, 21 (55a); Rashi on Num. 10:34.
291. Cf. TY Kilaim IX, 3; Ketuvot XII, 3. TB Bava Batra 74b.
292. Cf. Zohar I, 24b.
293. Cf. Deut. 7:1; Jos. 24:11; Lev. R. 17:5; Rashi on Gen. 15:19. Cf. also TB Zevahim 118b; Ketuvot 28a. Rashi on Num. 26:53. Cf. also R. Pinhas HaLevi Horowitz, *Panim Yafot*, on Deut. 7:1-6.
294. Cf. Deut. 8:8; TB Berakhot 37a; Zohar I, 157a.
295. Cf. Rambam, *Mishneh Torah, Hilkhot Bikkurim*, III, 14. Moses implored God during *seven* days to let him enter the promised land. Cf. Shir HaShirim R. 1:13. "Jericho was shut up... but the Lord said to Joshua: 'See, I have given Jericho into your hand.... You shall march around the city, all the men of war, thus shall you march for six days, and *seven* priests shall bear *seven* trumpets of rams' horns — *shofrot yovlim*. On the *seventh* day you shall march around the city *seven* times, the priests blowing the trumpets. And when they sound a long blast with the rams' horns, as soon as you hear the sound of the trumpet, then all the people shall shout with a great shout; and the wall of the city will fall down flat, and the people shall go up every man straight before him'" (Josh. 6:1-5). Before the resurrection of the dead, God will sound the horn (the *shofar*) *seven* times. Cf. Otiyot DeRabbi Akiva, 10.
296. Cf. TB Megillah 23b. Cf. Hakdamat Tikkunei HaZohar, 16b; Tikkunei HaZohar, 10: 24.
297. Cf. Ps. 90:10; TB Ta'anit 23a; Moed Katan 28a. Num. R. 14:24; Zohar I, 55a; 140a; II, 133b; 235a: Cf. also Zohar I, 78b. Cf. also Avot V, 21.
298. Cf. Gen. 46:27; Exod. 1:4; Deut. 10:22; Zohar II, 189b.
299. Cf. Num. 11:16, 11:24; TY Megillah I, 9; Sukkah V, 1. TB Sukkah 56b; Megillah 9a; Sanhedrin 2a. Massekhet Sofrim I, 8; Num. R. 13:19; Zohar III, 20a; Tikkunei HaZohar, 21: 70.
300. Cf. Zohar I, 177a.
301. Cf. Num. R. 13:15; Zohar I, 26a; 47b; 54a; II, 110b; III, 20a; 216a. Tikkunei HaZohar, 21 (47b; 50b). There are also groups of seventy *mitzvot* (cf. Lev. R. 24:5).
302. Cf. Mishnah Shekalim V, 1; TY Megillah I, 9. TB Shabbat 88b; Sukkah 55a-b; Megillah 13b; Sotah 32a; 36b; Sanhedrin 17a. Num. R. 14:22, 21:22; Shir HaShirim R. 4:2; Eihah R. 1:24; Tanhuma, Pinhas 16; Pirkei DeRabbi

Eliezer 24; Zohar I, 177a; II, 59a; 146a; 187a; III, 20a; 24b; 54b; 103b; 213b. Tikkunei HaZohar, 6 (23a); 22 (64a).
303. Cf. Zohar I, 24b; 218a; II, 129a.
304. Cf. Num. R. 13:18. Solomon built the *Bet HaMikdash* during *seven* years. Cf. 1 Kings 6:38; Lev. R. 12:4. The doors of the eastern gate in Jerusalem bore *seven* names. Cf. TY Eruvin V, 1.
305. Cf. Zohar I, 218a; II, 129a.
306. The "creation" is "completed" through Abraham, father of the Jewish people and spiritual father of humanity (cf. Gen. 17:4); it "relies" on him from now on. The history of "creation" *BeiBaram* (Gen. 2:4) becomes identified with the name of Abraham (cf. Gen. R. 12:7; Zohar I, 3b; 25a; 86b; 105a; 128b). "God gave to Abraham *seven* blessings corresponding to the *seven* verses of the work of *creation*, where it says "it was good" (Num. R. 11:4; cf. Zohar I, 78a). Abraham was *seventy* years old when God was revealed to him (cf. Num. R. 14:23; cf. also Zohar I, 78b).
307. Cf. Num. R. 14; Zohar I, 5b. Cf. Zohar II, 16b; 123a; 160b; 216a; III, 223b; 263a. Cf. Sefer HaBahir, 94; *Ba'al HaTurim* on Num. 11:16.
308. Cf. Zohar II, 207b; Tikkunei HaZohar, 24.
309. Cf. Zohar I, 5b; Zohar II, 207b.
310. Cf. Rashi on Lev. 25:18, 27:35. Cf. TB Nazir 32b. See also TB Bava Batra 75a; Zohar II, 35b; Tikkunei HaZohar, 21 (43a), regarding the periods of seventy years in the history of "returns" of natural phenomena.
311. Cf. TB Sanhedrin 99a; Zohar II, 6b-7a-b.
312. Cf. *Ma'assei Torah* 15.
313. Cf. Num. R. 14:24.
314. Cf. Rashi and Ramban on Lev. 25:2; Rabbeinu Bahya on Lev. 25:10 (II, p. 565). Cf. Maharsha on TB Sanhedrin 97a.
315. Cf. Gen. 2:3.
316. Cf. Lev. 25:13.
317. Cf. Ps. 90:4; TB Sanhedrin 97a; Num. R. 14:24; Zohar I, 261a; II, 17a.
318. R. Avraham Ben David ("the Rabad"), Rabbeinu Bahya, R. Yitshak Arama, Abrabanel, R. Ovadya Bartenora.
319. Rambam, R. Moshe Cordovero and, in part, Rashi, on TB Avodah Zarah 9a and Maharsha on TB Sanhedrin 97a.
320. Cf. Pirkei DeRabbi Eliezer 51; TB Berakhot 32a.
321. The Messiah will show *seven* miraculous things to Israel. Cf. Yalkut Shim'oni *in fine*; see also TB Rosh HaShanah 21b.
322. Cf. Mishnah Tamid VII, 4. See R. Ovadya Bartenora and *Tiferet Yisrael* ad loc. Cf. TB Berakhot 32a; Rosh HaShanah 21b; 31a; TB Sanhedrin 97a; Avodah Zarah 9a. Avot DeRabbi Nathan 1; Pirkei DeRabbi Eliezer 18, 51; Tana Devei Eliyahu Rabba 2. Cf. Zohar I, 4a; 125a; II, 10a; 20b; III, 9b; 16a; 142a. Otiyot DeRabbi Akiva, 2. Zohar Hadash, Bereshit 16; Tikkunei Zohar Hadash, Shir HaShirim 61. Cf. Ibn Ezra on Exod. 31:13; Recanati, Bereshit, p. 8b; Behar, p. 31a. Cf. Ramban on Gen. 2:3 and Lev. 25:2. Cf. Rabbeinu Bahya on Gen. 2:2-3:1 (pp. 53-54); on Lev. 25:2-10 (II, pp. 563-66). Cf. R. Yitshak Arama, *Bereshit*, IV, pp. 38-39; Abrabanel on Lev. 25. Cf. R. Yossef Gikatilla, *Sha'arei Orah*, 22-23; R. Moshe Cordovero, *Shiur Komah*, 83. Cf. Rambam, *Mishneh Torah*, *Hilkhot Teshuvah*, VIII, 8 and Rabad ad loc. Cf.

Rambam, *Moreh Nevukhim*, II, 28-29. Cf. *Sefat Emet*, II, pp. 66, 88, 91. Cf. Esther Starobinski-Safran, *Sabbats. années sabbatiques et jubilés* (thoughts on the exegesis of Leviticus 25, in *Mélanges*, E. Bréguet, Genève, 1975).
323. Cf. Tikkunei HaZohar, 30 (75b).
324. Zohar II, 184a. Cf. also Zohar I, 153b-154a, where the thoughts regarding the number seven and its developments arise from interpreting the biblical verse "And Jacob loved Rachel; and he said: I shall serve thee seven years for Rachel" (Gen. 29:18).
325. Cf. TB Sanhedrin 98a; TY Ta'anit I, 1; Shir HaShirim R. 8:16; Zohar I, 117b.
326. Cf. Lev. 8:33, 12:2, 13:4, 13:21, 23:15, 23:34. Cf. Dan. 9:24-27. Cf. TB Nazir 32b; Gen. R. 54:5; Lev. R. 24:5; Midrash Tadsheh, 6. Cf. Pirkei DeRabbi Eliezer 51; Rabbeinu Bahya on Gen. 2:3 (I, p. 54). Cf. Rashi on Lev. 25:18, 25:27, 25:35; HaGra on Isa. 11:1.
327. Cf. Avot III, 19.
328. Cf. Lev. R. 30:2; Num. R. 15:8; Tanhuma, Beha'alotkha 7; Shoher Tov, 16:2; Pirkei DeRabbi Eliezer 16.
329. Cf. Num. 7:13. Mishnah Orlah III, 7; Yoma I, 1; Avot V, 10; Menahot III, 6-7; Ohalot I, 1; Parah III, 1. TB Eruvin 19a; Pessahim 113b; Rosh HaShanah 17a; Megillah 14a; Moed Katan 20a-b; Ketuvot 59b; Sotah 10b; Sanhedrin 90a; Zevahim 98a; Menahot 27a; Niddah 31b; 83a. Massekhet Kallah IV. Avot DeRabbi Nathan, 36, 37. Pirkei DeRabbi Eliezer 11, 16, 53. Pesikta Zutarta, VaYera 20:16. Gen. R. 18:3, 52:13, 65:6, 89:7. Lev. R. 30:2. Num. R. 4:21, 14:5, 20:5, 20:16. Tanhuma, VaYeshev 6; Tsav 1; Balak 11. Shoher Tov, 11:6. Zohar I, 23b; 38a; 40a; 41a; 62b; 216b; II, 18a; 150b; 199b; 202b; 216b; 263a; III, 61a; 127a; 301a. Zohar Hadash, Bereshit 7b. Cf. Gen. 41; Zohar I, 204a. Cf. Num. 23:1; *Shem MiShemuel, Bemidbar*, p. 348. Cf. Gen. 4:15, 4:24; Ps. 79:12; Prov. 6:31; Ps. 12:7; Isa. 30:26.
330. Cf. Avot V, 8; Avot DeRabbi Nathan, 8:1; TB Megillah 15b; Yoma 54a; Gittin 57a. Tana Devei Eliyahu Rabba 30; Exod. R. 9:12, 14:3; Lev. R. 11:2; Num. R. 10:5, 14:24; Deut. R. 7:10. Tanhuma, Va'era 13; Kedoshim 15. Zohar II, 18a; Rashi on Lev. 23:18, 26:35; *Kli Yakar* on Lev. 27:23-24.
331. Cf. TB Moed Katan 20a; 27b; 28a; Massekhet Semahot III, 9; Avot DeRabbi Nathan, 32:1; Gen. R. 3:6, 27:7, 32:10; Tanhuma, Shemini 1.
332. Cf. Num. R. 11:4; cf. Zohar I, 78a.
333. Cf. TB Ketuvot 7b; Zohar III, 266b; Tikkunei HaZohar, 47 (84a). Cf. also Zohar III, 28b; Tikkunei HaZohar, 70 (124a). Cf. *Likkutei Moharan*, I, 31, p. 44a. Cf. Gen. R. 64:7; Pirkei DeRabbi Eliezer 35; the patriarchs dug *seven* wells. Cf. Tanhuma, Vezot HaBerakhah 1: Israel received *seven* blessings. Regarding the seven blessings in connection with the reading of the *Shema*, reading the Torah and the festival of Sukkot, see TB Berakhot 11a; 29a; Megillah 21a. Lev. R. 30:2.
334. Cf. TB Bava Kama 100b; Kohelet R. 1:3; Tanhuma, Pekkudei 3; Shoher Tov, 92:2; Zohar I, 146b.
335. Cf. Zohar I, 247a.
336. Cf. Sifrei Devarim 15 (Deut. 1:15), p. 68a; Massekhet Kallah VIII; Tossefta Berakhot VI, 5; TY Berakhot I, 5; Avot VI, 8; Avot DeRabbi Nathan, 37:8-9; Tana Devei Eliyahu Zuta 17; Lev. R. 30:2; Shoher Tov, 6:1; Zohar Hadash, Bereshit 8a; Rashi on Deut. 1:15.

337. Cf. Avot V, 10; Avot DeRabbi Nathan, 37:4; TY Berakhot IX, 5; Sotah V, 5. TB Sotah 22b.
338. Cf. TB Sanhedrin 56b; Avodah Zarah 2b. Gen. R. 34:7; Exod. R. 30:6; Shir HaShirim R. 1:16. Rabbeinu Bahya on Exod. 20:17 (II, p. 201).
339. See *Sefer HaHinukh* (Eshkol ed., Jerusalem, 5721/1950), pp. 374-77.
340. Cf. Avot V, 10; Tossefta Bava Kama VII, 3; Mekhilta Mishpatim, Messikhta DeNezikin 13 (Exod. 22:1), p. 96a; Pesikta Zutarta, Mishpatim 22; TB Pessahim 113b; Sanhedrin 9a. Deut. R. 8:7.
341. Cf. Avot V, 8; TY Ta'anit IV, 5; Megillah I, 12. TB Beitsa 25b; Yevamot 40a; 103a. Sanhedrin 60b. Lev. R. 22:6; Num. R. 9:7, 14:5; Eihah R. 2:5; Petihta DeEihah Rabbati, 23; Tanhuma, Nasso 1; Massekhet Derekh Erets Zuta 6; Rashi on Lev. 26:15; idem on TB Temurah 28b. Zohar II, 150b.
342. Cf. Prov. 26:25; Gen. R. 65:6; *Be'er Avraham*, p. 115. HaGra on Prov. 26:25 (*Mishlei*, Pardess ed., Tel-Aviv, p. 156). The Gra (R. Eliyahu of Vilna) sees in the *sheva toevot*, the *seven* abominations, the root of *shivim toevot*, the *seventy* abominations of the idolators.
343. Cf. TB Sukkah 52a; Zohar I, 18a; II, 263a; Zohar Hadash, Ruth 79a.
344. Cf. TB Berakhot 17a; Avot DeRabbi Nathan, 1; Zohar I, 135b; II, 83a.
345. Cf. TB Avodah Zarah 3a; Kohelet R. 1:36.
346. Cf. Zech. 14:7; Zohar II, 17a. Cf. also Ps. 139:16; Tana Devei Eliyahu Rabba 1.
347. Cf. R. Avraham of Sochaczew, *Avnei Nezer*, p. 112.
348. Cf. Ps. 12:7; Rashi on TB Rosh HaShanah 21b.
349. Cf. Recanati, Yitro, p. 9a.
350. Cf. Zohar II, 222b.
351. Cf. Zohar III, 176b.
352. Cf. *Be'er Avraham*, pp. 146, 184.
353. Cf. Zohar Hadash, Bereshit 16; R. Moshe Cordovero, *Shiur Komah*, 83.
354. Cf. Gen. R. 19:13; Num. R. 13:4; Shir HaShirim R. 5:1. Cf. also Gen. R. 54:5.
355. Cf. Isa. 54:9.
356. Cf. Rabbeinu Bahya on Exod. 20:1 (II, p. 184). Cf. also Gen. 21:31, 27:33.
357. Cf. *Sefer HaZohar Im Perush HaSulam*, IV, Yitro, p. 135 (529); Zohar Hadash, Toldot 27a; Rabbeinu Bahya on Exod. 20:8 (II, p. 198). Cf. also Ramban on Gen. 24:1.
358. The whole history of Israel is a painful process of *Kiddush HaShem*, of the "sanctification of the name" of God; it should lead to messianic times of *Kiddush HaShem*, in creative joy. The prayer of *Kaddish* which consecrates *Kiddush HaShem* and prepares and glorifies the reign of God, is recited in public by the *hazan*, *seven* times a day (cf. Shoher Tov, 6:1).
359. Cf. Tossefta Berakhot III, 14; TY Berakhot VIII, 1; Shabbat XV, 3. TB Berakhot 21a; 29a; Tanhuma, VaYera 1; cf. also TB Yoma 87b.
360. Cf. TY Berakhot VIII, 1.
361. Cf. Lev. R. 9:7; Tanhuma, Emor 14.
362. Cf. Ps. 119:164; Tossefta Berakhot VI, 5. TY Berakhot I, 5.
363. Cf. Zohar Hadash, Lekh Lekha 30b.
364. Cf. TB Bava Batra 75a, Pesikta Rabbati, 38a; Pirkei DeRabbi Eliezer 12; Zohar II; 245a; Rashi on Isa. 4:5.
365. Cf. Zohar I, 247a; cf. also TB Sanhedrin 38b.

366. Cf. Num. R. 20:5.
367. The festival which the Torah calls Hag HaMatsot, "festival of unleavened bread," we call Pessah. We sing God's praises and God sings Israel's praise. God sings Israel's praise: "They baked of the dough which they had brought out of Egypt, *ugot matsot*, unleavened cakes, for it was not leavened, because they were thrust out of Egypt and could not tarry, neither had they prepared for themselves any provisions" (Exod. 12:39); this is why the Torah calls this festival *Hag HaMatsot*, "feast of the unleavened bread," thus to praise Israel and to show its merits, celebrating its faith. And we call this feast *Pessah*, for in this way we praise God: "You shall say, It is the sacrifice of the Lord's Passover — *Zevah Pessah*, for He passed over — *passah* — the houses of the people of Israel in Egypt, when he slew the Egyptians but spared our houses" (Exod. 12:27). R. Levi Yitshak of Berditchev, *Kedushat Levi*, pp. 37a-b.
368. Cf. also Zohar I, 8a. In messianic times "seven groups of *tsaddikim* — just people — will welcome the presence of the *Shekhinah*." (Lev. R. 30:2). See also Zohar I, 261a-b.

Selected Bibliography

I. LISTING OF AUTHORS

A

Aboab, R. Yitshak	14th cent.
Abramski, R. Yehezkel	1886-1976
Abrabanel, Don Yitshak	1437-1508
Abudarham, R. David ben Yosef	13th-14th cent.
Aderet, R. Shelomo ben Avraham (Rashba)	1235-1310
Albo, R. Yossef	1380-1444
Alkabets, R. Shelomo	1505-1584
Alshekh, R. Moshe	c.1508-1600
Anav, R. Tsidkiyah ben Avraham HaRofe	1230-1300
Arama, R. Yitshak ben Moshe	1420-1494
ben Asher, R. Ya'akov (Ba'al HaTurim)	1275-1340
Ashkenazi, R. Tsevi (Hakham Tsevi)	1658-1718
Ashlag, R. Yehuda Halevi	1886-1955
Attar, R. Hayyim	1696-1743
R. Avraham, ben David (ibn David) (Rabad I of Tolédo)	1110-1180
R. Avraham, ben David of Posquíeres (Rabad III)	1120-1197
Azikri (Azkari), R. Eliezer ben Moshe	1533-1600
Azulay, R. Hayyim Yossef David (Hida)	1724-1806

B

Ba'al Shemtov, R. Yisrael	1698-1760
Ba'alei HaTossafot	12th-13th cent.
Babad, R. Yossef of Tarnopol	1800-1874
Baghdad, R. Yossef Hayyim of	1832-1909
Bahya ben Asher, Rabbeinu	1260-1340
Bahya ben Yossef ibn Pakuda, Rabbeinu	11th cent.
Berditchev, R. Levi Yitshak of	1740-1809
Berlin, R. Naftali Tsevi Yehuda of Volozhin (Netsiv)	1817-1893
Bartenora, R. Ovadyah of	c.1445-1510
Bloch, R. Yossef Yehuda (the Sabba of Tels)	1860-1930
Bratslav, R. Nahman of	1772-1811
Bratslav, R. Nathan (disciple of R. Nahman)	1780-1845

C

Chehanov, R. Avraham of	1789-1875
Coucy, R. Moshe of (Semag)	13th cent.
Czernowic, R. Hayyim of	19th cent.

D

R. David ben Zimra, (Radbaz)	1479-1589
Dessler, R. Eliyahu Eliezer	1891-1954
Duran, R. Shim'on ben Tsemah (Rashbatz)	1361-1444
Dynow, R. Tsevi Elimelech of	1785-1841

E

Edels, R. Shemuel Eliezer HaLevi (Maharsha)	1555-1631
Eibeschutz, R. David Shelomo	18th-19th cent.
Eibeschutz, R. Yonathan	1690-1764
Emden, R. Ya'akov	1697-1776

F

Falk, R. Ya'akov Yehoshua	1680-1756
Figo, R. Azariah	1579-1647
Finkel, R. Nosson Tsevi (the Sabba of Slobodka)	1849-1927

G

Galante, R. Shemuel HaLevi	18th-19th cent.
Gaon, Rabbeinu Sa'adya ben Yossef	882-942
Gerondi, Rabbeinu Nissim (Ran)	1290-1375
Gerondi, Rabbeinu Yonah	1180-1263
Gor (Guer, Gora Kalvaria), R. Yitshak Meir of	1789-1866
Gur, R. Yehuda Arie Leib of (Sefat Emet)	1847-1905

H

HaKohen, R. Yisrael Meir (Kagan) of Radin (Hafets Hayyim)	1838-1933
Hakono, R. Nehunya ben	c. 2nd cent.
HaLevi, R. Aharon of Barcelona	1215-1293
HaLevi, R. Avraham ben David	20th cent.
HaLevi, R. David ben Shemuel (Taz)	1586-1667
HaLevi, R. Yehudah	1075-1141
Halberstam, R. Hayyim of Zanz	1793-1876
HaMalakh, R. Avraham	1739-1776
Harlap, R. Ya'akov Moshe	1883-1951
HeHassid, R. Yehuda	1150-1217
Heller, R. Yomtov Lippman	1579-1654

Hirsch, R. Shimshon Raphael   1808-1888
Hoffman, R. David Tsevi   1843-1921
Horowitz, R. Pinhas HaLevi of Offenbach   1730-1805
Horowitz, R. Shmuel Shmelke of Nikolsburg   1726-1778
Horowitz, R. Yossef of Novhardok (HaSaba)   1848-1919
Horowitz, R. Yeshayahu HaLevi (Shelah)   1565-1630

I

Ibn Ezra, R. Avraham   1092-1167
Isserles, R. Moshe (Rema)   1525-1572

K

Karo, R. Yossef (Beit Yossef)   1488-1575
Kimhi, R. David (Radak)   1160-1235
Kohen, R. Meir Simha of Dvinsk   1843-1926
Koretz, R. Pinhas of   1726-1791
Kotsk, R. Menahem Mendel of   1787-1859
Koznitz, R. Yisrael, Maggid of   1733-1814
Kook, R. Avraham Yitshak Hakohen   1863-1935
Kranz, R. Ya'akov, Maggid of Dubno   1741-1804
Kutno, R. Yehoshua of   1820-1893

L

Landau, R. Yehezkel   1713-1793
Levovitch, R. Yeruham HaLevi   20th cent.
R. Loew, ben Bezalel (Maharal MiPrague)   1515-1609
Lunschitz, R. Shelomo Ephraim   1550-1610
Luria, R. Yitshak (HaAri HaKadosh)   1534-1572
Luzzatto, R. Moshe Hayyim (Ramhal)   1707-1746
Luzzatto, R. Shemuel David (Shedal)   1800-1865
Lyzhansk, R. Elimelech   1717-1786

M

ben Maimon, R. Moshe (Rambam, Maimonides)   1135-1204
Malbim, R. Meir Leibush   1809-1879
Margaliyot, R. Reuven   20th cent.
ben Manoah, R. Hizkiyahu   13th cent.
Meklenburg, R. Ya'akov Tsevi   1785-1865
ben Meir, R. Shemuel (Rashbam)   1080-1158
Meiri, R. Menahem   1249-1315
Metz, R. Eliezer ben R. Shemuel of   1115-1198
Mezerich, R. Dov Baer, Maggid of   1704-1772
Mezhibuzh, R. Baruch of   1757-1810

N

ben Nahman, R. Moshe (Ramban, Nahmanides) — 1194-1270

O

Ostrow, R. Yehoshua ben Shlomo Yehuda Leib of — 19th cent.

P

Polonnoye, R. Ya'akov Yossef of — 1704-1784
Pshiskhah, R. Simha Bunem of — 1765-1827

R

Recanati, R. Menahem — 13th-14th cent.
Rozin (Rosen), R. Yossef (the Gaon of Rogachov) — 1858-1936

S

Safran, R. Avinoam Bezalel — 20th cent.
Safran, R. Bezalel Ze'ev (HarBaz) — 20th cent.
Safran, R. Yossef — 20th cent.
Sarna, R. Yehezkel — 20th cent.
Schneerson, R. Shneur Zalman of Lyady (Tanya) — 1745-1813
Seforno, R. Ovadya — 1475-1550
Segal, R. David HaLevi (Turei Zahav)
Seville, Rabbeinu Yomtov ben Avraham (Ritva) — 14th cent.
Slonim, R. Abraham of — 1804-1883
Shapira, R. Kalonymos — 20th cent.
Sofer, R. Moshe (Hatam Sofer) — 1763-1839
Sochaczew (Sochatchov), R. Avraham of — 1839-1910
Sochaczew, R. Shemuel — 20th cent.
Soloveichik, R. Yitshak Ze'ev HaLevi of Brisk — 1887-1959
Soloveichik, R. Yossef Dov Baer HaLevi — 1820-1892
Starobinski-Safran, Esther — 20th cent.
Sudylkow, R. Moshe Hayyim Ephraim of — 1740-1800
Sperling, R. Avraham Yitshak (Ish Shuv) — 19th cent.

T

de Trani, R. Moshe ben Yossef (Mabit) — 1500-1580
de Trani, R. Yossef (Maharit) — 1568-1639

V

Vienna, R. Yitshak ben R. Moshe of — 13th cent.
Vilna, R. Eliyahu, Gaon of (HaGra) — 1720-1797
Vital, R. Hayyim — 1542-1620

W

Worms, R. Eliezer ben R. Yehuda of (HaRokeah)   1165-1230

Y

Yitshaki, R. Shelomo ben Yitshak (Rashi)   1040-1105
Yomtov ben Avraham Ishbili, Rabbeinu (Ritvo)   1240-1325

Z

Ziv, R. Simha Zissel, (the Sabba of Kelm)   1824-1898

II. PUBLISHED WRITINGS

Abrabanel (Abravanel), Pirush Al HaTorah, 3 vol., Jerusalem 5724 (1964).
Abudarham, by R. David Yossef Abudarham, Amsterdam 5486 (1725).
Aderet Eliyahu, by R. Eliyahu of Vilna (GRA), Tel-Aviv, n.d.
Akeidat Yits-hak, by R. Yits-hak Arama, Pressburg 1849, Lemberg 1868.
Arvei Nahal, by R. David Shelomo Eibeschütz, Lemberg 5624 (1864).
Avnei Nezer, by R. Avraham of Sokhatchov, Jerusalem 5733 (1973).
Avodat Yisrael, by R. Yisrael of Kozhnits, Jerusalem 5715 (1956).

Ba'al HaTurim, by R. Ya'akov ben Asher, *in* the Pentateuch with Commentaries, Vilna 5659 (1899).
Rabbeinu Bahya, commentary on the Torah, 3 vol., ed. Chavel, Jerusalem 5726-5728 (1966-1968).
Be'er Avraham, by R. Avraham of Slonim, Jerusalem 5730 (1970).
Be'er HaGola, by Maharal, R. Löw ben Bezalel, Tel-Aviv 5715 (1955).
Be'er Mayim Hayim, by R. Hayim of Tchernowitz, *in* the Pentateuch with Commentaries, Lemberg 1869.
Beit Avraham, by R. Avraham of Slonim, Jerusalem 5729 (1969).
Beit HaLevi, by R. Yossef Dov Ber HaLevi, Warsaw 5644 (1884).
Ben Ish Hai, by R. Yossef Hayim of Baghdad, Jerusalem 5732 (1972).
Benei Yehoyada, by R. Yossef Hayim of Baghdad, 3 vol., Jerusalem 5724-5725 (1964-1965).
Bertinoro, commentary by R. Ovadia Bertinoro, *in* Mishnayot.
Bina Leltim, by R. Azariah Figo, Warsaw 5668 (1908).
Bi'ur HaGRA al HaRaya Mehemna, by R. Eliyahu the Gaon of Vilna, Jerusalem 5735 (1975).
Bi'ur HaGRA al Sefer Mishlei, by R. Eliyahu the Gaon of Vilna, Tel-Aviv, n.d.

Bi'ur HaGRA al Sifra DiTseni'uta, by R. Eliyahu the Gaon of Vilna, Vilna 1882.
Bi'urei HaGRA al Agadot, by R. Eliyahu the Gaon of Vilna, Israel 5731 (1971).
B'nei Issakhar, by R. Tsevi Elimelekh of Dynov, Israel, n.d.
B'nei Issakhar, Haggada shel Pessah, by R. Tsevi Elimelekh of Dynov, Jerusalem 5733 (1973).
Butsina DiNehora, by R. Barukh of Mezhibozh, Lemberg 5644 (1884).

Da'at Hokhma U-Mussar, by R. Yeruham HaLevi Levovitz, Jerusalem 5732 (1972).
Da'at U-Tevuna, by R. Yossef Hayim of Baghdad, Ben Ish Hai, Jerusalem 5725 (1965).
Da'at Torah, by R. Yeruham HaLevi Levovitz, Jerusalem 5736 (1976).
Daliyot Yehezkel, by R. Yehezkel Sarna, 2 vol., Jerusalem 5735 and 5736 (1975 and 1976).
Degel Mahneh Ephraim, by R. Moshe Hayim Ephraim of Sudylkov, Pietrkow 5672 (1912).
Derashot HaRaN, by Rabbeinu Nissim Gerondi, Lemberg 5571.
Derashot MaHaRaL MiPrague, by R. Löw ben Bezalel, Jerusalem 5728 (1968).
Derekh Hayim, by MaHaRaL, R. Löw ben Bezalel, Tel-Aviv, n.d.
Divrei Eliyahu, by HaGRA, R. Eliyahu the Gaon of Vilna, Jerusalem, n.d.
Divrei Hayim, by R. Hayim Halberstam of Sanz, Munkacz 1877.
Divrei Shemuel, by R. Shemuel Shmelke Horowitz, of Nikolsburg, Jerusalem 5734 (1974).
Doreish LeTsion, by R. Bezalel Ze'ev Safran, Seini 5693 (1933).

Eish Kodesh, by R. Kalonymos Shapira, Jerusalem 5720 (1960).
Eits Hayim, by R. Hayim Vital, Lemberg 1864.
Eits Hayim, MeHaAri HaKadosh, ed. Ashlag, Jerusalem 5690 (1930).
Emet VeEmuna, by R. Menahem Mendel of Kotsk, Jerusalem 5708 (1948).

Gevurot Hashem, by MaHaRaL, R. Löw ben Bezalel, Tel-Aviv 5715 (1955).

Ha'amek Davar, by R. Naftali Tsevi Yehuda Berlin, of Volozhin (Netsiv), 5 vol., Jerusalem 5719 (1959).
HaEmuna HaRama, by R. Avraham ben David HaLevi, Berlin 1919.
Hafets Hayim, by R. Yisrael Meir HaKohen of Radin, Jerusalem 5727 (1967).
Hafets Hayim al HaTorah, by R. Yisrael Meir HaKohen of Radin, New York 5703 (1943).
Hafets Hayim al Siddur HaTefillah, by R. Yisrael Meir HaKohen of Radin, Jerusalem 5729 (1969).
Hakdamat HaRaMBaM LePirush HaMishna, by Rabbeinu Moshe ben Maimon, Jerusalem 5721 (1961).
HaKetav VeHaKabala, by R. Ya'akov Tsevi Meklenburg, Frankfurt am Main 1880.

HaMeiri al Massekhet Shabbat, by R. Menahem Meiri, Vienna 5622 (1862).
Hazonei HaGeula, by R. Avraham Yits-hak HaKohen Kook, Jerusalem 5701 (1941).
Hessed LeAvraham, by R. Avraham HaMal'akh, Jerusalem 5732 (1972).
Hiddushei HaRaMBaN, by R. Moshe Ben Nahman, Jerusalem 1928-29.
Hiddushei HaRaShBA, by R. Shelomo ben Avraham Adret, Warsaw 1883.
Hiddushei HaRIM, by R. Yits-hak Meir of Gur, Warsaw 1875.
Hiddushei HaRITVA, by Rabbeinu Yomtov Ben Avraham of Seville, Slavita 5621 (1861).
Hiddushei Hatam Sofer al Sugyot HaShass, by R. Moshe Sofer, Munkacz 5662 (1902).
Hiddushei Maran HaRIZ, by R. Yits-hak Ze'ev HaLevi, Jerusalem 5723 (1963).
Hiddushei U-Biurei HaGRA, by R. Eliyahu the Gaon of Vilna, 5734 (1974).
Hizkuni, by R. Hizkiyahu ben Manoah, Vilna 5640 (1879).
Hokhma U-Mussar, by R. Simha Zissel Ziv, the Sage of Kelm, II, Jerusalem 5724 (1964).
Hovot HaLevavot, by Rabbeinu Bahya ibn Pakuda, Vienna 1853.

Ibn Ezra al HaTorah, R. Avraham ibn Ezra, *in* the Pentateuch with Commentaries, Vilna 5659 (1899).
Iggerot HaRaiyah, by R. Avraham Yits-hak HaKohen Kook, Jerusalem 5722 (1961).
Iggerot HaRaMBaM, by Rabbeinu Moshe ben Maimon, Jerusalem 5720 (1910).
Iggerot Tsafun, by R. Shimshon Raphael Hirsch, Tel-Aviv 5708 (1948).

Kad HaKemah, by Rabbeinu Bahya ben Asher, Lemberg 5640 (1880).
Kedushat Levi, by R. Levi Yitshak of Berdytchev, Munkacz 5623.
Keli Yakar, by R. Shelomo Ephraim Lunschitz, *in* the Pentateuch with Commentaries, Vilna 5659 (1899).
Kissei Rahamim, by R. Hayim Yossef David Azulai (HIDA), Ungvar 1868.
Kitvei Rabbeinu Moshe ben Nahman (RaMBaN), ed. Chavel, 2 vol., Jerusalem 5723-5724 (1963-1964).
Kol Eliyahu, by R. Eliyahu, the Gaon of Vilna, Jerusalem, n.d.
Kuzari: Sefer HaKuzari, by R. Yehuda HaLevi, ed. Even-Shemuel, Tel-Aviv 5733 (1972).

Lehem Min HaShamayim, by R. Hayim Yossef David Azulai (HIDA), Livorno 1845.
Likkutei Amarim, by R. Shneior Zalman of Liady — see *Tanya*.
Likkutei HaGRA, by R. Eliyahu, the Gaon of Vilna, Israel 5731 (1971).
Likkutei MoHaRaN, by R. Nahman of Bratslav, Jerusalem 5729 (1969).
Likkutei Tefillot, by R. Nahman of Bratslav, Jerusalem 5717 (1957).
Likkutei Torah, by the Ari HaKadosh, R. Yits-hak Luria, Jerusalem 5732 (1972).

Madreigat HaAdam, by R. Yossef Horowitz of Novaradok, Jerusalem 5730 (1970).

Maggid Davarav LeYaʻakov, by R. Dov Ber of Mezrytch, ed. Schatz-Uffenheimer, Jerusalem 5736 (1976).
Malbim, R. Meir Leibush Malbim, *HaTorah VeHaMitsvah*, Pentateuch with Commentaries, Vilna 5682 (1922); Mikra'ei Kodesh, *NaKh*, Warsaw 5634 (1874).
Medicine and Judaism, by Avinoam Bezalel Safran, Tel-Aviv 1971.
Mefaneiah Tsefunot, by R. Yossef Rozin, the Gaon of Rogatchov, New York 5720 (1960).
Mehir Yayin, by R. Moshe Isserles, Cracow 5641.
Mekhilta, ed. Weiss, Vienna 1865.
Mekhilta de Rabbi Shimʻon ben Yohai, ed. Epstein-Melamed, Jerusalem 5715 (1955).
Mei HaShiloah, by R. Mordekhai Yossef of Izhbitsa, Jerusalem 5716 (1956).
Mei Marom, by R. Yaʻakov Moshe Harlap, *Missaviv LiShmoneh Perakim LaRaMBaM*, Jerusalem 5710 (1950); II, 5713 (1953); V, 5717 (1957); VI, 5723 (1963); VII, 5729 (1969); VIII, 5729 (1969); *Haggada Shel Pessah*, 5715 (1955).
Menorat HaMaor, by R. Yits-hak Aboab, Metz 5589.
Meshekh Hokhma, by R. Meir Simha Kohen of Dvinsk, Jerusalem 5714 (1954).
Messilat Yesharim, by R. Moshe Hayim Luzzatto (RaMHaL), Tel-Aviv 5717 (1956).
Midbar Kedeimot, by R. Hayim Yossef David Azulai (HIDA), Jerusalem 5717 (1957).
Midrash Aggada, ed. S. Buber, Vienna 5654 (1894).
Midrash HaGadol, Sefer Shemot, ed. Hoffmann, Berlin 5674 (1914).
Midrash HaGadol, Sefer VaYikra, ed. Rabinowitz, New York 5690.
Midrash Lekah Tov, Vilna 5644 (1884).
Midrash Pinehas, by R. Pinehas of Koretz, Warsaw 1876.
Midrash Rabba, Vilna 5671 (1911).
Midrash Simha, by R. Simha Bunim of Prszyshka, 2 vol., Jerusalem 5735 (1975).
Midrash Tanhuma, New York-Berlin 5684 (1924).
Midrash Tanhuma HaKadum VeHaYashan, Vilna 5645 (1885).
Midrash Tannaim, Sefer Devarim, ed. Hoffmann, Berlin 5668-5669 (1908-1909).
Midrash Tehillim, Shoheir Tov, Vilna 5651 (1891).
Mikhtav MeEliyahu, by R. Eliyahu Eliezer Dessler, 3 vol., Jerusalem 5719 (1959); 5723 (1963); 5724 (1964).
Minhat Hinnukh, by R. Yossef Babad, Vilna 5672 (1912).
Mishna: Shisha Sidrei Mishna, ed. Albeck, Jerusalem 5719 (1958).
Mishna Berura, by R. Yisrael Meir HaKohen of Radin (Hafets Hayim), Jerusalem 5724 (1964).
Mishneh Torah, Yad HaHazakah, by RaMBaM, Rabbeinu Moshe ben Maimon, Vilna 5660 (1900).
Moreh Nevukhim, by RaMBaM, Rabbeinu Moshe ben Maimon (Maimonides), ed. Even-Shemuel, Jerusalem 5719 (1959); ed. Kafeh, Jerusalem 5732 (1972).

Mussar Avikha, by R. Avraham Yits-hak HaKohen Kook, Jerusalem 5731 (1971).

Nahal Kedumim, by R. Hayim Yossef David Azulai (HIDA), *in* Pentateuch with Commentaries, Lemberg 1869.
Nefesh HaHayim, by R. Hayim of Volozhin, Vilna 5634 (1874).
Ne'ot HaDesheh, by R. Avraham of Sokhatchov, Tel-Aviv 5734 (1974).
Netivot Olam, by R. Shemuel HaLevi Galante, Lemberg 5567 (1807).
Netivot Olam, by MaHaRaL, R. Löw ben Bezalel, 2 vol., Tel-Aviv 5716 (1956).
Noam Elimelekh, by R. Elimelekh of Lizensk, ed. Nigal, 2 vol., Jerusalem 5738 (1978).

Od Yossef Hai, by R. Yossef Hayim of Baghdad (Ben Ish Hai), Jerusalem 5718 (1958).
Ohel Ya'akov, by R. Ya'akov Kranz, the Maggid of Dubno, Warsaw 1874.
Olat Re'iyah, by R. Avraham Yits-hak HaKohen Kook, 2 vol., Jerusalem 5709 and 5722 (1949 and 1962).
Olelot Ephraim, by R. Shelomo Ephraim Lunschitz, Amsterdam 5470 (1710).
Or HaHayim, by R. Hayim ibn Attar, *in* Pentateuch with Commentaries, Vilna 5659 (1899).
Or HaTsafun, by R. Nathan Tsevi Finkel, the Sage of Slobodka, 2 vol., Jerusalem 5719 (1958) and 5728 (1968).
Or Zarua, by R. Yits-hak ben R. Moshe of Vienna, Jerusalem 5647 (1887).
Orot, by R. Avraham Yits-hak HaKohen Kook, Jerusalem 5721 (1961).
Orot HaKodesh, by R. Avraham Yits-hak HaKohen Kook, 3 vol., Jerusalem 5710, 5723, 5724.
Orot HaRe'iyah, by R. Avraham Yits-hak HaKohen Kook, Jerusalem 5730 (1970).
Orot HaTeshuva, by R. Avraham Yits-hak HaKohen Kook, Jerusalem 5685 (1925).
Orot HaTorah, by R. Avraham Yits-hak HaKohen Kook, Jerusalem 5733 (1973).

Peirush HaGRA al Massekhet Avot, Jerusalem, n.d.
Peirushei MaHaRaL MiPrag LaAggadot HaShass, by R. Löw ben Bezalel, I, Jerusalem 5718 (1958); II, 5719 (1959); III, 5720 (1960); IV, 5723 (1963).
Peirushei Rabbeinu Yona Gerondi al Massekhet Avot, Jerusalem 5726 (1966).
Peirushei HaTorah LeRabbi Yehuda HeHassid, ed. Lange, Jerusalem 5735 (1975).
Penei Yehoshua, by R. Ya'akov Yehoshua Falk, Warsaw 5636-5643.
Der Pentateuch, Hirsch, Frankfurt am Main 1893.
Pesikta DeRav Kahana, ed. Mandelbaum, 2 vol., New York 5722 (1962).
Philon of Alexandria, De fuga et inventione, by Esther Starobinski-Safran, Paris 1970.
Pit-hei Hokhma, by R. Moshe Hayim Luzzatto (RaMHaL), Cracow 5640 (1880).

Die Psalmen, Hirsch, Frankfurt am Main 1898.

RaDaK: Peirush al HaTorah, by R. David Kimhi, ed. Kamelhar, Jerusalem 5730 (1970).

RaMBaM — see *Mishneh Torah*.

RaMBaN: Peirush al HaTorah, Rabbeinu Moshe ben Nahman, 2 vol., ed. Chavel, Jerusalem 5727-5728 (1967-1968).

RaShBaM, commentary by R. Shemuel ben Meir, *in* Pentateuch with Commentaries, Vilna 5659 (1899).

RaShI, the basic, standard Commentary on the Pentateuch; with English translation; ed. Silbermann, Jerusalem 5733 (1973).

Recanati, kabbalistic commentary on Pentateuch by R. Menahem Recanati, Lemberg 5640 (1880).

ReMA: R. Moshe Isserles, *in* Shulhan Arukh.

Romemot El, Peirush al Sefer Tehillim, by R. Moshe Alsheikh, Amsterdam 5455 (1695).

Ruah Hayim al Pirkei Avot, by R. Hayim of Volozhin, Jerusalem, n.d.

Seder Eliyahu Rabba VeEliyahu Zuta, Lemberg 5630 (1870). See *Tanna Devei Eliyahu Rabba*.

Sefat Emet, by R. Yehuda Arieh Leib of Gur, 5 vol., Jerusalem 5731 (1971).

Sefer Abudarham — see *Abudarham*.

Sefer HaBahir, Vilna 1883.

Sefer Bereishit, Meforash, by R. David Tsevi Hoffman, Bnei-Brak 1969-1971.

Sefer HaEmuna VeHaHashgaha, by R. Eliyahu, the Gaon of Vilna, Israel, n.d.

Sefer HaEmunot VeHaDe'ot, by Rabbeinu Sa'adya Gaon, Warsaw 5673 (1913).

Sefer Hafla'ah, by R. Pinhas HaLevi Horowitz, Offenbach.

Sefer HaHinnukh, ascribed to R. Aharon HaLevi of Barcelona, Jerusalem 5721 (1961).

Sefer HaIkkarim, by R. Yossef Albo, Lemberg 1866.

Sefer HaKuzari, by Rabbi Yehuda HaLevi — see *Kuzari*.

Sefer HaMakneh, by R. Pinhas HaLevi Horowitz, Offenbach.

Sefer HaMiddot, by R. Nahman of Bratslav, Bnei-Brak 5730 (1970).

Sefer HaMitsvot, by RaMBaM, Rabbeinu Moshe Ben Maimon, Jerusalem 5732 (1972).

Sefer Mitsvot Gadol (SeMaG), by R. Moshe of Coucy, Vilna 5660 (1900).

Sefer HaOra, by Rabbeinu Shelomo Yits-haki (RaShI), ed. S. Buber, Lemberg 5665 (1905).

Sefer HaPardes, by Rabbeinu Shelomo Yits-haki (RaShI), ed. Ehrenreich, Budapest 5684 (1924).

Sefer Haredim, by R. Eleazar Azikri, Venice 1601.

Sefer HaRoke-ah, by R. Eleazar of Worms, Fano 1505.

Sefer Hassidim, by R. Yehuda HeHassid, ed. Margaliot, Jerusalem 5724 (1964).

Sefer Tehillim, im Peirush Romemot El, by R. Moshe Alsheikh — see *Romemot El*.

Sefer Tehillim, im Peirush R. Shimshon Raphael Hirsch — see *Hirsch*.
Sefer Torat Kohanim — see *Sifra*.
Seforno, R. Ovadia Seforno, *in* Pentateuch with Commentaries, Vilna 5659 (1899).
SeMag — see *Sefer Mitsvot Gadol*.
Sha'arei HaAvoda, by Rabbeinu Yona Gerondi, Bnei-Brak 5727 (1967).
Sha'ar HaShamayim, Siddur by SheLaH HaKadosh, Jerusalem 5733 (1973).
Shabbat·HaArets, by R. Avraham Yits-hak HaKohen Kook, Jerusalem 5732 (1972).
SheDaL, Pirush al HaTora, by R. Shemuel David Luzzatto, Tel-Aviv 5732 (1971).
She'eilot U-Teshuvot Hakham Tsevi, by R. Tsevi Ashkenazi, Amsterdam 1712.
She'eilot U-Teshuvot HaRaDBaZ, by R. David ben Zimra, Warsaw 5642 (1882).
She'eilot U-Teshuvot HaRaShBa, by R. Shelomo ben Avraham Adret, Lemberg 5571, Vienna 5572.
She'eilot U-Teshuvot HaRBaZ, by R. Bezalel Ze'ev Safran, I, Warsaw 5690 (1930); II, Jerusalem 5722 (1962).
She'eilot U-Teshuvot Hatam Sofer, Heilek Yore De'a, by R. Moshe Sofer, Pressburg 5620 (1860). See *Hiddushei Hatam Sofer*.
She'eilot U-Teshuvot MaBIT, by R. Moshe ben Yossef di Trani, Lemberg 5621 (1861).
She'eilot U-Teshuvot MaHaRIT, by R. Yossef Trani, Venice 1629.
She'eilot U-Teshuvot Noda BiYehuda, by R. Yehezkel Landau, Warsaw 1880.
She'eilot U-Teshuvot Yeshu'ot Malko, by R. Yehoshua of Kutno — see *Yeshu'ot Malko*.
She'eilot DeRav Aha'i Gaon, Dhyrenfurt 5546 (1786).
SheLaH HaKadosh, Shenei Luhot HaB'rit, by R. Yeshayahu HaLevi Horowitz, 3 vol., Jerusalem 5730-5732 (1970-1972).
Shelosha Sefarim Niftahim, by R. Moshe Hayim Luzzatto (RaMHaL), Cracow 5640 (1880).
Shem MiShemuel, by R. Shemuel of Sokhatchov, Jerusalem 5734 (1974).
Shem MiShemuel, Haggada shel Pessah, by R. Shemuel of Sokhatchov, Jerusalem 5725 (1965).
Shibbolei HaLekket, by R. Tsidkiyahu ben R. Avraham HaRofei/Anav, ed. S. Buber, Vilna 5647 (1887).
Shirei R. Yehuda HaLevi, New York 5705 (1944).
Shi'urei Da'at, by R. Yossef Yehuda Bloch of Telz, Cleveland-New York 5724 (1964).
Shoher Tov — see *Midrash Tehillim*.
Shulhan Arukh, by R. Yossef Karo, Lemberg 5661 (1900).
Siddur Beit Ya'akov, by R. Ya'akov Emden, Zhitomir 5641 (1881).
Siddur HaGeonim VeHaMekubalim, ed. Weinstock, Jerusalem 5730-5731 (1970-1971).
Siddur Hircsh, by R. Samson R. Hirsch, Jerusalem-New York 5732 (1972).

Siddur Ishei Yisrael, by R. Eliyahu the Gaon of Vilna, Jerusalem 5728 (1968).
Siddur Rabbeinu Shelomo MiGarmaisa (Worms), ed. Herschler, Jerusalem 5732 (1971).
Siddur Shaʻar HaShamayim, by the SheLaH HaKadosh, R. Yeshayahu HaLevi Horowitz, Jerusalem 5733 (1973).
Siddur Shaʻarei Ratson, by R. Nahman of Bratslav, ed. Kenig, Bnei-Brak, n.d.
Siddur Tseluta d'Avraham, by R. Avraham of Tchehanov, Tel-Aviv 5716 (1956) and 5722 (1961).
Sifra Devei Rav — Torat Kohanim, ed. Weiss, Vienna 1862.
Sifra — Torat Kohanim, ed. Finkelstein, New York 5717 (1956).
Sifra DiTseni'uta, im Bi'ur HaGRA, Vilna 1882.
Sifra DiTseni'uta, im Peirush HaGRA, Jerusalem, n.d.
Sifre, BaMidbar, Devarim, *im Hagahot HaGRA*, ed. Zuckermann, Vilna 1866.
Sifre Deve Rav, ed. Friedmann, Vienna 1864.

Taʻamei HaMitsvot, by R. Hayim Vital, *in Likkutei Torah d'Ari HaKadosh*, Jerusalem 5732 (1972).
Talmud Bavli, Vilna 5657 (1897).
Talmud Yerushalmi, Vilna 5682 (1922).
Tanna Devei Eliyahu Rabba and *Tanna Devei Eliyahu Zuta*, Lemberg 5630 (1870).
Tanya, by R. Shneiur Zalman of Liady, Kfar Habad-New York 5726 (1966).
TaShBeTs, by R. Shimʻon bar Tsemah Duran, Amsterdam 5498.
TaZ: Turei Zahav, by R. David ben Shemuel HaLevi, *in Shulhan Arukh*.
Tehillim, im Peirush Romemot El, by R. Moshe Alsheikh — see *Romemot El*.
Tehillim, im Peirush R. Samson Raphael Hirsch, Jerusalem 5731 (1971).
Tiferet Yisrael, by R. Löw ben Bezalel (MaHaRaL), Tel-Aviv 5714 (1954).
Toledot Adam, by R. Yehoshua of Ostrova, Josefov 5635.
Toledot Yaʻakov Yossef, by R. Yaʻakov Yossef of Polonnoye, Jerusalem 5722 (1962).
Torat Kohanim — see *Sifra*.
Tosefot Yomtov, by R. Yomtov Lipman Heller, *in* Mishnayot.
Tossefta, im Peirush Hazon Yehezkel, by R. Yehezkel Abramsky, Seder Kodashim, II, Jerusalem 5737 (1977).
Tossefta KiFshuta, Im Bi'ur R. Shaul Lieberman, New York 5715-5722 (1955-1962).
Tsafenat Pane-ah, by R. Yaʻakov Yossef of Polonnoye, Pietrkov 5644 (1844).
Tsafenat Pane-ah, by R. Yossef Rozin, the Gaon of Rogatchov, Jerusalem 5736 (1976).
Tsafenat Pane-ah, al HaTorah, by R. Yossef Rozin, the Gaon of Rogatchov, Jerusalem 5720-5725 (1960-1965).
TseLaH: Tsiun LeNefesh Haya, al Massekhet Berakhot, by R. Yehezkel Landau, Lemberg 5636 (1876).
Turim, by R. Yaʻakov ben Asher, Vilna 5660 (1900).

Yad HaHazakah, by RaMBaM — see *Mishneh Torah*.
Yalkut Re'uveni, Warsaw 5652 (1892).
Yalkut Shim'oni, Vilna 5669 (1909).
Yemei MaHarNaT, by R. Nathan, disciple of R. Nahman of Bratslav, II, New York 5725 (1965).
Yeshu'ot Malko, She'eilot U-Teshuvot, by R. Yehoshua of Kutno, Pietrkov 5687 (1927).
Yessod HaAvoda, by R. Avraham of Slonim, Jerusalem 5719 (1959).

Zohar, im Peirush HaSulam, by R. Yehuda HaLevi Ashlag, Erets Israel, n.d.

GLOSSARY

AGGADAH: The sequel to those parts of the Bible which include stories and chronicles, sayings of the wise and moral instructions, and the admonitions and consolations of the prophets — as opposed to HALAKHAH.

ALIYAH (Heb. "ascent"): (1) A "calling up" to the reading of the Scroll of the Law in the synagogue during worship. (2) The immigration of Jews to Israel.

AMIDAH (Heb. "standing"): The main, central part of every prayer service, said silently, standing. In the weekday services it contains nineteen benedictions (originally eighteen; one was added later); also known as *tefillah* ("prayer") and *shemoneh esrei* ("eighteen").

AMORA (from Heb./Aram. *amar*=speak): Title given to the Jewish scholars in the third to sixth centuries who authored the GEMARA in ERETS YISRAEL and Babylonia (pl. AMORAIM).

ARAVAH: Willow; one of the four species of vegetation used on Sukkot (the Feast of the Tabernacles), together with the ETROG, LULAV and HADAS.

ASARAH BE-TEVET: The tenth day of the month of TEVET, a fast day mourning mainly the besieging of Jerusalem (586 BCE) by Nebuchadnezzar, king of Babylonia (II Kings 25:1).

AV: Fifth month of the Jewish calendar year, and eleventh of the civil, corresponding approximately to July-August.

BAR: Aramaic for "son of"; frequently appearing in personal names.

BARAITA: Teachings of the TANNAIM not incorporated into the MISHNAH (pl. BARAITOT).

BEIT HAMIDRASH: School for higher rabbinic learning where students gather for study, discussion, and prayer. Can be in a synagogue.

BEN: Hebrew for "son of"; frequently appearing in personal names.

BERACHAH: A set form of words of thanks and praise to God said before eating or performing a MITZVAH, after witnessing natural phenomena, or as part of a prayer.

CHABBAD: Initials of *Chochma Bina Va-Daat* (Heb. for "wisdom, understanding, and knowledge"). Name of the Lubavitch movement, founded by Rabbi Schneor Zalman of Lyadi.

CHANUKAH: Eight-day celebration (Kislev 25-Tevet 2) commemorating the victory of Judah the Maccabee over Antiochus Epiphanes and the rededication of the Temple and altar.

CHASSID: Follower of a Chassidic movement.

CHASSIDEI ASHKENAZ: The members of a medieval pietist movement in Germany that stressed asceticism, humility, and moral law.

CHASSIDISM: A religious and social movement founded by R. Israel Baal Shem Tov in the eighteenth century which taught that purity of heart was more essential than study.

CHIDDUSH: (lit. "innovation" or "novel thought"): In the plural, *chiddushei*, it denotes a commentary on the Talmud or later rabbinic works that attempts to derive new facts or principles from the implications of the text.

COHEN: Priest appointed by God to perform the service in the Temple. After the golden calf incident, these duties were assigned to the tribe of Levi.

DEVEIKUT: Intense love of God.

DIASPORA: (lit. "dispersion"): the countries outside the Land of Israel that became the locations of Jewry's exile.

DIN: A law (secular or religious) or a judgment.

ERETS YISRAEL: The Land of Israel.

ERUV: A technical arrangement which, by Rabbinic law, permits either carrying inside a city or walking a certain distance outside a city on the Sabbath, or cooking for the Sabbath on a festival day falling on a Friday.

ETROG: A citron; one of the four species of vegetation used on Sukkot (the Feast of the Tabernacles), together with the LULAV, ARAVAH, and HADAS.

EVEN HA'EZER: One of the four parts of the *Arba'ah Turim* and Shulhan Arukh that governs the life of observant Jewry.

GALUT: Exile of Jews from the Land of Israel.

GAON: Intellectual leader of the Babylonian Jewish community in the post-Talmudic period, who explained the language of the Bible and Talmud and made religious decisions; in later usage, a Torah genius.

GEMARA: The Talmud, q.v.

HALAKHAH (pl. HALAKHOT): Normal, definitive law; denotes also the legal part of talmudic and later Jewish literature, in contrast to *Haggadah* or AGGADAH, the non-legal elements.

HALLEL: Psalms 113-18, recited in Jewish prayers on certain festivals and occasions.

HAVDALAH: Ceremony marking the end of the Sabbath.

HOLOCAUST: The persecution and genocide of six million European Jews by the Nazis (1933-1945).

HOSHANAH RABBAH: The seventh day of Sukkot, when the judgment on a person's life, that was made on the Day of Atonement, becomes irrevocable. Extra prayers are accompanied by the beating of willow branches on the ground.

HOSHEN MISHPAT: One of the four parts of the *Arba'ah Turim* and SHULHAN ARUKH that deals with civil law and administration.

KABBALAH: The mystical tradition in Judaism.
KADDISH: A well-known Jewish liturgical doxology.
KAVANAH: The devotion and concentration of thought with which a Jew should conduct his religious actions and prayers.
KETUBAH: Marriage contract that stipulates the obligations of the bridegroom toward his bride.
KIDDUSH: Ceremonial blessing recited over wine on the Sabbath and festivals.
KIDDUSH HASHEM: an act of martyrdom or strict integrity that reflects creditably on Jews in the eyes of others.
KINAH (pl. KINOT): Dirge over the dead in Biblical, mishnaic, and talmudic times. Later extended to lamentations over the fate of the nation. Said on Ninth of Av and at other times.
KNESSET YISRAEL: Communal organization of Jewish groups in Israel during the time of the British Mandate.

LULAV: Palm branch; one of the four species of vegetation used on Sukkot (the Feast of Tabernacles), together with the ETROG, ARAVAH, and HADAS.

MAARIV: The evening prayer.
MAGGID: Name given to any popular preacher in Poland.
MENORAH: Candelabrum. One with seven branches was used in the Tabernacle and Temples. One with eight branches is used on CHANUKAH.
MIDRASH: Method of finding new meaning, in addition to the literal one, in the Scriptures. Some volumes deal with legal questions (*Midrash Halachah*), while others teach through narrative and ethical lessons (*Midrash Aggadah*).
MINCHAH: The afternoon prayer.
MISHNAH: Legal codification containing the core of the Oral Law, compiled by Rabbi Judah HaNasi around 200 CE.
MISHNAYOT: Paragraphs of the MISHNAH.
MITZVAH: A positive Torah or rabbinic injunction. Act of piety or charity.
MUSSAF: Supplementary service said on the Sabbath, Rosh Chodesh, and certain festivals when an additional sacrifice was offered in the Temple.
MUSSAR: Traditional ethical literature.
MUSSAR MOVEMENT: Moral movement that developed in the latter part of the nineteenth century among Orthodox Jewish groups in Lithuania, founded by Rabbi Israel Lipkin (Salanter).

NETZITZOT: Mystical term for Divine sparks that are in all people and things.
NISAN: First month of the religious year, seventh of the civil, it corresponds approximately to March-April.

OMER: The first cutting during the barley harvest, which was offered in the Temple as a sacrifice on the second day of Passover.
OMER, SEFIRAT HA-: The counting of forty-nine days from the day on

which the OMER was first offered in the Temple (16 Nisan) until SHAVUOT. It is a period of semi-mourning for historical reasons.

ORAH HAYIM: One of the four parts of the *Arba'ah Turim* and SHULHAN ARUKH, dealing with daily conduct, including prayers, Sabbath, and holidays.

PESSAH: Passover (15 Nisan).

POSSEK (pl. POSSEKIM): An outstanding Jewish scholar who renders decisions on what is permitted or forbidden by Jewish law.

PURIM: Festival commemorating the rescue of Persian Jewry through the mediation of Esther from Haman's threat of annihilation. Celebrated in some places on 14 Adar and in some on 15 Adar.

RABBAN: Variant form of "rabbi" given as title of honor to outstanding scholars during early mishnaic times, and especially to heads of the Sanhedrin.

RESPONSUM (pl. RESPONSA): Written replies given to questions on all aspects of Jewish law by qualified authorities.

ROSH HASHANAH: Two-day festival at the beginning of the month of Tishri. It is known as the Day of Judgment, when Hashem decrees the fate of each man.

ROSH YESHIVAH: Chief scholar who heads a YESHIVA.

SANHEDRIN: Assembly of seventy-one ordained scholars which, till the middle of the fourth century, functioned both as the Supreme Court and as the legislature. It denotes also the Jewish assembly called by Napoleon (1806).

SEDER: Ceremony observed in the Jewish home on the first night (outside Israel, first two nights) of Passover, when the *Haggadah* is recited.

SEFER TORAH: Rolled manuscript of the Pentateuch, portions of which are read to the congregation during certain synagogue services.

SHA-DAI: Divine name, often used in kabbalistic formulas, and placed on the outside of mezuzahs.

SHAVUOT: The last of the three pilgrim festivals, observed on 6 Sivan, which was the season of the wheat harvest. It commemorates the giving of the Ten Commandments on Mount Sinai.

SHEKHINAH: the presence of God in the world.

SHEMA: Proclamation of belief in the absolute unity of God, recited twice daily in worship: consists of Deut: 6:4-9, 11:12-21; Num. 15:37-41. (The first part is recited again at night before retiring.)

SHEMINI ATZERET: The last day (in the Diaspora the last two days) at the end of the Sukkos festival. It is considered a separate period of celebration.

SHIVA: The seven days of mourning following the burial of a member of one's immediate family.

SHOFAR: A ram's horn blown during synagogue services in the month of Elul, on Rosh HaShanah, at the end of Yom Kippur, and on other occasions.

SHULHAN ARUKH: (lit. "the Prepared Table"): The authoritative code of law for Jewish life and religious practice, written by R. Joseph Caro, 1564-5.
SIDDUR: The volume containing the daily Hebrew prayers (as opposed to the *Mahzor*, which contains the holiday prayers).
SIMHAT TORAH: The festival day marking the annual completion of the reading of the Pentateuch in the synagogue. It is observed on SHEMINI ATZERET (but outside Israel on the day following).
SIVAN: Ninth month of the Jewish civil year, and third of the religious one. Corresponds approximately with June-July.
SUKKAH: Booth erected for the Feast of Tabernacles when, for seven days, Jews "dwell" or, at least, eat in it (Lev. 23:42).

TALLIT: A "prayer cape"; a four-cornered garment with TZITZIT knotted on each corner in accordance with the Biblical prescription (Num. 15:37-41).
TALMUD (Heb. "teaching"): a collection of discussions on the MISHNAH by generations of scholars and Sages at a good number of Torah academies, from 200 to 500 CE. The *Talmud Yerushalmi* arose from such discussions and study in the Land of Israel, and the *Talmud Bavli* similarly in Babylonia.
TALMUD TORAH: Term applied generally to Jewish Torah study. Also denotes Jewish religious schools that also teach secular studies.
TAMMUZ: Tenth month of the Hebrew civil year and fourth of the religious year, corresponding approximately to June-July.
TANNA (pl. TANNAIM): A scholar and teacher, mentioned in the MISHNAH or BARAITA, living during part of the first two centuries CE.
TARGUM: Aramaic translation of the Bible.
TEFILLIN: Phylacteries, i.e., two black leather boxes attached to leather straps, containing four portions of the Pentateuch written on parchment (Exod. 13:1-16; Deut. 6:4-9; 11:13-21).
TEVET: Fourth month of the Hebrew civil year and tenth of the religious year. Corresponds approximately to December-January.
TIKKUN (Heb. "repair"): (1) A selection of Biblical, mishnaic and kabbalistic passages formulated by the Kabbalists for reading on certain occasions, mainly at night; (2) a mystic term designating the restoration of proper order and true unity in the *sefirot* after any spiritual "havoc" produced in the cosmos.
TISHA BE-AV: The Ninth of Av. Fast day mourning the destruction of the First and Second Temples.
TISHRI: First month of the Jewish civil year and seventh of the religious. Coincides approximately with September-October.
TOKHAHAH: Passages of reprimand (Lev. 26, Deut. 28:15-69) to Israel from God, warning them what will happen if they do not keep His commandments. Words of reprimand to someone.
TORAH: The Pentateuch, read from parchment scroll during certain synagogue services (the Written Torah); and denotes also the collection of traditional Jewish literature which arose from and around it (the Oral Torah).

TOSAFISTS: French and German scholars of the twelfth - fourteenth centuries who supplemented Rashi's commentary on the TALMUD

TOSAFOT: Critical and explanatory notes on the TALMUD, written by the TOSAFISTS.

TOSEFTA: A supplement to the MISHNAH which gives alternative versions for some paragraphs, elucidations of others, plus some independent material.

TZADDIK: A righteous man, outstanding for his faith and piety; denotes also the leader of a group of Chassidim.

TZIMTZUM: Mystical doctrine which states that God contracts from Himself into Himself, leaving a vacuum in which Creation (of the material world) can take place.

TZITZIT: Tassels knotted a special way on the four corners of a TALLIT (Num. 15:37-41).

YESHIVAH: Jewish traditional school devoted primarily to the study of the Talmud and rabbinic literature.

YISHUV: A settlement, specifically the Jewish community in Israel during the pre-Independence War period.

YOM KIPPUR: Day of Atonement. A solemn fast day observed on 10 Tishri during which Jews cleanse themselves from sin by means of repentance.

YOREH DE'AH: One of the four parts of the *Arba'ah Turim* and SHULHAN ARUKH, dealing with dietary laws and other matters.

ZOHAR: The chief work of the KABBALAH, mostly a mystical commentary on the Pentateuch.

TABLE OF CONTENTS

FOREWORD ix
PREFACE xi

PART I

THE INNER NATURE OF ISRAEL

CHAPTER 1

PEOPLE OF ISRAEL AND LAND OF ISRAEL:
Israel, "heart of the nations"/Erets-Yisrael, "soul of the universe" 1

The basic ideas of Judaism, 1. — Israel, God's possession, 1. — Israel is the people of God because it senses that it is in relationship with Him, 3. — A holy people and a community of the holy people by keeping the Torah, 4. — The Torah, God's spiritual instrument for the creation of the world, and the *mitzvot*, man's practical instrument for the perfection of the world, 5. — The People of Israel and the Land of Israel, foreseen together in the Creator's plan, deserved to be chosen by God, 6. — The People of Israel is called man because it is the life force of man; The Land of Israel, Erets-Yisrael, is called the Land because it is the life force of the Earth, 7. — The authenticity of the Torah of Israel can only be declared in Erets-Yisrael, 9. — It is on his return to Erets-Yisrael that Jacob acquires the name Israel, 10. — Because it neglected the Torah, the people of Israel were forced temporarily to leave Erets-Yisrael; nevertheless, it remains Israel's possession, 11. — In Exile, Israel underwent a painful apprenticeship to the Torah and the *mitzvot*, 13. — The "root" of every being is inherent in the name which it bears, 15. — God deliberately puts His name into that of Israel. Their common name reveals the common nature of their historical identity, 17. — Israel bears the name of Erets-Yisrael and Erets-Yisrael bears the name of Israel, 19. — The concept of a people based on the concept of the people of Israel, 20. — Every nation can become a people of God like Israel, 21. — The Torah, Israel and Erets-Yisrael, issuing from a trans-historical world, descend to a temporal world and aspire to return to their source after accomplishing their historical mission, 23. — The outside world has difficulty in comprehending the inner nature of the Torah, Israel and Erets-Yisrael, 24. — Which of the three categories — Torah, Israel or Erets-Yisrael — should take precedence?, 26. — The appearance of Israel/Erets-Yisrael as a bonded unit marks the beginning of the open history of humanity and of the earth, 27. — Divine Presence and human freedom, 30. — By helping Israel to be Israel and by helping Erets-Yisrael to be Erets-Yisrael, the nations of the world help God to save them, 32. — The physical covenant of circumcision and the spiritual covenant of the

Torah express the full bond between God, the Torah, Israel and Erets-Yisrael, 34. — The Torah, Israel and Erets-Yisrael are primordial elements, conceived before the creation of the world, 35. — The *tnai*, the Divine "condition," governs the life of the Torah, Israel and Erets-Yisrael, 37. — The impossibility of destroying Israel, 38. — The Divine love for Israel is a love of the world, 39. — Israel, the man and people of *teshuvah*, shows men and peoples the way of the "return" to God, 40. — Israel can never forget itself because it is linked to God who keeps it in a state of permanent awareness, 43. — The unique character of Israel is beneficial to all those who are honestly prepared to benefit from it, 45. — The *reshit*, the beginning, virtually contains the *ahrit*, the outcome, 46. — God does not cease revealing Himself through the *reshit*, 47. — The historical, universal and exceptional importance of the simultaneous manifestation of the three *reshit*, 48. — The House of Israel is "a nation unlike others" and "a land unlike others," 51. — Holiness and the sanctification of the Land of Israel, 52. — The recognition by the "nations of the world" of the specificity and legitimacy of the bond between the Torah, Israel and Erets-Yisrael, 54. — Solidarity of Israel and shared responsibility of the Jewish People, 55. — Contemporary reflections, 57.

Chapter 2A

Exile and Redemption:
Galut — Exile — a specifically Jewish phenomenon/its universal cosmic reference and its meta-historical dimension 59

The unique nature of the Galut and of the history of Israel, 59. — Exile and diaspora, 60. — Israel's slavery in Egypt, prototype of all the exiles, 62. — A punishment disproportionate to the sin, 63. — Punishment and love, 64. — Galut (exile) and Israel's continuing survival, 66. — "Sufferings of love," 69. — Galut and purification, 73. — Responsibility of Israel's persecutors, 74. — "Nevertheless, do not regard your oppressor with horror," 78. — The lesson to be learned from the slavery in Egypt: "You shall love the stranger as yourself," 80. — Jews grieve over the sufferings endured by their oppressors, 82. — During the feast of Passover, Israel celebrates its deliverance from Egypt and not the Egyptian's defeat, 84. —

Chapter 2B

The Galut — Israel's Exile:
Divine providence and human liberty 91

Essential reality and final objective, 91. — Between the times of the beginning and the fulfillment, between Genesis and the Messiah — Abraham, 92. — The Jewish Galut, a mission to the universe, 93. — Israel's election and Israel's Galut, 95. — The dialectic of the Galut: Divine coercion and human freedom, 96. — The dialectic of the Galut: from Talmud to Tosafot, from the Maharal to the Gaon of Rogachev, 99. —

Gezerah Min HaShamayim and *Koah HaBehirah Alei Adamot*: "The Divine Decree from Heaven" and man's "Freedom of Choice on Earth," 106. — The *gezerah* is a *hok*, a law. The *hok* of Galut, Torah and Nature, 113. — Interrogation and silence, 115. — The *tsaddik*, the righteous man, suffers in sympathy with God's suffering, 116. — The Galut and its task of unifying the Torah, Nature and History, 117. — *Geulah* through Galut: Galut leading to *geulah*, 119. — Galut, the cause of the *geulah*, 121. — Galut, the preparation for the *geulah*, 122. — The school of the Galut, 124. — Galut and *geulah*: want and plenty, 125. — Nocturnal visions foretell the Galut, 126. — The darkness of the night and the rising of the sun, 127. — Good is the final objective of the Galut, 129. — Divine power and mercy, 130. — *HaRahum Umakdim Rahamim LeRogez*, 131. — Veil and transparency, 131. — From Golah to *geulah*, from exile to redemption, 133.

CHAPTER 3

JERUSALEM, HEART OF ISRAEL, HEART OF THE WORLD 135

Jerusalem, the place where God and man, God and Israel, meet, 135. — When he leaves Jerusalem, man transports God into the world, 137. — When he turns his heart towards Jerusalem, man, especially the Jew, hallows the whole earth, 137. — Jerusalem, made sacred in the first place by the will of God, is afterwards hallowed by the merits of man, 139. — Yerushalayim, a plural form: shows the holiness of that city is due to the collaboration of God and man, 141. — If man neglects his share of this task of cooperation, God withdraws into His heavens, 142. — Israel faithfully carries Jerusalem in its heart, retains its identity in exile thanks to Jerusalem, 142. — The phenomenon of Israel is expressed in the phenomenon of Jerusalem, 144. — Jerusalem personifies the unity of Israel, 144.

CHAPTER 4

JEWISH TIME: SABBATICAL TIME 147

The Torah teaches the right use of time, 147. — "Respect the Shabbat of your God as if all your work were already done," 148. — By virtue of its identification with the Torah and with the Shabbat Israel becomes a cosmic factor, 149. — The Shabbat will be what one has succeeded in making of it during the "preparation" period, 157. — The days of the week do not even have names of their own; they all refer to the Shabbat, 152. — Our possessions belong to us to the extent to which we recognize that we belong to God, 143. — The Shabbat enables everyone to feel that they are equals for at least one-seventh of their lives, 153. — The *mitzvah* of Shabbat observance is equivalent to all other *mitzvot* of the Torah, 154. — Three proclamations of the Shabbat: (1) the Shabbat of the primordial time; (2) the Shabbat of the giving of the Torah; (3) the Shabbat of the time to come, 155. — *Shabbat kodesh* hallowed by God will henceforth be "sanctified" by man via the *kiddush*, 156. — The marriage contract between the Shabbat and Israel is written in the Torah, 158. — The children of Israel live the Shabbat in their home, 159. — In the Sabbatical law, tenderness and severity, freedom and discipline dwell together in mutual harmony, 160. — Two key words govern the Halakhah of the Shabbat: *zakhor* and *shamor*, 161. — "The nations of the world" have only adopted the "idea" of a day of rest, 162. — The Messianic Shabbat will be the result of the sum total of the *Shabbatot* kept by Israel, 163.

Chapter 5

Jewish Identity:
   Being and becoming a Jew/individual and community 165

Having been "made" initially by Another, the Jew is in a position "to remake himself," 165. — The Jew does not submit to his identity: he cherishes it as a vocation, 165. — A duty to become a Jew this very day as if he were not yet a Jew yesterday, 166. — No claim to a Jewish identity without a claim to the Torah and the *mitzvot*, 167. There is no Jew "who has not reserved a *mitzvah* for himself," 167. — A *mitzvah* is never isolated, 168. — So many *mitzvot*: hence their observance by so many different Jews, 169. — Shared responsibility with other Jews because of the *mitzvot*, 169. — Jewish identity only when one "does not separate himself from the ways of the community," 170. — Every Jew is responsible for the Judaism of his fellow believers, 170. — The Jewish soul is inexhaustible in essence, 170. — Israel is always the same, 171.

PART II

THE INNER SPIRIT OF ISRAEL

Chapter 1

The People of Israel and the Land of Israel 173

The people of God; the terms of a dialectic; internal dynamic and external repercussions; complementary themes and categories, 173. — The relation between the Torah and Israel, between the letters of the Torah and the Jews; the symbolic value of the numbers six, sixty and six hundred thousand, 176.

Chapter 2

Exile and Redemption 181

The Hebrew verb *gur* means "to sojourn" in a place both as a stranger and as an inhabitant; the Jew is a "stranger and an inhabitant," both in the countries of other nations, in the Diaspora, and in his own country, Erets-Yisrael; man, par excellence Jewish, the Jew, par excellence man, is both "stranger and inhabitant" on this earth, 181. — The *Sukkah* — "dwelling" — in both wilderness and Eretz-Yisrael; the dwelling of the Jew on earth; to be erected by nations in time to come to lead to the *Sukkah* of bliss "in the world to come", 183.

CHAPTER 3

JERUSALEM, HEART OF ISRAEL, HEART OF THE WORLD 203

Jerusalem, center of the world, 203. — The world is virtually contained in Jerusalem, 204. — Jerusalem is the Sanctuary, 204. — The Jew prays towards Jerusalem, 204. — Sinai and Moriah: Sinai is the place of God's word and man's listening; Moriah-Jerusalem is the place of the mutual quest of God and man, 205. — The *Akedah* of Yitshak, never the "Sacrifice of Isaac," 207. — Seeing and fearing; fear and love; fear and peace of mind, 208. — A "holy" place is determined by God's sovereign will but only partially shown by Him to man; it is man who is called upon freely to identify it and "sanctify" it, 210. — The meeting of the inward spirit of Abraham and that of the Promised Land; the descendants of Abraham are chosen by God's providence, 211. — Search and discovery, 212. — Choice and confirmation; the original choice of God and the actual choice by man, 213. — Holiness and sanctification; Divine choice and human choice, 214. — Man is the true holy place that God desires, 217. — The Divine salvation of the heavenly Jerusalem depends on the human salvation of the earthly Jerusalem, 218. — God does not question man about his territorial position but concenring his moral position, 219. — אַיֶּכָּה and אֵיכָה: "Where are you?" — "How I pity you!" 219. — Galut, a specific dimension of Jewish history; Jerusalem, the memory of Israel, 220. — The choice of David was made with the choice of Jerusalem in mind, 222. — Identity of Jerusalem and Israel; Israel is called Zion, 223. — The *Aliyah*, the "ascent": the Jewish people's history is always the history of the "ascent" to Erets-Yisrael and in particular to Jerusalem, 225. — In Jerusalem, the city of *shalom*, Peace, God is served with Joy; in Jerusalem, the city of *Shelemut*, Perfection, man must be perfect before his God, 228. — Jerusalem — salvation and justice, salvation and truth; salvation and return to Zion, 229. — Unity of Jerusalem, Israel and God, 230. — The universal, messianic vocation of Jerusalem, the "Throne of the Lord," 234. — Tsion and Yerushalayim; Zion and Jerusalem, 235.

CHAPTER 4

SURVEY OF "JEWISH TIME, SABBATH TIME" 239

Shabbat: Source and prerequisite of holiness, 239. — God and Israel create the Shabbat, its Divine holiness and its hallowing by man, 240. — God, the

Shabbat and Israel, 240. — *Ner Shabbat*, "The Shabbat candle," the privilege of the Jewish wife, 240. — The prayer of the "sanctification" of the Shabbat, 243. — Observance of the Shabbat is organized by the married couple together, 244. — The Shabbat home is a place of heavenly glory, 245. — Respect for God, for the Shabbat and for one's parents, 245. — It is Jacob's example which the whole family of Israel follows in celebrating the Shabbat, 246. — *Oneg Shabbat* — the delight of the Shabbat, 246. — Shabbat/Pessah/sanctuary. Holy day and Holy place. The power and the leniency of the Shabbat laws, 249. — *Pikkuah Nefesh*, safeguarding human life, takes priority over observance of the Shabbat laws, 250. — Shabbat observance and the precariousness of the "leisure civilization," 253. — The Shabbat and a weekly day of rest, 254. — The Jewish Shabbat and the Mesopotamian day of rest; the "delight of the Shabbat," and the sorrow of the *Shappatu*, 254. — The Shabbat prayers contain no petitions, 255. — The three Shabbat prayers and the three Shabbat meals, 255. — By celebrating the Shabbat, man saves himself from settling into the materialist conditions brought about by continuous work, 257. — Shabbat, the day of knowledge, 258. — Word and Action: Word and Witness, 258. — Speech: *Ma'amar* and *Dibbur*, 259. — God is distant yet near: *Hu* and *Atta*, "He" and "Thou"; He and you, 259. — The Jew is a servant of God during the week and a son of God on the Shabbat, 260. — Awe of the Shabbat and love of God, 260. — The Shabbat as a personal experience of the creative and providential revelation of God, 261. — The Shabbat of the Covenant with Israel precedes the Shabbat of the Creation, 262. — The covenant of circumcision and the Shabbat, 262. — Manna, sign of the Shabbat, 262. — The gift of Shabbat came before the gift of the Torah, 265. — Torah, Shabbat and Israel, 266. — The Shabbat of the individual and the Shabbat of the community, 266. — The consummation of the Divine Shabbat is the product of collaboration between God and Man, 267. — Each hour is irreplaceable, 268. — The days of the week are included in the Shabbat, 269. — The Shabbat, demarcated externally, is immeasurable in depth, 269. — The Shabbat, a day of revelation and discovery, 270. — The Shabbat: wholly day, wholly light, 271. — The unity of the Shabbat, 271. — In the Sabbatical, Messianic Age, the diversified world will return to its source and its unity, 271. — By the number seven the Creation, the Torah, Israel and the Shabbat are bound to one another, 272. — The significance of the number seven in the history of the world and the history of Israel, 272.

REFERENCES, SOURCES AND NOTES	281
SELECTED BIBLIOGRAPHY	445
GLOSSARY	459